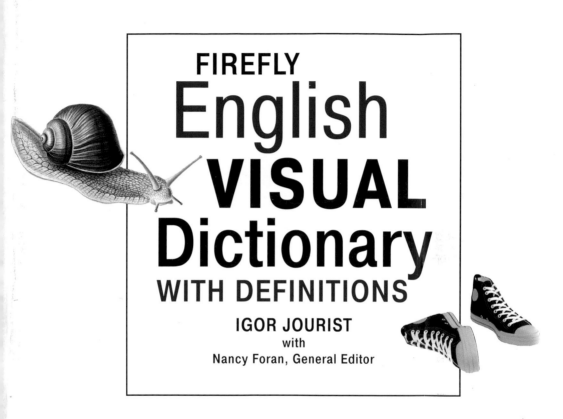

FIREFLY
English
VISUAL
Dictionary

WITH DEFINITIONS

IGOR JOURIST

with

Nancy Foran, General Editor

FIREFLY BOOKS

A FIREFLY BOOK

Published by Firefly Books Ltd. 2015
Illustrations and basic text © 2015 Jourist Verlag GmbH, Hamburg
Text adaptations for this publication © 2015 Firefly Books Ltd.

First printing

Publisher Cataloging-in-Publication Data (U.S.)
Jourist, Igor.
Firefly visual dictionary : with definitions / Igor Jourist with Nancy Foran, general editor.
[792] pages : color illustrations ; cm.
Includes index.
Summary: Divided into fourteen subject areas, this dictionary provides detailed and
accurate illustrations of thousands of items, from everyday objects to highly specialized
equipment.
ISBN-13: 978-1-77085-620-2
1. Picture dictionaries, English. 2. English language – Dictionaries. I. Foran,
Nancy, editor. II. Title. III. Visual dictionary.
423.17 dc23   PE1629.J576 2015

Library and Archives Canada Cataloguing in Publication
Jourist, Igor, author
Firefly visual dictionary : with definitions / Igor Jourist ; with Nancy Foran, general editor.
Includes index.
ISBN 978-1-77085-620-2 (bound)
1. Picture dictionaries, English. 2. English language–
Dictionaries. I. Foran, Nancy, editor
PE1629.J68 2015   423'.17   C2015-903103-6

Published in the United States by
Firefly Books (U.S.) Inc.
P.O. Box 1338, Ellicott Station
Buffalo, New York 14205

Published in Canada by
Firefly Books Ltd.
50 Staples Avenue, Unit 1
Richmond Hill, Ontario L4B 0A7

Illustrations, terminology and production: Jourist Verlags GmbH, Hamburg

jourist

Cover design: Jacqueline Hope Raynor
Printed in China

LIST OF CHAPTERS

CONTENTS

HOW TO USE THE DICTIONARY

Subtheme
The 14 themes are divided into more specific subjects, which group related objects together.

Indicator
These lines link the vocabulary with the specific part of the illustration that is being identified.

Topic
Some subthemes are divided into topics, which are more specific and more closely related groupings.

Subtopic
Subtopics are the smallest, most specific and most closely related groupings.

HOUSEHOLD FURNISHINGS
Furniture

Sofas
Different styles of upholstered seats with arms and a back, long enough to accommodate more than one person.

sectional sofa
A sofa separated into sections that can be moved to change the configuration.

backrest
The raised portion behind the seat of a chair or sofa, on which one may lean backwards.

seat cushion
A stuffed pad placed on top of a chair to provide comfortable support for sitting.

leg
A support attached to the bottom of a piece of furniture to stabilize or raise it.

arm
The raised portion at the side of a chair or sofa, providing a place for one to rest their arms.

ottoman
A small piece of furniture, usually upholstered and without back or arms, often used as stool or footstool.

loveseat
A sofa designed to hold only two people.

bench
A piece of furniture that is not fully upholstered, designed to seat two or more people.

chaise longe
An elongated cushioned seat that is designed to allow one to stretch out in a half-lying, half-sitting position.

Object illustration
A detailed illustration of the object being defined; for some illustrations, several parts are identified and defined.

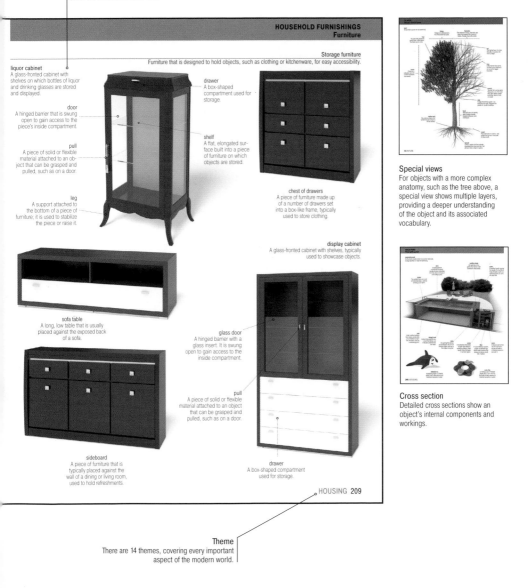

Storage furniture
Furniture that is designed to hold objects, such as clothing or kitchenware, for easy accessibility.

liquor cabinet
A glass-fronted cabinet with shelves on which bottles of liquor and drinking glasses are stored and displayed.

door
A hinged barrier that is swung open to gain access to the piece's inside compartment.

pull
A piece of solid or flexible material attached to an object that can be grasped and pulled, such as on a door.

leg
A support attached to the bottom of a piece of furniture; it is used to stabilize the piece or raise it.

drawer
A box-shaped compartment used for storage.

shelf
A flat, elongated surface built into a piece of furniture on which objects are stored.

chest of drawers
A piece of furniture made up of a number of drawers set into a box-like frame, typically used to store clothing.

display cabinet
A glass-fronted cabinet with shelves, typically used to showcase objects.

sofa table
A long, low table that is usually placed against the exposed back of a sofa.

glass door
A hinged barrier with a glass insert. It is swung open to gain access to the inside compartment.

pull
A piece of solid or flexible material attached to an object that can be grasped and pulled, such as on a door.

sideboard
A piece of furniture that is typically placed against the wall of a dining or living room, used to hold refreshments.

drawer
A box-shaped compartment used for storage.

HOUSING 209

Special views
For objects with a more complex anatomy, such as the tree above, a special view shows multiple layers, providing a deeper understanding of the object and its associated vocabulary.

Cross section
Detailed cross sections show an object's internal components and workings.

Theme
There are 14 themes, covering every important aspect of the modern world.

NATURE

animal cell
A microscopic structure that
is the fundamental biological
building block of animal life.

ribosome
An organelle that
synthesizes proteins.

endoplasmic reticulum
A network of flattened
membranes that can be the site
of either protein or lipid synthesis.

nuclear envelope
A double-layered
membrane that
surrounds the nucleus.

mitochondrian
An organelle that
synthesizes a cell's
energy.

nucleolus
The site of ribosome
synthesis.

centriole
An organelle involved
in cell division.

Golgi apparatus
An organelle that
modifies and packages
proteins. It is also called
a Golgi body.

lysosome
A membranous
organelle that destroys
waste within the cell.

cytoplasm
A gel-like substance that
allows suspension of the
organelles of a cell.

cell membrane
A semipermeable membrane
that is involved in cellular
transport and communication
between cells.

red blood cell
The most common type of
blood cell. It is the main means
of delivering oxygen to the
various tissues of the body.

hemoglobin
The iron-containing
metalloprotein that transports
oxygen throughout the body in
red blood cells.

ovum
A female reproductive egg cell that
is one of the largest cells in the
human body. It can be visible to the
naked eye.

cytoplasm
A gel-like substance within a
cell membrane that contains a
mixture of proteins, RNA and
small organic molecules.

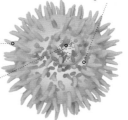

corona radiata
The innermost layer of
the cumulus oophorus. It
is formed by follicle cells
adhering to an oocyte.

cytoplasm
A gel-like substance
within a cell membrane
that contains a mixture of
proteins, RNA and small
organic molecules.

iron
An important component
of hemoglobin that
helps transport oxygen
in the body. It also helps
maintain healthy cells.

nucleus
A membrane-enclosed
organelle found in
eukaryotic cells that
contain most of the
cell's genetic material.

back
The area of a horse's body that is formed by the length of its vertebral column.

barrel
The area of a horse's body that is formed mostly by the ribs. It contains the major internal organs.

withers
The highest part of a horse's back. It is located at the base of the neck and above the shoulders.

mane
Long hair that grows along the top of a horse's neck.

Arabian horse
A type of horse that is bred for its swiftness and compact frame. It originated on the Arabian Peninsula.

loin
The area of a horse's body between the last rib and the croup.

crest
The upper area of a horse's neck, where the mane grows. It is more prominent in some species of horses.

poll
The area of the poll joint directly behind a horse's ears. It can be flat or protruding.

croup
The area of a horse's body that extends from the top of the hip to the dock. It is also called a rump.

forelock
The hair that grows at the top of a horse's forehead. It is sometimes called the foretop.

dock
This part of a horse's body consists of skin and muscles that cover the tailbone.

forehead
An area of a horse's face and head, between the ears and above the eyes and top of the nose.

buttock
The area of a horse's body that connects its hind legs to its torso.

nostril
One of two holes in a horse's nose that allows it to breathe and smell its environment.

tail
The part of a horse's body that includes the dock and long hair.

thigh
The upper part of a horse's hind leg. It is located between the stifle and the hips.

muzzle
The area of a horse's face that consists of its mouth and jaw bones.

stifle
The joint that connects a horse's thigh to its tibia. It is comparable to the human knee.

lip
One of two fleshy parts that line the opening of a horse's mouth.

elbow
The joint that connects a horse's forearm to its humerus.

gaskin
A large muscle between the hock and stifle of a horse's hind leg. It is comparable to the human calf.

cheek
The area of a horse's face below the eyes and between the mouth and the right or left ear.

neck
The area of a horse's body that contains the cervical part of its spine. It connects the head to the torso.

hock
The joint between the cannon and the upper part of a horse's hind leg.

knee
The joint that connects a horse's cannon to its forearm.

chest
The area of a horse's body between its neck and belly. It contains the heart and lungs.

pastern
The part of a horse's foot between the fetlock joint and the hoof.

shoulder
The joint that connects a horse's foreleg to its body. It contains three bones: clavicle, scapula and humerus.

fetlock joint
The joint located between the pastern and the cannon of a horse's hind leg. It is sometimes called an ankle.

belly
The body cavity between a horse's ribcage and hips. It contains most of the digestive system.

cannon
A bone that extends from the knee to the fetlock joint. It helps support the bones of the knee.

coronet
A band of soft tissue on a horse's foot that contains the cells necessary to produce its hooves.

forearm
The part of a horse's foreleg that is located between the elbow and the knee.

flank
The area of a horse's body between the ribcage and the hind leg.

hoof
The tip of a specialized toe of a horse's foot. It has a tough outer covering.

white-tailed deer
A common type of deer with brownish fur and a white underside of its tail. The males grow large, branched antlers.

shoulder
The joint that connects a deer's foreleg to its body. It contains three bones: clavicle, scapula and humerus.

back
The area of a deer's body that is formed by the length of its vertebral column.

loin
The area of a deer's body between the last rib and the rump.

rump
The area of a deer's body that extends from the top of the hip to the tail. It is also called a croup.

tail
The part of a deer's body that includes the tailbone.

thigh
The upper part of a deer's hind leg.

main beam
The long, central branch of a deer's antlers. Points branch from the main beam.

point
A tip that protrudes from the main beam of a deer's antlers.

burr
A ring of bone at the base of a mature deer's antler. It connects to the pedicle.

ear
A deer's sensory organ for hearing.

antler
A bony outgrowth of the skull. Antlers are grown and shed every year.

nape
The upper part of a deer's neck.

muzzle
The area of a deer's face that consists of its mouth and jaw bones.

cheek
The area of a deer's face below the eyes and between the mouth and the right or left ear.

nose
The deer's sensory organ for smell, and the area of the face through which air is taken in.

mouth
The area of a deer's face through which food is taken in.

chest
The area of a deer's body between its neck and belly. It contains the heart and lungs.

neck
The area of a deer's body that contains the cervical part of its spine. It connects the head to the torso.

dewclaw
The functionless inner toe located higher up on a deer's leg.

hock
The joint between the cannon and the upper part of a deer's hind leg.

flank
The area of a deer's body between the ribcage and the hind leg.

hoof
The tip of a specialized toe of a deer's foot. It has a tough outer covering.

belly
The body cavity between a deer's ribcage and hips. It contains most of the digestive system.

cannon
A bone that extends from the knee to the fetlock joint. It helps support the bones of the knee.

elbow
The joint that connects a deer's forearm to its humerus.

knee
The joint that connects a deer's cannon to its forearm.

antelope
A deer-like animal characterized by upward-rising horns. It is found throughout Africa and parts of Asia.

alpine ibex
A grayish brown species of mountain goat with large, curved horns. It is found in the European Alps.

reindeer
A type of deer that is found in the Arctic and sub-Arctic regions of the northern hemisphere.

elk
A large animal with large antlers. It is found worldwide.

gazelle
A type of antelope with curved horns and a light brown or white coat. It is found in Africa and parts of Asia.

moose
A large animal with large antlers, found in northern regions of North America, Europe and Asia.

musk ox
A large animal with a shaggy
coat and curved horns. It is
found in northern regions of
North America.

buffalo
A large, shaggy, brownish
mammal with curved horns. It
originated in Asia.

bison
A large, shaggy, brown mammal
with horns. It originated in the
grasslands of North America.

tapir
A herbivorous, nocturnal animal
with a prehensile snout. It is found
in Central and South America
and Asia.

goat
A domesticated farm animal with backward-curving horns and a beard.

bighorn sheep
A brown mountainous sheep with a white rump and very large, curved horns.

cashmere goat
Any breed of goat that produces fine and soft cashmere wool.

western roe deer
A small, reddish brown deer found in cold climates. It is found in Europe and parts of Asia.

mule
The offspring of a horse and a donkey. It is typically sterile and is used for labor.

rhinoceros
A large, grayish and thick-skinned animal with one or two horns. It is found in Africa and Asia.

hippopotamus
A large, semiaquatic mammal with thick, gray skin and large tusks. It is found in Africa.

giraffe
A tall, light brown mammal with brown spots. It has a long neck and legs and is found in Africa.

Asian elephant
A large, herbivorous animal that has a prehensile trunk and long tusks. It can be found in Southeast Asia.

dromedary camel
A camel that has one hump on its back and is known for being swift. It is found in Asia, Africa and eastern Europe.

Bactrian camel
A camel that has two humps on its back. It is currently endangered and is found only in some parts of Asia.

llama
A land mammal whose most prominent features are its long neck and soft fleece coat that varies in color.

zebra
This horse-like animal is known for its black and white stripes. Zebras live in large herds in Africa.

cow
A domesticated female farm
animal that is known for the
milk it produces.

donkey
A domesticated farm animal
with long ears.

wild boar
A wild pig with prominent
tusks and grayish-brown
fur. It originated in Europe,
central Asia and North Africa.

pig
A domesticated farm animal
with pink skin, bristly hairs
and a short and flat snout.

sheep
A domesticated farm animal
with a thick, wooly coat that
is often light in color.

polar bear
A large Arctic bear that lives on ice packs. It feeds on seals and is known for its swimming abilities.

black bear
An omnivorous, forest-dwelling bear with dark, shaggy fur. It is found in North America.

giant panda
A large, black-and-white bear that feeds mostly on bamboo. It is found in China.

grizzly bear
A large omnivorous bear. It is found in western North America.

cougar
A large wild cat with light brown fur. It is also known as a mountain lion.

chest
The area of a cougar's body between its neck and belly. It contains the heart and lungs.

ear
A cougar's sensory organ for hearing.

cheek
The area of a cougar's face below the eyes and between the mouth and the right or left ear.

eye
A cougar's sensory organ for vision. The eye detects light and movement.

shoulder
The joint that connects a cougar's foreleg to its body. It contains three bones: clavicle, scapula and humerus.

upper arm
The part of a cougar's foreleg that is located between its elbow and shoulder.

back
The area of a cougar's body that is formed by the length of its vertebral column.

elbow
The joint that connects a cougar's forearm to its humerus.

forehead
The area of a cougar's face and head between the ears and above the eyes and top of the nose.

ribcage
The large, curved bones in a cougar's chest that protect its lungs and heart and give structure to its body.

flank
The area of a cougar's body between the ribcage and the hind leg.

stop
The part of a cougar's face that is located between its eyes and above its nose.

tail root
The area of a cougar's body where the base of its tail connects to the rest of its body.

nasal dorsum
The long upper ridge of a cougar's nose. It contains olfactory tissue, which is used for smelling.

buttock
The area of a cougar's body that connects its hind legs to its torso.

whiskers
Large, specialized hairs on a cougar's muzzle that allow for tactile sensing.

tail
The part of a cougar's body that includes the tailbone.

muzzle
An area of a cougar's face that consists mainly of its nose, mouth and jaw bones.

nose
The cougar's sensory organ for smell, and the area of the face through which air is taken in.

hind leg
One of a cougar's four legs, found at the back of its body.

paw
The part of a cougar's foreleg that has digits and claws.

hock
The joint between the foot and the upper part of a cougar's hind leg.

dewclaw
The functionless inner toe located slightly higher up on a cougar's foreleg.

belly
The body cavity between a cougar's ribcage and hips. It contains most of the digestive system.

foreleg
One of a cougar's four legs, found at the front of its body.

forearm
Part of the foreleg, between the elbow and shoulder.

digit
An elongated and usually jointed part of a cougar's paw.

claw
A pointed, sharp and curved nail that is located on the tips of a cougar's digits.

pastern
The part of a cougar's leg between the first joint and the paw or foot.

wolf
A wild dog with thick fur and a long snout. It is found in North America, Europe and Asia.

cheetah
A large wild cat with round black spots on its fur. It is the fastest running land animal and is found mainly in Africa.

lion
A large wild cat with fur that ranges from light to dark brown. It is found in Africa and Asia.

jackal
A nocturnal wild dog that is known to scavenge and hunt in packs. It is found in Africa and parts of Asia.

lynx
A wild cat with a short tail and tufts of fur on the tips of its ears.

spotted hyena
A wild dog with spots
on its reddish-brown or
grayish brown fur. It is
found in Africa.

striped hyena
A wild dog with stripes
on its grayish-brown fur.
It is found in Africa and
parts of Asia.

snow leopard
A large wild cat with dark
spots on its grayish fur. It
is found in the mountains
of Asia.

tiger
A large wild cat with
stripes on its orange-
brown fur. It is found in
the forests of Asia.

jaguar
A large wild cat with spots
on its yellow-brown fur. It is
found in South America and
parts of North America.

otter
A semiaquatic mammal with webbed feet. Its main prey is fish, shellfish and aquatic invertebrates.

badger
A burrowing, omnivorous, nocturnal mammal with a black face that has white markings.

stoat
A small, carnivorous mammal with brown fur. It is found in North America, Europe and Asia.

polecat
A small, carnivorous mammal with dark brown fur and a dark mask on its face.

skunk
A small mammal with dark fur and white stripes. It sprays a pungent-smelling liquid when threatened.

racoon
A small grayish mammal with black facial markings and a striped tail. It is known for scavenging.

jungle cat
A medium-sized wild cat with small tufts of fur on the tips of its ears. It is found mainly in Southeast Asia.

marten
A small, omnivorous mammal with a bushy tail and fur that ranges from yellowish to dark brown.

wolverine
A carnivore that resembles a small bear. It is found in northern regions of the northern hemisphere.

wildcat
A small wild cat with a bushy tail and brown and black markings on its fur. It is found in Europe, Asia and Africa.

red fox
A wild dog with a bushy tail and a reddish coat. It is found mainly in the northern hemisphere.

gray seal
An aquatic mammal that lives near coastal regions and is known for its incredibly thick fur.

fur seal
An aquatic mammal with thick fur and webbed flippers. It is found in the Southern Ocean and along the Pacific coast.

walrus
A large aquatic mammal with long tusks and thick gray skin. It is found in northern regions.

sea lion
An aquatic mammal that lives in large colonies along the coasts of the Pacific Ocean.

bulldog
A breed of dog with short legs, a muscular frame and a flat, square and wrinkled face.

rottweiler
A breed of dog with a large, muscular body.

Siberian husky
A large breed of dog with thick fur and a bushy tail. It varies in color, although it is typically gray and white.

collie
A breed of dog that typically has long, thick fur, a long snout and is known to be intelligent.

dachshund
A breed of dog with short legs, a long body and a long snout. It is a natural hunter of rodents.

poodle
A breed of dog with a fluffy, curly coat. Poodles are known to be good swimmers.

German shepherd
A large breed of dog with black and brown fur. It is notable for working with police officers and blind people.

golden retriever
A large breed of dog with a long, light brown coat. It is commonly used as a hunting dog.

dalmatian
A breed of dog that is white with black spots. It is known for its high endurance.

Chihuahua
A breed of dog with a small body and large eyes and ears. The Chihuahua originated in Mexico.

Labrador retriever
A breed of dog with thick, short hair. It ranges in color from light yellow to dark brown to black.

croup
The area of a dog's body that extends from the top of the hip to the base of the tail.

loin
The area of a dog's body between the last rib and the croup.

nose
The dog's sensory organ for smell, and the area of the face through which air is taken in.

nasal dorsum
The long, upper ridge of a dog's nose. It contains olfactory tissue, which is used for smelling.

stop
The part of a dog's face that is located between its eyes and above its nose.

eye
A dog's sensory organ for vision. The eye detects light and movement.

hip
A dog's pelvic bone, which connects the hind leg with the torso at the hip joint.

back
The area of a dog's body that is formed by the length of its vertebral column.

ear
A dog's sensory organ for hearing.

flank
The area of a dog's body between the ribcage and the hind leg.

nostril
One of two holes in a dog's nose that allows it to breathe and smell its environment.

withers
The highest part of a dog's back. It is located at the base of the neck and above the shoulders.

thigh
The upper part of a dog's hind leg. It is located between the knee and the hips.

muzzle
An area of a dog's face that consists mainly of its nose, mouth and jaw bones.

tail
The part of a dog's body that includes the tailbone.

neck
The area of a dog's body that contains the cervical part of its spine. It connects the head to the torso.

belly
The body cavity between a dog's ribcage and hips. It contains most of the digestive system.

dewlap
The folds of loose skin located below a dog's lower jaw.

knee
The joint that connects a dog's thigh to the lower part of its leg.

flews
The lateral parts of a dog's upper lip that hang over the outside of its mouth.

hock
The joint between the foot and the knee of a dog's hind leg.

philtrum
The vertical groove between the two halves of a dog's upper lip that extends upward along the nose.

wrist
A group of bones between the metacarpal bones and the forearm. It is also called a carpus.

toe
The part of a dog's paw or foot that contains three phalanx bones: proximal, middle and distal.

shoulder
The joint that connects a dog's foreleg to its body. It contains three bones: clavicle, scapula and humerus.

chest
The area of a dog's body between its neck and belly. It contains the heart and lungs.

elbow
The joint that connects a dog's forearm to its humerus.

forearm
The part of a dog's foreleg that is located between the elbow and the wrist.

pastern
The part of a dog's leg between the wrist and paw or hock and foot.

claw
A pointed, sharp and curved nail that is located on the tips of a dog's toes.

stopper pad
A foot pad located on the back of a dog's foreleg. It is also known as a carpal pad.

British shorthair
One of the most ancient breeds of domesticated cats. They typically have a bluish-gray coat and copper eyes.

forehead
An area of a cat's face and head, between the ears and above the eyes and top of the nose.

nose
The cat's sensory organ for smell, and the area of the face through which air is taken in.

upper eyelid
The eyelid above a cat's eye.

superciliary whiskers
Large, specialized hairs that are located just above a cat's eyes. They are used to interpret sensory information.

ear
A cat's sensory organ for hearing.

eye
A cat's sensory organ for vision. The eye detects light and movement.

nictitating membrane
A translucent eyelid that removes debris from the eye. It opens and closes horizontally.

philtrum
The vertical groove between the two halves of a cat's upper lip; it extends upward along the nose.

lower eyelid
The eyelid under a cat's eye.

lip
One of two fleshy parts that line the opening of a cat's mouth.

cheek
The area of a cat's face below the eyes and between the mouth and the right or left ear.

mystacial whiskers
Large, specialized hairs on a cat's muzzle that allow for tactile sensing.

muzzle
An area of a cat's face that consists mainly of its nose, mouth and jaw bones.

mandible
The lower jaw of a cat's mouth. It is also called the jawbone.

shoulder
The joint that connects a cat's foreleg to its body. It contains three bones: clavicle, scapula and humerus.

chest
The area of a cat's body between its neck and belly. It contains the heart and lungs.

forearm
The part of a cat's foreleg that is located between the elbow and shoulder.

neck
The area of a cat's body that contains the cervical part of its spine. It connects the head to the torso.

fur
The cat's coat, which covers its entire exterior and consists of hair. It keeps the animal warm.

wrist
A group of bones between the metacarpal bones and the forearm. It is also called a carpus.

toe
The part of a cat's paw or foot that contains three phalanx bones: proximal, middle and distal.

pastern
The part of a cat's foreleg between the wrist and paw.

tail
The part of a cat's body that includes the tailbone.

Norwegian forest cat
A breed of cat that is larger than the average domesticated cat and has glossy, long fur.

Russian blue
A breed of domestic cat that has grayish-blue fur, green eyes and large, pointed ears.

Maine coon
A breed of cat with a large bone structure and long fur. It is the largest breed of domesticated cat.

Persian cat
A breed of cat with long fur and a round head. It comes in a variety of colors.

Siamese cat
A breed of cat with light-colored fur and blue eyes. It originated in Asia.

rabbit
A herbivorous mammal with long ears and a fluffy tail. It burrows and can jump long distances.

cheek
The area of a rabbit's face below the eyes and between the mouth and the right or left ear.

eye
A rabbit's sensory organ for vision. The eye detects light and movement.

forehead
An area of a rabbit's face and head, between the ears and above the eyes and top of the nose.

ear
A rabbit's sensory organ for hearing.

whiskers
Large, specialized hairs on a rabbit's muzzle that allow for tactile sensing.

nape
The upper part of a rabbit's neck.

muzzle
An area of a rabbit's face that consists mainly of its nose, mouth and jaw bones.

shoulder
The joint that connects a rabbit's foreleg to its body. It contains three bones: clavicle, scapula and humerus.

nose
The rabbit's sensory organ for smell, and the area of the face through which air is taken in.

back
The area of a rabbit's body that is formed by the length of its vertebral column.

mouth
The area of a rabbit's face through which food is taken in.

flank
The area of a rabbit's body between the ribcage and the hind leg.

neck
The area of a rabbit's body that contains the cervical part of its spine. It connects the head to the torso.

knee
The joint that connects the upper and lower parts of a rabbit's hind leg.

chest
The area of a rabbit's body between its neck and belly. It contains the heart and lungs.

rump
The area of a rabbit's body that extends from the top of the hip to the base of the tail.

foreleg
One of a rabbit's four legs, found at the front of its body.

paw
The part of a rabbit's foreleg that has digits and claws.

tail
The part of a rabbit's body that includes the tailbone.

elbow
The joint that connects the upper and lower parts of a rabbit's foreleg.

hind leg
One of a rabbit's four legs, found at the back of its body.

hock
The joint between the foot and the upper part of a rabbit's hind leg.

toe
The part of a rabbit's paw or foot that contains three phalanx bones: proximal, middle and distal.

belly
The body cavity between a rabbit's ribcage and hips. It contains most of the digestive system.

hare
A fast land mammal with long ears and long hind legs. It is similar in appearance to a rabbit.

koala
A herbivorous marsupial with thick gray hair, sharp claws and no tail. It originated in Australia.

head
The part of a koala's body that contains the brain, eyes, ears, nose and mouth.

cheek
The area of a koala's face below the eyes and between the mouth and the right or left ear.

ear
A koala's sensory organ for hearing.

eye
A koala's sensory organ for vision. The eye detects light and movement.

mouth
The area of a koala's face through which food is taken in.

nose
The koala's sensory organ for smell, and the area of the face through which air is taken in.

chest
The area of a koala's body between its neck and belly. It contains the heart and lungs.

forelimb
One of a koala's four limbs, found at the front of its body.

opposable digit
The first and second digits of a koala's forepaw are opposable to its other digits and allow for grasping objects.

hind limb
One of a koala's four limbs, found at the back of its body.

digit
An elongated and usually jointed part of the paw or foot.

forepaw
The part of a koala's forelimb that has digits and claws.

claw
A pointed, sharp and curved nail that is located on the tips of most of a koala's digits.

hind paw
The part of a koala's hind limb that has digits and claws.

kangaroo
A herbivorous marsupial with a long, thick tail and large ears. It moves by hopping on its powerful hind legs.

opossum
A marsupial with a long, bald tail and an opposable digit on each of its hind feet. It can be found in North America.

tail
The part of a mouse's body that includes the tailbone.

hind limb
One of a mouse's four limbs, found at the back of its body.

fur
The mouse's coat, which covers the entirety of its body's exterior and consists of hair. It keeps the animal warm.

house mouse
A common, grayish brown rodent with a pointed snout and a long, thin tail.

ear
A mouse's sensory organ for hearing.

eye
A mouse's sensory organ for vision. The eye detects light and movement.

hind paw
The part of a mouse's hind limb that has digits and claws.

digit
An elongated and jointed part of a mouse's paw or foot.

forelimb
One of a mouse's four limbs, found at the front of its body.

forepaw
The part of a mouse's front limb that has digits and claws.

claw
A pointed, sharp and curved nail that is located on the tips of a mouse's digits.

whiskers
Large, specialized hairs on a mouse's muzzle that allow for tactile sensing.

nose
The mouse's sensory organ for smell, and the area of the face through which air is taken in.

field vole
A small, herbivorous rodent with a short tail and grayish brown fur. It is found in Europe.

brown rat
A large, brownish-gray rodent with a long tail. It is also known as the Norway rat and is found in urban areas.

porcupine
A large rodent whose coat contains defensive quills. It is found in regions throughout the world.

red-rumped agouti
A large forest-dwelling rodent that is found in South America. It is also called the Brazilian agouti.

beaver
A semiaquatic rodent with a large, flat tail and powerful front teeth. It is found in North America, Europe and Asia.

muskrat
A semiaquatic rodent with short, thick fur, a long, scaly tail and webbed feet. It originated in North America.

chinchilla
A small rodent with grayish fur and a long, bushy tail. It is found in South America.

gray squirrel
An omnivorous, brownish-gray mammal with a bushy tail. It is found in North America.

marmot
A burrowing rodent that is found in mountainous areas of North America, Europe and Asia.

guinea pig
A domesticated rodent that varies in color. It originated in South America.

hamster
A small domesticated rodent with a short tail and large cheek pouches. They are common pets.

jerboa
A nocturnal, hopping desert rodent that is known to have excellent hearing.

chipmunk
A burrowing and ground-dwelling type of squirrel that has cheek pouches to collect and hold food materials.

Monotremes

platypus
A semiaquatic mammal that lays eggs and has brown fur, a large bill and webbed feet.

humpback whale
A large whale with a curved back and very long fins. It is known for slapping the water with its tail and fins.

killer whale
An aquatic mammal with large teeth and a dorsal fin. It is also known as an orca whale.

caudal fin
The fin found at the end of the whale's vertebral column. It facilitates motion and steering.

caudal peduncle
The narrow part of a whale's body, located immediately in front of the caudal fin.

dorsal fin
A fin that is located on a whale's back. A humpback whale's dorsal fin is small and curved.

blowhole
One of two nostril-like holes found on a humpback whale's head, used in breathing.

rostrum
The upper jaw and snout of the humpback whale. This region of the whale's body allows it to manipulate its mouth.

mouth
The area of a whale's head through which food is taken in.

median notch
The indentation between the two parts of a whale's caudal fin.

pectoral fin
One of two fins on either side of a whale's body, used to control direction during swimming.

eye
A whale's sensory organ for vision. The eye detects light and movement.

throat groove
One of multiple grooves found on a whale's throat that help filter the water the whale takes in while feeding.

tubercle
One of multiple rounded projections located on the humpback whale's snout that improve fluid flow.

dolphin
An aquatic mammal with an elongated snout. It is an extremely intelligent and social animal.

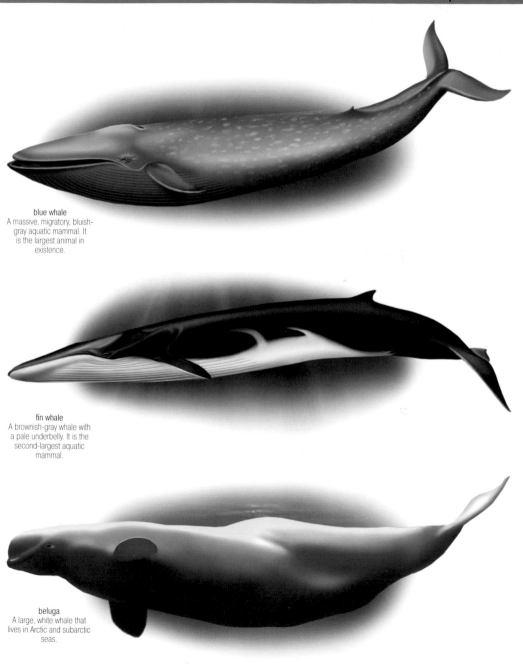

blue whale
A massive, migratory, bluish-gray aquatic mammal. It is the largest animal in existence.

fin whale
A brownish-gray whale with a pale underbelly. It is the second-largest aquatic mammal.

beluga
A large, white whale that lives in Arctic and subarctic seas.

Galápagos tortoise
A herbivorous turtle that can live a very long time. It is the largest living tortoise in existence.

costal scute
One of multiple bony plates of a tortoise's shell that protect its skeletal structure.

carapace
The upper part of a tortoise's shell. It includes dermal armor, scutes and the ribcage.

vertebral scute
The uppermost bony plate of a tortoise's shell, which protect its skeletal structure.

neck
The area of a tortoise's body that contains the cervical part of its spine. It connects the head to the body.

eye
A tortoise's sensory organ for vision. The eye detects light and movement.

horny beak
The sharp beak that is located on the tortoise's upper jaw. It is also known as the rhamphotheca.

marginal scute
One of multiple bony plates of a tortoise's shell that protect its skeletal structure.

mouth
The area of a tortoise's face through which food is taken in.

pygal plate
The most posterior part of a tortoise's body.

scale
A thin, hardened plate that is part of the outer layer of a tortoise's skin.

leg
One of a tortoise's four limbs.

claw
A pointed, sharp and curved nail that is located on the tips of a tortoise's digits.

plastron
The flat part of a tortoise's shell, located on the underside of its belly.

Blanding's turtle
A turtle with a bright yellow chin and throat. It is found in North America and is currently endangered.

green sea turtle
A large aquatic turtle with green flesh under its carapace. It is found in tropical and subtropical oceans.

chameleon
A lizard that is known for its
ability to change color.

iguana
A herbivorous lizard that is
green and has spines along
its back.

monitor lizard
A large, carnivorous
lizard with a long neck,
long claws and a long
tail. They are found
around the world.

gecko
A nocturnal, insectivorous
lizard that is known
for its adhesive feet.

common wall lizard
A small lizard that varies
in color. It is found in
North America and
Europe.

Cuban crocodile
A crocodile that is smaller
but more aggressive than
other species of crocodiles.
It is found only in Cuba.

caiman
A small crocodile that is
found in Central and South
America.

alligator
A large, crocodile-like
animal with thick skin and
sharp teeth. It originated in
North America.

Nile crocodile
A large crocodile that is
found in Africa. It is the
second-largest reptile in
existence.

Snakes

Reptiles with extendable jaws and no limbs or eyelids. Some species are venomous, and all vary in length.

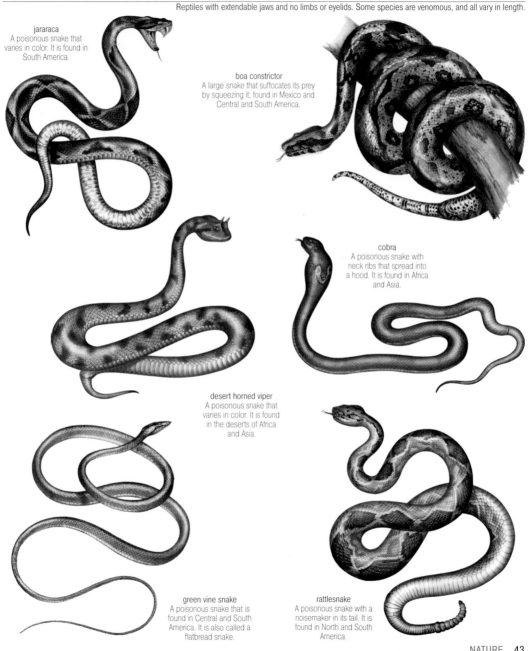

jararaca
A poisonous snake that
varies in color. It is found in
South America.

boa constrictor
A large snake that suffocates its prey
by squeezing it; found in Mexico and
Central and South America.

cobra
A poisonous snake with
neck ribs that spread into
a hood. It is found in Africa
and Asia.

desert horned viper
A poisonous snake that
varies in color. It is found
in the deserts of Africa
and Asia.

green vine snake
A poisonous snake that is
found in Central and South
America. It is also called a
flatbread snake.

rattlesnake
A poisonous snake with a
noisemaker in its tail. It is
found in North and South
America.

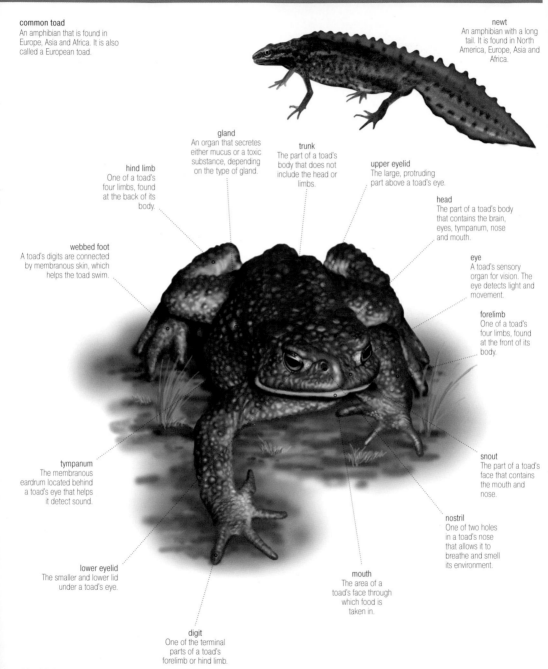

common toad
An amphibian that is found in Europe, Asia and Africa. It is also called a European toad.

newt
An amphibian with a long tail. It is found in North America, Europe, Asia and Africa.

gland
An organ that secretes either mucus or a toxic substance, depending on the type of gland.

hind limb
One of a toad's four limbs, found at the back of its body.

trunk
The part of a toad's body that does not include the head or limbs.

upper eyelid
The large, protruding part above a toad's eye.

head
The part of a toad's body that contains the brain, eyes, tympanum, nose and mouth.

webbed foot
A toad's digits are connected by membranous skin, which helps the toad swim.

eye
A toad's sensory organ for vision. The eye detects light and movement.

forelimb
One of a toad's four limbs, found at the front of its body.

tympanum
The membranous eardrum located behind a toad's eye that helps it detect sound.

snout
The part of a toad's face that contains the mouth and nose.

nostril
One of two holes in a toad's nose that allows it to breathe and smell its environment.

lower eyelid
The smaller and lower lid under a toad's eye.

mouth
The area of a toad's face through which food is taken in.

digit
One of the terminal parts of a toad's forelimb or hind limb.

salamander
An amphibian with scaleless, smooth skin that has bright marks and is moist to the touch.

cane toad
A large toad that originated in Central and South America. It is highly toxic if ingested.

common frog
A frog that varies in color. It is found in Europe and parts of Asia.

tree frog
It is usually lime green, sometimes with a translucent underbelly; found in Central and South America.

edible frog
A frog that is found in Europe and is commonly eaten.

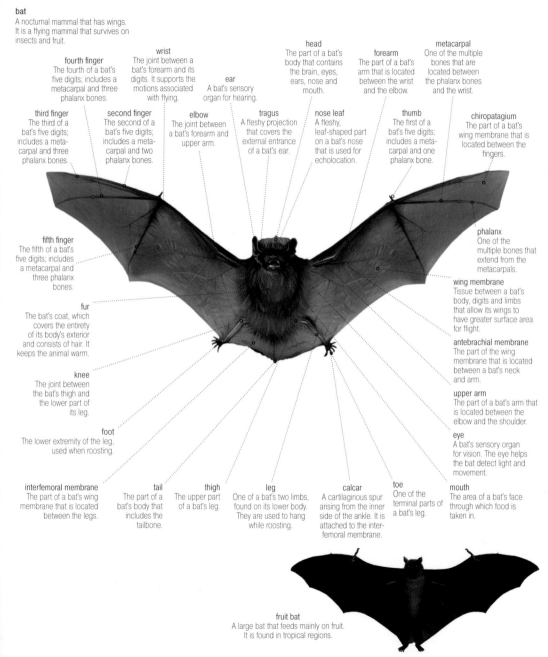

bat
A nocturnal mammal that has wings. It is a flying mammal that survives on insects and fruit.

fourth finger
The fourth of a bat's five digits; includes a metacarpal and three phalanx bones.

wrist
The joint between a bat's forearm and its digits. It supports the motions associated with flying.

head
The part of a bat's body that contains the brain, eyes, ears, nose and mouth.

forearm
The part of a bat's arm that is located between the wrist and the elbow.

metacarpal
One of the multiple bones that are located between the phalanx bones and the wrist.

third finger
The third of a bat's five digits; includes a metacarpal and three phalanx bones.

second finger
The second of a bat's five digits; includes a metacarpal and two phalanx bones.

elbow
The joint between a bat's forearm and upper arm.

ear
A bat's sensory organ for hearing.

tragus
A fleshy projection that covers the external entrance of a bat's ear.

nose leaf
A fleshy, leaf-shaped part on a bat's nose that is used for echolocation.

thumb
The first of a bat's five digits; includes a metacarpal and one phalanx bone.

chiropatagium
The part of a bat's wing membrane that is located between the fingers.

phalanx
One of the multiple bones that extend from the metacarpals.

fifth finger
The fifth of a bat's five digits; includes a metacarpal and three phalanx bones.

wing membrane
Tissue between a bat's body, digits and limbs that allow its wings to have greater surface area for flight.

fur
The bat's coat, which covers the entirety of its body's exterior and consists of hair. It keeps the animal warm.

antebrachial membrane
The part of the wing membrane that is located between a bat's neck and arm.

knee
The joint between the bat's thigh and the lower part of its leg.

upper arm
The part of a bat's arm that is located between the elbow and the shoulder.

foot
The lower extremity of the leg, used when roosting.

eye
A bat's sensory organ for vision. The eye helps the bat detect light and movement.

interfemoral membrane
The part of a bat's wing membrane that is located between the legs.

tail
The part of a bat's body that includes the tailbone.

thigh
The upper part of a bat's leg.

leg
One of a bat's two limbs, found on its lower body. They are used to hang while roosting.

calcar
A cartilaginous spur arising from the inner side of the ankle. It is attached to the interfemoral membrane.

toe
One of the terminal parts of a bat's leg.

mouth
The area of a bat's face through which food is taken in.

fruit bat
A large bat that feeds mainly on fruit. It is found in tropical regions.

mole
A small, insectivorous and burrowing rodent with a long snout, short fur and long claws.

head
The part of a mole's body that contains the brain, eyes, ears, nose and mouth.

eye
A mole's sensory organ for vision. Some moles have very limited vision, and some moles are totally blind.

body
The main torso area of the mole; it contains and protects the animal's inner organs.

snout
The part of a mole's face that contains the mouth and nose.

fur
The mole's coat, which covers the entirety of its body's exterior and consists of hair. It keeps the animal warm.

tail
The part of a mole's body that includes the tailbone.

finger
One of the terminal parts of a mole's forelimb.

claw
A pointed, sharp and curved nail that is located on the tips of a mole's fingers and toes.

forelimb
One of a mole's four limbs, found at the front of its body.

toe
One of the terminal parts of a mole's hind limb.

hind limb
One of a mole's four limbs that is found at the back of its body.

hedgehog
A brownish, nocturnal mammal that has spines on its back and can roll itself into a ball.

pangolin
A mammal that has a long snout, a long tongue and is covered in overlapping scales. It is found in Asia and Africa.

giant anteater
A large, insectivorous mammal with long fur, a long snout, large claws and a bushy tail.

armadillo
An omnivorous, nocturnal animal that has long claws and is covered in boney plates. It originated in South America.

Japanese macaque
A whitish brown monkey with cheek pouches and a short tail. It originated in Japan.

muzzle
An area of a macaque's face that consists mainly of its nose, mouth and jaw bones.

superciliary arch
The bony ridge on a macaque's face that is located above its eyes. It is also known as the brow ridge.

fur
The macaque's coat, which covers the entirety of its body's exterior and consists of hair. It keeps the animal warm.

face
The front area of a macaque's head, from its forehead to its chin.

knee
The joint that connects the upper and lower parts of a macaque's leg.

nose
The macaque's sensory organ for smell, and the area of the face through which air is taken in.

arm
One of a macaque's four limbs, found at the front of its body.

mouth
The area of a macaque's face through which food is taken in.

hand
A prehensile and multi-fingered extremity of each arm. They are used to grab objects and to assist with balance.

opposable digit
The first digit of a macaque's arm is opposable to its other digits and allows for grasping objects.

leg
One of a macaque's four limbs that is found at the back of its body.

digit
An elongated and usually jointed part of the hand or foot.

foot
The lower extremity of the leg; it is used for walking and balance and has numerous bones and muscles.

nail
A hardened covering at the tips of a macaque's digits.

chimpanzee
An intelligent and tree-dwelling ape with black hair and large ears. It is found in Africa.

baboon
A yellowish-brown monkey with strong jaws. It is found in Africa and Asia.

lemur
A nocturnal primate with short, wooly hair and a long tail. It is found in Madagascar.

lion tamarin
A small monkey with a
mane that surrounds its
face. It is found in the rain
forests of Brazil.

orangutan
A large, orange-brown, hairy
ape with long arms and
dark skin. It is found in Asia.

red howler monkey
A small monkey that is known for
its loud vocalization. It is found in
South America.

slow loris
A nocturnal primate with
large eyes and distinctive
markings on its face. It is
found in Asia.

mandrill
A medium-sized monkey
with a very colorful face and
body. It is found in Africa.

gorilla
A large, dark ape with
broad shoulders. It is found
in Africa.

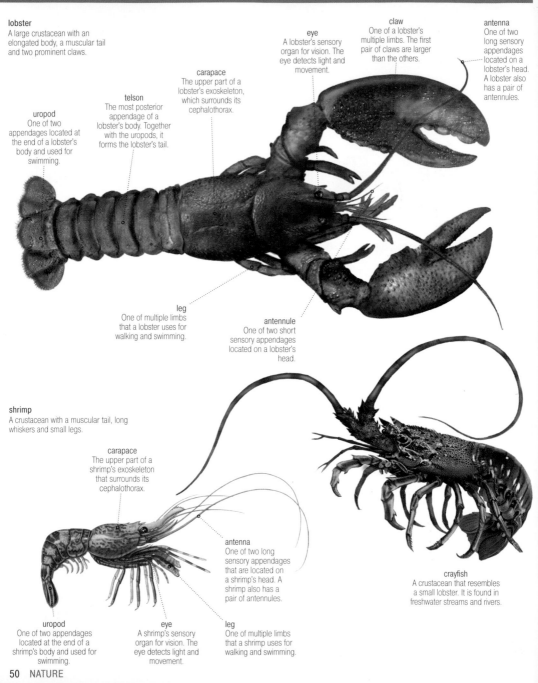

lobster
A large crustacean with an elongated body, a muscular tail and two prominent claws.

eye
A lobster's sensory organ for vision. The eye detects light and movement.

claw
One of a lobster's multiple limbs. The first pair of claws are larger than the others.

antenna
One of two long sensory appendages located on a lobster's head. A lobster also has a pair of antennules.

carapace
The upper part of a lobster's exoskeleton, which surrounds its cephalothorax.

telson
The most posterior appendage of a lobster's body. Together with the uropods, it forms the lobster's tail.

uropod
One of two appendages located at the end of a lobster's body and used for swimming.

leg
One of multiple limbs that a lobster uses for walking and swimming.

antennule
One of two short sensory appendages located on a lobster's head.

shrimp
A crustacean with a muscular tail, long whiskers and small legs.

carapace
The upper part of a shrimp's exoskeleton that surrounds its cephalothorax.

antenna
One of two long sensory appendages that are located on a shrimp's head. A shrimp also has a pair of antennules.

crayfish
A crustacean that resembles a small lobster. It is found in freshwater streams and rivers.

uropod
One of two appendages located at the end of a shrimp's body and used for swimming.

eye
A shrimp's sensory organ for vision. The eye detects light and movement.

leg
One of multiple limbs that a shrimp uses for walking and swimming.

mackerel
A surface-dwelling, predatory fish found in North and South America, Europe and Asia.

trout
A freshwater fish that is widely fished. It is found in North America, Europe and Asia.

carp
A freshwater fish that has barbels around its mouth and is commercially fished.

haddock
A bottom-dwelling fish that is widely used for food. It lives in the Atlantic ocean.

perch
An edible freshwater fish with a high, spiny dorsal fin. It is found in North America, Europe and Asia.

largemouth bass
A freshwater fish that is used for food. It is found worldwide.

damselfish
A saltwater fish that is often brightly colored. Some species live in freshwater.

tilapia
A fish that is widely used for food and is found worldwide. Most species live in freshwater.

snout
The part of a skate's body that contains the mouth and sensory organs.

skate
A large cartilaginous fish that is known to rest on the ocean floor to ambush its prey.

eye
A skate's sensory organ for vision. The eye detects light and movement.

spiracle
A round opening that is located behind a skate's eyes. It is used for breathing.

sole
A bottom-dwelling fish that is widely used for food. It is found worldwide.

pelvic fin
One of two fins found on either side of a skate's cloaca that maintain stability during swimming.

pectoral fin
One of two fins found on either side of a skate's body that is used to control direction during swimming.

caudal fin
The fin found at the end of the vertebral column. It facilitates motion and steering.

cod
A bottom-dwelling fish with a whisker-like projection on its chin. It is found in cold marine water.

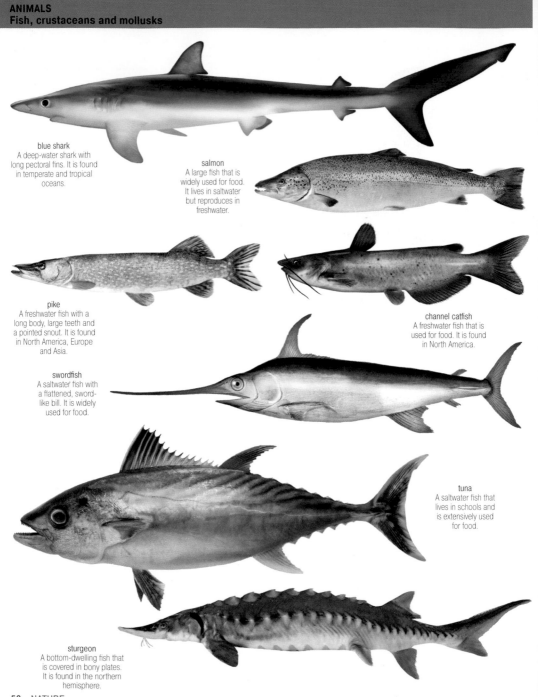

blue shark
A deep-water shark with long pectoral fins. It is found in temperate and tropical oceans.

salmon
A large fish that is widely used for food. It lives in saltwater but reproduces in freshwater.

pike
A freshwater fish with a long body, large teeth and a pointed snout. It is found in North America, Europe and Asia.

channel catfish
A freshwater fish that is used for food. It is found in North America.

swordfish
A saltwater fish with a flattened, sword-like bill. It is widely used for food.

tuna
A saltwater fish that lives in schools and is extensively used for food.

sturgeon
A bottom-dwelling fish that is covered in bony plates. It is found in the northern hemisphere.

mantle
An area of the octopus's body that can draw and expel water. It can also change color to fool predators.

siphon
A muscular, tube-like part of an octopus's mantle that aims water to help with swimming.

eye
The octopus's sensory organ for vision. The eye detects light and movement.

octopus
A mollusk with two eyes and eight appendages. It is known for its ability to expel ink.

arm
An octopus's flexible limb, used for grasping and movement.

sucker
A muscular part of an octopus's arm that allows attachment, grasping and tasting.

crab
A crustacean with stalked eyes and a pair of chelipeds. Depending on the species, it lives in water or on land.

eyestalk
A protruding structure on a crab's head that allows the eyes to be extended for better vision.

antenna
One of two short sensory appendages located on a crab's head. A crab also has antennules.

leg
One of multiple limbs that a crab uses for walking and swimming.

cheliped
A crab's limb that has a claw.

carapace
The upper part of a crab's exoskeleton that surrounds its cephalothorax.

Eurasian jay
A bird with a crested crown and pink-brown feathers that is native to Eurasia.

crown
The uppermost area of a bird's head. Some species have a crest on their head.

nape
The upper part of a bird's neck.

shoulder
The joint that connects a bird's wing to its body. It contains three bones: clavicle, scapula and humerus.

back
The area of a bird's body that is formed by the length of its vertebral column.

scapular feathers
The feathers that originate on a bird's shoulder.

auricular region
The area of a bird's head that covers the opening of the ear.

tertial feathers
The innermost of the large feathers on a bird's wing.

forehead
The area of a bird's face below the crown and above the eyes and bill.

secondary feathers
The feathers that originate on a bird's ulna. They are located between the primaries and the tertials.

eye
A bird's sensory organ for vision. The eye detects light and movement.

flank
The area of a bird's body between its belly and the underside of its wings.

upper mandible
The upper part of a bird's bill.

primary feathers
The large feathers that originate on a bird's metacarpals. They are the main flight feathers.

lower mandible
The lower part of a bird's bill.

upper-tail covert feathers
The small feathers above a bird's tail.

tongue
A bird's tongue is involved in tasting, eating and manipulating objects.

lore
The area that is located between the eye and the bill.

tail feathers
The feathers that originate on a bird's tail.

chin
The area that is located above the throat and below the bill.

under-tail covert feathers
The small feathers under a bird's tail.

malar region
The area that is located in front of and below a bird's eyes.

belly
The lowest surface of a bird's body.

foot
The lower extremity of the leg, used for walking.

greater covert feathers
The feathers that overlap the secondaries.

throat
The front part of a bird's neck, sometimes with a characteristic pattern or color.

toe
The part of a bird's leg that contains three phalanx bones: proximal, middle and distal.

hind toe
A toe at the back of a bird's foot that allows perching and grabbing objects.

tarsus
The part of a bird's leg between the foot and the tibia and fibula. It is also called a shank.

breast
The front area of a bird's body, often with a characteristic pattern or color.

claw
A pointed, sharp and curved nail located on the tips of a bird's toes.

median covert feathers
The feathers that overlap the greater coverts.

Eurasian siskin
A songbird with yellow and greenish feathers. It is found in Europe and Asia.

bullfinch
A songbird that varies in color and has a strong bill. It is found worldwide.

common swift
A medium-sized bird with short legs and a short, forked tail. It is found in Europe, Asia and Africa.

greater titmouse
A small woodland bird with a short, strong bill. It is found in Europe and Asia.

pigeon
A songbird with a stout body, a small head and short legs.

blue jay
A medium-sized bird with blue and white feathers, and a crest on its head. It is known to be noisy.

red-backed shrike
A carnivorous bird with a reddish back, hooked bill and a black mask.

woodpecker
A bird with a strong bill for drilling and drumming on trees. It has a sticky tongue to extract food.

hummingbird
A very small bird that is often brightly colored and beats its wings extremely fast.

black-capped chickadee
A small bird with light brown sides and distinctive black and white markings on its head and throat.

kingfisher
A brightly colored bird with a long, sharp bill for catching fish.

barn swallow
A small bird with a reddish forehead, chin and throat and a deeply forked tail.

cockatiel
A crested Australian bird that has a grayish body and characteristically orange cheeks.

American goldfinch
A songbird with a black forehead and a bright yellow body. It is common in fields and gardens.

cardinal
A songbird with a crest and a strong bill.

American robin
A songbird with a reddish breast and a gray-brown body. It is known for its melodious singing.

American crow
A black bird with a strong bill that is known to be very intelligent. It is common in human-inhabited areas.

thrush
A songbird with brown feathers and a spotted throat and breast. They are known for their melodious singing.

nightingale
A songbird that is known for its beautiful song. It sings during the day and at night.

sparrow
A common, small, brownish-gray songbird with a strong, short bill.

starling
A songbird that is known for its ability to imitate the sounds of other birds.

owl
A nocturnal bird of prey with large eyes and a hooked bill. It can vary widely in size and color.

stork
A large wading bird with very long legs, a long neck and a long bill.

partridge
A bird that varies in color and spends much of its time on the ground.

gyrfalcon
A bird of prey that lives on Arctic coasts. It is the largest species of falcon in existence.

condor
A very large scavenger bird with
a featherless head and dark
feathers.

ruffed grouse
A medium-sized bird with
barred, brown or gray
feathers. It lives in mixed
forests.

bald eagle
A large, white-headed bird
of prey.

rooster
A male chicken. It is common
in agricultural settings.

ostrich
A flightless bird with long
legs, a long neck and two
toes on each foot.

sharp-tailed grouse
A medium-sized bird with
barred, brown feathers and
a pointed tail. It lives in
grassland areas.

peacock
The male bird has large,
bright blue and green
tail feathers that have
eye-like markings on
their tips.

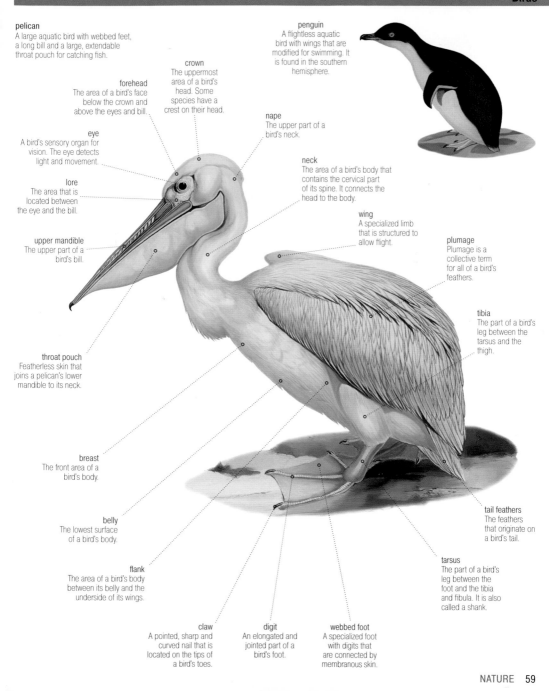

pelican
A large aquatic bird with webbed feet, a long bill and a large, extendable throat pouch for catching fish.

penguin
A flightless aquatic bird with wings that are modified for swimming. It is found in the southern hemisphere.

crown
The uppermost area of a bird's head. Some species have a crest on their head.

forehead
The area of a bird's face below the crown and above the eyes and bill.

nape
The upper part of a bird's neck.

eye
A bird's sensory organ for vision. The eye detects light and movement.

neck
The area of a bird's body that contains the cervical part of its spine. It connects the head to the body.

lore
The area that is located between the eye and the bill.

wing
A specialized limb that is structured to allow flight.

plumage
Plumage is a collective term for all of a bird's feathers.

upper mandible
The upper part of a bird's bill.

tibia
The part of a bird's leg between the tarsus and the thigh.

throat pouch
Featherless skin that joins a pelican's lower mandible to its neck.

breast
The front area of a bird's body.

tail feathers
The feathers that originate on a bird's tail.

belly
The lowest surface of a bird's body.

tarsus
The part of a bird's leg between the foot and the tibia and fibula. It is also called a shank.

flank
The area of a bird's body between its belly and the underside of its wings.

claw
A pointed, sharp and curved nail that is located on the tips of a bird's toes.

digit
An elongated and jointed part of a bird's foot.

webbed foot
A specialized foot with digits that are connected by membranous skin.

albatross
A seabird with webbed feet for swimming and long wings for gliding.

mallard duck
An aquatic bird with a flat bill and webbed feet.

tern
A shorebird with a forked tail, a pointed bill, and long, narrow wings.

gull
A shorebird with whitish-gray feathers that is known for scavenging and being noisy.

swan
An aquatic bird with a long neck, black legs and webbed feet.

flamingo
A wading bird with a long neck, long legs and characteristically pink plumage.

goose
An aquatic bird with a flat bill, a long neck and webbed feet.

heron
A wading bird with long legs, a long neck and a long bill.

Arachnids
Invertebrates with a hard exoskeleton, segmented body and eight legs.

femur
The third segment of a scorpion's limb. It is typically the longest and strongest segment.

mesosoma
The first part of the opisthosoma.

telson
The most posterior part of a scorpion's body. It contains the aculeus and the poison glands.

scorpion
An arachnid that is known for its pincers and its poisonous stinger. It lives in warm and dry regions.

patella
The fourth segment of a scorpion's limb. It is located between the femur and the tibia.

aculeus
The stinger. The scorpion injects poison through the aculeus.

pedipalp
One of the first two of a scorpion's limbs. They originate on the prosoma.

metasoma
The second part of the opisthosoma. It contains the telson and the aculeus.

chela
A pincer-like claw that is located on a pedipalp. It is used for attack and defense.

trochanter
The second segment of a scorpion's limb. It is located between the coxa and the femur.

leg
One of the multiple legs, which originate on the prosoma.

chelicerae
Pincer-like appendages that are used to rip food into smaller pieces.

prosoma
The most anterior segment of the body, which contains the head, chelicerae, pedipalps and legs.

tarsus
The terminal segment of a pedipalp.

tibia
The second-last segment of a scorpion's limb.

black widow
A poisonous spider with a characteristic red hourglass shape on its abdomen. It is found worldwide.

ladybird spider
A spider often identified by its bright red abdomen spotted with large black dots. It is found in Europe.

water spider
A spider that spins webs to form air-filled chambers for breathing. It is the only spider that lives underwater.

tick
A small arachnid that is known to bury its head into an animal's body to feed on its blood.

European garden spider
This spider specializes in spinning orb webs. It is found in North America and Europe.

crab spider
A spider with long forelegs. It is commonly seen moving in a sideways motion, similar to a crab.

tarantula
A large and often hairy spider. It is found worldwide.

woodlouse spider
A spider with a shiny abdomen that feeds only on woodlice. It is found worldwide.

Beetles

Insects whose forewings are modified into harder sheaths that protect the hind wings.

Hercules beetle
A type of rhinoceros beetle that is found in tropical areas. The male beetles have two long horns.

elytron
One of two forewings that are modified into wing sheaths.

suture
The line or groove that separates the wings.

scutellum
The triangular area on the upper surface of the thorax, behind the pronotum.

compound eye
The organ for vision; it is made up of many units, which each sense part of what is being viewed.

hind leg
The back-most of the beetle's six legs, which all originate on the thorax.

pronotum
The hardened plate on the first segment of the thorax.

pronotal horn
A large horn that originates on the pronotum.

cephalic horn
A large horn that originates on the head.

tarsus
The terminal segment of a beetle's leg.

tibia
The second-last segment of a beetle's leg, located between the tarsus and the femur.

head
The most anterior segment of the body. It contains the eyes, mouthparts and antennae.

middle leg
The central of the beetle's six legs, which all originate on the thorax.

mouthparts
Paired appendages that are used for feeding.

femur
The third segment of a beetle's leg. It is typically the longest and strongest segment.

palpus
One of two sensory appendages that are located in the area of the mouthparts.

spur
A spur improves a beetle's grip on its prey and on various surfaces.

abdomen
The most posterior segment of the body.

thorax
The middle segment of the body. It is located between the head and the abdomen.

foreleg
The front-most of the beetle's six legs, which all originate on the thorax.

claw
Claws improve a beetle's grip on various surfaces.

antenna
One of two sensory appendages that are located on a beetle's head.

shard beetle
A dung beetle that is known for placing dung in its burrow before it lays eggs.

whirligig beetle
A beetle that swims on the surface of water and has two pairs of compound eyes.

burying beetle
A beetle that buries carrion to feed its larvae.

Carabus problematicus (Lat.)
A black beetle with a blue pronotum and blue elytral margins. It is found in Europe.

furniture beetle
A wood-boring beetle that lays its eggs in cracks of wood. Its larvae are known to destroy furniture.

Sagra buqueti (Lat.)
An iridescent beetle with strong hind legs. It is found in Southeast Asia.

black vine weevil
A black, flightless beetle whose elytra are fused together. It is found in North America and Europe.

cockchafer
A brownish beetle that is known to damage foliage and roots. It is found in Europe.

ladybug
A small beetle that has red wings with black spots.

thick-legged flower beetle
An elongated beetle with a shimmery green body. It is found in Europe.

rhinoceros beetle
A large beetle with two prominent horns. It is found worldwide.

stag beetle
A large beetle with mandibles that resemble antlers. It is found in Europe.

Colorado potato beetle
A beetle with black and yellow stripes. It is known to destroy potato crops.

rose chafer
A green or copper-colored beetle that feeds on flowers and is found in North America and Europe.

goliath beetle
A very large beetle with distinctive black and white markings. It is found in Africa.

larch ladybug
A beetle with light to dark brown wings. It is found in North America and Europe.

dung beetle
A large beetle that feeds exclusively on dung. It is found worldwide.

flower beetle
A beetle that is often greenish in color and is seen on or near flowers. It is found worldwide.

golden scarab beetle
A gold-colored beetle that is found only in Central America.

Butterflies and moths

Insects with a proboscis and wings that are covered in scales and are often colorful and patterned.

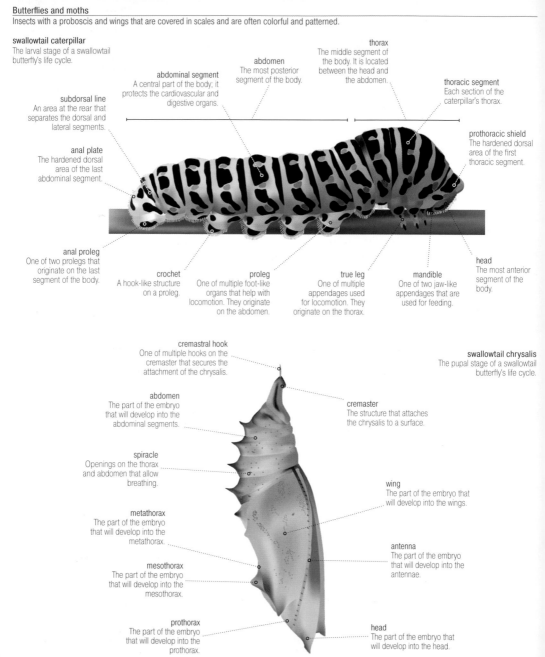

swallowtail caterpillar
The larval stage of a swallowtail butterfly's life cycle.

thorax
The middle segment of the body. It is located between the head and the abdomen.

abdomen
The most posterior segment of the body.

abdominal segment
A central part of the body; it protects the cardiovascular and digestive organs.

thoracic segment
Each section of the caterpillar's thorax.

subdorsal line
An area at the rear that separates the dorsal and lateral segments.

prothoracic shield
The hardened dorsal area of the first thoracic segment.

anal plate
The hardened dorsal area of the last abdominal segment.

anal proleg
One of two prolegs that originate on the last segment of the body.

crochet
A hook-like structure on a proleg.

proleg
One of multiple foot-like organs that help with locomotion. They originate on the abdomen.

true leg
One of multiple appendages used for locomotion. They originate on the thorax.

mandible
One of two jaw-like appendages that are used for feeding.

head
The most anterior segment of the body.

cremastral hook
One of multiple hooks on the cremaster that secures the attachment of the chrysalis.

swallowtail chrysalis
The pupal stage of a swallowtail butterfly's life cycle.

abdomen
The part of the embryo that will develop into the abdominal segments.

cremaster
The structure that attaches the chrysalis to a surface.

spiracle
Openings on the thorax and abdomen that allow breathing.

wing
The part of the embryo that will develop into the wings.

metathorax
The part of the embryo that will develop into the metathorax.

antenna
The part of the embryo that will develop into the antennae.

mesothorax
The part of the embryo that will develop into the mesothorax.

prothorax
The part of the embryo that will develop into the prothorax.

head
The part of the embryo that will develop into the head.

tiger swallowtail
A yellow and black butterfly with long tails on its hind wings. It is found in North America.

club
The thickened ends of a butterfly's antennae.

scape
The base of a butterfly's antenna.

pedicel
The second of three segments of a butterfly's antenna.

flagellum
The third of three segments of a butterfly's antenna.

head
The most anterior segment of the body. It contains the eyes, mouthparts and antennae.

antenna
One of two sensory appendages that are located on a butterfly's head.

thorax
The middle segment of the body. It is located between the head and the abdomen.

labial palpus
A jointed sensory appendage that is part of a butterfly's mouthparts.

costa
The most anterior edge of a butterfly's wing.

compound eye
The organ for vision; it is made up of many units, which each sense part of what is being viewed.

forewing
One of two wings that are located in front of the smaller hind wings.

apex
The anterior corner of a butterfly's wing.

wing vein
Tubular pathway that carries oxygen and supports the wings.

outer margin
The outer edge of an Old World Swallowtail's triangular-shaped wing that is typically black in color.

wing cell
An area of the wing that is surrounded by veins.

tornus
The posterior corner of a butterfly's wing.

inner margin
A component of the wing of a butterfly that Is located between colored stripes and helps to confuse predators.

hind wing
One of two wings that are located behind the larger forewings.

base
The region of the Swallowtail butterfly's body that is responsible for connecting its wings to its thorax.

hind wing tornus
The back corner of a butterfly's hind wing.

abdomen
The most posterior segment of the body.

abdominal segment
One of the 10 abdominal segments of a Swallowtail butterfly that is responsible for housing various organs.

eyespot
A marking that resembles an eye. It deceives potential predators.

Adonis blue
A butterfly with bright blue wings. It is found in Europe and Asia.

clothes moth
A small moth whose larvae feed on fabric and that is known to damage clothing.

lappet moth
A small, brown moth that has a hairy appearance. It is found worldwide.

cabbage white
A medium-sized butterfly with white wings. It is found worldwide.

silkmoth
A moth that is used in the production of silk. It is a domesticated moth that originated in Asia.

monarch butterfly
A large butterfly with orange and black markings. It feeds on milkweed and is found worldwide.

buff-tip
A large gray moth with cream-colored tips; it resembles a broken twig when at rest.

scarce swallowtail
A multicolored butterfly with long tails on its hind wings. It is found in Europe.

brimstone
A butterfly with bright yellow wings. It is found in South America, Europe, Africa and Asia.

Apollo
A mountain species of butterfly with pale wings and red eyespots. It is found in Europe and central Asia.

luna moth
A pale green moth with long tails on its hind wings.

black-veined white
A butterfly with white wings and black veins that feeds on fruit trees. It is found in North America, Europe and Asia.

blue morpho
A large butterfly with bright blue wings. It is found in North, South and Central America.

Brahmin moth
A large moth with brown and black patterns on its wings. It is found in Asia.

divana diva
A moth with blue and black wings that is commonly mistaken for a butterfly. It is found in Central America.

purple emperor
A large butterfly with purple-blue wings. It is found in Europe and Asia.

Hercules moth
A very large, brown moth with long tails on its hind wings. It is found in Australia and New Guinea.

spear-marked black moth
A wetland moth with black-and-white wings. It is found in the northern hemisphere.

Wasps and wasp-like insects

Insects whose larger forewings are attached to their smaller hind wings by hooks.

wasp
A winged insect with a narrow waist and a large stinger. It can be recognized by its black and yellow stripes.

wing
A specialized appendage that allows a wasp to fly.

tergum
The thick, plate-like portion of the dorsal segments of a wasp's abdomen.

metathorax
The last segment of the thorax.

mesothorax
The middle segment of the thorax. It is located between the prothorax and the metathorax.

thorax
The middle segment of the body. It is located between the head and the abdomen.

abdomen
The most posterior segment of the body.

wing cell
An area of the wing that is surrounded by veins.

wing vein
Tubular pathway that carries oxygen and supports the wings.

prothorax
The first segment of the thorax.

aculeus
The stinger. The wasp injects poison through the aculeus.

vertex
The most anterior and widest part of a wasp's head.

hind leg
The back-most of the wasp's six legs, which all originate on the thorax.

ocelli
One of multiple simple eyes on a wasp's head.

claw
Claws improve a wasp's grip on various surfaces.

antenna
One of two sensory appendages that are located on a wasp's head.

tibia
The second-last segment of a wasp's leg. It is located between the metatarsus and the femur.

coxa
The first segment of a wasp's leg.

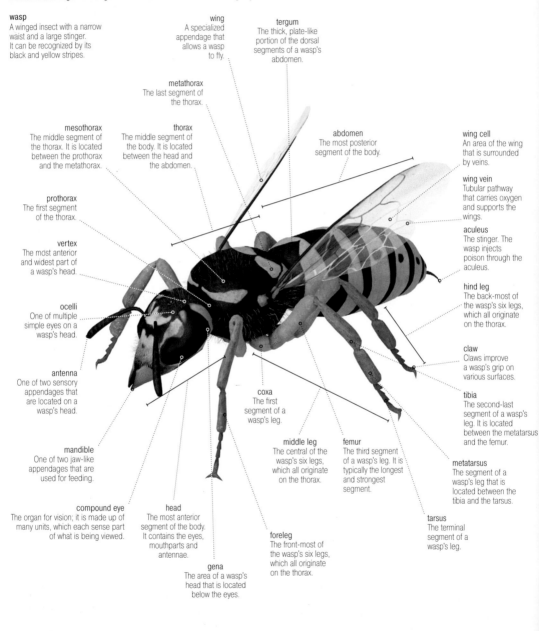

mandible
One of two jaw-like appendages that are used for feeding.

middle leg
The central of the wasp's six legs, which all originate on the thorax.

femur
The third segment of a wasp's leg. It is typically the longest and strongest segment.

metatarsus
The segment of a wasp's leg that is located between the tibia and the tarsus.

compound eye
The organ for vision; it is made up of many units, which each sense part of what is being viewed.

head
The most anterior segment of the body. It contains the eyes, mouthparts and antennae.

foreleg
The front-most of the wasp's six legs, which all originate on the thorax.

tarsus
The terminal segment of a wasp's leg.

gena
The area of a wasp's head that is located below the eyes.

ant
A small insect that forms large colonies. It can lift many times its own body weight.

buff-tailed bumblebee
One of the largest bumblebees. It originated in Europe but has been introduced in other parts of the world.

hornet
A large insect with a wide head. It is found mostly in the northern hemisphere.

red wood ant
A reddish-brown ant that builds large mounds in grasslands. It is found in North America, Europe and Asia.

honey bee
A black-and-yellow insect that collects nectar and is commonly farmed for producing honey.

mud dauber
An insect that builds its nest using mud.

True flies
Insects that have only one pair of functional wings.

horsefly
A medium-sized fly that is commonly known for biting and annoying humans and livestock.

common housefly
The most common fly in human-inhabited areas. It is known to carry diseases.

flesh fly
A fly that is oviparous and lays larvae on decaying matter, dung or in open animal wounds.

little housefly
A fly that is smaller than a common housefly and has a slender and agile body.

blackfly
A fly that commonly feeds on the blood of mammals and can carry serious diseases.

blowfly
A metallic blue, green or black fly. It feeds on dung and decaying animal flesh.

mosquito
A long-legged flying insect. Female mosquitoes feed on animal blood and can transmit diseases.

tsetse fly
A fly that feeds on animal blood and can carry serious diseases.

Neoptera
Insects that can fold their wings over their abdomen.

mantis
A large flying insect with a long, thin body and characteristic raptorial forelegs.

tegmen
Modified forewings that shield the flying hind wings.

metathorax
The last segment of the thorax.

mesothorax
The middle segment of the thorax. It is located between the prothorax and the metathorax.

prothorax
The first segment of the thorax.

antenna
One of two sensory appendages that are located on the head.

flying hind wing
One of two wings that a mantis uses for flight.

eye
A mantis's sensory organ for vision. The eye detects light and movement.

coxa
The first segment of a mantis's leg.

head
The most anterior segment of the body. It contains the eyes, mouthparts and antennae.

abdomen
The most posterior segment of the body.

mouthparts
Paired appendages that are used for feeding.

trochanter
The second segment of a mantis's leg. It is located between the coxa and the femur.

spur
Spurs improve a mantis's grip on its prey. The mantis has multiple spurs.

tibia
The second-last segment of a mantis's leg. It is located between the tarsus and the femur.

femur
The third segment of a mantis's leg. It is typically the longest and strongest segment.

raptorial foreleg
One of a mantis's legs that is modified for capturing prey.

tarsus
The terminal segment of a mantis's leg.

louse
A tiny, flightless, parasitic insect that feeds on the blood of most animals.

flea
A small, wingless, jumping insect that feeds on the blood of mammals and birds.

termite
An ant-like insect that lives in large colonies in mounds of dirt. It is known to voraciously eat wood.

grasshopper
A plant-eating insect with long hind legs that are specialized for jumping.

locust
A species of grasshopper that has a swarming phase in its life cycle. Locust swarms can be very destructive to crops.

Madagascar hissing cockroach
A large cockroach that is characterized by the hissing sound it makes. It originated in Madagascar.

earwig
An insect that has pincer-like appendages on its abdomen and segmented antennae. It is found worldwide.

stinkbug
An insect that varies in color and emits a strong odor when it's disturbed.

firebug
A bright red insect with distinctive black markings. It is found in North America, Europe and Asia.

American cockroach
A large, winged insect that can carry diseases. It is found worldwide.

Odonata

A variety of carnivorous insects that includes both dragonflies and damselflies.

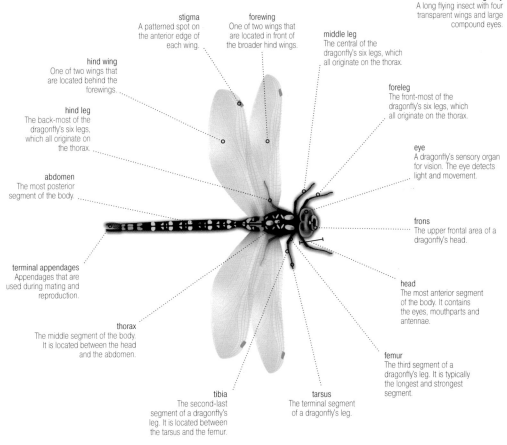

dragonfly
A long flying insect with four transparent wings and large compound eyes.

stigma
A patterned spot on the anterior edge of each wing.

forewing
One of two wings that are located in front of the broader hind wings.

middle leg
The central of the dragonfly's six legs, which all originate on the thorax.

hind wing
One of two wings that are located behind the forewings.

foreleg
The front-most of the dragonfly's six legs, which all originate on the thorax.

hind leg
The back-most of the dragonfly's six legs, which all originate on the thorax.

eye
A dragonfly's sensory organ for vision. The eye detects light and movement.

abdomen
The most posterior segment of the body.

frons
The upper frontal area of a dragonfly's head.

terminal appendages
Appendages that are used during mating and reproduction.

head
The most anterior segment of the body. It contains the eyes, mouthparts and antennae.

thorax
The middle segment of the body. It is located between the head and the abdomen.

femur
The third segment of a dragonfly's leg. It is typically the longest and strongest segment.

tibia
The second-last segment of a dragonfly's leg. It is located between the tarsus and the femur.

tarsus
The terminal segment of a dragonfly's leg.

Worms and worm-like insects

Worms are tube-like invertebrates that are flexible, have no limbs and commonly live underground.

millipede
A long insect with two pairs of legs on most of its body segments. It feeds on dead leaves.

earthworm
A segmented worm that lives in soil or leaf matter. It is found worldwide.

plant cell
A microscopic structure that is the fundamental biological building block of plant life.

chloroplast
A membranous organelle that is the site of photosynthesis. It contains chlorophyll.

ribosome
An organelle that synthesizes proteins.

vacuole
A large, membranous organelle that contains water and other substances.

cell wall
A strong layer surrounding the cell that maintains the cell's shape and protects the organelles.

plasmodesma
A tubular extension of the cell membrane that connects the cytoplasm of adjacent cells.

Golgi apparatus
An organelle that modifies and packages proteins. It is also called a Golgi body.

nucleolus
The site of ribosome synthesis.

nucleus
A membranous organelle that contains the genetic material of a cell.

endoplasmic reticulum
The site of protein or lipid synthesis, depending on the presence of ribosomes.

cytoplasm
A gel-like substance that allows suspension of the organelles of a cell.

mitochondrion
A membranous organelle that synthesizes energy for a cell.

coffee
A tropical flowering plant whose seeds are grown commercially and sold as coffee beans.

coffee bean
The seed of the coffee plant. Coffee beans are commonly roasted and used to make coffee.

leaf
A part of a plant that is often thin and flat, and the site of energy production for the plant.

branch
The part of a woody plant that grows out of its trunk and often bears smaller branches, leaves, fruits or seeds.

trunk
The main axis of a woody plant; it helps transfer nutrients between roots and leaves.

lavender
A small, aromatic, silvery green shrub commonly used in perfumes and medicines.

oat
A type of grass that is grown for its seeds as food. It is often sold as rolled oats and as livestock feed.

cotton
A plant that is grown commercially for the soft, white, fibrous material that it produces.

grape
A woody vine that produces fruits that are commonly used for wine production.

vine shoot
The vine's climbing branch, which supports the grapes.

fruit
The grape plant produces sweet fruits called grapes. They typically ripen at the end of a summer season.

leaf
A part of a plant that is often thin and flat, and the site of energy production for the plant.

trunk
The main axis of a woody plant; it helps transfer nutrients between roots and leaves.

support
A structural framework that is commonly used by gardeners to structurally support climbing plants.

tea
An evergreen shrub that is grown commercially for its leaves, which are steeped to produce a hot drink.

sunflower
A tall flowering plant that has large yellow flowers with large black seeds in the center.

soybean
A small leguminous plant that is grown commercially for its seeds, which are high in protein.

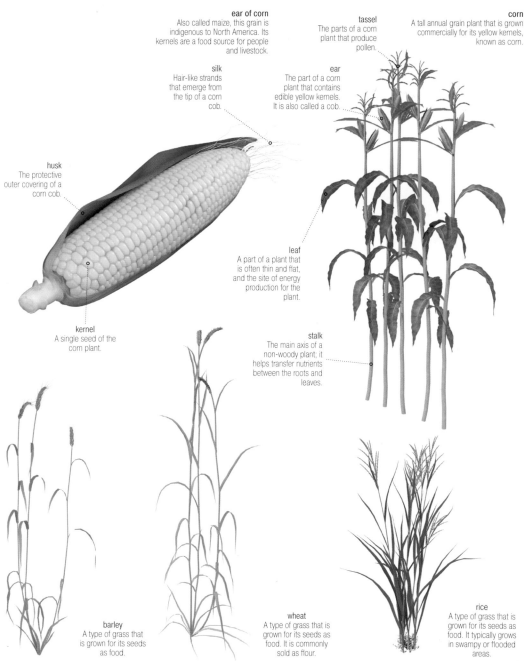

ear of corn
Also called maize, this grain is indigenous to North America. Its kernels are a food source for people and livestock.

tassel
The parts of a corn plant that produce pollen.

corn
A tall annual grain plant that is grown commercially for its yellow kernels, known as corn.

silk
Hair-like strands that emerge from the tip of a corn cob.

ear
The part of a corn plant that contains edible yellow kernels. It is also called a cob.

husk
The protective outer covering of a corn cob.

leaf
A part of a plant that is often thin and flat, and the site of energy production for the plant.

kernel
A single seed of the corn plant.

stalk
The main axis of a non-woody plant; it helps transfer nutrients between the roots and leaves.

barley
A type of grass that is grown for its seeds as food.

wheat
A type of grass that is grown for its seeds as food. It is commonly sold as flour.

rice
A type of grass that is grown for its seeds as food. It typically grows in swampy or flooded areas.

geranium
A plant that is grown for its flowers, which vary in color.

flower
The flower contains the reproductive parts of a plant.

petal
One of several modified leaves of a flower. Petals are often colorful, to attract pollinators.

flower bud
An undeveloped part of a plant that eventually develops into a flower.

stalk
The main axis of a non-woody plant; it helps transfer nutrients between the roots and leaves.

leaf
A part of a plant that is often thin and flat, and the site of energy production for the plant.

marigold
A plant that is grown for its flowers, which are usually yellow or orange.

calla lily
A plant with arrow-shaped leaves and a colorful spathe that is commonly mistaken for a flower.

hydrangea
A shrubby plant with rounded flowerheads that can be white, pink, purple or blue.

Fruits and vegetables
Plants that are grown for their nutritional value. They are eaten cooked or raw.

strawberry
A low-growing flowering plant that is grown for its sweet fruit.

flower
The flower contains the reproductive parts of a plant.

unripe berry
A berry that is still undeveloped and is usually green or greenish.

leaf
A part of a plant that is often thin and flat, and the site of energy production for the plant.

stem
A part of a plant that facilitates the transfer of nutrients between roots and leaves.

berry
A rounded, fleshy fruit that has no core structure and may have many small seeds.

broccoli
A vegetable from the cabbage family that is grown for its edible green flowerheads.

lettuce
A vegetable from the daisy family that is grown for its crunchy, delicate leaves.

cauliflower
A vegetable from the cabbage family that is grown for its edible white flowerheads.

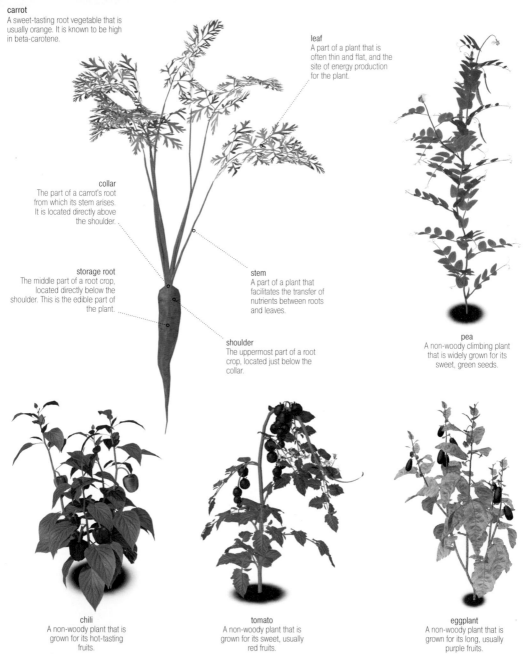

carrot
A sweet-tasting root vegetable that is usually orange. It is known to be high in beta-carotene.

leaf
A part of a plant that is often thin and flat, and the site of energy production for the plant.

collar
The part of a carrot's root from which its stem arises. It is located directly above the shoulder.

storage root
The middle part of a root crop, located directly below the shoulder. This is the edible part of the plant.

stem
A part of a plant that facilitates the transfer of nutrients between roots and leaves.

shoulder
The uppermost part of a root crop, located just below the collar.

pea
A non-woody climbing plant that is widely grown for its sweet, green seeds.

chili
A non-woody plant that is grown for its hot-tasting fruits.

tomato
A non-woody plant that is grown for its sweet, usually red fruits.

eggplant
A non-woody plant that is grown for its long, usually purple fruits.

zucchini
A long, dark green squash. It ripens from early to late summer and is commonly called a summer squash.

squash
A plant that is grown for the flesh and seeds of its fruit. It is commonly called a winter squash.

watermelon
A plant that produces melons that are known for their sweet flesh, which is usually red.

cantaloupe
A plant that produces melons that are known for their sweet, orange flesh. It is also called muskmelon.

onion
A plant that is grown mainly for its edible bulb, which is composed of multiple white or yellowish layers.

cucumber
A plant that is grown for its cylindrical green fruit.

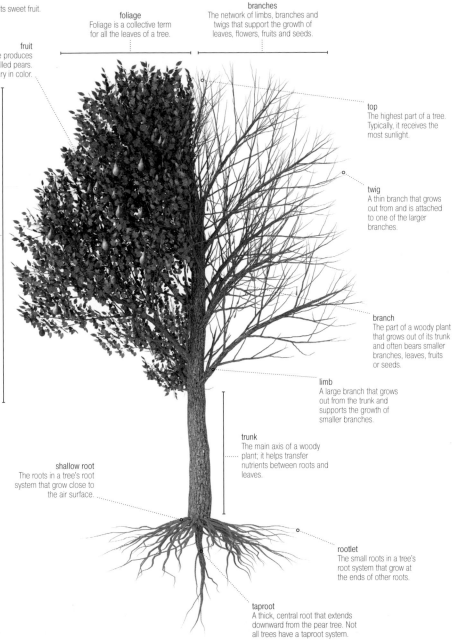

pear
A tree that is grown for its sweet fruit.

foliage
Foliage is a collective term for all the leaves of a tree.

branches
The network of limbs, branches and twigs that support the growth of leaves, flowers, fruits and seeds.

fruit
The pear tree produces sweet fruits called pears. The fruits vary in color.

top
The highest part of a tree. Typically, it receives the most sunlight.

twig
A thin branch that grows out from and is attached to one of the larger branches.

crown
Crown is a collective term for a tree's branches and leaves.

branch
The part of a woody plant that grows out of its trunk and often bears smaller branches, leaves, fruits or seeds.

limb
A large branch that grows out from the trunk and supports the growth of smaller branches.

trunk
The main axis of a woody plant; it helps transfer nutrients between roots and leaves.

shallow root
The roots in a tree's root system that grow close to the air surface.

rootlet
The small roots in a tree's root system that grow at the ends of other roots.

taproot
A thick, central root that extends downward from the pear tree. Not all trees have a taproot system.

American sycamore
A deciduous tree with palmate leaves and fruit that often hangs on the tree in the winter.

English oak
A large tree with large leaves that produces acorns. It is found in Europe.

apple
A deciduous fruit tree with flowers that vary in color.

holly
A shrub with dark green leaves, white flowers and red fruits.

palm tree
A tree that grows in tropical, subtropical and warm temperate regions.

European aspen
A deciduous tree with round, toothed leaves. It is found in Europe, Asia and Africa.

red oak
A very large deciduous tree that is known for its red and brown leaves in autumn.

ash
A deciduous tree that has leaves with multiple thin leaflets.

sugar maple
A large deciduous tree that is known for its bright range of colored leaves in autumn. It is also called hard maple.

rubber tree
A tree that produces latex, used in the production of natural rubber. It is grown commercially in Asia and Africa.

olive
An evergreen tree that produces fruits called olives. It originated in Europe, Asia and Africa.

large-leaf linden
A deciduous tree with heart-shaped leaves and fragrant flowers.

black alder
A small deciduous tree that grows in wet habitats.

hawthorn
A large deciduous shrub with white flowers and red fruits. It has long thorns on its trunk.

ginkgo tree
A deciduous tree with fan-shaped leaves. It originated in Asia.

American beech
A large deciduous tree
that produces edible
nuts and has smooth,
gray bark.

chestnut
A deciduous tree
that produces edible
brown nuts. It is found
worldwide.

silver birch
A deciduous tree that
grows in dry, sandy soil.
It originated in Europe
and Asia.

hornbeam
A deciduous tree with
drooping flowers and
winged nuts. It is found
in North America,
Europe and Asia.

juniper
An evergreen shrub with sharp, needle-like leaves and dark blue fruits.

western red cedar
An evergreen tree with flat green leaves and small brown cones. It is found worldwide.

Caucasian fir
A large evergreen tree with flat, needle-like leaves and brown cones. It originated in Asia.

English yew
An evergreen tree with flat, needle-like leaves and fleshy red cones.

Colorado blue spruce
An evergreen tree with
bluish-green, needle-like
leaves and hanging cones.

Italian cypress
An evergreen tree with
thick foliage and grayish
bark. It is known to live
for a long time.

red pine
An evergreen tree with
needle-like leaves that grow in
bunches of two. It is known to
live for a long time.

Norway spruce
An evergreen tree with
green, needle-like leaves
and hanging cones.

white pine
An evergreen tree with
elongated cones and
needle-like leaves that
grow in bunches of five.

rhododendron
A shrub that is grown for its showy flowers. It can be evergreen or deciduous, depending on the species.

flower
The flower contains the reproductive parts of a plant.

leaf
A part of a plant that is often thin and flat, and the site of energy production for the plant.

trunk
The main axis of a woody plant; it helps transfer nutrients between roots and leaves.

branch
The part of a woody plant that grows out of its trunk and often bears smaller branches, leaves, fruits or seeds.

golden bamboo
A plant from the grass family that is harvested as a wood product. It is known to grown very rapidly.

magnolia
A small deciduous tree with creamy, white or pinkish flowers.

structure of a flower
The main parts of a flower, which contain the reproductive parts of a plant.

filament
The stalk of the stamen. It terminates at the anther.

stigma
The sticky end of a pistil that catches pollen grains.

style
The stalk of the pistil. It terminates at the stigma.

petal
One of several modified leaves of a flower. Petals are often colorful, to attract pollinators.

anther
The part of a flower that contains pollen, which contains the plant's male sex cells.

receptacle
The thickened end of a peduncle to which petals and sepals are attached.

ovule
Ovules contain the female sex cells. A seed develops when a female sex cell is fertilized.

sepal
Leaf-like parts that surround and protect the petals.

peduncle
The stalk that supports the flower.

ovary
The part of a flower that contains ovules, which contain the plant's female sex cells.

rose
A deciduous shrub that has thorns and leaves with glossy leaflets. Its flowers vary in color.

amaryllis
A bulbous flowering plant with large flowers that vary in color.

pistil
The female reproductive organ of a flower. It includes the stigma, style and ovary.

corolla
Corolla is a collective term for all the petals of a flower.

petal
One of several modified leaves of a flower. Petals are often colorful to attract pollinators.

thorn
A sharp outgrowth of the outer layers of the stem. It helps the rose hang on to other plants to grow over them.

leaf
A part of a plant that is often thin and flat, and the site of energy production for the plant.

stamen
The male reproductive organ of a flower. It includes the anther and filament.

stem
A part of a plant that facilitates the transfer of nutrients between roots and leaves.

hyacinth
A bulbous flowering plant with bell-shaped flowers that vary in color.

daisy
A flowering plant with large white flowers with yellow centers. It is found worldwide.

carnation
A flowering plant with sweet-scented flowers that vary in color.

iris
A flowering plant that can be bulbous or rhizomatous. It has narrow, sword-shaped leaves and large flowers.

bird of paradise
A flowering plant with distinct, brightly colored flowers.

Asiatic lily
A bulbous plant that is known for its showy flowers in a wide variety of colors.

crocus
A bulbous flowering plant with long, thin leaves and large, brightly colored flowers.

bromeliad
A plant that has elongated leaves. Both leaves and flowers vary in color.

peony
A shrub that is known for its large flowers that vary in color.

orchid
A plant with flowers that are
often difficult to cultivate
but very fragrant.

gerbera daisy
A plant from the daisy
family that is known for
its large flowers that vary
in color.

gladiolus
A bulbous plant with
narrow, sword-shaped
leaves and brightly
colored flowers.

tulip
A bulbous flowering
plant with elongated
leaves and brightly
colored flowers.

Houseplants

dragon tree
A palm-like plant with elongated trunks
and long, narrow leaves.

leaf
A part of a plant that
is often thin and flat,
and the site of energy
production for the plant.

cactus
A drought-tolerant plant that
varies greatly in appearance.
It is known to have a shallow
root system.

soil
The organic mate-
rial, dirt and rock
particles in which
plants grow.

trunk
The main axis of
a woody plant; it
helps transfer nutrients
between roots and
leaves.

pot
A container, typically
ceramic or plastic,
that is filled with soil
and used for growing
houseplants in.

sago palm
A palm-like plant with stiff,
dark green leaves and a
thick, shaggy trunk.

weeping fig
A tree with drooping branches
and shiny leaves.

ivy
A climbing plant that is
grown for its ease of care.

croton
A plant that is grown for its
broad red, yellow and green
leaves.

fern
A non-flowering plant that
reproduces by spores that
grow on the underside of
the leaves.

fan palm
A palm tree with large,
palmate leaves.

Aquatic plants

lotus
An aquatic plant that
is known for its large,
vibrantly colored flowers.

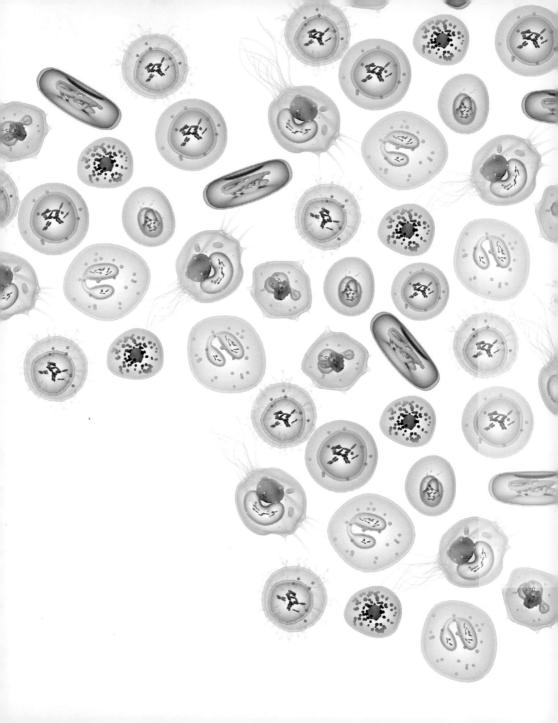

HUMAN BEING

anterior view of female body
The exterior portions of a female body's structure, as viewed from the front.

nose
A protuberance of the face that contains the olfactory mucosa. It is used for smelling and breathing.

eye
The sensory organ for vision. The eye detects light and converts it into electro-chemical impulses in neurons.

ear
An auditory organ located on both sides of the head.

mouth
The opening of the face through which food is taken in and speech is emitted.

cheek
An area of the face situated below the eyes and between the nose and the right or left ears.

chin
An area of the the jaw that protrudes from the area below the mouth and stretches to above the neck.

neck
The part of the body containing the cervical portion of the human spine; it connects the head to the torso.

shoulder
A region made up of three bones: the clavicle, scapula and humerus. It is where a human arm connects to the body.

armpit
Also known as the axilla, this is the area of the human body located under where the arm connects to the shoulder.

nipple
A pigmented structure on the breasts surrounded by the areola. In women, breast milk is delivered via the nipple.

breast
The upper ventral region of the torso; it bears mammary glands to secrete milk for feeding infants.

navel
A scar on the abdomen also known as the umbilicus or belly button; the attachment site of the umbilical cord.

thorax
Located between the neck and the abdomen, this area contains the heart, lungs and thymus gland.

abdomen
The region between the thorax and the pelvis; it contains major viscera (stomach, intestines, liver, spleen and pancreas).

groin
The pubic area located at the junction of the torso and legs. It covers an array of muscles and internal organs.

vulva
The external female genital organ that is responsible for containing many major and minor anatomical structures.

mons pubis
An area of fat that is responsible for protecting the pubis bone. It is located between the abdomen and the vulva.

knee
A joint between the thigh and calf. It connects the femur to the tibia in the leg.

ankle
The joint that connects the foot with the leg.

toe
One of the digits of the human foot that comprises three phalanx bones: the proximal, middle and distal.

foot
The extremity at the end of the leg; used for standing and walking.

posterior view of female body
The exterior portions of a female body's
structure, as viewed from the back.

hair
A protein filament that
commonly grows from the
follicles located throughout the
dermis. It provides warmth.

wrist
The region between the
forearm and hand; it
contains the carpus, or
carpal bones.

nape
The area at the back
of the neck.

head
The uppermost part of the
human bod,y comprising
the eyes, ears, nose and
mouth. It also contains the
skull and brain.

elbow
A hinged joint, located
mid-arm, that allows
movement of the
forearm and hand.

hand
The extremity found
at the distal end of
each human arm,
containing the fingers.
They are used to
manipulate objects.

neck
The part of the body containing the
cervical portion of the human spine;
it connects the head to the torso.

arm
One of the five main appendages
of the human body. It connects
the hand to the shoulder blade.

torso
The central part of the
body, from which the
neck and limbs extend.

forearm
The structural and distal
area of the upper limb. It is
located between the elbow
and the wrist.

shoulder blade
Also called the scapula, this
bone connects the humerus
with the clavicle.

back
The area of a human's body
that is formed by the length
of the vertebral column. It
facilitates movement.

loin
The area of the human body just
above the pelvis on the lower portion
of a person's back.

waist
The section of the abdomen that is
situated between the rib cage and
hips and allows various movements.

buttock
Two rounded layers of fat
superimposed on the gluteus
maximus and gluteus medius
muscles.

hip
The joint between the femur and
acetabulum of the pelvis that
supports the weight of the body.

thigh
The area of the leg between the
pelvis and the knee; it contains the
femur bone.

calf
The back region of the lower leg that
contains a pair of muscles called the
gastrocnemius and the soleus.

leg
One of two lower limbs of the body,
principally involved in facilitating
locomotion.

heel
Containing the calcaneus, the heel
forms the back point of support in the
foot when standing or moving.

foot
The extremity at the end of the leg;
used for standing and walking.

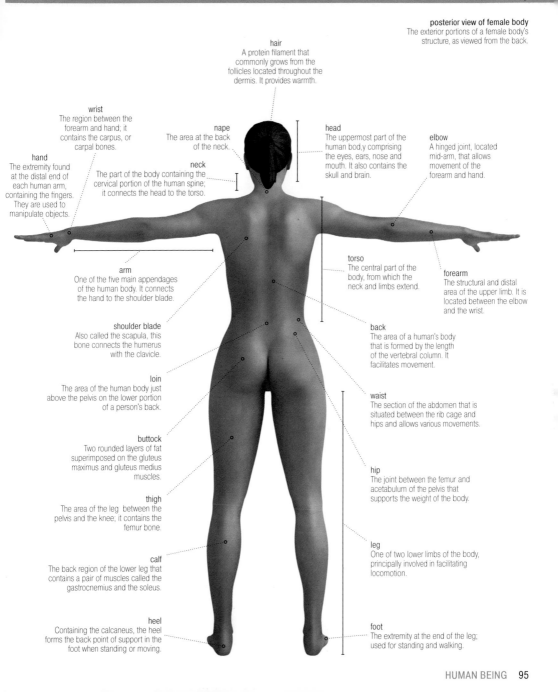

anterior view of male body
The exterior portions of a male body's structure, as viewed from the front.

forehead
An area of the face and head marked by the hairline and the supraorbital ridge. It can be found above the eyes.

face
The front part of the head, forehead to chin; a key component of emotional expression.

temple
The space on the side of the head behind the eyes, above the skull's temporal bone.

Adam's apple
A laryngeal prominence that is formed by the two laminae of the thyroid cartilage as they surround the larynx.

ear
An auditory organ located on both sides of the head.

shoulder
A region made up of three bones: the clavicle, scapula and humerus. It is where the arm connects to the body.

armpit
Also known as the axilla, this area of the body is located under where the arm connects to the shoulder.

nipple
A pigmented structure on the breasts surrounded by the areola.

thorax
Located between the neck and the abdomen, this area contains the heart, lungs and thymus gland.

breast
Similar to a female's breast, with the main difference being that the male breast does not contain mammary glands.

navel
A scar on the abdomen also known as the umbilicus or belly button. It is the attachment site of the umbilical cord.

abdomen
An area of the body that is located between the thorax and pubis. It houses the digestive system.

groin
The pubic area located at the junction of the torso and legs. It covers an array of muscles and internal organs.

pubic region
The lowest area of the abdomen, below the navel.

penis
The external male reproductive organ that also serves as a urinal duct. It is found in the pubic region.

scrotum
A dual-chambered protuberance of skin and muscle in males that contains the testicles and is divided by a septum.

ankle
The joint that connects the foot with the leg.

knee
The joint between the thigh and calf. It connects the femur to the tibia in the leg.

instep
The arched region located at the top of the foot, between the toes and ankle.

foot
The extremity at the end of the leg; used for standing and walking.

toe
One of the digits of the human foot that comprises three phalanx bones: the proximal, middle and distal.

posterior view of male body
The exterior portions of a male body's structure, as viewed from the back.

hair
A protein filament that commonly grows from the follicles located throughout the dermis. It provides warmth.

head
The uppermost part of the human body, comprising the eyes, ears, nose and mouth. It contains the skull and brain.

nape
The area at the back of the neck.

hand
The extremity found at the distal end of each human arm, containing the fingers. They are used to manipulate objects.

neck
The part of the body containing the cervical portion of the human spine; it connects the head to the torso.

arm
One of the five main appendages of the body. It connects the hand to the shoulder blade.

elbow
A hinged joint, located mid-arm, that allows movement of the forearm and hand.

shoulder blade
Also called the scapula, this bone connects the humerus with the clavicle.

forearm
The structural and distal area of the upper limb. It is located between the elbow and the wrist.

wrist
The region located between the forearm and hand; it contains the carpus, or carpal bones.

back
The area of the body that is formed by the length of the vertebral column. It facilitates mobility.

waist
The section of the abdomen between the rib cage and hips; it allows various movements.

torso
The central part of the body, from which the neck and limbs extend.

loin
The area of the human body situated just above the pelvis on the lower portion of a person's back.

hip
The joint between the femur and acetabulum of the pelvis that supports the weight of the body.

buttock
Two rounded layers of fat superimposed on the gluteus maximus and gluteus medius muscles of the human body.

posterior rugae
Also known as the inter-gluteal cleft, this is the deep, slender crease between the two buttocks.

thigh
The area of the leg located between the pelvis and the knee; it contains the femur bone.

leg
One of two lower limbs of the body; it is principally involved in facilitating locomotion.

calf
The back region of the lower leg that contains a pair of muscles called the gastrocnemius and the soleus.

heel
Containing the calcaneus, the heel forms the back point of support when a human is standing or moving.

foot
The extremity at the end of the leg; used for standing and walking.

anterior view of main muscles
The muscular system, responsible for providing movement and producing force, as viewed from the front.

trapezius
A large and superficial muscle located on the back that functions to move the scapulae and support the arm.

pectoralis major
A large, fan-shaped muscle of the chest that is primarily responsible for movement of the shoulder joint.

brachial
A muscle located in the upper arm and that serves to assist the biceps brachii in flexing at the elbow.

deltoid
The muscle forming the rounded contour of the shoulder. It is the prime mover of arm abduction along the frontal plane.

pronator teres
A muscle located mainly in the forearm that, along with the pronator quadratus, serves to pronate the forearm.

biceps brachii
The two-headed muscle located on the upper arm between the shoulder and the elbow. It facilitates arm movements.

brachioradial
A back compartment muscle in the forearm innervated by the radial nerve. It flexes the forearm at the elbow.

external oblique
The largest and most superficial of the three flat muscles on the lateral and anterior parts of the abdomen.

long palmar
A slim and fusiform muscle found on the medial side of the flexor carpi radialis. It is supplied by the median nerve.

abdominal rectus
Either of two muscles running vertically along the anterior abdominal wall. Also known informally as lower abdominals.

tensor of fascia lata
A muscle of the thigh that assists with movement of the gluteus maximus.

sartorius
The longest muscle in the human body; it runs down the length of the thigh in the anterior compartment.

long adductor
A skeletal muscle of the thigh and one of the adductor muscles of the hip. Its main function is to adduct the thigh.

lateral vastus
The largest part of the quadriceps femoris; it helps extend the leg.

femoral rectus
One of the four quadriceps muscles, situated in the middle of the frontal area of the thigh.

medial vastus
A muscle situated medially in the thigh. It functions to extend the knee and is part of the quadriceps muscle group.

peroneus longus
A superficial muscle in the lateral compartment of the leg that acts to tilt the foot away from the body.

anterior tibial
A muscle located near the shin on the lateral side of the tibia. It helps to allow inversion of the human foot.

short extensor of toes
Muscles that produce movement of the toes and are located beneath the tendons of the long extensors.

long fibular
A superficial muscle that tilts the foot away from the body.

long extensor of toes
A pennate muscle that extends the four small toes and dorsally flexes the foot.

semispinalis capitis
A muscle located in the upper and back part of the neck; it helps extend and rotate the head.

occipitalis
A thin and rectangular segment of muscle that is located on the back part of the human skull.

posterior view of main muscles
The muscular system, responsible for providing movement and producing force, as viewed from the back.

splenius of head
A broad and strap-like muscle in the back of the neck involved in simple movements, such as shaking the head.

triceps of arm
These muscles are principally involved with facilitating the extension of the elbow.

brachioradial
A muscle on the lateral side of the forearm that assists the elbow in flexing.

teres minor
A narrow muscle of the rotator cuff that is attached to the head of the humerus, which it helps to rotate.

trapezius
A large and superficial muscle located on the back that functions to move the scapulae and support the arm.

short radial extensor of wrist
A muscle whose main responsibility is to facilitate the extension and abduction of the wrist toward the radius.

ulnar extensor of wrist
A skeletal muscle located on the ulnar side of the forearm that acts to extend and adduct at the carpus.

anconeus
A short extensor muscle of the forearm on the posterior aspect of the elbow joint; it assists in elbow extension.

common extensor of fingers
The muscle that is located in the posterior forearm and is used to extend the medial four digits of the hand.

ulnar flexor of wrist
Also known as the flexor carpi ulnaris, this muscle in the forearm flexes and adducts the hand.

teres major
One of seven scapulohumeral muscles of the upper limb. It is a medial rotator and abductor of the humerus.

latissimus dorsi
A flat dorso-lateral muscle located on the torso. It is posterior to the arm and partially covered by the trapezius.

infraspinatus
One of the four muscles of the rotator cuff. It is a thick muscle, occupying the main part of the infraspinatous fossa.

external oblique
The largest and the most superficial of the three flat muscles on the lateral and anterior parts of the abdomen.

gluteus maximus
The largest and most superficial of the gluteal muscles. It extends the acetabulofemoral joint and manipulates the thigh.

adductor magnus
A group of muscles in the hip and thigh regions that are used to abduct, flex and rotate the thigh medially.

vastus lateralis
The largest part of the quadriceps femoris; it helps extend the leg.

biceps of thigh
Also known as the biceps femoris, these are the posterior femoral muscles of the caudolateral section of the thigh.

semitendinosus
A muscle located in the back of the thigh and in one of the hamstrings. It facilitates the flexing of the knee joint.

semimembranosus
A muscle located medially in the back of the thigh that helps to extend the hip joint and flex the knee joint.

gracilis
The most superficial muscle on the medial side of the thigh. It adducts, medially rotates and flexes the hip.

gastrocnemius
A powerful, superficial, bipennate muscle in the back part of the lower leg, mostly used in running and similar motions.

short fibular
The muscle assisting in plantar flexion and eversion of the foot. It lies under the fibularis longus, though it is smaller.

facial muscles
Also known as mimetic muscles, these are the muscles located under facial skin. They control facial expressions.

zygomaticus major muscle
A facial muscle that facilitates facial expressions. It is used to manipulate the mouth.

frontalis
A variety of muscle that covers the forehead. It facilitates facial expressions.

temporal muscle
A large muscle that helps raise and lower the jaw.

risorius
A facial muscle that is used to create facial expressions. It extends through the fascia.

procerus muscle
A small, pyramid-shaped muscle located over the central part of the nose. It helps pull the eyebrows down.

masseter
One of the various muscles used for mastication. It is a thick quadrilateral muscle consisting of two heads.

orbicularis oculi
This muscle of the human face facilitates the closing of the eyelids.

occipitalis
A thin and rectangular segment of muscle on the back part of the human skull.

nasalis muscle
A muscle that functions similarly to a sphincter. It is the muscle responsible for flaring the nostrils.

sternocleidomastoid
Also known as the sternomastoid, this is a large segment of muscle located on the side of the human neck.

zygomaticus minor
A muscle that extends from the malar bone. It facilitates facial expressions.

platysma muscle
A large and superficial muscle that extends up through the length of the neck and into the chin and cheeks.

orbicularis oris
A series of muscles that surround the lips of the face and are used to close the mouth and pucker the lips.

trapezius muscle
A large and superficial muscle that projects up from the occipital bone. It helps to support the arm.

mentalis
One of two muscles located below the bottom lip of the face. It helps to raise and lower the position of the chin.

depressor labii inferioris muscle
A facial muscle that helps lower the bottom lip during speech or facial expressions.

sternothyroid muscle
Also known as the sternothyreoideus, this muscle is in the lower neck and arises from the ribs.

depressor anguli oris muscle
A facial muscle that is principally involved in producing frowns. It projects forth from the mandible.

stratum lucidum
A thin layer of dead skin cells in the epidermis, located between the stratum granulosum and stratum corneum layers.

stratum corneum
The outermost epidermal layer, consisting of 15 to 20 layers of dead cells.

skin section
The various layer of human skin, seen at the cellular level.

neuron
A nerve cell that processes and transmits information through electrical and chemical signals in synapses.

epidermis
The outermost layers of skin cells and the largest organ in the body. This layer of skin protects human muscles.

melanocyte
A melanin-producing cell found throughout the stratum basale, uvea, inner ear, meninges, bones and heart.

cell body
Also called the soma, this is the bulbous end of a neuron; it contains and protects a cell's nucleus.

dermis
A layer of skin between the epidermis and subcutaneous tissues that is made of fibroblasts, macrophages and adipocytes.

dendrite
The branched projection of a neuron, along which impulses received from other cells are transmitted to the cell body.

axon
Also known as a nerve fiber, this is a projection of a nerve cell that directs electrical impulses away from the cell.

subcutaneous tissue
The skin's base layer, located deep within the dermis. It is made mostly of fat.

nerve ending
The end point of a cable-like bundle of axons that function as cutaneous receptors and detect pain.

adipose tissue
A loose type of connective tissue that contains stored cellular fat and is primarily composed of adipocytes.

microvillus
Cellular membrane protrusions involved in absorption, secretion, cellular adhesion and mechanotransduction.

hepatocyte
A fundamental type of tissue cell consisting of up to 85 percent of the liver's cytoplasmic mass.

mitochondrion
A membrane-bound organelle found in most eukaryotic cells. They supply cells with adenosine triphosphate.

macrophage
A white blood cell that consumes and digests cellular debris and microbes in a process called phagocytosis.

centriole
A cylindrical cell structure usually composed of a protein called tubulin that is found in most eukaryotic cells.

nucleus
A membrane-enclosed organelle found in eukaryotic cells that contain most of the cell's genetic material.

nucleus
The control center of a cell, which contains most of the cell's genetic material.

rough endoplasmic reticulum
A network of tubular membranes within the cytoplasm of the cell, which bears cisternae studded with ribosomes.

lysosome
A membrane-bound cell organelle containing hydrolitic enzymes. They are capable of breaking down most biomolecules.

engulfed antigen
Cellular debris, foreign substances, microbes and cancer cells that are in the midst of phagocytosis.

vacuole
A membrane-bound organelle containing inorganic and organic molecules, such as ingested materials.

anterior view of skeleton
The physical structure of bones that make up the internal framework of a human body, as viewed from the front.

frontal bone
The bone that forms the front part of the skull and the upper part of the eye sockets.

temporal bone
A bone at the sides and base of the skull. It is lateral to the temporal lobes of the cerebrum.

maxilla
One of two bones that are fused to form a hinge-like structure. It forms the upper jaw and palate of the mouth.

zygomatic bone
Also called the cheek bone, this is the bone that articulates with the maxilla and the temporal bone, among others.

clavicle
Also known as the collarbone, this is a horizontal, flat bone that acts as a strut between the scapula and the sternum.

mandible
This is the lower jawbone. It holds the lower teeth in place for chewing.

scapula
Also called the shoulder blade, this bone connects the humerus with the clavicle.

ribs
Long, curved bones that form a cage to protect the lungs, heart and other internal organs of the thorax.

sternum
A long, flat, bony plate that connects the rib bones via cartilage and protects the chest organs.

humerus
A long bone in the arm running from the shoulder to the elbow. It connects to the scapula at its proximal end.

floating rib
The two lowermost rib pairs, so-called because they are attached to the vertebrae and not to the sternum.

ulna
One of the two long bones that provide structure to the forearm. This bone is prismatic in shape.

spinal column
A cavity protecting the spinal cord made from a bony skeletal structure formed by bones called vertebrae.

radius
One of the two large bones in the forearm. It extends from the lateral side of the elbow to the thumb side of the wrist.

ilium
The uppermost broad bone and largest of the three bones that make up the pelvis. It supports the flank.

coccyx
Also known as the tailbone, this is the final segment of the spinal column. It is composed of several fused vertebrae.

sacrum
A triangular bone at the base of the spine and at the upper part of the pelvic cavity between the hip bones.

femur
The most proximal bone of the human leg and the only bone in the thigh. It is the heaviest bone in the human body.

patella
A thick, flat, triangular bone that is also known as the kneecap. It protects the surface of the human knee joint.

tibia
Also known as the shinbone, this is the larger and stronger of the two bones in the leg below the knee.

fibula
Also known as the calf bone, it is a leg bone that projects below the tibia and forms the lateral part of the ankle joint.

posterior view of skeleton
The physical structure of bones that make up the internal framework of a human body, as viewed from the back.

occipital bone
A lower skull bone that has an opening through which the cranial cavity connects with the vertebral canal.

parietal bone
One of two bones located in the human skull that help to form the sides and roof of the human cranium.

atlas
The most superior cervical vertebra of the spine. It is the vertebra that supports the head.

cervical vertebrae
The seven upper vertebrae in the spinal column, located in the neck; they facilitate head movement.

axis
This is the second cervical vertebra of the spine. It facilitates pivot-like movements of the head.

head of humerus
The proximal end of the humerus. It has a large, rounded head, joined by the neck and two eminences.

acromion
The bony process that is attached to the clavicle and extends in a lateral fashion.

thoracic vertebrae
The 12 vertebrae that are found throughout the middle section of the vertebral column.

spine of scapula
Also known as the scapular spine, this is a prominent plate of bone located on the scapula. It separates two fossa.

false ribs
The five bottom pairs of ribs, which indirectly connect to the sternum via the cartilage of other ribs or remain floating.

scapula
Also called the shoulder blade, this bone connects the humerus with the clavicle.

lumbar vertebrae
The five vertebrae between the rib cage and the pelvis. This is the largest segment of the vertebral column.

lateral epicondyle
A tuberculated eminence of the elbow joint; it helps muscles attach to ligaments.

sacrum
A triangular bone at the base of the spine and at the upper part of the pelvic cavity between the hip bones.

olecranon
A bony eminence at the proximal end of the ulna in the forearm. It projects behind the elbow.

greater trochanter
A large, irregular, quadrilateral eminence that is located at the proximal end of the femur.

medial epicondyle
A large, convex eminence that is attached to the tibial collateral ligament with the knee joint.

ischium
Forming the lower and back part of the hip bone, this bone is below the ilium and behind the pubis.

greater trochanter
A large, irregular, quadrilateral eminence that is located at the proximal end of the femur.

lateral condyle of femur
One of two projections on the distal end of the femur. It is more prominent in its antero-posterior diameter.

head of femur
The ball-shaped and most proximal part of the femur. Supported by the neck, its surface is smooth and coated with cartilage.

neck of femur
A flattened, pyramidal area of bone on the femur, connecting the femoral head with the femoral shaft.

medial condyle of femur
One of two projections located on the distal end of the femur bone that facilitate locomotion.

calcaneus
Also called the heel bone, it is the largest of the tarsal bones and the largest bone of the foot.

talus
A bone in the tarsus group, forming the lower part of the ankle joint. It is also called the ankle bone.

shoulder bones
A region made up of three bones: the clavicle, scapula and humerus. It is where the arm connects to the body.

head of humerus
The proximal end of the humerus. It consists of a large, rounded head joined by the neck and two eminences.

humerus
A long bone in the arm, running from the shoulder to the elbow. It connects to the scapula at its proximal end.

clavicle
Also known as the collarbone, this is a horizontal, flat bone that acts as a strut between the scapula and the sternum.

scapula
Also called the shoulder blade, this is the bone that connects the humerus with the clavicle.

foot bones
The inner structural components of the foot, comprising 26 bones and 33 joints.

fibula
Also known as the calf bone, it is a leg bone that projects below the tibia and forms the lateral part of the ankle joint.

tibia
Also known as the shinbone, this is the larger and stronger of the two bones in the leg below the knee.

metatarsus
A group of five long bones found in the foot between the tarsal bones and the phalanges of the toes.

lateral malleolus
A prominence located on the exterior lateral side of the ankle. It is formed around the lower end of the fibula.

tarsus
A cluster of seven bones that form the ankle and top of the foot.

intermediate cuneiform
A tarsal bone of the foot. It articulates proximally with the second metatarsal.

phalanges
A series of bones that form the structure of the five toes.

navicular
A bone in the tarsus group that forms the lower part of the ankle joint. It is also called the ankle bone.

proximal phalanx
Any one of the bones found within the first group of phalanges, located in the proximal aspect of the foot.

calcaneus
Also called the heel bone, it is the largest of the tarsal bones and the largest bone of the foot.

cuboid
One of the seven tarsal bones of the foot. Located on the lateral side, it connects the foot and the ankle.

lateral cuneiform
A small tarsal bone of the foot, situated between the navicular posteriorly and the third metatarsal bone proximally.

metatarsal
One of five long bones found in the foot between the tarsal bones and the phalanges of the toes.

middle phalanx
One of four bones positioned between the distal and proximal phalanges. It is not present in the thumb.

distal phalanx
Any of the small distal bones located in the third row of phalanges at the furthest points of human toes and fingers.

hand bones
27 bones organized into five main groups: carpals, metacarpals, proximals, intermediates, distals and phalanges.

middle phalanx
One of four bones positioned between the distal and proximal phalanges. It is not present in the thumb.

distal phalanx
Any of the small distal bones in the third row of phalanges, at the furthest points of human toes and fingers.

phalange
A group of bones that form the structure of the five fingers.

metacarpus
The five metacarpal bones in the hand between the phalanges and the carpus.

hamate
A carpal bone in the hand and wrist, noticeable by its wedge shape and a hook-like projection from its palmar surface.

carpus
The cluster of bones in the wrist, between the radius and ulna, that connect the hand to the forearm.

pisiform
A small, knobby, pea-shaped sesamoid-type of bones found in the proximal row of the carpus.

triquetral
One of the eight carpal bones located in the wrist on the medial side of the proximal row of the carpus.

lunate
A carpal bone in the hand at the center of the proximal row of carpal bones. It is distinguished by its deep concavity.

ulna
One of the two long bones that provide structure to the forearm. This bone is prismatic in shape.

radius
One of the two large bones in the forearm. It extends from the lateral side of the elbow to the thumb side of the wrist.

scaphoid
One of the carpal bones of the wrist; it helps form the carpal tunnel.

capitate
The largest of the carpal bones in the hand. It is at the center of the wrist, near the third metacarpal.

trapezoid
The smallest carpal bone, in the distal row of the wrist.

trapezium
A carpal bone forming the radial border of the carpal tunnel, marked by a deep groove on its surface.

metacarpal
A group of five bones in the hand, between the wrist and the fingers.

proximal phalanx
Any one of the bones found within the first group of phalanges, located in the proximal aspect of the foot.

knee
A joint between the thigh and calf.
It connects the femur to the tibia
in the leg.

femur
The most proximal bone of the
leg and the only bone in the
thigh. It is the heaviest bone
in the body.

medial condyle of femur
One of two projections located on
the distal end of the femur bone
that facilitate locomotion.

lateral condyle of femur
One of two projections on the
distal end of the femur. It is
more prominent in its antero-
posterior diameter.

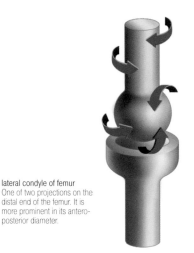

ball-and-socket joint
A freely moving joint in which a
ball on the head of one bone
fits into the round cavity of
another bone.

hinge joint
A joint with articular surfaces that
are molded to each other so as to
permit motion only on one plane.

fibula
Also known as the calf bone, it is
a leg bone that projects below
the tibia and forms the lateral
part of the ankle joint.

tibia
Also known as the
shinbone, this is the larger
and stronger of the two
bones in the leg below
the knee.

pivot joint
A synovial joint where the axis
of a convex articular surface is
parallel with the longitudinal axis
of the bone.

elbow
A hinged joint, located mid-arm, that
allows movement of the forearm
and hand.

humerus
A long bone in the arm, running
from the shoulder to the elbow.
It connects to the scapula at its
proximal end.

lateral epicondyle of humerus
A tuberculated eminence
of the elbow joint that helps
muscles attach to ligaments.

ulna
One of the two long bones that
provide structure to the forearm.
This bone is prismatic in shape.

radius
One of the two large
bones in the forearm. It
extends from the lateral
side of the elbow to the
thumb side of the wrist.

olecranon
A bony eminence at
the proximal end of the
ulna in the forearm.
It projects behind the
elbow.

condyloid joint
A synovial joint that receives a
rounded protuberance, called a
condyle, into an elliptic cavity.

saddle joint
A type of joint that forms between bones
with articulating surfaces; it consists of
concave and convex surfaces.

gliding joint
A synovial joint that permits sliding
or gliding movements in the plane of
articular surfaces.

spinal column
A cavity protecting the spinal cord, made from a structure formed by bones called vertebrae.

atlas
The most superior cervical vertebra of the spine. It is the vertebra that supports the head.

cervical vertebrae
The seven upper vertebrae in the neck. They facilitate head movements.

axis
This is the second cervical vertebra of the spine. It facilitates pivot-like movements of the head.

transverse process
A tiny, bony projection off the sides of each vertebra; it functions as a site of attachment for muscles and ligaments.

thoracic vertebrae
The 12 thoracic vertebrae that can be found throughout the middle section of the spinal column.

axis
This is the second cervical vertebra of the spine. It facilitates pivot-like movements of the head.

intervertebral disk
A fibro-cartilaginous joint between adjacent vertebrae in the spine. Each acts as a type of shock absorber.

lumbar vertebrae
The five vertebrae between the rib cage and the pelvis. This is the largest segment of the spinal column.

atlas
The most superior cervical vertebra of the spine. It is the vertebra responsible for supporting the head.

sacrum
A triangular bone found at the base of the spine and at the upper part of the pelvic cavity between the hip bones.

coccyx
Also known as the tailbone, this is the final segment of the spinal column. It is composed of several fused vertebrae.

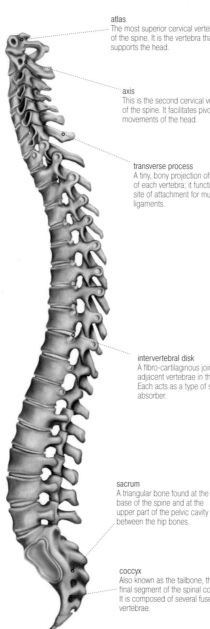

sacrum
A triangular bone found at the base of the spine and at the upper part of the pelvic cavity, between the hip bones.

lumbar vertebra
One of the five vertebrae between the rib cage and the pelvis. This is the largest segment of the vertebral column.

sacrum
A triangular bone found at the base of the spine and at the upper part of the pelvic cavity between the hip bones.

coccyx
Also known as the tailbone, this is the final segment of the spinal column. It is composed of several fused vertebrae.

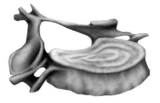

cervical vertebra
One of seven upper vertebrae in the neck. It facilitates head movement.

vertebral arch
A circle of bone around the spinal canal composed of a floor at the back of the vertebra and a roof, where two laminae join.

thoracic vertebra
Any of the 12 bones of the backbones, or spinal column. The ribs are attached here.

articular process
Projections of the vertebra that fit with an adjacent vertebra. The region of contact is called the articular facet.

vertebral foramen
The opening formed by a neural arch in vertebrae, through which the spinal cord passes to create the spinal canal.

transverse process
A tiny, bony projection off the sides of each vertebra; it functions as a site of attachment for muscles and ligaments.

spinous process
A bony projection on the back of each vertebra; it attaches muscles to ligaments.

vertebral body
The largest part of a vertebra that is cylindrical in shape. The body is convex from side to side.

adult's skull
A framework of bones in the head that provides the structure of the human face and protects the brain.

parietal bone
One of two bones located in the skull that help to form the sides and roof of the cranium.

coronal suture
A dense and fibrous connective tissue joint that separates the frontal and parietal bones.

frontal bone
The bone that forms the front part of the skull and the upper part of the eye sockets.

squamous suture
A connecting joint in the skull that connects the temporal bone to the parietal bone.

sphenoid bone
An unpaired bone of the neurocranium situated in the middle of the skull, toward its frontal aspect.

nasal bone
One of two small, oblong bones that shape and form the bridge of the human nose.

lambdoid suture
A fibrous connective tissue joint found on the back of the skull. It links the parietal bones with the occipital bone.

zygomatic bone
Also called the cheek bone, this is the bone that articulates with the maxilla and the temporal bone, among others.

anterior nasal spine
A pointed, bony projection of the human skull found at the front portion of the intermaxillary suture.

occipital bone
A bone at the lower part of the skull with an opening through which the cranial cavity connects with the vertebral canal.

maxilla
One of two bones that are fused to form a hinge-like structure. It forms the upper jaw and palate of the mouth.

temporal bone
A bone located at the sides and base of the skull. It is lateral to the temporal lobes of the cerebrum.

mastoid process
A conical prominence projecting out from the undersurface of the mastoid part of the temporal bone.

external auditory canal
A mostly bony tube that runs from the outside of the head to the eardrum membrane.

styloid process
A pointed bone process that extends down from the skull and is located directly below the ear.

mandible
This is the lower jawbone. It holds the lower teeth in place for chewing.

child's skull
A framework of bones in a child's head that provides the structure of the face and protects the brain.

anterior fontanelle
The large fontanelle at the intersection of the sagittal, coronal and frontal suture of an infant's cranial vault.

parietal bone
One of two bones located in the skull that helps to form the sides and roof of the cranium.

coronal suture
A dense and fibrous connective tissue joint that separates the frontal and parietal bones of the skull.

posterior fontanelle
The triangular break that is formed at the junction of the sagittal and lambdoidal sutures in the skull.

frontal bone
The bone that forms the front part of the skull and the upper part of the eye sockets.

occipital bone
A bone at the lower part of the skull with an opening through which the cranial cavity connects with the vertebral canal.

mastoid fontanelle
Membranous break on either side of the skull, found at the mastoid angle of the parietal, temporal and occipital bones.

sphenoidal fontanelle
An anatomical feature of the infant skull, made of soft membranous gaps between the cranial bones.

teeth and skull
Small, calcified, whitish structures located in the jaw and the skeletal structure that supports the face.

nasal bone
One of two small, oblong bones that form the bridge of the human nose.

palate
The roof of the mouth. It separates the mouth from the nasal cavity, directly above it.

zygomatic bone
Also called the cheek bone, this is the bone that articulates with the maxilla and the temporal bone, among others.

isthmus of fauces
Also known as the oropharyngeal isthmus, this part of the oropharynx is behind the mouth cavity.

second molar
The tooth that is located distally from both the mandibular first molars of the mouth. They are used for grinding.

first molar
Also known as six-year tooth, it is located on the lower arch of the mouth. Its main functions are grinding or chewing.

second premolar
The tooth that is located distally from both the mandibular first premolars of the human mouth.

first premolar
The tooth located on the bottom jaw that is similar to a small canine tooth and is used for tearing and chewing.

maxilla
One of two bones that are fused to form a hinge-like structure. It forms the upper jaw and palate of the mouth.

uvula
Also known as palatine uvula, this is a fleshy hanging structure that extends from the back of the soft palate.

canine
Any of the four large, pointed teeth.

molars
The most posterior and complicated type of tooth; its primary function is to grind food during chewing.

premolars
The eight transitional teeth of the human mouth that are located between the canine and molar teeth.

central incisor
The front teeth located on the upper premaxilla and on the lower mandible. There are eight in total.

tongue
A fleshy organ in the mouth; it is used for tasting, licking and swallowing.

lateral incisor
Two maxillary teeth located laterally from the maxillary central incisors and mesially from the maxillary canines.

incisors
The eight narrow-edged frontal teeth in the premaxilla above and on the mandible below. They help to cut food.

gum
The mucosal soft tissue over the mandible and maxilla inside the lining of the mouth and surrounding the teeth.

mandible
This is the lower jawbone. It holds the lower teeth in place for chewing.

cross section of molar
The internal structures of a molar tooth.

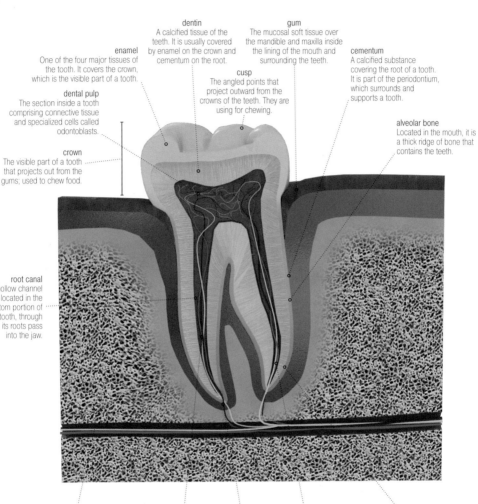

dentin
A calcified tissue of the teeth. It is usually covered by enamel on the crown and cementum on the root.

gum
The mucosal soft tissue over the mandible and maxilla inside the lining of the mouth and surrounding the teeth.

enamel
One of the four major tissues of the tooth. It covers the crown, which is the visible part of a tooth.

cusp
The angled points that project outward from the crowns of the teeth. They are using for chewing.

cementum
A calcified substance covering the root of a tooth. It is part of the periodontium, which surrounds and supports a tooth.

dental pulp
The section inside a tooth comprising connective tissue and specialized cells called odontoblasts.

alveolar bone
Located in the mouth, it is a thick ridge of bone that contains the teeth.

crown
The visible part of a tooth that projects out from the gums; used to chew food.

root canal
The hollow channel located in the bottom portion of a tooth, through which its roots pass into the jaw.

blood vessel
One of two bones that are fused at an intermaxillary suture. It forms the upper jaw and palate of human mouth.

periodontal ligament
Tubular components of the circulatory system that transport blood throughout the body.

dental plexus
The anatomic space at the terminal end of the root of a tooth. It allows blood to enter the tooth.

nerve
A cable-like bundle of fibers that transmit impulses of sensation to the spinal cord or brain.

apex
The terminal pointed end at the root of a tooth; it contains the apical foramen.

upper lobe
The upper two segments of each lung. They facilitate respirational processes.

trachea
A tube in the respiratory system connecting the pharynx and larynx to the lungs that allows the passage of air.

respiratory organs
The system of organs and biological structures that are used when a person breathes in and out.

left lung
The left of two organs whose main function is to transport oxygen into the bloodstream and release carbon dioxide.

right lung
The right of two organs whose main function is to transport oxygen into the bloodstream and release carbon dioxide.

lower lobe
The area at the lower segments of both lung's bases.

larynx
An organ that provides a passage for air to the lungs and houses the vocal cords.

middle lobe
The smallest lobe, in the middle of the right lung. It is unique to the right lung, as the left lung lacks this lobe.

epiglottis
A flap of elastic cartilage at the entrance of the larynx, which is depressed when swallowing to cover the trachea.

hyoid bone
A horseshoe-shaped bone in the neck, between the chin and the thyroid cartilage.

diaphragm
A skeletal muscle extending across the bottom of the rib cage. It plays a major role in the breathing process.

thyroid membrane
Also known as the hyothyroid membrane, this is a fibro-elastic segment of membrane that is attached to the thyroid.

lungs
The two organs that transport oxygen into the bloodstream and release carbon dioxide.

thyroid cartilage
A structure in and around the trachea that contains and protects the larynx.

tracheal ring
A semicircular ring of hyaline cartilage occupying the anterior two-thirds of the circumference of the trachea.

lobe bronchus
Airway passages in the respiratory tract extending from a primary bronchus to a segmental bronchus and into the lungs.

trachea
A tube that connects the pharynx and larynx to the lungs; it allows the passage of air.

terminal bronchiole
The last part of the non-respiratory conducting airway, which divides into respiratory bronchioles.

main bronchus
One of two airway passages in the respiratory tract that are used to conduct air into the lungs via the trachea.

principal arteries
The major blood vessels that deliver oxygen-rich blood to the body, from the heart.

subclavian artery
One of the major arteries in the upper thorax, below the clavicle, that supplies blood to the arms.

axillary artery
A large blood vessel that transports oxygenated blood from the heart to the various pertinent regions of the body.

common carotid artery
Arteries located on both the left and right sides of the body that supply the head and neck with oxygenated blood.

aortic arch
A part of the aorta that curves above the heart. It supplies blood to the brachiocephalic trunk and various arteries.

ulnar artery
The primary blood vessel that is responsible for carrying oxygenated blood in the middle of the forearm.

brachial artery
A major blood vessel of the upper arm that extends from the axillary artery to beyond the teres major muscle.

radial artery
The main artery of the side of the forearm. It supplies oxygenated blood to the arm and hand.

renal artery
A branch of the abdominal aorta, which supplies the kidneys with blood.

pulmonary artery
The artery that is responsible for moving deoxygenated blood from the right ventricle to the lungs.

abdominal aorta
The primary artery in the abdominal cavity. It begins at the diaphragm and extends downward.

thoracic aorta
A section of the aorta that helps carry blood to most of the body.

common iliac artery
One of two large arteries that originate from the aortic bifurcation, at the fourth lumbar vertebra.

internal iliac artery
The main artery supplying the walls and viscera of the pelvis, buttocks and reproductive organs with blood.

peroneal artery
An artery that carries blood from the popliteal artery to the top part of the leg and dorsal surface of the foot.

femoral artery
A large artery in the thigh entering from behind the inguinal ligament as a continuation of the external iliac artery.

anterior tibial artery
Also known as the peroneal artery, it branches off the posterior tibial artery and supplies blood to the side of the leg.

dorsalis pedis
A blood vessel in the upper surface of the foot; it carries oxygenated blood to the top of the foot.

principal veins
The various fundamental veins that supply oxygenated blood through the body.

internal jugular vein
A paired vein that returns blood from the brain and superficial parts of the face and neck back to the heart.

external jugular vein
A major vein of the head that receives most of the blood from the exterior of the cranium and the deep parts of the face.

subclavian vein
A major vein in the upper thorax, below the clavicle, that directly follows the subclavian artery.

axillary vein
A large blood vessel that carries blood from the front of the thorax, axilla and upper limbs to the heart.

cephalic vein
A superficial vein in the upper limbs that is connected with the basilic vein via the median cubital vein at the elbow.

basilic vein
A large superficial vein found within the upper limbs that helps to export blood from the hands and forearms.

pulmonary vein
Any of four large blood vessels that receive oxygenated blood from the lungs and drain into the left atrium of the heart.

superior vena cava
A wide, short vein that carries deoxygenated blood from the upper half of the body to the right atrium of the heart.

superior mesenteric vein
A vein that drains the small intestine; it is behind the neck of the pancreas.

renal vein
This vein drains the kidney and carries the blood that has been purified by the kidney.

common iliac vein
A vein in the abdomen that drains blood from the lower limbs.

inferior vena cava
The major vein that carries deoxygenated blood into the right atrium of the heart from the lower half of the body.

femoral vein
A blood vessel accompanying the femoral artery. It begins at the adductor canal and ends at the inguinal ligament.

popliteal vein
A vein carrying blood from the knee to the thigh. This vein is formed at the junction of the venae comitantes.

small saphenous vein
A superficial vein of the back of the leg that travels the length of the ankle and continues up the back of the calf.

great saphenous vein
A large, subcutaneous, superficial vein; it is the longest vein in the body.

heart
A muscular organ located behind the breastbone in the chest that pumps blood throughout the circulatory system.

aortic arch
A part of the aorta that curves above the heart. It supplies blood to the brachiocephalic trunk and various arteries.

pulmonary trunk
A vessel arising from the right ventricle, which extends upward and divides into the pulmonary arteries.

left pulmonary vein
One of four large blood vessels that receive oxygenated blood from the left lung and drain into the left atrium of the heart.

superior vena cava
A wide, short vein that carries deoxygenated blood from the upper half of the body to the right atrium of the heart.

right pulmonary vein
One of two large blood vessels that receive oxygenated blood from the right lung and drain into the heart's left atrium.

inferior vena cava
The major vein that carries deoxygenated blood into the right atrium of the heart from the lower half of the body.

aorta
The main artery in the body that originates from the left ventricle of the heart. It extends down to the abdomen.

cross section of heart
The principal organ of the circulatory system. It is responsible for constantly pumping blood throughout the body.

right atrium
One of four chambers of the heart, found in the upper right portion of the organ. It helps pump blood.

superior vena cava
A wide, short vein that carries deoxygenated blood from the upper half of the body to the right atrium of the heart.

aortic arch
This is a portion of the aorta that projects upward toward the trachea's left side.

pulmonary trunk
A blood vessel that extends upward from the right ventricle of the heart; it separates into the pulmonary arteries.

right pulmonary artery
One of the pulmonary arteries that is responsible for moving deoxygenated blood from the right ventricle to the lungs.

left pulmonary artery
One of the pulmonary arteries that is responsible for moving deoxygenated blood from the left ventricle to the lungs.

right pulmonary veins
Large blood vessels that receive oxygenated blood from the right lung. They drain into the left atrium of the heart.

aortic valve
A semilunar valve within the heart. It allows blood to leave the heart at certain pressures.

pulmonary valve
This valve separates the aorta and left ventricle; it prevents blood from flowing back into the ventricle.

tricuspid valve
Also known as the right atrioventricular valve, this valve is between the right ventricle and atrium.

left pulmonary vein
Large blood vessels that receive oxygenated blood from the left lung. They help circulate blood through the body.

endocardium
The inner layer of tissue that surrounds the inner chamber of the heart. It protects the heart's inner structure.

left atrium
One of four chambers; it is in the upper left and helps to pump blood.

right ventricle
The lower right chamber of the heart. It stores and releases blood that is collected from the atrium.

mitral valve
A valve in the heart that has two flaps. It is between the left ventricle and the left atrium.

inferior vena cava
The major vein that carries deoxygenated blood into the right atrium of the heart from the lower half of the body.

left ventricle
The lower left chamber of the heart. It stores and releases blood that is collected from the atrium.

interventricular semptum
A rigid wall that separates the lower chambers of the heart. It has thin and thick muscular sections.

papillary muscle
One of the various muscles in the human heart. It connects to the atrioventricular valves.

myocardium
The middle layer of muscle in the center of the heart. It facilitates pumping actions.

anterior view of brain
The front parts of the human cerebrum, which coordinates functions, movements, sensations and thought.

cerebral cortex
The outer layer of the cerebrum that plays a key roles in memory, attention, perceptual awareness and consciousness.

longitudinal fissure
A large, deep groove between the medial surfaces of the cerebral hemispheres.

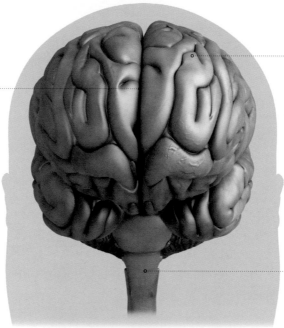

medulla oblongata
A bulbous area in the lower half of the brain stem; contains the control centers for the heart and lungs.

posterior view of brain
The back parts of the human cerebrum, which coordinates functions, movements, sensations and thought.

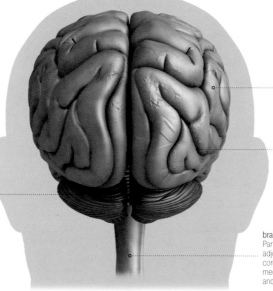

gyrus
A ridge on the cerebral cortex that is usually surrounded by one or more sulci, depressions or grooves.

sulcus
The depression or groove located within the cerebral cortex of the brain.

cerebellum
A region of the brain tucked underneath the cerebral hemispheres that plays an important role in motor control.

brain stem
Part of the brain that adjoins with the spinal cord. It contains the medulla oblongata, pons and midbrain.

thalamus
A mass in the human brain responsible for pain perception and relaying sensory information.

corpus callosum
A wide and flat bundle of neural fibers that connect the brain's left and right cerebral hemispheres.

septum pellucidum
A triangular, thin, vertical membrane that separates the anterior horns of the left and right lateral brain ventricles.

fornix
A C-shaped bundle of fibers; carries signals from the hippocampus to the hypothalamus.

cross section of brain
The internal parts of the human cerebrum, which coordinates functions, movements, sensations and thought.

cerebrum
The largest part of the brain; it contains the cerebral cortex and subcortical structures and controls voluntary motions.

cerebellum
A region of the brain tucked underneath the cerebral hemispheres that plays an important role in motor control.

medulla oblongata
A bulbous area in the lower half of the brain stem; contains the control centers for the heart and lungs.

pons
A bulbous band of nerve fibers on the ventral surface of the brain stem, located above the medulla and below the midbrain.

lateral view of brain
The top of the human cerebrum, including the cerebral cortex and subcortical structures, which control voluntary motions.

frontal lobe
Located at the front of each cerebral hemisphere, it is responsible for thinking, decision making and planning.

temporal lobe
The lobe of the cerebral cortex involved with language and sensory input.

cerebellum
A region of the brain tucked underneath the cerebral hemispheres that plays an important role in motor control.

parietal lobe
One of four major lobes of the cerebral cortex.

occipital lobe
One of the four major lobes of the cerebral cortex in the brain. It is the visual processing center of the brain.

main structure of nervous system
The various nerves branches that comprise the structure of the human nervous system.

brain
The center of the nervous system and the most complex organ in the body. It exerts control over other organs.

cranial nerves
The nerves that emerge from the brain and brain stem, as opposed to spinal nerves, which emerge from the spinal cord.

ulnar nerve
A nerve that runs near the ulna bone. It is directly connected to the little finger and the adjacent half of the ring finger.

brachial plexus
A network of nerves that runs from the spine throughout the entirety of the neck, axilla and upper arms.

digital nerve
Any of the branches of the median nerve or the ulnar nerve that run through regions of the fingers and the thumb.

intercostal nerve
Ventral branches of the thoracic nerves extending along the lower margin of the ribs in the subcostal grooves.

radial nerve
The nerve that supplies the medial, lateral and long heads of the triceps brachii muscle, found in the arm.

spinal nerves
A long, thin, tubular bundle of nervous tissue and support cells. It is protected by three layers of spinal meninges.

spinal cord
A tubular bundle of nervous tissue that connects nearly all parts of the body to the brain.

femoral nerve
The largest branch of the lumbar plexus, arising from the dorsal divisions of the ventral rami of the lumbar nerves.

sciatic nerve
The longest nerve in the human body, as it begins in the lower back and runs through the buttocks to the lower limbs.

lymphatic organs
A network of vessels that carry a clear fluid, called lymph, throughout the body. It supports the immune system.

cervical lymph nodes
Oval-shaped organs of the lymphatic system that facilitate the proper functioning of the immune system.

thymus
Two identical lymphoid organs that produce T cells for the immune system, located in front of the heart.

thoracic lymph nodes
Two lymph glands that are located in the thorax. They work closely in conjunction with other organs.

spleen
Located in the left upper quadrant of the abdomen, this organ plays an important role within the immune system.

thoracic duct
The largest lymphatic vessel, also known as the left lymphatic duct or the alimentary duct.

intestinal lymph nodes
Bodily vessels that are used to receive lymph from the liver, stomach, spleen, pancreas and small intestine.

inguinal lymph nodes
A type of lymph node in the inguinal region. It is critical to the immune system.

popliteal lymph nodes
Six or seven nodes of the lymphatic system located in the legs, near the knees and around the popliteal fossa.

breast
The upper ventral region of a human female's torso, which bears mammary glands to secrete milk for feeding infants.

lactiferous duct
A system of branches connecting the mammary gland to the tip of the nipple. It helps to carry milk to the nipple.

lactiferous sinus
A constrained, spindle-shaped opening of the lactiferous duct, where it enters the nipple of the breast.

mammary gland
The organ that is situated in the breast of a female and produces milk to feed newborn infants.

female reproductive organs
The internal genital structures of a female; includes the ovaries, fallopian tubes, uterus and vagina.

common iliac artery
One of two large arteries that originate from the aortic bifurcation, at the fourth lumbar vertebra.

ovary
An ovum-producing reproductive organ in the female reproductive system that is analogous to testes in males.

uterus
Also known as the womb, this is the major female reproductive organ and where a fetus develops during gestation.

ureter
Tubes made of smooth muscle fibers that move urine from the kidneys to the urinary bladder.

urinary bladder
The organ on the pelvic floor that collects the urine excreted by the kidneys before disposal by urination.

fallopian tube
One of two fine tubes lined with ciliated epithelia. It allows the passage of an egg from the ovary to the uterus.

urethra
A tube that is used for the removal of fluids from the bladder, which occurs in females via the urethral orifice.

vagina
A fibromuscular tubular sex organ of the female genital tract extending from the vulva to the uterus.

urinary bladder
The organ on the pelvic floor that collects the urine excreted by the kidneys before disposal by urination.

penis
The external male reproductive organ, which also serves as a urinal duct. It is found in the pubic region.

testicle
Components of the male reproductive system whose primary function is to produce sperm and testosterone.

glans penis
The sensitive bulbous structure at the distal end of the penis, commonly known as the head of the penis.

male reproductive organs
A system of organs that facilitate sexual reproduction. In males, the main organs are the penis and testicles.

prostate
A compound tubuloalveolar exocrine gland of the male reproductive system that surrounds the urethra below the bladder.

vas deferens
The cord-like structure in males that carries sperm from the testicles to urethra.

bulbocavernous muscle
One of the superficial muscles of the perineum. It is responsible for covering the bulbs of human reproductive organs.

epididymis
An elongated organ located behind the testes that is responsible for storing sperm cells while they mature.

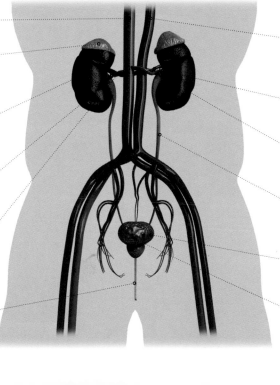

inferior vena cava
The major vein that carries deoxygenated blood into the right atrium of the heart from the lower half of the body.

adrenal gland
One of the glands of the endocrine system that releases hormones as a response to stressors.

right kidney
An organ at the back of the abdominal cavity; it excretes urine and regulates fluids.

renal hilum
The depression and opening on the medial side of the kidney through which renal vessels enter and leave.

renal vein
This vein drains the kidney and carries the blood that has been purified by the kidney.

urethra
A tube used for the removal of fluids from the bladder; this occurs in males via the penis.

urinary organs
Also known as the renal system, this is the body's drainage system, which removes urine.

abdominal aorta
This is the primary artery in the abdominal cavity. It begins at the diaphragm and extends downward.

renal artery
A branch of the abdominal aorta, which supplies the kidneys with blood.

left kidney
An organ at the back of the abdominal cavity; it excretes urine and regulates fluids.

ureter
The tubes made of smooth muscle fibers that move urine from the kidneys to the bladder.

detrusor urinae
The muscle found in the wall of the bladder. It relaxes to allow the bladder to store urine and contracts to release urine.

urinary bladder
The organ on the pelvic floor that collects the urine excreted by the kidneys before disposal via urination.

anterior view of digestive system
The system that converts digested food into energy. This view shows the front of the relevant organs.

liver
A vital organ and gland that has many functions, including detoxification processes.

esophagus
A fibro-muscular tube that connects the mouth to the stomach and pushes food from the pharynx to the stomach.

stomach
A muscular, hollow and dilated part of the digestive system between the esophagus and the duodenum.

gallbladder
A small organ just beneath the right lobe of the liver that stores bile before releasing it into the small intestine.

large intestine
The last part of the digestive system. Its function is to absorb water from fecal matter before it is excreted via the anus.

small intestine
The region of the gastrointestinal tract that follows the stomach and precedes the large intestine.

vermiform appendix
A narrow, blind tube connected to the cecum. It is at the junction of the small intestine and the large intestine.

anus
The opening in the fold between the buttocks; where solid waste leaves the body.

posterior view of digestive system
The system that converts digested food into energy.
This view shows the back of the relevant organs.

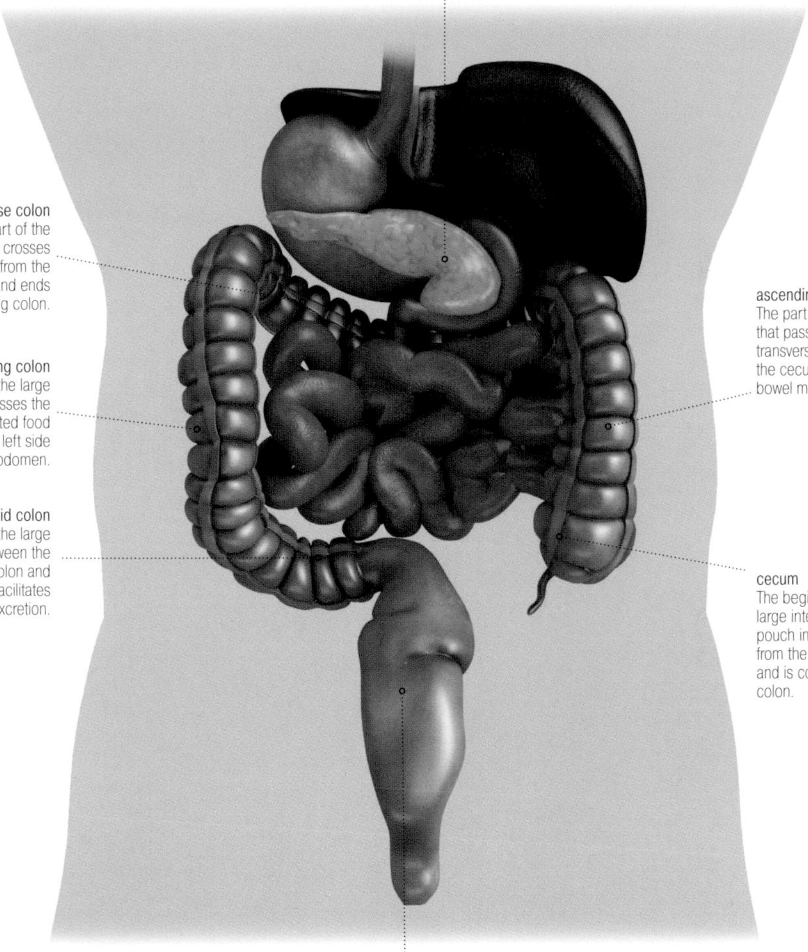

pancreas
A glandular organ of the
digestive and endocrine
systems that produces
hormones, such as insulin
and glucagon.

transverse colon
The longest part of the
colon, which crosses
the abdomen from the
ascending colon and ends
at the descending colon.

ascending colon
The part of the colon
that passes between the
transverse colon and
the cecum. It facilitates
bowel movements.

descending colon
The part of the large
intestine that passes the
remains of digested food
downward on the left side
of the abdomen.

sigmoid colon
A region of the large
intestine between the
descending colon and
the rectum. It facilitates
excretion.

cecum
The beginning of the
large intestine. It is a
pouch into which chyme
from the ileum empties
and is connected to the
colon.

rectum
The last straight
segment of the large
intestine. It begins at
the sigmoid colon and
concludes at the anus.

female endocrine system
A system of the human body comprising glands that secrete hormones directly into the circulatory system.

thyroid gland
A large endocrine gland; it secretes hormones that regulate growth and development.

heart
A muscular organ located behind the breastbone in the chest that pumps blood throughout the circulatory system.

liver
A vital organ and gland of the digestive system that has a wide range of functions, including detoxification processes.

adrenal gland
A small endocrine gland responsible for releasing steroid hormones and epinephrine.

pancreas
A glandular organ of the digestive and endocrine systems that produces hormones, such as insulin and glucagon.

kidney
An organ at the back of the abdominal cavity that excretes urine, regulate fluids and behaves as an endocrine gland.

ovary
An ovum-producing reproductive organ in the female reproductive system that is analogous to testes in males.

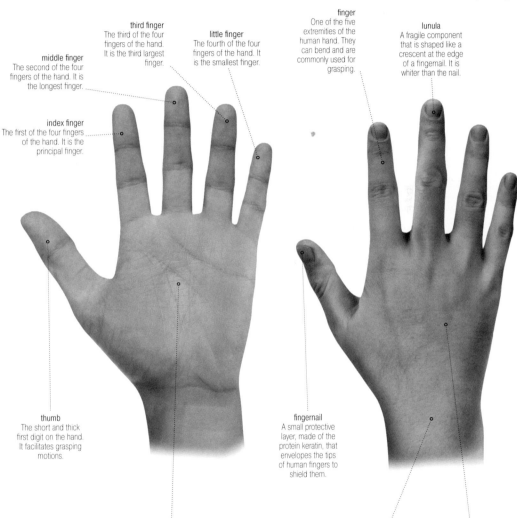

hand
The extremity at the distal end of each arm, containing the fingers; used to manipulate objects.

third finger
The third of the four fingers of the hand. It is the third largest finger.

little finger
The fourth of the four fingers of the hand. It is the smallest finger.

finger
One of the five extremities of the human hand. They can bend and are commonly used for grasping.

lunula
A fragile component that is shaped like a crescent at the edge of a fingernail. It is whiter than the nail.

middle finger
The second of the four fingers of the hand. It is the longest finger.

index finger
The first of the four fingers of the hand. It is the principal finger.

thumb
The short and thick first digit on the hand. It facilitates grasping motions.

fingernail
A small protective layer, made of the protein keratin, that envelopes the tips of human fingers to shield them.

palm
Also known as the volar, this is the soft inner pad of the hand. It is structured to readily grasp objects.

wrist
The joint connecting the hand and the forearm; it contains the carpus, or carpal bones.

back
The hard, bony portion of the hand that is covered in hair follicles.

ear
The internal and external parts of an ear, which is the auditory organ for hearing and comprehending sounds.

posterior semicircular canal
A part of the ear providing directional balance; it detects head rotations on the saggital plane.

lateral semicircular canal
A part of the ear providing directional balance; it detects vertical head movements.

malleus
A bone within the middle ear. It serves to connect the incus with the surface of the eardrum.

external acoustic meatus
The canal located within the external ear. It comprises both cartilage and bone, and extends from the auricle.

superior semicircular canal
A part of the ear providing directional balance; it detects head rotations on the anterior-posterior axis.

vestibular nerve
A sensory nerve in the ear; it transmits messages from vestibular hair cells.

cochlear nerve
A sensory nerve located within the cochlea; it transmits auditory signals to the brain.

cochlea
A spiral-like cavity located within the inner ear that comprises bone and through which sound waves pass.

vestibule
An egg-shaped structure found within the ear; it facilitates the passage of certain veins.

eustachian tube
Also known as the auditory tube, this is an area of the ear that connects the nasopharynx to the middle ear.

stapes
A bone within the middle ear. It helps to facilitate the conduction of sound into the ear.

incus
A bone within the middle ear. It is anvil-like in shape and is one of the ear's three ossicles.

eardrum
Also known as the tympanic membrane, this is an aspect of the human ear that transmits sound to ossicles in the ear.

auricle
The external and visible structure of the ear. It funnels sound inward to the auditory organs.

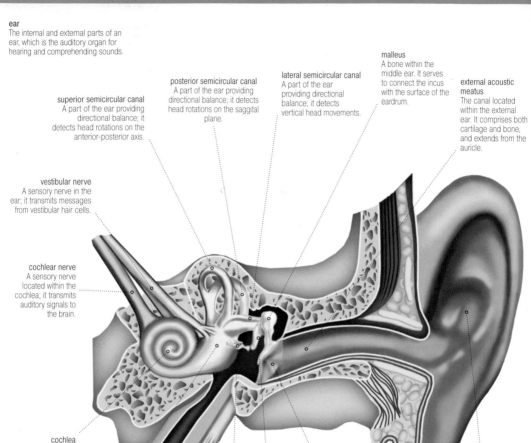

pupil
A hole in the center of the iris. Its shape allows light to readily enter the human retina.

eyelash
Hairs that grows around the rim of the eye to protect it from small debris.

eye
The sensory organ for vision. The eye detects light and converts it into electro-chemical impulses in neurons.

iris
A small and circular structure found at the center of the eye. It helps to control how much light hits the retina.

upper eyelid
A small flap of skin that can extend or retract over the top of the eye. It is used to blink or to shield the eye.

lachrymal carunkel
Also known as the lacrimal caruncle, this is a small pinkish nodule at the inner corner of the eye.

conjuctiva
The inner lining of the eyelids. It surrounds the sclera and ensures the eye stays lubricated.

sclera
The outer layer of the eye; it is characteristically white.

lower eyelid
A small flap of skin that can extend or retract over the bottom of the eye. It is used to blink or to shield the eye.

superior rectus muscle
An extraocular muscle that is innervated and can be found within the human orbit. It helps to raise the eye.

choroid
Also known as the choroid coat, this vascular layer of the eye is situated between the retina and the sclera.

eyeball
The round part of the eye, located in the socket and behind the eyelid.

sclera
The outer layer of the eye; it is characteristically white.

retina
A layer of tissue that is light sensitive and can be found surrounding the inner portion of the human eye.

lens
A biconvex structure within the eye that refracts and focuses light onto the retina.

pupil
A hole in the central aspect of the iris. Its shape allows light to readily enter the human retina.

optic nerve
Also called the second cranial nerve, this is a sensory nerve that transports visual data to the brain.

cornea
The transparent front of the human eye. It encases the anterior chamber, pupil and iris and refracts light.

vitreous humor
A transparent, jelly-like material within the eye, behind the lens.

ciliary body
An aspect of the eye that contains the ciliary muscle. It helps to anchor the lens and keep it in place.

suspensory ligament
A specialized ligament below the eyeball that hoists and supports the eye.

aqueous humor
A transparent, jelly-like liquid that has a low concentration of protein. It maintains eye pressure.

HEALTH AND MEDICINE

angiography room
A radiology facility designed to take X-ray images of blood vessels.

radiologist
A medical imaging specialist who uses radiography, ultrasound and MRI to help diagnose injury or illness.

C-arm crawler carriage
The movable C-shaped segment of a radiographic image intensifier scanner.

mattress
A pad placed on a support, bed frame or incubator tray.

video monitor
An electronic visual display for images and data.

camera housing
A structure that protects the internal components of the image intensifier's camera.

image intensifier
A device used to convert low intensity X-rays to visible light in order to make an image.

angiography machine
A medical imaging device that uses contrast agents in the bloodstream to see inside blood vessels and organs.

height-adjustable pedestal
A vertically adjustable stand for a patient support table.

scrub nurse
A peri-operative nurse who assists a surgeon during surgery.

X-ray tube
A vacuum tube capable of producing X-rays. It is commonly used to create CAT scan images.

non-movable C-arm track
The stationary C-shaped section of a radiographic image intensifier.

patient support table
A surface designed to safely position a patient during medical procedures.

surgical drape
A sterile covering used during medical procedures.

collimator housing
A protective compartment that contains the device that narrows the beam of particles or waves during imaging.

support arm
A support for the weight of an angiography machine's C-arm crawler carriage.

MRI (magnetic resonance imaging) room
A specialized room fitted with radio frequency shielding and an MRI scanner.

file cabinet
A piece of office equipment used to organize and store paper documents in file folders.

technician's room
A control and observation room located behind special glass that protects from radiation.

screened glass
Shielding or leaded glass that protects from radiation. It is transparent, so occupants can observe the procedure.

display device
An electrical screen where information is shown for observational and diagnostic purposes.

MRI scanner
A magnetic resonance imaging scanner; it uses magnetic fields and radio waves to examine the body.

procedure room
A room inside a medical facility for a specific test or other medical use.

computer with image-capturing hardware
A computer used to view images created by an MRI scanner.

motorized table
A table moved by a motor and designed to accommodate diagnostic procedures.

pedestal
A structural component used to support the motorized table of an MRI scanner.

scanning tube
A long, hollow device that takes sliced images of body tissue and uses them to build a 2-D or 3-D model.

operating room
A sterile room where surgery occurs.

surgical mask
A surgical nose and mouth covering, which protects the sterile operating room environment from bacteria.

multi-movement pendant
A device that suspends lights and monitors in various positions.

ceiling light
A light installed in the ceiling of a room.

video monitor
An electronic visual display for images and data.

scrub nurse
A peri-operative nurse who assists a surgeon during surgery.

anesthesiologist
A medical doctor specializing in anesthesia.

operating light
A special light that illuminates the examination or operating area.

instrument cart
A movable tray fitted with wheels; used to store medical instruments.

patient
A person receiving medical treatment.

surgical drape
A sterile covering used during surgery or other medical procedures.

adjustable stool
A seat without a back or armrests that can be raised or lowered using a small lever.

patient monitor
A screen that displays patient data, such as blood pressure and heart rate.

operating table
A flat surface designed to safely position patients during surgical procedures.

surgeon
A medical doctor specializing in surgery within a given field of medicine, such as orthopedics or urology.

hospital room
A medical room that accommodates one, two or several patients.

nurse call button
A push button near a hospital bed so a patient can alert a nurse or other staff member that help is needed.

privacy screen
A fixed or movable partition used to divide a room for privacy.

over-bed light
A light source located above a bed to illuminate a small area so as not to disturb others.

IV (intravenous) stand
A vertically adjustable stand on wheels used to support a gravity drip device.

medical utility table
A stainless steel table fitted with wheels and used to store instruments and supplies.

bedside table
A small piece of furniture positioned beside a bed so that personal effects may be readily reached.

adjustable hospital bed
A bed that can be raised or lowered with levers or a remote control.

wall light
A light source fitted on a hospital room wall.

intensive care unit
Also called a critical care unit, the ICU provides specialized care to people with life-threatening conditions.

numeric fields
Numbers that represent measurable bodily functions, such as vital signs.

waveform fields
A type of graph used to show the shape and form of a signal, such as a heartbeat.

patient monitor
A screen that displays patient data, such as blood pressure and heart rate.

patient connection panel
A panel of ports where electrical cables attached to the patient are connected.

cart
A buggy for a patient monitor or other equipment.

bedside table
A small piece of furniture positioned beside a bed so that personal effects may be readily reached.

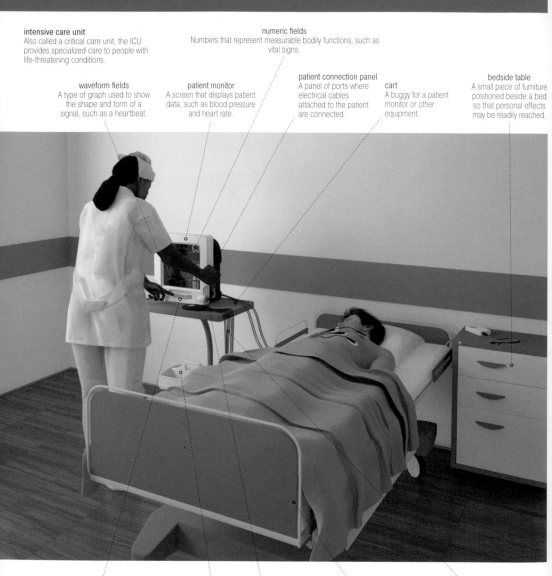

function buttons
Buttons that control the various functions of a patient monitor.

utility basket
A container used to store materials or waste.

trim knob
A knob on a patient monitor that allows the operator to scroll through various menu options.

adjustable hospital bed
A bed that can be raised or lowered with levers or a remote control.

cables
Wires that carry electrical current from a patient to a monitoring device.

physical therapy room
A room with examination tables and fitness equipment so that patients can recover from injuries.

physical therapist
A health care professional who helps patients improve their strength and mobility.

treatment table
A firm surface where a patient can be examined.

fitness ball
An exercise ball constructed of soft elastic material and filled with air.

bolster
A long, thick pillow that is typically placed under other pillows for additional neck or back support.

adjustable stool
A seat without a back or armrests that can be raised or lowered using a small lever.

treadmill
A piece of exercise equipment for walking or running in place.

gynecological examination room
A medical room where a gynecologist receives and treats patients.

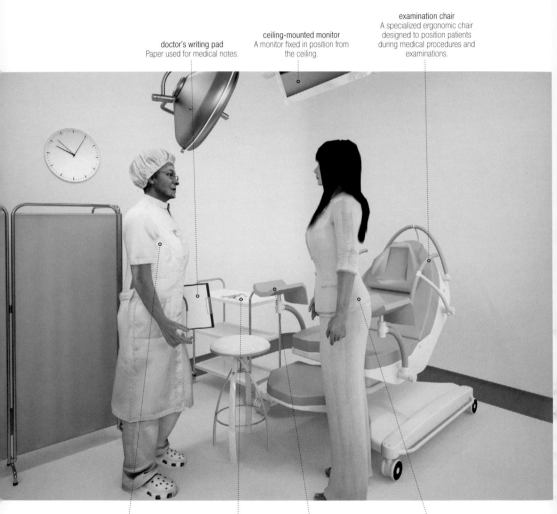

examination chair
A specialized ergonomic chair designed to position patients during medical procedures and examinations.

ceiling-mounted monitor
A monitor fixed in position from the ceiling.

doctor's writing pad
Paper used for medical notes.

gynecologist
A doctor who specializes in the female reproductive system.

instrument cart
A movable tray fitted with wheels; used to store medical instruments.

leg support
A support frame for a patient's legs during gynecological examinations.

patient
A person receiving medical treatment.

anesthesia monitor
A screen that displays a patient's vital signs when the patient is under anesthesia.

neonatal intensive care unit
A specialized area where babies who are born premature or have congenital anomilies or illnesses can be treated.

incubator
A piece of medical equipment that maintains environmental conditions suitable for ill or premature newborns.

canopy
The protective and insulated covering of an incubator, which maintains temperature and humidity levels.

porthole
An opening in an incubator canopy that allows a health care worker to safely access a newborn's body.

mattress
A pad placed on a support, bed frame or incubator tray.

newborn
A recently born baby.

mattress tray
A flat support surface for an incubator's mattress.

display panel
An electrical screen where information is shown for observational and diagnostic purposes.

height-adjustment foot pedals
Foot-controlled levers that allow hands-free vertical adjustment of an incubator.

neonatologist
A medical doctor specializing in the care of newborns, especially ill or premature newborns.

dressing container
A stainless steel drum used to sterilize, store and transport instruments and dressings.

underpad
Soft foam used to provide cushioning.

control and information panel
The graphical user interface (GUI) for operating a device. It is used to display and manipulate collected data.

two-tier medical utility cart
A stainless steel buggy fitted with two trays for instruments and supplies.

dental room
A room that contains specialized equipment for procedures done on teeth and gums.

emesis basin
A shallow, bean-shaped basin used in medical facilities to collect waste materials.

dental chair
A specialized ergonomic chair designed to position patients during dental procedures and examinations.

operating light
A special light that illuminates the examination or operating area.

delivery system
A movable module designed for easy access to dental instruments during dental procedures.

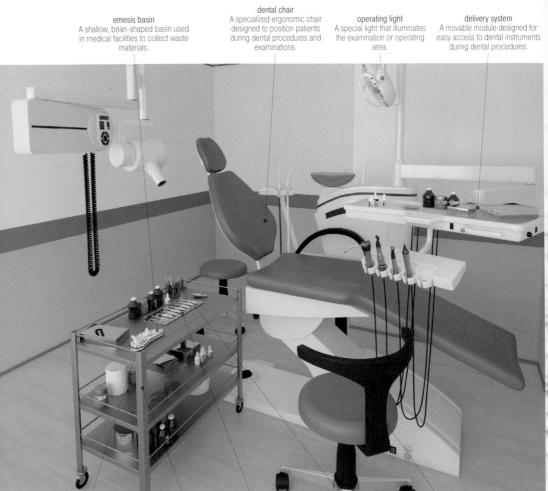

dental mirror
A dental instrument that allows a dentist to see inside a person's mouth.

Mayo instrument stand
A movable instrument tray often positioned adjacent to a dental chair.

work tray
A rectangular plate with raised edges that holds dental instruments or other items.

dental tweezers
A small instrument used like a pair of pincers to pick up and move small objects during dental procedures.

adjustable stool
A seat without a full back or armrests that can be raised or lowered using a small lever.

psychotherapy room
An office where a psychotherapist,
psychiatrist or psychologist treats
patients.

therapy couch
A couch used in therapy settings so
that a patient may sit comfortably.

therapist's chair
A seat where a therapist sits during
therapy sessions.

therapist's notes
Pertinent patient details written by a
therapist.

infant warmer
A heating device to warm newborns.

heating device
A device that uses electricity to produce heat to warm a newborn.

shelf
A flat surface for placing items.

surface for the baby
The area where the newborn is placed.

drawer
A storage compartment that slides in and out of a larger chest.

protective glass
A wall of glass used to protect a newborn from falling off an infant warmer.

doctor
A licensed practitioner of medicine.

wheel
A circular part that rotates on a bearing and allows the warmer to easily be moved.

incubator
A piece of medical equipment that maintains environmental conditions suitable for ill or premature newborns.

pediatric examination table
A specialized table designed to safely position an infant during a medical examination.

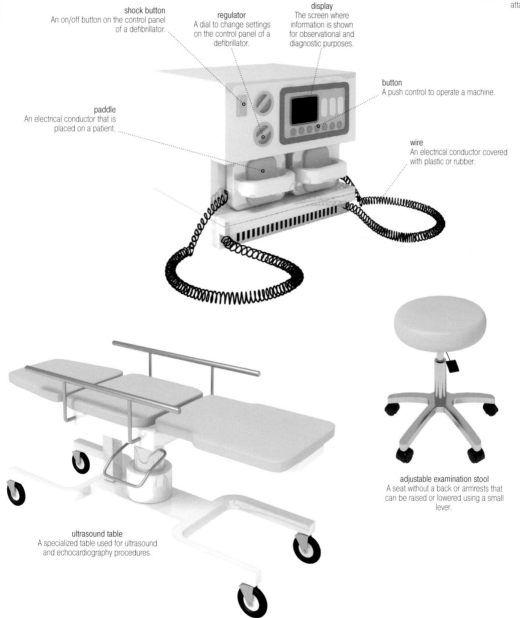

manual defibrillator
A device that uses an electrical shock to start the heart, usually after a heart attack.

shock button
An on/off button on the control panel of a defibrillator.

regulator
A dial to change settings on the control panel of a defibrillator.

display
The screen where information is shown for observational and diagnostic purposes.

button
A push control to operate a machine.

paddle
An electrical conductor that is placed on a patient.

wire
An electrical conductor covered with plastic or rubber.

adjustable examination stool
A seat without a back or armrests that can be raised or lowered using a small lever.

ultrasound table
A specialized table used for ultrasound and echocardiography procedures.

electric hospital bed
A bed that can be repositioned from
flat to upright using electrical power.

side rail
A steel rail designed to keep a patient from
falling off a hospital bed.

mattress
A pad placed on a support,
bed frame or incubator tray.

base
The foundation of an electric
hospital bed. It connects
the wheels and adjustment
pedals to the bed.

adjustment pedal
A foot control used to lower, raise or tilt an
electric hospital bed.

wheel
A circular part that rotates on a
bearing and allows the bed to
easily be moved.

hospital bed
A bed for a patient; usually fitted with
wheels.

IV (intravenous) stand
A vertically adjustable stand on wheels
used to support a gravity drip device.

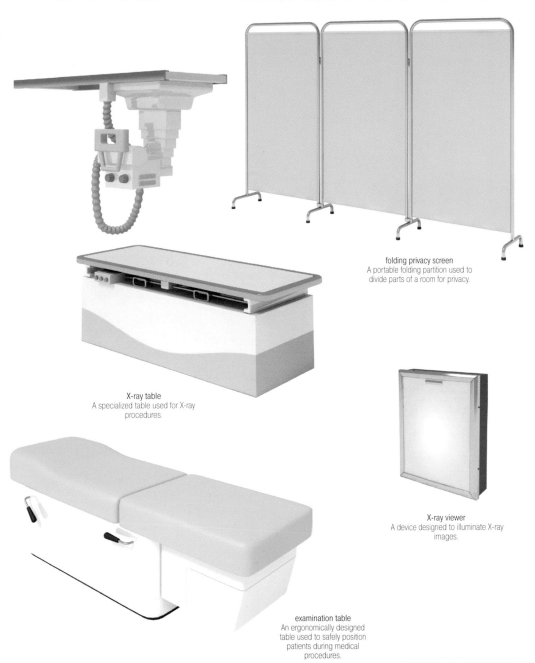

folding privacy screen
A portable folding partition used to divide parts of a room for privacy.

X-ray table
A specialized table used for X-ray procedures.

X-ray viewer
A device designed to illuminate X-ray images.

examination table
An ergonomically designed table used to safely position patients during medical procedures.

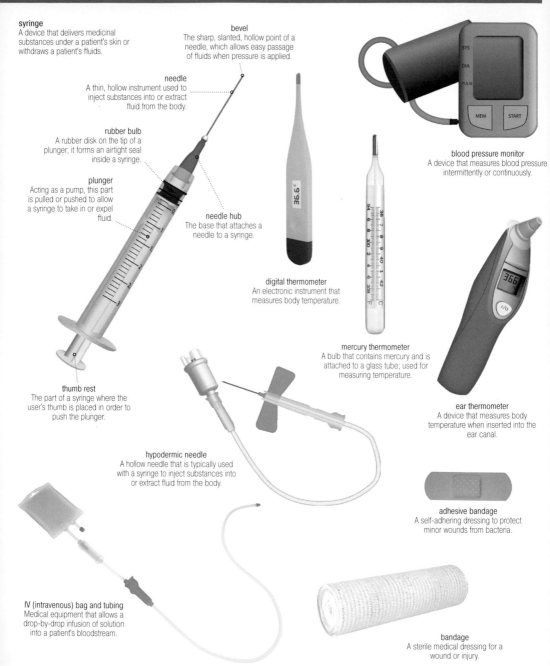

syringe
A device that delivers medicinal substances under a patient's skin or withdraws a patient's fluids.

bevel
The sharp, slanted, hollow point of a needle, which allows easy passage of fluids when pressure is applied.

needle
A thin, hollow instrument used to inject substances into or extract fluid from the body.

rubber bulb
A rubber disk on the tip of a plunger; it forms an airtight seal inside a syringe.

plunger
Acting as a pump, this part is pulled or pushed to allow a syringe to take in or expel fluid.

needle hub
The base that attaches a needle to a syringe.

digital thermometer
An electronic instrument that measures body temperature.

mercury thermometer
A bulb that contains mercury and is attached to a glass tube; used for measuring temperature.

blood pressure monitor
A device that measures blood pressure intermittently or continuously.

ear thermometer
A device that measures body temperature when inserted into the ear canal.

thumb rest
The part of a syringe where the user's thumb is placed in order to push the plunger.

hypodermic needle
A hollow needle that is typically used with a syringe to inject substances into or extract fluid from the body.

adhesive bandage
A self-adhering dressing to protect minor wounds from bacteria.

IV (intravenous) bag and tubing
Medical equipment that allows a drop-by-drop infusion of solution into a patient's bloodstream.

bandage
A sterile medical dressing for a wound or injury.

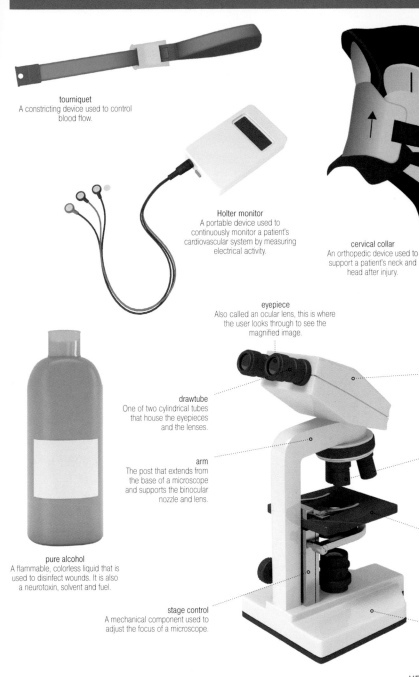

tourniquet
A constricting device used to control blood flow.

Holter monitor
A portable device used to continuously monitor a patient's cardiovascular system by measuring electrical activity.

cervical collar
An orthopedic device used to support a patient's neck and head after injury.

eyepiece
Also called an ocular lens, this is where the user looks through to see the magnified image.

microscope
A laboratory instrument used to see very small objects, such as cells.

binocular nozzle
The tube that connects the objective lens with the eyepiece.

drawtube
One of two cylindrical tubes that house the eyepieces and the lenses.

arm
The post that extends from the base of a microscope and supports the binocular nozzle and lens.

objective lens
The lens located over the slide or sample being viewed.

pure alcohol
A flammable, colorless liquid that is used to disinfect wounds. It is also a neurotoxin, solvent and fuel.

stage
The tray where slides or samples are placed.

stage control
A mechanical component used to adjust the focus of a microscope.

base
The foundation of a microscope.

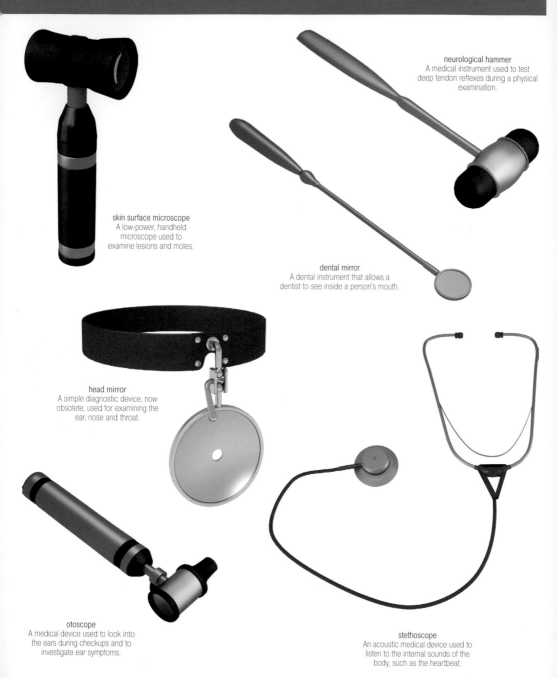

skin surface microscope
A low-power, handheld microscope used to examine lesions and moles.

neurological hammer
A medical instrument used to test deep tendon reflexes during a physical examination.

dental mirror
A dental instrument that allows a dentist to see inside a person's mouth.

head mirror
A simple diagnostic device, now obsolete, used for examining the ear, nose and throat.

otoscope
A medical device used to look into the ears during checkups and to investigate ear symptoms.

stethoscope
An acoustic medical device used to listen to the internal sounds of the body, such as the heartbeat.

pills
An oral dose of medication in tablet, caplet or biodegradable capsule form.

capsule
A small case of gelatin or other digestable substance that is designed to store medication.

suppository
Medication inserted into the rectum and absorbed by the bloodstream.

tablet
A small, circular pill made of condensed powder.

caplet
A cylindrical pill made of condensed powder; it is typically a higher dose than a tablet.

syrup
A thick, often sticky liquid medication.

ampule
A hermetically sealed glass vial or vessel used to store solution for hypodermic injection.

metered-dose inhaler
A handheld device capable of delivering a specific amount of medication in aerosol form for inhalation.

auto-injector
A spring-loaded syringe designed to deliver a single dose of medication, typically in the thigh or buttocks.

nasal spray
Any liquid medication that can be atomized and inhaled through the nose.

ointment
A topical cream rubbed on the skin, usually to heal a wound and reduce pain or discomfort.

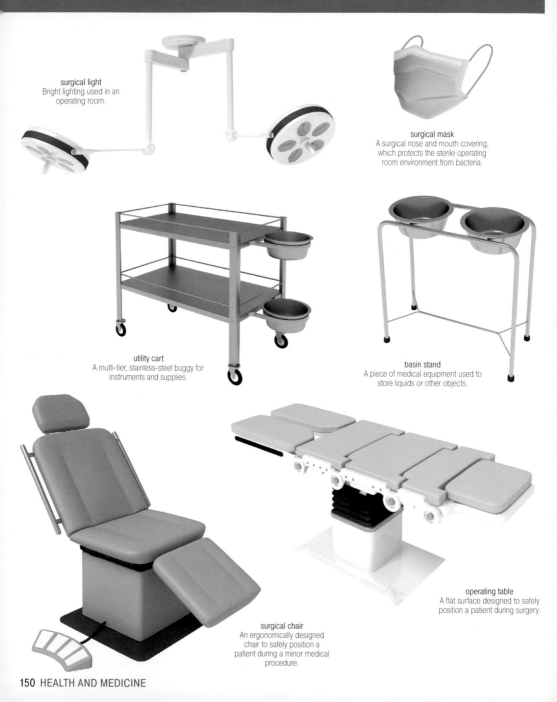

surgical light
Bright lighting used in an operating room.

surgical mask
A surgical nose and mouth covering, which protects the sterile operating room environment from bacteria.

utility cart
A multi-tier, stainless-steel buggy for instruments and supplies.

basin stand
A piece of medical equipment used to store liquids or other objects.

surgical chair
An ergonomically designed chair to safely position a patient during a minor medical procedure.

operating table
A flat surface designed to safely position a patient during surgery.

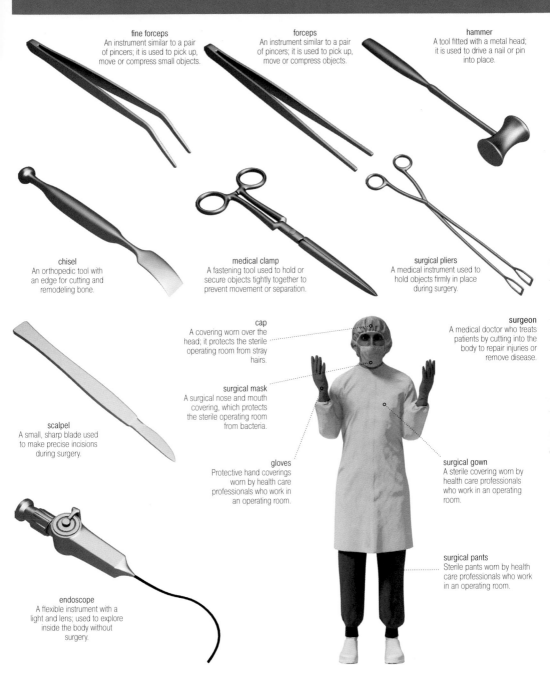

fine forceps
An instrument similar to a pair of pincers; it is used to pick up, move or compress small objects.

forceps
An instrument similar to a pair of pincers; it is used to pick up, move or compress objects.

hammer
A tool fitted with a metal head; it is used to drive a nail or pin into place.

chisel
An orthopedic tool with an edge for cutting and remodeling bone.

medical clamp
A fastening tool used to hold or secure objects tightly together to prevent movement or separation.

surgical pliers
A medical instrument used to hold objects firmly in place during surgery.

cap
A covering worn over the head; it protects the sterile operating room from stray hairs.

surgeon
A medical doctor who treats patients by cutting into the body to repair injuries or remove disease.

surgical mask
A surgical nose and mouth covering, which protects the sterile operating room from bacteria.

scalpel
A small, sharp blade used to make precise incisions during surgery.

gloves
Protective hand coverings worn by health care professionals who work in an operating room.

surgical gown
A sterile covering worn by health care professionals who work in an operating room.

surgical pants
Sterile pants worn by health care professionals who work in an operating room.

endoscope
A flexible instrument with a light and lens; used to explore inside the body without surgery.

four-wheel walker
A walking support frame for those injured or disabled.

handle
An ergonomically designed handgrip to push a four-wheel walker.

brake lever
A hand control used to stop or lock wheels.

basket
A storage compartment.

wheel
A circular part that rotates on a bearing and allows the wheelchair to move easily.

brake cable
A flexible wire used to lock the back wheels of a four-wheel walker.

caster
A wheel that can swivel in any direction to provide greater ease of movement.

quad cane
A walking stick with a base of four legs, which offer extra balance and support.

Fritz cane
A walking stick with an ergonomically designed handle.

four-wheel electric scooter
A power-operated mobility aid similar to a motor scooter and fitted with a swiveling seat.

offset cane
A walking stick that provides extra balance and support for those with gripping problems.

underarm crutch
A walking support held against the ribcage; it has a padded handgrip and support that goes in the armpit.

electric wheelchair
A wheelchair powered by an electric motor rather than by manual power.

back
Soft fabric that supports a seated person's back.

handle
An ergonomically designed handgrip to push a wheelchair.

control stick
The electric mechanism by which the person controls the wheelchair's movements.

armrest
A padded or upholstered arm on a wheelchair or other seat.

seat
A surface for sitting.

electric drive
A transmission system that provides power to the rear wheels of a wheelchair.

wheel
A circular part that rotates on a bearing and allows the walker to move easily.

footboard
Foldaway platforms that support the feet of someone in a wheelchair.

caster
A wheel that can swivel in any direction to provide greater ease of movement.

forearm crutch
Also known as a Lofstrand crutch, this is a crutch with a cuff at the top to fit the forearm.

back
Soft fabric that supports a seated person's back.

clothing guard
A panel on the side of a wheelchair; it protects the user's clothes from dirt or spray from the wheel.

wheelchair
A chair with large wheels that is designed to make disabled people mobile.

handle
An ergonomically designed handgrip to push a wheelchair.

arm
Part of the metal frame of a wheelchair, extending from the back to the front wheels.

armrest
A padded or upholstered arm on a wheelchair or other seat.

seat
A surface for sitting.

push rim
A circular handrail fitted to the wheel; it allows the wheels to be turned by hand, propelling the wheelchair.

caster
A wheel that can swivel in any direction to provide greater ease of movement.

hub
The center of a wheel, which consists of an axle, bearings and hub shell.

footrest
A foldaway platform that supports the feet of someone in a wheelchair.

large wheel
Resembling a bicycle wheel, this is one of two large back wheels on a wheelchair.

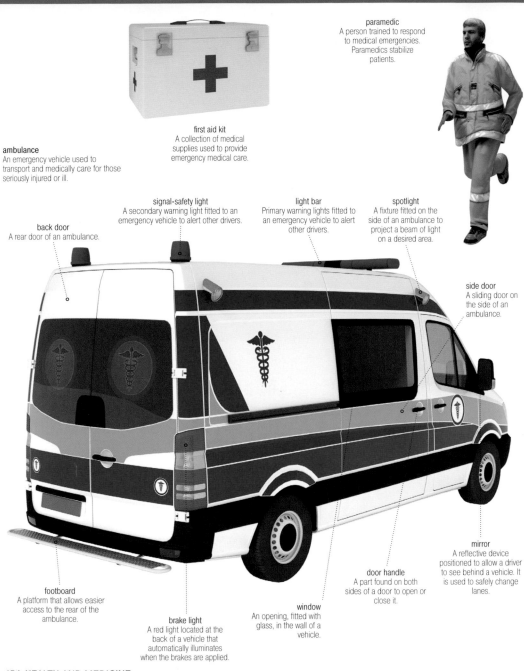

first aid kit
A collection of medical supplies used to provide emergency medical care.

paramedic
A person trained to respond to medical emergencies. Paramedics stabilize patients.

ambulance
An emergency vehicle used to transport and medically care for those seriously injured or ill.

signal-safety light
A secondary warning light fitted to an emergency vehicle to alert other drivers.

light bar
Primary warning lights fitted to an emergency vehicle to alert other drivers.

spotlight
A fixture fitted on the side of an ambulance to project a beam of light on a desired area.

back door
A rear door of an ambulance.

side door
A sliding door on the side of an ambulance.

mirror
A reflective device positioned to allow a driver to see behind a vehicle. It is used to safely change lanes.

footboard
A platform that allows easier access to the rear of the ambulance.

door handle
A part found on both sides of a door to open or close it.

brake light
A red light located at the back of a vehicle that automatically illuminates when the brakes are applied.

window
An opening, fitted with glass, in the wall of a vehicle.

stretcher
An apparatus used to move injured patients who require medical care.

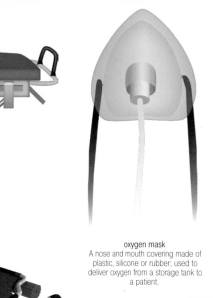

oxygen mask
A nose and mouth covering made of plastic, silicone or rubber; used to deliver oxygen from a storage tank to a patient.

support
The structural component of a stretcher, which provides a framework for the bed.

stretcher
An apparatus used to move injured individuals who require medical care.

foot
The end of a stretcher opposite the handles.

bed
A fabric panel fitted to the support of a stretcher.

handle
An ergonomically designed handgrip to carry a stretcher.

bag valve mask
A manual resuscitation device that provides positive pressure ventilation to patients who need help breathing.

bag
The inflatable reservoir of a bag valve mask.

adapter
A device used to attach two parts, such as a bag to a mask.

mask
The part of a bag valve mask that covers the mouth and nose of a patient.

HOUSING

ground floor of house
The main floor of the building.

refrigerator
A household appliance with an insulated compartment kept artificially cool for the storage of perishable foods.

kitchen
The room in a house where food is prepared and usually stored.

cabinets
A set of cupboards with shelves and hinged doors, typically found in the kitchen and used for storage.

powder room
A room for personal hygiene purposes, usually containing only a sink and a toilet, and commonly used by visitors.

stairs
A series of steps leading from one level of a building to another.

breakfast bar
A long counter in a kitchen, usually accommodated by bar stools, at which meals, often informal ones, are served.

bar stool
A seat supported on tall pedestals or legs, usually padded and without backs, most often placed around a bar.

dining room
A room or defined space, most often adjacent to the kitchen, designated for formal meals.

mailbox
A compartment designed to receive private postal deliveries.

dining table
A table usually made to accommodate six or more people, designed for formal meals.

picture
Images captured on paper in the form of photographs or artwork and framed for display purposes.

dining chair
A style of chairs with tall upright backs and without arms, typically matching a large table designed for formal meals.

front door
The main entrance to a house or other building.

front steps
A set of stairs leading to the main entrance of a house or other building.

doorbell
A bell or chimes that can be rung by a person outside of a building, usually by a push button, to signal their presence.

patio
A paved outdoor space adjoining a residence, generally used for recreation or dining.

patio umbrella
A canopy attached to a pole and used to provide shade over outdoor furniture.

fence
An upright structure, typically of wood or wire, enclosing an area of property.

flower bed
A built-up area of soil in which flowers are cultivated outdoors.

banister
A structure fixed to the side of a staircase; it is composed of upright pieces to support the handrail, which is gripped for balance.

shelf
A flat, elongated surface built onto or into a wall for the storage or display of small objects.

sofa
A fully upholstered seat with arms and a back, long enough to accommodate three or more people.

coffee table
A piece of furniture, usually long and low, designed to be placed in front of a sofa or easy chairs.

living room
A gathering space in a home; it often contains upholstered furniture and a television.

television
An electronic broadcast system that displays picture and sound for entertainment.

retaining wall
A structure used to hold back dirt or water.

ottoman
A small piece of furniture, usually upholstered and without a back or arms, often used as a stool or footstool.

gate
An opening in a fence or wall secured with a movable barrier, usually hinged.

car
A four-wheeled, engine-powered vehicle that is designed for road travel and carries a small number of people.

paver
A brick or concrete block used to create a driveway, path, patio or other outdoor area.

shrub
Small, woody plants often situated around the perimeter of a property for decorative or privacy purposes.

lawn
An area of grass that is mowed regularly and kept neat, usually surrounding a residence.

sandbox
A shallow pit or raised box filled with sand for children to play in, usually found outdoors.

second floor of house
The level immediately above the ground-level floor of a building.

closet
A small area enclosed by doors; used to store clothing and shoes.

bathroom
A room for personal hygiene purposes, usually containing a bathtub, shower, sink and toilet.

hall
A long, narrow area with doors that lead to individual rooms.

dressing room
A room designed for changing clothing; it usually contains a mirror and clothes closets.

master bedroom
A room where the heads of the household sleep; it usually contains a closet, bed and storage furniture.

balcony
A platform built on the outside of a building, above ground level; it can be accessed from inside.

bistro set
A small table with two matching chairs, usually placed on a balcony or patio for casual, intimate seating.

railing
A fence or barrier, typically made of wood, metal or glass, around the perimeter of a balcony to prevent falling.

bathroom
A room for personal hygiene purposes, usually containing a bathtub, shower, sink and toilet.

child's bedroom
A room where a child sleeps; usually contains a closet, bed and dressers.

nursery
A room where a baby sleeps; it contains a crib, changing table and other accessories.

security camera
A surveillance device mounted on the outside of a building; it transmits live or static images to a monitor inside.

exterior of house
The house's envelope and the surrounding property.

balcony
A platform built on the outside of a building, above ground level; it can be accessed from inside.

roof
The topmost covering of a building.

roof hatch
A hinged barrier that can be opened to access the area under the roof of a building.

front door
The main entrance to a house or other building.

porch
A platform at the entrance to a building, often covered by an overhang and accessed by a short flight of steps.

patio umbrella
A canopy attached to a pole, used to provide shade over outdoor furniture.

patio
A paved, outdoor space adjoining a residence, generally used for recreation or dining.

bistro set
A small table with two matching chairs, usually placed on a balcony or patio for casual, intimate seating.

flower bed
A built-up area of soil in which flowers are cultivated outdoors.

lawn
An area of grass that is mowed regularly and kept neat, usually surrounding a residence.

sandbox
A shallow pit or raised box filled with sand for children to play in, usually found outdoors.

fence
A upright structure, typically of wood or wire, enclosing an area of property.

ventilation shaft
A passage constructed under the roof of a building to allow air circulation.

solar panel
A sheet of silicon-based material that absorbs radiation from the sun in order to convert it into electricity.

security camera
A device mounted on the outside of a building; it transmits live or static images to a monitor inside.

garage door
A barrier that can be moved to gain access to a garage; usually a large sheet of metal that can be rolled or swung up.

car
A four-wheeled, engine-powered vehicle that is designed for road travel and carries a small number of people.

hedge
Outdoor vegetation used to provide decoration, privacy or shade.

retaining wall
A structure used to hold back dirt or water.

gate
An opening in a fence or wall secured with a movable barrier, usually hinged.

driveway
A short, paved area leading from a main road to the garage or entrance of a residence.

apartment building
A tall residential building with a number of contained residences on each floor.

facade
The primary outer face of a building into which the main entrance is built, usually facing the main road.

penthouse
An apartment on the top floor of an apartment building, typically luxurious and with a nice view.

balcony door
A barrier that can be moved to gain access to a balcony; often a full-length sliding pane of glass.

balcony
A platform built on the outside of a building, above ground level; it can be accessed from inside.

balcony railing
A fence or barrier, typically made of wood, metal or glass, around the perimeter of a balcony to prevent falling.

resident
A person who lives in a building and can claim rights to a specified space within the building.

window
A sheet of glass or other transparent or opaque material fixed into the wall of a building as a source of natural light.

intercom
An electrical device next to the entrance of a building that allows communication with a party indoors.

main entrance
The primary entry and exit to a building; it often has an overhang and a security system.

satellite dish
A bowl-shaped object fixed to the outside of a building; it is fitted with an antenna to receive communications signals.

antenna
A device designed to transmit or receive communications signals, usually for radio or television.

patio umbrella
A canopy attached to a pole, used to provide shade over outdoor furniture.

patio
A paved outdoor space adjoining a residence, generally used for recreation or dining.

living room
A gathering space in a home; it often contains upholstered furniture and a television.

book
A bound set of printed, written or illustrated sheets of paper.

fruit bowl
A concave vessel used to hold and display fruit, like apples and oranges.

bookshelf
Thin slabs of rigid material, usually fixed horizontally to a wall or frame, to display books and other objects.

sofa
A fully upholstered seat with arms and a back, long enough to accommodate three or more people.

magazine
A printed work that is issued on a periodical basis; it contains articles and images about a specific topic.

coffee table
A piece of furniture, usually long and low, designed to be placed in front of a sofa or easy chairs.

remote control
An apparatus that emits electronic signals to manipulate the functions of an electronic device from a distance.

DVD
A compact digital disc that is used to store large amounts of data, usually in the form of audiovisual recordings.

DVD player
A machine that reads the data from a DVD and relays it onto a television or computer screen.

television
An electronic broadcast system that displays picture and sound for entertainment.

shelf
A flat, elongated surface built onto or into a wall for the storage or display of small objects.

cushion
A large upholstered pillow that is placed on a chair or sofa to make it more comfortable.

armchair
A chair with armrests, usually with a cushioned back and seat and sometimes upholstered.

ottoman
A small piece of furniture, usually upholstered and without a back or arms, often used as a stool or footstool.

potted plant
Vegetation grown in a pot indoors, usually for decorative purposes.

master bedroom
A room where the heads of the household sleep; it
usually contains a closet, bed and storage furniture.

curtain
One of a pair of pieces of fabric hung
over a window; they can be drawn
together for privacy.

light fixture
A device that artificially
illuminates an area.

photograph
A picture taken by camera,
transfered to light-sensitive
material or stored digitally.

nightstand
A small piece of furniture,
usually with drawers or
shelves, that sits next to the
head of a bed.

rug
A covering made of thick,
woven material that only
covers a section of floor.

book
A bound set of printed,
written or illustrated sheets
of paper.

bed
A piece of furniture for
lying upon to sleep, usually
consisting of a frame raised
from the floor and a mattress.

pillow
A cushioned support for the head, usually
rectangular, that is stuffed with a soft
material such as foam or feathers.

light switch
A small device on a wall used to control the
flow of electricity to light fixtures, usually by
moving it up or down.

closet door
A barrier that can be moved to gain access
to a closet, usually structured as a hinged or
sliding sheet of wood with a knob.

telephone
An electronic device used to
communicate with another
person through speech and
across a distance.

electrical outlet
A set of holes in a wall leading
to a power source into which an
electrical plug connected to a
device can be inserted.

hardwood floor
A type of flooring composed
of narrow slats of wood fitted
tightly together lengthwise to
form a flat surface.

bathroom
A room for personal hygiene purposes, usually containing a bathtub, shower, sink and toilet.

recessed light
A lighting fixture that is installed in the ceiling of a room.

shower cubicle
A small, enclosed area in the bathroom, equipped with a showerhead, where one can clean oneself.

tile
A piece of clay, stone or glass; used to create a surface on a floor or wall.

bath towel
A large piece of absorbent material used to dry the body after bathing or showering.

faucet
A device with handles or knobs that can be turned to adjust the flow of water from a pipe.

shampoo
A liquid soap that is formulated specifically for cleaning the hair on one's head.

bathtub
A large basin fitted with a tap and a drain, usually made of porcelain or plastic, that is filled with water for bathing.

bath mat
A small rug made of an absorbent material that covers a section of floor next to a bathtub or shower.

window
A sheet of glass or other transparent or opaque material fixed into the wall of a building as a source of natural light.

toilet
A fixture used to flush bodily waste into a sewer or septic system.

mirror
A glass surface used to view one's appearance.

fan
A vent built into the wall or ceiling of a room to expel an accumulation of moisture or steam to the outside environment.

medicine cabinet
An enclosed cupboard mounted on the wall of a bathroom, usually over a sink, to hold personal hygiene products.

soap dish
A small, shallow container that sits on the edge of a washing fixture, such as a sink or tub, to hold a bar of soap.

faucet
A device with handles or knobs that can be turned to adjust the flow of water from a pipe.

toothbrush
A hygiene tool consisting of bristles, which is used to clean the teeth.

toothbrush holder
A cup designed to hold toothbrushes, often with a lid with slots into which individual toothbrushes can be placed.

lotion
A thick, smooth substance that can be applied to the hands and rest of the body to moisturize the skin.

sink
A basin fitted with a tap and a drain, usually made of porcelain or other hard, smooth, material.

hand towel
A small piece of absorbent material used to dry the hands after washing.

floor
The surface of a room on which people walk and most furniture and fixtures sit.

toilet paper
Soft, absorbent paper, usually in the form of small sheets on a roll, used to wipe oneself after using the toilet.

toilet brush
A bristeled cleaning tool used to scrub the inner bowl of a toilet.

wastebasket
A small container used to collect garbage, often fitted with a lid that can be opened with a foot pedal.

vanity
A bathroom structure that houses the sink and features a countertop. It also stores items.

girl's room
A room where a female child sleeps.

wall decal
A decorative image that can be affixed to a wall.

clock
A device that measures and displays time in hours, minutes and seconds.

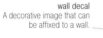

photograph
A picture taken by camera and transfered to light-sensitive material or stored digitally.

chest of drawers
A piece of furniture with a number of storage areas set into a box-like frame, typically used to store clothing.

pillow
A cushioned support for the head, usually rectangular, that is stuffed with a soft material such as foam or feathers.

sheets
Sections of soft cloth, usually rectangular, used to cover the mattress of a bed and the person sleeping on it.

bed
A piece of furniture for lying upon to sleep, usually consisting of a frame raised from the floor and a mattress.

wallpaper
A decorative paper that can be applied to walls in vertical strips.

picture
Images captured on paper in the form of photographs or artwork and framed for display purposes.

lamp
A light fixture, usually with a short pedestal and a shade, designed to sit on a flat surface, such as a nightstand.

toy
An object that is made for a child to play with, often with bright colors and moving parts.

nightstand
A small table that sits next to the head of a bed, usually containing drawers or shelves to hold small objects.

hardwood floor
A type of flooring composed of narrow slats of wood fitted tightly together lengthwise to form a flat surface.

throw rug
A small, woven piece of material that covers a small area of a floor; it can be easily moved.

nursery
A room where a baby sleeps; it contains a crib, changing table and other accessories.

baby lotion
A moisturizing cream formulated for an infant's soft, sensitive skin.

shelf
A flat, elongated surface built onto or into a wall for the storage or display of small objects.

changing table
A padded platform that provides a surface on which to lay a baby for hygienic activities such as changing diapers.

toy
An object that is made for a child to play with, often with bright colors and moving parts.

curtain
One of a pair of pieces of
fabric hung over a window;
they can be drawn together
for privacy.

floor lamp
A light fixture set atop a
long pedestal or pole that
is designed to stand on the
floor of a room.

rocking chair
A chair with semi-circular
pieces on either side to
allow a rocking motion when
one is seated.

pillow
A cushioned support for the
head, usually rectangular,
that is stuffed with a soft
material such as foam or
feathers.

rug
A covering made of thick,
woven material that only
covers a section of floor.

crib
A bed designed for an infant
or very small child, usually
with latticed or railed sides
to prevent falling.

Children's furniture
Household furnishings designed specifically for small children or infants.

changing table
A padded platform that provides a surface on which to lay a baby for hygienic activities such as changing diapers.

knob
A ball-shaped handle.

drawer
A box-shaped compartment in a piece of furniture; used for storage.

leg
A support attached to the bottom of a piece of furniture to stabilize or raise it.

shelf
A flat, elongated surface built into a piece of furniture, on which objects are stored.

armoire
A tall, freestanding piece of furniture with long doors; used to store clothing.

high chair
An elevated chair fitted with a front tray in which a small child can be seated for feeding.

back
The rear surface of an object, such as a chair or other piece of furniture, that makes up part of its frame.

desk and chair
A table designed for written or computer work, along with a seat designed for one person.

desk
A piece of furniture with a large, flat surface on which work can be performed.

tray
A flat container, usually with a raised rim and sometimes with handles, most often used to carry food and drink.

seat
A flat surface on which a person may sit, for example, as part of a chair or sofa.

leg
A support attached to the bottom of a piece of furniture to stabilize or raise it.

footrest
A small, protruding platform on a tall chair or stool where the feet can be placed when they cannot touch the floor.

chair
Seats for one person that have backs and may or may not have armrests.

frame
A structure comprising several pieces of rigid material, such as wood, fixed together to form a specific shape.

bunk bed
A piece of furniture consisting of two beds, one mounted over the other.

drawer
A box-shaped compartment in a piece of furniture; used for storage.

safety rail
A fence or barrier, typically made of wood, metal or glass, around the edge of a platform to prevent falling.

pillow
A cushioned support for the head, usually rectangular, that is stuffed with a soft material such as foam or feathers.

ladder
A structure of two upright bars and a set of horizontal steps; used for cimbing up or down.

mattress
A large, stuffed pad for sleeping on; it is covered with material and often reinforced internally with springs.

crib
A bed designed for an infant or very small child, usually with latticed or railed sides to prevent falling.

slat
A thin, narrow piece of wood or metal that creates a barrier, such as around a child's bed.

mattress
A large, stuffed pad for sleeping on; it is covered with material and often reinforced internally with springs.

drawer
A box-shaped compartment in a piece of furniture; used for storage.

bed
A piece of furniture for lying upon to sleep, usually consisting of a frame raised from the floor and a mattress.

kitchen
A room with major appliances, a sink and countertops, where meals are prepared.

picture
Images captured on paper in the form of photographs or artwork and framed for display purposes.

clock
A device that measures and displays time in hours, minutes and seconds.

refrigerator
A household appliance with an insulated compartment kept artificially cool for the storage of perishable foods.

microwave
A small oven used to heat foods using electromagnetic waves.

breakfast bar
A long counter in a kitchen, usually accommodated by bar stools, at which meals, often informal ones, are served.

bar stool
A seat supported on a tall pedestal or legs, usually padded and without a back, most often placed at or around a bar.

oven
A large kitchen appliance used to cook foods, usually by baking or broiling.

coffee machine
A kitchen appliance that is used to brew fresh coffee, usually using coffee grounds in a drip filter.

wine fridge
A refrigerated cabinet in which wine bottles can be placed to be kept cool.

range hood
A fan built into the wall or ceiling of a room; used to expel steam or smoke.

wine glass
A vessel used for drinking wine and usually made of glass.

canister
A cylindrical container usually made of glass with a screw-on lid; used to store dry goods.

cup
A small, bowl-shaped vessel for drinking hot liquids.

faucet
A device with handles or knobs that can be turned to adjust the flow of water from a pipe.

cabinet
A series of shelving units that is built onto a wall and covered with hinged doors.

cooktop
A cooking appliance composed of hot plates or burners, usually built into a countertop.

countertop
A smooth, raised surface at which one works in the kitchen.

dishwasher
A kitchen appliance into which soiled kitchenware, such as dishes and cutlery, can be stacked to be washed automatically.

sink
A basin fitted with a tap and a drain, usually made of porcelain, metal or other hard, smooth material.

tiled floor
A floor with a surface covered in squares of clay, ceramic, porcelain or stone.

Large appliances

Large machines designed for use in the home, such as to keep food fresh or clean dishes.

refrigerator
An appliance with an insulated compartment kept artificially cool for the storage of perishable foods.

shelf
A flat, elongated surface built into an appliance, on which objects are stored.

egg tray
A compartment with indented cups for storing eggs.

refrigerator compartment door
A hinged barrier that is swung open to gain access to the primary chilled compartment.

handle
The part of the appliance that is held by the hand to open and close the door.

side-by-side refrigerator and freezer
A refrigerator with two doors that swing outward to either side, one of which is usually to the freezer compartment.

freezer compartment
The section of a refrigerator used to store and keep foods frozen.

microwave
A small oven used to heat foods using electromagnetic waves.

crisper
A specialized compartment that is designed to store vegetables and keep them fresh.

drawer
A box-shaped compartment used for storage.

handle
The part of the appliance that is held by the hand to open and close the door.

clock timer
A device that measures or controls the length of time an appliance is in use; often equipped with a sound alert.

freezer compartment door
A hinged barrier that is swung open to gain access to the freezer section.

window
The clear glass section one looks through to see inside and monitor the cooking of food.

turntable
A circular, rotating plate; food is placed on the plate and spun to be cooked evenly.

cooktop
An electrical cooking appliance with hot plates or burners; usually built into or placed atop a kitchen countertop.

door
A barrier, usually hinged, that is used to gain access to the microwave's cooking compartment.

control panel
An area containing switces or dials that allow the user to operate the device.

ventilation duct
A tubular length of metal suspended over an appliance and used to channel steam outside.

range hood
A fan built into the wall or ceiling of a room; used to expel steam or smoke.

power button
A small lever that can be flipped or pressed to turn the electrical connection between a source and a device on or off.

dishwasher
An appliance into which soiled kitchenware, such as dishes and cutlery, is stacked and then washed automatically.

handle
The part of the appliance that is held by the hand to open and close the door.

control knob
A knob that can be adjusted to select the cycle or other operation on the appliance.

screen
A plate of resistant material, such as glass or metal, to create a barrier.

indicator light
A tiny light built into an appliance to signal the active running or completion of the machine's cycle.

door
A hinged barrier that is swung open to gain access to the washing compartment.

filter
A thick, woven mesh of porous fibers over the opening of a ventilation device to capture residue.

display
A lit panel that provides information, such as the selected function or cycle of operation.

gas range
A cooking appliance consisting of an oven and stove combination that is powered solely by natural gas or propane.

burner
A circular, perforated piece of metal designed to concentrate flames to a small area on a gas-powered stovetop.

cooktop control knob
A knob that adjusts the amount of gas being released to a burner; used to control the cooking temperature.

handle
The part of the appliance that is held by the hand to open and close the door.

oven control knob
A dial on an oven that can be turned to adjust its function, for example, from bake to broil.

electric range
A cooking appliance consisting of an oven and stove combination that is powered solely by electricity.

oven
The compartment on a range that is used to bake or broil foods.

Small appliances
Machines and devices that automate simple household tasks.

espresso machine
A kitchen appliance that is used to brew a fresh concentrated coffee called espresso.

pressure gauge
An indicator that displays the level of pressure built up inside the main compartment.

cup-warming tray
A heated, flat pan of metal on which a drinking vessel, such as a cup or mug, can be placed to be warmed.

group head
The part of an espresso machine in which coffee is mixed with hot water and dispensed into a drinking vessel.

water tank
A container that holds water to be used in the operation of an appliance.

filter holder
A conical closed container designed to hold the filter and coffee grounds in a coffee machine.

spout
A small tube that channels liquid into a stream, making it easy to pour.

coffee grinder
A kitchen appliance that is used to reduce coffee beans into grounds.

handle
A heat-resistant handgrip that is used when handling the filter basket.

steam nozzle
The open end of the steam wand; it expels steam to create foam.

automatic drip coffeemaker
An appliance that is used to brew fresh coffee, using coffee grounds in a drip filter.

lid
The covering for the top of the filter compartment.

water-level indicator
A transparent strip of material on the side of the water chamber that shows the level of water within.

drip tray
A flat pan that collects any spilled liquid.

basket
A closed container designed to hold the filter paper and coffee grounds.

pot lid
A covering made of a heat-resistant material so it can be handled.

lid-release button
A small protrusion that is depressed to unlock and open the lid.

handle
The part of the pot that is grasped with the hand so the pot can be held.

pot
A large, sometimes insulated, vessel with a spout, handle and tight-fitting lid.

warming plate
A heated, flat plate of metal on which the pot can be placed to be warmed.

water reservoir
The compartment on an appliance that holds a store of water.

blender
An appliance with a vessel and blades attached to a motor; used to mix ingredients.

juicer
An appliance into which fruits or vegetables are inserted to have the juice squeezed from them and collected.

pusher
A blunt cylindrical tool that is used to press food into a mincing or grinding appliance.

feed tube
A vertical opening through which ingredients are pressed or poured into an appliance.

filter
A mesh of porous fibers or a grid of metal or plastic that is placed over an opening to separate solids from liquids.

lid
The covering for the top of a container; it can be hinged or freely lifted off.

motor housing
A hard outer casing enclosing the motor.

pulp container
The vessel used to collect solid elements of the fruits or vegetables.

spout
A small tube that channels liquid into a stream, making it easy to pour.

power button
A small lever that can be flipped or pressed to turn the electrical connection between a source and a device on or off.

safety latch
A rod that can be raised or lowered to lock or unlock the main compartment.

immersion blender
A handheld kitchen tool with small rotating blades; used to blend ingredients together.

electric kettle
A metal or plastic vessel with a spout, lid and handle that can be plugged into an electrical outlet for boiling water.

electric citrus juicer
A machine that is used to extract the liquid from citrus fruits.

reamer
The central protruding piece onto which fruit is pushed to extract the juice.

spout
A small pinched piece that channels liquid into a stream, making it easy to pour.

lid
The covering for the top of the pot; usually hinged.

lid-release button
A small protrusion that can be depressed to unlock and open the lid of a container.

strainer
A device with small holes used to separate solids from liquids.

spout
A small pinched piece that channels liquid into a stream, making it easy to pour.

power switch
A small lever that can be flipped or pressed to turn the electrical connection between a source and a device on or off.

handle
The part of a tool, machine or object that is held by the hand to pull or control it.

juice-level indicator
A transparent strip of material on the side of the jug of a juicer showing the level of juice within.

motor housing
A hard outer casing enclosing the motor.

bowl
A container attached to the appliance that collects and holds the liquid.

base
A flat or footed low platform on which the pot rests.

indicator light
A small light built into an appliance to signal an active electrical connection.

toaster oven
A kitchen appliance used to bake, toast or broil foods.

handle
The part of the appliance that is held by the hand to open and close the door.

display
A lit panel that provides information, such as the selected function or cycle of operation.

rack
A metal grid that can be slid onto side supports to raise cooking vessels off the bottom of the oven.

control button
A small protusion that allows the user to change the function or cycle.

temperature control
A rotating knob that can be turned to adjust the level of heat.

door
A barrier, usually hinged, that is used to gain access to the cooking compartment.

timer
A device that measures or controls the length of time the appliance will be in use.

deep fryer
An appliance used to fry foods, such as breaded chicken or doughnuts, in hot oil.

timer
A device that measures or controls the length of time an appliance is in use; often equipped with a sound alert.

control panel
The area on a device that allows the user to change its function, motion or response, using buttons or switches.

lid handle
A heat-resistant arm that can be grasped to open or close the cover.

lid
The covering for the top of the fryer; can usually be lifted off.

carrying handle
A piece of solid material that is attached at either end of the object so it can be moved more easily.

fryer basket handle
A heat-resistant handgrip attached to the fryer basket; it can be grasped to handle the basket.

viewing window
A small, clear pane that allows one to see into the appliance.

egg cooker
An electric kitchen appliance with cup-shaped compartments used to cook eggs within their shells.

slot
The opening in which slices of bread are placed to be browned by heating strips or coils.

toaster
A kitchen appliance into which slices of bread are placed to be heated and browned.

control buttons
Small protrusions that can be depressed to modify the operation of an appliance.

crumb tray
A shallow metal pan that catches crumbs.

lever
An object that, when depressed or lifted, acts on a pivot to move another object.

browning control
The dial that can be turned to adjust the intensity of the toasting, from dark to light.

table grill
An electric appliance used to cook foods on a metal framework.

waffle iron
A small appliance featuring hinged metal pans onto which batter is poured to cook waffles.

bread maker
An appliance that is specifically designed to prepare and bake bread products.

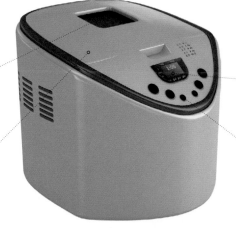

window
A transparent opening on top of the lid; it allows the bread to be viewed as it bakes.

liquid-crystal display (LCD)
The digital screen that shows settings, program information and a timer.

lid
The protective covering that seals the inner chamber during baking.

control buttons
Various switches that are pushed to change settings.

food processor
An appliance that is designed to finely mix or shred food materials within its bowl.

feed tube
A vertical opening through which ingredients are pressed or poured into an appliance.

bowl
The container in which foods are placed to be mixed or shredded.

handle
The gripping component of a food processor; it is held when handling the bowl.

blade
A metal disk with sharp projections that slice and mix ingredients.

motor housing
A hard outer casing enclosing the motor.

control pad
A switch that is turned to control the settings or speeds.

control buttons
Various switches that are used to change settings or speeds.

stand mixer
An appliance used to thoroughly mix liquid and powder ingredients together.

tilt-back head
The uppermost structural component; it is lifted to remove the beaters from the bowl.

beater
The component that rotates rapidly to thoroughly mix the ingredients.

dehydrator
A kitchen appliance used to remove most of the moisture from foods, to preserve them.

mixing bowl
The large, metallic bowl that fits in the base of a stand mixer. It holds the ingredients.

pusher
A blunt, cylindrical tool that is used to press food into a mincing or grinding appliance.

electric meat grinder
An electric appliance used to mince large pieces of solid meat into finer pieces.

feeder tray
A shallow pan that is fixed around the opening of an appliance to catch spillage or discharged contents.

feed tube
A vertical opening through which ingredients are pressed or poured into an appliance.

grinding plate
The flat, perforated piece of metal that shapes the meat into smaller pieces or sections.

knife housing
The long, tubular section that encloses the blades.

power switch
A small lever that can be flipped or pressed to turn the electrical connection between a source and a device on or off.

slow cooker
An appliance designed to gradually cook foods over a period of several hours.

motor housing
A hard outer casing enclosing the motor.

ceramic pot
The container in which foods are placed to be cooked; it rests in the base.

lid
The top covering for the ceramic pot.

sandwich toaster
A kitchen appliance with two folding hinged sections; bread is placed in between for heating and browning.

control pad
A dial located on the front of the slow cooker; it is used to alter settings.

heating base
The outer portion, which emits heat to the pot to cook foods.

table setting
An arrangement of dishes, glassware and silverware on a formal dining table.

dessert knife
A small utensil designated for use during the dessert course of a meal; it is used to cut foods.

tablecloth
A large piece of fabric or thin plastic that is placed over a table and under table settings as protection from spillage.

dessert fork
A small utensil designated for use during the dessert course of a meal.

bread-and-butter plate
A small dish to the left of the main plate; used for bread or dinner rolls.

butter knife
A utensil designated for spreading butter, often with a pointed tip for spearing butter pats.

dinner plate
The dish in a table setting used to hold foods, such as meats and vegetables, during the main course.

dinner fork
The utensil designated for the main course of a meal and usually the largest fork in a table setting.

salad fork
A utensil that is smaller than a dinner fork; designated for use during the salad course.

red wine glass
A stemmed vessel with a wide mouth, allowing oxidation of the wine, which improves the aroma and flavor.

candle
A mold of wax formed around a string that acts as a wick to be lit as a source of light.

candlestick
A decorative stand with a deep indentation in the top in which a candle is placed to stand upright.

white wine glass
A stemmed vessel with a narrow mouth, which limits the amount of oxidation of the wine.

ice bucket
An insulated vessel that can be filled with ice cubes and used to keep a bottle of wine cool.

champagne flute
A long-stemmed vessel with a narrow bowl and mouth to preserve the carbonation of a sparkling beverage.

napkin
A square piece of fabric or soft paper used to wipe one's lips or fingers during a meal; often laid on the lap.

teaspoon
A small utensil used for stirring beverages, such as coffee or tea.

soupspoon
A large utensil used to eat soup.

fish knife
A utensil designed to cut fish during a meal.

dinner knife
The cutting utensil used during the main course of a meal and usually the largest knife in a table setting.

Cutlery

Utensils, usually made of metal, that are used to bring food to the mouth when eating.

butter knife
A utensil designated for spreading butter, often with a pointed tip for spearing butter pats.

dessert knife
A small cutting utensil designated for use during the dessert course of a meal.

fish knife
A utensil designed to cut fish during a meal; it is smaller than a dinner knife.

dinner knife
The cutting utensil used during the main course; usually the largest knife in a table setting.

salad fork
A utensil designated for use during the salad course; it is smaller than a dinner fork.

dessert fork
A small utensil designated for use during the last course of a meal.

dinner fork
The utensil designated for use during the main course of a meal; usually the largest fork in a table setting.

teaspoon
A small utensil designated to stir beverages, such as coffee or tea, during a meal.

napkin ring
A decorative, circular piece of plastic, wood or other material used to hold a napkin in a folded or rolled position.

soupspoon
A utensil designated for eating foods with a large amount of liquid, such as soup.

Kitchen knives
Handheld instruments with blades; they are specifically designed to cut food.

knife set
A collection of cutting tools used to preparare food; they are often stored in a wooden block.

handle
The part of the knife that can be grasped in the hand.

heel
The part of a blade that forms the rear of the edge, extending horizontally from the handle to block the hand.

bolster
A piece of metal that reinforces the joint between the handle and the blade.

whetstone
A section of stone with a gritty surface, usually mounted on a platform or handle, used to sharpen the edge of blades.

back
The blunt edge of the blade, sometimes reinforced to maintain the blade's straightness.

blade
The sharpened metal portion of the knife.

knife block
A piece of wood with narrow slits where knives are stored, typically on a kitchen countertop.

sharpening steel
A handheld kitchen tool used to sharpen blades.

cutting edge
The sharpened side of the blade; used for slicing and chopping food.

point
The tip of the blade; it has been honed and can be used for piercing.

ham knife
A knife with a large, flat, rectangular blade used for carving meat, particularly ham.

carving knife
A knife typically with a long, wide blade designed for cutting meat into slices.

utility knife
A utensil with a medium-sized blade used for general purposes around the kitchen.

paring knife
A small utensil with a short blade used mainly for removing the peel from fruits or vegetables.

bread knife
A utensil designed for cutting bread; usually has a serrated blade.

cleaver
A knife with a large, heavy, flat rectangular blade, used mainly for butchering meat.

chef's knife
A knife with a long, narrow blade; mostly used for chopping.

zester
A handheld tool with a toothed edge; used to scrape the peel from citrus fruit.

Tableware
Vessels, often made of china or stoneware, on which food is served.

cereal bowl
A large cup in which cereal and other foods are served.

rice bowl
A tall cup in which rice is traditionally served.

soup bowl
A deep dish in which soup or stew is served; it holds about two cups of liquid.

rimmed plate
A flat dish, often with a flattened rim, made of china or stoneware and on which food is served.

fluted plate
A decorative dish with a flattened rim with slightly raised spines in a circular pattern, on which food is served.

vase
A container used to hold cut flowers for decoration, often elongated and made of a fragile material such as glass.

deep plate
A dish in the shape of a shallow bowl, typically used to serve foods in a sauce, such as pasta.

square plate
A flat dish with straight edges forming a square and often with a flattened rim, on which food is served.

vegetable bowl
A concave dish with a lid to keep foods hot; often placed in the center of a table during a meal.

mug
A cylindrical, deep cup with a thick handle, used for drinking hot liquids.

square tureen
A deep, box-shaped vessel that is fitted with a lid to keep foods hot while standing, typically for serving soup or stew.

platter
A large plate, usually oval, from which foods, such as sliced meats, are presented at the table and served.

dinner plate
A dish designed to hold foods during the main course, such as meats and vegetables.

dessert plate
A small dish designed to hold foods during the dessert course, such as cakes or pastries.

spoon rest
A small, elongated plate on which a spoon is placed after it has been used for serving, mainly to preserve a tablecloth.

dessert bowl
A deep dish designed to hold foods during the dessert course, such as puddings or compotes.

cup and saucer
A delicate handled vessel used for drinking hot liquids and a small, indented plate.

soup tureen
A deep, rounded vessel that is fitted with a lid to keep foods hot while standing, typically for serving soup or stew.

teapot
A lidded pot with a handle and elongated spout primarily used to steep and pour tea.

creamer
A small, decorative jug used to pour milk or cream into a hot beverage, such as tea or coffee.

sugar bowl
A small lidded pot, often fitted with handles on either side, used to hold sugar when serving tea or coffee.

Kitchen utensils
Devices that are designed to assist with the preparation and cooking of food.

cube slicer
A tool composed of a grid of thin wire used to cube foods, such as cheese, in one motion.

bowl
The container used to hold items to be weighed.

electronic kitchen scale
A device fitted with a bowl in which objects or substances can be placed and weighed.

fondue set
A heated pot and thin, long-handled forks used to cook or dip foods at the table.

burner
A container filled with fuel and lit with a flame in order to produce constant heat.

fondue pot
A vessel that is heated to melt foods, such as cheese or chocolate.

stand
A flat or footed low platform that acts as a base on which to rest an object.

fondue fork
A long, thin utensil with two small tines and a heat-resistant handle, used to pierce and dip foods into a hot liquid.

display
A lit panel that shows the weight measured.

platform
The flat surface that holds the bowl; the weight sensor is affixed below it.

bowl
A concave vessel used to hold foods.

corkscrew
A kitchen gadget fitted with a spiraled piece of metal, used to remove corks from bottles.

bread box
An enclosed container, usually with a hinged or roll-top lid, in which bread is stored to prolong its freshness.

tray
A flat container, usually with a raised rim and sometimes with handles, most often used to carry food and drink.

manual coffee grinder
An appliance used to reduce coffee beans into grounds by hand.

roll-top lid
A cover of a container that, when opened, slides into the container itself in a rolling motion.

pastry blender
A handheld tool used to cut ingredients
into each other; typically used when
making dough.

citrus juicer
A tool used to extract the
liquid from citrus fruit.

pot grabber
A piece of heat-resistant
material, such as silicone,
worn on the hand as
protection to allow handling
of hot vessels.

meat thermometer
A device used to
measure the internal
temperature of meat,
typically during cooking.

mezzaluna
A utensil composed of one or
two semi-circular blades; used
to chop herbs.

peeler
A utensil used to
remove the skin from
fruits and vegetables.

apple corer and slicer
A tool used to remove the core
of an apple and slice it in one
motion.

grater
A kitchen device consisting of
a sheet of metal punctured with
holes with raised, sharp edges
for grating foods.

pastry brush
A utensil with bristles designed
to spread liquids onto baked
goods and other foods.

milk frother
A tool with a long, thin rod
ending in a circular whisk;
used to agitate liquids, such
as milk, into a foam.

sieve
A tool made of framed wire
mesh; used to separate larger
particles from smaller ones or
solids from liquids.

cutting board
A flat piece of resilient material such as wood or plastic on which foods are sliced or chopped.

baking sheet
A large, flat tray of metal with a slightly raised rim used for cooking foods in an oven.

bottle carrier
A metal or plastic frame with a top handle, designed to hold cylindrical objects such as bottles.

baking rack
A metal grid with small feet on which baked goods, such as cookies or pies, are placed to cool.

measuring spoon
Small plastic spoons that are used to ensure exact quantities of ingredients during food preparation.

measuring cup
Small vessels used to ensure proper amounts of an ingredient.

funnel
A cone-shaped object that is used to transfer a liquid into a vessel with a narrow opening or mouth.

sifter
A mug-shaped kitchen tool with a squeeze handle and rotating bottom blades that separate particles from flour.

bottle opener
A kitchen tool used to remove bottle caps.

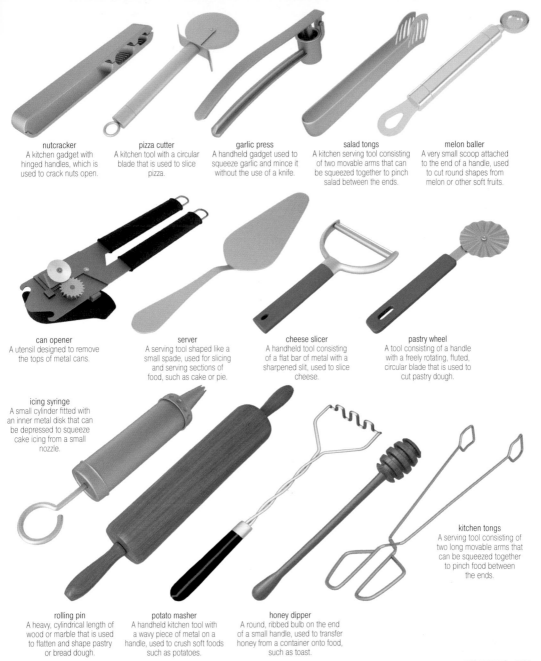

nutcracker
A kitchen gadget with hinged handles, which is used to crack nuts open.

pizza cutter
A kitchen tool with a circular blade that is used to slice pizza.

garlic press
A handheld gadget used to squeeze garlic and mince it without the use of a knife.

salad tongs
A kitchen serving tool consisting of two movable arms that can be squeezed together to pinch salad between the ends.

melon baller
A very small scoop attached to the end of a handle, used to cut round shapes from melon or other soft fruits.

can opener
A utensil designed to remove the tops of metal cans.

server
A serving tool shaped like a small spade, used for slicing and serving sections of food, such as cake or pie.

cheese slicer
A handheld tool consisting of a flat bar of metal with a sharpened slit, used to slice cheese.

pastry wheel
A tool consisting of a handle with a freely rotating, fluted, circular blade that is used to cut pastry dough.

icing syringe
A small cylinder fitted with an inner metal disk that can be depressed to squeeze cake icing from a small nozzle.

kitchen tongs
A serving tool consisting of two long movable arms that can be squeezed together to pinch food between the ends.

rolling pin
A heavy, cylindrical length of wood or marble that is used to flatten and shape pastry or bread dough.

potato masher
A handheld kitchen tool with a wavy piece of metal on a handle, used to crush soft foods such as potatoes.

honey dipper
A round, ribbed bulb on the end of a small handle, used to transfer honey from a container onto food, such as toast.

dish brush
A long handle with bristles on one end, designed to clean kitchenware, such as plates and cups.

skewer
A long, slender rod of metal with a sharp tip onto which food is threaded to hold it together during cooking.

meat tenderizer
A pounding tool used to soften or flatten slabs of meat prior to cooking.

ice cream scoop
A small spoon used to serve rounded portions of ice cream.

cooking utensil set
A collection of handheld tools used to prepare and serve food, often stored in a jar-shaped container.

spatula
A kitchen utensil with a slightly tilted, broad, flat head, used to flip food during cooking.

spaghetti server
A spoon-shaped utensil with a perforated head, rimmed with claws, used to scoop long noodles from cooking water.

serving spoon
A long-handled utensil with a large bowl used for stirring large quantities of a liquid-based food, such as stew.

egg ring
A circular band of metal into which an egg is cracked on a pan; the egg then cooks in a circular shape, with yolk intact.

slotted spatula
A utensil with a broad, flat head with slits; used to lift food and drain liquids while cooking.

wooden spoon
A long utensil made out of wood, most commonly used for stirring batter or liquid-based foods.

wooden spatula
A utensil made of wood with a broad, flat head; used to spread or stir thick liquids.

utensil cup
A container used to store kitchen tools in an upright position so their functions can be easily identified.

pepper mill
A handheld device used to grind whole peppercorns into fine pepper than can be sprinkled on food.

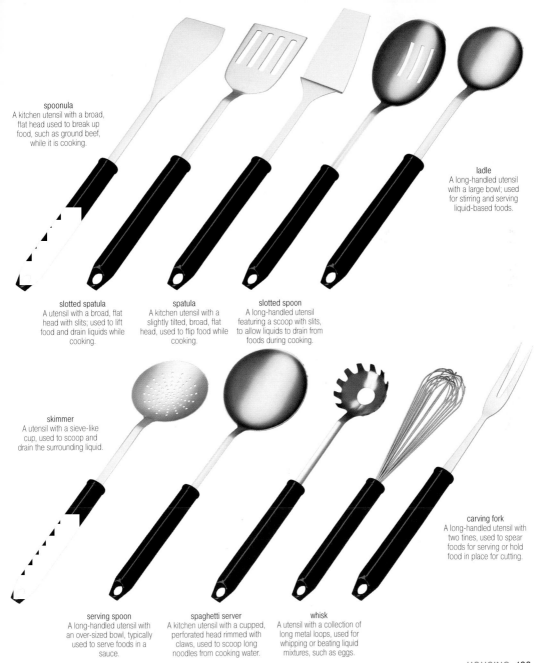

spoonula
A kitchen utensil with a broad, flat head used to break up food, such as ground beef, while it is cooking.

ladle
A long-handled utensil with a large bowl; used for stirring and serving liquid-based foods.

slotted spatula
A utensil with a broad, flat head with slits; used to lift food and drain liquids while cooking.

spatula
A kitchen utensil with a slightly tilted, broad, flat head, used to flip food while cooking.

slotted spoon
A long-handled utensil featuring a scoop with slits, to allow liquids to drain from foods during cooking.

skimmer
A utensil with a sieve-like cup, used to scoop and drain the surrounding liquid.

carving fork
A long-handled utensil with two tines, used to spear foods for serving or hold food in place for cutting.

serving spoon
A long-handled utensil with an over-sized bowl, typically used to serve foods in a sauce.

spaghetti server
A kitchen utensil with a cupped, perforated head rimmed with claws, used to scoop long noodles from cooking water.

whisk
A utensil with a collection of long metal loops, used for whipping or beating liquid mixtures, such as eggs.

coffee carafe
A large, insulated vessel with a spout, handle and tight-fitting lid, designed for serving coffee.

measuring cup
A vessel with a spout, marked with a column of measurements; used to measure liquids.

ice bucket
An insulated vessel with a tight-fitting lid, used to hold ice cubes and keep them frozen.

mold
A hollow, metal container formed into a decorative shape, used to bake fancy cakes and pastries.

mortar and pestle
A utensil consisting of a small, thick bowl and a heavy tool with a rounded end, used mainly for crushing spices.

plastic storage container
A box or bowl made of plastic, often translucent, with a sealing lid, typically used to store leftover food.

mixing bowl
Vessels used when combining ingredients; they are typically used when baking.

saucepan
A small kitchen pot with a single long handle and lid.

kettle
A large metal vessel with a spout and a lid, fitted with a handle and used for boiling water on an element.

pie dish
A round baking pan with raised edges that are sometimes fluted, usually made of metal or glass.

double boiler
A set of fitted saucepans that are placed into each other in order to delicately cook sauces or chocolate.

wok
A deep, bowl-shaped frying pan traditionally used in Asian cooking, such as stir frying.

skillet
A large pan with high sides, often made of cast iron; it is typically used for frying foods in hot fat or oil.

frying pan
A large, shallow pan with a long handle, often made of stainless steel; it is usually used for frying foods in hot oil.

casserole dish
A large, heavy cooking vessel, often oval in shape with a lid and handles at either end, used to cook foods in an oven.

stock pot
A large, deep cooking vessel with a lid, most often used to cook liquid-based foods, such as soup or stew.

colander
A deep metal bowl with perforated bottom and sides; used to drain liquid from foods like spaghetti.

salad spinner
A tool consisting of a plastic bowl with a nested spinning basket, to remove excess water from leafy vegetables.

loaf pan
A rectangular-shaped metal pan used for baking bread and other loaf-shaped foods.

roasting pan
A large, rectangular-shaped metal pan used to roast various foods, like turkey.

Glassware

A general term for vessels used for drinking and usually made of glass.

water glass
In a table setting, the cup that is designated for water, usually with a wide mouth.

white wine glass
A stemmed vessel with a narrow mouth, which limits the amount of oxidation of the wine.

champagne flute
A long-stemmed vessel with a narrow bowl and mouth to preserve the carbonation of a sparkling beverage.

Alsace glass
A vessel with a stem long enough to prevent the wide bowl from being touched or warmed by the hand.

decanter
A serving vessel, generally made of glass and used to serve wine.

cocktail glass
A small, stemmed vessel with a bell-shaped bowl, commonly used to serve mixed alcoholic beverages in small quantities.

champagne glass
A stemmed vessel with a shallow, wide bowl and wide mouth; it allows carbonation to emerge and tickle the nose.

sherry glass
A stemmed vessel with a tall, narrow bowl and narrow mouth to preserve the richness of a sweet wine.

brandy snifter
A vessel with a short stem, large bowl for swirling, and narrow mouth that directs a spirit to the tip of the tongue.

burgundy glass
A stemmed vessel with a wide mouth and large bowl; it enhances the flavor of a wine.

port glass
A vessel with a short stem and wide mouth, allowing greater oxidation, enhancing the aroma and flavor of the wine.

red wine glass
A stemmed vessel with a wide mouth, allowing oxidation of the wine, which improves the aroma and flavor.

liqueur glass
A very small, elongated vessel with a stem, traditionally used to serve sweet spirits, often during coffee service.

old-fashioned glass
A short, squat tumbler that is typically used to serve alcoholic beverages with ice cubes.

beer mug
A large, heavy tumbler with a handle made of thick glass; used to keep beer cold.

beer glass
A tall, slender, slightly fluted tumbler used for serving beer.

Tables

Furniture with a pedestal or legs supporting a flat surface.

console table
A small table, usually with a decorative carved design and drawers, that sits flush against or is fixed to a wall.

nightstand
A small table that sits next to the head of a bed, usually containing drawers or shelves to hold small objects.

dining table
A table usually made to accommodate six or more people, designed for formal meals.

writing desk
A small table that is designed specifically for writing and incorporates drawers for storing writing materials.

telephone table
A tall, small table with a surface just large enough to hold a telephone and a pad of paper, often with a drawer.

end table
A small piece of furniture, usually positioned next to an armchair or sofa and on which small objects are placed.

top
The upper surface of a structure, such as a table.

leg
A support attached to the bottom of a piece of furniture to stabilize or raise it.

tempered glass
Glass that has been molecularly altered to increase its strength and safety; often used for table surfaces.

patio table
A table, usually small and portable, designed for outdoor use, such as in a backyard.

base
The lowest section, which rests on the floor and carries the table's weight.

vanity
A small table, with or without drawers and often topped with a mirror, at which one sits to groom the face and hair.

coffee table
A piece of furniture, usually long and low, designed to be placed in front of a sofa or easy chairs.

Chairs

Seats for one person, with backs and with or without armrests.

bergère
A French armchair with an enclosed frame that is completely upholstered, including the back and arms.

leather armchair
A comfortable, padded chair that is upholstered with a material made from the cured or tanned skin of an animal.

back
The rear surface of an object, making up part of its frame.

arm
The raised portion at the side of a chair or sofa, providing a place for one to rest their arms.

seat
A flat surface on which a person may sit, for example, as part of a chair or sofa.

leg
A support attached to the bottom of a piece of furniture to stabilize or raise it.

armchair
A chair with arms with an upholstered seat and back.

Voltaire chair
An armchair with a very low seat and a high back.

stool
An armless and backless seat that usually rests on three or four legs, or on a pedestal.

easy chair
A big, cushy chair in the form of a sofa for one person.

cushioned armchair
A chair with open sides, padded on the back and arms, with the addition of a thick pad on the seat.

kitchen chair
An upright chair, usually without arms, designed to be placed at a kitchen table for eating.

folding chair
An upright chair that can be collapsed into a flat structure for easy storage.

stacking chair
An upright chair, usually without upholstery, with slightly splayed legs to allow one to be stacked onto another.

bar stool
A seat supported on a tall pedestal or legs, usually padded and without a back, most often placed at or around a bar.

rocking chair
A chair with legs that are fixed to semi-circular pieces on either side to allow a rocking motion.

back
The rear surface of an object, such as a chair or other piece of furniture, that makes up part of its frame.

dining chair
A seat with a tall, upright back and without arms, typically matching a large table designed for formal meals.

seat
A flat surface on which a person may sit, for example, as part of a chair or sofa.

upholstery
A covering for furniture, such as chairs and sofas, made of a soft, padded material.

director's chair
A folding chair with crossed legs and a seat and back made of a sturdy fabric.

front leg
The support that lies beneath the front edge of a piece of furniture with an obvious forward-facing design.

back leg
The support that lies beneath the back of a piece of furniture with an obvious forward-facing design.

Sofas

Different styles of upholstered seats with arms and a back, long enough to accommodate more than one person.

sectional sofa
A sofa separated into sections that can be moved to change the configuration.

backrest
The raised portion behind the seat of a chair or sofa, on which one may lean backwards.

seat cushion
A stuffed pad placed on top of a chair to provide comfortable support for sitting.

leg
A support attached to the bottom of a piece of furniture to stabilize or raise it.

arm
The raised portion at the side of a chair or sofa, providing a place for one to rest their arms.

ottoman
A small piece of furniture, usually upholstered and without back or arms, often used as a stool or footstool.

loveseat
A sofa designed to hold only two people.

chaise longe
An elongated cushioned seat that is designed to allow one to stretch out in a half-lying, half-sitting position.

bench
A piece of furniture that is not fully upholstered, designed to seat two or more people.

Storage furniture

Furniture that is designed to hold objects, such as clothing or kitchenware, for easy accessibility.

liquor cabinet
A glass-fronted cabinet with shelves on which bottles of liquor and drinking glasses are stored and displayed.

door
A hinged barrier that is swung open to gain access to the piece's inside compartment.

pull
A piece of solid or flexible material attached to an object that can be grasped and pulled, such as on a door.

leg
A support attached to the bottom of a piece of furniture; it is used to stabilize the piece or raise it.

drawer
A box-shaped compartment used for storage.

shelf
A flat, elongated surface built into a piece of furniture on which objects are stored.

chest of drawers
A piece of furniture made up of a number of drawers set into a box-like frame, typically used to store clothing.

display cabinet
A glass-fronted cabinet with shelves, typically used to showcase objects.

sofa table
A long, low table that is usually placed against the exposed back of a sofa.

glass door
A hinged barrier with a glass insert. It is swung open to gain access to the inside compartment.

pull
A piece of solid or flexible material attached to an object that can be grasped and pulled, such as on a door.

sideboard
A piece of furniture that is typically placed against the wall of a dining or living room, used to hold refreshments.

drawer
A box-shaped compartment used for storage.

vertical panel
A flat component that is inset vertically to form an interior wall.

top panel
A flat component that covers the top, end to end and front to back, of a piece of furniture.

wall unit
A piece of furniture composed of shelves, drawers and sometimes cupboards, designed to rest against the wall of a living room.

back panel
A flat component that covers the back, side to side and top to bottom, of a piece of furniture.

shelf
A flat, elongated surface built into a piece of furniture on which objects are stored.

side panel
The surface perpendicular to the front of a piece of furniture, such as a dresser or cabinet.

drawer
A box-shaped compartment in a piece of furniture or object; it is used for storage.

corner cabinet
A cupboard with shelves and a V-shaped backing, allowing it to be placed in the corner of a room.

bottom panel
A flat component that covers the bottom, end to end and front to back, of a piece of furniture.

armoire
A tall, free-standing piece of furniture with long doors like a closet, used to store clothing.

chiffonier
A tall, narrow chest of drawers, often incorporated with a series of open shelves or with cabinets.

bookcase
A set of shelves set in a frame or cabinet, used to hold and store books.

Domestic appliances
Household machines designed to assist with everyday chores, such as washing and ironing clothes.

control knob
A knob that can be adjusted to change the machine's cycle or temperature

dryer
A household appliance used to remove moisture from clothing or other materials, usually using warmed forced air.

start button
A small, protruding object that, when pressed by the user, will initiate the device's action.

drum
The cylindrical component of a washing machine, mounted to allow rotation; materials are placed inside to be washed.

door
A hinged barrier used to gain access to the appliance's drum.

control panel
Buttons that are used to change the machine's cycle or temperature.

front-loading washer
A household appliance used to clean clothing and other materials, such as bedding, using detergent and water.

lint trap
The part of a dryer that acts as a filter and traps lint as air is vented out during the drying cycle.

door
A hinged barrier used to gain access to the appliance's drum.

handle
The part of the door that is held in the hand to pull it open.

control knob
A knob that can be adjusted to change the machine's cycle or temperature.

iron
A handheld appliance with a heated base that is passed over clothing to smooth out wrinkles.

steam button
A small, protruding object that is pressed to release steam.

handle
The part that is held in the hand to move the iron.

delete term
A hard outer casing, usually with smooth surfaces, enclosing the appliance's inner workings.

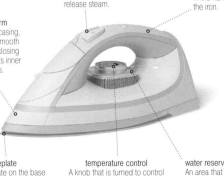

soleplate
The metal plate on the base of an iron that is heated; it is passed over clothing to remove creases.

temperature control
A knob that is turned to control the temperature to which it should be heated.

water reservoir
An area that holds water to be used in the appliance's operation.

top-loading washer
A household appliance used to clean clothing and other materials; it has a hinged lid on the top.

ceiling fan
A machine with flat, rotating blades, mounted to a ceiling and used to cool a room.

ceiling mount
The part that is used to attach the fan to the ceiling.

rod
A long metal cylinder that joins the rotating unit to the ceiling mount.

blade
A large, flat surface that generates wind when it rotates.

pedestal fan
A rotating blade mounted on a tall pole and used to cool a room.

blade
A large, flat surface that generates wind when it rotates.

motor housing
A hard outer casing enclosing the motor.

height adjustment
A part used to change the height of the fan.

oscillation control
A knob that is pushed or pulled to adjust whether the fan rotates.

motor housing
A hard outer casing that encloses the motor.

safety guard
The wire mesh plate covering the rotating blades of a fan to prevent contact.

speed control
A knob that is turned to adjust the speed at which the blades rotate.

stand
A rigid pole on which the motor housing is mounted.

ductless air conditioner
A unit capable of cooling a room or floor of a house but that does not require any internal ductwork.

base
The lowest section, which rests on the floor and carries the fan's weight.

canister vacuum cleaner
A household appliance that uses suction to collect small debris from the surface of an area, such as a floor or a rug.

power switch
A lever that can be flipped to turn a device's power on or off.

pipe
The metal tube attached to the end of a vacuum hose through which debris is sucked into the vacuum bag or compartment.

hose
A length of tubing that provides flexibility when maneuvering the handheld portion of the machine.

storage compartment release button
The button that can be pressed to open the section holding the collected debris.

handheld vacuum cleaner
A miniature vacuum that can be held in a single hand; used primarily for small areas and furniture.

wheel
A circular device that rotates on an axis and allows the object to be moved easily.

ventilation grille
An area of slits in a vacuum cleaner's housing that allows air heated by the motor to be released.

rug and floor brush
A piece that is secured to the end of a vacuum cleaner's suction tube to allow various types of debris to be picked up.

robotic vacuum cleaner
A small and self-propelled vacuum cleaner that is programmed to constantly roam and vacuum flooring.

upright vacuum cleaner
An electric device that, using suction, removes dirt and debris from flooring and carpets.

Audiovisual equipment

Household devices that are designed to produce images and related sounds for entertainment purposes.

television
An electronic broadcast system that displays picture and sound for entertainment.

screen
The flat panel on which images are displayed.

stand
A flat or footed low platform that acts as a base on which the television sits.

projector
An electronic device used to project and display images onto a large screen.

lens
A piece of glass that, by its shape, concentrates or disperses light rays, thereby capturing or modifying images.

control buttons
Objects that can be pushed to change the device's functions.

ventillation grille
An area of slits or holes that allows air heated by the motor or by electricity to be released.

lens shift lever
A part that can be rotated to adjust the positioning of the lens and adjust the focus of the image.

control panel
An area that contains buttons or switches or dials that allow the user to change the device's function.

satellite TV receiver
An electronic device that receives satellite signals from an outside antenna and converts the signals to a television screen.

vent
An area of slits or holes that allows air heated by the motor or by electricity to be released.

display
A lit panel that provides information, such as the selected function or channel.

card slot
The slit on a satellite television receiver into which the data card is inserted.

cover
A movable surface that is used to protect an underlying area or object.

sound system
A collection of speakers that are strategically placed in a room to produce the best surround sound from an entertainment device.

main speaker
An upright speaker in the shape of a column that stands next to or a distance in front of the main stereo unit.

subwoofer
A stereo speaker designed to produce sounds of very low bass frequencies.

stand
A rigid pole or column on which the operating portion of an appliance is mounted, such as on a floor fan, speaker or lamp.

surround speaker
An upright speaker on a stand that is situated a distance behind the main stereo unit.

base
The lowest section, which rests on the floor and carries the speaker's weight.

headphones
A pair of speakers that are joined by a headband and placed over the ears.

headband
A strip of material designed to wrap across the top of the head from ear to ear.

casing
An outer shell made of resistant material that protectively encloses the more delicate components of a device.

input button
On a remote control, the button that can be pressed to activate the reception of signals on an entertainment device.

remote control
An apparatus that emits electronic signals to manipulate the functions of an electronic device from a distance.

ear cushion
A padded material attached to headphones that is to be placed against the ear for comfort.

earphone
A mechanism that projects sound from a device and that usually contains an internal amplifier, such as in headphones.

standby button
A button on a remote control that can be pressed to pause the transmission of signals to an entertainment device.

image format button
On a remote control, the button that can be pressed to alter the display of the image on a television.

play button
On a remote control, the button that can be pressed to activate a recorded piece, such as a video.

volume control
Buttons on a remote control pressed to increase or decrease the level of sound being emitted from a device.

DVD player and amplifier
A machine that reads DVDs and a machine that amplifies the sound of the DVD being played.

DVD slot
A slit within the DVD player in which one places a DVD.

DVD player
A machine that reads the data from a DVD and relays it onto a television or computer screen.

control pad
The object on a device that allows the user to change its function, motion or response by touch.

channel scan button
Buttons on a remote control that move a television's reception from one channel to another, in sequence.

channel selector buttons
Numbered buttons on a remote control that can be used to select specific television channels.

control pad
The object on a device the allows the user to change its function, motion or response by touch.

amplifier
An electronic device that increases the power of signals, usually in the form of sound.

control panel
An area of a device often containing switces or dials, allowing the user to change the device's function.

volume control
A knob on an entertainment device that can be turned to increase or decrease the volume of sound being emitted.

function button
A button on a remote control that can be pressed to direct the remote control's signal from one device to another.

Lightbulbs

Small, glass-enclosed devices that are inserted into fixtures and produce light.

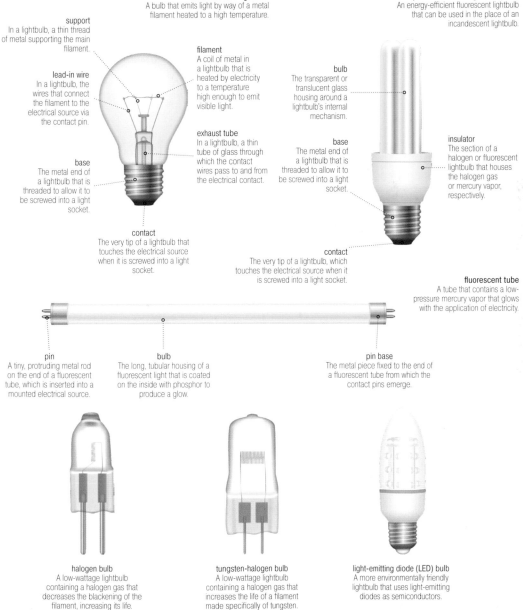

incandescent lightbulb
A bulb that emits light by way of a metal filament heated to a high temperature.

compact fluorescent lightbulb (CFL)
An energy-efficient fluorescent lightbulb that can be used in the place of an incandescent lightbulb.

support
In a lightbulb, a thin thread of metal supporting the main filament.

lead-in wire
In a lightbulb, the wires that connect the filament to the electrical source via the contact pin.

filament
A coil of metal in a lightbulb that is heated by electricity to a temperature high enough to emit visible light.

bulb
The transparent or translucent glass housing around a lightbulb's internal mechanism.

base
The metal end of a lightbulb that is threaded to allow it to be screwed into a light socket.

exhaust tube
In a lightbulb, a thin tube of glass through which the contact wires pass to and from the electrical contact.

base
The metal end of a lightbulb that is threaded to allow it to be screwed into a light socket.

insulator
The section of a halogen or fluorescent lightbulb that houses the halogen gas or mercury vapor, respectively.

contact
The very tip of a lightbulb that touches the electrical source when it is screwed into a light socket.

contact
The very tip of a lightbulb, which touches the electrical source when it is screwed into a light socket.

fluorescent tube
A tube that contains a low-pressure mercury vapor that glows with the application of electricity.

pin
A tiny, protruding metal rod on the end of a fluorescent tube, which is inserted into a mounted electrical source.

bulb
The long, tubular housing of a fluorescent light that is coated on the inside with phosphor to produce a glow.

pin base
The metal piece fixed to the end of a fluorescent tube from which the contact pins emerge.

halogen bulb
A low-wattage lightbulb containing a halogen gas that decreases the blackening of the filament, increasing its life.

tungsten-halogen bulb
A low-wattage lightbulb containing a halogen gas that increases the life of a filament made specifically of tungsten.

light-emitting diode (LED) bulb
A more environmentally friendly lightbulb that uses light-emitting diodes as semiconductors.

Light fixtures and lamps
Decorative household objects that emit light.

chandelier
An elaborate hanging light fixture with a number of arms for several lightbulbs, often decorated with glass or crystal pendants.

canopy
The cup or plate of a hanging light fixture that is mounted directly to the ceiling.

scroll
A curved decorative piece, on a chandelier for example, shaped to look like the loosely rolled end of a piece of paper.

hanger loop
A small, curved piece attached to the canopy of a ceiling light fixture from which the main lighting structure is hung.

bobeche
A small, decorative cup on a chandelier that separates the main hanging structure from the hanger loop.

spindle
A slender, tapered rod forming a part of the hanging structure of a chandelier.

ball
On a chandelier, a solid or hollow round sphere forming part of the hanging structure.

crystal pendant
A faceted piece of crystal or glass that refracts the light, usually tear-drop shaped, decorating a chandelier.

lightbulb
Small, glass-enclosed devices that are inserted into fixtures and produce light, such as in lamps or chandeliers.

arm
One of several branches that extend from the spindle and support the lightbulbs and crystals.

floor lamp
A light fixture set atop a long pedestal or pole that is designed to stand on the floor of a room.

chain
Small loops joined together to form a continuous string, sometimes with jewels or beads.

font
The cup that completes the hanging structure of a chandelier.

finial
An ornamental carved or molded piece that is placed on the end, top or corner of an object, such as a curtain rod or chandelier.

sconce
A light fixture that attaches to a wall and is often shaped like a candle or torch.

table lamp
A device that gives off light; it is often placed on a desk or table to light a small area.

lampshade
An open-ended hood that is placed over a lamp to temper or direct the light, often conical or bowl-shaped.

floor lamp
A light fixture set atop a long pedestal or pole that is designed to stand on the floor of a room.

ceiling mount
The cup or plate of a hanging light fixture that is attached directly to the ceiling.

hanging pendant
A light fixture that is mounted to the ceiling and suspends over a room.

wire
A thin filament of metal used to conduct electricity from a source to a device, covered in insulated tubing.

swivel arm
A supporting structure between an object and its stand that can be moved from side to side, such as on a lamp.

shade
An object that is placed over the bulb of a ceiling light fixture, the base of which may or may not be closed.

stand
A rigid pole or column on which the lighting mechanism is mounted.

base
The lowest section, which rests on the floor and carries the lamp's weight.

ceiling mount
The cup or plate of a hanging light fixture that is attached directly to the ceiling.

hanging track lighting
A fixture consisting of parallel supports suspended from the ceiling, in which lightbulbs are fitted in a line.

suspension wire
Long, sturdy threads of metal that are used to hang one object from another, such as a light fixture from its canopy.

ceiling fixture
A light fixture that is mounted to, suspend from, or is embedded in the ceiling of a room.

track
A structure consisting of parallel supports in which objects can be placed in a line, such as bulbs in track lighting.

lightbulb
Small, glass-enclosed devices that are inserted into fixtures and produce light, such as in lamps or chandeliers.

Electrical fittings
Objects and devices that deliver electricity from a source to an appliance or tool.

light socket
A device with an inner ribbed surface in which lightbulbs are screwed to connect to a source of electricity.

bracket
A protrusion that can be attached to mount an object or tool, such as on a light fixture to attach it to the ceiling or wall.

insulator
A section of an electrical tool or appliance, which is made of a material that does not conduct electricity.

cross section of a plug
The inner workings of an electrical plug.

clamp
A small piece of metal or plastic that is screwed in place fixing wires into position, such as in an electrical plug.

neutral wire
The wire that conducts electricity from a source to a device and completes a circuit.

cover
A hard outer casing that encloses the wires of the plug.

pin
The protrusion on an electrical plug that is inserted into an electrical socket.

cord
A wire covered or coated with an insulating material that directs electricity from a source to a device.

hot wire
The wire within the plug that has electricity coursing through it, as opposed to other neutral wires.

ground wire
An electrical wire, typically colored green, that is connected to a source of zero activity, most often the ground.

terminal
A small sharp pin of metal that is ribbed helically and can be turned by its head to be inserted into an object.

screw thread
A raised rib of material formed in a helix, such as on a pipe or in a cap, that allows it to be screwed to another object.

power outlet
A set of holes in a wall leading to a power source into which an electrical plug connected to a device can be inserted.

cover plate
A decorative frame designed to be placed around switches or sockets, hiding wires and rough edges in the wall.

socket contact
The small, circular space into which an electrical plug's pin is inserted.

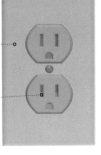

power bar
A block of electrical sockets attached to a single power cord; it allows multiple devices to be powered by an outlet.

switch
A small lever that can be flipped or pressed to turn the electrical connection between a source and a device on or off.

dimmer switch
A knob that is turned to control the brightness of an electric light and can be pressed to turn it on or off.

European power outlet
A set of holes in a wall leading to a power source into which an electrical plug connected to a device can be inserted.

European/round-pin plug
A device used to create an electrical connection between a source of power and a device. This design is prevalent in Europe.

flat mop
A cleaning tool with a long handle and a flat head to which a cloth or sponge is attached to wash floors.

mop
A cleaning tool made of long twisted fibers fixed to the end of a long handle, used to wash floors.

handle
The part of a tool, machine or object held by the hand to pull or control it.

broom
A cleaning tool, consisting of bristles on the end of a long handle, used to sweep debris from floors.

mop head
The flat, rectangular plate at the end of the long handle of a mop to which a sponge or mop cloth can be attached.

bucket
An open container with a handle, designed to carry objects or liquid.

scrub brush
A tool equipped with bristles, used for general cleaning.

dustpan
A flat receptacle with a handle, which is used to collect dust and debris being swept up by a broom.

wastebasket
An open container, often with a hinged lid, designed to collect and store garbage for disposal.

aquarium
A large tank that is filled with water, usually filtered and circulating, specifically designed to house fish and other sea life.

lighting hood
A piece of plastic or metal that covers a light source, usually a fluorescent tube, from end to end.

fish
A vertebrate animal that lives and breathes in water with the use of gills.

plant
Unit of vegetation, usually leafy, with its own root system.

decorative rock
A stone that is placed for aesthetic purposes in an aquarium or terrarium.

gravel
Finely crushed rock or stone often used to line pathways or the bottom of containers, such as an aquarium.

tank
The glass receptacle that holds water and houses the fish.

air pump
A device that continuously intakes and expels air in order to remove impurities, such as in an aquarium.

terrarium
A glass case, often with sand and rocks, designed to house reptiles.

ventilation screen
A protective sheet of mesh that covers the opening of a container to allow air to pass through, such as into a terrarium.

heating light
In a terrarium, a small fluorescent light used to heat the environment.

decorative background
A sheet of material designed to look like an animal's natural environment, often placed in a terrarium.

chameleon
A type of lizard with skin that changes color according to its environment and bulbous eyes.

driftwood
Branches or small logs found saturated with water; they typically dry into interesting shapes.

ventilation
A series of holes or slits set in the face of a container to allow the passage of air, such as on a terrarium.

base
The lowest section, which rests on the floor and carries the terrarium's weight.

plant
Unit of vegetation, usually leafy, with its own root system.

tank
The glass receptacle that houses the lizard.

latch
A small device used to hold a door closed by way of interlocking pieces, often with a small lever that can be turned.

swinging door
A hinged barrier that can be swung outwards to allow access to the interior of the terrarium.

water bowl
A small concave vessel that holds water for the pet to drink.

sand
A mixture of finely ground substances such as rock, silicon and shells, often used to line a terrarium.

hanging ring
A loop of rigid material, usually metal, attached to the top of an object to allow it to be suspended from a hook.

birdcage
An enclosure, typically made of wire and hung from a pole, used to house pet birds.

wire bar
A metal rod that frames the structure of the cage.

leash
A long strip of material such as leather, looped at one end to form a handle, used to lead an animal by its collar.

access door
A hinged barrier on an opening of a bird's cage to allow the animal to enter or exit the cage, or to allow feeding.

parrot
A colorful tropical bird that is a popular pet and can be trained to talk.

food and water bowls
Round, concave vessels that are designated specifically for the use of serving a pet's food and water.

feeding dish
A small container used to hold an animal's food, such as seeds for a pet bird.

perch
A seat or swing for a caged pet bird.

collar
A loop of material, such as leather or cloth, that encircles a dog's neck and to which tags or a leash can be attached.

muzzle
A device made of cloth or leather formed to fit over a dog's snout to prevent it from biting.

covered litter box
A hooded, plastic pan with raised edges that is filled with litter in which a cat may relieve itself.

pet carrier
A cage that is fitted with a carrying handle, used to transport small animals.

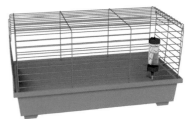

small animal cage
A structure of bars or wires used to house pets like hamsters or mice.

Curtain rods

Long, rigid poles mounted along the tops of windows and from which curtains are hung, often from rings encircling the rod.

wooden curtain rod
A long, rigid pole made of wood and from which curtains are hung.

ring
A small circular piece of rigid material, such as wood or metal, which encircles an object, such as on a curtain rod.

bracket
A protrusion, such as from a wall, that can be attached to mount an object or tool.

metal curtain rod
A long, rigid pole made of metal, mounted along the top of a window, from which curtains are hung.

rod
A long, rigid pole, often used as a support onto which objects can be threaded or hung.

eyelet
A small hook from which a curtain can be hung.

finial
An ornamental carved or molded piece that is placed on the end, top or corner of an object, such as a curtain rod or chandelier.

wrought iron curtain rod
A long, rigid pole made of wrought iron, mounted along the top of a window, from which curtains are hung.

double curtain rod
Two long, rigid poles mounted parallel to each other along the top of a window, from which two sets of curtains are hung.

curtain track
A curtain rod that is hidden by a decorative molding, usually made of wood or plaster.

Window treatments

Objects used to cover windows, to block light or provide privacy.

grommet curtains
Curtains with small holes sewn along the top, through which a curtain rod is passed, replacing the need for hooks.

grommet
A hole in the curtain material through which a rod can be inserted.

curtain rod
A long, rigid pole mounted along the top of a window, from which curtains are hung.

roll-up shade
A length of cloth or series of slats covering a window that, by means of a pulley, can be compressed upwards.

curtain
One of a pair of pieces of fabric hung over a window; they can be drawn together for privacy.

drapery
Pieces of fabric hung from the top of a window.

curtain rod
A long, rigid pole mounted along the top of a window, from which curtains are hung, often from rings encircling the rod.

valance
A short, decorative curtain or length of cloth hung along the top of a main curtain, often to hide curtain fittings.

sheer curtain
A drape made of a fine, see-through material that allows a small amount of light to enter a room.

swag
A decorative curtain or length of cloth that is fastened to a main curtain in swoops or drooping curves.

curtain
One of a pair of pieces of fabric hung over a window; they can be drawn together for privacy and to block outside light.

tab-top curtain
Curtains with a series of pockets across the top through which the curtain rod is threaded.

valance
A short, decorative curtain hung along the top of a main curtain, often to hide curtain fittings.

loose curtain
Curtains that only extend a short way past the base of a window, typically to the level of the top of a table.

roller shade
A covering made up of a length of cloth that can be rolled onto a pole fixed across the top edge of a window.

roman shade
A length of cloth covering a window that, by means of a pulley, can be folded into sections upwards.

headrail
The bar or pole across the top of a structure or device from which an object is hung, such as blinds from a window frame.

vertical blind
A series of slats that are hung vertically to cover a window and that, by means of a pulley, can be opened and closed.

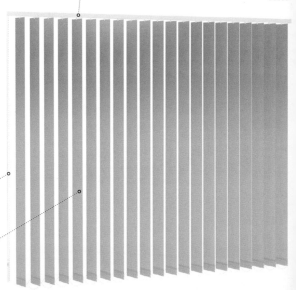

panel track blinds
A series of vertically hung strips of cloth covering a window that, by means of a pulley, can be slid sideways.

cord
A double length of thick string or thin chain that can be pulled to open or close the slats.

slat
The thin, overlapping sections of a window blind, usually made of light metal, plastic or stiffened cloth.

headrail
The bar or pole across the top of a structure or device from which an object is hung, such as blinds from a window frame.

blinds
A length of cloth or series of slats covering a window that, by means of a pulley, can be opended and closed.

lift cord
The length of rope or chain that is connected to a pulley device in the headrail of window blinds to raise them.

tilt wand
A long bar connected to a device in the headrail of window blinds that can be rotated to adjust the angle of the slats.

cord
On window blinds, a length of thick string that runs vertically, connecting the slats.

slat
The thin overlapping sections of a window blind, usually made of light metal, plastic or stiffened cloth.

kitchen curtains
Pieces of fabric hung from the top of a window, to the bottom edges, as decoration or to shield light.

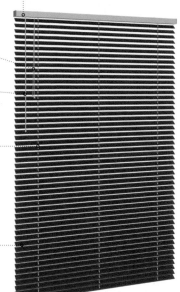

Linens
Household items made out of cloth, such as towels and bedding.

duvet
On a bed, a large, soft quilt or blanket, typically filled with feathers and used during sleep.

pillowcase
A cushioned support for the head, usually rectangular, that is stuffed with a soft material such as feathers.

bed linens
A set of various shapes of cloth to cover a bed, consisting of blankets, sheets and pillowcases.

sheet
On a bed, a large rectangular piece of soft cloth that covers the mattress or is laid underneath a blanket.

throw rug
A piece of material that covers a small area of a floor and can be easily moved.

brick house
A residential building whose outer construction is primarily made of hardened blocks of clay called bricks.

lintel
A horizontal supporting beam set across the top of a door or window.

roofing
The material used for covering the outer surface of a roof, such as shingles or tar, to protect it from weather.

plaster
A compound of lime, sand or cement, and water that is spread across an area, such as a wall, to form a smooth surface.

lawn
An area of grass around a house that is mowed regularly and kept neat.

tile
A piece of clay, stone or glass; used to create a surface on a floor or wall.

roof underlayment
A material, usually made of synthetic felt, that lies under the exterior roofing material as protection from moisture.

roof batten
Strips of wood, metal or plastic laid horizontally to provide a stable base for roofing.

ridge beam
The beam that runs horizontally across the peak of a roof as the upper portion of the supporting structure of the roof.

rafter
One of several beams that extend from the lower edge to the peak, creating a supporting structure.

attic floor
The floor of the area or room directly beneath the roof of a building.

ceiling joist
A heavy, horizontal beam set from wall to wall of a room to support the ceiling.

hardwood floor
A type of flooring composed of narrow slats of wood fitted tightly together lengthwise to form a flat surface.

underlay
A thin insulating material that lies between the subflooring and final flooring layers.

subfloor
A layer of particle board or plywood laid on a floor to create a smooth, flat surface on which to attach the top flooring.

floor joist
A beam set from wall to wall; a parallel series creates a raised area on which to lay flooring.

foundation
In construction, the lowest load-bearing part of a structure, typically below ground level.

footing
The supporting groundwork or base of a structure.

front porch
A platform at the entrance of a building, usually accessed by a short flight of steps.

front step
A small, raised platform on which one stands to reach a higher level, a series of which may form a staircase.

reinforced concrete house
A residential building whose main framework consists of concrete and steel girders.

fascia
A board or sheet of metal that caps the end of the rafters or may be used to hold the rain gutter.

window
A sheet of glass or other transparent or opaque material fixed into the wall of a building as a source of natural light.

lawn
An area of grass that is mowed regularly and kept neat, usually surrounding a residence.

front step
A small, raised platform on which one stands to reach a higher level, a series of which may form a staircase.

concrete
A building material that is made, usually, of sand, cement and water, and is poured to form a hardened platform.

self-leveling concrete
A layer of concrete poured onto an area to create a smooth surface on which to lay another material, such as tile.

attic
The area or room directly beneath the roof of a building.

wall
A continuous surface that extends from the floor to the ceiling of a building to separate areas into rooms.

rafter
One of several beams that extend from the lower edge to the peak, creating a supporting structure.

girder
A beam made of metal, such as iron or steel, forming part of the framework of a building.

corner support
A tall, upright structure or pillar, often made of stone or concrete, that supports another structure.

doorway
The opening in a wall that leads from one room to another, often hung with a barrier, called a door.

hardwood floor
A type of flooring composed of narrow slats of wood fitted tightly together lengthwise to form a flat surface.

underlay
A thin, insulating material that lies between the subflooring and final flooring layers.

subfloor
A layer of particle board or plywood laid on a floor to create a smooth, flat surface on which to attach the top flooring.

floor joist
A beam set from wall to wall; a parallel series creates a raised area on which to lay flooring.

foundation
In construction, the lowest load-bearing part of a structure, typically below ground level.

footing
The supporting groundwork or base of a structure.

front porch
A platform at the entrance of a building, usually accessed by a short flight of steps.

wooden-frame house
A residential building whose main framework consists of wooden beams and boards.

shingle
Thin, overlapping pieces of asphalt composite, slate, wood or metal that protect the roof of a building.

window opening
The hole cut from the interior to the exterior of a wall into which a window is to be fitted.

insulation
A sheet of material that prevents heat from escaping the interior of a building.

sheathing
A supporting outer layer of boards covering the ends of beams or joists on a building's structural frame.

gutter
A shallow trough running the length of an eave to collect and carry off rainwater and other debris, such as leaves.

stucco
A fine plaster that can be applied to surfaces, such as walls, and can be formed into decorative textures or shapes.

lawn
An area of grass that is mowed regularly and kept neat, usually surrounding a residence.

front step
A small, raised platform on which one stands to reach a higher level, a series of which may form a staircase.

tile
A piece of clay, stone or glass; used to create a surface on a floor or wall.

underlayment
A material, usually made of synthetic felt, which lies under the exterior roofing material as protection from moisture.

roof batten
Strips of wood, metal or plastic laid horizontally to provide a stable base for roofing.

purlin
A thin, horizontal beam laid across the underlayment of a roof to provide additional structural support for roofing.

ridge beam
The beam that runs horizontally across the peak of a roof as the upper portion of the supporting structure of the roof.

rafter
One of several beams that extend from the lower edge to the peak, creating a supporting structure.

tie beam
The horizontal beam that forms the base of a triangular truss in a pitched roof.

wall
A continuous surface that extends from the floor to the ceiling of a building to separate areas into rooms.

stud
A vertical beam in a wall to which surfacing materials, such as drywall, can be affixed.

hardwood floor
A type of flooring composed of narrow slats of wood fitted tightly together lengthwise to form a flat surface.

underlay
A thin, insulating material that lies between the subflooring and final flooring layers.

footing
The supporting groundwork or base of a structure.

subfloor
A layer of particle board or plywood laid on a floor to create a smooth, flat surface on which to attach the top flooring.

floor joist
A beam set from wall to wall; a parallel series creates a raised area on which to lay flooring.

foundation
In construction, the lowest load-bearing part of a structure, typically below ground level.

front porch
A platform at the entrance of a building, usually accessed by a short flight of steps.

lintel
A horizontal supporting beam set across the top of a door or window.

solid brick
A small, rectangular clay block, solid in structure. It is heavier and sturdier than other types of bricks.

perforated brick
A small, rectangular clay block, bearing three holes in its structure. It is lighter than other types of bricks.

concrete block
A large, rectangular brick used in construction, typically in the foundation of buildings.

paver
A style of brick that is specifically used for paving walkways or other outdoor areas.

board insulation
A board of pressed materials used to preserve a desired temperature in a building.

roof tiles
A roofing material used to protect a building from rain and snowfall.

tar paper
A flat and waterproof material that is set underneath sets of shingles to seal a roof from moisture.

foam weather stripping
A long and thin layer of material that can be used to seal a variety of different openings, such as windows.

flagstone
A generic variety of flat stone that is commonly used to build paved surfaces such as driveways.

asphalt shingles
Thin, overlapping pieces of asphalt that are placed on the roof of a building to prevent cold and leaks.

fireplace
A concrete or ceramic structure that is designed to safely foster and sustain a burning fire indoors.

mantle
A beam that supports the fireplace hood and also serves as a shelf to display small objects.

hood
A large metal encasing situated over the top of a fireplace; it directs and expels smoke.

corbel
An architectural projection that extends outward from the wall in order to support the weight of the hood.

lintel
A load-bearing component of the fireplace structure that is situated directly overhead the firebrick chamber.

jamb
A variety of brick that bears one rounded corner in order to provide a rounded surface at the edge of a wall.

firebrick back
The back side of the firebrick chamber; it is designed to contain and funnel heat up into the hood.

base
The large marble or concrete platform that forms a foundation for the structure of a fireplace and its hood.

frame
The metal frame of the firebrick chamber around which bricks are set in order to create the fireplace.

fire irons
Various types of fireplace utensils used to safely maintain fires.

tongs
A tool made of fire-resistant material that is used to grab, push and adjust burning logs.

poker
A rod made of fire-resistant material used to poke, push and adjust burning logs within the fireplace.

broom
A tool with bristles on the end, used to brush ashes left over from a fire into a shovel for disposal.

shovel
A scoop with a long handle that is used to scoop and discard ashes left over from fires.

wood racks
A small metallic structure that is placed near a fireplace and is used to neatly store wooden logs.

forced-air heating and air-conditioning system
A residential air-flow system that is designed to heat or cool a home through the use of forced air.

cold air register
A specialized mechanism that distributes cold air into a room.

attic vent
A small opening, typically on the upper part of a wall, that improves air flow.

thermostat
A device used to alter the level of heat or air conditioning.

insulation
A sheet of material usually built into a wall that prevents heat from escaping.

room air conditioner
A small air cooling unit positioned in the window of a room in order to generate cool air into the room.

cold air return
A type of duct system that is specifically used to disperse and remove cold air from within the residence.

furnace flue
Metal piping that is used to expel exhaust away from the furnace and outside the home.

humidifier
A machine that is designed to deliver moisture throughout a room or home.

main duct
A metal enclosure that is used to disperse and remove hot air from within a residence.

filter
A small component of the furnace system that catches and collects small particles, like dust, from the duct.

central air conditioner
An air-cooling unit located outside the home.

furnace
A residential heating device. It is usually placed in the basement and heats the entire house.

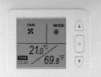

room thermostat
A device that is found on the wall of a room inside a residence and can be used to alter temperatures.

radiator thermostat
A device used to alter the level of heat.

column radiator
A type of residential heating device that emits heat that is generated from a heated reservoir of oil.

cover grille
A rectangular metal sheet that is placed over the inner components of a radiator to prevent fires.

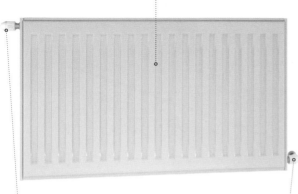

thermostat
The component that is used to adjust the temperature settings of the device.

hot-water outlet
An area of the column radiator where hot water can be expelled from the device during usage.

towel rail
A metallic apparatus that can be mounted on an inside or outside wall to neatly store or hang towels.

infrared heater
A devices that generates heat using electromagnetic radiation.

on/off switches
Small buttons located on the front face of a radiator. They are used to start and stop the device.

handle
A gripping component of the radiator that can be grabbed by the hand in order to move the device.

oil-filled radiant heater
A convection heating device bearing an oil reservoir that is electrically heated and emits heat.

pilot light
An area of a radiator where a flame is lit in order to ignite oil within the radiator.

fin
One of the thin and connected metal columns of a radiator; it radiates heat when activated.

control panel
An area of a radiator where the thermostat knob, pilot light and on/off switches are found.

thermostat
A knob located on the front of a radiator that allows the device's temperature to be altered.

vent
A small opening that expels hot air during use, preventing the unit from overheating.

power cord
A cable that can be plugged into a wall outlet in order to provide electricity to the radiator.

radiant heater
An electronic heating device that can be plugged into an outlet. It emits heat into a room.

cord storage
A small part that extends from the face of a radiator. The radiator's cord can be wrapped around it.

plumbing system
The collection of piping and structures that facilitates the transportation of waste and water from a household.

roof vent
A ventilation system designed to release steam to the exterior of the house.

vent stack
A vertical pipe running to the roof vent.

toilet
A bathroom device linked to a home's plumbing system; it collects and expels human waste.

tank
A hollow chamber that collects water between toilet usages in order to flush waste when a lever is pushed.

shower stall
A small, enclosed area in the bathroom, equipped with a showerhead, where one may clean oneself.

waste pipe
A pipe that is specifically designed to facilitate the transportation of waste products.

sink
A basin fitted with a tap and a drain, usually made of porcelain or other hard material, used to hold water.

main drain line
A large vertical pipe to which the plumbing fixtures connect and that transports the waste water from the home.

water heater
An appliance consisting of a tank, which stores water, and a heating unit, which warms the water for a home.

double kitchen sink
A variety of sink that is characterized as having two large bowls that can both be used simultaneously.

cold-water supply pipe
A series of piping that leads to and from the water heater; the pipes transport cool water.

dishwasher
An appliance into which soiled kitchenware, such as dishes and cutlery, can be stacked to be washed automatically.

drainpipe
A length of piping that is used to empty the washer of water in between cycles.

sewer drainpipe
The series of pipes that extends into the ground beneath a home and expels waste products.

washer
A household appliance used to launder clothing and other materials, such as bedding.

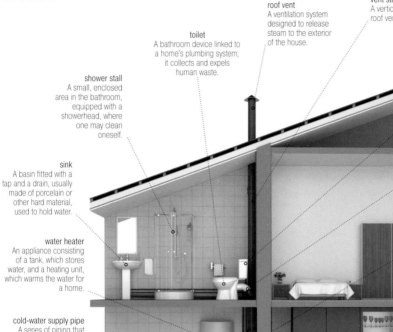

water service pipe
A pipe that brings water into a residence from an outside source.

hot-water supply pipe
A length of pipe that leads to and from the water heater.

hot-water riser
Piping that extends vertically into an upper floor to deliver hot water to a bathroom.

cold-water riser
Piping that extends vertically into an upper floor to deliver cold water to a bathroom.

handle
The lever that is adjusted to turn the water on and off.

spline
The series of intermittently spaced ridges that grip into the handle component in order to activate a faucet.

thread
A rubber-like component of a faucet that secures the tap valve to the spline component.

spout
The part that allows hot or cold water to be released into the sink.

nut
A tightening mechanism that is placed within a faucet in order to secure pertinent components.

ceramic disc
A small ceramic component of a faucet that is used to permit or prohibit water to pass.

tap valve
The valve that starts and stops the flow of water.

retaining ring
A fastening device made of steel or copper; used to secure components together.

O-ring
A rubber-like component that is used to prevent leaks around the spout.

cartridge faucet
A type of faucet that is characterized as having a cylinder that bears a valve that controls water flow.

disc faucet
A type of faucet that is characterized as having a spout lever located over a wide and cylindrical body.

setscrew
A colored screw that indicates which side releases cold water and which releases hot.

aerator body
The structural framework that serves to encase and protect an aerator insert

aerator insert
Also known as a tap aerator, this is a device located on the tip of the spout that releases air into the water.

cylinder
The component of a disc faucet that is encapsulated by the bonnet and stores various mechanisms.

post
The column found within the cylinder that mounts the cylinder to the bonnet.

handle
The lever that is adjusted to turn the water on and off.

bonnet
The structural component of a disc faucet that connects the handle to the spout sleeve.

mounting screw
The screw that is specifically designed to connect the bonnet to the frame of the cylinder.

aerator insert
Also known as a tap aerator, this is a device located on the tip of the spout that releases air into the water.

aerator body
A small metal cylinder that holds the aerator in place. It is screwed onto or inserted into the spout.

spout
The water dispensation component of a disc faucet. It is used to dispense water into the sink.

spout sleeve
The outer metallic casing of a spout. It stores and protects the spout's inner components.

spot shank
A component of a disc faucet that facilitates the transportation of water as it goes to the spout.

seal
Three small rubber rings that create airtight closures when connected to the cylinder.

water inlet
A cylindrical section through which water enters the faucet and can then be directed out the spout.

toilet
A fixture used to flush bodily waste into a sewer or septic system.

seat cover
The plastic or ceramic cover that can be lowered over the toilet bowl to minimize odor and bacteria.

seat
A cover that is placed atop the toilet bowl to provide a place for one to sit.

toilet bowl
The hollow chamber of a toilet that is specifically designed to collect and then flush waste products.

tank lid
The plastic or ceramic lid that is set atop the tank so as to store and protect its inner components.

flush handle
A small lever that can be pushed down to activate the flushing mechanism.

tank
An area of the toilet where water is stored between uses.

waste pipe
A pipe that is specifically designed to facilitate the transportation of waste products.

stem faucet
A type of faucet that is found in external environments. They are commonly used with gardening hoses.

handle
The component of a stem faucet that is manipulated by the hand to turn water on or off.

gland nut
A fastening mechanism that is designed to secure the handle to the packing.

packing
A piece or rubber or other non-porous material that prevents leaks within the faucet valve.

spindle
A component located within a stem faucet that contains the packing and washers.

thread
The small, raised metallic lines at the joints of a stem faucet that allow it to connect to other pipes.

stem washer
A small component located within a stem faucet that creates a seal in order to prevent water leaks.

ball valve
A valve that is characterized as having a hollow ball that is used to control the water flow.

handle
The gripping component of the ball valve; it can be turned by hand to adjust pressure.

thread
The small, raised metallic lines located at the joints of a ball valve that allow for pipe connections.

retaining ring
The component of a ball valve that is used to hold pressure but still permit flowage.

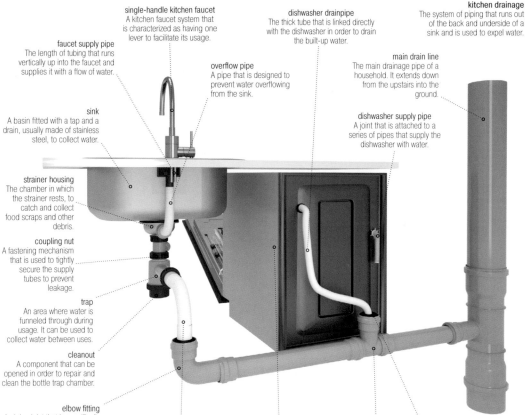

single-handle kitchen faucet
A kitchen faucet system that is characterized as having one lever to facilitate its usage.

dishwasher drainpipe
The thick tube that is linked directly with the dishwasher in order to drain the built-up water.

kitchen drainage
The system of piping that runs out of the back and underside of a sink and is used to expel water.

faucet supply pipe
The length of tubing that runs vertically up into the faucet and supplies it with a flow of water.

overflow pipe
A pipe that is designed to prevent water overflowing from the sink.

main drain line
The main drainage pipe of a household. It extends down from the upstairs into the ground.

sink
A basin fitted with a tap and a drain, usually made of stainless steel, to collect water.

dishwasher supply pipe
A joint that is attached to a series of pipes that supply the dishwasher with water.

strainer housing
The chamber in which the strainer rests, to catch and collect food scraps and other debris.

coupling nut
A fastening mechanism that is used to tightly secure the supply tubes to prevent leakage.

trap
An area where water is funneled through during usage. It can be used to collect water between uses.

cleanout
A component that can be opened in order to repair and clean the bottle trap chamber.

elbow fitting
A piping joint that is specifically designed to change the directional flow of water going down the drain.

kitchen sink drain hose
The length of hosing that allows water to be drained from the kitchen sink during the course of its use.

dishwasher
An appliance into which soiled kitchenware, such as dishes and cutlery, can be stacked to be washed automatically.

tee fitting
A piping joint that is characterized as being T-like in its shape. It has one large and one small chamber.

rubber gasket
A sealing mechanism that is used between the tee fitting and the dishwasher drain hose.

Various components commonly used in piping and plumbing systems.

double wye
A fitting that is characterized as being trident-like in shape. It bears three openings on one end.

cross
A type of piping joint that is characterized as being cross-like in shape. It has two intersecting chambers.

coupling
A joint that connects two smaller segments of piping.

45-degree elbow
A type of piping joint that is characterized as being bent at a 45-degree angle. It helps change directional flow.

tee connector
A type of piping joint that is characterized as being T-like in shape. It has one large and one small chamber.

connector coupling
A joint typically used to conjoin two segments of pipe that are different sizes.

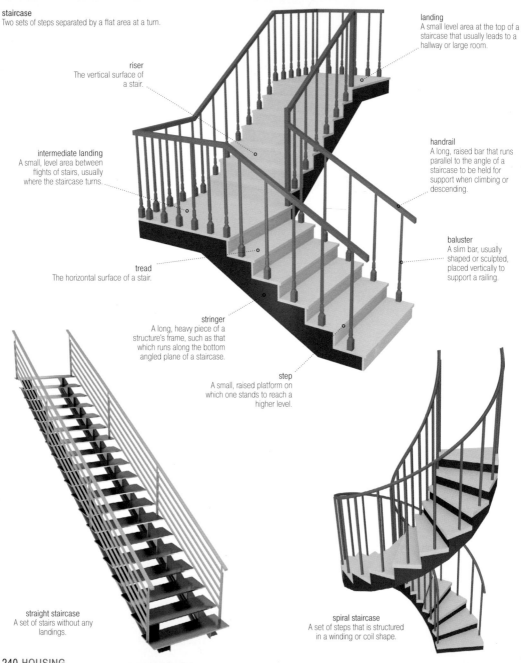

staircase
Two sets of steps separated by a flat area at a turn.

landing
A small level area at the top of a staircase that usually leads to a hallway or large room.

riser
The vertical surface of a stair.

handrail
A long, raised bar that runs parallel to the angle of a staircase to be held for support when climbing or descending.

intermediate landing
A small, level area between flights of stairs, usually where the staircase turns.

baluster
A slim bar, usually shaped or sculpted, placed vertically to support a railing.

tread
The horizontal surface of a stair.

stringer
A long, heavy piece of a structure's frame, such as that which runs along the bottom angled plane of a staircase.

step
A small, raised platform on which one stands to reach a higher level.

straight staircase
A set of stairs without any landings.

spiral staircase
A set of steps that is structured in a winding or coil shape.

Roofs
The topmost covering of a building.

shingles
The material used for covering the outer surface of a roof, such as shingles or tar, to protect it from weather.

sheathing
Sheets of a material, such as particle board or drywall, where the shingles are attached.

rafter
One of several beams that extend from the lower edge to the peak, creating a supporting structure.

gabled roof
A roof with an inverted V-shape frame that has an acute top angle to create a severe slant to the roof's surface.

ridge beam
The beam that runs horizontally across the peak of a roof as the upper portion of the supporting structure of the roof.

collar tie
A support beam that runs across the outer inverted V-shape of a slanted roof's frame.

side post
An upright support beam that runs from one side of the inverted V-shape of a slanted roof's frame to a rafter.

fascia
A board or sheet of metal that caps the end of the rafters or may be used to hold the rain gutter.

beam
A sturdy length of wood or metal that supports the structure of a roof.

rafter plate
A heavy piece of timber that runs the length of either side of the base of a roof's frame to which rafters are secured.

low-pitch roof
A roof with an inverted V-shape frame that has acute corner angles to create a shallow slant to the roof's surface.

gambrel roof
A pitched roof structure that incorporates two degrees of slant, one steeper than the other, on both sides of the roof.

roof construction
The layered components that make up the construction of a roof, such as rafters, insulation and underlayment.

underlay
A material, usually made of synthetic felt, that lies under the exterior roofing material as protection from moisture.

insulation
A sheet of material usually built into a wall that prevents heat from escaping.

rafter
One of several beams that extend from the lower edge to the peak, creating a supporting structure.

ridge beam
The length of metal or wood that runs horizontally across the peak of a roof, acting as the supporting structure.

ridge
The uppermost line of a peaked roof.

roofing
The material used for covering the outer surface of a roof, such as shingles or tar, to protect it from weather.

purlin
A thin, horizontal beam laid across the underlayment of a roof to provide additional structural support for roofing.

gutter
A shallow trough running the length of an eave to collect and carry off rainwater and other debris, such as leaves.

downspout
A pipe attached to the gutters of a building and extending downward to allow rainwater to be carried off.

fascia
A board or sheet of metal that caps the end of the rafters or may be used to hold the rain gutter.

roof lining
The lowermost layer in a roof's construction, placed above the ceiling to prevent moisture from entering the home.

beam
A sturdy length of material, such as wood or metal; many beams form the horizontal supporting structure of a roof.

flat roof
The structure forming the upper covering of a building, which is completely horizontal with no slant or pitch.

vent
A protected opening that is designed to release moisture collected on the roof's underside.

coping
A sheet of material, usually of metal, formed to cover the outer perimeter of a flat roof structure.

roof membrane
A layer of material applied to a roof, under shingles, to prevent leaks and help with water run-off.

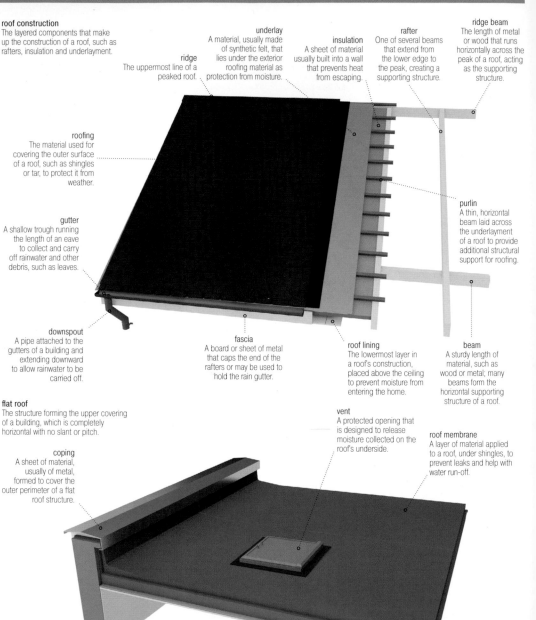

turbine vent
A tubular length of metal or plastic suspended over an appliance, designed to extract steam to the external environment.

ridge
The uppermost line of a peaked roof.

gutter
A shallow trough running the length of an eave to collect and carry off rainwater and other debris, such as leaves.

roofing
The material used for covering the outer surface of a roof, such as shingles or tar, to protect it from weather.

fan blade
A length of metal that rotates to improve the airflow created by the vent.

rotating cap
The end of a ventilation duct or chimney that protrudes from the roof of a building to the outdoors.

skirt
In construction, a smooth frame that is built around the perimeter of the base of a protruding section, such as a chimney.

flashing
A strip of metal that creates a seal at a juncture in a roof; often used on chimneys.

flue
A duct that extends to the exterior of a building to allow the escape of smoke or steam, such as from a fireplace.

Roof windows
Openings that are built into or extending upward from a roof, such as a skylight.

ridge
The uppermost line of a peaked roof.

shingle
Thin, overlapping pieces of asphalt composite, slate, wood or metal that protect the roof of a building.

skylights
A window built into the roof of a building, which provides natural light from the ceiling of a room.

dormer window
A window on a house, which is raised up from the main roof with its own framed structure and small roof.

window frame
The supporting structure of a window, usually made of wood or vinyl, forming one or more squares.

window
A sheet of glass or other transparent or frosted material fixed into the wall as a source of natural light.

gutter
A shallow trough running the length of an eave to collect and carry off rainwater and other debris, such as leaves.

facade
The primary exterior surface of the wall of a building, usually facing a main road.

swimming pool
A structure, usually made of concrete, that holds a large quantity of water for swimming.

deck
A raised platform constructed of planks, usually of wood, extending from the side of a house or surrounding a pool.

overflow drain
An opening in the gutter that allows water overflow to drain away.

gutter
A shallow trough running the length of an artificial body of water, such as a swimming pool, to carry off spill-over.

ladder
Two upright bars and a set of horizontal steps, used for cimbing up or down.

wall
A flat, vertical surface that makes up the side of a container or box-like structure, such as a swimming pool.

diving board
A plank that extends over a pool that allows one to bounce and dive into the water.

drain
An opening that allows excess liquid to be run off through a pipe, such as at the bottom of a pool.

pump
A mechanism that takes in water and cleans it, usually by filtering, then ejects it into the same or another space.

filter
In a pool filtration system, a layer of sand through which water continuously passes to remove small bits of debris.

hatch
A hinged barrier that can be opened to access an area or container beyond or beneath it.

inflatable toy
A plaything made of a flexible plastic that is filled with air and maintains buoyancy in water.

swim ring
An inflated tube of flexible plastic that is worn around the body to help a person to maintain buoyancy in water.

sauna
A small room that is heated and filled with steam and in which a person may relax and perspire for body cleansing purposes.

seat
A place where a person can sit; it can have a back or not and armrests or not.

bench
An elongated backless, armless seat for more than one person made of a hard substance such as wood or stone.

light
A mechanism that generates luminous energy to brighten a dark room or area.

thermometer
A device for measuring units of temperature.

bathrobe
A long, soft coat, usually belted and sometimes with a hood, that is typically worn before or after bathing.

sauna bucket
A wooden vessel accompanied by a ladle that is used to pour small amounts of water onto hot stones to create steam in a sauna.

bucket
An open container with a handle designed to carry a number of objects or an amount of liquid, usually made of plastic or wood.

ladle
A kitchen utensil, similar to a large spoon, used to scoop liquids from one vessel to another.

glass door
A barrier that can be moved to gain access to the inside of a space that accumulates steam or heat, such as a shower or sauna.

heater
A device that warms air or water through the conversion of electricity into heat energy or by the burning of a fuel.

towel
A piece of absorbent cloth used to dry one's body or hair.

laundry hamper
A container used to hold soiled linens or clothing until washing.

casing
An outer shell of resistant material that protects the more delicate components.

temperature pointer
The thin, tapered hand on the face of a thermometer that rotates to indicate a specific unit of temperature.

thermometer
A device for measuring units of temperature.

dial
The surface of a clock, or other measuring device, marked with specific units of measure in a concentric formation.

hygrometer pointer
The thin, tapered piece on the face of a hygrometer that rotates to indicate a specific unit of humidity.

deck chair
A folding, low-slung, outdoor chair, usually made of wood or a light metal, with a canvas seat and back.

bistro set
A small table with two matching chairs, usually placed on a balcony or patio for casual, intimate seating.

bistro table
A small table, often with a round top, that is placed on a patio or terrace and made of a material to withstand weather.

roof
The topmost covering of a building.

gazebo
A decorative outdoor structure in the shape of a rounded room with a roof but without walls.

table
A piece of furniture with a pedestal or legs supporting a flat surface on which to place objects.

bench
An elongated backless, armless seat for more than one person made of a hard substance such as wood or stone.

support beam
A long, sturdy length of rigid material, such as wood, that forms a load-bearing part of a structural frame.

floor
The lower surface of a room or outdoor structure, such as a shed or gazebo, on which one walks.

bistro chair
A small chair, often folding, that is placed on a patio or terrace and made of a material to withstand weather.

bench
An elongated outdoor piece of furniture designed to seat more than one person and made of a hard substance such as wood.

lounger
An elongated outdoor seat with an adjustable back designed to allow one to stretch out in a lying or sitting position.

sofa
An upholstered seat with arms at either side and a back, long enough to accommodate more than one person.

folding table
A table with legs that can be collapsed to lie flush against the underside of the top for easy storage and portability.

folding bench
A bench with legs that can be collapsed to lie flush against the underside of the seat for easy storage and portability.

porch swing
A bench that is suspended by ropes or chains, used for relaxing outoors.

bridge
A structure that spans an obstacle, such as a river or stream, to allow convenient passage from one side to the other.

patio umbrella
A canopy attached to a pole, used to
provide shade over outdoor furniture.

fountain
A decorative structure in a
pond or pool that pumps
water into the air in a spray or
cascade.

fence
An upright structure, typically of
wood or wire, enclosing an area
of property.

patio heater
An appliance that warms an
outdoor area; typically powered
by burning fuel.

reflector
A hood placed over the
flame to direct the heat
in a specific direction,
usually downward.

shade
A covering placed
over a light source to
temper or direct the
light, often conical or
bowl-shaped.

burner
An apparatus that is filled
with fuel and lit with a
flame in order to produce
constant heat.

sconce
A light fixture in the general
shape of a candle or torch
that is attached to a wall by a
decorative bracket.

ventilation hole
A slot or hole in a
closed container that
allows steam or smoke
to escape freely and air
to pass through.

propane tank housing
A protective casing that
holds and protects a
propane fuel source.

base
The lowest section,
which rests on the
ground and carries
the heater's weight.

decorative light
A light source used more
for decoration than a quality
source of light.

lamppost
An outdoor light fixture atop a
long column set into or fixed
onto the ground.

stake light
An outdoor light fixture atop
a short post or spike that is
usually driven into the ground
of a grassy area.

control pad
Dials located on the front of the barbecue that can be turned to alter temperature settings.

lid
The metallic casing that can be lowered over a grill in order to close in heat and cook food quickly.

barbecue
An outdoor grill, usually heated with propane or charcoal, primarily used to cook meat.

grill rack
The metal rack placed over the heat, where food is cooked.

meat
The flesh of an animal that is butchered and cooked as food.

gas cylinder
A container that holds the fuel used to initiate and sustain the flames on a barbecue.

wheel
A circular device that rotates on an axis and allows the object to be moved easily.

storage rack
The lowermost flat surface of the barbecue, used as a shelf to hold propane tanks.

outdoor fireplace
An outdoor fireplace, often made of fired clay or stone, which may be fitted with a grill for cooking.

grill
A metal grid onto which food is placed to be cooked over an open flame, such as on a barbecue.

hibachi
A small, portable outdoor grill, often round and fitted with a removable lid, that is set low to the ground for picnics or camping.

lid
The covering for the top of the grill.

electric grill
An electronic kitchen appliance that behaves like a barbecue but cooks food with heated elements rather than fuel.

bowl
The container into which coal or other fuels, such as wood chips, are laid out for burning.

barbecue utensils
Handheld implements used for cooking foods over a barbecue, such as tongs, a spatula and a long-handled fork.

fork
A utensil with two or more tines, used to pierce and manipulate food or to hold it in place when cutting.

knife
A handheld utensil with a sharp blade used for cutting.

basting brush
A kitchen tool with bristles, used to spread liquids onto foods being cooked or baked.

corn holder
A knob with a small, sharp spear or fork that is pierced into the end of a hot cob of corn, allowing it to be picked up.

tongs
A kitchen serving tool consisting of two movable arms that can be squeezed together to pinch items between the ends.

spatula
A kitchen utensil with a slightly tilted, broad, flat head, used to flip food while cooking.

scraper
A scraper featuring bristles that is used to scrape off burnt-on foods from a grill.

carrying case
A small or portable container, usually with two hinged covers and a handle, used for transporting small items.

skewer
A long, slender rod of metal with a sharp tip onto which food is threaded to hold it together during cooking.

TOOLS
Gardening tools

gardening gloves
Gloves made of a tough material, such as canvas or rubber, used to protect hands from dirt or injury when gardening.

wheelbarrow
A small cart with one large front wheel and two supporting legs, typically pushed by hand to cart objects.

leaf blower
A motorized gardening tool that forces air through a long nozzle, which is used to move leaves and debris.

snow scoop
An oversized shovel used to collect and displace snow.

plastic snow shovel
A tool with a large plastic scoop attached to a long handle; typically used to lift and toss snow.

metal snow shovel
A tool with a large metal scoop attached to a long handle; typically used to lift and toss snow.

leaf rake
A yard tool with bent, flexible prongs, used to collect and remove leaves from the ground.

level rake
A pole with a rigid comb-like metal structure on the end, used to level gravel, dirt or asphalt.

garden fork
A pole with a handle and four sharp tines, used to move long cut grasses.

hoe
A garden tool, consisting of a dull, flat blade attached to a long handle, used for tilling or aerating soil.

weeder
A gardening hand tool shaped like a small spade, used to remove unwanted plants.

hand rake
A handheld gardening tool with a claw, used to scrape away debris from a small area.

hand cultivator
A handheld gardening tool with a claw designed to loosen soil or scrape away debris over a small area.

double-headed hoe
A tool with a dull, flat blade on one side and a forked blade on the other, used to cultivate gardens.

pick
A heavy metal bar, pointed at one or both ends, used to break up materials such as rock.

spade
A gardening tool consisting of a broad blade and a long handle, used for digging dirt.

shovel
A tool with a long handle and broad, pointed scoop, used primarily for digging and displacing earth.

garden shears
A gardening hand tool shaped like a pair of scissors, designed to trim plants.

hand fork
A gardening hand tool, made up of sharp prongs attached to a handle, used for penetrating hard-packed soil.

garden trowel
A hand tool shaped like a shovel, used for digging areas of soil or for extracting unwanted plants.

pruning saw
A gardening tool made up of a sturdy blade mounted on a handle, used to cut through twigs and small branches.

ax
A hand tool with a sharp, heavy blade attached to a long handle; it is usually used for chopping wood.

pruning shears
A gardening hand tool shaped like a pair of scissors, designed to cut through tough plants, such as shrubs.

gas cap
A screw-on covering for the tank containing the fuel, most often gasoline, on a powered machine such as a chainsaw.

anti-vibration handle
On a chainsaw, a curved bar that can be grasped to direct the blade.

chainsaw
A handheld, motorized cutting tool with a notched chain that rotates rapidly around a flat blade.

safety switch
An attachment on a machine that can be flipped to instantly stop or shut down the motor.

chain brake
A protective shield on a chainsaw fixed between the front handle and the blade, which, when touched, stops the motor.

chain
A strip of flexible metal studded with teeth that rotates on the blade of a chainsaw.

accelerator trigger
An attachment on a machine that is squeezed to control the flow of fuel or other power to the motor.

handle
On a chainsaw, a curved bar that can be grasped to provide stability for the machine when in use.

guide bar
The flat panel of metal around which the chain of a chainsaw runs.

scythe
A tool with a curved blade, used for cutting long grass or grain in a sweeping motion.

tree pruner
A gardening tool made up of scissor-shaped blades at the end of a long pole, used for trimming tree branches.

lawn trimmer
A gardening tool that uses a rapidly rotating thin wire at the end of a long pole to cut the edges of areas of grass.

trigger
The small lever pressed by a finger to activate a mechanism.

guard
A protective shield that prevents fingers from touching the dangerous moving parts.

hedge trimmer
A handheld tool with a long, toothed blade, used to cut shrubbery and bushes in a yard.

lopping shears
A scissor-shaped gardening tool used to trim shrubs and bushes by squeezing two handles together.

handle
The part of a tool or machine that is held by the hand to pull or control it.

blade
The sharpened metal part; it is toothed on both edges and used for cutting.

lawn mower
A gas-powered or electric tool consisting of rotating blades; it is pushed across an area of grass to cut it.

grass catcher
The compartment on a lawnmower, in the form of a bag or tank, designed to collect grass clippings for later disposal.

handle
The part of a tool or machine that is held by the hand to pull or control it.

gas tank
The part of an engine in which fuel is stored and then propelled into the engine.

safety handle
A bar attached to a machine, in close proximity to the handle, that can be squeezed or pulled to activate the motor.

control lever
An attachment on a machine that can be flipped to control the flow of fuel or other power to the motor.

string trimmer
A tool with a thick, rigid plastic cord that is used to make precision cuts to grass and other low-growing vegetation.

air filter
A device on a machine that filters dust or other particles, preventing them from passing into the motor.

wheel
A circular device that rotates on an axis and found on the base of an object, allowing the object to be moved easily.

watering wand
A handheld device that can be attached to the end of a garden hose and has a head used to spray water.

impulse sprinkler
A device that is attached to a water source, used to spray water on an area of land, usually on a lawn.

oscillating sprinkler
A device that is attached to the end of a garden hose and turns, allowing water to be sprinkled across an area.

pistol nozzle
A handheld device attached to the end of a garden hose; it has a trigger to control the spray of water.

watering can
A portable container with a handle and perforated cap, used for watering plants.

garden hose
A coil of rubber tubing that can be attached to an outdoor tap, allowing water to be ejected at a distance.

hose reel
A contraption that is turned in order to coil a garden hose onto a cylindrical spindle, preventing kinks.

flaring tool
A tool used to widen the opening of a tube by compressing its wall.

wing nut
A fastening device that is threaded onto the end of a screw with the fingers by way of small protrusions on either side.

pipe wrench
A hand tool with large jaws that can be adjusted to fit the width of the object they are grasping.

clamp
A device used to tighten, strengthen or fasten objects together, usually constructed of a resistant material.

tube slot
The hole in a tube expander tool where a tube is placed to be expanded.

mount
The piece that supports the clamp and contains the tube slots.

pipe cutter
A hand tool with extremely sharp blades on handles that are squeezed in a scissor-like motion to cut through pipes.

plumber's snake
A thin coil of metal designed to snake through pipes to dislodge materials that have built up and created a blockage.

plunger
A device made up of a rubber cup on the end of a long handle, used to manipulate water pressure to clear blocked pipes.

tongue-and-groove pliers
A hand tool with serrated jaws formed in a V-shape, used to grasp and turn cylindrical or irregularly shaped objects.

pipe threader
A handheld device used to cut threads on the end of a pipe in order to allow it to be screwed into an object.

crescent wrench
A hand tool with large jaws that can be adjusted to fit the width of the object they are grasping.

jaw
One of two opposing hinged parts of the tool; when squeezed together, they pinch an object or material.

locking pliers
A handheld tool with a double handle ending in locking pincers for gripping or bending thin metal rods or wires.

measurement scale
A strip of metal or plastic notched with demarcations of progressive units of distance, such as inches.

handle
The part of a tool or machine that is held by the hand to pull or control it.

thumbscrew
A protruding piece of rigid material formed in a rounded shape that is rotated to bring two pieces of a device together.

hole
A hollowed-out section of any material, sometimes passing directly through an object.

slip-joint pliers
A handheld tool with a pivot point that can be used to increase the size range of the jaws.

faucet seat wrench
A hand tool that can be inserted into a valve to control the direction or rate of flow of liquid through a fitted pipe.

Allen wrench
A small hand tool with a head of a specific shape designed to fit into the same shape on the head of a bolt or screw.

socket set
A tool box that contains different varieties and sizes of sockets, together with a socket wrench.

combination wrench
A hand tool with one open end designed to grasp objects and a socket on the other end designed to fit over objects.

flare nut wrench
A hand tool with open ends designed to grasp nuts or bolts to be loosened or tightened.

box end wrench
A cylindrical wrench with a hexagonal end fitting, used when nuts and bolts are particularly hard to reach.

open end wrench
A hand tool with two open ends, usually set at different angles, designed to grasp objects such as nuts or bolts.

ratchet box end wrench
A hand tool with socket openings at either end, which may be fitted onto nuts or bolts to be turned in only one direction.

motor housing
A hard outer casing enclosing the motor of a tool or appliance.

circular saw
A handheld motorized tool with a circular blade; most often used to cut lengths of wood.

handle
The part of a tool, machine or object that is held by the hand to pull or control it.

jigsaw
An electrical saw with a thin, vertical blade used for cutting materials, such as wood, in precise, often curved, lines.

handle
The part of a tool, machine or object that is held by the hand to pull or control it.

blade
The sharpened cutting edge of a saw, which may be toothed.

blade guard
A protective component of a circular saw designed to shield the blade in order to prevent accidents.

blade
The sharpened metal part that is toothed on one edge and used for cutting.

motor housing
A hard outer casing enclosing and protecting the motor of a tool or appliance.

vent
An opening in a machine, usually in the form of slits, that allows air to flow through to cool the inner motor.

handle
The part of a tool, machine or object held by the hand to pull or control it.

blade
The sharpened metal part that is toothed on one edge and used for cutting.

frame
The fitting on a saw that allows the length of the blade available for cutting to be changed.

hacksaw
A cutting tool used primarily for cutting through metal.

bolt
A small, threaded pin of metal with a blunt end used to fasten one object to another and usually secured with a nut.

nut
A ring of metal that is threaded onto the end of a bolt, once it has been driven through a material, as a fastener.

wing nut
A fastening device that is threaded onto the end of a screw with the fingers, using small protrusions on either side.

table saw
A power tool with a blade mounted under a bench and projected through a slot; typically used to cut wood.

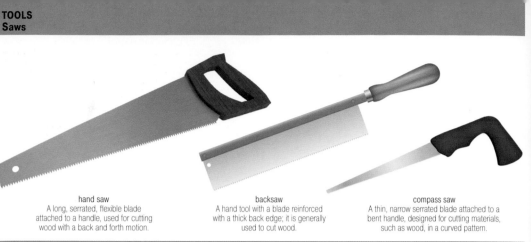

hand saw
A long, serrated, flexible blade attached to a handle, used for cutting wood with a back and forth motion.

backsaw
A hand tool with a blade reinforced with a thick back edge; it is generally used to cut wood.

compass saw
A thin, narrow serrated blade attached to a bent handle, designed for cutting materials, such as wood, in a curved pattern.

Sanding and polishing tools

electric grinder
A hand tool with a flat, mildly abrasive surface used to rub surfaces to make them smooth or glossy.

power cord
A long wire coated with an insulating material attached to a tool or an appliance that can be plugged into an outlet.

motor housing
A hard outer casing enclosing and protecting the motor of a tool or appliance.

orbital sander
An electrical tool with a flat, round piece of abrasive material that rotates and is used to smooth rough surfaces.

dust collection bag
A thick, woven mesh of porous fibers placed over the opening of a ventilation device to capture airborne residue.

belt sander
A tool with long, flat rotating strip of abrasive material that is used to smooth rough surfaces.

motor housing
A hard outer casing that encloses the motor of a tool or appliance.

fastening
A device that is used to attach one object to another, such as a filter onto an appliance or tool.

sanding pad
The flat, round piece of abrasive material that is used to smooth surfaces.

power cord
A long wire coated with an insulating material attached to a tool or an appliance that can be plugged into an outlet.

sanding belt
The long, flat strip of abrasive material that is wrapped around the rotating section of a belt sanding machine.

dust collection bag
An opening in a machine, usually in the form of slits, that allows air to flow through to expel waste gases.

pulley
A rod that is passed through the center of a wheel to maintain it in a fixed position, or to control its movement.

soldering iron
An electric hand tool with a metal tip that is heated and loaded with solder.

heating element
A piece of metal, such as on a soldering gun, that is heated electrically and touched to other objects to heat or melt.

soldering gun
An electric hand tool with a metal tip that is heated and loaded with solder.

solder
An alloy metal that melts at low temperatures, used to join materials.

handle
The part of a tool or machine that is held by the hand to pull or control it.

power switch
A lever or button that can be flipped or pressed to turn a device's power on or off.

power cord
A long wire coated with an insulating material attached to a tool or an appliance that can be plugged into an outlet.

Electrical tools

display
A lit panel that provides information about the voltage, current or resistence being tested.

multimeter
An electronic device used to measure voltage, current and resistence.

voltage tester
A sensory tool used to detect electric current in wires.

probe
A slender pin of metal connected to a handle that is inserted into areas to measure activities such as voltage.

tip
The pointed or tapering end of a slim, elongated object, such as a drill bit or a screwdriver.

insulation
On electrical tools, a material that does not conduct electricity, usually used on exposed portions of the tool.

insulated handle
The portion of a tool that is held in the hand, covered with material and does not conduct electricity.

clip
A small device attached to an object, which is used to fasten it to another object.

selector switch
A knob or lever that can be adjusted to change the function of a machine, such as on a multimeter.

wire stripper
A scissor-shaped hand tool used for cutting and removing the insulating coating of wires.

indicator light
A tiny light built into a sensory tool to indicate the presence or level of a substance, such as the voltage of an electrical source.

electric drill
A hand tool with a rotating tip used for making holes or setting screws.

speed selector switch
A small lever that can be adjusted to control the speed of a bit's rotation.

chuck
The component on the end the drill into which differently shaped bits can be inserted and clamped.

motor housing
A hard outer casing that encloses the motor of a tool or appliance.

bit
A cutting tool designed to create small holes of various shapes and sizes and fixed into the end of a drill.

trigger switch
A switch in the form of a trigger that is squeezed to start or stop a mechanism.

reversing switch
A small lever that can be adjusted to change the direction of the drill bit's rotation.

handle
The part of a tool or machine that is held by the hand to pull or control it.

auger bit
A small tool for boring holes in materials, such as wood, that is inserted and clamped into the end of a drill.

battery
In appliances or tools, a container of cells that convert chemical energy into a source of power.

battery
In appliances or tools, a container of cells that convert chemical energy into a source of power.

spade bit
A tool with cutting blades on either side of a center point, which is inserted and clamped into the end of a drill.

drill press
A machine tool used to bore holes into wood, metal or plastic.

hammer drill
An electric tool with a rotating tip that uses successive blows to bore holes; usually used for masonry or rock.

feed lever
Similar to a handle, this is turned by hand to bring the drill bit down into a piece of material, such as wood.

protective screen
A plate or sheet of resistant material, such as glass or metal mesh, creating a barrier in front of a potentially dangerous area.

twist drill bit
A tool designed to create small holes; it is fixed into the end of a drill.

motor housing
A hard outer casing enclosing the motor of a tool or appliance.

drill bit
A cutting tool designed to create small holes of various shapes and sizes, and is fixed into the end of a drill.

tip
The point of the bit, used for boring holes.

column
A rigid pole on which the operating portion of an appliance is mounted, such as on a floor fan, speaker or lamp.

table
A flat surface of a tool or appliance on which an object can be placed to be manipulated, such as on a drill press.

land
A raised rib of material formed in a helix, such as on a pipe or in a cap, that allows it to be screwed to another object.

flute
A narrow indentation that is used to direct the movement of a substance along its length, such as on a drill bit.

masonry drill bit
A small tool for boring holes in construction materials, such as brick or stone, that is clamped into the end of a drill.

base
The lowest section, which rests on the floor and carries the drill press's weight.

claw hammer
A handheld tool with one flat side for pounding and a clawed side for extracting nails.

claw
The curved end of a hammer, which is used to extract nails.

face
The blunt, pounding side on the head of a claw hammer.

shaft
A long, narrow rod that connects the operating mechanism of a tool to a handle.

handle
The part of a tool, machine or object held by the hand to pull or control it.

crowbar
A hand tool with a curved and sometimes bifurcated end, used as a lever to pry one material away from another.

masonry hammer
A handheld tool with a heavy head for pounding into brick and other stonework.

mallet
A type of hammer, usually with a wooden head, used to pound the end of another tool, such as a chisel.

nail gun
A mechanical device that forcefully ejects nails used for construction, eliminating the need for pounding.

electric stapler
A device that forcefully ejects staples, eliminating the need to pound them in by hand.

nail set
Tools placed on the head of a nail and then hit with a hammer in order to drive a nail below a surface.

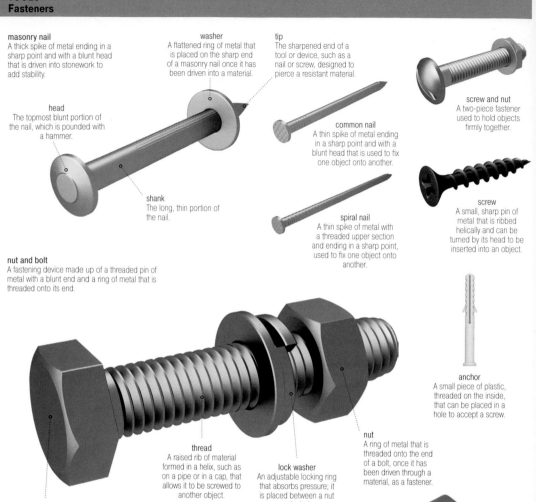

masonry nail
A thick spike of metal ending in a sharp point and with a blunt head that is driven into stonework to add stability.

washer
A flattened ring of metal that is placed on the sharp end of a masonry nail once it has been driven into a material.

tip
The sharpened end of a tool or device, such as a nail or screw, designed to pierce a resistant material.

screw and nut
A two-piece fastener used to hold objects firmly together.

head
The topmost blunt portion of the nail, which is pounded with a hammer.

common nail
A thin spike of metal ending in a sharp point and with a blunt head that is used to fix one object onto another.

screw
A small, sharp pin of metal that is ribbed helically and can be turned by its head to be inserted into an object.

shank
The long, thin portion of the nail.

spiral nail
A thin spike of metal with a threaded upper section and ending in a sharp point, used to fix one object onto another.

nut and bolt
A fastening device made up of a threaded pin of metal with a blunt end and a ring of metal that is threaded onto its end.

anchor
A small piece of plastic, threaded on the inside, that can be placed in a hole to accept a screw.

nut
A ring of metal that is threaded onto the end of a bolt, once it has been driven through a material, as a fastener.

thread
A raised rib of material formed in a helix, such as on a pipe or in a cap, that allows it to be screwed to another object.

lock washer
An adjustable locking ring that absorbs pressure; it is placed between a nut and a bolt.

head
The topmost blunt portion of the bolt, which is grasped to tighten the bolt.

cabinet hinge
A joint with a lever mechanism that is used to connect doors to pieces of furniture.

door hinge
A joint with a central pin that connects a door to a frame and allows the door to be swung open or shut.

C-clamp
A device used to tighten, strengthen or fasten objects together, usually constructed of a resistant material.

handle
The part of a tool or machine that is held by the hand to pull or control it.

screw
A helically ribbed rod that can be turned to pass through an object for fastening purposes, such as on a clamp.

head
The topmost blunt portion of a tool or device, such as on a nail for pounding or screw for gripping.

rod
A cylindrical, rigid piece on a tool or device, usually connecting two pieces together, such as the handle to the main section.

jaw
One of two opposing hinged parts of the tool; when squeezed together, they pinch an object or material.

vise
A tool consisting of strong, flat jaws that hold an object firmly in place.

handle
The part of the tool that is turned to tighten the jaws.

slotted screwdriver
A handheld tool with a flattened tip, used to thread screws through resistant materials.

Robertson (square) screwdriver
A type of screwdriver that has a square head. It is used with screws that have a square hole.

handle
The part of a tool or machine that is held by the hand to pull or control it.

Phillips screwdriver
A type of screwdriver that has a cross-shaped head. It is used with screws that bear a cross shape.

tip
The pointed or tapering end of a slim, elongated object, such as a drill bit or a screwdriver.

lubricant spray
A liquid applied to metal parts to keep them from seizing.

spiral screwdriver
A handheld tool that is used to thread screws through resistant materials to fix them together.

lineman's pliers
A handheld tool with a double handle ending in pincers for gripping, bending or cutting thin metal rods or wires.

precision screwdriver
A very small tool that is held between the fingers to thread tiny screws to affix objects, such as watch parts, together.

sledgehammer
A tool with a very heavy head attached to a handle, mainly used for breaking hard objects such as stone.

needle-nose pliers
A hand tool with two handles ending in tapered pincers, used to bend thin metal rods or wires.

caulking gun
A tool that is used to squeeze out a waterproof, gummy material from a nozzle to seal construction cracks or seams.

spring
A coiled piece of metal that retains its shape when squeezed or released, to provide tension or absorption of movement.

tube
A long, hollow cylinder made of a rigid material through which liquid, gaseous or viscous materials may flow or be squeezed.

plunger
The end that applies pressure to the tube of caulk so it comes out of the nozzle.

nozzle
The spout at the end of the tube; it helps direct the caulk.

handle
The part of a tool, machine or object that is held by the hand to pull or control it.

trigger
The small lever pressed by a finger to activate a mechanism or eject material from a tool.

roller grid
Used inside a paint bucket, a roller is dragged across it to remove excess paint.

heat gun
A handheld device that emits a stream of very hot air, used for drying or softening materials.

glass cutter
A tool with a sharp, flat piece of metal on a handle, used to score glass so it can be snapped.

paint tray
A shallow basin, often with a slant or with levels, designed to hold paint for a paint roller.

mason's trowel
A handheld tool shaped like a small spade, used for leveling, spreading and shaping mortar or concrete.

tuck pointer
A hand tool with a flat metal blade attached to a handle, used primarily for filling masonry joints with mortar or cement.

square trowel
A hand tool with a flat, metal plate attached to a handle, used primarily for smoothing mortar or cement.

digital caliper
An electronic tool that measures the thickness of materials.

framing square
A device with two straight perpendicular sides, often designed as a ruler, used to test or mark out right angles.

scraper
A hand tool with a moderately sharp flat edge, used to remove paint, dirt or other unwanted materials from a surface.

cement mixer
A machine with a revolving drum that is used to combine water and concrete mix.

platform stepladder
A ladder with built-in platforms on which objects, such as cans of paint, can be rested at an elevated height.

shelf
The section of a stepladder that maintains the integrity of the construction when it has been opened.

leg
A support attached to the ladder to raise it and stabilize it.

leg tip
A rubber cup attached to the end of the leg of an object that rests on the ground, such as a ladder, to prevent slippage.

extension ladder
A ladder that features sliding sections that can be moved to lengthen or shorten the ladder, as needed.

step
A horizontal surface interspersed between the two upright bars of a ladder, used for climbing.

spirit level
A device used to establish the specific angle, usually horizontal, of an object by the shift of a bubble within liquid.

tape measure
A narrow strip of metal used to measure lengths of material.

bricklayer's hammer
A tool with a heavy head sharpened at one end to form a chisel, attached to a handle, for working with stone or brick.

paintbrush
A handheld tool with bristles, used to spread paint on a surface.

paint sprayer
A handheld device with a nozzle to which a container of paint is attached to be evenly sprayed over a surface.

paint reservoir
A removable container attached to a paint sprayer that holds the paint and releases it only as the trigger is squeezed.

handle
The part of a tool or machine held by the hand to pull or control it.

paint roller
A rotating cylinder of absorbent material attached horizontally to a handle, used to spread paint over a surface.

trigger
The small lever pressed by a finger to activate a mechanism or eject material from a tool.

roller
A freely rotating cylindrical object that can be used to flatten or spread a material such as paint.

fluid adjustment screw
A knob on a paint sprayer that can be turned to control the pressure of the paint being emitted from the device.

nozzle
The spout at the end of a device that emits a liquid or gas, usually cylindrical in shape.

handle
The part of a tool or machine that is held by the hand to pull or control it.

FOOD

bacon
A fatty meat cut from the back, sides or belly of a pig, which is cured and traditionally cut in strips and fried.

bologna
Ground, seasoned meat encased in a cylindrical length of skin, which has been cooked for immediate consumption.

cooked sausage
Ground, seasoned meat encased in a cylindrical length of skin, which has been smoked and cooked for immediate consumption.

foie gras
A pâté of French origin made from the liver of a force-fed, fattened duck or goose.

breakfast sausage
Ground, seasoned meat encased in a cylindrical length of skin, which must be cured or cooked prior to consumption.

sausage meat
Ground, seasoned meat that has been smoked but should still be cooked.

kielbasa sausage
Ground, seasoned meat encased in a cylindrical length of skin, which has been cooked and only requires heating.

prosciutto
A ham of Italian origin that has been dry-cured; usually served in paper-thin slices.

bratwurst sausage
Ground, seasoned meat encased in a cylindrical length of skin, which must be cured or cooked prior to consumption.

salami
Ground, seasoned meat encased in a cylindrical length of skin and dehydrated in a salt mixture for immediate consumption.

pâté
A paste made of pureed or finely ground cooked meat, mixed with fat and seasonings.

wiener
A slender sausage of Austrian origin, made from very finely ground or pureed meat; usually served smoked or steamed.

Variety meats

beef liver
The butchered liver of a cow; often served fried with onions.

chicken liver
The liver of a chicken that has been specially butchered for human consumption; often served fried or made into pâté.

heart
The heart of an animal, most often beef or lamb, that has been butchered for human consumption.

kidney
The kidney of an animal, most often pork or lamb, that has been butchered for human consumption.

tongue
The tongue of an animal, most often beef, that has been butchered; usually boiled.

chicken
The most common domesticated fowl;
the meat, offal and eggs are frequently
consumed.

duck
A variety of water fowl that has a dark
meat with a richer flavor and texture
than chicken.

goose
A variety of water fowl larger than a
duck, but whose meat is similar to a
duck's in flavor and texture.

chicken breast
The breast meat from a butchered
chicken; known as white meat and
low in fat.

chicken leg
The leg from a butchered chicken;
known as dark meat, and high in fat.

chicken wing
The wing from a butchered chicken;
popularly served deep fried, seasoned
or with a sauce.

chicken egg
Eggs that are laid by chicken
hens. They are widely used
in savory and sweet dishes
worldwide.

Game

quail
A small, ground-dwelling bird; the
meat is dark and can be tough.

quail egg
A small egg, considered a delicacy; often served
raw as a garnish on other foods.

pheasant
A large, ground-dwelling bird; the
meat is dark and slightly fatty.

guinea fowl
A plump, ground-dwelling bird
native to Africa that has been
domesticated in many countries
for its eggs and meat.

rabbit
A lagomorph with long ears
and powerful hind legs, often
hunted for its fur and meat.

partridge
A plump, ground-dwelling bird native
to Eurasia; it is hunted primarily
for food.

Lamb
Flesh from an immature sheep that has been butchered and prepared for consumption.

cuts of lamb
Specific sections of flesh and bone from an immature sheep that has been butchered and prepared for consumption.

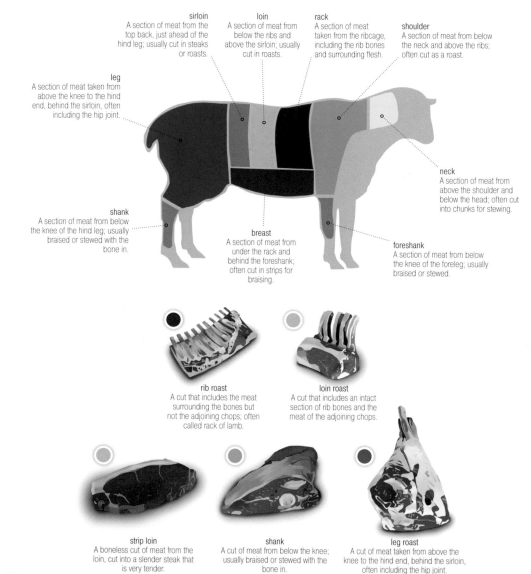

sirloin
A section of meat from the top back, just ahead of the hind leg; usually cut in steaks or roasts.

loin
A section of meat from below the ribs and above the sirloin; usually cut in roasts.

rack
A section of meat taken from the ribcage, including the rib bones and surrounding flesh.

shoulder
A section of meat from below the neck and above the ribs; often cut as a roast.

leg
A section of meat taken from above the knee to the hind end, behind the sirloin, often including the hip joint.

neck
A section of meat from above the shoulder and below the head; often cut into chunks for stewing.

shank
A section of meat from below the knee of the hind leg; usually braised or stewed with the bone in.

breast
A section of meat from under the rack and behind the foreshank; often cut in strips for braising.

foreshank
A section of meat from below the knee of the foreleg; usually braised or stewed.

rib roast
A cut that includes the meat surrounding the bones but not the adjoining chops; often called rack of lamb.

loin roast
A cut that includes an intact section of rib bones and the meat of the adjoining chops.

strip loin
A boneless cut of meat from the loin, cut into a slender steak that is very tender.

shank
A cut of meat from below the knee; usually braised or stewed with the bone in.

leg roast
A cut of meat taken from above the knee to the hind end, behind the sirloin, often including the hip joint.

Pork

Flesh from a pig that has been butchered and prepared for consumption.

cuts of pork

Specific sections of flesh and bone from a pig that has been butchered and prepared for consumption.

blade shoulder
Meat from the upper part of the shoulder, often including the blade bone and cut as a roast.

loin
Meat from the top of the ribcage, usually cut in cylindrical-shaped roasts.

leg
Meat from the hindquarters, including the upper portion; often referred to as ham.

arm shoulder
Meat taken from the lower part of the shoulder; often deboned and cut as a roast.

side
Meat taken from the side, below the ribcage and between the front and hind legs, including the belly.

pork hock
A cut of meat from below the knee to above the foot; often braised or boiled.

pork chop
A cut of meat from the loin; usually thick, roughly circular and trimmed of excessive fat.

spare ribs
A cut of meat from the lower section of the ribs; usually cooked as a slab, with the bones in.

blade steak
A boneless cut of meat from the butt; usually a flat steak for grilling or braising.

tenderloin
A boneless cut of meat from the loin, between the shoulder and leg, cut into a slender roast.

picnic roast
A cut of meat from the shoulder; often tied in a round shape and roasted or stewed.

Beef

Flesh from a cow that has been butchered and prepared for consumption.

cuts of beef

Specific sections of flesh and bone from a cow that has been butchered and prepared for consumption.

sirloin
A section of meat from the top back, just ahead of the hind leg; usually cut in steaks or roasts.

short loin
A section of meat from below the ribs and above the sirloin; usually cut in roasts.

rib
A section of meat from the ribcage, including the rib bones and surrounding flesh.

chuck
A section of meat from the neck and shoulders; often cut into steaks or roasts.

round
A section of meat taken from the hindquarters, including the upper portion of the hind leg.

brisket
A section of meat from the lower breast; often cut into roasts for braising.

flank
A section of meat from the belly, ahead of the hind leg; usually cut in thin steaks.

short plate
A section of meat from the belly, below the ribs; usually cut in slabs for braising or stewing.

shank
A cut of meat from below the knee of the leg; usually braised or stewed with the bone in.

skirt steak
A thick slice of meat from the diaphragm muscle in the short plate; flavorful but sinewy.

tenderloin roast
A large cut of meat most often taken from the round or sirloin and roasted.

sirloin steak
A thick slice of meat from the sirloin, sometimes with a section of bone; usually grilled or broiled.

round steak
A thick slice of meat from the rib section; it is well marbled with fat and very tender.

shank
A cut of meat from below the knee of the leg; usually cut in sections and braised or stewed with the bone.

rib eye steak
A thick slice of sinewy meat taken most often from the front sections of a cow, such as the brisket, and slow-cooked.

ground beef
Beef run through a grinder; usually formed into patties or balls, or used in sauces.

Chateaubriand
A thick cut of meat from the tenderloin filet; in the French tradition, prepared for two with a wine sauce.

back ribs
A cut of meat from the ribs, extending from the back; usually braised or stewed.

flank steak
A cut of meat from the most tender sections, such as the sirloin; usually braised or roasted.

rib roast
A cut of meat from the rib section, often the ribeye; usually baked slowly to bring out the flavor.

T-bone steak
A thick slice of meat from the short loin, with a T-shaped section of bone with meat on either side.

Veal

Flesh from an immature cow that has been butchered and prepared for consumption.

cuts of veal

Specific sections of flesh and bone from an immature cow that has been butchered and prepared for consumption.

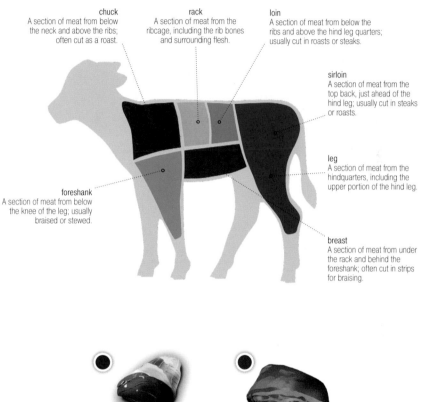

chuck
A section of meat from below the neck and above the ribs; often cut as a roast.

rack
A section of meat from the ribcage, including the rib bones and surrounding flesh.

loin
A section of meat from below the ribs and above the hind leg quarters; usually cut in roasts or steaks.

sirloin
A section of meat from the top back, just ahead of the hind leg; usually cut in steaks or roasts.

leg
A section of meat from the hindquarters, including the upper portion of the hind leg.

foreshank
A section of meat from below the knee of the leg; usually braised or stewed.

breast
A section of meat from under the rack and behind the foreshank; often cut in strips for braising.

blade roast
A cut of meat from the chuck, specifically from the shoulder blade; usually slow roasted in an oven.

breast
A cut of meat from the breast that tends to be tough and fatty; usually roasted with a sauce.

rib chop
A thick slice of meat from the rack that consists of the meat surrounding a rib bone.

shank
A cut of meat from the shank that includes a section of bone; usually braised or stewed.

cutlet
A thick slice of meat from the loin or leg, usually boneless; most often pan-seared or broiled.

Milk and cream
Drinkable foods that are derived from the milk of female mammals, such as cows, goats or sheep.

kefir
A sour drink originating from the Caucasus mountains in Eastern Europe, made of milk fermented by kefir grains.

cow's milk
A drinkable food that is sourced from the mammary glands of cows and processed for consumption.

goat's milk
A drinkable food that is sourced from the mammary glands of goats and processed for consumption.

lactose-free milk
Milk from which the naturally occurring sugar lactose has been removed for easier digestion.

sour cream
A thick, tangy product made by fermenting cream with lactic acid bacteria; often used as a condiment.

whipped cream
Cream with a high milk fat content that can be beaten to stiffen it; often sweetened for use in desserts.

yogurt
A thick, tangy product made by fermenting milk with bacterial culture; often sweetened or flavored.

evaporated milk
A canned milk, with over half of the water content removed, which is often sweetened and used for baking.

cream cheese
A mild, soft cheese, high in fat, that is consumed fresh but is also used in cooking, especially desserts.

butter
A dairy product made through the process of churning, which separates the fat from the milk or cream.

buttermilk
The thick, tart liquid left over from the process of churning butter from milk or cream.

Cheeses
A dairy product made of milk that has been curdled with the use of an enzyme and drained of its whey.

mozzarella
A mild, semi-soft Italian cheese traditionally produced from the curdled milk of water buffalo, easily melted in cooking.

cottage cheese
Small, solidified pieces of soured milk that form loose curds in whey, creating a creamy mixture.

Parmesan
A hard cheese from Parma, Italy, that is white to yellow and used as a flavorful topping.

Gouda
A popular aged yellow cheese made from cow's milk, often encased in a rind of wax, originating from the Netherlands.

Emmentaler
A variety of semi-hard cheese with a savory but mild flavor, originating from the Emmental valley in Switzerland.

cheddar
A hard, smooth cheese, often orange in color, that originates from Cheddar, in southern England.

American cheese
A type of processed cheese that has a very low melting point, usually sold sealed in a plastic wrap.

goat cheese
Soft cheese produced from goat's milk, usually with a tangier flavor than cheese made from cow's milk.

Gorgonzola
A cheese from Italy, often crumbly and salty, marked with distinctive, strongly flavored veins of blue mold.

Danish blue
A semi-soft, blue-veined cheese made from cow's milk, strong in both aroma and flavor, originating from Denmark.

brie
A soft cheese made from cow's milk and encased in a rind of white mold, originating from the Brie region of France.

smoked cheese
Cheese that has been cured with smoke; retains a smoky flavor and can be identified by its yellowish-brown outer skin.

Vegetarian dairy alternatives
Foods that have been processed to mimic dairy products but do not contain any animal-based ingredients.

tofu
The pressed curd produced from the coagulated milk of mashed soybeans, used primarily in Asian and vegetarian cooking.

margarine
A spreadable butter substitute made from refined vegetable oils, which may also be used for baking and cooking.

soy milk
A plant milk originating from Asia, which consists of an emulsion of ground, dried soybeans and water.

salmon roe
The egg mass removed from the
ovaries of a female salmon; commonly
used in Japanese cooking and
consumed raw.

caviar
The egg mass, most often black,
which is removed from the ovaries
of large fish, such as sturgeon, and
cured with salt.

mussel
A bivalve mollusk with an elongated
hinged shell, which is dark on the
outside and lined with a shiny nacre.

scallop
A bivalve mollusk with a ribbed, fan-
shaped, hinged shell that the animal
opens and closes rapidly to swim.

clam
A bivalve mollusk with a rounded
hinged shell. It is found in fresh or
salt water and may be cooked or
eaten raw.

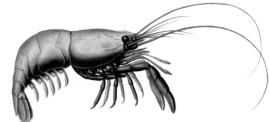

shrimp
A small decapod crustacean with an
elongated body and a long tail and
legs. It is often harvested in large
quantities.

snail
A land- or marine-dwelling gastropod
mollusk with a spiral enclosed shell;
collected as food in certain cultures.

fish
A cold-blooded animal that lives in the water and is harvested, or fished, worldwide for human consumption.

operculum
Also called gill cover, it is a flap of skin, often stiffened by a bony plate, that protects the gills.

spiny ray
A vertical fin located on the backs of some fish; protective spines protrude from it.

soft ray
A vertical fin located on the backs of some fish; it is rayed but does not contain spines.

head
The cranial portion of an animal; it contains the mouth and brain, usually defined from the rest of the body by a neck.

tail
The back portion of the body, which can be moved independently of the torso and is often an extension of the spine.

pectoral fin
A horizontal fin located on the sides, below the head, of some varieties of fish, which helps to control direction.

pelvic fin
A soft, vertical fin located on the bellies of some varieties of fish, which help to control direction.

scale
A small, hard plate attached to the skin of some fish and reptiles, which overlap to form a protective covering.

lateral line
A row of tubular sensory organs running the length of the head and side, which detect vibrations and pressure.

anal fin
A soft, vertical fin located on the bellies of some varieties of fish, between the anus and caudal fin.

caudal fin
The vertical fin that acts as an extension of the tail; used for propulsion through water.

smoked salmon
The flesh of a salmon that has been cured by smoking, distinctively pink in color and delicate in flavor and texture.

salmon fillet
A large piece of flesh that has been sliced by cutting lengthwise along the body, parallel to the spine.

salmon steak
A thick slice cut from the body of the fish, often perpendicular to the spine and including the skin and bones.

canned fish
The meat of a fish, such as tuna, which has been processed and preserved in a can, often with water, oil or sauce.

canned sardines
Very small fish that are preserved by canning. They are widely available in grocery stores.

Leaf vegetables

Plants from which the leaves and stems are harvested for consumption, most often green in color and high in vitamins.

red cabbage
A variety of cabbage known for its purple leaves, which may be eaten raw or cooked.

Brussels sprout
A variety of cabbage with small edible buds, which must be cooked carefully to avoid a pungent odor and flavor.

white cabbage
A vegetable with a compact, round head of edible leaves that are cut from a thick stem.

Belgian endive
A vegetable of the daisy family, with small, elongated, compact heads of bitter leaves; used in salads.

corn salad
A dark green, leafy herb of the daisy family, with a nutty flavor and soft texture; used in salads.

curly kale
A leafy vegetable with a loose mass of earthy-flavored, crinkled green leaves that resist wilting, even when overcooked.

garden sorrel
A silvery green, leafy herb with a slightly acidic flavor, used fresh in salads or dried as a seasoning.

Boston lettuce
A variety of lettuce with a loosely packed, rounded head of broad, light green leaves that are buttery in texture.

iceberg lettuce
A variety of lettuce with a compact head of light green leaves with a crunchy texture.

Chinese cabbage
A subspecies of the turnip with an elongated head of pale green leaves.

radicchio
A variety of chicory native to Italy, with a compact head of white-veined, purple leaves and a distinct bitter flavor.

arugula
A leafy herb of the mustard family, with long green leaves and a strong peppery flavor.

romaine lettuce
A flavorful variety of lettuce, with an elongated head of dark green leaves with firm ribs containing a mildly bitter milk.

green cabbage
A variety of cabbage with a tightly packed, round head of mildly flavored, wrinkly leaves in contrasting shades of green.

spinach
A leafy green that may be consumed either raw or cooked, the bitterness being determined by the darkness of the leaves.

bok choy
A variety of cabbage with thick, crunchy stems and long, smooth leaves; both parts are edible.

Bulb vegetables

Plants whose primary edible portions are considered to be root bulbs.

garlic
A plant with an edible bulb composed of extremely pungent fleshy sections, used in a variety of cuisines as a seasoning.

clove
A section that can be broken away from a garlic bulb; encased in a thin, flaky membrane that is removed prior to cooking.

yellow onion
A pungent bulb vegetable composed of concentric layers, rarely eaten on its own but commonly used to flavor dishes.

spring onion
A variety of onion with an underdeveloped root bulb, served raw or cooked along with its long, dark green shoots.

leek
A vegetable related to the onion, with a cylindrical bulb and long, flat leaves, which can all be eaten.

bear garlic
A wild variety of chives native to Europe and Asia, named because the brown bear likes its flavor.

chives
The smallest of the edible onions; a cluster of tubular green leaves, usually chopped and used as an herb.

red onion
A variety of onion with a mild flavor, often consumed raw and used as a garnish due to its vivid color.

Inflorescence vegetables

Plants whose primary edible portions are considered to be flowers or buds.

broccoli
A variety of cabbage with a head of firm, immature flower buds, usually green, which can be eaten as a vegetable.

cauliflower
A variety of cabbage with a large head of firm, immature flower stalks, usually white, which can be eaten as a vegetable.

artichoke
A variety of thistle native to the Mediterranean, with a large flower bud of fleshy scales; edible when immature.

Seaweed

A term for marine dwelling plants, usually large algae that live near the seabed and are found in a variety of colors.

nori
An edible seaweed that is usually dried then pressed into sheets or used as a seasoning, most often in sushi dishes.

sea lettuce
An edible green algae with fronds resembling leaves; eaten raw or cooked, often in soups and salads.

Fruit vegetables
Plants whose primary edible portions are considered to be the fruit, which contains the seeds.

olives
Small oval fruits with a firm, slightly bitter flesh, which are harvested from trees and often pressed to produce oil.

black olive
The fruits of an olive tree, which are picked when fully ripe then preserved, often by pickling or drying.

green olive
The fruits of an olive tree, which are picked before they are fully ripe then preserved, usually in a brine.

avocado
A fruit native to Mexico and Central America, with a large pit and creamy, pale green flesh encased in a leathery skin.

tomatoes on the vine
Tomatoes which are allowed to ripen while still on the vine and sold in vine-held clusters of fruit.

vine
The climbing, woody stem or runner of a plant from the grape family and to which the fruit is attached.

zucchini
An elongated variety of summer squash with a smooth, dark green skin.

pattypan squash
A small, saucer-shaped summer squash with scalloped edges, at its best when immature, as it tends to toughen as it grows.

okra
A variety of mallow plant, with seed pods that can be eaten when immature and contain a natural thickening agent.

green chili pepper
A long, thin, green pepper, often milder than red, whose heat varies greatly depending on the variety.

tomato
The juicy, edible fruit of the tomato plant, which comes in many varieties and is used in a wide variety of dishes.

red chili pepper
A long, thin, red pepper, often hotter than green, whose heat varies greatly depending on the variety.

buttercup squash
A winter squash with orange flesh and dark green skin; similar in flavor to sweet potatoes.

pumpkin
A squash with orange flesh and skin; traditionally used in sweet and savory fall dishes.

acorn squash
A dark green, deeply ridged winter squash with mild, slightly sweet yellow to orange flesh.

yellow pepper
A pepper that is more mature and sweeter than a green pepper, but less mature and sweet than a red one.

sweet pepper
A variety of sweet pepper with a hollow seeded interior and crisp flesh that comes in various colors.

red pepper
The most mature and sweetest pepper; it is the same as the green pepper, but has been allowed more time to ripen.

green pepper
A sweet pepper that is green when immature but changes color from yellow to orange to red as it matures and sweetens.

eggplant
A vegetable with hearty flesh and, typically, dark purple rind; used in Mediterranean dishes as a meat substitute.

cucumber
A cylindrical vegetable from the gourd family, with a watery flesh and dark green skin, usually eaten raw or pickled.

Root vegetables

Plants whose primary edible portions are considered to be the root, usually harvested from beneath the soil.

carrot
A plant with a long, tapering root, eaten raw and crisp or cooked; traditionally orange but found in a variety of colors.

carrot tops
The leafy tops that grow above the soil; usually discarded when cooking but often fed to animals.

beet
A plant with edible leaves and taproot; usually deep red in color with a sweet, earthy flavor.

horseradish
A tapered, white vegetable with a pungent odor and hot flavor; usually grated and used as a condiment.

radish
A small, spherical vegetable with a red skin, crunchy texture and spicy flavor; usually eaten raw in salads.

black radish
A vegetable with a black skin and white inner flesh, with a hot, bitter flavor, somewhat similar to horseradish.

parsnip
A cream-colored root vegetable that is closely related to parsley and carrots.

watermelon radish
A root vegetable related to the turnip, with a white skin, deep pink flesh and a mild peppery flavor.

turnip
A root vegetable whose round, white bulb and leaves can be consumed, both of which have a mild peppery flavor.

rutabaga
A root vegetable with a purplish skin and yellow inner flesh, which originated as a cross between a cabbage and a turnip.

daikon
An elongated white radish with a mild flavor, often pickled or salted and dried.

Stalk vegetables

Plants whose primary edible portions are considered to be the stalk between the root and leaves.

rhubarb
A plant with large leaves and edible green to red stems, which are notably tart and usually sweetened when cooked.

fennel
A flowering plant related to celery, with a large bulb and stalks eaten as vegetables and leaves used as herbs.

asparagus
A large, feathery plant of the lily family, with long, narrow shoots harvested in the spring, when young.

celery
A plant of the parsley family with branch-like, succulent, pale green stalks that can be eaten raw or cooked.

Tuber vegetables

Plants whose primary edible portions are considered to be the root or growth that is found beneath the soil.

Jerusalem artichoke
The edible tuber of the Jerusalem artichoke sunflower, which is neither from Jerusalem nor in the artichoke family.

kohlrabi
A variety of cabbage whose leaves and sweet, bulbous stem can be consumed raw or cooked.

potato
A tuber vegetable high in starch and mild in flavor, considered to be one of the most important food crops.

sweet potato
A starchy, slightly elongated tuber vegetable with a bright, pink-orange flesh and sweet flavor.

Legumes

Plants that produce edible seeds contained in pods, such as beans or peas, and are often grown agriculturally.

white kidney bean
Large, white, highly nutritious kidney-shaped beans that are dried for storage and rehydrated by soaking or cooking.

black-eyed pea
A medium-sized, white bean grown worldwide in crops and noted for its distinctive black spot.

chickpea
A legume that is mild in flavor and high in protein, often used in soups or salads and to make hummus.

lentil
Very small, round, flattened legumes that come in a variety of colors and are usually dried and split for storage.

adzuki bean
A small bean, usually red, which is often used in Asian cooking by mashing it into a sweetened paste.

red kidney bean
Large, red, highly nutritious kidney-shaped beans that are dried for storage and rehydrated by soaking or cooking.

pinto bean
Beans that are high in starch yet buttery in texture, with a mild flavor that works well with many other foods.

peanut
A bean with underground pods that contain one to three edible seeds, mostly eaten as a nut.

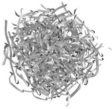

mung bean
A small, green legume native to India, which is used most often in Southeast Asian cuisine and cultivated for sprouts.

green bean
Long, thin pods that are harvested when still immature; known for their sweetness and crispness, eaten raw or cooked.

pea
Spherical green seeds harvested from pea pods, usually sweet and succulent; eaten raw or cooked.

bean sprouts
The sprouting seeds of beans, usually mung beans; popular in Asian cuisine.

porcini mushroom
An edible boletus mushroom widely found in woodlands, with a thick, rounded brown cap and a rich, nutty flavor.

stem
The elongated portion of a mushroom that emerges from the ground or is fixed to a food source and supports the cap.

cap
The top portion, usually rounded, that is upheld by the stem and often has gills on its underside.

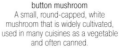

oyster mushroom
A common edible mushroom that is named for its shape, similar to an oyster shell, and which grows on the wood of trees.

enoki mushroom
A thin-stemmed variety of white mushroom native to Japan, which grows in clusters on the trunks of enoki trees.

cremini
A variety of tan or brown-capped button mushroom, which, when allowed to mature after picking, is called a portobello.

button mushroom
A small, round-capped, white mushroom that is widely cultivated, used in many cuisines as a vegetable and often canned.

chanterelle
A fragrant, yellow-orange woodland mushroom with a funnel-shaped cap, leathery appearance and mild peppery flavor.

honey mushroom
A wild mushroom that grows mainly on the roots of trees and should not be consumed raw, due to potential toxicity.

morel
A variety of wild mushroom whose brown cap is covered in ridges and pits, giving it a sponge-like appearance.

wood ear
A dark, rubbery fungus that grows on fallen trees, sold after it has been dried into wrinkled shapes resembling ears.

truffle
An underground woodland fungus, highly prized in the culinary world and often found with the aid of trained dogs or pigs.

russula
A brightly colored type of mushroom that includes many different species, only some of which are edible.

saffron milk cap
A wild mushroom that exudes a milky latex from its gills when cut or torn; often fried in butter with garlic.

shiitake
A small, edible mushroom native to East Asia, which is frequently used as a meat substitute.

slippery jack
A variety of edible mushroom known for its buttery texture and distinctive brown cap, which becomes slimy when wet.

bay bolete	red aspen bolete	birch bolete	suede bolete
A highly sought-after wild mushroom with a porous stem, round brown cap and deep flavor; often picked young.	A wild mushroom with a deep red cap; classified as edible, though its levels of toxicity are debated.	An edible mushroom that grows around birch trees, with a rounded brown cap that has a porous rather than gilled underside.	An edible mushroom that has a downy surface on its rounded cap; rarely used on its own.

Nuts

walnut
An edible wrinkled tree nut made up of two halves enclosed in a hard shell which is contained in a green fruit.

shell
The hard protective casing that surrounds an edible fruit seed known as a nut.

almond
The oval, edible seed of the almond tree, which grows in a woody shell and is used in various forms of cuisine.

hazelnut
The edible fruit of the hazel tree; it grows in a hard brown shell and is often used in desserts.

coconut
The large seed of a coconut tree, made up of a hard brown shell surrounding a white, edible flesh and a clear liquid.

pine nut
Small, edible seeds produced by pine trees; often ground into a paste and used in sauces.

Brazil nut
The three-sided edible seed of the Brazil nut tree, which has a woody shell, a buttery texture and a light flavor.

cashew
The kidney-shaped edible nut of the cashew tree, which is roasted and shelled, eaten as is or used in cooking.

macadamia nut
The edible nut of the Australian macadamia tree, which is usually gently roasted prior to consumption.

chestnut
Nuts with a smooth brown shell produced by several varieties of trees in the beech family, which are roasted for eating.

pistachio
The edible seed of the pistachio tree, which is encased in a hard shell that partially splits with roasting.

pecan
An edible tree nut made up of two halves enclosed in a hard shell; similar to a walnut but sweeter.

black mustard
The small, round seed of the
black mustard plant, with a very
strong flavor; mainly used in
Indian cuisine.

black pepper
The dried fruit of a flowering
vine; often ground and
used as a seasoning and in
medicines.

caraway
A small fruit, often mistaken
for a seed, that is similar to
anise in flavor and used in
many cuisines worldwide.

cardamom
A strong, aromatic spice
made from the seed pods of
plants in the ginger family.

white pepper
The dried fruit of a flowering
vine in the Piperaceae family,
with the husk removed, ground
and used as a seasoning.

cinnamon
An aromatic spice formed
from the bark of several
varieties of tree, which has
been dried and rolled, then
often ground.

bird's eye chili pepper
A small, long, thin red
pepper popular in Southeast
Asian cuisine. It is quite hot.

dried chili
Chili peppers that have been
preserved through dehydration
and can be crumbled or
rehydrated in soup or sauce.

ginger
A root that imparts a strong, spicy
flavor; often used in Asian cuisine
and desserts.

ground pepper
Peppercorns that have been
run through a grinder; a
commonly used flavoring.

jalapeño
A medium-sized green chili pepper
that turns bright red when mature;
very hot and used mainly in
Mexican cuisine.

juniper berry
A female seed cone from
a juniper bush; often dried
and used to flavor foods
and spirits.

nutmeg
The edible seed of a tree of
the *Myristica* genus; ground
as a warm-flavored spice
for foods.

paprika
A spice created by drying
sweet red chili peppers and
then grinding them into a
powder.

pink peppercorn
The partially ripe berry of a
schinus bush, native to Peru,
which is ground and used as
a milder substitute for pepper.

poppy seed
The small seeds from an
opium poppy flower, which
can be used whole or ground
or pressed to produce oil.

clove
Dried, edible flower buds
from a tree of the Myrtaceae
family, with a strong flavor.

saffron
The dried stigma of a crocus
flower, known as the most
expensive spice; also used
as a food coloring.

white mustard
The hard, round seed of
some mustard plants;
used whole to flavor and
pickle foods or ground as a
seasoning.

cayenne pepper
A hot chili pepper said to have
therapeutic value, usually
dried and ground to a powder
and used as a spice.

table salt
A crystalline mineral used as a
preservative and to enhance
the flavor of foods.

turmeric
A bright yellow, aromatic Asian
spice made from the dried and
powdered stem of a plant in
the ginger family.

sea salt
A coarse salt that is removed
from seawater through the
process of evaporation and
retains other trace minerals.

curry powder
An aromatic mixture of powdered
spices whose composition varies
widely, depending on the region
where it is produced.

anise
A plant of the parsley family with a flavor similar to licorice.

basil
An herb native to tropical Asia that is now widely used in a variety of cuisines, often in sauces or as a garnish.

bay leaf
An inedible, dried leaf from the bay tree, commonly used to add flavor and fragrance to cooked dishes.

caper
The edible, unripened flower buds of the caper bush, native to the Mediterranean; often pickled.

cilantro
A pungent herb of the carrot family, whose leaves and seeds are used to flavor dishes across many national cuisines.

dill
An herb closely related to celery, used fresh or dried to flavor many foods, including seafood, pickles and dips.

rosemary
A fragrant herb of the mint family, with small, needle-like leaves used medicinally and to flavor foods and perfumes.

fennel
A flowering plant related to celery, with a large bulb and stalks eaten as vegetables, and leaves used as herbs.

garden cress
A fast-growing herb with a sharp peppery flavor, related to watercress and mustard.

parsley
A small, leafy plant that is highly versatile and can be used as an herb, spice, vegetable or palate cleanser.

lemongrass
A tall, coarse grass grown in tropical regions, inedible in itself, but which releases a lemon-scented oil when bruised.

mint
An invasive herb that grows in temperate regions, with a sweet flavor and a cooling effect on the palate.

mugwort
An aromatic herb of the daisy family, which is consumed primarily for its medicinal properties rather than as food.

sage
A savory herb of the mint family, with silvery green leaves and a peppery flavor.

thyme
A decorative herb of the mint family, used either fresh or dried, both medicinally and to flavor foods.

tarragon
An intensely flavored herb of the daisy family, with narrow leaves that are used fresh or dried, often in French cuisine.

oregano
An herb from the mint family,
whose leaves impart greater
flavor when dried.

purple basil
A basil that is milder in flavor
than green basil; used for
its aroma in cooking and
perfumes.

lemon balm
An herb closely related to
mint, most often used in
deserts or steeped in teas
for a calming effect.

Tea and coffee

black tea
A highly oxidized, strongly flavored
variety of tea made from the fully
fermented leaves of the *Camellia
sinensis* shrub.

herbal tea
Tea or other dried leaves infused with
flavors or combined with dried fruits,
flowers, herbs or spices.

green coffee bean
Unroasted coffee beans; contain high
levels of chlorogenic acid and are
used in weight-loss supplements.

ground coffee
Roasted coffee beans that have been
run through a grinder in preparation
for brewing.

instant coffee
Roasted, ground coffee beans that are
brewed to extract the flavor; the liquid
is freeze-dried into a soluble powder.

oolong tea
A Chinese tea made from the partially
fermented leaves of the *Camellia
sinensis*, which have been sun-dried
and twisted.

green tea
A minimally oxidized, slightly bitter variety
of tea made from the unfermented
leaves of the *Camellia sinensis* shrub.

white tea
A minimally oxidized variety of tea
made from the unfermented young
leaves of the *Camellia sinensis* shrub.

roasted coffee bean
Green coffee beans that have been heated
to change their chemical properties and
flavor, in preparation for grinding.

wheat
A cereal grain cultivated worldwide; used to produce flour, beer and animal feed.

rye
A cereal grain similar to wheat, used to produce flour for bread, varieties of whiskey and animal feed.

corn
A large cereal grain that is a staple in many indigenous cuisines and comes in many varieties and colors.

rice
A swamp-grown cereal grain that forms the base diet of many cultures around the world, particularly in Asia.

buckwheat
A plant whose grain-like seeds are often milled into flour as a gluten-free alternative to wheat flour.

quinoa
The edible, starchy seed of an herb native to the Andes; eaten as a grain and high in protein.

millet
A cereal grain with small seeds that are used primarily to make flour, alcoholic drinks and animal feeds.

oats
A popular cereal grain used to make foods such as granola, breakfast cereal and baked goods.

spelt
A cereal grain related to common wheat, sold as a health food.

barley
A widely cultivated cereal grain often added to bread dough, eaten as a substitute for rice and used to brew beer.

wild rice
The edible seeds of the aquatic grasses of the genus *Zizania*, harvested by knocking the seeds out with wooden poles.

Flour
A fine powder that is produced from finely ground plant parts, such as grains or seeds, mainly used to make bread.

bulgur
A whole grain cereal high in fiber, made from the parboiled groats of various types of wheat, most often durum.

couscous
Small granules made of crushed and steamed semolina, originating in North Africa and still a staple food there.

all-purpose flour
A form of finely milled white flour that is highly versatile and can be used in most recipes that call for flour.

semolina
The coarsely milled and purified middlings of durum wheat, often used to make pastas and breakfast cereals.

Tropical fruits

Fruits that are grown in the hot region between the Tropics of Cancer and Capricorn, such as bananas or papayas.

banana
An elongated, soft pulpy tropical fruit with a thick skin that changes from green to yellow or red as it ripens.

flesh
The inner portion of a fruit, usually covered with a skin or rind, in which seeds are embedded.

papaya
A melon-like fruit native to the American tropics, with an orange-yellow flesh and a thick, inedible greenish skin.

flesh
The inner portion of a fruit, usually covered with a skin or rind, in which seeds are embedded.

skin
The outer covering of a fruit, which can be edible, such as on an apple, or should be removed, such as on a banana.

seeds
The embryonic stage of plants, which will grow if allowed to germinate; some are edible.

lychee
A tropical tree fruit native to China, with a sweet, slimy flesh enclosed in a rough skinand containing a large stone.

carambola
A tropical fruit that resembles a star when sliced and can be eaten whole or used in desserts and sauces.

cherimoya
A tropical American fruit with smooth, uniquely flavored, creamy flesh encased in a scaly, green skin.

durian
A tropical fruit native to Southeast Asia, with a foul-smelling, custard-like flesh covered with a hard, spiny rind.

fig
A bulb-shaped fruit of the mulberry family; high in sugar and often used in sauces and jams or dried.

guava
An American fruit of the myrtle family, with a pink, strongly sweet-smelling flesh covered with green skin.

Asian pear
A tropical fruit native to Japan and China that has a crisp, juicy texture and flavor similar to apples.

horned melon
A tropical melon native to Africa, with an orange skin covered with spines and tart, green, gelatinous flesh.

membrane
A thin, flexible sheet in living organisms that acts as a lining or barrier, such as around the seed chambers of a fruit.

pomegranate
A tropical fruit native to North Africa and western Asia with a hard red skin enclosing multiple edible seed chambers.

skin
The outer portion of a fruit or vegetable.

aril
An extra covering on a seed. It is often colored and hairy or fleshy.

pineapple
A large, juicy, fruit that is sweet and tart; eaten on its own, used in desserts or juiced.

feijoa
A fruit native to South America, the size of a hen's egg, with a flavor like pineapple with a touch of mint.

kiwifruit
A tropical berry native to China, with a fuzzy brown skin, soft, green flesh and a flavor similar to strawberries.

mango
A stone fruit native to Asia, with a flesh that is eaten ripe, or can be preserved or pickled when green.

mangosteen
A tropical fruit native to southeastern Asia, with a thick, deep purple rind and segments of sweet, juicy, white flesh.

dragon fruit
A colorful tropical fruit that grows on a species of cactus, with a mildly sweet flesh similar in texture to kiwi.

persimmon
A fruit of the trees of the genus Diospyros; it resembles a tomato but has a sweeter flavor.

passion fruit
A fruit of the passion flower, native to South America, with a sweet, aromatic flavor and jelly-like, seedy texture.

rambutan
A tropical fruit with a tentacled skin and inner white flesh that is sweet and sour like a grape but gummy in texture.

tamarillo
A tropical fruit native to South America that looks somewhat like a tomato but with a firmer, sweeter flesh.

Citrus fruits
Fruits from flowering plants of the rue family, often with a stippled rind and a segmented juicy pulp high in vitamin C.

clementine
A citrus fruit that is a hybrid between a mandarin and an orange with a deep orange rind and very few, if any, seeds.

leaf
A flat appendage on the stem or stalk of a vascular plant; it is responsible for photosynthesis.

rind
The outer skin of a fruit or vegetable, which can be eaten, such as on an apple, or must be removed, such as on a banana.

segment
A section that can be separated from the larger fruit; they are enclosed in separate membranes.

orange
A citrus fruit with an orange peel and pulp that may be bitter or sweet and is high in vitamins and antioxidants.

lime
A green tropical citrus fruit whose juice is tart but less sour than a lemon; often used in sauces and drinks.

grapefruit
A large citrus fruit bred as a cross between a pomelo and an orange, which may be tart or sweet, depending on the variety.

lemon
A popular citrus fruit that is too sour to be consumed on its own but is often added to desserts, sauces and marinades.

blood orange
A variety of orange named for its deep red pulp, with a sweet juice that is less acidic than that of traditional oranges.

tangerine
A small citrus fruit closely related to the mandarin orange, with a looser peel and milder flavor than a sweet orange.

citron
A large, fragrant citrus fruit with very little juice but with a thick, flavorful rind that is candied or pickled.

kumquat
A small fruit with an edible peel that can be very tart if not fully ripe; often candied and used in desserts.

bergamot
A citrus fruit shaped like an orange but with a flavor and color more similar to a lemon.

Berries

Fleshy growths produced from a single flower with a single ovary that may be eaten as food, usually small and sweet.

cranberry
A smooth red berry with a tough texture and bitter flavor; often prepared as a sweetened sauce or juice.

red grape
A red berry that grows in clusters on vines; some varieties are used to make red wines.

white grape
A pale green berry that grows in clusters on vines; some varieties are used to make white wines.

red currant
A small red berry with a glossy, smooth skin and tart-sweet flavor; often used in jams and wines.

cloudberry
A tart, pale red berry made up of a number of drupelets, similar to a raspberry, with a creamy texture when fully ripened.

gooseberry
A round, smooth fruit, usually green, that looks and tastes like a sour grape and grows on a large, straggly bush.

strawberry
A highly aromatic fruit high in antioxidants, known for its bright color, juicy flesh and boldly sweet flavor.

raspberry
A fragrant red berry of the rose family, which is often consumed fresh and commonly made into jams and desserts.

blackberry
A sweet and slightly tart berry, similar to a raspberry but dark purple; used in pies, jams and wines.

black currant
A dark purple, very tart berry with glossy skin; often sweetened for use in jams and juice.

blueberry
A sweet berry extremely high in antioxidants, which turns deep indigo when ripe, with a slightly tart and bitter skin.

cape gooseberry
A tart berry native to South America that grows within a papery bladder and has a smooth, orange skin when ripe.

elderberry
A small, dark purple berry, native to Europe, which is often used for medicinal purposes and in wine-making.

lingonberry
A small, bright red Scandinavian berry that is extremely tart and is usually sweetened to be used as a sauce or spread.

Melons

Fruits produced by flowering plants of the gourd family, usually large and round with a hard rind and sweet flesh.

cantaloupe
A sweet variety of muskmelon with bright orange flesh and a rough, netted rind, slightly stringy in texture.

watermelon
A melon with a high concentration of water; usually with red flesh and a green rind.

yellow watermelon
A variety of watermelon with yellow flesh and a flavor similar to the traditional red variety, but sweeter.

honeydew melon
A mild yet sweet variety of muskmelon, with pale green flesh and a smooth, whitish rind, juicy and soft in texture.

canary melon
A variety of sweet honeydew melon with pale green flesh and a yellow, bumpy rind, juicy and soft in texture.

Pome fruits

Fruits from flowering plants, usually trees, with a thin, usually edible skin, pulpy flesh and multiple seed chambers.

pear
A sweet, slightly gritty pome fruit found in green, yellow and red varieties, with a rounded base tapering to the stem.

stalk
The thin stem that connects a fruit, leaf or flower to the main supporting structure of a plant.

red apple
A sweet and sometimes tart, round pome fruit cultivated worldwide in numerous varieties.

leaf
A flat appendage on the stem or stalk of a vascular plant that is primarily responsible for photosynthesis.

flesh
The inner portion of a fruit, usually covered with a skin or rind, in which seeds are embedded.

seed
The embryonic stage of plants, which will grow if allowed to germinate; some are edible.

skin
The outer covering of a fruit, which can be edible, such as on an apple, or should be removed, such as on a banana.

stamen
Remnants of the flower that remain on the fruit once the flower has dropped off and the fruit has matured.

loquat
A small, yellow, acidic fruit with large seeds, native to China and Japan; grows on an ornamental evergreen shrub.

green apple
A generic name for any variety of apple that has green skin.

ya pear
A fragrant pear native to Northern China, with a whitish skin that tastes like a combination of rose and pineapple.

Stone fruits

Also called a drupe, a fruit, such as a peach or plum, with a flesh surrounding a hard casing of a single large seed.

apricot
A bright orange-yellow fruit that looks like a small peach, with a flesh rich in vitamins.

plum
A small oval stone fruit with a smooth purple, yellow or reddish skin and a juicy flesh surrounding a flat, pointed pit.

peach
A stone fruit with yellow, juicy, sweet flesh and a slightly fuzzy, pinkish-yellow skin, native to northwest China.

nectarine
A stone fruit that is genetically similar to a peach but with a smooth skin without fuzz.

black cherry
A variety of cherry native to eastern North America, with a deep red color and sharper flavor than other cherries.

Saturn peach
A variety of white-fleshed peach native to China, which is somewhat doughnut-like in shape.

seed
The embryonic stage of plants, which will grow if allowed to germinate; some are edible.

acerola
A tropical stone fruit with a strong resemblance to a cherry, which has an extremely high concentration of vitamin C.

greengage
A variety of European plum with a light green skin and a pale flesh, whose flavor carries notes of honey.

cherry
A small stone fruit with varieties that range from yellow to bright red to nearly black, and from tart to sweet.

sour cherry
A variety of cherry native to Eurasia that is more acidic than a sweet cherry, with a tart flavor.

date
A sweet, soft fruit that grows on a palm tree and is often dried to a chewy consistency and a brown color.

aioli
A French sauce consisting of a base of olive oil, lemon juice and egg yolks, traditionally flavored with garlic.

barbecue sauce
A sauce originating in the United States with many regional variants; used with meat.

salsa
A spicy sauce made with tomatoes and onions, popular in Mexican and Tex-Mex cuisine.

mustard
A sauce used primarily on salads that consists of oil, vinegar and some combination of seasonings, depending on region.

Italian dressing
A sauce used primarily on salads that consists of oil, vinegar, garlic and a combination of Italian seasonings.

ketchup
A sweet and tangy sauce usually used as a condiment, made by combining pureed tomatoes with vinegar, salt and sugar.

mayonnaise
A creamy sauce made from a mixture of egg yolks and oil, which is stabilized with vinegar or a strong citrus juice.

French dressing
A pungent sauce usually used as a condiment, made by combining ground mustard seeds with water, salt and lemon juice.

harissa
A North African sauce made with various chili peppers combined with oil and other seasonings into a paste.

pesto
An Italian sauce, typically for pasta, made of crushed basil leaves, garlic, olive oil, pine nuts and Parmesan cheese.

rémoulade
A sauce used mostly on salad or seafood, consisting of an aioli base combined with herbs and other seasonings.

sambal oelek
A spicy sauce from Indonesia and Malaysia, consisting of various chili peppers combined with brown sugar and seasonings.

tomato paste
A thick sauce made from tomatoes that have been cooked to remove moisture until a sweet paste is formed.

tamarind paste
A sauce made from the sweet-sour pulp contained in the pods of the tamarind, a tree native to Asia and North Africa.

wasabi
A paste made from a Japanese root, similar to horseradish; used mostly as a condiment for raw fish.

tomato puree
A sauce made by cooking, blending and straining tomatoes of their seeds and skin, usually with no other ingredients.

balsamic vinegar
An Italian vinegar created through the reduction of a grape juice, often used as a condiment and in salad dressings.

cider vinegar
A variety of vinegar produced from fermented apple cider; used in salads, sauces and marinades.

chili oil
An Asian condiment that consists of vegetable oil that has been infused with hot chili peppers.

white wine vinegar
A variety of low acidity vinegar that has been produced by fermenting white wine, such as champagne, in wooden barrels.

soy sauce
An Asian sauce made with fermented soybean paste; used as a condiment or seasoning.

white vinegar
A versatile, acidic liquid made from fermented ethanol; often used as a condiment and in pickling.

Oils

sunflower oil
An oil created by pressing the seeds of the sunflower; used mainly for cooking and in cosmetics.

walnut oil
An obtained by pressing English walnuts; mainly used as a condiment for salads and for polishing furniture.

soybean oil
An oil extracted from soybean seeds, widely used in cooking but also as a base for inks and paints.

sesame oil
An oil produced by pressing sesame seeds, generally used to season foods and for medicinal purposes.

corn oil
An oil thought to lower blood cholesterol, extracted from the germ of corn; mainly used for frying.

olive oil
An oil created by pressing fresh olives; considered a healthy oil and used as a condiment and in cooking.

peanut oil
An oil extracted from peanuts, popular due to its health benefits.

pumpkin seed oil
An oil produced by pressing pumpkin seeds, with a flavor that runs from nutty to bitter; often used on salad.

spaghetti
A long, thin, cylindrical Italian noodle made from wheat, which can be accompanied by a wide variety of sauces.

lasagna
An Italian pasta in the form of flat, wide strips, which are most often layered with sauce, cheese, vegetables and meat.

udon
A long, thin Japanese noodle made from wheat flour; often served in a flavored broth.

cannelloni
A large, tubular Italian pasta that is usually filled with meat or cheese, covered in sauce and baked.

ramen
A long, thin, curled Chinese wheat noodle usually served in a broth with other ingredients.

tagliatelle
A flat, long Italian noodle that is ribbon-like once cooked and can easily support a hearty sauce.

rice noodles
Noodles that are made with rice flour, usually cut in long, thin strands; they appear slightly translucent.

fusilli
A short, corkscrew-shaped Italian noodle made from durum wheat, which holds sauce well in its spirals.

penne
A small, tube-shaped Italian pasta with diagonally cut ends, whose name is derived from the Latin word for quill.

conchiglie
A type of Italian pasta that resembles a seashell, often colored with natural pigments, such as tomato or squid ink.

rigatoni
A tube-shaped Italian pasta often served with a meat sauce, due to its ability to hold the morsels of meat.

gnocchi
Bite-size Italian dumplings that can be created from a number of different ingredients, such as potatoes or semolina.

ravioli
An Italian pasta that consists of two small sheets of pasta dough pressed together with a filling between them.

tortellini
An Italian pasta that is shaped like a small ring or belly button and is usually filled with meats and cheeses.

farfalle
A delicate Italian pasta well known for its shape, whose name comes from the Italian word for butterfly.

baguette
A form of white bread originating in France, which is shaped into a long, narrow loaf and often torn rather than sliced.

crust
The outer, harder surface on a loaf of bread, which was exposed directly to the heat when baked.

multi-grain bread
A baked good whose base ingredients are flour and water, into which various grains and seeds are added.

slice
A small portion of food with a flattish shape that is cut from a larger item, such as a loaf of bread.

sunflower seed
The embryonic stage of the sunflower, which can be roasted, shelled and eaten as food, often in baked goods.

white bread
A light-colored bread whose dough is made from wheat flour that has had the bran and germ removed during milling.

toast
A slice of bread that has been exposed to heat, such as the radiant heat of a toaster, turning it brown and crisp.

challah
A white bread containing eggs that is braided before baking; traditionally eaten on the Jewish Sabbath.

bagel
A dense bread made from yeasted wheat dough shaped into a hand-sized ring, which is boiled prior to baking.

pretzel
A type of bread made of a dense dough that has been shaped into a hand-sized knot and coarsely salted before baking.

stuffed pastry
A baked good made of a delicate dough that has been folded to contain a filling, such as mincemeat, prior to baking.

whole wheat roll
Fist-sized loaves of bread made from flour that contains all parts of the wheat grain, often with other grains added.

coarse rye bread
A type of rye bread made with coarsely milled whole rye flour, giving it a dark hue and more robust flavor.

sourdough bread
A type of bread made from rye flour, typically heavier than wheat bread.

jelly doughnut
A soft sweet dough that is formed into a ball and injected with a fruit jelly then cooked in hot fat.

powdered sugar
A sugar produced by grinding standard white sugar into a fine powder; often used to decorate cakes.

doughnut
A soft, sweet dough that is formed into a thick ring, cooked in hot fat and often decorated with icing or toppings.

sugar cookie
A small, crisp baked good made primarily from sugar, eggs, milk and flour.

chocolate cookie
A small, crisp baked good made primarily from sugar, eggs, milk, flour and chocolate, giving it a dark, rich flavor.

kifli
A type of traditional European bread roll made from yeast dough, formed into a crescent shape.

Spritzkuchen
A German fried pastry similar to a doughnut, with a spiral pattern.

butter cookie
A thin baked good made with butter that has a very mild but rich flavor.

layer cake
A dessert made with fruit or cream between sheets of spongy, sweet cake; often frosted.

jelly roll
A thin, flat, spongy cake that is spread with jelly and then rolled before baking.

bread roll
A small loaf, often round, designed as a single serving of bread as an accompaniment to a meal or used for a sandwich.

oatmeal cookie
A small baked good made primarily with oatmeal and often containing dried fruits, such as raisins.

vatrushka
An Eastern European pastry consisting of a ring of dough filled with quark and, sometimes, bits of fruit or raisins.

croissant
A flaky, crescent-shaped pastry with a buttery flavor and light texture, which originated in Vienna.

waffle
Batter that is cooked between two heated plates with a ridged design, to create the signature woven pattern.

rusk
Bread that is hardened by baking it twice; often given to babies to gnaw when they are teething.

cheesecake
A dessert consisting of a thick creamy layer made with sugar and soft cheese that usually sits on a thin graham crust.

fruit sauce
Cooked, jellied fruits and their syrup used to top various foods, particularly desserts, such as cheesecake.

Bundt cake
A type of traditional European cake that has been baked in a ring-shaped pan with fluted sides.

cupcake
A baked good that consists of a small cake topped with icing or cream, often decorated with various toppings.

fruit tartlet
A small, individual pie shell filled with custard or cream and topped with pieces of fruit, most often berries.

cherry tart
A baked good consisting of an open or lidded pastry shell that is filled with sweetened cherries.

blueberry pie
A large pie crust filled with berries and sugar that produce a sweet syrup during the baking process.

banana bread
A baked good made with a base of bananas, often with dried fruits or nuts, that is served as a dessert or snack.

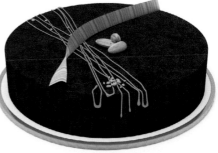

cake
A classic dessert made from a base of flour, eggs and sugar that is baked and often served decorated.

chocolate torte
A rich, creamy chocolate cake, often flavored with extracts, such as almond, orange or hazelnut.

ice cream cone
Ice cream that is placed in the open end of a dry, waffle-type cone of pastry so that it may be eaten without a spoon.

sundae
A dessert made of balls of ice cream placed in a dish and topped with ingredients, such as syrups or whipped cream.

wafer
Decorative, thin cookies that have been rolled into tubes, occasionally filled with chocolate or cream.

chocolate sauce
A thick chocolate sauce that is served warm over desserts, such as cake or ice cream.

ice cream
A frozen dessert food made from milk or cream, flavored with ingredients such as chocolate or fruit.

cone
A dry, waffle-like pastry shaped like a tapering tube, designed to hold ice cream so that it may be eaten by hand.

crushed nut
A piece of nut that has been ground into small pieces and used as a food topping or ingredient.

scoop of ice cream
A round ball of ice cream that is created by using a rounded spoon to separate it from the main product.

dessert
A sweet dish that is served at the end of a meal, traditionally with coffee or tea.

fruit coulis
A thick, syrupy sauce made from pureed fruit;,often topping a cake.

panna cotta
A custard-like Italian dessert made with cream, egg whites and honey, cooked in a double-boiler; often served with a sauce.

sundae glass
A glass with fluted edges designed to hold scoops of ice cream with sauces and toppings.

jar
A cylindrical glass container with a wide mouth and secure lid; primarily used to store foods.

jam
A mixture produced by cooking chunks of fruit with their juice, sugar and added pectin to produce a gelling effect.

whipped cream
A cream with a high milk-fat content that has been sweetened and beaten until it is stiff and fluffy.

honey
A sweet, sticky food produced by honeybees from flower nectar; used as a spread and sugar substitute.

rubber seal
A rubber ring attached to the lid of a jar, which aligns with the mouth of the jar to create an air-tight seal.

lid
The covering for the top of a container.

candy-coated chocolates
Small pieces of chocolate
covered with thin shells of sugar
candy, usually in bright colors.

sugar cubes
Sugar that has been mixed with
a small amount of sugared water,
formed into cubes and dried prior to
packaging.

chocolate truffle
A soft candy made of chocolate, butter
and sugar, often with a liqueur-flavored
center, and coated with cocoa.

hard candy
A sweet created by boiling sugar with
corn syrup and flavoring, then drying it
into bite-sized shapes.

sugar crystals
A candy created by allowing a
concentrated sugar syrup to crystallize
into hard masses.

chocolate coating
Chocolate that has been
melted to a liquid consistency
then poured over another
food, such as fruit or candy.

chocolate candy
A type of bite-sized sweet that is made
up of a filling, such as nougat, which is
covered with chocolate.

wrapper
A disposable covering,
usually made from paper
or plastic, that is placed
around a food item to
protect it from the air.

gummy candy
A candy made of a sweetened liquid
solidified with a collagen derivative,
most often flavored and brightly
colored.

filling
An ingredient or mixture
enclosed by another food,
for example, the inside of
a pie or candy.

Chocolate

A confectionery substance made from roasted and ground cocoa seeds, usually combined with a sweetener.

cocoa
The base ingredient for chocolate,
produced from roasted and
ground cocoa beans; often used
in baked goods.

aerated chocolate
Melted chocolate turned into
foam by adding carbonated
gas; when cooled it retains the
bubbles.

dark chocolate
Chocolate with a high
percentage of cocoa versus milk
and sugar, giving it a dark color
and bitter flavor.

milk chocolate
Chocolate with a low percentage of cocoa versus milk and
sugar, giving it a creamy texture
and sweet flavor.

white chocolate
A candy created from cocoa
butter, sugar and milk, giving it
a texture similar to chocolate
made from cocoa.

hot dog
A boiled or grilled weiner served in a bun and typically topped with various condiments.

mustard
A condiment that consists mainly of ground mustard seeds; known for its tangy flavor and bright yellow color.

hot dog bun
A small piece of bread that is especially shaped to hold a weiner.

wiener
A small sausage link, usually served in a bun. It is generally made from pork or beef.

Greek salad
A salad made of olives, tomatoes, red onion, feta cheese and an herb vinaigrette.

pizza
An Italian flat bread that is covered with sauce and cheese, and often meats and vegetables, and baked in an oven.

crust
The outer ridge of dough on a pizza, which is exposed directly to the heat when baked, creating a crispy rim.

chips
Vegetables, often potatoes, sliced finely, fried until crisp; often seasoned and eaten as a snack or meal accompaniment.

toppings
Ingredients that are placed on top of another food item as a garnish, such as meats and vegetables on a pizza.

french fries
A long, thin cut of potato that is usually deep-fried and salted or seasoned before serving.

slice of pizza
A wedge from a pizza, served as an individual portion; often sold as such in fast food restaurants.

pizza peel
A large, flat board made of wood with a circular indentation and small handle used for serving an entire pizza.

cola
A carbonated beverage, usually sweet and flavored and served cold.

chips and dip
A common hors d'oeuvre and snack consisting of chips and a sauce to dip them in.

salsa
A thick, coarse tomato sauce, often spicy, that is served with Mexican and Tex-Mex cuisine.

sandwich
A hand-held food made of ingredients such as cold cuts or sliced cheese, placed between two slices of bread.

wrap
A hand-held food made of ingredients such as chopped vegetables or meats, rolled in soft, unleavened bread.

coffee
A beverage brewed from roasted and ground coffee beans, served hot or cold and often flavored with cream and sugar.

hamburger
A patty made of ground beef, usually grilled or fried, served in a bun.

popcorn
Corn kernels that have been heated until they burst open; often salted or seasoned and eaten as a snack.

doner kebab / shawarma / gyro
Meat seasoned with spices and cooked on a vertical rotisserie, then shaved off and served in a flatbread.

breakfast cereal
A combination of cereals, dried fruits and nuts, often sweetened with honey and usually eaten with milk.

milk
A drinkable food that is derived from the milk of female mammals, such as cows, goats or sheep.

rolled oats
De-husked oat groats that have been steamed and rolled flat, often eaten as a cereal or used in baked goods.

blueberry
A sweet berry extremely high in antioxidants, which turns deep indigo when ripe, with a slightly tart and bitter skin.

soft-boiled egg
An egg boiled long enough to set the whites yet leave the yolk runny; often served at breakfast.

cream of vegetable soup
A soup with a cream base instead of a broth, in which various vegetables are blended into a smooth consistency.

olive oil
A type of oil created by pressing whole, fresh olives; considered a healthy oil and used as a condiment and in cooking.

fried egg
A fresh egg that is cracked into a pan and fried in hot oil or fat; often served as a breakfast food with toast.

appetizer
A small course that is served before the main meal. It often consists of bread and butter or oil.

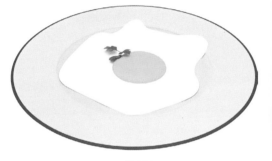

bread
A baked good whose base ingredients are flour and water, into which various seasonings and grains may be incorporated.

dipping bowl
A shallow bowl designed to hold a sauce or oil, into which pieces of food can be dunked before eating.

green olive
The fruit of an olive tree, which is picked before it is fully ripe then preserved, usually in a brine.

black olive
The fruit of an olive tree, which is picked when fully ripe then preserved, often by pickling or drying.

serving board
A portable surface, often made from plastic, wood or glass, on which foods are served.

tomato soup
A soup made with crushed or pureed tomatoes seasoned with herbs and spices, such as garlic and basil.

breast
A white meat cut from below the neck and between the wings; low in fat with a tendency to be dry.

leg
An appendage that facilitates movement on land; the meat is dark and juicy.

roast turkey
A large domestic bird that is seasoned and often stuffed with vegetables and bread then roasted.

stuffing
A mixture of bread or other starchy food and herbs and spices that is stuffed and baked inside poultry or other meat.

spaghetti and sauce
Spaghetti served with a thick Italian sauce made with tomatoes, herbs, spices and sometimes ground meat.

wing
An appendage on an animal used to facilitate movement through the air; also as a cut of meat.

hors d'oeuvre
A small assembly of bread or pastry with savory and decorative ingredients designed to be eaten with the fingers.

spaghetti
A long, thin, cylindrical Italian noodle made from wheat, which may be accompanied by a wide variety of sauces.

skewer
A slender length of metal or wood with a sharp tip, onto which food is threaded to hold it together for eating or cooking.

bocconcini
A mild semi-soft Italian cheese traditionally produced from the curdled milk of water buffalo, formed into a small round.

grated cheese
A firm cheese that has been run over a grater or through a mill to produce shreds.

tomato sauce
A thick Italian pasta sauce made with tomatoes and flavored with various herbs and spices, often with meat.

whipped cream
A cream with a high milk fat content that has been sweetened and beaten until it is stiff and fluffy.

pancakes
Flat, rounded cakes made by frying batter in hot oil, often served with jam or syrup as a breakfast food.

basil
An herb originating in tropical Asia and now widely used in a variety of cuisines, often in sauces or as a garnish.

crouton
A square of bread that has been toasted in an oven to a crunchy consistency, often used as a garnish for other foods.

cherry tomato
A variety of sweet tomato, roughly the size and shape of a cherry, which is often eaten raw in salads.

pancake
A flat, rounded cake made by frying batter in hot oil.

green tea
A minimally oxidized, slightly bitter variety of tea made from the unfermented leaves of the *Camellia sinensis* shrub.

teapot
A lidded pot with a handle and elongated spout, used to steep and pour tea.

sushi
A traditional Japanese food made of a combination of ingredients rolled with vinegared rice, often in a skin of seaweed.

rice
A swamp-grown cereal grain that forms the base diet of many cultures around the world, particularly in Asia.

avocado
A fruit with a large pit and creamy, pale green flesh. Often used as a sushi filling.

tea
A beverage, served hot or cold, produced by steeping the prepared leaves from various plants in boiled water.

tea bowl
A large cup without a handle, sometimes with a lid, in which tea is served and raised to the lips with both hands.

nori
An edible seaweed that is usually dried then pressed into sheets or used as a seasoning, most often in sushi dishes.

tobiko (flying fish roe)
The egg mass that is removed from the ovaries of a flying fish, commonly used in sushi.

chopsticks
Originating in Asia, two slender, tapering sticks that are held together in one hand and used as an eating utensil.

chopstick
One of a pair of two slender, tapering sticks used as an eating utensil.

gari (pickled ginger)
Pickled ginger that is traditionally served with sushi.

soy sauce
A sauce made with fermented soybean paste; used as a condiment or seasoning, primarily in Chinese and Japanese cuisine.

chow mein
Pasta made from rice or wheat flour and formed into long, thin strands, usually eaten with chopsticks.

chopstick rest
A small, indented block on which a diner rests their chopsticks when not eating, to prevent them from touching the table.

chopstick
One of a pair of two slender, tapering sticks used as an eating utensil.

miso soup
A soup made with a paste of fermented soybeans that contains small squares of firm tofu and bits of seewead.

fortune cookie
A crispy, wafer-thin cookie that is folded around a small piece of paper printed with a prediction or wise saying.

cappuccino
An Italian coffee made by combining espresso and hot milk, often topped with steamed-milk foam.

espresso
A very strong form of Italian coffee created by forcing a small amount of boiling water through rich coffee grounds.

black tea
A highly oxidized, strongly flavored variety of tea made from the fully fermented leaves of the *Camellia sinensis* shrub.

hot chocolate
A hot beverage made by melting shaved or powdered chocolate in hot water or milk.

creamer
A small, decorative jug typically used to pour milk or cream into a hot beverage, such as tea or coffee.

coffee
A beverage brewed from ground roasted coffee beans; served hot often flavored with cream and sugar.

milkshake
A combination of milk, ice cream and often fruit or a flavored syrup, blended to form a thick, cold beverage.

straw
A long, flexible, plastic tube that is placed into a drink and used to suck up the liquid.

fruit
Fleshy growths from the ovaries of flowering plants, usually sweet.

beverage with ice and lime
A liquid for human consumption that has been cooled with ice and flavored with lime.

lemonade
A beverage produced by pressing the liquid out of lemons, often sweetened with sugar.

pineapple juice
A beverage produced by pressing the liquid out of pineapples.

orange juice
A beverage produced by pressing the liquid out of oranges; usually contains pulp.

peach juice
A beverage produced by pressing the liquid out of peaches.

pomegranate juice
A beverage produced by pressing the liquid out of pomegranate seeds.

apple juice
A beverage produced by pressing the liquid out of apples; usually pasteurized.

grape juice
A beverage produced by pressing the liquid out of grapes.

tomato juice
A beverage produced by pressing the liquid out of tomatoes; often thickened with puree and salted.

bottled water
Water that has been filtered to remove excess chemicals or minerals then bottled for sale as a beverage.

cap
A round, threaded lid that is screwed onto the end of a tubular opening, such as on a bottle.

label
A paper or film of plastic printed with product identification and information and stuck on packaging.

barcode
A series of lines of varying widths that can be scanned by a machine into a computer and translated into information.

sparkling water
Naturally carbonated water that is sourced from an above- or below-ground spring and bottled for sale.

still mineral water
Uncarbonated water that is sourced from a natural mineral spring and contains dissolved minerals, such as salts.

canned pop
A variety of carbonated beverage, usually sweetened, that is stored in a metallic can and is popular worldwide.

wine stopper
A small item used to plug a wine bottle after it has been opened, preserving the flavor of the wine.

red wine
An alcoholic beverage produced by fermenting dark-colored grapes, giving it a red color and a slightly bitter flavor.

white wine
An alcoholic beverage produced by fermenting pale grape pulp, giving it a golden color and fruity flavor.

champagne
A sparkling wine produced from twice-fermented white grapes grown in the Champagne region of France.

cognac
A variety of brandy, an alcoholic beverage made from distilled wine, specifically produced in the Cognac region of France.

whiskey
An alcoholic beverage created by fermenting and distilling grain mash then aging it in charred white oak casks.

vodka
A liquor produced from distilled grains or potatoes; it is flavorless, but flavors are sometimes added to it.

garnish
An item used to enhance the flavor or appearance of a food or beverage.

cocktail
A mixed alcoholic beverage with at least two different ingredients, such as a spirit with a juice or soda.

beer
An alcoholic beverage made from yeast-fermented, malted cereal grains and flavored with hops or other ingredients.

cocktail glass
A small-stemmed glass with a bell-shaped bowl, used to serve mixed alcoholic beverages in small quantities.

CLOTHING AND ACCESSORIES

fashion show
An event at which the latest clothing designs are modeled for an audience, often by live models.

truss
A complex structure comprised of one or more pieces of rigid material, such as wood or metal, fixed to form a support.

spotlight
A lamp that emits a concentrated beam of light that is focused on a specific location or person, usually on a stage.

designer
A person who manages the designing, fabric choices, and adjustments to new garments based on societal trends.

cameraman
A person who specializes in the operation of a camera, usually to record a public event for broadcasting.

video camera
An electronic device designed to capture, record and, sometimes, transmit images of the surrounding proceedings.

audience
Assembled spectators or listeners at a public event, such as a play, movie or fashion show.

WEEK
LONDON · MILAN

sign
A decorative banner with words or images, mounted for public viewing to provide information on products or events.

model
A person who has been professionally trained to physically display clothing and accessories.

photographer
A person who operates a camera to capture still photographs, often at a show or event for later publication.

uplight
Lights embedded into or placed on the floor to illuminate people or objects from below, often on the edge of a stage.

runway
An elevated, narrow walkway that runs down the center of an audience and on which models walk to display fashions.

wardrobe
A tall free-standing piece of furniture with long doors, such as on a closet, designed to store clothing and accessories.

door
A hinged, sliding or revolving barrier that provides access to an enclosed area.

accessories drawer
A box-shaped compartment intended for the storage of accessories.

handle
A piece of solid or flexible material attached to an object that may be grasped to carry, pull, or otherwise control it.

drawer
A storage compartment that slides out of a piece of furniture.

shelf
A flat, elongated surface built into a piece of furniture on which objects are stored.

rod
The bar or pole across the top of a structure from which objects, such as clothes hangers in a wardrobe, may be hung.

clothing
Garments made of various flexible materials that are worn on the body for warmth, modesty and fashion.

box
A container with flat sides designed to store or carry objects, often with a fitted lid which may be hinged.

shoe
A foot covering, usually made from leather or canvas with a sturdy sole, that does not typically extend above the ankle.

shoe cabinet
A wide shelf, usually in a closet or wardrobe, on which shoes are stored and displayed for ease of selection.

bifold door
A door with two vertical sections that are hinged together and fold onto each other when opened, often on a closet.

mirror
A reflective surface usually composed of glass coated on one side with a metal compound.

closet
A small recess in a room enclosed by a door that is used for the storage of personal or household items.

glass door
A wall made of glass that separates a section of a room from another and can be slid to one side.

drawer
A box-shaped compartment in a piece of furniture that is usually set on runners so that it may be slid out easily.

coat
A thick outer garment made of an insulating, durable material, such as wool or leather, that is worn outdoors for warmth.

collar
A slightly raised strip of fabric that is sewn around the neck of a garment as decoration or to keep the neck warm.

sleeve
The part of a garment that covers the arm, fully or partially.

pocket
A small pouch sewn into a garment for carrying small objects.

jacket
A garment for the upper body that is made of a thick durable material and is worn outdoors.

button
A small piece of hard material, often round, that is pushed through a corresponding slit to hold clothes together.

trench coat
A weather-resistant double-breasted, military-style coat with wide lapels and a belt that is cinched aroud the waist.

fleece jacket
A type of jacket made from a soft, warm material with a texture that resembles wool, often with a short collar.

sweat suit
A matching combination of a loose-fitting sweatshirt or jacket and pants, worn during exercise or relaxation.

MEN'S CLOTHES
Suits and formal accessories

bow tie
A wide length of ribbon, typically worn by men, that is tied around the neck and fashioned into a bow for formal events.

vest
A fitted vest held together with buttons down the front that is worn over a shirt and under the jacket of a suit.

double-breasted jacket
A jacket with wide front flaps folding over each other and two columns of buttons, one of which is decorative.

suit
A combination of trousers and jacket worn for formal or semiformal events, or for business.

necktie
A length of decorative fabric that is tied in a knot around the neck and under the collar of a shirt.

Pants

jeans
Casual, durable pants made out of denim, traditionally dyed blue but available in many colors and styles.

waistband
A strip of material sewn along the upper opening of pants to fit them to the waist.

belt
A narrow strip of leather that is secured around the waist with a buckle.

punch hole
A hollowed-out section of material into which the buckle's hinge fits to secure the belt.

belt loop
Small strips of material that are sewn around the perimeter of a waistband to form loops to hold a belt in place.

belt loop
Small strips of material that are sewn around the perimeter of a waistband to form loops to hold a belt in place.

pocket
A small pouch sewn into the general design of a piece of clothing or a bag, in which small objects may be carried.

zipper
A flexible fastening device made of two lengths of cloth with interlocking plastic or metal teeth joined with a slide.

buckle
A metal frame and hinged pin used to secure the two ends of a belt.

pant leg
The tubular section on a pair of pants that covers or partially covers the leg down from the crotch.

Bermuda shorts
A style of semi-casual pants worn by both sexes, also known as dress shorts, with legs that fall to just above the knee.

suspenders
Straps that are designed to be worn over the torso and fasten to pants to keep them up.

pants
A piece of clothing that is designed to cover each leg separately, and fits over the buttocks and around the waist.

hoodie
A casual, loose-fitting top with long sleeves and a hood, usually made of a thick cotton.

sweatshirt
A comfortable, usually loose-fitting, garment for the upper body with long sleeves.

three-button sweater
A comfortable, usually loose-fitting, knitted garment for the upper body with a row of three buttons at the neck.

zip-front cardigan
A knitted sweater that is fastened at the front by a zipper.

sweater
A comfortable, usually loose-fitting, knitted garment for the upper body that provides warmth, often worn over a shirt.

zip hoodie
A casual, thick sweatshirt with a front zipper and a hood.

cardigan
A knitted long-sleeved sweater with an open front that is closed with a zipper or buttons, designed specifically for men.

dress shirt
A formal button-up shirt with long sleeves.

button
A small piece of hard material, often round, that is pushed through a corresponding slit to hold clothes together.

collar
A slightly raised strip of fabric that is sewn around the neck of a garment as decoration or to keep the neck warm.

sleeve
The part of a garment that covers the arm, fully or partially.

plaid shirt
A garment with a checkered design that is worn over the upper body, often with buttons and a collar.

cuff
A fold at the end of a long sleeve, often created from a separate strip of fabric and fastened with a button.

polo shirt
A short-sleeved top with a collar and usually a short row of buttons at the neck, often worn to play certain sports.

short sleeve
A sleeve of a garment that does not extend below the elbow, usually meant to be worn in warm weather.

V-neck
A style of neckline that forms a V-shape, opening from the throat and tapering to a point on the chest.

T-shirt
A casual, collarless shirt with short sleeves that is made of a light, soft material and pulled over the head.

double-pocket shirt
A collared shirt with pockets sewn onto the breast, often with buttoned flaps, designed to hold small items like pens.

short-sleeved shirt
A garment that is worn over the upper body, with short sleeves, buttons down the front and a collar.

swim briefs
A style of legless, fitted swimsuit made from a light material, often worn for water sports.

trunks
Swimsuit shorts, usually loose-fitting, made from a light material designed to be worn by men.

square-cut trunks
Fitted swimsuit shorts made from a light material designed to be worn by men when engaged in water sports.

boxer shorts
A style of men's underwear shaped like fitted shorts with legs that extend over a portion of the upper thighs.

briefs
A style of men's underwear shaped like legless shorts that fit snugly over the buttocks.

socks
Fitted garments made of knitted wool or cotton that cover the feet and usually extend over the ankle.

ribbed top
The uppermost section of a sock, which is knit with small ripples and often with elastic for added support.

leg
The elongated part of a sock or stocking that extends above the ankle and is traditionally elasticized.

long underwear
A style of fitted underwear in the shape of footless stockings and made from an insulating material for warmth.

heel
The part of a sock or stocking that covers the heel of the foot and is often reinforced against wear.

foot
The part of a sock or stocking that covers the foot from the heel to the toe and from the sole to the ankle.

toe
The part of a sock or stocking that covers the toes and is often reinforced against wear.

sole
The part of a sock or stocking that covers the bottom of the foot and is often reinforced against wear.

undershirt
A fitted shirt, with or without sleeves, made of an insulating material that is worn under outer clothing for warmth.

trench coat
A weather-resistant double-breasted, military-style coat with wide lapels and a belt that is cinched around the waist.

button
A small piece of hard material, often round, that is pushed through a corresponding slit to hold clothes together.

collar
A slightly raised strip of fabric that is sewn around the neck of a garment as decoration or to keep the neck warm.

belt
A narrow strip of sturdy cloth or leather that encircles the waist and is usually secured with a buckle.

sleeve
The part of a garment that covers the arm, fully or partially.

parka
A warm jacket, often with a hood, designed for cold weather.

biker jacket
A classic fitted leather jacket with metal stud or zipper accents, often worn by motorcyclists.

peacoat
A short double-breasted woolen coat with wide lapels, traditionally worn by sailors.

poncho
An outer garment made of a single piece of cloth with a center hole that is pulled over the head to rest on the shoulders.

fur coat
A warm coat made from the fur pelts of animals, such as beaver, fox or ermine, considered to be luxurious.

wool coat
A warm coat made from finely woven
wool fibers, usually taken from sheep,
goats or alpacas.

denim jacket
A casual, durable jacket made out
of denim, traditionally dyed blue but
available in many colors and styles.

double-breasted overcoat
A short double-breasted woolen coat
with wide lapels, traditionally worn
by sailors.

sheepskin jacket
A coat made from the skin of a sheep
with the suede as the outer layer and
the fleece as the lining for warmth.

overcoat
A weather resistant double-breasted,
military-style coat with wide lapels and
a belt that is cinched around the waist.

down coat
A warm, puffy coat with the soft
feathers of a duck or goose stuffed
between layers of nylon material.

maternity pants
A style of pants with an elastic waistband that allow it to expand with the growing belly of a pregnant woman.

belt loop
Small strips of material that are sewn around the perimeter of a waistband to form loops to hold a belt in place.

waistband
A strip of material sewn along the top of pants to fit them to the waist.

pocket
A small pouch sewn into the general design of a piece of clothing or a bag, in which small objects may be carried.

seam
A thin line that is formed where two pieces of fabric are sewn together, the stitching being hidden on the underside.

pant leg
The tubular section on a pair of pants that covers or partially covers the leg down from the hip.

slim-fit pants
A style of pants that are fitted closely to the skin, often made of a material threaded with elastic to make it stretchy.

jeggings
A style of jeans that are fitted closely to the skin, made of denim combined with spandex to make it stretchy.

wide-leg pants
A style of pants that fit snugly around the waist but loosely around the legs, often designed to be worn over boots.

bell-bottomed jeans
A style of jeans that originally became popular in the 1960s, in which the legs get progressively wider toward the ankle.

straight-leg jeans
A style of jeans that have no tapering or flare in the cut of the legs, often fitted snugly over boots.

slim-fit jeans
A style of jeans that are fitted closely to the skin, often made of denim threaded with elastic to make it stretchy.

shorts
A style of casual pants with legs cut well above the knee, often worn for exercising, sports or in warm weather.

spaghetti strap dress
A dress with very thin straps, usually worn in warm weather or as evening wear.

sheath dress
A dress that closely skims the body and can be worn as daywear or evening wear, depending on the style.

strap
A strip of fabric that passes over the shoulder to hold a sleeveless garment in place.

draped neckline
A style of neckline that hangs in loose folds, most often found on clothing designed for women.

belt
A narrow strip of sturdy cloth or leather that encircles the waist and is usually secured with a buckle.

skirt
The portion of a dress that extends below the waistline, although the waistline may not be defined.

halter dress
A style of sleeveless dress with straps that fasten behind the neck, leaving the upper back bare.

drop-waist dress
A style of loose-fitting dress with a skirt that begins at the hip rather than the waist.

shirtdress
A short-sleeved dress that has a collar and usually a short row of buttons at the neck, often loose-fitting and soft.

A-line dress
A dress that is fitted at the hips and gradually widens at the base, creating a shape similar to the letter A.

sleeve
The part of a garment that covers the arm, fully or partially.

jersey dress
A dress made of a soft knitted fabric that can be draped or fitted to the body.

strapless gown
A dress without straps. It is held up by the internal structure and can be formal or casual.

maxi skirt
A style of long, flowing skirt that extends to touch the tops of the feet; it can be formal or casual.

jumpsuit
A one-piece outfit that combines a top and pants, usually loose-fitting and made of a soft, comfortable material.

sundress
A lightweight, loose-fitting dress, often sleeveless, that is worn in warm weather.

V-neck
A style of neckline on a garment that forms a V-shape, opening from the throat and tapering to a point on the chest.

cap-sleeve dress
A dress with short sleeves that only cover the shoulders.

bodice
The part of a dress that is above the waist, surrounding the torso and shoulders.

skirt
The portion of a dress that extends below the waistline, although the waistline may not be defined.

wedding dress
A formal dress worn by a bride, traditionally white and with a long skirt, and usually adorned with lace and embroidery.

pencil skirt
A style of close-fitting skirt that has a narrow, straight cut.

maxi dress
A style of dress with a long, flowing skirt that extends to the tops of the feet; it can be formal or casual.

minidress
A close-fitting short dress that typically ends well above the knee.

short-sleeved shirt
A shirt specifically designed for a woman with short sleeves, often with decorative features or patterns.

sleeve
The part of a garment that covers the arm, fully or partially.

button
A small piece of hard material, often round, that is pushed through a corresponding slit to hold clothes together.

bolero
A style of women's jacket designed without lapels or a collar and that often does not fully close across the front.

tunic sweater
A comfortable, usually loose-fitting, knitted garment for the upper body that extends below the hips.

tank top
A garment worn on the upper body without sleeves and usually without a collar.

ruffled top
A style of woman's shirt with layers of gathered fabric forming ruffles, which may extend the length of the garment.

spencer
A style of jacket with long sleeves and ending at the hips or waist, worn for semi-formal events or business.

peasant blouse
A woman's loose top with long, wide sleeves and often with embroidery at the neck in the style of European peasants.

blouse
A loose top in the style of a shirt, typically worn by women only.

blazer
A style of jacket with long sleeves and lapels, ending just below the waist, worn for semi-formal events or business.

batwing-sleeve top
A style of sleeve that is very wide at the armhole and fitted at the wrist, usually cut as one piece with the body.

pocket
A small pouch sewn into a garment for carrying small objects.

long cardigan
A knitted long-sleeved sweater with an open front that is closed with a zipper or buttons and extends below the hips.

T-shirt
A casual, collarless shirt with short sleeves that is made of a light, soft material and pulled over the head.

polo shirt
A short-sleeved top that has a collar and often a short row of buttons at the neck, designed specifically for women.

three-quarter sleeve top
A casual garment worn on the upper body, with long sleeves that extend just past the elbow.

short cardigan
A knitted long-sleeved sweater with an open front that is closed with a zipper or buttons and ends above the hips.

sweater vest
A comfortable, usually loose, sleeveless knitted garment worn over a shirt, which is buttoned or pulled over the head.

elastic-waist top
A loose-fitting women's blouse that is gathered at the waist and often at the ends of the sleeves by sewn-in elastic.

cover-up
A style of tunic, often made of an absorbent fabric, worn over a swimsuit as protection from the sun or for modesty.

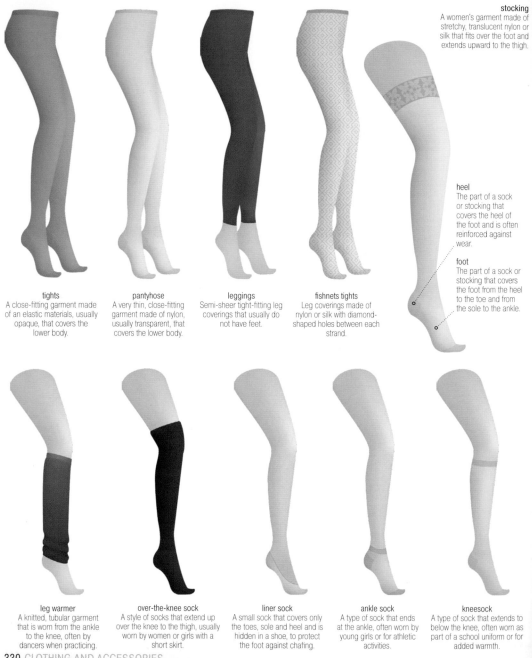

stocking
A women's garment made of stretchy, translucent nylon or silk that fits over the foot and extends upward to the thigh.

heel
The part of a sock or stocking that covers the heel of the foot and is often reinforced against wear.

foot
The part of a sock or stocking that covers the foot from the heel to the toe and from the sole to the ankle.

tights
A close-fitting garment made of an elastic materials, usually opaque, that covers the lower body.

pantyhose
A very thin, close-fitting garment made of nylon, usually transparent, that covers the lower body.

leggings
Semi-sheer tight-fitting leg coverings that usually do not have feet.

fishnets tights
Leg coverings made of nylon or silk with diamond-shaped holes between each strand.

leg warmer
A knitted, tubular garment that is worn from the ankle to the knee, often by dancers when practicing.

over-the-knee sock
A style of socks that extend up over the knee to the thigh, usually worn by women or girls with a short skirt.

liner sock
A small sock that covers only the toes, sole and heel and is hidden in a shoe, to protect the foot against chafing.

ankle sock
A type of sock that ends at the ankle, often worn by young girls or for athletic activities.

kneesock
A type of sock that extends to below the knee, often worn as part of a school uniform or for added warmth.

corselet
A garment that combines a corset and bra; worn to enhance the bosom and make the torso appear slimmer.

shoulder strap
A strip of fabric that passes over the shoulder to hold a sleeveless garment in place.

cup
The part of a bra in which the breast rests and is sometimes shaped or lifted with padding or special stitching.

zipper
A flexible fastening device made up of two lengths of cloth with interlocking plastic or metal teeth joined with a slide.

dressing gown
A type of women's nightwear made of soft, thin material and often decorated with lace or ribbons.

camisole and briefs
A matching set of undergarments consisting of a sleeveless undershirt and low-cut panties, also worn as nightwear.

baby-doll
A type of women's negligee that is very loose-fitting, usually sleeveless, and extends only to below the buttocks.

corset
A very tightly fitted undergarment worn by women to squeeze the body into a smooth shape, hiding bulges.

body shaper
A tight-fitting undergarment that is pulled on and incorporates a bra, corset and panties.

slip
A woman's undergarment worn under a dress to allow it to hang more smoothly or to protect the skin from chafing.

push-up bra and panties
A set of undergarments consisting of panties and a matching bra with padding to lift the breasts.

shoulder strap
A strip of fabric that passes over the shoulder to hold a sleeveless garment in place.

bra
A woman's undergarment with cups to support the breasts, held with straps over the shoulders and fastened around the torso.

cup
The part of a bra in which the breast rests and is sometimes shaped or lifted with padding or special stitching.

waistband
A strip of material sewn along the top of pants to fit them to the waist.

panties
Legless underpants that are designed for women or girls, often decorated with patterns or lace trim.

sweat suit
A matching combination of a loose-fitting sweatshirt and pants with an elasticized waist, worn during exercise or leisure.

sports bra
A garment designed to provide additional support to women's breasts during vigorous exercise.

nightgown
A type of women's nightwear in the shape of a long, loose-fitting dress, usually pretty and made of a soft material.

teddy
A one-piece garment incorporating a bra and panties made of lace or spandex and snaps at the legs or on the back.

pajamas
A loose-fitting set of shirt and pants made of soft material for sleeping or lounging, worn by both men and women.

garter belt
A woman's undergarment that fits around the waist with hanging fasteners that hold up stockings.

garter
The hanging fasteners that hang from the belt; they hold up stockings.

camisole
A tight-fitting top with thin shoulder straps that can be worn as an undergarment or on its own.

bra and thong set
A bra and panties set that matches in color, size, shape and style.

nursing bra
A bra with cups that may be folded down individually to allow a mother to nurse without removing the garment.

bathrobe
A long, soft indoor coat, usually belted, that is typically worn before or after bathing.

Swimwear

tankini
A two-piece swimsuit that covers the tummy; it has a top resembling a tank top and a bottom resembling panties.

one-piece swimsuit
A garment designed to be worn while swimming that covers the torso and buttocks, made from a stretchy material.

sarong
A long piece of cloth that is worn as a garment by wrapping it around the body and tucking edges in to secure them.

bikini
A two-piece swimsuit that exposes the tummy; it has a top resembling a bra and a bottom resembling panties.

diaper bag
A large storage bag used to hold all the needs of a baby, such as diapers, bottles and clothing.

baby sling
A length of cloth that is wrapped around the body and in which a baby is secured close to the chest.

cloth baby carrier
A pair of shoulder straps attached to a supporting structure in which a baby is carried close to the body.

bib
A piece of material that rests on the chest and is secured around the neck, worn by babies to catch spills when eating.

nursing pillow
A soft U-shaped cushion on which a baby may be rested to elevate them and steady their head for ease of nursing.

hooded towel
A soft towel fitted with a small hood used to wrap a baby in after bathing to both dry and keep them warm.

pacifier
A rubber or plastic nipple that is placed in a baby's mouth, encouraging a calm, sucking reflex.

pacifier clip
A piece of fabric or elastic used to attach a pacifier to the clothing or seat of an infant so it does not fall.

teething ring
An object made of rubber or plastic on which a baby may bite when teething to soothe their sore gums.

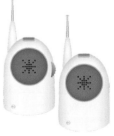

baby monitor
A two-way radio system that allows parents to hear an infant from another room.

backpack baby carrier
A baby carrier for the back consisting of a cloth seat in which a baby is placed.

baby bouncer
A small bed on rockers in which a baby may be strapped to be gently rocked, simulating movements of the womb.

harness
A clasp designed to secure a safety belt, allowing a person or baby to be strapped in securely.

stroller
A cushioned bed or chair that is attached to a structure on wheels in which a baby is placed and pushed along.

handle
A piece of solid or flexible material attached to an object that may be grasped to carry, push or otherwise control it.

hood
A covering for an object or an opening to protect it from weather.

wheel
A circular object fixed to the base of a structure that rotates on an axis to allow for easy movement on a surface.

lightweight stroller
A cushioned bed or chair that is attached to a structure on wheels in which a baby is placed and pushed along.

basket
An open storage compartment fixed to the carriage.

brake
A rubberized device that impedes the rotation of a wheel to bring it to, or keep it at, a standstill.

play mat
A mat on which an infant is placed on their back to play with suspended, colorful toys that often make sounds.

toy
An object for a child to play with.

baby bathtub
An oval basin, sometimes fitted with cushions and toys, that is filled with a shallow amount of water to bathe a baby.

tub
An open container, usually round or oval and made of plastic, in which the baby is washed.

mat
A small, padded piece of cloth that is laid on the floor for kneeling or lying upon, often for an infant.

potty chair
A small, portable chair that is used by small children who are being toilet trained.

disposable diaper
A form-fitting piece of absorbent material that is placed over a baby's bottom and front to catch urine and feces.

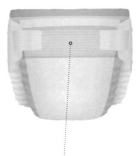

onesie
A small article of clothing, specifically designed for babies, with an opening flap near the diaper area.

toilet seat reducer
A toilet seat for small children, with a closed front and a smaller opening; it fits over a standard toilet seat.

fastener
Flaps of adhesive material on the back section of a diaper that stick to the front when wrapped around a baby.

tongue
The flap of material under the laces or buckles of a shoe that allows for different levels of tightness.

backstay
The reinforced rear portion of a shoe or boot; it covers the back of the foot from the sole to the ankle.

dress shoes
A type of black leather shoe that is designed to be worn during formal occassions.

quarter
The section of a shoe that covers the sides of the foot from the sole to the laces and from the backstay toward the toe.

lace
A thin strip of material, often waxed, that is strung through the eyelets of a shoe to join two sides together.

sole
A piece of material attached to the bottom of a shoe, made of a durable material to withstand wear.

heel
A piece of material attached to the sole of a shoe that raises the heel of the foot off the ground.

toe cap
Reinforced material that protects the toes, usually made of stiff leather or steel.

sneaker
A style of comfortable sports shoe made of a soft material, usually cloth, with rubber soles and laces.

basketball shoe
A style of shoe made of canvas that was once worn to play basketball but is now worn for fashion.

cross-trainer
A style of athletic shoe designed to be worn for both indoor and outdoor sporting activitites.

high-top sneaker
A style of sneaker that extends up over the ankle, commonly worn to play basketball.

oxford
A common style of men's shoe, usually made of leather, with laces and a slight tapering toward the toe.

hiking boot
A style of boot designed for hiking, with a reinforced, gripping rubber sole, a hard toe and laces.

boat shoes
A style of casual, lace-up shoe made of cloth or leather with gripping rubber soles designed to prevent slippage on boats.

moccasins
A style of casual, slip-on shoe, usually made of suede, that is sometimes adorned with tassels or beads.

insole
A piece of padding in the rough shape of a foot, which is inserted into a shoe for added comfort.

slippers
A style of comfortable, slip-on shoe worn indoors, often backless and made of cloth or soft leather.

shoe tree
A hard structure in the rough shape of a foot, which is inserted into a shoe to keep its shape when not being worn.

shoehorn
A length of curved metal or plastic that is held against the inner heel of a shoe to allow the foot to slip in easily.

boot tree
A contraption that is inserted into the leg of a boot to prevent it from becoming misshapen when not being worn.

shoe brush
A flat configuration of soft bristles that are used to clean and shine shoes, often used with shoe polish.

shoe polish
A waxy, waterproof substance that is massaged onto leather shoes to produce a shine and maintain their condition.

ankle-strap sandals
A style of high-heeled or flat sandal with a strap that is fastened entirely around the ankle.

heel
A piece of material attached to the sole of a shoe that raises the heel of the foot off the ground.

platform pumps
A style of women's shoe with a long, narrow heel, usually over an inch long, a thick sole and a tapered toe.

strap
A strip of flexible material, such as cloth or leather, with a fastener that is used to secure one object to another.

platform
The thick sole of a platform shoe, which supports the foot.

toe
The front portion of a shoe or boot, which covers the toes and is sometimes reinforced.

sole
A piece of material on the bottom of a shoe, made of a durable material to withstand wear.

ballet flats
A style of slip-on shoe fashioned after a soft ballet slipper with a very thin heel and made of a soft material.

high-heeled boot
A style of women's boot with an elongated, narrow heel, usually over an inch long, and a fitted boot shaft.

high-heeled sandal
A style of women's sandal with an elongated, narrow heel, usually over an inch long, and a number of straps.

sandal
A lightweight, open-toed shoe with straps attaching the sole to the foot.

slippers
A style of comfortable, slip-on shoe worn indoors, often backless and made of cloth or soft leather.

peep-toe ankle boot
A style of women's high-heeled boot that only extends to just above the ankle and has a small opening at the toe.

peep-toe flat
A style of slip-on shoe with a very thin heel and a small opening at the toe.

biker boots
A style of boot made of sturdy leather with metal accents, designed to be worn when driving a motorcycle.

ankle boots
A style of boot that only extends to just above the ankle, usually high-heeled.

wedge boot
A style of high-heeled boot where the height of the heel is formed by a block of material.

peep-toe pump
A style of women's slip-on shoe with a high heel and a small opening at the toe.

pump
A style of women's slip-on shoe, usually made of leather, with a low-cut front and a high heel.

wedge sandal
A style of women's sandal where the height of the heel is formed by a solid block of material.

pom-pom
A fuzzy ball made of short knit fibers that is attached to the top of a hat.

stocking cap
A style of knitted hat that fits closely to the head and often adorned with a pom-pom.

sun hat
A style of hat with a wide brim designed to protect the head from overheating and the scalp and face from sun damage.

hatband
A length of material or ribbon that encircles the base of the crown of a hat, often with decorative items attached.

crown
The part of a hat above the band that covers the head and that can be structured or close-fitting.

brim
The part of a hat that extends horizontally from the perimeter of the crown to protect the face from weather.

straw hat
A lightweight, brimmed hat made of woven straw or reeds that is traditionally worn as protection from the sun.

fedora
A soft felt hat with a curled brim and a creased crown, designed for men.

cloche
A close-fitting, bell-shaped hat designed for women.

cap
A brimless hat with a visor that extends out above the face for shade and protection from weather.

scarf
A strip of soft fabric worn around the neck for warmth or decoration, specifically designed for women.

flatcap
A type of cap with a crown that slouches over the front visor, usually made of cloth.

earflap cap
A warm hat made from real or artificial fur with material that covers the ears; usually worn in cold climates.

baseball cap
A visored cap traditionally worn by baseball players with a stiff, round crown, often adorned with stitching.

gloves
Articles of clothing that are specifically designed to be worn around the hands to keep them warm.

fingerless gloves
An article of clothing for the hands that is designed to keep the palm and tips of the fingers exposed.

umbrella
A device made from fabric stretched across a collapsible frame mounted on a short pole, carried as protection from rain.

ring
The small, circular piece on an umbrella's shank that may be moved up and down to expand or collapse the frame.

canopy
The piece of fabric that makes up the protective covering of an umbrella, usually made of a treated nylon taffeta.

shank
The pole that holds up the main structure of an umbrella to allow it to be carried above the head.

spreader
Long, thin pieces of metal set in a circular pattern to the canopy of an umbrella to support its domed shape.

garment bag
A long bag in which clothing can be laid flat then folded with the bag to avoid excess creasing.

backpack
A sturdy bag, usually made of a weatherproof material, that is carried on the back with shoulder straps.

handle
The elongated length of rigid material that is held in the hand.

briefcase
A flat, rectangular case, typically made of leather, used for carrying books and papers.

telescopic umbrella
A type of umbrella with a handle and frame that can be collapsed and slipped into a nylon sleeve.

retractable handle
A handle that may be slid in or out of the object to which it is attached, such as on a piece of luggage.

suitcase
A large piece of luggage, often rectangular and made of a sturdy fabric, used to store personal items when traveling.

carry-on bag
A piece of luggage small enough to be stored in the overhead compartment or under the seat of a plane.

handle
A piece of solid or flexible material attached to an object that may be grasped to carry, pull, or otherwise control it.

zipper
A flexible fastening device made up of two lengths of cloth with interlocking plastic or metal teeth joined with a slide.

pocket
A small pouch sewn into the general design of a piece of clothing or a bag, in which small objects may be carried.

strap
A strip of flexible material, such as cloth or leather, with a fastener that is used to secure one object to another.

pocket
A small pouch sewn into the front-facing design of a piece of clothing or a bag, in which small objects may be carried.

cell-phone case
A small sleeve in which a cell phone is carried to protect it from scratches, inadvertent calls and general wear.

document case
A flat, folding piece of reinforced leather in which documents may be carried to protect them from dirt or creasing.

checkbook holder
A type of wallet in the shape of and in which a checkbook may be carried to protect it from dirt or tearing.

key case
A small, folding piece of leather or vinyl fitted with small hooks on which keys can be strung to keep them together.

card case
A type of wallet with several flat pockets designed to carry cards, such as credit cards, identification or memberships.

coin purse
A small pouch with a clasp or zip closure used to carry coins or other small items, such as travel tokens.

underarm portfolio
A case, usually made of leather, with a large flap and without a handle, used to carry documents and other papers.

wallet
A folded piece of leather or vinyl fitted with various slots used to carry money and cards.

clutch
A small, hard purse without a strap or handle that is grasped in the hand, often carried on formal occasions.

writing case
A flat, folding case, usually with a wrap-around zipper, that holds a large notepad and often a pen.

evening bag
A small decorative bag made of rich fabric, carried by women on formal occasions.

passport holder
A type of wallet designed to carry a passport when traveling to protect it from creasing and moisture.

backpack purse
A type of purse, usually made of leather, with shoulder straps that allow it to be carried on the back.

shoulder bag
A purse with one or two long straps that are slung over the shoulder in order to leave the hands free.

men's bag
A bag designed specifically for men, often made of leather, in which necessities, such as a wallet or keys, are carried.

carrier bag
An environmentally-friendly, reusable bag made of plastic or treated fabric used primarily for grocery shopping.

schoolbag
A sturdy bag, usually made of a weatherproof material, that is carried on the back with shoulder straps.

sea bag
A type of backpack purse with a length of cord or leather threaded around the opening that is tightened to close it.

handbag
A small bag used especially by a woman to carry everyday personal items such as money and keys.

vanity bag
A hard-sided piece of luggage fitted with interior pockets and sleeves designed to hold cosmetics and toiletries.

drawstring bag
A type of purse with a length of cord or leather threaded around the opening, which is tightened to close it.

laptop bag
A square satchel with padding designed to carry a laptop, usually with a shoulder strap and handles.

tote purse
A rectangular purse in which larger items may be carried, often when traveling.

attaché case
A hard, often lockable, case that can be used to store and transport paper and other materials.

pocket watch
A small clock with a flip lid that is carried in the pocket and often attached by a chain to a buttonhole.

analogue watch
A traditional style of watch on which moving hands point to numbers that represent hours and minutes.

watchband
A strap on a watch, often made of leather, that holds the clockface and encircles the wrist to hold it in place.

case
An outer shell made of resistant material that protectively encloses the more delicate components.

crown
A small knob that can be rotated to adjust the time, date or other indicators.

hour hand
The short hand on the dial of a clock or watch, which marks the hours of a day.

face
The section of a watch on which the time, sometimes with the date, is displayed, either digitally or with a dial.

ring
A small, circular loop of rigid material attached to an object as a fixed point to which another object may be joined.

minute hand
The long hand on the dial of a clock or watch, which marks the minutes of an hour.

second hand
A long hand on the dial of a clock or watch that marks the seconds of a minute.

chain
A series of small metal loops joined together to form a continuous string, often used to suspend or connect objects.

women's watch
A small clock that is attached with a band around the wrist and is often decorative.

digital watch
A modern style of watch on which the time is displayed in numerals, rather than with a dial.

nose pad
A small oval piece of plastic or rubber on the inner frame of eyeglasses that sits on the bridge of the nose.

bridge
The central section that connects and suspends the lenses over the eyes.

temple
The part that sits over the ear; it is usually slightly curved or bent and sometimes coated.

sunglasses
Eyeglasses with tinted lenses that are worn to protect the eyes from damaging ultraviolet sun rays.

frame
The rigid structure on a pair of eyeglasses that holds the lenses in place and to which the earpieces are attached.

lens
A piece of glass or plastic formed or treated to alter or diffuse light as it reaches the cornea, altering vision.

eyeglasses
A frame that rests on the ears and nose and that holds lenses, shaped to correct vision, in front of the eyes.

half-rimmed glasses
A style of glasses where only the top or bottom half of the lenses is enclosed by the frame.

clip-on sunglasses
A style of sunglasses with tinted lenses that are clipped onto eyeglasses for protection from the sun.

bifocal lens
A lens with two distinct focal powers, one that corrects distance vision and one that corrects near vision.

opera glasses
A small pair of binoculars that may be held easily in one hand, specifically designed for use at the theater.

monocle
A single corrective lens that is held in position using the muscles surrounding the eye, usually for brief periods.

soft contact lenses
Thin, flexible lenses made of a material containing water that are placed directly onto the eyes to correct vision.

hard contact lenses
Thin, rigid lenses made of a gas-permeable material that are placed directly onto the eyes to correct vision.

disposable contact lenses
Contact lenses that are only worn for a day or two then replaced with a new pair, designed for convenience.

lens case
A container with two small compartments in which soft contact lenses are bathed in a cleaning solution when not worn.

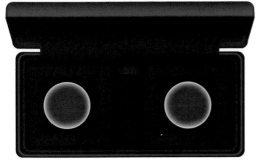

antique lens case
A container with two small compartments in which hard contact lenses were bathed in a cleaning solution when not worn.

multipurpose solution
A liquid that is put into a contact lens case to disinfect, moisten and remove built-up protein from contact lenses.

lubricant eye drops
A solution that is put in the eye in small drops to relieve dryness and discomfort resulting from contact lens use.

cleaning cloth
A small piece of fabric cloth that is used to clean smudges off of the lenses of glasses.

glasses cord
A small fabric cord that is often stretchy and can be attached to the ends of glasses to fasten them to the body.

glasses case
A small, rigid container with a soft lining shaped to hold a pair of eyeglasses to protect them from damage.

oval cut
A rounded cut with a standard number of 69 facets, named after the Latin word "ovum," meaning egg.

pear-shaped cut
A gem cut shaped like a sparkling tear drop that combines features of the Marquise and oval cuts, usually for small gems.

marquise cut
A French cut that is named after the word for "little boat," in the shape of an oval with pointed ends.

baguette cut
A long, rectangular step cut that is mostly used for side stones as it is not known for its brilliance or sparkle.

tapered baguette cut
A gemstone cut that has two long sides that taper inward to form a trapezoid.

Flanders cut
A gemstone cut that was created in Belgium in the 1980s and is known for bearing 61 different facets.

princess cut
A gemstone cut that is square or rectangular in shape.

heart cut
A gemstone cut that creates a diamond that appears to be heart shaped.

emerald cut
A gem cut in a rectangular shape with cropped corners and outer step cuts, first noted in 1477 in Austria.

step cut
A style of gem cut, most often square or rectangular, with straight facets around the sides of a flat face.

trilliant cut
A gemstone cut that is triangular in shape with 43 or more facets.

radiant cut
A gemstone cut that is characterized as being either rectangular or square and having up to 73 facets.

brilliant full cut
Diamonds with 57 or 58 facets, mathematically determined to be the standard required for maximum brilliance.

hexagonal cut
A variety of gemstone cut with six edges.

trillion cut
A gemstone cut that was designed in Amsterdam. It is triangular in shape and bears 44 facets.

diamond
A precious stone consisting of a clear, crystalline form of carbon; the hardest natural substance known to man.

amethyst
A precious stone consisting of a purple variety of crystallized quartz.

aquamarine
A precious stone consisting of a clear, light blue or green variety of beryl; named for its resemblance to ocean water.

tourmaline
A semiprecious stone consisting of a complex crystalline silicate, some of which appear to change color with light.

blue topaz
A precious stone consisting of an aluminum silicate found in pale varieties, such as blue or pink, as well as colorless.

ruby
A precious stone consisting of a form of translucent corundum, found in varying shades of red.

emerald
A precious stone consisting of a bright green, transparent variety of beryl, found in many countries around the world.

garnet
A semiprecious stone consisting of a silicate mineral, usually deep red but also found in yellow, green or purple.

sapphire
A precious stone consisting of a form of transparent corundum, usually blue but may be any color except red.

quartz crystal
A mineral consisting of silicon dioxide found in a variety of colors and considered to have healing powers.

malachite
A semiprecious stone, opaque and bright green with variegated bands, consisting of a copper carbonate.

moonstone
A semiprecious stone consisting of a pearly white alkali feldspar, considered to have mystical powers.

jade
A hard, typically green semiprecious stone consisting of the minerals jadeite or nephrite.

onyx
A semiprecious variety of translucent agate that is characterized by parallel bands of different colors.

opal
A semiprecious stone consisting of hydrated silica, usually milky white with an iridescent play of different colors.

ivory
An opaque, hard, whitish substance composed of dentin, found in the tusks of elephants, walruses and narwhals.

lapis lazuli
A semiprecious stone consisting of a combination of several minerals, resulting in an opaque, bright blue substance.

turquoise
A semiprecious stone consisting of a hydrated copper aluminum phosphate, opaque and ranging from blue to green.

tigereye
A semiprecious stone consisting of a variety of yellow-brown quartz, veined and with a silky luster resembling an eye.

agate
A semiprecious stone consisting of a hard variety of striped chalcedony that comes in a variety of colors.

tiara
A jeweled ornamental band that sits on top of a woman's head, worn on formal occasions or by young girls.

charm bracelet
A loose bracelet of silver or gold chain with small ornaments that often represent important events or memories.

cuff
A thick, open-ended bracelet made of a rigid material that is worn loose on the wrist.

leather bangle
A piece of jewelry that is made of leather and is slipped over the hand.

locket
A small ornamental case with a hinged lid, often used to hold a tiny photograph, that is worn on a necklace.

rhinestone
An imitation diamond made of rock crystal, glass or acrylic, used in jewelry and often to decorate clothing.

cameo
A typically oval piece of jewelry with an image carved in relief set on a background of a contrasting color.

choker
A necklace that fits closely around the neck, often with a decorative accent at the base of the throat.

pearl necklace
A strand of lustrous, small spheres that are produced by bivalve mollusks, primarily oysters and worn around the neck.

brooch
An ornament that is attached to clothing with a hinged pin and catch, usually on the chest or at the base of the throat.

filigree pendant
A pendant made of ornamental wire, often silver or gold, formed into an intricate pattern.

pendant
An ornament, often including a gem set in a precious metal, that is designed to hang from a necklace.

navel ring stud
An ornamental piece of metal that is designed to be worn in the belly button.

silver pendant
A pendant made entirely out of a semiprecious, grayish-white metal that, when polished, has a pronounced shine.

jewelry box
A box fitted with smaller compartments and often a mirror on the inside lid, designed to store various types of jewelry.

screw earring
Earrings that are attached to the lobe with a small clamp that is screwed and tightened.

drop earring
Earrings that hang down from the lobe and are typically inserted into a piercing with a small hook.

stud
Earrings that are inserted into a piercing with a post and are held in place with a separate backing.

hoop earring
Earrings that are shaped as hoops with a thinner section that slides into a piercing and fits into the hoop.

Men's jewelry

tie bar
An ornamental clip, usually in the shape of a long, flat rectangle, worn to hold a tie in place on the front of a shirt.

cuff link
A decorative device that fastens the sides of a shirt cuff together.

tiepin
A long, straight pin, usually with a sheath for the sharp point, that is worn to hold a tie to a shirt.

Rings

band
A simple ring in gold, silver or platinum that has little to no adornment, typically worn as a wedding ring.

class ring
A style of ring with a thick band holding a circular gem or design, worn to symbolize high school or college graduation.

engagement ring
A ring given as a symbol of a promise to be wed, often with a slim band and a centered precious stone.

platinum ring
A band made of a precious silvery-white metal that is noncorroding and virtually unoxidizable.

solitaire ring
A style of ring with a slim band and a setting containing a single precious stone, often given as an engagement ring.

wedding ring
Rings, usually simple matching bands, that are exchanged by the partners during a wedding ceremony.

signet ring
A style of ring with a thick band carved with initials, a seal or a monogram or set with a symbolic stone.

powder blush
A variety of cosmetic application that is placed on the cheeks and is usually different in color than a user's skin tone.

mirror
The small reflective piece of glass that allows users to view themselves as they apply powder blush.

blush
A colored pigment, often in powder form and tones of pink, that is applied to the face to highlight the cheekbones.

makeup brush
A small collection of soft fibers attached to the end of a handle that is used to apply powdered forms of makeup.

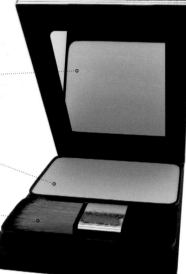

compact
A small case with a hinged lid containing a facial powder, applicator and mirror that is usually carried in a purse.

eye shadow
A colored pigment, often in powder form, that is applied to the eyelids and, sometimes, below the eyebrows.

powder puff
A small, round piece of a soft material that is used to apply loose face powder to the skin.

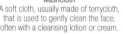

washcloth
A soft cloth, usually made of terrycloth, that is used to gently clean the face, often with a cleansing lotion or cream.

loose eye shadow
A colored pigment in powder form that is applied to the eyelids and, sometimes, below the eyebrows.

makeup remover pad
Small, round, disposable pieces of absorbent cotton sponge used to apply, blend or remove makeup, lotion or cream.

pressed face powder
Face powder that has been slightly moistened to create a semi-solid substance that may be smoothly applied to the skin.

face cream
A thick lotion that is applied to the face to soften and moisten the skin and minimize wrinkles.

loose face powder
A soft powder, usually with skin-toned pigments, that is applied to the face to minimize pores and remove shine.

makeup remover
A liquid cleanser, often with a softening agent and a fresh scent, formulated to remove makeup without water.

brow brush and lash comb
A beautician's instrument consisting of a tiny, two-sided comb used to shape and form eyebrows and eyelashes.

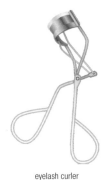

eyelash curler
A handheld instrument with a metal clamp that squeezes and bends the upper eyelashes upward toward the brow.

cotton swab
Small pieces of cotton attached to either end of a short stick, used for cosmetic, medicinal and hygienic purposes.

tweezers
A cosmetic tool with two small movable parts that may be squeezed together to pinch and remove unwanted hairs.

lip gloss
A thick liquid or waxy substance with little or no pigment that is applied to the lips to give them a glossy finish.

eye cream
A lotion that is applied to the thin skin around the eyes to minimize wrinkles, shadows or other imperfections.

concealer
A flesh-toned liquid or soft pencil used to cover specific blemishes, such as pimples or dark spots, on the face.

lipstick
A pigmented waxy solid, usually in a pink or red shade and in the form of a stick, that is applied to the lips.

lip balm
A waxy, colorless substance that is applied to the lips to heal or prevent chapping or as a protection against the sun.

loose powder brush
A small collection of soft fibers attached to the end of a handle that is used to apply powdered forms of makeup.

liquid eye shadow
A colored pigment in moistened powder form that is applied to the eyelids and, sometimes, below the eyebrows.

liquid eyeliner
A colored pigment in liquid form that is applied to the outline of the eyes, near the lashes, to make them stand out.

mascara
A thick, dark liquid that is applied to the eyelashes with a small brush to darken, lengthen and thicken them.

fan brush
A brush used to gently apply powder or blush in wide, sweeping strokes so that foundation makeup is not disturbed.

lip brush
A makeup brush with a small, narrow collection of bristles, used to apply a cream lipstick or gloss to the mouth.

lip liner
A soft pencil used to define the outline of the lips prior to the application of a complementary shade of lipstick.

eyebrow pencil
A soft pencil used to shade in or alter the shape of the eyebrows, often used for sparse or uneven eyebrows.

liquid foundation
A cosmetic lotion with a skin-toned pigment that is applied to the face to mask skin imperfections.

Manicure and pedicure

nail polish
A colored varnish that is painted on toenails and fingernails for decoration as well as to protect the nail plate.

nail polish remover
An organic solvent, often containing acetone and a nail conditioner, that is used to remove nail polish.

cuticle nippers
A type of short scissor with horizontal blades that is used to safely and painlessly trim cuticles or hangnails.

nail clippers
A small cutting tool with horizontal blades, used to cut and trim fingernails, toenails and hangnails.

safety scissors
Scissors with ends that are blunted to prevent accidental stabbing of the skin around fingers and toes.

toenail scissors
Small, thick scissors with very sharp blades used to cut and trim tough toenails.

nail scissors
Small scissors that are used with either hand to cut and trim nails, primarily on the fingers.

cuticle scissors
Small, slightly curved scissors designed to clip away dry skin from around the nail bed of fingers and toes.

nail file
A flat metal stick with an abrasive surface that is run over the edges of nails to sculpt and smooth them.

nail scissors
A specialized type of manicure tool that is used to cut fingernails and to remove hang nails.

manicure set
A set of manicure tools that are designed to perform a wide variety of tasks related to grooming the fingernails.

nail shaper
A specialized manicure tool that is designed to help shape and form fingernails.

case
The container in which all of the utensils of the manicure set can be safely stored.

cuticle nippers
A stick with a blunt, curved end that is used to push excess cuticle growth back and away from the nail bed.

tweezers
A cosmetic tool with two small movable parts that may be squeezed together to pinch and remove unwanted hairs.

nail file
A flat, metal stick with an abrasive surface that is run over the edges of nails to sculpt and smooth them.

emery board
A strip of hard material coated with an abrasive substance that is run over the edges of nails to sculpt and smooth them.

cuticle pusher
A stick with a blunt, curved end that is used to push excess cuticle growth back and away from the nail bed.

cuticle trimmer
A stick with a small, sharp V-shaped end that is used to trim off layers of dry skin from the cuticle or nail line.

nail whitening pencil
A soft pencil used to whiten the tips of nails to give them the appearance of a French manicure.

electric shaver
An electric device for shaving, with oscillating or rotating blades behind a metal guard, which are passed over the skin.

head
The portion of an electric razor that contains the blades and that can be removed or opened for cleaning.

housing
A hard outer casing made of metal or plastic enclosing the inner workings, such as the motor.

power button
A small object that may be pressed to turn the electrical connection between a source and a device on or off.

flexible power cord
A coiled wire coated with an insulating material that is attached to a device and plugged into an outlet.

shaving cream
A thick lather that is contained under pressure in a canister and can be ejected as needed for shaving.

disposable razor blade
A device that closely cuts facial and body hairs, used only a few times then thrown out.

aftershave
A lotion or gel, often scented and containing an astringent, that is applied to the skin after shaving.

disposable razor
A tool with an exposed blade that is dragged over an area of the body to completely shave off hair then is thrown away.

men's razor
A shaving tool that bears multiple blades and is used to efficiently cut and groom facial and bodily hairs.

cleaning brush
A small, narrow length of bristles used to clean bits of hair from an electric razor.

head
The uppermost portion of the razor, which connects the blades to the handle.

precision trimmer
A small blade located on the lower aspect of the floating head that helps to cut and trim the shortest of hairs.

hair clippers
An electric shaver fitted with a wide-toothed comb that rests against the skin to regulate the length of hair being cut.

blade
The flat, sharp strip of metal on the head of a razor that is used to cut hairs from the skin.

lubricating strip
A small component that turns helps to loisturize the skin.

epilator
An electrical device that grasps and pulls out unwanted body hairs without damaging the surrounding skin.

shaving brush
A thick, soft collection of bristles attached to a short handle that is used to lather the face before shaving.

blade
The metal portion that has been sharpened on one edge; it is used to cut hairs from the skin.

straight razor
A foldable razor with a long blade and a handle that produces the closest possible shave.

handle
The length of rigid material that is held in the hand when the razor is in use.

pivot
The point where the two pieces are connected, it allows the pieces to move in a scissoring motion.

Hair care

curling iron
An electric tool with a long heated rod around which hair is twirled and clamped to produce waves or curls.

clamp lever
A bent extension on the clamp that is used to lift and lower it.

indicator light
A small light built into the device that is illuminated to show an active electrical connection.

clamp
A curved, blunt blade that holds a section of hair so that it can be wrapped around the barrel.

handle
The length of rigid material that is held in the hand when the device is being used.

power switch
A small lever that is flipped to turn the electrical connection between a source and the device on or off.

air inlet grille
A plastic grid that facilitates the suction of air when the device is in use.

barrel
The long, heated rod on a curling iron around which hair is wrapped or twirled to form a curl or wave.

cool tip
A small piece on the outermost tip of the barrel that can be touched while the iron is in use.

headband
A decorative strip of material that wraps across the top of the head from ear to ear, holding hair back from the face.

blow-dryer
An electric device that emits a continuous blast of heated air that is used to quickly dry or shape wet hair.

fan housing
A hard outer casing made of metal or plastic enclosing the inner workings of the fan.

handle
The length of rigid material that is held in the hand when the device is being used.

barrel
The component of a curling iron that becomes heated so as to temporarily create hair curls.

barrette
A small clip used to hold a section of hair; typically bar-shaped and decorative.

selector switch
A small lever on an electrical device that may be flipped or pressed to change its function, motion or response.

air outlet grille
The cylindrical spout at the end of the device through which the hot air escapes.

electric cord
A long wire coated with an insulating material attached to a device or an appliance which may be plugged into an outlet.

straightening iron
An electric device consisting of two heated, flat plates between which hair is pressed to remove curls.

self-grip roller
A small tube covered with short bristles around which a section of hair is twirled and held to produce a curl.

roller
A small tube around which a section of hair is twirled and held in place with a clip to produce a curl.

hair tie
A band of stretchy rubber covered with thread or material, used to hold gathered hair together.

hair gel
A gooey, semi-solid substance, often scented, that is applied to hair and allowed to stiffen to hold the hair in place.

hair spray
A liquid polymer solution that is sprayed onto the hair and allowed to dry to hold the hair in place.

hair conditioner
A creamy solution that is applied to wet hair after it has been washed to moisturize it and prevent tangles.

hair dye
A solution that is applied to hair to permanently or temporarily change its color.

shampoo
A liquid soap specially formulated to cleanse hair, often scented and incorporating natural oils and nutrients.

mousse
A thick foam, often scented, that is applied to hair and allowed to dry to give shape and body to the hair.

single-edged thinning scissors
A pair of scissors with one notched blade that leaves some hair uncut; used to create particular styles.

double-edged thinning scissors
A pair of scissors with notched blades that leave some hair uncut.

tooth
The protrusion created between two notches and usually found in a series, such as on a notched blade.

shank
The extending shaft to which the handle is attached.

pivot
The point at which the two pieces are connected; it allows them to move crosswise.

hair-cutting scissors
Scissors with narrow, sharp blades specifically designed to cut hair with precision, usually used by professionals.

ring-handle
A rounded loop at the end of each shank and operated with the index finger and thumb.

bobby pin
A small, folded strip of material, usually metal or plastic, which is used to hold a section of hair in place.

hairpin
A small device with two thin metal prongs used to hold artificial sections of hair, such as wigs, to natural hair.

alligator hair clip
Two lengths of metal or plastic held in place with a springed pivot that are used to keep hair in place.

rake comb
A style of wide-toothed comb primarily used to remove tangles from wet or damp hair, or to comb textured hair.

quill brush
A style of brush with a large number of closely packed bristles used to remove tangles and add volume to hair.

vent brush
A style of brush with slits in the head, used to remove tangles and give volume to hair while using a hairdryer.

round brush
A cylindrical styling brush used to add volumizing curl or wave to hair while blowing it dry.

tint brush
A brush used to spread a color solution on hair, from the roots to the tips or only on specific sections.

wave clip
Two pieces of plastic with interlocking, long teeth held in place with a springed pivot, used to grasp hair.

hair pick
A type of comb with widely spaced long teeth at the end of a short handle, used to fluff hair with a jabbing motion.

paddle brush
An all-purpose brush with a large head and many bristles, used to smooth and add natural shine to hair.

tail comb
A style of comb with a long, tapering handle that is used to separate hair into sections.

pitchfork comb
A type of comb that combines a teaser comb on one end of the handle with a hair pick on the other end.

barber comb
A general-purpose comb used for very short hair, often with teeth spaced widely on one half and narrowly on the other.

teaser comb
A comb with teeth of varying lengths used to backcomb hair into loose tangles that add artificial volume.

battery-operated toothbrush
A toothbrush with oscillating or vibrating bristles that is powered with a small, often rechargeable, battery.

bristles
Short, stiff hairs, either natural or synthetic, that are closely packed onto a surface, used for brushing or scrubbing.

on/off button
A small object that can be pressed to start or to stop the device.

charger base
An electric device that supports an object in a standing position while its battery is charged.

toothbrush
A small collection of tightly packed synthetic bristles at the end of a long handle, used for cleaning the teeth.

gum stimulator
A specialized dental tool that is used to remove plaque and improve gum health.

dental floss
A soft thread, which can be waxed or flavored, used to clean food and plaque from between the teeth.

toothpaste
A paste or gel with agents, often containing fluoride, formulated for cleaning teeth.

mouthwash
A cleanser, usually alcohol-based and often with a whitening agent, used to rinse the mouth of debris and freshen breath.

sanitary pad
Elongated pieces of absorbent material that are placed in a woman's panties to catch and absorb menstrual discharge.

tampon
A piece of absorbent material that is inserted into the vagina to catch and absorb menstrual discharge.

pantyliner
Thin, elongated pieces of absorbent material that are placed in a woman's panties to absorb small amounts of discharge.

wipe
Disposable pieces of cloth moistened with a hypo-allergenic, often scented, solution used to clean the skin.

natural sponge
A scrubbing material made from the porous surface of a marine creature, usually used to scrub one's skin.

synthetic sponge
A scrubbing material made from a porous synthetic compound that can be used for household or physical cleaning.

toilet paper
Absorbent soft paper, usually in the form of small sheets on a roll, used to wipe oneself after using the toilet.

wax strip
A piece of cloth or paper coated with wax and pressed to an area of skin to catch hold of and remove hair.

soap dish
A small ceramic container that is used in washrooms to store hard soap between uses.

soap
A skin-cleaning substance, usually a compound of natural oils or fats combined with an alkali, that lathers with water.

loofah
A scrubbing material made from the dried fibrous skeleton of a marrow-like tropical fruit, used to scrub the skin.

condom
A thin rubber sheath worn over the penis during sexual intercourse to prevent pregnancy and infection.

depilatory cream
A cosmetic lotion with a strong chemical that weakens the base of hairs enough to remove them from the body.

sunscreen
A lotion that contains sun-blocking ingredients that is applied to the skin as protection against burning.

bronzer
A lotion or powder that contains organic dyes of brown or gold that is applied to the skin to darken it.

liquid soap
A liquified form of skin-cleaning soap that is often mixed with a disinfectant and dispensed from a pump bottle.

eau de parfum
A diluted form of perfume containing less oils than true perfume, thereby releasing a lower concentration of scent.

bubble bath
A scented liquid soap that is poured into the bathtub as it is filling with water to create bubbles.

shower gel
A body-cleaning, moisturizing soap, usually scented, in a gel form; most commonly used in the shower.

spray-on deodorant
An aerosol spray, often scented, that is applied to the armpits to prevent unpleasant body odors.

eau de toilette
A highly diluted form of perfume with a high alcohol content, formulated to freshen and lightly scent the skin.

nail brush
A wooden or plastic block covered with bristles, used to buff dead skin and dirt off the body and nails.

moisturizer
A thick lotion that is applied to the skin, primarily to moisturize it but often also to lightly scent it.

solid deodorant
A gelled or solid substance that is applied to the armpits to prevent unpleasant body odors.

bath bomb
A scented mass, often spherical, that dissolves and fizzes when placed in a bath.

toiletry bag
A small case, usually lined with plastic, used to carry small personal hygiene items.

bath sheet
An oversized towel that can be wrapped around the entire body after bathing or showering.

exfoliating glove
A glove made of absorbent cloth that is worn for washing the body, often with an abrasive section for exfoliating.

bath towel
A large piece of absorbent material used to dry the body after bathing or showering.

washing symbols
Small images that are sewn or printed on a tag in an article of clothing to provide washing instructions.

do not wash
A laundry symbol advising that the article of clothing should not come in contact with water and only be dry-cleaned.

hand wash
A laundry symbol advising that the article of clothing should not be washed in a machine, only delicately by hand.

wash in warm water
A laundry symbol advising that the article of clothing should not be washed at high temperatures.

drying symbols
Small images that are sewn or printed on a tag in an article of clothing to provide drying instructions.

tumble dry at any heat
A laundry symbol advising that the article of clothing can be tumble dried at any setting.

tumble dry at low heat
A laundry symbol advising that the article of clothing should be tumble dried only on a low setting.

tumble dry at medium heat
A laundry symbol advising that the article of clothing can be tumble dried on a medium setting.

do not tumble dry
A laundry symbol advising that the article of clothing should not be dried in a machine.

ironing symbols
Small images that are sewn or printed on a tag in an article of clothing to provide ironing instructions.

iron at low setting
A laundry symbol advising that the article of clothing should only be ironed on a low setting.

iron at medium setting
A laundry symbol advising that the article of clothing should be ironed on a medium setting to effectively remove wrinkles.

iron at high setting
A laundry symbol advising that the article of clothing needs to be ironed on a high setting to effectively remove wrinkles.

do not iron
A laundry symbol advising that the article of clothing should not be ironed due to the nature of the material.

bleaching symbols
Small images that are sewn or printed on a tag in an article of clothing to provide bleaching instructions.

use any bleach
A laundry symbol advising that the article of clothing may be bleached with any kind of bleaching product.

use non-chlorine bleach only
A laundry symbol advising that the article of clothing should only be bleached with a bleaching product free of chlorine.

do not bleach
A laundry symbol advising that the article of clothing should not be bleached.

dry cleaning
Small images that are sewn or printed on a tag in an article of clothing to advise whether the item can be dry-cleaned.

dry clean
A laundry symbol advising that the article of clothing can be dry cleaned but does not necessarily need to be.

do not dry clean
A laundry symbol advising that the article of clothing should not be dry cleaned.

SOCIETY

parents and children
Children are cared for by adult guardians, the parents; together they form a family.

parents
The people legally responsible for the upbringing of a child or children, whether biological or adopted.

grandparents and grandchildren
The parents of a child's mother or father; the children of that mother or father.

grandparents
The parents of a daughter or son's mother or father.

father
A male parent of a child, whether biological or through adoption.

grandfather
The father of a daughter or son's mother or father.

grandmother
The mother of a daughter or son's mother or father.

mother
A female parent of a child, whether biological or through adoption.

daughter
A female child related to her parents by birth or adoption.

son
A male child related to his parents by birth or adoption.

granddaughter
A daughter of a mother or father's daughter or son.

grandson
A son of a mother or father's daughter or son.

children
The offspring, whether male or female, of a parent or parents.

grandchildren
The children of a mother or father's daughter or son.

brothers and sisters
Male and female offspring of the same parents; also called siblings.

twins
Two people produced at the same birth, including identical, fraternal and unusual twinnings, such as conjoined.

baby
A newborn or recently born human who is completely reliant on an adult's care.

brother
A male child in relation to his other sibling(s).

sister
A female child in relation to her other sibling(s).

stages of life: female
The progressive steps in a female's lifetime, from infancy to adulthood.

stages of life: male
The progressive steps in a male's lifetime, from infancy to adulthood.

woman
A human adult female, no longer a minor, who is fully responsible for her own care.

girl
A human school-aged female, a minor, under the care of a parent or guardian.

toddler
A human infant under the care of a parent or guardian.

toddler
A human infant, under the care of a parent or guardian.

boy
A human school-aged male, a minor, under the care of a parent or guardian.

man
A human adult male, no longer a minor, who is fully responsible for his own care.

Body types
The various forms of bodily characteristics, in terms of size and proportion.

overweight
A person who is of higher than average weight for their height and bone structure.

average
A person who is considered to be of normal weight for their height and bone structure.

slim
A person who is considered to be under the normal weight for their height and bone structure.

athletic
A person who is considered to be fit and active, often with a well-defined musculature.

classroom
A room in an educational institution in which people are taught, usually at the same level or on the same subject.

teacher
A person who provides education by instructing others.

blackboard
A flat, hard surface, usually of a dark color and mounted on a classroom wall, for the purpose of writing on with chalk.

globe
A spherical representation of the Earth, usually with labels naming areas of land, water and their boundaries.

chair
A seat that includes a back, designed for individual use.

teacher's desk
A fairly large desk, usually situated at the front of a classroom, designated for the personal use of the teacher.

student
A person receiving education by means of being instructed, often in a classroom setting.

chalk
A soft limestone, or facsimile thereof, typically formed into light-colored sticks and used to write on a blackboard.

bulletin board
A flat surface mounted on a wall to which notices may be pinned or otherwise attached for general viewing.

bookcase
A piece of furniture made up of a series of shelves on which books and other small items may be displayed or stored.

desk
A table with a worktop, typically including small drawers for storing materials such as paper and pens.

lecture hall
An open chamber that is typically found in conference halls and universities that is used for giving lectures.

desk
A table with a worktop, typically including small drawers for storing materials such as paper and pens.

blackboard
A flat, hard surface, usually of a dark color and mounted on a classroom wall, for the purpose of writing on with chalk.

professor
Someone who works at a college or university, providing educational lectures and grading students.

seat
A space where a student sits to listen to the lecture; often equipped with a writing surface.

podium
A stand with a flat, slanted top on which a teacher or professor can rest printed materials during a lecture or lesson.

slanted top
A flat upper surface at a slight angle, to facilitate viewing notes or other material.

shelf
A flat, elongated surface built into a piece of furniture or an appliance, on which objects are stored.

metal frame
Several pieces of metal that are fixed or molded together to form a primary supporting structure.

leg
A piece of rigid material attached to the bottom of a piece of furniture to raise it from the ground or stabilize it.

microphone
A device that amplifies vocalizations so they can be projected over a larger area.

decorative grille
A sheet of metal or plastic mesh affixed to an object for aesthetic purposes.

student
A person who is receiving education by means of being instructed, usually in reference to a classroom setting.

dais
A raised platform on which a person providing a lecture can stand to be better seen by the audience.

doors
A basic structural component of the facility that serve as a means of entering and leaving the room.

step
One of a series of declining platforms that provide access to the lower levels of the lecture hall facility.

aisle
A walkway between seating areas, along which one can pass to reach one's row and seat.

school supplies
A collection of items used by a student to assist them with their educational studies, such as pens, paper, ruler, etc.

ruler
A narrow, flat strip of material, such as metal or plastic, marked with linear measurements such as inches or centimeters.

fountain pen
A writing implement that contains a reservoir of ink that flows continuously to a thin split metal nib when writing.

marker
A writing implement that contains a reservoir of ink that flows continuously to a nib made of compressed fibers.

scissors
A cutting tool composed of two blades attached on top of each other by a central pin and ending in finger loops.

ballpoint pen
A writing implement that contains a reservoir of ink that flows around a tiny sphere that serves as a nib when writing.

podium
A stand with a flat slanted top on which a teacher or professor can rest printed materials during a lecture or lesson.

whiteboard
A large board with a smooth white surface that can be used as a writing surface or to display projected images.

pencil holder
A cup or jar designated to hold writing supplies such as pencils, pens, rulers, etc.

residential neighborhood
An area that is almost entirely covered with residential buildings, such as houses, apartments, and condos.

high-rise apartment building
A tall building with numerous floors, usually containing several apartments on each floor.

intersection
The juncture at which two roads cross each other, often with traffic control indicators, such as lights or stop signs.

parking lot
A piece of land designated as a place to temporarily leave vehicles, often paved and marked with individual spots.

townhouse
A house in a row of houses that are attached to each other on one or both sides, often including a small yard.

front yard
The area between the front of a residence and a public sidewalk or road, usually manicured with landscaping.

low-rise apartment building
A building that is only a few stories high, usually containing several apartments on each floor.

house
A fully detached home containing one or more stories on a lot that usually includes a front and back yard.

coffee shop
A small restaurant that specializes in coffee and other hot beverages, also offering light meals or snacks.

swimming pool
A structure built into or above the ground that holds a large quantity of water for swimming.

hotel
A building or complex containing rooms for rent, often also offering conference spaces, dining and other facilities.

road
A strip of land that usually extends for a significant distance, designated for vehicular traffic.

shopping mall
A sizable building or complex containing a variety of retail stores, often also including restaurants and seating.

warehouse
A spacious building, usually with one level, in which goods are stored prior to shipping to retail outlets to be sold.

truck
A large motor vehicle with a closed or open storage area used to transport loads of materials or equipment.

tennis court
A flat, rectangular area of ground, marked with lines and cut in half by a low net, on which tennis is played.

baseball field
A large, flat area of ground marked with lines on which baseball is played, usually with a seating area for spectators.

recreation center
A specialized facility where a wide variety of recreational activities are conducted for youth and adults.

pond
A small body of water that may be naturally occurring or formed artificially, such as in a park.

car
An engine-powered vehicle with four wheels, designed for road travel, that carries a small number of people.

billboard
A large outdoor advertising poster that is mounted well off the ground or on the side of a building for high visibility.

street light
An outdoor light fixture atop a tall post situated along the edge of a roadway, sidewalk, bikepath or other route.

trash can
An open container, often with a hinged lid, designed to collect and store waste for later disposal.

bench
An elongated outdoor piece of furniture designed to seat more than one person and made of a hard substance such as wood.

downtown
The area of a town or city in which commercial and business services are most concentrated.

crane
A large machine used to move heavy materials by suspending them from a long arm, usually for construction.

restaurant
A business establishment that specializes in serving food.

museum
A facility that specializes in collecting and preserving historical or artistic artifacts for viewing by the public.

helipad
A flat area on the ground or on the roof of a large building designated for the landing and takeoff of helicopters.

helicopter
A type of aircraft operated by way of overhead rotors that create lift, propulsion and maneuverability.

construction site
An area of land where work is being carried out in order to build, tear down or repair a structure.

skyscraper
A very tall, narrow building of numerous floors, usually occupied by business offices or residential units.

building
A structure composed of walls, floors and a roof used for purposes such as residences, offices and other facilities.

container
A large box, usually made of metal, that is placed outside to store materials for shipping or waste.

truck
A large motor vehicle with a closed or open storage area used to transport loads of materials or equipment.

cement truck
A truck with a large drum mounted on its back that contains cement and revolves to keep the mixture consistent.

satellite dish
A bowl-shaped object fixed to the outside of a building, fitted with an antenna to receive communications signals.

solar panel
A sheet of silicon-based material that absorbs radiation from the sun in order to convert it to electricity.

car
An engine-powered vehicle with four wheels, designed for road travel, that carries a small number of people.

road
A strip of land that usually extends for a significant distance, designated for vehicular traffic.

hospital
A medical facility that contains specialized equipment for the treating of injured or ill people.

supermarket
A large store, primarily stocked with food and beverages.

antenna
A slender rod at the top of which an antenna is mounted, usually on the roof of a building or vehicle.

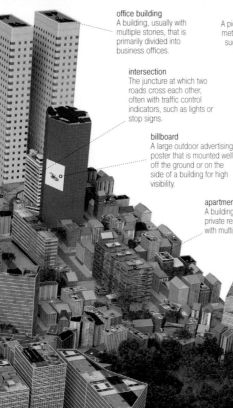

office building
A building, usually with multiple stories, that is primarily divided into business offices.

visor
A piece of curved plastic or metal that covers an object such as a light to direct or concentrate the beam.

traffic light
A set of red, yellow and green lights programmed to change automatically to control the flow of traffic.

store
A business establishment that sells goods, such as clothes or books.

intersection
The juncture at which two roads cross each other, often with traffic control indicators, such as lights or stop signs.

red light
The traffic light that indicates to come to a stop just before the intersection.

pedestrian light
A set of stop and go lights mounted on the corner of an intersection that indicate when it is safe to walk across a road.

billboard
A large outdoor advertising poster that is mounted well off the ground or on the side of a building for high visibility.

yellow light
The traffic light that indicates to proceed with caution or, if possible, come to a stop just before the intersection.

green light
The traffic light that indicates to proceed.

apartment building
A building divided into private residences, typically with multiple floors.

pedestrian call button
A button that is pressed to activate the pedestrian light at the next changing of the traffic light at an intersection.

city hall
A facility where a variety of administrative, legal and governmental activities are conducted.

pedestal
A tall upright column, usually made of concrete or metal, at the top of which a set of traffic lights is mounted.

post office
A facility that specializes in receiving and transporting mail to local residences and business establishments.

library
A facility that specializes in collecting textual resources so as to provide book loaning services to the public.

park
An outdoor public recreational space full of natural vegetation such as grass, trees and flowers.

factory
An industrial building or complex for uses such as manufacturing, processing and assembling products.

penthouse
A suite on the top floor of a tall building, typically luxurious and with a good view.

shopping mall
A space containing a variety of retail stores, often also including restaurants and seating.

cosmetics store
A store specializing in makeup and other cosmetics, typically also selling related items such as grooming products.

maintenance worker
A person employed to maintain a building or complex, attending to repairs and general upkeep.

sporting goods store
A store specializing in sporting equipment, sportswear, sporting accessories and other sporting goods.

jewelry store
A store specializing in jewelry such as rings, necklaces and bracelets.

skylight
A series of glass windows that serves to provide a transparent view of the skyline above the facility.

travel agency
A commercial establishment that provides travel services, such as flight and hotel arrangements.

railing
A waist-height barrier structure, typically made of wood, metal or glass, used to prevent falling.

potted plant
A plant displayed for decoration, kept in a pot and situated attractively.

bridge
A structure that spans an obstacle or an open space to allow convenient passage from one side to the other.

clothing store
A store specializing in clothing, typically also selling accessories such as belts, hats and bags.

housewares store
A store specializing in household items such as dishware, small appliances, bathroom items and decorations.

vending machine
A machine automated to sell items such as snacks and drinks.

security guard
A person employed to detect and report criminal activity and to be available to address general safety concerns.

bench
An elongated piece of furniture designed to seat more than one person and made of a hard substance such as wood.

menswear store
A store specializing in men's clothing, typically also selling men's accessories such as belts, hats and ties.

department store
A large store primarily stocked with a variety of household items.

trash can
An open container, often with a hinged lid, designed to collect and store waste for later disposal.

customer
A person who seeks the services of a commercial establishment, such as a shopper in a retail store or a diner in a restaurant.

information stand
A panel on a stand in a central location of a large building that provides information, such as a map of the facility.

toy store
A store specializing in children's toys, such as plush animals, games, dolls and puzzles.

electronics store
A store specializing in electronics, such as computers, phones, speakers and related accessories.

lighting store
A store specializing in lighting fixtures and accessories, such as lamp shades and bulbs.

information display
A lit panel that provides information, such as a map of shops in a mall.

coffee shop
A small restaurant that specializes in coffee and other hot beverages, also offering light meals or snacks.

newsstand
A store specializing in newspapers and magazines, typically also selling drinks and snacks.

automated teller machine (ATM)
A machine that provides automated banking services, such as dispensing cash and depositing checks.

bakery
A store specializing in goods baked on-site, such as breads, pastries and cakes.

table and chairs
A piece of furniture supporting a flat surface on which to place objects, with accompanying seats.

baby-changing room
A small, private room in a public building designated for changing a baby's diaper.

restroom
A room providing washing and toilet facilities for public use.

janitor
A person employed to keep a building or complex clean and tidy.

supermarket
A store that sells a wide variety of foods and beverages.

baked goods
Dough-based oven-cooked goods, such as breads, pastries and cakes, often made from wheat flour.

drinks fridge
A refrigerator designated for the storage of cold beverages.

display freezer
A refrigerated cabinet for displaying frozen foods.

prepared foods
Ready-to-eat foods that require only unpacking and sometimes reheating.

frozen foods
Foods kept below freezing for longer storage or due to their nature, such as ice cream.

locker
A small closet where clothes and personal belongings can be locked away while shopping.

drinks
Beverages that are packaged for portability and easy consumption.

security guard
A person employed to detect and report criminal activity and to be available to address general safety concerns.

conveyor belt
A flat, wide strip of rubber formed in a slowly rotating loop to move objects from one end of a counter to the other.

cashier
A person employed to carry out retail transactions.

chair
A seat that includes a back, designed for individual use.

counter
A smooth, raised surface used for serving customers in a retail establishment.

basket
A container with an open top and handles, usually constructed of woven plastic or metal, used to carry small objects.

customer
A person who seeks the services of a commercial establishment, such as a shopper in a retail store or a diner in a restaurant.

railing
An upright structure, typically made of wood, metal or glass, used to separate one area from another.

store entrance/exit
The primary doorway of a retail establishment.

anti-theft sensor
A panel that detects a small magnet on an object that has not been removed at time of purchase, setting off an alarm.

fruits and vegetables
A collection of foods that are grown in the ground or on trees or bushes, such as apples, carrots and potatoes.

shopping cart
A large, wheeled basket that can be pushed through a store to hold items to be purchased.

magazine stand
A tall, circular rack on which magazines are stood upright for display and ease of selection by customers.

newspaper and magazine rack
A tall rack with shelves on which publications are stood upright for display and ease of selection by customers.

dairy products
Foods that are made by processing milk, such as cheese, yogurt and pasteurized milk in cartons or bags.

deli counter
A refrigerated cabinet displaying cheeses and cooked meats that are sliced fresh and packaged upon request.

box
A container with flat sides, often made of cardboard, that can be filled with objects for temporary storage.

scale
A device used to measure the weight of an object.

stockroom
An enclosed room in a retail establishment, inaccessible to customers, designated for the storage of goods prior to sale.

shelves
Thin slabs of rigid material fixed horizontally to a wall or frame in order to store or display items.

salesclerk
A person employed to assist customers in finding items and carrying out transactions.

roll-up door
A barrier made up of a series of slats that may be moved upward against the ceiling to gain access to an enclosed area.

wooden pallet
A small wooden structure that is used to stack and collect materials in warehouse and market settings.

doors
A set of sliding, hinged or revolving barriers at the entrance to a space.

pallet truck
A device consisting of two long, horizontal prongs that can be slid under heavy objects to lift and move them.

stocker
A person employed to handle the allocation of inventory from stock room to sales display.

bakery
A place where dough-based, oven-cooked goods are prepared.

fish and seafood
Water-dwelling creatures that have been prepared for human consumption.

shelves
Thin slabs of rigid material fixed horizontally to a wall or frame in order to store or display items.

plastic bag
A small plastic bag composed of recyclable materials that is commonly used in markets to collect products.

paper grocery bag
A large pouch made of paper that is used to carry goods purchased from a supermarket.

reusable grocery bag
A large pouch made of plastic or cloth, usually fitted with handles, used to carry objects.

coffee house
A small restaurant that specializes in coffee and other hot beverages, also offering light meals or snacks.

menu display
A panel, often lit and wall mounted, that provides information about the foods and beverages for sale.

restroom
A room providing washing and toilet facilities for public use.

customer
A person who seeks the services of a commercial establishment, such as a shopper in a retail store or a diner in a restaurant.

counter
A smooth, raised surface, such as those used by bartenders and baristas for serving.

chair
A seat that includes a back, designed for individual use.

bakery
A store where dough-based, oven-cooked goods are prepared and sold.

door
A sliding, hinged or revolving barrier at the entrance to a space.

salesclerk
A person employed to assist customers in finding items and carrying out transactions.

refrigerated display case
A refrigerated cabinet with a glass front that allows the contents, most often foods, to be seen by customers.

counter
A smooth, raised surface used to conduct business with customers.

cake
A baked good made from flour, eggs and milk, usually sweet and often decorated with frosting.

storefront sign
A decorative panel with words and/or images, mounted on the front of a store to provide information, such as the name.

exhaust fan
A fan built into the wall or ceiling of a room to expel an accumulation of moisture or steam to the outside environment.

pendant light
A light fixture that is mounted to suspend from the ceiling of a room.

barista
A person employed to prepare specialty coffee drinks and other hot beverages.

waitress
A female person employed in a restaurant to take and deliver customer orders of food and beverages.

table
A piece of furniture supporting a flat surface on which to place objects.

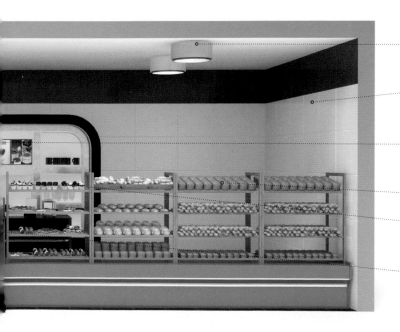

light
A source of electric illumination such as a lamp or fixture.

tile
A slim slab of material used as flooring or cladding, typically made of ceramic or composite.

menu display
A panel, often lit and wall mounted, that provides information about the foods and beverages for sale.

bread loaf
A baked good made from flour and liquid, typically leavened with yeast.

bread roll
A small, round bread loaf designed for a single serving.

customer
A person who seeks the services of a commercial establishment, such as a shopper in a retail store or a diner in a restaurant.

cosmetics store
A retail establishment that sells products for the body, mainly for beauty or skin care, such as makeup and lotions.

mirror
A reflective surface, usually composed of glass coated on one side with a metal compound.

display
A collection of items for sale arranged on a surface in a retail store.

store manager
The employee responsible for the store's overall operations, including staff, customer service and merchandise.

computer
An electronic device used for storing and processing data, such as sales and inventory at a store.

counter
A smooth, raised surface used for serving customers in a retail establishment.

electronics store
A retail establishment that sells electronic equipment and accessories, such as radios, computers and cell phones.

tablet
A self-contained computer that includes the required circuitry, battery and touch-screen monitor in one portable unit.

monitor
A screen that projects still and moving images transmitted from an electronic device, such as a computer.

cellular phone
A portable, cordless telephone that operates via cellular radio signals and can be used over a wide area.

counter
A flat, raised surface over which a customer consults with a sales assistant.

light
A source of electric illumination such as a lamp or fixture.

shampoo
A thick liquid that is specially designed to clean human hair.

sales assistant
A person employed to assist customers in finding items and carrying out transactions.

customer
A person who seeks the services of a commercial establishment, such as a shopper in a retail store or a diner in a restaurant.

perfume
An odorous material that is very pleasant to the nose and is applied to the body so as to provide fragrance.

lipstick
A variety of cosmetic application that is meant to be applied to the lips so as to alter and magnify their color.

light
A source of electric illumination such as a lamp or fixture.

display
Furniture on which a collection of items for sale is arranged in a retail store.

sales assistant
A person employed to assist customers in finding items and carrying out transactions.

customer
A person who seeks the services of a commercial establishment, such as a shopper in a retail store or a diner in a restaurant.

laptop
A portable computer consisting of a monitor and keyboard attached with hinges that can be folded onto each other.

clothing store
A store specializing in clothing, typically also selling accessories such as belts, hats and bags.

hooks
Curved or looped pieces of metal that are attached to a wall and from which items can be hung.

curtain
A piece of fabric hung in front of a fitting room; it can be drawn to provide privacy.

hangers
Shoulder-shaped pieces of stiff material over which clothing can be draped and hung from a rod or hook.

fitting room
A small room in a clothing store in which a customer can try on clothing before making a decision to purchase it.

bench
A small, low piece of furniture that can be used as a seat or table, made of a hard substance such as wood or plastic.

full-length mirror
A reflective surface, usually composed of glass coated on one side with a metal compound, that is mounted on a wall.

display table
A table showcasing a collection of arranged items for sale in a retail store.

clothes rod
A long, mounted rod on which a number of hangers can be arranged for the display of clothing.

mannequin
A form used to display clothes.

shelves
Thin slabs of rigid material fixed horizontally to a wall or frame in order to store or display items.

checkout computer
A specialized computer device that is designed to process merchant transactions.

sales and merchandise area
The sales floor, where items are displayed and customers are assisted with their purchase decisions.

counter
A flat, raised surface over which a sales assistant conducts business with a customer.

bar
An establishment or area in a restaurant in which the primary fare served is alcoholic beverages and light snacks.

draft beer taps
Small taps attached to pipes through which beer from kegs can be poured directly.

patron
A person who visits a restaurant or other establishment that provides a service for a fee.

waitress
A woman employed to serve customers food and beverages directly at tableside.

bar counter
A long, smooth raised surface at which patrons sit in a bar to consume beverages.

bar stool
A seat supported on a tall pedestal or legs, usually padded and without a back, most often placed at or around a bar.

liquor bottle
Glass containers filled with spirits or other alcoholic beverages. They are usually displayed behind a bar.

coffee machine
An applicance used to brew fresh coffee, fitted with a flat, heated pan of metal on which cups can be warmed.

point-of-sale computer
A specialized computer device that is designed to ring up and process merchant transactions.

wine rack
A space fitted with compartments that hold wine bottles for display and easy access.

bartender
A person employed in a bar to prepare and serve beverages, usually alcoholic, from behind the bar counter.

rack of glasses
An assortment of glasses stacked and ready for use.

napkin dispenser
A small box that holds a stack of napkins that are dispensed individually from an open side.

refrigerator
An appliance with an insulated compartment kept artificially cool for the storage of perishable items.

restaurant
An establishment with a number of tables at which people can be served food and drinks for a fee.

grand piano
A large musical instrument with horizontal strings that are struck with hammers attached to a keyboard.

walk-in cooler
A small room kept at a low temperature in which perishable goods are stored, such as foods in a restaurant.

storage room
A small room in which goods are kept for later use, such as non-perishable supplies in a restaurant.

bus cart
A small table on wheels for carrying away used tableware in a restaurant.

kitchen
The room or area in a restaurant where food is prepared and plated for serving.

chef
A person who has been professionally trained to prepare food in a restaurant.

prep table
A smooth, raised surface where a chef prepares ingredients before cooking.

piano bar
A room or defined space in a restaurant or bar where patrons can listen to a piano player while eating and drinking.

bar counter
A long, smooth raised surface at which patrons sit in a bar to consume beverages.

bartender
A person employed in a bar to prepare and serve beverages, usually alcoholic, from behind the bar counter.

range hood
An appliance that is suspended over a stovetop, fitted with a fan to extract steam or smoke to the outdoors.

restroom
A room providing washing and toilet facilities for public use.

banquette
A long bench fitted against a wall in front of which tables are placed.

sink
A basin fitted with a tap and drain to collect water, usually made of metal or another hard, smooth material.

waitress
A woman employed to serve customers food and beverages directly at tableside.

dining room
A room or defined space in a restaurant containing seating arrangements at which customers are served.

checkroom attendant
A person employed to handle the temporary storage of customers' items in the checkroom.

checkroom
A room for temporary storage of customers' items, such as outerwear, large packages and strollers.

bar
An establishment or area in a restaurant in which the primary fare served is alcoholic beverages and light snacks.

headwaiter
A person employed in a restaurant to handle reservations and oversee the service staff and operations.

headwaiter station
A narrow, raised stand at which the headwaiter of a restaurant conducts business such as reservations.

bar stool
A seat supported on a tall pedestal or legs, usually padded and without a back, most often placed at or around a bar.

patron
A person who visits a restaurant or other establishment that provides a service for a fee.

menu stand
A narrow stand with a screen or page that lists the available fare, often including photos.

fast-food restaurant
A restaurant, usually with a counter and take-out services, that serves food that can be prepared quickly and easily.

cash register
A machine for monetary transactions with customers; often includes a drawer for cash and a terminal for card payments.

beverage dispenser
A small tap attached to a pipe through which a beverage, such as soda, can be poured directly into a cup.

menu board
A panel mounted on a wall that provides information about the foods available in an eatery.

salt and pepper shakers
Small vessels fitted with tops that have been perforated with tiny holes, used to sprinkle salt and pepper over food.

counter
A smooth raised surface from which customers in a retail establishment are served.

napkin dispenser
A small box that holds a stack of napkins that are dispensed individually from an open side.

waitress
A woman employed to serve customers food and beverages directly at tableside.

glasses
Drinking vessels made from, or partially made from, glass material.

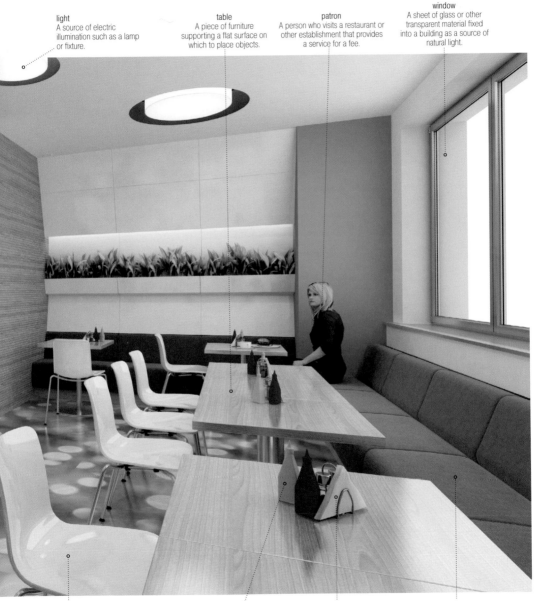

light
A source of electric illumination such as a lamp or fixture.

table
A piece of furniture supporting a flat surface on which to place objects.

patron
A person who visits a restaurant or other establishment that provides a service for a fee.

window
A sheet of glass or other transparent material fixed into a building as a source of natural light.

chair
A seat that includes a back, designed for individual use.

squeeze bottle
A plastic bottle fitted with a small-mouthed nozzle that can be squeezed to dispense condiments.

napkin holder
A small holder for a stack of napkins, designed for use by a single table of patrons.

banquette
A long bench fitted against a wall in front of which tables are placed.

reception
An area immediately past the front entrance of an establishment, where guests and visitors are serviced.

newspaper
A periodic publication, usually consisting of large folded sheets, containing informative articles and advertisements.

mural
A work of art painted or otherwise executed directly onto a wall, typically large in scale.

sofa
An upholstered seat with arms at either side and a back, long enough to accommodate more than one person.

potted plant
A plant displayed for decoration, kept in a pot and situated attractively.

entrance to stairs
A doorway leading to a stairway that allows access to other floors in a building.

table
A piece of furniture supporting a flat surface on which to place objects.

armchair
An upholstered, cushioned chair with arms.

luggage cart
A platform set on wheels, sometimes with raised sides, used to transport suitcases and other luggage.

porter
A person employed to carry items, such as luggage, for hotel guests.

elevator
A compartment attached to cables and a pulley mechanized to move people or cargo from floor to floor in a building.

elevator call button
A button that is pressed to signal that an elevator car is required on that floor.

guest
A patron in a hotel or other establishment offering overnight accommodations.

key cabinet
A set of labeled shelves built into the wall behind the reception counter in a hotel for the storage of room keys.

front desk clerk
A person who checks hotel guests into their rooms and provides other customer service duties.

RECEPTION

front entrance
The primary doorway into a building, usually facing the main road.

suitcase
A sturdy, typically rectangular container with a handle, in which items are stored when traveling.

trash can
An open container, often with a hinged lid, designed to collect and store waste for later disposal.

magazine stand
A tall, circular rack on which magazines are stood upright for display and ease of selection.

chair
A seat that includes a back, designed for individual use.

hotel room
A large closed chamber within a hotel that includes a sleeping area and a bathroom.

ventilation fan
A fan built into the wall or ceiling of a room to expel an accumulation of moisture or steam to the outside environment.

toilet paper
Absorbent, soft paper, usually in the form of small sheets on a roll, used to wipe oneself after using the toilet.

toilet
A washroom fixture with a seat and bowl, used to flush bodily waste down a pipe leading to a sewer or septic system.

flush buttons
Buttons that activate the toilet's flushing mechanism to various degrees, such as half-flush and full-flush.

toilet brush
A long handle with a bristly formation on the end used to clean the inner bowl of a toilet.

bathtub
A large basin fitted with a tap and a drain, usually made of porcelain or plastic, that is filled with water for bathing.

trash can
An open container, often with a hinged lid, designed to collect and store waste for later disposal.

towel
A piece of absorbent cloth used to remove moisture from one's body or hair.

mirror
A reflective surface usually composed of glass coated on one side with a metal compound.

sink
A basin fitted with a tap and drain to collect water, usually made of porcelain or another hard, smooth material.

bath mat
A small rug made of an absorbent material that covers a section of floor next to a bathtub, shower or sink.

front door
The main entrance to a space.

tiled floor
A floor clad with tiles, usually in a room that produces an accumulation of moisture or steam.

coat hook
A short, knobbed rod set into a wall from which outerwear or handbags can be hung.

shelf
A thin slab of rigid material fixed horizontally to a wall or frame in order to store items.

shower enclosure
An enclosed or partially enclosed space for containing the spray of water while showering.

closet
A small, enclosed recess in a room, typically used for everyday storage.

night table
A small table, usually with small drawers or shelves, that sits next to the head of a bed.

book
A set of printed pages bound together along a seam and sandwiched between covers made of a thicker paper.

newspaper
A periodic publication, usually consisting of large folded sheets, containing informative articles and advertisements.

bed
A piece of furniture composed of a mattress raised off the floor by a sturdy frame.

telephone
A communications device that converts acoustic vibrations to electrical signals, which in turn are converted to sound.

wall sconce
A light fixture attached to a wall by a decorative bracket.

remote control
An apparatus that emits electronic signals to manipulate the functions of an electronic device from a distance.

vase with flowers
A container holding cut flowers for decoration, often elongated and made of a fragile material such as glass.

curtain
A piece of fabric hung from the top of a window that can be drawn to form a shield from exterior light.

rug
A woven piece of material that covers an area of floor.

blanket
A soft fabric sheet that hotel guests use to keep warm at night. They are cleaned daily or between guest stays.

desk
A table with a worktop, typically including small drawers for storing materials such as paper and pens.

television
A device that transmits visual images to a screen and produces the corresponding sound via electrical waves.

desk chair
A chair used to accompany a desk.

laptop
A portable computer consisting of a monitor and keyboard attached with hinges that can be folded onto each other.

desk lamp
A small lamp that is placed on a table or desk to light a small area for close activities, such as reading or writing.

auditorium
A large room designed to accommodate events such as lectures, panel discussions and debates.

projector screen
A large sheet of firm, white material onto which images from a projector are displayed.

head table
A long table placed at the front of a room, usually on a raised platform, at which the people seated are the focal point.

podium
A stand with a flat, slanted top on which a speaker can rest printed materials during a presentation.

microphone
A device that amplifies vocalizations so that they can be projected over a larger area, such as for a lecture or concert.

gooseneck
A flexible arm that can be bent to adjust the position of the device's head.

grille
A section of wire mesh placed over a sensitive area of a device to protect it from external matter.

dais
A raised platform at the front of a large room on which the head table or podium is placed for the primary speakers.

indicator light
A tiny light built into an appliance to signal i'ts actively running.

power switch
A small switch that can be flipped or pressed to turn the electrical connection between a source and a device on or off.

control button
A button that is pressed to control a device's functions.

base
The lowest section of a structure, which rests on the ground or a surface or is supported by legs or a pedestal.

microphone
A device that amplifies vocalizations so that they can be projected over a larger area, such as for a lecture or concert.

video camera
An electronic device designed to capture moving images.

simultaneous interpretation booth
A booth in which translators listen to proceedings and simultaneously interpret the speech for foreign parties.

soundproof window
A sheet of tempered glass covering an opening in a room that has been treated to prevent the passage of sound.

conference table
A table in a conference hall that is fitted with a microphone and built-in power outlet to accommodate a participant.

desk chair
A seat with a back and sometimes armrests that can be used when sitting at a desk.

door
A rectangular entryway that allows conference attendees to readily enter or exit the hall as needed.

floor
The lower surface of a room or structure, kept dry and level to facilitate unimpeded walking.

Police department

A municipal service responsible for law enforcement and general public peacekeeping.

police officer
A person employed by the government to uphold the law, detect and prevent crime, and maintain overall public peace.

pocket
A small pouch sewn into the general design of a piece of clothing, in which small objects may be carried.

pistol
A small firearm that may be held in one hand, often kept in a holster attached to a belt on the body.

belt
A narrow length of sturdy cloth or leather that encircles the waist and is usually secured with a buckle.

holster
A pocket attached to a belt designed to securely hold a gun in a position in which it can be easily and quickly removed.

cap
A brimless hat with a visor that extends out above the face for shade and protection from weather.

jacket
A piece of outerwear designed to protect the upper body from cold, weather or other intrusive elements, such as fire.

buckle
A device used to secure the two ends of a belt; composed of a metal frame and hinged pin that fits into holes in the belt.

pants
A piece of clothing that is designed to cover each leg entirely and separately, over the buttocks and around the waist.

boot
A sturdy type of footwear that extends over the ankle, often over part of the leg, often tightened with laces.

POLICE

police car
A vehicle used by law enforcement personnel, fitted with equipment such as sirens and a scanner.

windshield
A large sheet of transparent, tempered glass covering the front window of a vehicle or aircraft.

light bar
A set of lights fitted atop an emergency vehicle that produces intermittent bursts of illumination in a pattern.

window
A sheet of tempered glass to provide visibility and as a source of natural light.

headlight
A light situated above the front bumper of a vehicle, used for illumination while driving in the dark.

bull bar
A strong metal frame attached to the front bumper of a vehicle to provide reinforcement against impact.

grille
A sheet of metal mesh on the front of a vehicle, covering the radiator to prevent debris from entering the engine.

door
A barrier that can be moved to gain access to an enclosed space, such as a vehicle.

bumper
A thick, protruding lip across the end of a vehicle designed to lessen the effect in case of impact.

rotor blade
A long, flat length of metal attached to a motor that causes it to rotate at great speed, such as on a helicopter.

rotor hub
The central part at the top of a helicopter, where the driveshaft and blades connect.

police helicopter
A helicopter that is specifically used by and designed for law enforcement agents; equipped with surveillance devices.

fuselage
The main physical structure, or shell, of an aircraft.

anti-torque tail rotor
Small rotating blades on the tail that provide additional control of movement and loft.

horizontal stabilizer
A horizontal structure on the tail assembly that is usually fixed and provides stability while flying.

searchlight
A powerful beam that is sent sweeping across a large area from above, often to assist in a search for lost persons.

door
A barrier that can be moved to gain access to an enclosed area, such as a helicopter fuselage.

skid
A long runner attached to the undercarriage of a helicopter that acts as the landing gear when at rest on the ground.

tail boom
A long portion of the fuselage of a helicopter extending back from the main body for balance and maneuverability.

mirror
A reflective surface usually composed of glass coated on one side with a metal compound.

windshield
A large sheet of transparent, tempered glass that is mounted as a vertical barrier in front of the handlebars of a motorcycle.

police motorcycle
A motorcycle that is equipped with a siren and computer and is used by law enforcement personnel.

beacon
A light, often colored, mounted on the rear of a vehicle that produces intermittent bursts of illumination in a pattern.

handlebars
Grips used to steer a two-wheeled vehicle by hand, attached via a series of bars to the front wheel.

seat
A flat surface designated for sitting.

fender
A sheet of metal curved to fit the wheel well of a vehicle to minimize splashing from the wheel.

crash bar
A curved rod attached vertically to the side of a motorcycle to prevent crushing in the case of falling over on the side.

footrest
A short, protruding rod on the lower side of a motorcycle where one's foot can be rested while in motion.

tire
An inflated ring-shaped wheel component made of rubber that connects the vehicle with the road, providing traction.

Fire department

A municipal service that is responsible for the emergency response to fires and other life-threatening situations.

firefighter
A person employed by a municipal government to fight fires and assist in other life-threatening emergency situations.

helmet
A hat made of a rigid material, such as plastic, designed to provide protection to the head in case of impact.

face mask
A device designed to protect the firefighter's face from water, fire, steam and other hazards.

reflective band
A strip of material sewn onto clothing that is highly reflective of light to be clearly visible in darkness.

turnouts
A water- and fire-resistant garment that firefighters wear to protect themselves.

rubber boot
A type of footwear made of water-resistant rubber that completely encloses the feet, ankles and calves.

storage compartment
A closed container built into another object for storage, such as on a fire truck to hold tools or first-aid supplies.

rearview mirror
A mirror mounted on a vehicle that allows the driver to see a reflection of the area beside and behind the vehicle.

fire truck: front view
A vehicle designed and equipped to deal with fires and other emergencies.

light bar
A set of lights fitted atop an emergency vehicle that produces intermittent bursts of illumination in a pattern.

blind-spot mirror
An extra mirror that is mounted on a vehicle, for example from the corner of the roof, to allow greater visibility.

grille
A sheet of metal mesh on the front of a vehicle covering the radiator to prevent debris from entering the engine.

spotlight
A powerful light beam mounted onto an emergency vehicle, such as a fire truck.

front step
A platform firefighters use to climb on and off the front pumper.

front outrigger
A device that can be deployed to stabilize the fire truck when the ladders are raised.

grab handle
A metal loop attached to the side of the truck that firefighters can grasp to stabilize themselves when climbing aboard.

650

water cannon
A pipe that emits a forceful jet of water, used by a fire truck to battle serious fires.

suction hose
A hollow tube through which water flows from the fire truck or a fire hydrant.

fire truck: back view
The rear view of a vehicle that is designed and equipped to deal with emergencies, in particular fires.

spotlight
A powerful light beam mounted onto an emergency vehicle, such as a fire truck.

storage compartment
A closed container built into another object for storage, such as on a fire truck to hold tools or first-aid supplies.

brake light
A red light above the rear bumper of a vehicle that is automatically lit by use of the brake pedal.

outrigger
A device on the fire truck's frame that can be deployed to support and stabilize the center of the vehicle.

window
A sheet of glass or other transparent material fixed into a structure as a source of natural light.

ladder
A structure made of two upright bars and a series of narrow steps evenly interspersed for climbing.

rear outrigger
A device on the fire truck's frame that can be deployed to support and stabilize the rear of the vehicle.

light
A source of electric illumination, a fixture such as on an emergency vehicle.

beacon
A light, often colored, mounted on the rear of a vehicle that produces intermittent bursts of illumination in a pattern.

step
A small, raised platform on which one stands to reach a higher level, a series of which can form a staircase.

storage compartment
A closed container built into another object for storage, such as on a fire truck to hold tools or first-aid supplies.

door
A barrier that can be moved to gain access to an enclosed space, such as a vehicle.

hydrant intake
A spout that is used to funnel water from a source such as a fire hydrant to the fire truck's tank.

control valve
A valve that can be adjusted to control the flow of water through the firefighter's hoses.

elevating cylinder
A device that operates under pressure to lift the fire truck's ladder and help keep it stable.

fire hydrant
An upright, brightly colored water pipe fixed into the street, designated strictly for use by emergency officials.

Information signs
Small placards displaying words or pictures to provide information for the public.

telephone
A sign to advise people of the location of a telephone.

post office
A sign to advise people of the location of a post office.

currency exchange
A sign to advise people of the location of currency exchange services.

first aid
A sign to advise people of the location of medical supplies or care.

lost and found
A sign to advise people of the location of services for lost items.

checkroom
A sign to advise people of the location of temporary storage services.

baggage lockers
A sign to advise people of the location of lockers for storing items such as luggage.

down escalator
A sign to advise people of the location of the downward-bound escalator.

up escalator
A sign to advise people of the location of the upward-bound escalator.

stairs
A sign to advise people of the location of stairs or a stairwell.

elevator
A sign to advise people of the location of an elevator.

men's restroom
A sign to advise people of the location of a men's restroom.

women's restroom
A sign to advise people of the location of a women's restroom.

restroom
A sign to advise people of the location of a restroom for public use.

baby changing area
A sign to advise people of the location of an area, typically enclosed, for changing diapers.

waiting room
A sign to advise people of the location of an area for waiting for one's turn to receive service.

information
A sign to advise people of the location of information services, such as tourist information.

lodging
A sign to advise people of the location of accomodations for lodging, such as a hotel.

airport
A sign to advise people of the location of an airport, whether domestic or international.

litter barrel
A sign to advise people of the location of a litter barrel, for disposing of trash.

taxi stand
A sign to advise people of the location of a taxi stand.

bus stop
A sign to advise people of the location of a bus stop, such as for a local or intercity bus.

ground transportation
A sign to advise people of the location of ground transportation services such as taxis and shuttle buses.

train station
A sign to advise people of the location of transportation by rail, whether passenger or freight train.

ferry terminal
A sign to advise people of the location of a terminal for transportation by water.

car rental
A sign to advise people of the location of services for renting vehicles.

restaurant
A sign to advise people of the location of an eatery.

coffee shop
A sign to advise people of the location of a coffee shop.

bar
A sign to advise people of the location of a bar.

baggage claim
A sign to advise people of the location of baggage handling services, whether automated or staffed.

parking
A sign to advise people of the location of a parking lot, whether automated or staffed.

smoking area
A sign to advise people of the location of a zone uniquely designated for smoking.

wheelchair access
A sign to advise people of the location of facilities, such as a restroom or entrance, accessible by wheelchair.

tent camping
A sign to advise people of the location of facilities for camping with a tent.

trailer camping
A sign to advise people of the location of facilities for camping with a trailer.

hospital
A sign to advise people of the location of a hospital, whether limited or full-service.

picnic area
A sign to advise people of the location of a picnic area, whether open-air or under a roof.

fire extinguisher
A sign to advise people of the location of a fire extinguisher, typically within a glass cupboard.

service station
A sign to advise people of the location of a service station, whether automated or staffed.

Wi-Fi zone
A sign to advise people of the location of an area offering access to a Wi-Fi signal, whether free or for a fee.

campfire area
A sign to advise people of the location of a spot uniquely designated for campfires.

automatic teller machine (ATM)
A sign to advise people of the location of an automated banking machine.

dog-walking area
A sign to advise people of the location of an area ideal for walking dogs.

swimming area
A sign to advise people of the location of an area where swimming is permitted and safe.

drinking water
A sign to advise people that the water source designated by the sign is potable.

video surveillance
A sign to advise people that video surveillance is being conducted, whether by a single or multiple cameras.

hiking trail
A sign to advise people of the location of a trail for hiking and similar activities.

auto mechanic
A sign to advise people that there is a mechanic available on the premises to service and repair vehicles.

Hazard signs

Small placards displaying words or pictures to warn the public of hazardous substances present.

corrosive to skin and metals
A sign that warns people that a substance is corrosive.

gases under pressure
A sign that warns people of an item that contains gases under pressure.

flammable materials, self-reactives, organic peroxides
A sign that warns people of a substance that can ignite or emit flammable gases.

explosives, self-reactives
A sign with an image of a detonation to warn people of the presence of substances that may explode.

aquatic toxicity
A sign that warns people that a substance could damage organisms if exposed to an aquatic environment.

oxidizers
A sign that warns people of a substance that is a danger when exposed to air.

health hazard
A sign that warns people that a substance is poisonous to humans.

acute toxicity
A sign that warns people that a substance is lethal to humans.

Workplace safety signs

Small placards displaying words or pictures to warn workers and visitors that precautionary measures are required.

eye protection
A sign to advise people that protective eyewear is required in the area indicated.

respiratory system protection
A sign to advise people that a protective device for the respiratory system is required in the area indicated.

foot protection
A sign to advise people that foot protection is required in the area indicated.

hand protection
A sign to advise people that hand protection is required in the area indicated.

head protection
A sign to advise people that head protection is required in the area indicated.

protective clothing
A sign to advise people that protective clothing is required in the area indicated.

face shield
A sign to advise people that a face shield is required in the area indicated.

ear protection
A sign to advise people that ear protection is required in the area indicated.

Warning signs
Small placards displaying words or pictures to warn the public of hazardous conditions.

poison
A sign to warn people that the indicated substance is poisonous to humans.

radioactive
A sign to warn people that the indicated substance is radioactive.

irritant
A sign to warn people of the presence of substances that can adversely affect health.

flammable
A sign to warn people of the presence of substances that are highly flammable.

magnetic field
A sign to warn people of the presence of magnetic material or a moving electric charge.

high voltage
A sign to warn people of the presence of exposed electrical currents.

slippery
A sign to advise people that a surface is unsafe to walk upon due to slippery conditions.

corrosive to skin and metals
A sign to warn people that the indicated substance causes chemical burns to skin and metals.

Prohibition signs
Small placards displaying words or pictures to warn the public of actions that are strictly prohibited.

not drinking water
A sign to advise people that the water supply indicated is not potable.

cell phone use prohibited
A sign to advise people that the use of cell phones is strictly prohibited in the area indicated.

no open flame
A sign to advise people that open flames are dangerous in the area indicated and are thus prohibited.

photography prohibited
A sign to advise people that photography is strictly prohibited in the area indicated.

no smoking
A sign to advise people that smoking is strictly prohibited in the area indicated.

pets prohibited
A sign to advise people that animals are strictly prohibited from entering the area indicated.

no access
A sign to warn people that entering a particular area is strictly prohibited and considered trespassing.

stop
A sign used in industrial settings to indicate that access to the specified area is prohibited.

Emergency signs

Small placards displaying words or pictures to provide information for the public during an emergency.

first aid
A sign to advise people of the location of first-aid medical care or supplies.

emergency telephone
A sign to advise people of the location of a telephone that can be used for emergency calls.

assembly point
A sign to advise people of the location in which to gather during an emergency.

automated external defibrillator (AED)
A sign to advise people of the location of an available defibrillator in case of cardiac emergency.

eye wash station
A sign to advise people of the location of an eye wash station.

doctor
A sign to advise people of the location of emergency medical assistance.

in case of emergency break glass
A sign to advise people of the method of access to a lever that sets off an alarm, such as in case of fire.

emergency exit
A sign to advise people of the location of an exit used only in case of emergency.

Fire safety signs

Small placards displaying words or pictures to provide information for the public in case of fire.

fire hose
A sign to advise people of the location of an emergency water hose to use in case of fire.

ladder
A sign to advise people of the location of a ladder designated for use only in case of emergency.

fire extinguisher
A sign to advise people of the location of a fire extinguisher, typically kept in a glass cabinet.

fire alarm
A sign that advises people of the availability of a fire alarm that can be manually activated.

fire-fighting equipment
A sign to advise people of the location of protective equipment that can be used in case of a fire.

emergency phone
A sign to advise people of the location of a telephone that can be used for emergency calls.

directional arrow
A sign to direct people along the designated path of evacuation in case of an emergency.

Asia

The largest continent, both in land mass and population, located in the eastern and northern hemispheres.

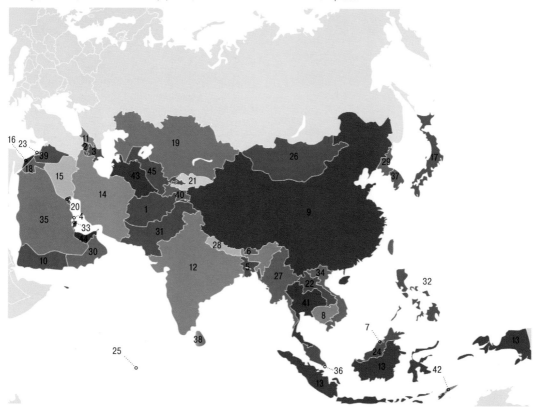

Afghanistan
The flag of Afghanistan, a landlocked country located across Central and South Asia, whose capital is Kabul.

Armenia
The flag of Armenia, a country along the borders of Western Asia and Eastern Europe, whose capital is Yerevan.

Azerbaijan
The flag of Azerbaijan, a country along the borders of Eastern Europe and Western Asia, whose capital is Baku.

Bahrain
The flag of Bahrain, a small archipelago country off the Western shores of the Persian Gulf, whose capital is Manama.

Bangladesh
The flag of Bangladesh, a country in South Asia containing the world's largest delta, whose capital is Dhaka.

Bhutan
The flag of Bhutan, a country in South Asia, whose capital is Thimphu.

Brunei
The flag of Brunei, a sovereign state on the island of Borneo in Southeast Asia, whose capital is Bandar Seri Begawan.

Cambodia
The flag of Cambodia, a country at the south of the Indochina Peninsula in Southeast Asia, whose capital is Phnom Penh.

Republic of China
The flag of the Republic of China, a large country in East Asia, whose capital is Beijing.

Yemen
The flag of Yemen, a country in the southwestern part of the Arabian peninsula, whose capital is Sana'a.

11
Georgia
The flag of Georgia, a country located along the borders of Western Asia and Eastern Europe, whose capital is Tbilisi.

12
India
The flag of India, a large country located in South Asia, whose capital is New Delhi.

13
Indonesia
The flag of Indonesia, a country consisting of islands across Southeast Asia and Oceania, whose capital is Jakarta.

14
Iran
The flag of Iran, a country in Western Asia with coastlines on the Caspian Sea and Indian Ocean, whose capital is Tehran.

15
Iraq
The flag of Iraq, a country in Western Asia with an outlet on the Persian Gulf, whose capital is Baghdad.

16
Israel
The flag of Israel, a country in Western Asia on the Mediterranean Sea.

17
Japan
The flag of Japan, an island nation in East Asia in the Pacific Ocean, whose capital is Tokyo.

18
Jordan
The flag of Jordan, a country in Western Asia located east of the Jordan River, whose capital is Amman.

19
Kazakhstan
The flag of Kazakhstan, a country that extends from the Caspian Sea to the Altai Mountains, whose capital is Astana.

20
Kuwait
The flag of Kuwait, a country in Western Asia on the northwestern coast of the Persian Gulf, whose capital is Kuwait City.

21
Kyrgyzstan
The flag of Kyrgyzstan, a mountainous country in Central Asia, whose capital is Bishkek.

22
Laos
The flag of Laos, a landlocked country in Southeast Asia, whose capital is Vientiane.

23
Lebanon
The flag of Lebanon, a country in Western Asia with a coastline on the Mediterranean Sea, whose capital is Beirut.

24
Federation of Malaysia
The flag of the Federation of Malaysia, a country in Southeast Asia, whose capital is Kuala Lumpur.

25
Maldives
The flag of Maldives, an archipelago country situated in the Indian Ocean and Arabian Sea, whose capital is Malé.

26
Mongolia
The flag of Mongolia, a landlocked country in East-Central Asia, whose capital is Ulan Bator.

27
Myanmar
The flag of Myanmar, a country in Southeast Asia on the Bay of Bengal, whose capital is Naypyidaw.

28
Nepal
The flag of Nepal, a country in the Himalayas of South Asia, whose capital is Kathmandu.

29
North Korea
The flag of North Korea, a country located in the northern part of the peninsula of Korea, whose capital is Pyongyang.

30
Oman
The flag of Oman, a country situated at the mouth of the Persian Gulf in Southwest Asia, whose capital is Muscat.

31
Pakistan
The flag of Pakistan, a country on the Arabian Sea in South Asia, whose capital is Islamabad.

32
Philippines
The flag of the Philippines, an island country in Southeast Asia in the Pacific Ocean, whose capital is Manila.

33
Qatar
The flag of Qatar, a country in Western Asia on the western coast of the Persian Gulf, whose capital is Doha.

34
Vietnam
The flag of Vietnam, the easternmost country on the Indochina Peninsula in Southeast Asia, whose capital is Hanoi.

35
Saudi Arabia
The flag of Saudi Arabia, a country that spans most of the Arabian peninsula, whose capital is Riyadh.

36
Singapore
The flag of Singapore, an island country in Southeast Asia, whose capital is Singapore City.

37
South Korea
The flag of South Korea, a country located in the southern part of the peninsula of Korea, whose capital is Seoul.

38
Sri Lanka
The flag of Sri Lanka, an island country in South Asia in the north Indian Ocean, whose capital is Colombo.

39
Syria
The flag of Syria, a country in Western Asia on the eastern Mediterranean Sea, whose capital is Damascus.

40
Tajikistan
The flag of Tajikistan, a country in Central Asia mostly consisting of mountains, whose capital is Dushanbe.

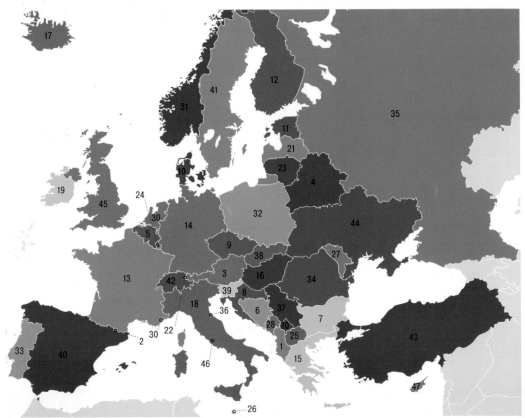

Thailand
The flag of Thailand, a country at the center of the Indochina Peninsula in Southeast Asia, whose capital is Bangkok.

East Timor
The flag of East Timor, a country on an island in the southern part of the Malay Archipelago, whose capital is Dili.

Turkmenistan
The flag of Turkmenistan, a country situated between the Caspian Sea and Afghanistan, whose capital is Ashgabat.

United Arab Emirates
The flag of the United Arab Emirates, a country in the southeast of the Arabian Peninsula, whose capital is Abu Dhabi.

Uzbekistan
The flag of Uzbekistan, a country in Central Asia, south and southeast of the Aral Sea, whose capital is Tashkent.

Europe
A continent located on the westernmost peninsula of Eurasia.

1

Albania
The flag of Albania, a country in Southeastern Europe, whose capital is Tirana.

2

Andorra
The flag of Andorra, a small country in the Pyrenees of Southwestern Europe, whose capital is Andorra la Vella.

3

Austria
The flag of Austria, a country located in the Alps of Central Europe, whose capital is Vienna.

4

Belarus
The flag of Belarus, a largely forested country in Eastern Europe, whose capital is Minsk.

5

Belgium
The flag of Belgium, a country in Western Europe on the southern shore of the North Sea, whose capital is Brussels.

6

Bosnia and Herzegovina
The flag of Bosnia and Herzegovina, a country in Southeastern Europe, whose capital is Sarajevo.

7

Bulgaria
The flag of Bulgaria, a country on the western shores of the Black Sea, whose capital is Sofia.

8

Croatia
The flag of Croatia, a country situated along the borders of Central and Southeastern Europe, whose capital is Zagreb.

9

Czech Republic
The flag of the Czech Republic, a country in Central Europe, whose capital is Prague.

10

Denmark
The flag of Denmark, a country in Northern Europe and including many islands, whose capital is Copenhagen.

11

Estonia
The flag of Estonia, a country in the Baltic region of Northern Europe, whose capital is Tallinn.

12

Finland
The flag of Finland, a country in Northern Europe, whose capital is Helsinki.

13

France
The flag of France, a country in Western Europe with several overseas regions and territories, whose capital is Paris.

14

Germany
The flag of Germany, a country overlapping Western and Central Europe, whose capital is Berlin.

15

Greece
The flag of Greece, a country in Southern Europe and including many islands, whose capital is Athens.

16

Hungary
The flag of Hungary, a country in Central Europe, whose capital is Budapest.

17

Iceland
The flag of Iceland, an island country located just south of the Arctic Circle, whose capital is Reykjavik.

18

Italy
The flag of Italy, a peninsular country in Southern Europe, whose capital is Rome.

19

Ireland
The flag of Ireland, an island country in the North Atlantic, whose capital is Dublin.

20

Kosovo
The flag of Kosovo, a country in Southeastern Europe, whose capital is Pristina.

21

Latvia
The flag of Latvia, a country in the Baltic region of Northern Europe, whose capital is Riga.

22

Liechtenstein
The flag of Liechtenstein, a small alpine country in Central Europe, whose capital is Vaduz.

23

Lithuania
The flag of Lithuania, a country on the southeastern shore of the Baltic Sea in Northern Europe, whose capital is Vilnius.

24

Luxembourg
The flag of Luxembourg, a small country in Western Europe.

25

Macedonia
The flag of Macedonia, a country in the central Balkan peninsula in Southeast Europe, whose capital is Skopje.

26

Malta
The flag of Malta, an archipelago country in Southern Europe in the Mediterranean Sea, whose capital is Valletta.

27

Moldova
The flag of Moldova, a landlocked country in Eastern Europe, whose capital is Chisinau.

28

Monaco
The flag of Monaco, a small country on the French Riviera in Western Europe, whose capital is Monaco.

29

Montenegro
The flag of Montenegro, a country on the Adriatic Sea in Southeastern Europe, whose capital is Podgorica.

30

Netherlands
The flag of the Netherlands, a country in Western Europe and with Caribbean islands, whose capital is Amsterdam.

Norway
The flag of Norway, a Scandinavian country in Northern Europe, parts of the Arctic and Antarctica, whose capital is Oslo.

Poland
The flag of Poland, a country in Central Europe, whose capital is Warsaw.

Portugal
The flag of Portugal, a country in westernmost Europe on the Iberian peninsula, whose capital is Lisbon.

Romania
The flag of Romania, a country in Southeastern and Central Europe on the Black Sea, whose capital is Bucharest.

Russia
The flag of Russia, a country spanning Northern Asia and Eastern Europe, whose capital is Moscow.

San Marino
The flag of San Marino, a small country in Europe surrounded by Italy, whose capital is the City of San Marino.

Serbia
The flag of Serbia, a landlocked country along the borders of Central and Southeast Europe, whose capital is Belgrade.

Slovakia
The flag of Slovakia, a country in Central Europe, whose capital is Bratislava.

Slovenia
The flag of Slovenia, a mountainous country in southern Central Europe on the Adriatic Sea, whose capital is Ljubljana.

Spain
The flag of Spain, a country in Southwestern Europe on the Iberian Peninsula, whose capital is Madrid.

Sweden
The flag of Sweden, a Scandinavian country in Northern Europe, whose capital is Stockholm.

Switzerland
The flag of Switzerland, a country in Western and Central Europe, whose capital is Bern.

Turkey
The flag of Turkey, a country primarily in Western Asia and partly in Southeastern Europe, whose capital is Ankara.

Ukraine
The flag of Ukraine, a country in Eastern Europe situated north of the Black Sea, whose capital is Kiev.

United Kingdom
The flag of the United Kingdom of Great Britain and Northern Ireland, a country whose capital is London.

Vatican City
The flag of Vatican City, a country and the seat of government of the Roman Catholic Church, whose capital is Vatican City.

Cyprus
The flag of Cyprus, a large island country in the Eastern Mediterranean Sea, whose capital is Nicosia.

Africa
A continent that stretches from northern to southern temperate zones, spanning either side of the equator.

Algeria
The flag of Algeria, a country in North Africa on the Mediterranean coast, whose capital is Algiers.

Angola
The flag of Angola, a country in Southern Africa, whose capital is Luanda.

Benin
The flag of Benin, a sub-Saharan country in West Africa, whose capital is Porto-Novo.

Botswana
The flag of Botswana, a country in Southern Africa, whose capital is Gaborone.

Burkina Faso
The flag of Burkina Faso, a landlocked country in West Africa, whose capital is Ouagadougou.

Burundi
The flag of Burundi, a landlocked country in Southeast Africa, whose capital is Bujumbura.

Cameroon
The flag of Cameroon, a country in Central Africa, whose capital is Yaoundé.

Cape Verde
The flag of Cape Verde, an island country off the coast of Western Africa in the Atlantic Ocean, whose capital is Praia.

Central African Republic
The flag of the Central African Republic, a landlocked country in Central Africa, whose capital is Bangui.

Chad
The flag of Chad, a country in Central Africa, whose capital is N'Djamena.

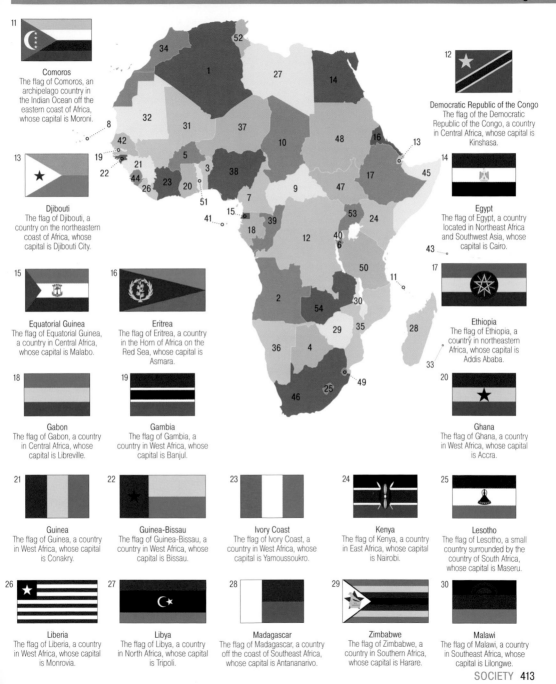

11 Comoros
The flag of Comoros, an archipelago country in the Indian Ocean off the eastern coast of Africa, whose capital is Moroni.

13 Djibouti
The flag of Djibouti, a country on the northeastern coast of Africa, whose capital is Djibouti City.

15 Equatorial Guinea
The flag of Equatorial Guinea, a country in Central Africa, whose capital is Malabo.

16 Eritrea
The flag of Eritrea, a country in the Horn of Africa on the Red Sea, whose capital is Asmara.

18 Gabon
The flag of Gabon, a country in Central Africa, whose capital is Libreville.

19 Gambia
The flag of Gambia, a country in West Africa, whose capital is Banjul.

12 Democratic Republic of the Congo
The flag of the Democratic Republic of the Congo, a country in Central Africa, whose capital is Kinshasa.

14 Egypt
The flag of Egypt, a country located in Northeast Africa and Southwest Asia, whose capital is Cairo.

17 Ethiopia
The flag of Ethiopia, a country in northeastern Africa, whose capital is Addis Ababa.

20 Ghana
The flag of Ghana, a country in West Africa, whose capital is Accra.

21 Guinea
The flag of Guinea, a country in West Africa, whose capital is Conakry.

22 Guinea-Bissau
The flag of Guinea-Bissau, a country in West Africa, whose capital is Bissau.

23 Ivory Coast
The flag of Ivory Coast, a country in West Africa, whose capital is Yamoussoukro.

24 Kenya
The flag of Kenya, a country in East Africa, whose capital is Nairobi.

25 Lesotho
The flag of Lesotho, a small country surrounded by the country of South Africa, whose capital is Maseru.

26 Liberia
The flag of Liberia, a country in West Africa, whose capital is Monrovia.

27 Libya
The flag of Libya, a country in North Africa, whose capital is Tripoli.

28 Madagascar
The flag of Madagascar, a country off the coast of Southeast Africa, whose capital is Antananarivo.

29 Zimbabwe
The flag of Zimbabwe, a country in Southern Africa, whose capital is Harare.

30 Malawi
The flag of Malawi, a country in Southeast Africa, whose capital is Lilongwe.

Mali
The flag of Mali, a country in West Africa, whose capital is Bamako.

Mauritania
The flag of Mauritania, a Saharan country in North Africa, whose capital is Nouakchott.

Mauritius
The flag of Mauritius, a country in the Indian Ocean off the coast of Africa, whose capital is Port Louis.

Morocco
The flag of Morocco, a country in North Africa, whose capital is Rabat.

Mozambique
The flag of Mozambique, a country in Southeast Africa, whose capital is Maputo.

Namibia
The flag of Namibia, a country in Southern Africa, whose capital is Windhoek.

Niger
The flag of Niger, a country in West Africa, whose capital is Niamey.

Nigeria
The flag of Nigeria, a country in West Africa, whose capital is Abuja.

Republic of the Congo
The flag of the Republic of the Congo, an equatorial country in Central Africa, whose capital is Brazzaville.

Rwanda
The flag of Rwanda, an equatorial country in Central and East Africa, whose capital is Kigali.

São Tomé and Príncipe
The flag of São Tomé and Príncipe, an archipelago country in the Gulf of Guinea; its capital is São Tomé.

Senegal
The flag of Senegal, a country in West Africa, whose capital is Dakar.

Seychelles
The flag of Seychelles, an archipelago country in the Indian Ocean; its capital is Victoria.

Sierra Leone
The flag of Sierra Leone, a country in West Africa, whose capital is Freetown.

Somalia
The flag of Somalia, a country in the Horn of Africa, whose capital is Mogadishu.

South Africa
The flag of South Africa, a country at the south tip of Africa, whose capitals are Pretoria, Cape Town and Bloemfontein.

South Sudan
The flag of South Sudan, a country in Northeastern Africa, whose capital is Juba.

Sudan
The flag of Sudan, a country in North Africa in the Nile Valley, whose capital is Khartoum.

Swaziland
The flag of Swaziland, a country in Southern Africa, whose capitals are Lobamba and Mbabane.

Tanzania
The flag of Tanzania, a country in East Africa, whose capital is Dodoma.

Togo
The flag of Togo, a small sub-Saharan country in West Africa, whose capital is Lomé.

Tunisia
The flag of Tunisia, the northernmost country in Africa, whose capital is Tunis.

Uganda
The flag of Uganda, an equatorial country in East Africa, whose capital is Kampala.

Zambia
The flag of Zambia, a landlocked country in Southern Africa, whose capital is Lusaka.

North America

A continent in the northern and western hemispheres, bordered by the Arctic, Atlantic and Pacific Oceans.

Antigua & Barbuda
The flag of Antigua & Barbuda, twin islands between the Caribbean Sea and Atlantic Ocean, whose capital is Saint John's.

Bahamas
The flag of the Bahamas, an island country in the Atlantic Ocean southeast of the U.S., whose capital is Nassau.

Barbados
The flag of Barbados, an island country in the northern Atlantic Ocean, whose capital is Bridgetown.

Belize
The flag of Belize, a country in Central America, whose capital is Belmopan.

Canada
The flag of Canada, a country in northern North America, whose capital is Ottawa.

Costa Rica
The flag of Costa Rica, a country in Central America, whose capital is San José.

Cuba
The flag of Cuba, the largest island in the Caribbean, whose capital is Havana.

Dominica
The flag of Dominica, an island country in the Caribbean, whose capital is Roseau.

Dominican Republic
The flag of the Dominican Republic, a country on the Caribbean island of Hispaniola, whose capital is Santo Domingo.

El Salvador
The flag of El Salvador, the smallest country in Central America, whose capital is San Salvador.

Grenada
The flag of Grenada, an island country in the Caribbean, whose capital is St. George's.

Guatemala
The flag of Guatemala, a country in Central America, whose capital is Guatemala City.

Haiti
The flag of Haiti, a country on the Caribbean island of Hispaniola, whose capital is Port-au-Prince.

Honduras
The flag of Honduras, a country in Central America, whose capital is Tegucigalpa.

Jamaica
The flag of Jamaica, an island country in the Greater Antilles of the Caribbean, whose capital is Kingston.

Mexico
The flag of Mexico, a country in southern North America, whose capital is Mexico City.

Nicaragua
The flag of Nicaragua, the largest country in Central America, whose capital is Managua.

Panama
The flag of Panama, the southernmost country in Central America, whose capital is Panama City.

Saint Kitts-Nevis
The flag of Saint Kitts-Nevis, a two-island country in the West Indies, whose capital is Basseterre.

Saint Lucia
The flag of Saint Lucia, an island country in the Caribbean, bordering the Atlantic Ocean, whose capital is Castries.

Saint Vincent and the Grenadines
The flag of Saint Vincent and the Grenadines, an archipelago country in the Caribbean, whose capital is Kingstown.

United States of America
The flag of the United States of America, located in the middle of North America, whose capital is Washington, D.C.

South America

A continent in the western and southern hemispheres, mostly in the tropics.

Argentina
The flag of Argentina, a country in southeastern South America, whose capital is Buenos Aires.

Bolivia
The flag of Bolivia, a country in western-central South America, whose capital is La Paz.

Chile
The flag of Chile, a long, narrow country in South America on the Pacific Ocean, whose capital is Santiago.

Ecuador
The flag of Ecuador, a country in northwestern South America, including the Galápagos Islands, whose capital is Quito.

Paraguay
The flag of Paraguay, a landlocked country in South America, whose capital is Asunción.

Venezuela
The flag of Venezuela, a country in northern South America, whose capital is Caracas.

Brazil
The flag of Brazil, the largest country in South America, whose capital is Brasília.

Colombia
The flag of Colombia, a country in northwest South America, whose capital is Bogotá.

Guyana
The flag of Guyana, a country in the northeast of South America, whose capital is Georgetown.

Peru
The flag of Peru, a country in western South America, whose capital is Lima.

Suriname
The flag of Suriname, a country in northeastern South America, whose capital is Paramaribo.

Trinidad and Tobago
The flag of Trinidad and Tobago, a twin-island country off South America in the Caribbean, whose capital is Port of Spain.

Uruguay
The flag of Uruguay, a country in southeastern South America, whose capital is Montevideo.

Australia and Oceania
Islands in the South Pacific; the smallest of the seven traditional continents.

Australia
The flag of Australia, a country including the mainland Australian continent and islands, whose capital is Canberra.

Federated States of Micronesia
The flag of the Federated States of Micronesia, an island nation in the Western Pacific Ocean, whose capital is Palikir.

Fiji
The flag of Fiji, an island country in the South Pacific Ocean, whose capital is Suva.

Kiribati
The flag of Kiribati, an island country in the central tropical Pacific Ocean, whose capital is South Tarawa.

Marshall Islands
The flag of the Marshall Islands, a country in the northern Pacific Ocean, whose capital is Majuro.

Nauru
The flag of Nauru, the smallest island country in the South Pacific, whose capital is Yaren.

New Zealand
The flag of New Zealand, an island country in the southwestern Pacific Ocean, whose capital is Wellington.

Palau
The flag of Palau, an island country in the western Pacific Ocean, whose capital is Ngerulmud, Melekeok State.

Papua New Guinea
The flag of Papua New Guinea, an Oceanian country on the island of New Guinea, whose capital is Port Moresby.

Samoa
The flag of Samoa, an Oceanian country made up of islands in the South Pacific Ocean, whose capital is Apia.

Solomon Islands
The flag of the Solomon Islands, an Oceanian country east of Papua New Guinea, whose capital is Honiara.

Tonga
The flag of Tonga, a Polynesian archipelago country in the southern Pacific Ocean, whose capital is Nuku'alofa.

Tuvalu
The flag of Tuvalu, a Polynesian island country in the Pacific between Hawaii and Australia, whose capital is Funafuti.

Vanuatu
The flag of Vanuatu, an Oceanian island country in the South Pacific Ocean near New Guinea, whose capital is Port Vila.

International organizations
Organizations with a membership composed of various countries across the world, founded for specific purposes.

United Nations
An international organization established to promote intergovernmental cooperation, primarily to prevent a world war.

European Union
A political and economic union of European countries, with free trade among members and uniform tariffs for outsiders.

International Olympic Committee
A Swiss non-profit non-governmental organization with international members dedicated to organizing the Olympic Games.

money counter
A machine used to count paper money or coins quickly and accurately.

function keys
One of several buttons used to choose various options, such as the account and the amount of the transaction.

deposit slot
The area of the automatic teller machine where financial deposits may be inserted so as to be processed.

automatic teller machine (ATM)
A computerized terminal that can be used to deposit or withdraw money or to check account details.

LEXI24 Cashpoint

Cashpoint
Please insert your card

dollar
The typographical representation that refers to the American dollar.

euro
The typographical representation that refers to the European euro.

pound
The typographical representation that refers to the British pound.

alphanumeric keypad
A type of keyboard that is used by patrons to input numbers or letters in the device.

cash dispenser
The area of the automatic teller machine where notes are dispensed to the user of the machine.

card reader slot
The area of the automatic teller machine where an individual's debit or credit card may be inserted.

check
A form of legal tender that can be cashed at a bank or similar financial facility. It is guaranteed with a signature.

financial institution
A graphical representation of the banking organization upon which an order of payment is drawn.

date of issue
The date on which the funds can be withdrawn from the account.

stack of bills
A collected assortment of bills that are neatly amassed together to facilitate ease of transportation.

LEXI24

DATE 2014/02/25

PAY TO THE ORDER OF   A. X. Corporation $ 100.00

one hundred dollars only   DOLLARS

John Smith
AUTHORIZED SIGNATURE

00164464 4641 0473 7089

payee
The name of the person who is designated as the receiver of the funds being withdrawn.

signature of drawer
The signature of the person to whom the account belongs, who is authorizing the withdrawal.

amount of currency
The exact amount of money that can be withdrawn from the account.

FEDERAL BANK
100
E31119560F
ONE HUNDRED DOLLARS

paper money
Legal tender in the form of strips of paper. Common denominations include 5, 10, 20, 50 and 100.

50 PENNIES 50¢

roll of pennies
A stack of one hundred pennies that are encased in a cylinder of paper to provide ease of transportation.

chip
The small elecrtonic chip that processes and transmits credit card transactions.

card number
The series of numbers on the front of the card that are used to identify accounts.

credit card: front view
A view of the front side of the credit card. This is the area of the card that displays the credit card number.

magnetic strip
The thin magnetic strip located on the back of the credit card that allows the card to be read.

credit card: back view
A view of the back side of the credit card. This is the area of the card that contains the magnetic strip.

cardholder's name
The area below the card number where the cardholder's name is printed for identification purposes.

expiration date
The area of the credit card where the card's expiration date is listed to serve as a reminder.

holder's signature
The area located on the back of the credit card where the cardholder's name is to be signed.

security code
A security confirmation number that is located on the back of the card. It is used to authorize purchases.

electronic payment terminal
A small electronic and portable device that merchants use to read and process credit cards for payment.

transaction receipt
A small slip of paper on which the details of the transaction are outlined.

display
A small plastic bag composed of recyclable materials that is commonly used in markets to collect products.

debit card
A specialized variety of transaction card that is linked to a bank account and bears no line of credit.

operation key
One of several buttons used to choose various options, such as the account from which to take the payment.

alphanumeric keypad
A type of keyboard that is used by patrons to input numbers or letters in the device.

credit card
A small plastic card used as for payments based on a specific loan agreement with a financial instituion.

card reader slot
The area of the electronic payment terminal that is used to read a card to process payment.

pistol
A firearm that can be held in one hand, often kept in a holster.

front sight
A small raised piece on the tip of the barrel of a gun that is aligned with a rear sight when aiming.

barrel
The component of the pistol that is designed so that a bullet may be spun and propelled through its chamber.

takedown lever
A small metal piece on the side of a gun that can be moved outward to block, or inward to release, the slide.

rear sight
A small raised piece on the rearmost end of a gun with a slit that is aligned with the foresight when aiming.

hammer
A small piece on a gun that is drawn back and swung forward when the trigger is pulled to initiate the firing mechanism.

muzzle
The opening at the end of a gun's barrel from which the bullet or other projectile is ejected with great force.

slide
A section along a pistol barrel that can be pushed to load a bullet into fire ready position.

trigger
A protruding piece on a device that can be squeezed to set off a mechanism, often to eject material, such as on a gun.

safety catch
A small piece on a gun that can be depressed to lock the firing mechanism when the gun is not in use.

magazine
A hollow device that slides into the pistol's butt; it holds the cartridges and feeds them into the barrel.

trigger guard
A thin metallic shield that surrounds the periphery of the rifle's trigger so that the gun cannot be accidentally fired.

grip panel
A patterned section on the grip of a gun to provide traction for the hand to prevent slippage.

cartridge case
The tubular section of a cartridge which contains the gunpowder.

magazine catch
A small protrusion on a gun that can be pressed to eject the clip from the magazine for reloading.

butt
The part of a pistol that is held when aiming and firing.

magazine
A hollow device that slides into the pistol's butt; it holds the cartridges and feeds them into the barrel.

bullet
The pointed or rounded end of a large projectile that is ejected from a firearm and is sometimes designed to detonate on impact.

cylinder
A round section on a revolver which holds bullets in individual slots and rotates to move a bullet into firing position.

barrel
The elongated, cylindrical piece on a firearm through which the bullet or cartridge travels before being fired from the muzzle.

front sight
A small raised piece on the tip of the barrel of a gun that is aligned with a rear sight when aiming.

revolver
A handgun with a cylinder that rotates to place a bullet into firing position.

hammer
A small piece on a gun which is drawn back and swung forward when the trigger is pulled to initiate the firing mechanism.

muzzle
The opening at the end of a gun's barrel from which the bullet or other projectile is ejected with great force.

butt
The part of a gun that is held when aiming and firing; it often has finger grooves.

trigger guard
A strip of metal that creates a frame around the trigger of a firearm to prevent accidental contact with the trigger.

trigger
A protruding piece on a device that can be squeezed to set off a mechanism, often to eject material, such as on a gun.

front sight housing
A small raised piece on the tip of the barrel of a gun that is aligned with a rear sight when aiming.

gas tube
Slits or holes in a rifle that allow the accumulation of heat and gases to be released.

rear sight
A small, raised piece toward the back of a gun that is aligned with the foresight when aiming.

trigger
A protruding piece on a device that can be squeezed to set off a mechanism, often to eject material, such as on a gun.

safety lever
A small piece on a rifle that can be adjusted to lock or adjust the behavior of the firing mechanism.

assault rifle
A long-barreled firearm that ejects bullets one after another in rapid bursts as long as the trigger is depressed.

barrel
The elongated, cylindrical piece on a firearm through which the bullet or cartridge travels before being fired from the muzzle.

handguard
The section of a rifle between the barrel and the trigger that is held to keep the muzzle raised and aimed.

pistol grip
The section near the butt of a rifle, close to the trigger, that is held when aiming and firing.

stock
The rearmost part of a rifle, often made of wood, which rests against the shoulder when firing.

cartridge
A small enclosed tube that contains gunpowder and is capped with a pointed nose that detonates upon impact.

bullet
A small projectile that is ejected from a firearm and is sometimes designed to detonate on impact.

magazine
A hollow device that holds the cartridges and feeds them into the barrel.

cartridge case
The tubular section of a cartridge that contains the gunpowder.

primer
The blunt end of a cartridge which is struck by the hammer of a firearm, such as a rifle.

assault rifle with folding stock
A long-barreled firearm that ejects bullets one after another in rapid bursts as long as the trigger is depressed.

light machine gun
A long-barreled firearm that can eject bullets one after another in rapid bursts or fire single bullets.

rocket-propelled grenade (RPG) and launcher
A long-barreled weapon designed to launch small bombs by means of propulsion created by fuel combustion.

breech
The end of the bore of a weapon which can be opened for the insertion of a projectile or other material, such as fuel.

rear grip
A secondary grip that is held when aiming and firing to provide extra stability.

optical sight
A rear sight that is digitalized to provide information regarding aim and distance.

barrel
The elongated, cylindrical piece on a firearm through which the bullet or cartridge travels before being fired from the muzzle.

front sight
A small raised piece on the tip of the barrel of a gun that is aligned with a rear sight when aiming.

trigger
A protruding piece on a device that can be squeezed to set off a mechanism, often to eject material, such as on a gun.

grenade
A small bomb that is typically thrown by hand or launched from a propulsive weapon.

front grip
The section near the trigger that is held when aiming and firing.

shotgun
A long-barreled weapon designed to expel small projectiles, such as bullets, at relatively short range.

sniper rifle
A powerful long-barreled firearm designed for precision even at long range.

optical sight
A small telescope, usually with crosshatch markings, mounted on a weapon to allow maximum precision aiming.

rear sight
A small, raised piece toward the back of a gun that is aligned with the foresight when aiming.

barrel
The elongated, cylindrical piece on a firearm through which the bullet or cartridge travels before being fired from the muzzle.

front sight
An aiming component that allows the shooter to target objects at a distance.

stock
The rearmost part of a rifle, often made of wood, which rests against the shoulder when firing.

trigger
A protruding piece on a device that can be squeezed to set off a mechanism, often to eject material, such as on a gun.

magazine
A hollow device that holds the cartridges and feeds them into the barrel.

handguard
The section of a rifle between the barrel and the trigger that is held to keep the muzzle raised and aimed.

flash hider
A device attached to the muzzle that reduces the visibility of the flash when firing.

combat submachine gun
A lightweight automatic firearm that can be held in one hand, that ejects bullets for as long as the trigger is held.

submachine gun
A lightweight automatic firearm, shot from the shoulder or hip, that ejects bullets for as long as the trigger is held.

aerial bomb
A large bomb that is mounted on the belly of an aircraft to be released during flight.

primary pull ring
A round loop of metal that is attached to the grenade and pulled to detonate the mechanism.

stun grenade
A grenade that is designed to disorient a person with a flash and loud noise, rather than to harm them physically.

secondary pull ring
A triangular loop of metal that is attached to the grenade and pulled to detonate the mechanism.

safety lever
A metal rod on a stun grenade that is set in place to prevent accidental initiation of the detonation mechanism.

mine
A disk-shaped bomb that is set into the ground and triggered when stepped on.

body
An outer casing enclosing the entire framework and workings of an item.

charge
The volatile substance in a weapon, such as explosive gunpowder in a cartridge or grenade.

missile
A long, narrow weapon containing explosive material that is self-propelled or directed via remote control to a target.

soldier
A member in an army.

helmet
A hat made of a rigid material, such as plastic, designed to provide protection to the head in case of impact.

special forces soldier
A member in an army who is trained for specific tactical combat situations.

helmet
A hat made of a rigid material, such as plastic, designed to provide protection to the head in case of impact.

pistol
A small firearm that may be held in one hand, often kept in a holster attached to a belt on the body.

glove
A snug-fitting protective covering for a person's hand.

balaclava
A protective covering for a person's face.

bulletproof vest
Tight-fitting clothing that has been reinforced with bulletproof materials to protect the torso from being punctured.

bulletproof vest
Tight-fitting clothing that has been reinforced with bullet-proof materials to protect the torso from being punctured.

belt
A narrow length of sturdy cloth or leather that encircles the waist and is usually secured with a buckle.

pistol
A small firearm that can be held in one hand, often kept in a holster attached to the body.

holster
A fitted holder designed to securely carry a gun so that it can easily and quickly be removed.

pocket
A small pouch sewn into a piece of clothing, in which small objects can be carried.

holster
A pocket attached to a belt designed to securely hold a gun in a position in which it may be easily and quickly removed.

camouflage uniform
A suit of clothing that is patterned in neutral colors to allow the wearer to blend in with natural surroundings.

boot
A sturdy type of footwear that extends over the ankle, often over part of the leg, often tightened with laces.

boot
A sturdy type of footwear that extends over the ankle, often over part of the leg, often tightened with laces.

camouflage uniform
A suit of clothing that is patterned in neutral colors to allow the wearer to blend in with natural surroundings.

tent
A formed sheet of weatherproofed canvas that is stretched over a frame to create a temporary shelter.

wall
The piece or structure forming the upper covering of a shelter or building.

guy line
A rope or other material used to tie down an object.

window vent
On a tent, an opening covered with mesh to provide air flow for internal ventilation.

mosquito net
Fine mesh used to cover open spaces, such as a window vent on a tent, to prevent the entry of insects.

turret
The upper structure on a tank; it houses the guns and can be entirely rotated to aim combat fire.

periscope
A long tube fitted with mirrors that extends upward from an enclosed area to reflect images of the exterior surroundings.

main battle tank (MBT)
An armored vehicle designed for situations of intense combat fire.

armor
Sheets of reinforced metal fixed to a vehicle to prevent damage from artillery fire, gunfire, debris and other dangers.

cannon
A large automatic gun that fires shells from a tank or aircraft.

headlight
A light above the front bumper of a vehicle, the purpose of which is to provide illumination when driving in the dark.

wheel
One of several round devices that propel the track forward or backward, thereby moving the tank.

hatch
A hinged barrier that can be opened to access an area or container beyond or beneath it.

track
A length of metal belts that form an endless loop around a series of wheels to allow movement over rough terrain.

infantry fighting vehicle (IFV)
An armored vehicle designed to transport military personnel in combat situations and to provide fire support.

heavy tank
A heavily armored vehicle designed to resist and return intense combat fire.

high mobility multipurpose wheeled vehicle (humvee)
A highly customizable type of military vehicle that can be used for troop transports and combat.

shield
A broad piece of metal or similar material used to provide protection by deflecting advancing objects.

machine gun
A long-barreled firearm that ejects bullets for as long as the trigger is held down.

air intake
A cylindrical pipe that extends from the engine compartment of a vehicle to let in air without debris.

hood
The hinged, flat, horizontal piece of a vehicle's frame that covers the engine.

reflector
A piece of reflective material on a vehicle that deflects lights from other vehicles in order to identify them.

turn signal
A light set to the side on the nose of a vehicle that flashes to indicate the vehicle is going to turn in that direction.

grille
A sheet of metal mesh on the front of a vehicle covering the radiator to prevent debris from entering the engine.

headlight
A light above the front bumper of a vehicle, the purpose of which is to provide illumination when driving in the dark.

tow hook
A sturdy metal hook protruding from the end of a vehicle to which objects can be fastened and hauled.

front bumper
A thick, protruding lip across the front end of a vehicle, designed to lessen the effect in case of impact.

tire
An inflated ring-shaped wheel component made of rubber that connects the vehicle with the road, providing traction.

armor
Thick structural plates that are welded to the tank to make it stronger and better able to resist attack.

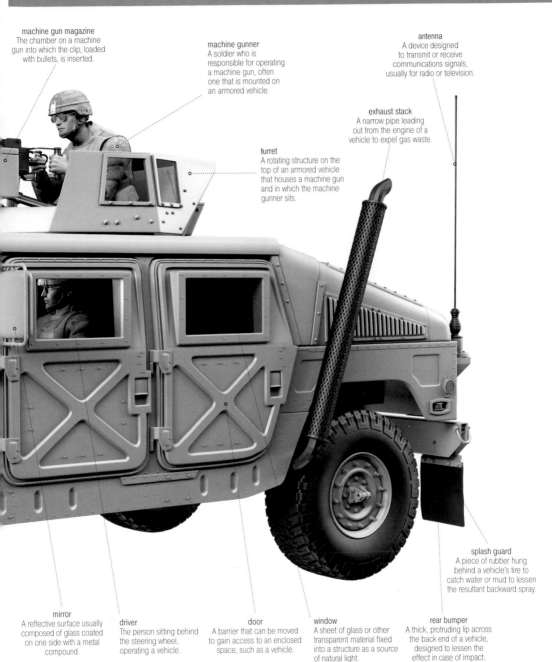

machine gun magazine
The chamber on a machine gun into which the clip, loaded with bullets, is inserted.

machine gunner
A soldier who is responsible for operating a machine gun, often one that is mounted on an armored vehicle.

antenna
A device designed to transmit or receive communications signals, usually for radio or television.

exhaust stack
A narrow pipe leading out from the engine of a vehicle to expel gas waste.

turret
A rotating structure on the top of an armored vehicle that houses a machine gun and in which the machine gunner sits.

mirror
A reflective surface usually composed of glass coated on one side with a metal compound.

driver
The person sitting behind the steering wheel, operating a vehicle.

door
A barrier that can be moved to gain access to an enclosed space, such as a vehicle.

window
A sheet of glass or other transparent material fixed into a structure as a source of natural light.

rear bumper
A thick, protruding lip across the back end of a vehicle, designed to lessen the effect in case of impact.

splash guard
A piece of rubber hung behind a vehicle's tire to catch water or mud to lessen the resultant backward spray.

humvee: bottom view
A rugged vehicle, usually armored and
equipped with firearms, designed to be
driven over rough terrain.

tire
An inflated ring-shaped
wheel component made
of rubber that connects
the vehicle with the road,
providing traction.

suspension arm
A structure that supports
the wheels of a vehicle
on their axles and
absorbs shock from
contact with the road.

transmission
The mechanism
that transfers power
generated by a vehicle's
engine to the wheels.

armor
Sheets of reinforced
metal fixed to the
underside of a vehicle
to prevent sharp debris
from damaging the
undercarriage.

muffler
A part of a vehicle's
exhaust system that is
designed to dampen
the sound produced by
an internal-combustion
engine.

driveshaft
A rotating rod
that connects the
transmission of a vehicle
to the wheels to provide
torque and rotation.

exhaust pipe
A narrow pipe leading
out from the engine of a
vehicle to expel gas waste.

differential
A mechanism on a vehicle
that allows one wheel to
rotate faster than the other
as is necessary when
making a turn.

splash guard
A piece of rubber hung
behind a vehicle's tire
to catch water or mud
to lessen the resultant
backward spray.

ladder frame
A main support structure
for the underside of a
vehicle shaped like a
ladder with two outer bars
and smaller inner ones.

rear bumper
A thick, protruding lip across
the back end of a vehicle,
designed to lessen the effect
in case of impact.

tow hook
A sturdy metal hook protruding
from the end of a vehicle to
which objects can be fastened
and hauled.

truck
A large motor vehicle with a closed or open storage area used to transport loads of materials or equipment.

Czech hedgehog
A structure made of angled metal pieces with protruding ends placed to prevent military tanks from accessing an area.

dish antenna
A specialized audio-transmission device that is utilized to beam radio signals over vast distances.

satellite
A structure that has been launched into Earth's orbit to collect and transmit data such as surveillance intel.

load-bearing frame
A structure comprising several pieces of rigid material, fixed together to form a specific shape able to bear weight.

parabolic reflector
The large parabolic dish surrounding the receiving mechanism of an antenna that allows signal waves to be collected.

transreceiving dish
A device designed to transmit or receive communications signals, usually for radio or television.

feed horn
A small horn antenna that carries radio waves between transmitters and receivers.

solar panel
A sheet of silicon-based material that absorbs radiation from the sun in order to convert it to electricity.

elevation adjustment
The mechanism on a large antenna's structure that can be operated to raise or lower the dish.

azimuth adjustment
The mechanism on a large antenna's structure that can be operated to rotate the dish from side to side on an axis.

transmission dish
A specialized parabolic dish that collects and carries radio waves to the appropriate receivers.

railing
An upright structure, typically made of wood, metal or glass, used to separate one area from another, often to prevent falling.

stairs
A series of steps that allow access to upper and lower levels of a structure.

Airplanes

Motorized flying vehicles with wings that are fixed in place and with a weight greater than the displaced air.

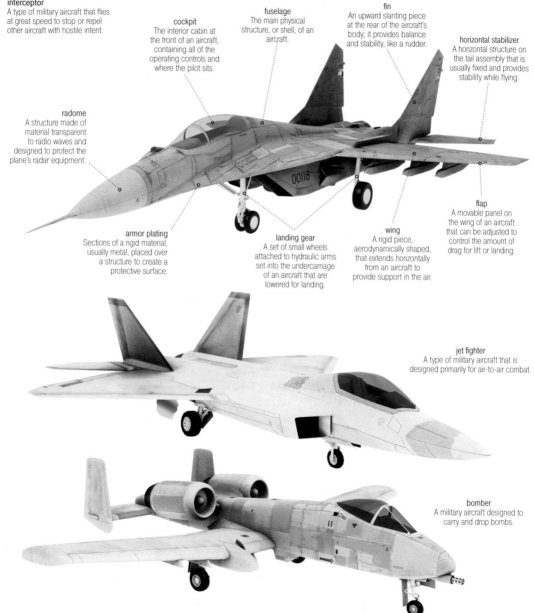

interceptor
A type of military aircraft that flies at great speed to stop or repel other aircraft with hostile intent.

cockpit
The interior cabin at the front of an aircraft, containing all of the operating controls and where the pilot sits.

fuselage
The main physical structure, or shell, of an aircraft.

fin
An upward slanting piece at the rear of the aircraft's body; it provides balance and stability, like a rudder.

horizontal stabilizer
A horizontal structure on the tail assembly that is usually fixed and provides stability while flying.

radome
A structure made of material transparent to radio waves and designed to protect the plane's radar equipment.

armor plating
Sections of a rigid material, usually metal, placed over a structure to create a protective surface.

landing gear
A set of small wheels attached to hydraulic arms set into the undercarriage of an aircraft that are lowered for landing.

wing
A rigid piece, aerodynamically shaped, that extends horizontally from an aircraft to provide support in the air.

flap
A movable panel on the wing of an aircraft that can be adjusted to control the amount of drag for lift or landing.

jet fighter
A type of military aircraft that is designed primarily for air-to-air combat.

bomber
A military aircraft designed to carry and drop bombs.

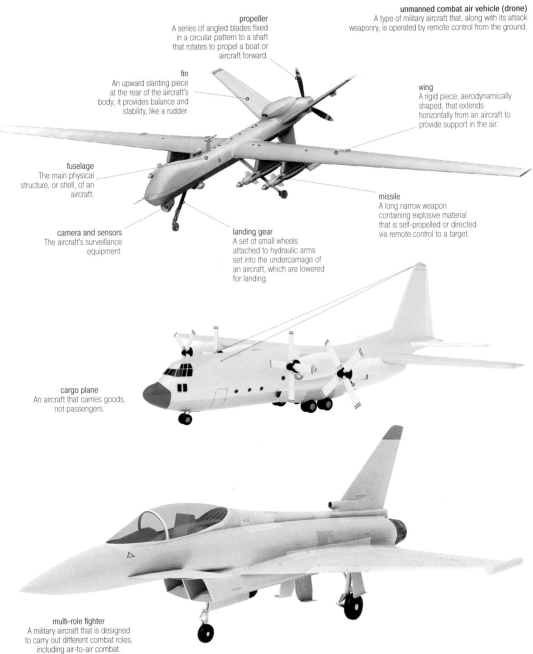

propeller
A series of angled blades fixed in a circular pattern to a shaft that rotates to propel a boat or aircraft forward.

unmanned combat air vehicle (drone)
A type of military aircraft that, along with its attack weaponry, is operated by remote control from the ground.

fin
An upward slanting piece at the rear of the aircraft's body; it provides balance and stability, like a rudder.

wing
A rigid piece, aerodynamically shaped, that extends horizontally from an aircraft to provide support in the air.

fuselage
The main physical structure, or shell, of an aircraft.

missile
A long narrow weapon containing explosive material that is self-propelled or directed via remote control to a target.

camera and sensors
The aircraft's surveillance equipment.

landing gear
A set of small wheels attached to hydraulic arms set into the undercarriage of an aircraft, which are lowered for landing.

cargo plane
An aircraft that carries goods, not passengers.

multi-role fighter
A military aircraft that is designed to carry out different combat roles, including air-to-air combat.

Helicopter

A type of aircraft operated by way of overhead rotors that create lift, propulsion and maneuverability.

utility helicopter: side view

A general-purpose helicopter that can be used in a combat role, as a medical evacuation vehicle or to transport troops.

rotor hub
The central part at the top of a helicopter, where the driveshaft and blades connect.

engine
A mechanized machine that converts power, such as produced by fuel combustion, into locomotion.

window
A sheet of glass or other transparent material fixed into a structure as a source of natural light.

rotor blade
A long, flat length of metal attached to a motor, which causes it to rotate at great speed, such as on a helicopter.

fuselage
The main physical structure, or shell, of an aircraft.

cockpit
A large sheet of transparent, tempered glass covering the front window of a vehicle or aircraft.

cockpit door
The door leading to the internal cabin of an aircraft containing the operating controls and the pilot's seat.

landing window
A somewhat circular opening at the nose of the helicopter that can be used by pilots to monitor landings.

landing gear
A set of small wheels attached to hydraulic arms set into the undercarriage of an aircraft; they are lowered for landing.

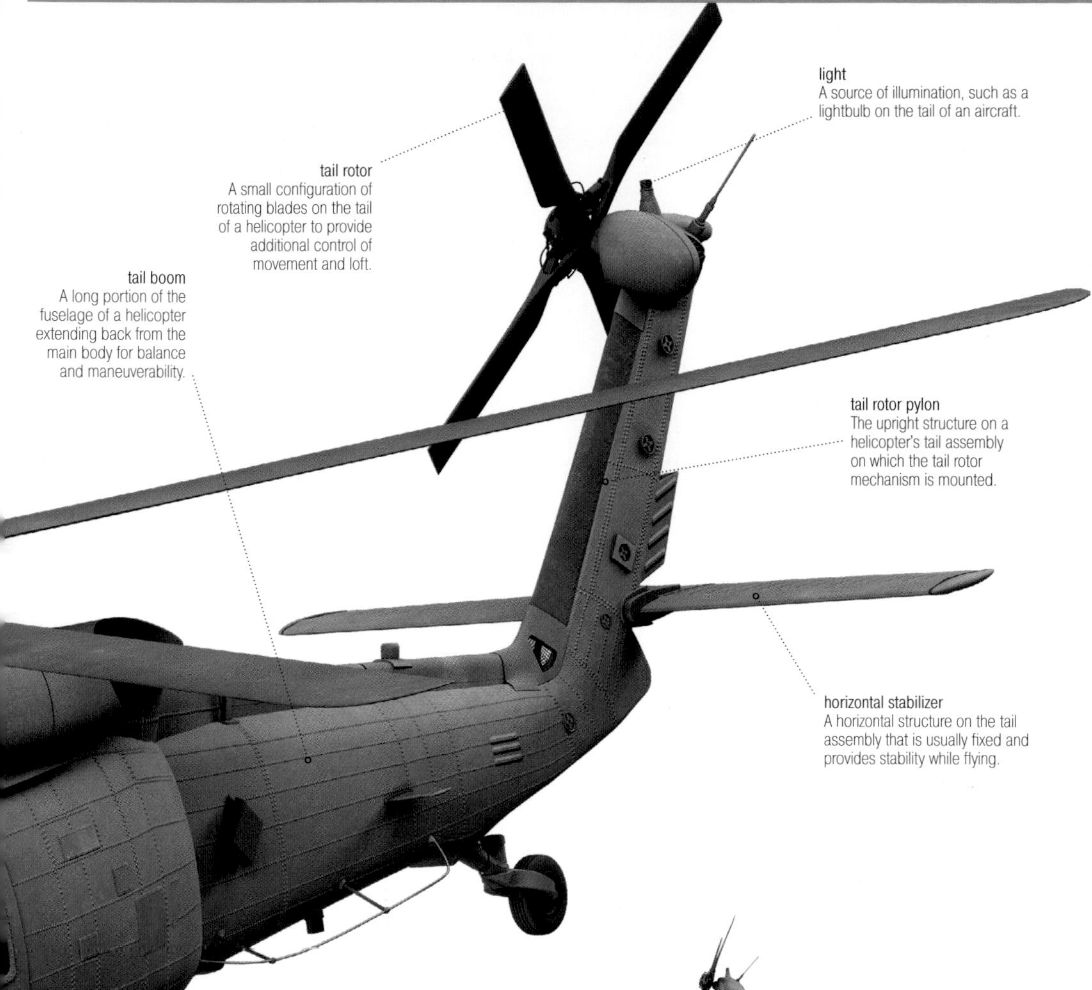

light
A source of illumination, such as a
lightbulb on the tail of an aircraft.

tail rotor
A small configuration of
rotating blades on the tail
of a helicopter to provide
additional control of
movement and loft.

tail boom
A long portion of the
fuselage of a helicopter
extending back from the
main body for balance
and maneuverability.

tail rotor pylon
The upright structure on a
helicopter's tail assembly
on which the tail rotor
mechanism is mounted.

horizontal stabilizer
A horizontal structure on the tail
assembly that is usually fixed and
provides stability while flying.

step
A small, raised platform used
to reach a higher level.

wheel
A circular device fixed to the
base of an object that rotates
on an axis to allow it to be
moved easily on a surface.

helicopter: front view
A type of aircraft with overhead
rotors that create lift, propulsion
and maneuverability.

cockpit
The interior cabin at the front of a helicopter, containing all of the operating controls and where the pilot sits.

windshield
A large sheet of transparent, tempered glass covering the front window of a vehicle or aircraft.

windshield wiper
A thin, narrow blade covered with rubber that sweeps across the windshield to wipe away moisture, such as rain.

control stick
An upright structure connected to the controls of a helicopter that can be maneuvered by hand to adjust the flight.

instrument panel
A large panel in an aircraft with displays of various operational components, and buttons to change those operations.

display
A lit panel in a vehicle or aircraft that displays information, such as the time, altitude or level of fuel.

anti-torque pedal
A flat lever that changes the tail rotor blade pitch, thereby controlling the aircraft's direction.

gauge
An indicator that displays the level of contents in a closed compartment, such as the pressure or amount of gases.

center console
A panel of buttons and levers in the cockpit of a helicopter that can be adjusted to alter the aircraft's response.

passenger cabin
The interior cabin of a helicopter, containing seating for a number of passengers.

anchor point
A clasp designed to secure a safety belt to a portion of a seat, allowing a person to strap themselves in securely.

window
A sheet of glass or other transparent material fixed into a structure as a source of natural light.

safety belt
A length of stiff, reinforced material that is passed over the body and secured to the seat of a vehicle or aircraft.

seat
A flat surface designated for sitting, such as an aircraft passenger seat.

search and rescue (SAR) helicopter
A helicopter that is equipped with the components of a ground ambulance, designed to find and save persons in trouble.

transport helicopter
A helicopter that is designed to carry a number of people, in the way of an airborne bus.

attack helicopter
An armored helicopter equipped with weaponry designed to attack and destroy enemy targets at close range.

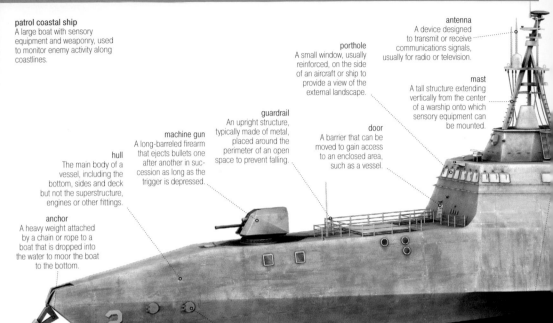

patrol coastal ship
A large boat with sensory equipment and weaponry, used to monitor enemy activity along coastlines.

antenna
A device designed to transmit or receive communications signals, usually for radio or television.

porthole
A small window, usually reinforced, on the side of an aircraft or ship to provide a view of the external landscape.

mast
A tall structure extending vertically from the center of a warship onto which sensory equipment can be mounted.

machine gun
A long-barreled firearm that ejects bullets one after another in succession as long as the trigger is depressed.

guardrail
An upright structure, typically made of metal, placed around the perimeter of an open space to prevent falling.

door
A barrier that can be moved to gain access to an enclosed area, such as a vessel.

hull
The main body of a vessel, including the bottom, sides and deck but not the superstructure, engines or other fittings.

anchor
A heavy weight attached by a chain or rope to a boat that is dropped into the water to moor the boat to the bottom.

hatch
A hinged barrier that can be opened to access an area or container beyond or beneath it.

radar
A device that emits high-frequency electromagnetic waves toward moving objects to calculate their location.

submarine
A large type of military watercraft designed to be completely submerged and travel underwater for long periods.

antenna
A device designed to transmit or receive communications signals, such as for radio or sonar navigation.

periscope
A long tube fitted with mirrors that extends upward from a submarine to reflect images from above the water's surface.

upper rudder
A flat piece attached vertically to the stern of a boat to assist with directional steering.

conning tower
A structure on the dorsal surface of a submarine in the shape of a tower from which the antenna and periscope emerge.

propeller
A series of angled blades fixed in a circular pattern to a shaft that rotates to propel a boat or aircraft forward.

torpedo tube
The cylindrical chamber from which torpedoes may be stored and fired at command during operations.

conning tower
The armored and raised platform that projects upward from the submarine's body. It is used for navigation.

missile tube
A depression on the surface of a submarine in which a torpedo or missile is stored and from which it may be launched.

torpedo
A self-propelled missile that is usually launched under water from a ship or submarine and which detonates on impact.

life buoy
An inflated object made of rubber or some other buoyant material that can be used to stay afloat.

helicopter hangar
A large, partially enclosed space used to house helicopters, such as on a military ship.

helicopter flight deck
A flat area on the stern of a large ship designated for the landing and takeoff of helicopters.

helicopter
A type of aircraft operated by way of overhead rotors that create lift, propulsion and maneuverability.

life raft
A small boat, usually made of inflatable rubber and equipped with oars, used to evacuate a ship in case of emergency.

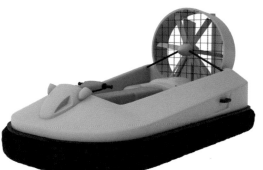

lifeboat
A boat stored on the side of a large ship that can be lowered into the water in case of an emergency evacuation.

davit
A small crane mounted on the side of a large ship used to lower a lifeboat into the water.

hovercraft
A type of small boat that travels above the water by way of a force of air propelled downward.

fast attack craft
A small military boat, often painted in camouflage and armed with missiles, a gun or torpedoes; they patrol coastlines.

propeller
A series of angled blades fixed in a circular pattern to a shaft that rotates to propel a boat or aircraft forward.

blade
One of the slightly slanted, flat pieces that fan out from the hub of a propeller and rotate to create forward thrust.

shaft
A rod that connects a propeller to the transmission of a boat to transfer power from the engine to rotate the propeller.

hub
The central point of a propeller from which the blades fan out and which is attached to the shaft.

main deck
The uppermost complete deck on a naval vessel; it runs the full length and width of the ship.

aircraft carrier
An enormous ship with a runway built onto its deck that enables aircraft to take off and land.

radar
A device that emits high-frequency electromagnetic waves toward moving objects to calculate their location.

hull
The main body of a vessel, including the bottom, sides and deck but not the superstructure or other fittings.

helicopter
A type of aircraft operated by way of overhead rotors that create lift, propulsion and maneuverability.

081

helicopter flight deck
A helicopter landing pad located on the deck of a ship.

anchor
The massive steel weight that is positioned at the front of the carrier and can be dropped to tether the ship.

jet blast deflector
A safety barrier that deflects the exhaust from jet engines to prevent damage to the ship and injury to crew.

elevator
A mechanism consisting of a platform attached to a hydraulic system designed to move large objects from one level to another.

porthole
A small window, usually reinforced, on the side of an aircraft or ship to provide a view of the external landscape.

lower deck
A deck of a ship that is located directly above the hold and at a lower level than an upper deck.

aircraft
A machine designed for flight, such as an airplane or helicopter.

anchor
A heavy weight tethered by a chain or rope, dropped into the water to moor the boat.

flight deck
On an aircraft carrier, the deck painted with a runway that enables aircraft to take off and land

arm
A raised, elongated portion of an object, such as a piece attached to the shank of an anchor.

shank
The central rod of an anchor, to which the arms and the securing chain are attached.

barrel
A large, cylindrical container, usually made of a bouyant material such as wood or plastic and fitted with a lid.

palm
The flattened, widened portion at the end of an arm of an anchor.

ARTS AND
ARCHITECTURE

band
A group of people who sing and play instruments, sometimes in front of an audience and sometimes for a recording.

block of lights
Lights that can produce various colors and patterns and are used to illuminate large areas of a stage.

parabolic aluminized reflector light
A lamp that emits a concentrated beam of light that is focused on a specific location or person, usually on a stage.

guitarist
A person who plays the guitar, either electric or acoustic.

electric guitar
A solid-body stringed instrument with pickups that convert sounds into electrical signals that can be amplified.

loudspeaker
A device that amplifies and projects sound to an audience.

cable
A thick electrical cord designed to transmit a large amount of electricity, such as for sound and lighting on a stage.

monitor
A speaker that is placed at the edge of the stage and directed toward the performers to help them hear themselves.

synthesizer
An electronic keyboard instrument that combines different frequencies to produce a wide variety of sounds.

keyboardist
A person who plays keyboard instruments.

audio engineer
A professional who controls the sounds produced by instruments and voices during a performance or recording session.

singer
A person who sings.

drummer
A person who plays the drums and other types of percussion instruments.

drum kit
A specific collection of drums and cymbals that are used to set the rhythm and beat for a piece of music.

bassist
A person who plays a bass guitar.

trussing
A complex structure of rigid material, such as wood or metal, that is fixed together to form a support.

console
A control panel used to manipulate sounds, including voices and instruments.

chair
A seat for one person with a back and that may or may not have arms.

laptop computer
A portable computer consisting of a monitor and keyboard attached with hinges.

table
A piece of furniture with a pedestal or legs supporting a flat surface on which objects can be placed.

bass guitar
A guitar-like electric instrument with four thick strings that produce notes in the lower register.

stage
A large, raised platform on which people, such as actors or musicians, perform in front of an audience.

movie theater
A public building in which movies are shown on a large screen to a paying audience for entertainment.

exit
A doorway to leave a room or building.

console
A control panel used to manipulate sounds, including voices and instruments.

screen
A large, white surface used to display images from a projector.

stage
A large raised platform in front of the screen, sometimes used for presentations.

carpet
Fibrous material laid on a floor to muffle sound.

seat
A space in which an audience member sits.

ticket collector
A worker who verifies and collects admittance stubs.

trash can
A waste container.

popcorn
Heated corn kernels that have burst open and are often served buttered and salted.

table and chairs
Furniture for sitting and eating, often placed outdoors on a patio or indoors in a lobby.

film projector
A machine that shoots pictures from film onto a screen, creating an image in continuous motion.

digital projector
An electronic device designed to project a digital image or video onto a screen or wall.

counter
The surface of a concession stand, where customers are served.

projector
A device used to display images on a screen.

projection booth
A small room, situated behind an audience, from which a movie is projected onto a movie screen.

concession stand
A service area where customers can purchase beverages and snacks.

vendor
A person employed to prepare and serve beverages and snacks.

mixing console
An electronic device used to manipulate sound during a performance, including individual voices and instruments.

volume unit meter
A visual representation of the volume level of the sound that is being monitored by the meter.

fader
A knob that can be slid along a slot in a mixing console to gradually increase or decrease the volume.

beverages
A liquid that has been prepared for human consumption.

voltage divider (potentiometer)
A knob that can be turned to allow certain sound frequencies to be brought forward or pushed back.

power LED
A small light built into an appliance that illuminates to show an active electrical connection.

vending machine
An automated machine that sells goods, such as snacks or drinks.

restroom
A public washroom.

movie poster
A decorative banner with words and images to promote a movie.

bench
Public seating for more than one person, usually made of wood or metal.

entrance
A doorway to enter a room or building.

escalator
A moving set of stairs.

box office
A booth where tickets can be bought.

lobby
A space immediately inside a building entrance, often furnished with comfortable chairs and tables.

television show
A performance, program or other production that is broadcast for information, education or entertainment.

stage
A large raised platform on which people, such as actors or musicians, perform in front of an audience.

desk
The flat surface at which the host of the television program sits.

scenery
Designs and structures placed on a stage to set a mood and context for a performance.

host
A person who leads a television show, introducing and interviewing guest stars.

monitor
A flat screen that projects images transmitted from an electronic device, such as a computer.

guest
A person, usually well-known, who participates on an ad-hoc basis in a television show, often as an interviewee.

chair
A seat for one person with a back and that may or may not have arms.

electric guitar
A solid-body stringed instrument with pickups that convert sounds into electrical signals that can be amplified.

drum kit
A collection of drums, cymbals and other percussion instruments that are played, usually to set the rhythm and beat.

microphone
A device that converts sound waves into electrical signals that can be amplified, transmitted or recorded.

television studio
An indoor area that houses the production of a television show, which is recorded or broadcast live.

scenery
Structures at the back of a stage to set a mood or atmosphere or to create a context for the performance.

light
A lamp that emits a beam of light.

monitor
A flat screen that projects images transmitted from an electronic device, such as a computer.

truss
A support structure of rods or beams.

host
A person who leads a television show, introducing and interviewing guest stars.

cable
A thick electrical cord.

microphone
A device that amplifies voices, so they may be projected over a large area.

cameraman
A person who specializes in the operation of a camera, usually to record a public event or show for broadcasting.

script
Speech and movement directions that have been written for an actor or television personality to follow.

stage
A large raised platform on which people, such as actors or musicians, perform in front of an audience.

guest
A person, often famous, participating as a one-time member of a television talk show or game show.

singer
A person skilled at singing; often a professional.

musician
A talented instrument player; usually a professional.

director
A person who gives instructions to the actors, guests and crew of a television or theater production.

camera
An electronic device designed to capture and record images and sound for broadcasting.

audience member
A person watching a show or event in person.

stage
A large raised platform on which people, such as actors or musicians, perform in front of an audience.

light
An electrical source of illumination that is used to brighten or highlight specific areas of the stage.

proscenium
The walls and floor, often fitted with lights, that frames the stage, separating it from the audience.

stage curtain
A large piece of heavy fabric that can be drawn across or lowered to hide the stage from the audience.

actress
A woman who performs a scripted work, either in front of an audience or on camera.

orchestra pit
A sunken area in front of the stage in which the orchestra sits, so as not to detract from the performance on stage.

orchestra conductor
A person who stands in front of an orchestra to guide the musicians' playing with arm movements and a baton.

beam
Horizontal strips of fabric that can be lowered to hide the upper part of the stage so the audience cannot see it.

backdrop
A large piece of painted cloth or other structure hung at the back of a stage as part of the overall scenery.

actor
A man who performs a scripted work, either in front of an audience or on camera.

stage
The main part of the stage floor, where the artists perform.

audience
The group of people, usually seated, who watch a musical, theatrical or other performance.

theater
A public building that hosts live
theatrical and musical performances.
It often has tiered seating for the
audience.

mezzanine
A curved deck of seating that
projects over the orchestra
seats.

balcony
A deck of curved seating built
along the walls above the
mezzanine.

seat
Where an audience member
sits; the price varies
depending on its position
relative to the stage.

orchestra
The first level of seats, on
the ground floor of the
theater.

opera glasses
An optical magnification device, usually easily held in one hand, that is designed for use at the theater.

flamenco dancer
A man or woman who dances in the flamenco style, a classical dance originating in the Andalusian region of Spain.

lens
A piece of glass that has been formed or treated to alter or diffuse light as it reaches the cornea, altering vision.

ruffled sleeve
A sleeve with multiple layers of frilled material, sometimes worn by dancers to complement arm movements.

focusing wheel
A wide, ridged ring between the eyepieces of a pair of binoculars or opera glasses that is spun to sharpen the view.

ruffled skirt
A long skirt with multiple layers of frilled material, sometimes worn by dancers to complement leg movements.

body
The hard outer casing that encloses the inner workings of a device.

handle
A piece of solid or flexible material attached to an object so that it can be grasped and held.

maang tikka
A type of Indian hair jewelry that follows the central part of the hair and dangles over the forehead.

Indian dancer
A man or woman who performs choreographed dances to traditional Indian music and in an ornate costume.

bindi
A decorative mark or small piece of jewelry, often red, worn in the middle of the forehead, primarily by Hindu women.

nose ring
A large hoop of silver or gold, sometimes adorned with stones or beads, that Indian women traditionally wear.

actor
A person who performs a scripted work, either in front of an audience (a play) or on camera (for movies or television).

panja bracelet
A style of Indian bracelet made of gold, silver or colored beads that is joined to a finger ring by a chain.

costume
Garments worn by actors or other performers for a particular role.

bangle
A loose, rigid bracelet that women often wear stacked up the arm.

choli
A traditional Indian blouse that is cut above the midriff and is traditionally worn under a sari.

dupatta
A traditional Indian woman's scarf made of fine material with many colors, patterns and other adornments.

lehenga
A long, colorful skirt with many adornments and patterns that is traditionally worn by Indian women.

first position of the arms
A position with the feet held heels together and toes pointing out, and the arms down and rounded (called bras bas).

leotard
A stretchy, tight-fitting garment that covers the torso and ends at the top of the thighs.

tights
A thin, flexible, tight-fitting garment that extends from the waist to the ankles and allows dancers to move freely.

ballet shoes
Soft shoes made of cloth or silk designed specifically for ballet, often tied to the feet with ribbons around the ankle.

arabesque on pointe
The arabesque position in which the dancer is standing on the tips of the toes of the supporting leg.

jeté
A ballet move in which the dancer leaps from one foot to the other by throwing one leg forward.

front attitude on pointe
The attitude position in which the dancer stands on the tips of the toes of one leg with the other leg extended forward.

grand jeté
A ballet move in which the dancer makes a huge leap from one foot to the other by throwing one leg forward.

second position of the arms
A basic ballet position of the arms, in which the arms are held out to the sides and slightly lower than horizontal.

third position of the arms
A basic ballet position of the arms, in which one arm is brought forward and raised from the second position.

fourth position of the arms
A basic ballet position of the arms, in which both arms are slightly rounded, one held out and the other raised.

fifth position of the arms
A basic ballet position of the arms, in which both arms are rounded and held over the head with the hands apart.

backward attitude on pointe
A basic ballet position in which the dancer stands on one leg with the other leg extended and slightly bent at the knee.

retiré on pointe
A basic ballet position in which the dancer bends one leg, turns it to the side and points the toes at the supporting knee.

pas de bourrée
A ballet move consisting of a series of three quick steps in which one foot always leads.

arabesque
A basic ballet position in which the dancer stands on one leg with the other leg extended behind in a straight line.

ballet moves
Fundamental movements performed in ballet that carry the dancer from one part of the stage to another.

back bend
A ballet move in which the dancer throws back the upper body and one straightened leg while bending the supporting leg.

entrechat
A ballet move consisting of a vertical jump in which the dancer crosses or beats the legs together before landing.

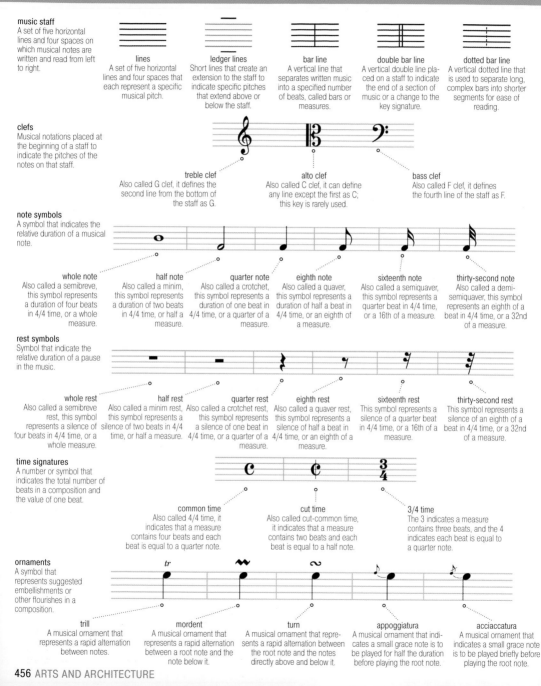

music staff
A set of five horizontal lines and four spaces on which musical notes are written and read from left to right.

lines
A set of five horizontal lines and four spaces that each represent a specific musical pitch.

ledger lines
Short lines that create an extension to the staff to indicate specific pitches that extend above or below the staff.

bar line
A vertical line that separates written music into a specified number of beats, called bars or measures.

double bar line
A vertical double line placed on a staff to indicate the end of a section of music or a change to the key signature.

dotted bar line
A vertical dotted line that is used to separate long, complex bars into shorter segments for ease of reading.

clefs
Musical notations placed at the beginning of a staff to indicate the pitches of the notes on that staff.

treble clef
Also called G clef, it defines the second line from the bottom of the staff as G.

alto clef
Also called C clef, it can define any line except the first as C; this key is rarely used.

bass clef
Also called F clef, it defines the fourth line of the staff as F.

note symbols
A symbol that indicates the relative duration of a musical note.

whole note
Also called a semibreve, this symbol represents a duration of four beats in 4/4 time, or a whole measure.

half note
Also called a minim, this symbol represents a duration of two beats in 4/4 time, or half a measure.

quarter note
Also called a crotchet, this symbol represents a duration of one beat in 4/4 time, or a quarter of a measure.

eighth note
Also called a quaver, this symbol represents a duration of half a beat in 4/4 time, or an eighth of a measure.

sixteenth note
Also called a semiquaver, this symbol represents a quarter beat in 4/4 time, or a 16th of a measure.

thirty-second note
Also called a demi-semiquaver, this symbol represents an eighth of a beat in 4/4 time, or a 32nd of a measure.

rest symbols
Symbol that indicate the relative duration of a pause in the music.

whole rest
Also called a semibreve rest, this symbol represents a silence of four beats in 4/4 time, or a whole measure.

half rest
Also called a minim rest, this symbol represents a silence of two beats in 4/4 time, or half a measure.

quarter rest
Also called a crotchet rest, this symbol represents a silence of one beat in 4/4 time, or a quarter of a measure.

eighth rest
Also called a quaver rest, this symbol represents a silence of half a beat in 4/4 time, or an eighth of a measure.

sixteenth rest
This symbol represents a silence of a quarter beat in 4/4 time, or a 16th of a measure.

thirty-second rest
This symbol represents a silence of an eighth of a beat in 4/4 time, or a 32nd of a measure.

time signatures
A number or symbol that indicates the total number of beats in a composition and the value of one beat.

common time
Also called 4/4 time, it indicates that a measure contains four beats and each beat is equal to a quarter note.

cut time
Also called cut-common time, it indicates that a measure contains two beats and each beat is equal to a half note.

3/4 time
The 3 indicates a measure contains three beats, and the 4 indicates each beat is equal to a quarter note.

ornaments
A symbol that represents suggested embellishments or other flourishes in a composition.

trill
A musical ornament that represents a rapid alternation between notes.

mordent
A musical ornament that represents a rapid alternation between a root note and the note below it.

turn
A musical ornament that represents a rapid alternation between the root note and the notes directly above and below it.

appoggiatura
A musical ornament that indicates a small grace note is to be played for half the duration before playing the root note.

acciaccatura
A musical ornament that indicates a small grace note is to be played briefly before playing the root note.

accidentals
Symbols on the left of a note that modify that note's pitch for the rest of the measure.

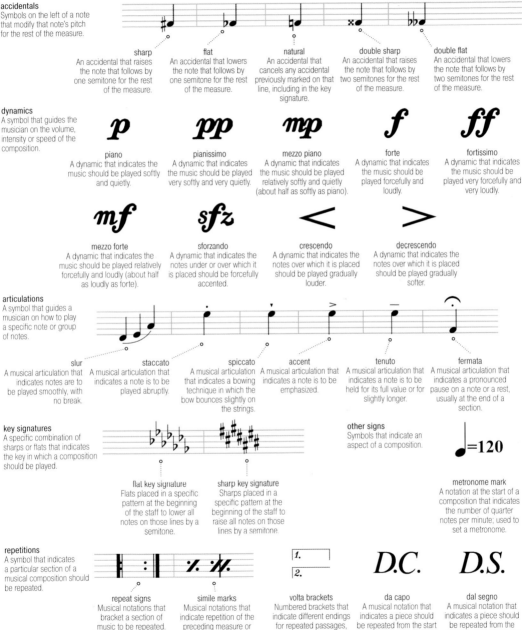

sharp
An accidental that raises the note that follows by one semitone for the rest of the measure.

flat
An accidental that lowers the note that follows by one semitone for the rest of the measure.

natural
An accidental that cancels any accidental previously marked on that line, including in the key signature.

double sharp
An accidental that raises the note that follows by two semitones for the rest of the measure.

double flat
An accidental that lowers the note that follows by two semitones for the rest of the measure.

dynamics
A symbol that guides the musician on the volume, intensity or speed of the composition.

piano
A dynamic that indicates the music should be played softly and quietly.

pianissimo
A dynamic that indicates the music should be played very softly and very quietly.

mezzo piano
A dynamic that indicates the music should be played relatively softly and quietly (about half as softly as piano).

forte
A dynamic that indicates the music should be played forcefully and loudly.

fortissimo
A dynamic that indicates the music should be played very forcefully and very loudly.

mezzo forte
A dynamic that indicates the music should be played relatively forcefully and loudly (about half as loudly as forte).

sforzando
A dynamic that indicates the notes under or over which it is placed should be forcefully accented.

crescendo
A dynamic that indicates the notes over which it is placed should be played gradually louder.

decrescendo
A dynamic that indicates the notes over which it is placed should be played gradually softer.

articulations
A symbol that guides a musician on how to play a specific note or group of notes.

slur
A musical articulation that indicates notes are to be played smoothly, with no break.

staccato
A musical articulation that indicates a note is to be played abruptly.

spiccato
A musical articulation that indicates a bowing technique in which the bow bounces slightly on the strings.

accent
A musical articulation that indicates a note is to be emphasized.

tenuto
A musical articulation that indicates a note is to be held for its full value or for slightly longer.

fermata
A musical articulation that indicates a pronounced pause on a note or a rest, usually at the end of a section.

key signatures
A specific combination of sharps or flats that indicates the key in which a composition should be played.

flat key signature
Flats placed in a specific pattern at the beginning of the staff to lower all notes on those lines by a semitone.

sharp key signature
Sharps placed in a specific pattern at the beginning of the staff to raise all notes on those lines by a semitone.

other signs
Symbols that indicate an aspect of a composition.

metronome mark
A notation at the start of a composition that indicates the number of quarter notes per minute; used to set a metronome.

repetitions
A symbol that indicates a particular section of a musical composition should be repeated.

repeat signs
Musical notations that bracket a section of music to be repeated. One repeat sign indicates repetition from the start.

simile marks
Musical notations that indicate repetition of the preceding measure or measures, depending on the number of slashes.

volta brackets
Numbered brackets that indicate different endings for repeated passages, often played on different instruments.

da capo
A musical notation that indicates a piece should be repeated from the start to the coda mark or, if noted, to the end.

dal segno
A musical notation that indicates a piece should be repeated from the segno mark to the coda or, if noted, to the end.

upright piano
An instrument with a vertical soundboard and metal strings, which are struck by hammers connected to the keyboard.

cabinet
The wooden outer structure that encloses the strings and hammers and improves the instrument's accoustics.

upper panel
The front-facing, upper vertical surface of the cabinet, behind which the strings and hammers lie.

lid
The uppermost horizontal surface of a piano, which can be hinged open or freely lifted off to tune the strings.

music stand
A small ledge above the keyboard on which sheet music or other scores can be propped up.

fallboard
A movable lid that may be slid or folded out to cover and protect the keyboard of a piano from dust when not in use.

key
A white or black lever that is pressed with the fingers to make a hammer strike a string, producing a note.

keybed
The sunken area that protrudes from the front of the cabinet and supports the keyboard.

leg
A wooden column that stabilizes the instrument and supports the weight of the keyboard.

keyblock
Pieces of wood at each end of the keyboard, forming part of the cabinet.

lower panel
The front-facing, lower vertical surface of the cabinet, behind which the bridges and soundboard lie.

toe block
Pieces of wood under the legs of an upright piano that provide structural support below the keyboard.

soft pedal
The left foot lever; it reduces the hammers' impact, making the notes softer.

muffler pedal
The middle foot lever; it sustains or stifles vibrations, depending on the hammers' position.

damper pedal
The right foot lever; it prolonges the hammers' vibrations and the notes' duration.

cursor buttons
Small buttons on the panel that can be pressed to control and modify the sound, as shown in the LCD.

synthesizer
An electronic keyboard instrument that combines different frequencies to produce a wide variety of sounds.

liquid-crystal display (LCD)
A screen that shows information about the instrument's settings and operations.

dial
A knob that can be rotated to select which function to modify; the relevant function will be shown in the LCD.

system buttons
Buttons that allow the player to select the instrument's main functions and access sounds stored in its memory.

pitch switch
A lever that gradually adjusts the pitch of the sound into a higher or lower register.

function buttons
Buttons on the panel that perform specific tasks, such as warping, blending and playback properties.

sequencer buttons
A series of buttons that reproduce melodies and rhythms based on prerecorded sounds and music.

top board
The large board that protects the inner workings; it is raised during play.

grand piano
An instrument with a horizontal soundboard and metal strings, struck by hammers connected to a keyboard.

music stand
A small ledge built onto the front of a piano above the keyboard on which musical scores can be propped upright.

top board front
The front section of the main lid, which can be grasped to open or close the lid.

keyboard
The series of black and white keys that are pressed to produce sound, either electronically or via strings.

lyre post
One or two bars that extend down from the main body of a grand piano to support the pedal box.

top board prop
A long bar that holds the lid of a grand piano open, displaying the inner workings and improving the sound quality.

piano bench
The bench on which someone sits to play the piano.

cast iron frame
A rigid inner structure on a grand piano that sustains the integrity of its shape, particularly during transport.

leg
A piece of rigid material attached to the bottom of an instrument to raise it from the ground or stabilize it.

damper pedal
The right foot lever; it prolongs the hammers' vibrations and the notes' duration.

caster
A small, swiveling wheel attached to the bottom of a large object to make it easier to move.

pedal box
The casing that holds and protects the pedals and their mechanism.

muffler pedal
The middle foot lever; it sustains or stifles vibrations, depending on the hammers' position.

harpsichord
A keyboard instrument similar to a grand piano, but with two keyboards and strings that are plucked rather than struck.

soft pedal
The left foot lever; it reduces the hammers' impact, making the notes softer.

electric organ
An organ that uses electronics, not pipes, to produce sounds.

drum kit
A specific collection of drums and cymbals that are used to set the rhythm and beat for a piece of music.

drumhead
The membrane stretched across the drum and struck with sticks; it can be tightened or loosened to adjust the pitch.

ride cymbal
A standard cymbal on most drum kits; usually placed on the drummer's dominant side and struck in a sustaining rhythm.

high-hat cymbal
A pair of cymbals mounted one of top of the other on a stand; clashed via a foot pedal.

tom-tom
A pair of small drums originally designed to be beaten with the hands but now common to modern drum kits.

crash cymbal
A large single cymbal mounted on a stand and struck with a stick, mallet or brush.

bass drum
A large two-headed drum that is mounted on its side and struck with a soft pedal-controlled mallet.

rim
The metal hoop that holds the head taut; drummers sometimes strike it with the side of their stick.

superior cymbal
The upper cymbal on a hi-hat; it is clashed down and held on the inferior cymbal via a foot pedal.

tenor drum
A large double-headed drum that is mounted on three integrated legs.

stool
An armless and backless seat that is sometimes height adjustable and usually rests on three or four legs.

inferior cymbal
The lower cymbal on a hi-hat; it remains stationary, and the superior cymbal is clashed down onto it.

leg
A rigid support that raises the drum off the ground and stabilizes it.

tripod stand
A solid base with three adjustable, folding legs that can support heavy items.

bass drum hammer
A metal rod with a large, soft head; used to strike a bass drum, producing a rich, booming sound.

pedal
A lever that is pressed with the foot to make the mallet strike the membrane.

high-hat stand
An adjustable, rigid structure with a foot pedal; the hi-hat is mounted on it.

lug
A piece on the side that holds a wire that connects the upper and lower rims; used to adjust the head's tension.

snare drum
A double-headed drum that has a set of wire rattles stretched across the inside of one of the heads.

stand
The rigid piece on which the bass drum and pedal sit.

cymbals
Slightly concave metal disks that are struck together or with a stick to create a loud clashing sound.

triangle
A piece of metal, usually steel, that is bent into a triangular shape and struck with a rod to produce a ringing tone.

tambourine
A shallow handheld drum fitted with small metal disks around its shell that jangle when the instrument is struck.

drumsticks
Long, thin sticks with rounded heads that are used to strike percussion instruments, such as drums.

sleigh bells
A series of hollow metal balls containing small pendulums or pellets that jingle when agitated.

gong
A large metal disk with a turned rim that is hung from a frame and struck with a mallet to produce loud reverberations.

wire brush
A variation of drumsticks that have heads of stiff wire bristles that are brushed over drums or cymbals.

castanets
Small concave pieces of wood held in the fingers and played by clicking them together; popular in Latin music.

tubular bells
An orchestral instrument made up of a hanging row of gradually longer metal tubes that are struck to produce notes.

xylophone
An instrument consisting of a row of progressively longer wooden bars that each produce a note of the scale when struck.

vibraphone
A percussion instrument, with two rows of tuned metal bars connected to tubular resonators, that produces a vibrato sound.

bongos
Two small connected drums that are held between the knees and struck with the hands and fingers in rapid patterns.

bass drum hammer
A mallet, with a large, soft head, used to beat a bass drum to produce a rich booming sound.

mallet
Metal or wooden rods with large, soft heads that are used to strike a drum to produce a rich, booming sound.

djembe
A drum of African origin that is shaped like a goblet, tuned with ropes and played by beating with the hands.

kettledrum
A large, bowl-shaped drum; the head's tension is adjustable, changing the pitch. It is struck with mallets.

tension rod
A knob on the side of that drum that is used to adjust the tension of the head to change the pitch.

drum head
The flat membrane that is struck with a mallet; it can be tightened or loosened to adjust the pitch.

counterhoop
A metal hoop that is tightened around the drum to stretch the drumhead and keep it in place.

caster
A small, swiveling wheel that is attached to the bottom of the a large object to make it easier to move.

bass drum
A large, two-headed drum that is placed on its side and struck with a soft mallet, which may be attached to a foot pedal.

Brass instruments
Wind instruments made of brass or other metal; sound is produced by vibrating the lips and blowing into them.

bell brace
One of typically three vertically set rods that hold the bell section of a trombone in a curve over the slide section.

bell lock ring
A small metal ring on the slide section of a trombone that controls the depth to which it is slid into the bell section.

trombone
A brass instrument held over the shoulder and played by blowing into the mouthpiece and sliding the valve.

counterweight
A round weight on the tuning slide that helps to balance the instrument over the shoulder while it is played.

bell
The flared end of a wind instrument; its design optimizes the instrument's sound.

tuning slide
A small slide at the back of a trombone that is adjusted to modify the pitch of the instrument before playing.

slide bumper
A small rubber knob that is fitted onto the end of the slide to protect it from being bumped and dented.

water key
A small valve on a wind instrument that may be opened to allow the moisture that accumulates to drain.

mouthpiece
The opening on a wind instrument where the lips are pressed to blow air through a reed or into or across a tube.

second slide brace
A horizontally placed bar on the slide section of a trombone that is grasped to move the slide in and out.

slide
A telescoping mechanism that is used to lengthen or shorten the instrument to lower and raise the pitch.

French horn
A coiled brass instrument; sound is made and varied by vibrating the lips against the mouthpiece and pressing the keys.

trumpet
A brass instrument with a flared bell and only three valves; it relies greatly on air pressure to produce different notes.

tuning slide
The primary slide on a French horn; it can be adjusted to modify the overall pitch of the instrument before playing.

mouthpiece
The opening on a wind instrument where the lips are pressed to blow air through a reed or into or across a tube.

mouthpiece receiver
The narrow pipe that leads from the mouthpiece to the main tubing of some brass instruments, such as a French horn.

valve slide
One of three small slides on a French horn that can be adjusted to modify the pitch of the instrument before playing.

valve key
A small lever that is pressed and released to open and close an air valve on a wind instrument, such as a French horn.

bell
The flared end of a wind instrument; its design optimizes the instrument's sound.

bell pipe
The final section of tubing on a wind instrument; it ends in the bell and its length affects the acoustics.

rotary valve
Small circular plugs on some wind instruments, such as a French horn, that are rotated to change the range of pitch.

thumb key (fourth lever)
An air valve lever on a French horn that is operated by the thumb to change the instrument's flat pitch between F and B.

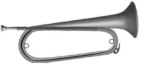

bugle
A brass instrument without valves; the player produces different notes by varying the air pressure when blowing.

tuba
A large instrument with three to six valves and a broad bell that produces the lowest notes in the brass family.

saxhorn
A brass instrument with a mellow quality. There are seven types of saxhorn, differentiated by their root notes.

euphonium
A brass instrument with a coiled conical tube and large bell; it produces notes in the baritone range.

cornet
A valved brass instrument similar to a trumpet but with a shorter, partly conical tube.

Woodwind instruments

Tubular instruments made of wood or metal; sound is produced by blowing against a reed or through a hole.

saxophone
A single-reed brass instrument that is widely used in jazz and other popular music genres.

octave key
A key on the curve of the neck of a saxophone that can be pressed to raise the pitch of the notes by an octave.

mouthpiece
The opening on a wind instrument where the lips are pressed to blow air through a reed or into or across a tube.

neck
The curved section between the mouthpiece and the body; it allows the instrument to be played in a vertical position.

reed
A thin, flat piece, usually made of cane, that vibrates in the mouthpiece of some woodwind instruments to produce sound.

neck cork
A ring of cork that is glued to the neck of a saxophone and holds the mouthpiece firmly in place.

ligature
A clamping device designed to hold a reed firmly in the mouthpiece of a woodwind instrument, such as a saxophone.

recorder
A simple woodwind instrument with a whistle mouthpiece and a conical tube with holes that are covered with the fingers.

bell
The flared end of a wind instrument; its design optimizes the instrument's sound.

shoe
The supporting structure that holds the tubes in place and by which the instrument may be held.

panpipe
An ancient instrument made of a linked row of pipes of varying lengths, played by blowing across the top.

key
A small pad on a woodwind instrument that can be held down to adjust the air column to create a different pitch.

key guard
A small metal piece that keeps the keys from shifting while being played and protects them from damage.

key/finger button
A small button on a woodwind instrument that can be pressed to hold down a key without touching the pad.

bow
The U-shaped section at the bottom of a saxophone; it connects the bell to the body, so the bell faces outward.

thumb rest
A small tab that is supported by the thumb to help keep the instrument balanced when it is played.

tube
A hollow pipe made of a material that readily vibrates, such as metal or wood, and produces sound with the passage of air.

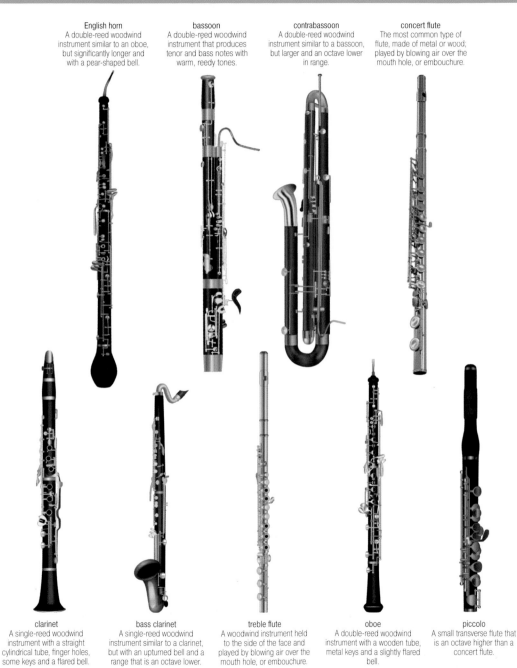

English horn
A double-reed woodwind instrument similar to an oboe, but significantly longer and with a pear-shaped bell.

bassoon
A double-reed woodwind instrument that produces tenor and bass notes with warm, reedy tones.

contrabassoon
A double-reed woodwind instrument similar to a bassoon, but larger and an octave lower in range.

concert flute
The most common type of flute, made of metal or wood; played by blowing air over the mouth hole, or embouchure.

clarinet
A single-reed woodwind instrument with a straight cylindrical tube, finger holes, some keys and a flared bell.

bass clarinet
A single-reed woodwind instrument similar to a clarinet, but with an upturned bell and a range that is an octave lower.

treble flute
A woodwind instrument held to the side of the face and played by blowing air over the mouth hole, or embouchure.

oboe
A double-reed woodwind instrument with a wooden tube, metal keys and a slightly flared bell.

piccolo
A small transverse flute that is an octave higher than a concert flute.

cello
A large stringed instrument that is played with a bow, held between the knees and resting on the floor.

scroll
The spiral-shaped ornamental design that is carved into the end of the pegbox.

head
The top section of the bow, which is bent perpendicular to the stick, holding the hairs away from the stick.

tip
The part that holds the hairs to the bow, allowing them to be attached, detached and replaced.

violin and bow
A stringed instrument that is held against the shoulder and under the chin and played with a horsehair rod, called a bow.

pegbox
The section at the top of the neck where the pegs are attached.

nut
A small notched bar at the end of the neck that seperates the strings and raises them off the fingerboard.

hair
Long, fine horse hairs or synthetic fibers that are strung onto the bow and drawn across the strings to produce sound.

peg
A device that adjusts the tightness of a string, which affects the sound produced.

ribs
The thin pieces of wood that form the sides of the body.

belly
A stringed instrument body that bows out slightly from the center, creating a larger hollow and more reverberation.

top bout
The upper part of the hollow body; can be tapped to create different sounds or to keep the beat.

purfling
A decorative strip around the edge of the body; it is often painted or stained a different color or inlaid.

string
A long, thin length of gut, nylon or metal that is bowed or plucked to create sound through vibrations.

fingerboard
The flattened section on the neck; it's where the strings are pressed to produce different notes.

stick
The wooden part of a bow, along which the hair is stretched; it is curved and flexible.

waist
The two indented curves in the middle of the hourglass-shaped hollow body.

handle
The area at the base of the stick that is held between the thumb and fingers when playing.

C string
The first and thickest string on a cello, traditionally tuned to two octaves below middle C.

frog
A device near the end closest to the bowing hand; it slides to adjust the tension of the hairs.

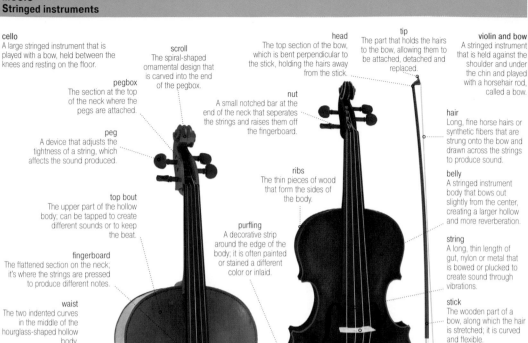

G string
The second string, traditionally tuned to G in the second octave below middle C, or a fourth above the first string.

chin rest
A piece of molded plastic or shaped wood that is propped under the chin when playing.

screw
A device that tightens and loosens the hairs to help create specific sounds or play different instruments.

D string
The third string, traditionally tuned to D in the first octave below middle C, or a fourth above the second string.

bridge
A small device on the body that holds the strings and helps transmit vibrations to the soundboard.

A string
The fourth string, traditionally tuned to A in the first octave below middle C, or a fourth above the third string.

F hole
The two curled holes in the soundboard; designed to improve the volume and tone of the sound.

tailpiece
A piece of wood or plastic to which the lower ends of the strings are attached, keeping them separate and in order.

bottom bout
The two lower curves of the hourglass-shaped hollow body.

end spike
A point on which the instrument balances on the ground, allowing it to be spun, twisted and turned when performing.

tailpiece
A knob on the tailpiece of a stringed instrument which is turned to minutely adjust the tension of a connected string.

bow
A length of wood along which fine hairs are stretched; used to play classical stringed instrument.

double bass
The largest and lowest-pitched classical bowed string instrument, usually played in a standing position.

tuning pin
A pin that is turned to adjust the tightness of the string, which affects the sound produced.

harp
An instrument with a triangular frame and strings of varied lengths, played by plucking the strings with one's fingers.

neck
The upper section of the harp; its curved design controls the lengths of the strings.

crown
The top section of the pillar; it is often elaborately carved and decorated with paint or even jewels.

shoulder
The curved section that connects the neck to the soundboard.

string
A long, thin length of gut, nylon or metal that creates sound through vibrations.

pillar
A column that frames out the structure and that contains part of the pedals' mechanism.

sound box
The large hollow body of the instrument; it amplifies the sound vibrations from the strings.

soundboard
The thin, flexible top layer of the body.

pedestal
The base that sits on the floor and where the pillar and soundboard meet.

foot
A support that protrudes from the base and keeps the instrument stable while it is being played.

viola
A four-stringed instrument that is larger than a violin and a fifth lower in tone.

pedal
A lever activated by the foot that raises or lowers the tone of the note created by the string.

electric upright bass
An electronically amplified version of a double bass, with a lightweight body.

electric violin
A violin designed to be electronically amplified.

bass guitar
A guitar-like electric instrument with four thick strings that produce notes in the lower register.

tuning peg
A device that adjusts the tightness of a string, which affects the sound produced.

electric guitar
A solid-body stringed instrument with pickups that convert sounds into electrical signals that can be amplified.

headstock
The upper end of the neck, where the tuning pegs are attached and the strings are wound.

position marker
A piece of wood, plastic or other material inlaid in the fingerboard to indicate proper string placement.

nut
A small notched bar at the end of the neck that seperates the strings and raises them off the fingerboard.

headstock
The widest part of the neck, at the end; the tuning pegs are attached to it.

fret
Thin bars at specific intervals that, when a string is pressed, shorten its length to produce a specific note.

neck
The elongated part that extends from the body; where the strings are pressed by fingers when playing.

twelfth fret marker
A special mark used to indentify the 12th fret, which is one full octave above the pitch of the open string.

fingerboard
The flattened section on the neck; it's where the strings are pressed to produce different notes.

neck pickup
The pickup that is closest to the neck of the guitar

middle pickup
The pickup that is in the middle of the pickguard.

strap button
A small peg to which a band of leather or other material can be attached so the guitar can easily be held while playing.

bridge pickup
The pickup that is closest to the bridge of the guitar.

cutaway
A section on the upper bout of a guitar which has been carved or molded inversely to the body to create a horn.

whammy bar
A device that raises and lowers the bridge, adjusting the strings tension, changing the notes' pitch.

pickguard
A piece of plastic material that protects the body of the guitar from scratches or wear from the pick.

pickup selector
A switch that allows the player to select which vibrations to amplify and which to suppress to adjust the sound.

string
A long, thin length of gut, nylon or metal that is plucked or strummed to create sound through vibrations.

tone control
A knob that adjusts the frequency of the electric signals of the notes; controls the tone of the guitar.

pickup
A device that captures strings' vibrations, turning them into electric signals that can be amplified.

volume control
A knob that controls how loud or quiet the instrument sounds.

output jack
The plug that transmits the electric signals from the guitar to the amplifier.

bridge
The bar on the lower body of a guitar that holds the strings in place; can sometimes be adjusted to alter the sound.

body
The instrument's main structure; all of the components are attached to it and it houses the electrical components.

peg
A device that adjusts the tightness of a string, which affects the sound produced.

headstock
The widest part of the neck, at the end; the tuning pegs are attached to it.

acoustic guitar
A hollow-bodied instrument with 6 or 12 strings played by plucking or strumming, without electrical amplification.

nut
A small notched bar at the end of the neck that seperates the strings and raises them off the fingerboard.

fret
Thin bars at specific intervals that, when a string is pressed, shorten its length to produce a specific note.

neck
The elongated part that extends from the body; where the strings are pressed by fingers when playing.

distortion pedal
A foot pedal that is connected between an electric guitar and an amplifier that, when pressed, alters the sound produced.

heel
A small piece of wood that attaches the neck to the body and adds stability.

ribs
The thin pieces of wood that form the sides of the body.

rosette
A decorative border around the guitar's sound hole.

sound hole
A hole in the soundboard that amplifies the strings' vibrations, improving the sound's volume and quality.

semi-acoustic guitar
An acoustic guitar that can be amplified and is played while connected to an electronic source.

string
A long, thin length of gut, nylon or metal that is plucked or strummed to create sound through vibrations.

purfling
A decorative strip around the edge of the body; it is often painted or stained a different color or inlaid.

bridge
A bar on the lower body that holds the strings and helps them return to their neutral position when not being played.

soundboard
The thin, flexible top layer of the body.

amplifier
A speaker that can be plugged directly into the body of an electric instrument to increase the volume of the sound.

guitar case
A hard or soft container for storing a guitar. It often has compartments for picks and other accessories.

concertina
An instrument, similar to an
accordion, with handheld
bellows and small side keys
to produce notes.

harmonium
A small reed organ with
bellows that are pumped
with the feet.

melodica
A small handheld keyboard,
with reeds, played by
blowing into a mouthpiece
and pressing keys.

harmonica
A small mouth organ with
chambers and metal reeds
that vibrate when the
player inhales and exhales,
producing sound.

accordion
A large wind instrument with
handheld bellows, a keyboard
and side keys that are pressed to
produce different sounds.

bayan
A Russian instrument,
similar to an accordion, with
buttons to produce notes.

Australian instruments

Musical instruments that were developed by Aboriginal Australians before colonization.

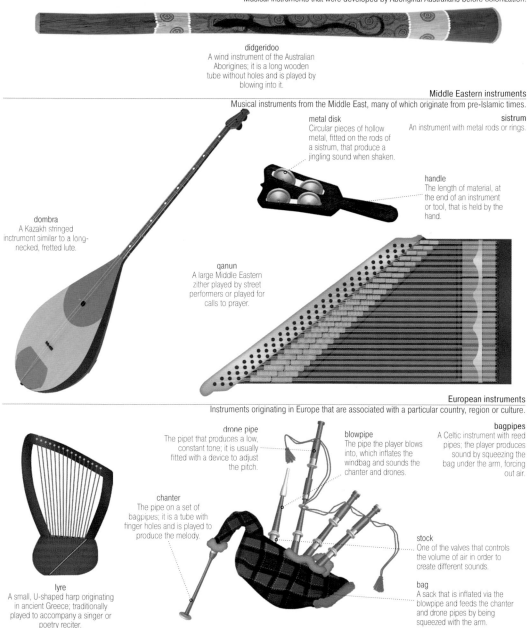

didgeridoo
A wind instrument of the Australian Aborigines; it is a long wooden tube without holes and is played by blowing into it.

Middle Eastern instruments

Musical instruments from the Middle East, many of which originate from pre-Islamic times.

metal disk
Circular pieces of hollow metal, fitted on the rods of a sistrum, that produce a jingling sound when shaken.

sistrum
An instrument with metal rods or rings.

handle
The length of material, at the end of an instrument or tool, that is held by the hand.

dombra
A Kazakh stringed instrument similar to a long-necked, fretted lute.

qanun
A large Middle Eastern zither played by street performers or played for calls to prayer.

European instruments

Instruments originating in Europe that are associated with a particular country, region or culture.

drone pipe
The pipet that produces a low, constant tone; it is usually fitted with a device to adjust the pitch.

blowpipe
The pipe the player blows into, which inflates the windbag and sounds the chanter and drones.

bagpipes
A Celtic instrument with reed pipes; the player produces sound by squeezing the bag under the arm, forcing out air.

chanter
The pipe on a set of bagpipes; it is a tube with finger holes and is played to produce the melody.

stock
One of the valves that controls the volume of air in order to create different sounds.

lyre
A small, U-shaped harp originating in ancient Greece; traditionally played to accompany a singer or poetry reciter.

bag
A sack that is inflated via the blowpipe and feeds the chanter and drone pipes by being squeezed with the arm.

mandolin
An instrument in the lute family with a pear-shaped body and double sets of strings, played by plucking with a pick.

string
A long, thin length of gut, nylon or metal used to make sounds when plucked, strummed or pulled.

body
The main part of an instrument. Many stringed instruments have bodies that taper toward the top.

headstock
The widest part of the neck, at the end; the tuning pegs are attached to it.

bridge
A small device on a stringed instrument to hold the strings and help transmit vibrations.

tailpiece
A piece of wood or plastic, on the lower end of a stringed instrument, to which the ends of the strings are attached.

barrel organ
An instrument, similar to an organ, played by turning a crank.

bowed psaltery
An Irish musical instrument similar to a zither. It has a small, triangular body and is played with a bow.

body
The main part of the instrument; it is hollow, which amplifies the sound vibrations

soundboard
The thin, flexible top layer of the body.

hitch pins
Small pins that secure the strings along the edge of body; the bow is drawn in between them when playing.

bridge
A small device on the body that holds the strings and helps transmit vibrations to the soundboard.

tuning pin
Pins that secure the strings along the bottom; turning adjusts the tightness, which affects the sound.

balalaika
A Russian stringed instrument with a triangular body and three strings that are plucked with the fingers or a pick.

string
A long, thin length of gut, nylon or metal that creates sound through vibrations.

psaltery bow
A curved length of wood along which fine hairs are stretched; used to play a stringed instrument.

zither
A traditional stringed instrument that does not have a neck; it is popular in Germany and Austria.

African instruments

Musical instruments originating from Africa, often associated with particular traditions or rituals.

African conga
A tall, narrow drum that is shaped like a barrel, has a low tone and is played by beating with the hands.

kora
A West African stringed instrument that is played by plucking and is made of a cut calabash gourd and cow skin.

American instruments

Musical instruments originating from the Americas and that are associated with specific regions or traditions.

banjo
A stringed instrument developed by colonial African-Americans. Its body consists of a membrane stretched over a frame.

quena
A traditional flute of the Andes, played by natives during worship or important ceremonies.

tuning peg
A device that adjusts the tightness of a string, which affects the sound produced.

headstock
The widest part of the neck, at the end; the tuning pegs are attached to it.

nut
A small notched bar at the end of the neck that seperates the strings and raises them off the fingerboard.

neck
The elongated part that extends from the body; where the strings are pressed by fingers when playing.

fifth-string peg
A peg on the neck of a banjo that is turned to adjust the tension of the fifth string, traditionally a drone string.

resonator
A plate on the back of the head that is designed to project sound and make the instrument louder.

tone ring
An assembly that holds the head tight, which helps clarify and project the sound.

head
The thin membrane that acts as a soundboard on a banjo; usually made of animal skin or plastic.

bridge
A small device on the lower body that holds the strings and helps transmit vibrations to the soundboard.

bandola
A small, pear-shaped stringed instrument from Venezuela or Colombia. It is similar to a mandolin but has a short neck.

charango
A small guitar from the Andes region of South America, traditionally made from the shell of an armadillo.

armrest
A rigid piece on the rim of the head that prevents the player's arm from damaging the head.

tailpiece
A piece of wood or plastic to which the lower ends of the strings are attached, keeping them separate and in order.

Asian instruments

Musical instruments originating in Asia and traditionally classified into families based on their primary material.

guzheng
A Chinese zither-like instrument that sits on a stand. It is plucked with nail picks traditionally made of turtle shell.

bridge
A small device on the body that holds the strings and helps transmit vibrations to the soundboard.

bass side
The section of strings that produce lower notes and are situated further from the player.

fixed bridge
A straight bar near the heads that holds the strings and helps transmit vibrations to the soundboard.

tail
The decorative end, which can be designed in a variety of shapes and colors.

soundboard
The thin, flexible top layer of the body.

treble side
The section of strings that produce higher notes and are situated closest to the player.

stand
A rigid structure used to raise an object off the ground; often made of joined poles or bars.

head
The squared off end; it is shaped like a box and has a hinged lid that allows access to the tuning pegs.

dholak
A two-headed South Asian hand drum, with one side tuned lower using a black tuning paste placed on the head.

jew's harp
An ancient instrument that has a long reed held in a frame; it is placed between the teeth and plucked with the tongue.

guqin
A Chinese zither, without frets, played for worship or meditation.

shehnai
A traditional Pakistani double-reed instrument. It has a low pitch and is made of wood and metal.

staple
The part that holds the instrument stable and together and allows the player to move freely while playing.

ivory needle
A small needle made of ivory that dangles on a thread from a shehnai and is used to clear the mouthpiece of saliva.

finger hole
One of several small holes on a wind instrument that are covered and uncovered with the fingers to create different notes.

bell
The flared end of a wind instrument; its design optimizes the instrument's sound.

double reed
Two thin, flat pieces that vibrate in the mouthpiece of some woodwind instruments, such as an oboe, to produce sound.

huqin
A Chinese fiddle, usually with only two strings and a geometrically shaped sound box covered with snakeskin or wood.

pipa
A shallow-bodied, four-stringed Chinese lute that plays high notes.

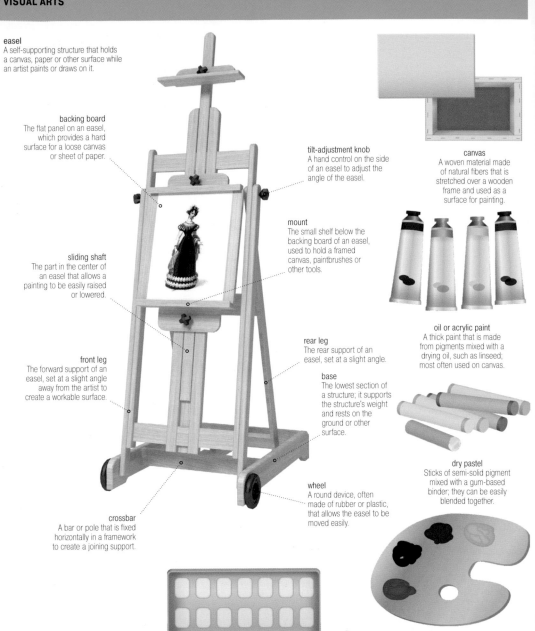

easel
A self-supporting structure that holds a canvas, paper or other surface while an artist paints or draws on it.

backing board
The flat panel on an easel, which provides a hard surface for a loose canvas or sheet of paper.

tilt-adjustment knob
A hand control on the side of an easel to adjust the angle of the easel.

canvas
A woven material made of natural fibers that is stretched over a wooden frame and used as a surface for painting.

mount
The small shelf below the backing board of an easel, used to hold a framed canvas, paintbrushes or other tools.

sliding shaft
The part in the center of an easel that allows a painting to be easily raised or lowered.

oil or acrylic paint
A thick paint that is made from pigments mixed with a drying oil, such as linseed; most often used on canvas.

rear leg
The rear support of an easel, set at a slight angle.

base
The lowest section of a structure; it supports the structure's weight and rests on the ground or other surface.

front leg
The forward support of an easel, set at a slight angle away from the artist to create a workable surface.

dry pastel
Sticks of semi-solid pigment mixed with a gum-based binder; they can be easily blended together.

crossbar
A bar or pole that is fixed horizontally in a framework to create a joining support.

wheel
A round device, often made of rubber or plastic, that allows the easel to be moved easily.

watercolor
Thinner paints made of pigment and water. They are sheer, very blendable and often fade over time.

palette
Hand tool used to hold multiple paints or to mix together different paints before putting them onto the canvas.

airbrush
An electronic device used
for spraying paint onto
a canvas by means of
compressed air; particularly
useful for shading.

wax crayon
Sticks made of pigmented
wax that can be rubbed
across paper or another
surface and are very
blendable.

brush
Fine bristles attached to a
stick in a rounded formation
and cut to create a point;
used for painting small
details.

flat brush
Fine bristles attached to
a stick in a rectangular
formation and cut evenly
across the top; used for
painting large areas.

colored pencil
A long, thin rod of hard
pigment that is encased in
wood and sharpened at one
end for drawing or writing.

gouache
A type of watercolor paint
that is blended with a
gluelike substance to create
a heavy, opaque effect
when applied.

oil pastel
A drawing medium similar
to dry pastel sticks, but
blended with non-drying oil
and wax, allowing bolder
shading.

turpentine
An essential oil used to clean
brushes so they can be reused and
to thin oil paints.

Mosaic work
An art form that involves creating a design with small pieces of colored glass or tile set in mortar, cement or glue.

glue
An adhesive used to secure
something, the composition
of which varies depending
on the materials being
glued.

tessera
Small pieces of colored glass, tile
or stone that are fit together into a
design and glued to a surface or
set in mortar.

mosaic
A design created with small
pieces of colored-glass or tile set
in mortar, cement or glue.

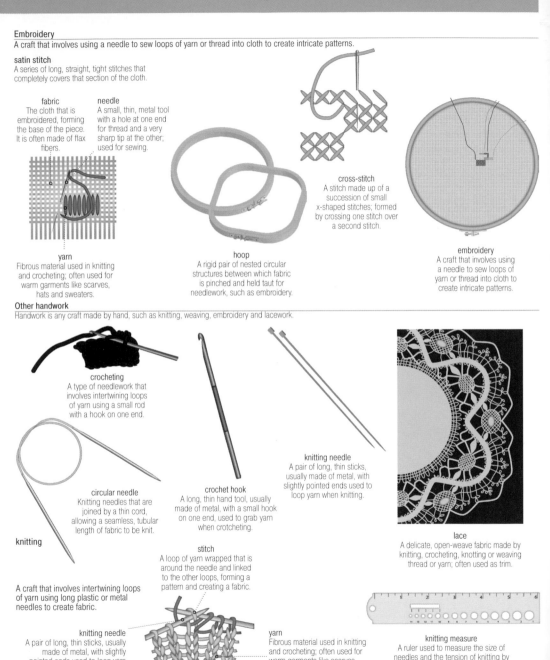

Embroidery

A craft that involves using a needle to sew loops of yarn or thread into cloth to create intricate patterns.

satin stitch

A series of long, straight, tight stitches that completely covers that section of the cloth.

fabric
The cloth that is embroidered, forming the base of the piece. It is often made of flax fibers.

needle
A small, thin, metal tool with a hole at one end for thread and a very sharp tip at the other; used for sewing.

cross-stitch
A stitch made up of a succession of small x-shaped stitches; formed by crossing one stitch over a second stitch.

yarn
Fibrous material used in knitting and crocheting; often used for warm garments like scarves, hats and sweaters.

hoop
A rigid pair of nested circular structures between which fabric is pinched and held taut for needlework, such as embroidery.

embroidery
A craft that involves using a needle to sew loops of yarn or thread into cloth to create intricate patterns.

Other handwork

Handwork is any craft made by hand, such as knitting, weaving, embroidery and lacework.

crocheting
A type of needlework that involves intertwining loops of yarn using a small rod with a hook on one end.

circular needle
Knitting needles that are joined by a thin cord, allowing a seamless, tubular length of fabric to be knit.

crochet hook
A long, thin hand tool, usually made of metal, with a small hook on one end, used to grab yarn when crotcheting.

knitting needle
A pair of long, thin sticks, usually made of metal, with slightly pointed ends used to loop yarn when knitting.

lace
A delicate, open-weave fabric made by knitting, crocheting, knotting or weaving thread or yarn; often used as trim.

knitting
A craft that involves intertwining loops of yarn using long plastic or metal needles to create fabric.

stitch
A loop of yarn wrapped that is around the needle and linked to the other loops, forming a pattern and creating a fabric.

knitting needle
A pair of long, thin sticks, usually made of metal, with slightly pointed ends used to loop yarn when knitting.

yarn
Fibrous material used in knitting and crocheting; often used for warm garments like scarves, hats and sweaters.

knitting measure
A ruler used to measure the size of needles and the tension of knitting by showing the number of stitches per inch.

Sewing

A craft that involves stitching thread into cloth to create or repair a garment or textile object.

thread take-up lever
A tension-regulating lever through which the upper thread is run before it is threaded through the needle.

thread guide
A metal tab that directs the thread toward the thread take-up lever.

arm
It hangs over the base, connects the head to the column and houses part of the machine's drive mechanism.

sewing machine
An electronic machine that sews faster and more accurately than hand sewing.

pressure dial
A mechanism used to adjust the pressure of the presser foot on the fabric, ensuring the needle moves smoothly.

bobbin winder
A metal pin that can spin a bobbin wheel so it can be quickly loaded with thread from the main spool.

spool release lever
A small lever that releases the spool so it can reloaded with thread or changed to a different thread.

head
The portion of a sewing machine that contains the intricate mechanism that controls the needle's movements.

handwheel
A large wheel on the side of a sewing machine that may be rotated to manually lift or lower the needle.

zipper
A flexible fastening device made up of two lengths of cloth with interlocking plastic or metal teeth joined by a slide.

needle plate
A metal plate with a hole through which the needle passes to pick up the bobbin thread.

pincushion
A small cushion that holds the sharp ends of pins and needles for use when sewing.

needle
A small, thin, metal tool with a hole at one end for thread and a very sharp tip at the other; used for sewing.

flat bed
The surface over which the fabric moves as it is sewn.

switch
A small device that is flipped to the right or left to turn a source of illumination on or off.

display
A lit panel that provides information such as the stitch width and stitch selected.

needle threader
A small device with a thin wire that is used to pull a length of thread or yarn through the small hole on a needle.

snap
A fastening made of interlocking disks, one socket shaped and one ball shaped, that snap together.

thimble
A metal or plastic protector worn on the index or middle finger when sewing by hand, usually when pushing the needle.

tape measure
A ruler used to measure lengths and widths of fabric, often when taking circular or curved measurements.

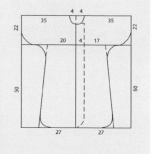

sew-through buttons
Circular fasteners made of glass, plastic, resin or stone with holes through which they can be stitched to fabric.

hook and eye
A fastening device consisting of small twists of metal that fit into each other.

pattern
Detailed drawing of the cuts required to the fabric when sewing, indicating options for pleats and sewing lines.

fabric
A woven sheet of natural or synthetic fibers used to create garments, soft furnishings, upholstery or other items.

safety pin
A bent pin that forms a spring and has a protective covering that holds the pointy end of the pin when it is closed.

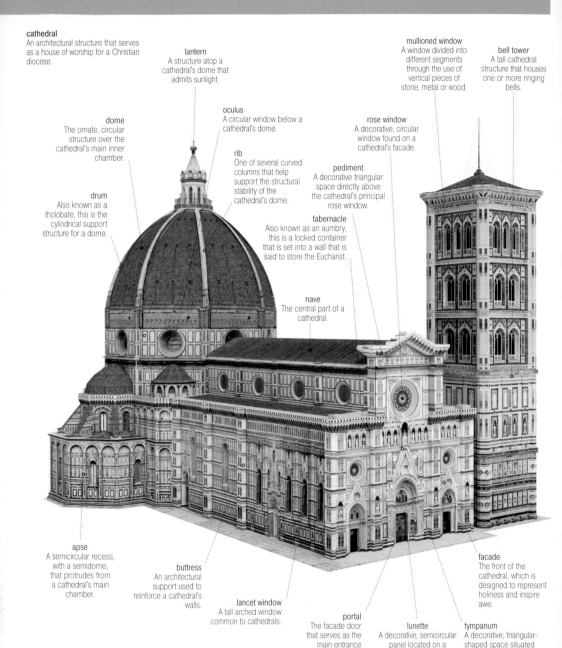

cathedral
An architectural structure that serves as a house of worship for a Christian diocese.

lantern
A structure atop a cathedral's dome that admits sunlight.

mullioned window
A window divided into different segments through the use of vertical pieces of stone, metal or wood.

bell tower
A tall cathedral structure that houses one or more ringing bells.

dome
The ornate, circular structure over the cathedral's main inner chamber.

oculus
A circular window below a cathedral's dome.

rose window
A decorative, circular window found on a cathedral's facade.

drum
Also known as a tholobate, this is the cylindrical support structure for a dome.

rib
One of several curved columns that help support the structural stability of the cathedral's dome.

pediment
A decorative triangular space directly above the cathedral's principal rose window.

tabernacle
Also known as an aumbry, this is a locked container that is set into a wall that is said to store the Eucharist.

nave
The central part of a cathedral.

apse
A semicircular recess, with a semidome, that protrudes from a cathedral's main chamber.

buttress
An architectural support used to reinforce a cathedral's walls.

lancet window
A tall arched window common to cathedrals.

portal
The facade door that serves as the main entrance for visitors to a cathedral.

lunette
A decorative, semicircular panel located on a cathedral's facade.

facade
The front of the cathedral, which is designed to represent holiness and inspire awe.

tympanum
A decorative, triangular-shaped space situated above a cathedral's main entrance.

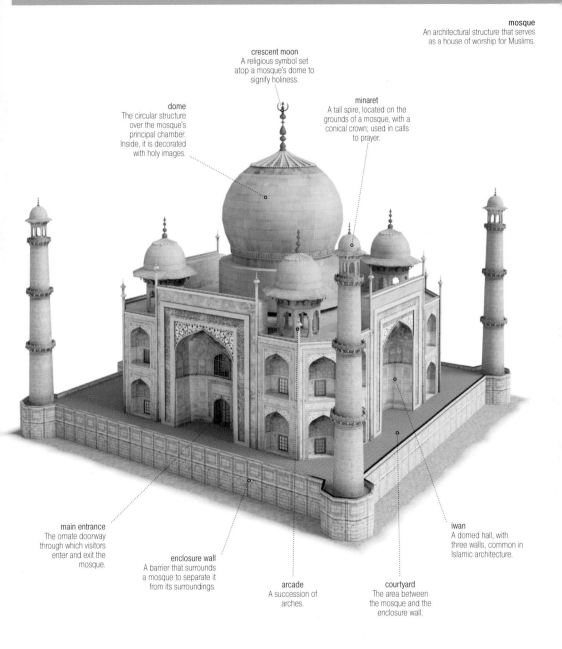

mosque
An architectural structure that serves
as a house of worship for Muslims.

crescent moon
A religious symbol set
atop a mosque's dome to
signify holiness.

minaret
A tall spire, located on the
grounds of a mosque, with a
conical crown; used in calls
to prayer.

dome
The circular structure
over the mosque's
principal chamber.
Inside, it is decorated
with holy images.

main entrance
The ornate doorway
through which visitors
enter and exit the
mosque.

enclosure wall
A barrier that surrounds
a mosque to separate it
from its surroundings.

arcade
A succession of
arches.

courtyard
The area between
the mosque and the
enclosure wall.

iwan
A domed hall, with
three walls, common in
Islamic architecture.

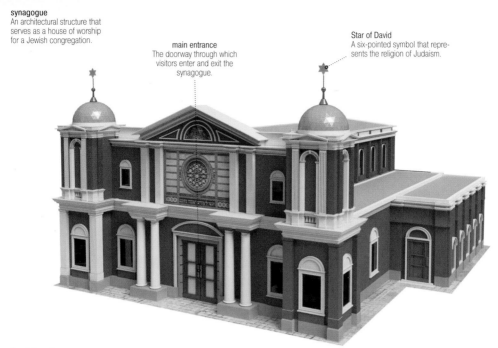

synagogue
An architectural structure that serves as a house of worship for a Jewish congregation.

main entrance
The doorway through which visitors enter and exit the synagogue.

Star of David
A six-pointed symbol that represents the religion of Judaism.

Greek temple
An architectural structure that served as a place of worship and culture in ancient Greece.

tile
Marble slabs used to create the roofing of the temple.

frieze
A decorated panel found above the Greek temple's columns.

architrave
Also known as an epistyle, this is a beam positioned atop the columns of the Greek temple.

euthynteria
The uppermost portion of the Greek temple's foundation. It supports the weight of the entire temple.

stylobate
The top step of the Greek temple, where the temple's columns are placed.

peristyle
Also known as a tetrastoon, this is a court surrounded by columns, a common feature of ancient Greek architecture.

column
A vertical support structure.

entablature
A superstructure in classical architecture that consists of architrave, frieze and cornice. It is supported by columns.

medieval castle
A fortified structure prevalent throughout Europe in the Middle Ages.

battlement
An accessible area of a curtain wall, where defenders can scout enemy positions or fire missiles.

keep
A fortified tower within the walls of a castle.

bailey
The courtyard found within a castle's walls.

flanking tower
A fortified tower projecting from a curtain wall.

storehouse
A storage structure located inside the castle's walls.

gate
A door, located at the castle's entrance, that can be opened or closed.

machicolation
A floor opening used to release stones and other objects upon outside attackers.

arena
The area of a Roman amphitheater where events, such as chariot races, take place.

curtain wall
A fortified partition that joins two towers of a castle.

drawbridge
A bridge that can be lowered or raised from a castle's walls in order to permit or prohibit entrance.

Roman amphitheater
An architectural structure that served as an arena for contests and spectacles in ancient Rome.

engaged Corinthian column
A wall-embedded column, common to classical architecture, characterized by a flared capital.

engaged Ionic column
A wall-embedded column, common to Greek architecture, characterized by a capital with a scroll-like design.

arcade
A series of arches that creates a covered area.

Corinthian pilaster
An ornamental structure created on the surface of a wall to give the appearance of a column.

engaged Doric column
A wall-embedded column, common to Greek architecture, characterized by a smooth capital and a grooved shaft.

SPORTS

soccer field
A rectangular playing field on which the game of soccer is played, with a goal net at either end.

fourth official
The assisstant to the assistant referee, often charged with managing substitutions and other technical areas.

entrance gate to field
The opening through which players and other personnel can enter and exit the soccer field from an exterior area.

coach
A person trained to provide technical guidance, strategy and mentorship to athletes during training and competition.

substitutes' bench
Area where players sit when they are not playing, but are available when needed to sub into the game.

on-field scoreboard
The electronic panel that displays the current score of the event. It is designed to be readily visible.

stands
The area in a soccer stadium where spectators sit to watch the game.

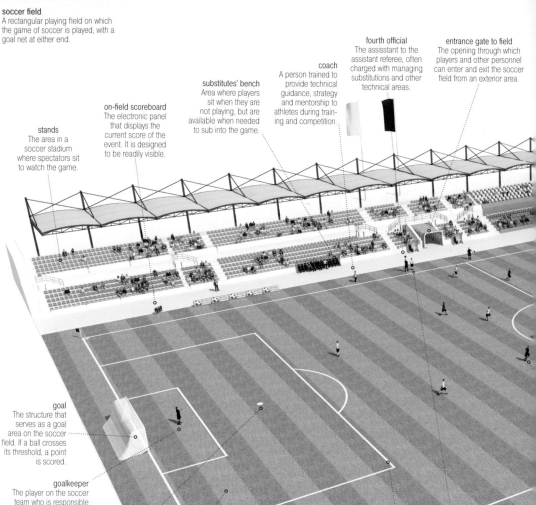

goal
The structure that serves as a goal area on the soccer field. If a ball crosses its threshold, a point is scored.

goalkeeper
The player on the soccer team who is responsible for protecting the goal and stopping the ball from entering.

penalty spot
The place on a soccer pitch where penalty kicks are taken after a serious foul has occurred.

penalty area
The area of the pitch where any violations against forwards result in a penalty kick.

substitute player
A player who does not start off in the game, but who can join it to replace another player later.

penalty area marking
The three lines that mark the boundaries of the penalty area on the soccer pitch.

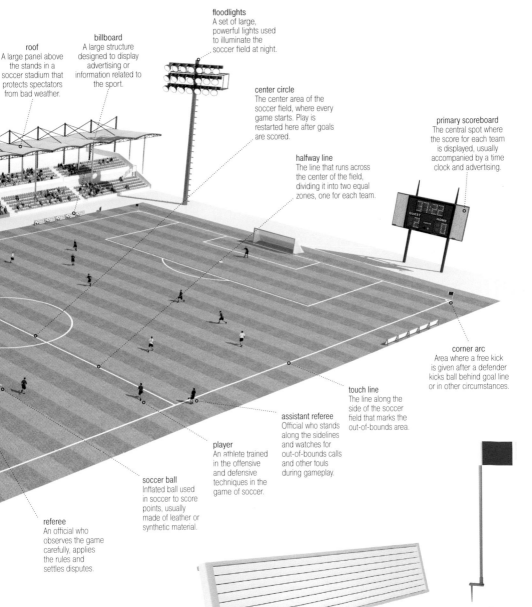

roof
A large panel above the stands in a soccer stadium that protects spectators from bad weather.

billboard
A large structure designed to display advertising or information related to the sport.

floodlights
A set of large, powerful lights used to illuminate the soccer field at night.

center circle
The center area of the soccer field, where every game starts. Play is restarted here after goals are scored.

primary scoreboard
The central spot where the score for each team is displayed, usually accompanied by a time clock and advertising.

halfway line
The line that runs across the center of the field, dividing it into two equal zones, one for each team.

corner arc
Area where a free kick is given after a defender kicks ball behind goal line or in other circumstances.

touch line
The line along the side of the soccer field that marks the out-of-bounds area.

assistant referee
Official who stands along the sidelines and watches for out-of-bounds calls and other fouls during gameplay.

player
An athlete trained in the offensive and defensive techniques in the game of soccer.

soccer ball
Inflated ball used in soccer to score points, usually made of leather or synthetic material.

referee
An official who observes the game carefully, applies the rules and settles disputes.

billboard
A large structure designed to display advertising or information related to the sport.

corner flag
A signaling device that marks the corner where the boundary lines of the soccer field connect.

soccer ball
An Inflated ball made of leather or synthetic material, used in the game of soccer to score points.

seam
The intricate stitching that holds the soccer ball together to prevent it from being torn apart during play.

hexagon
A geometric patch on a soccer ball, which forms a pattern with the pentagon patches to make a perfect sphere.

cover
The protective surface material of the soccer ball, made of leather or another soft and durable material.

pentagon
A geometric patch on a soccer ball, which forms a pattern with the hexagon patches to make a perfect sphere.

coach's board
A clipboard used by the coach, on which they draw plays and illustrate tactics related to the game of soccer.

soccer ball machine
Machine used to funnel, sort, move and guide balls through a series of pulleys, gears and other mechanical devices.

soccer field diagram
A drawing of the soccer field on the coach's board, on which game plans can be outlined.

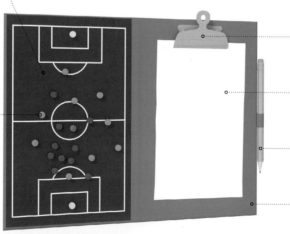

clip
A spring device that holds paper sheets on a clipboard.

paper
Thin sheets of material made from wood pulp, which is used for writing and drawing upon.

marker
A small object that is used to represent a player on the soccer field diagram.

pencil
A writing device made from graphite or other material and is used to record information on paper.

clipboard
A board with a clip, which is used to hold papers and provide a hard surface for writing.

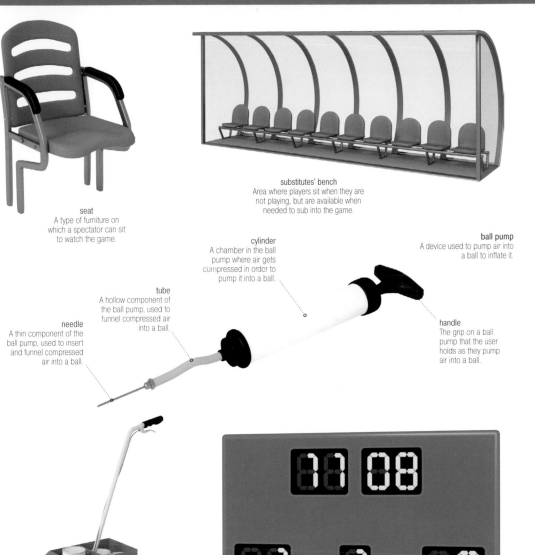

seat
A type of furniture on which a spectator can sit to watch the game.

substitutes' bench
Area where players sit when they are not playing, but are available when needed to sub into the game.

cylinder
A chamber in the ball pump where air gets compressed in order to pump it into a ball.

ball pump
A device used to pump air into a ball to inflate it.

tube
A hollow component of the ball pump, used to funnel compressed air into a ball.

needle
A thin component of the ball pump, used to insert and funnel compressed air into a ball.

handle
The grip on a ball pump that the user holds as they pump air into a ball.

field marker
A specialized rolling cart that leaves a powder trail, paint or other marking material to create lines on the field.

scoreboard
The electronic panel that displays the current score of the event. It is designed to be readily visible.

Referee's equipment
The equipment used by the referee to signal official calls and communicate with players.

referee's shelter
An enclosed area on the sidelines where the referee is protected from the weather while they watch the game.

frame
The steel structure that forms the shape of the referee's shelter.

desk
A flat, horizontal piece of furniture on which objects can be placed.

protective covering
Transparent material on the referee's shelter that shields the person inside from bad weather.

red card
A red card held up by a referee to signal an extreme penalty for a player, who is removed from the game.

seat
A chair where a referee can sit while observing the game.

yellow card
A yellow penalty card held up by a referee that signals a player has been given a penalty for a foul.

substitution board
A flat, electronic board that is used to display the numbers of players who are either leaving play or substituting.

stopwatch
Timing device that measures time very precisely in minutes, seconds and fractions of seconds.

whistle
A small device that makes a high-pitched sound to signal when play should stop.

Soccer player and equipment
An athlete trained to play soccer, and his uniform and protective gear.

shin guard
A protective pad designed to fit securely over an athlete's lower leg to protect it during play.

soccer player
An athlete trained in the offensive and defensive techniques in the game of soccer.

jersey
Stretchy uniform covering the top of an athelete's body, often featuring the team colors and player's number.

shorts
Short pants that cover only the top part of the leg and allow unrestricted movement.

goalkeeper's glove
A flexible, padded glove for a goalkeeper, made with textured material to make it easier to grasp the ball.

tongue
A flap of material underneath the laces on the cleat shoe, over which the laces crisscross.

lace
Length of string used to join two sides of a shoe together to hold it tightly to the foot.

soccer cleats
Shoes worn to play soccer, with rubber spikes on the bottom to help grip the terrain of the soccer field.

stud
A small spike attached to the cleat shoe to provide superior traction and reduce slipping on the turf.

heel
The part of the cleat shoe that covers the back end of the athlete's foot.

toe
The front part of the cleat shoe, where the toes are encased by hard plastic, leather or other material.

American football field
A specially designed field for playing American football. The field has two end zones and two field goal stands.

referee
An official who observes the game carefully, enforces the rules and settles disputes.

team area
The area on the football field where coaches, assistants and substitute players stand during gameplay.

line judge
An official whose duties include timekeeping, signaling stoppages and supervising kickoffs.

end zone
The area where a touchdown is scored when a player enters it with the ball.

billboard
A large structure designed to display advertising or information related to the sport.

concession stand
An outlet where refreshments can be purchased, including popcorn and drinks.

50-yard line
Line that is 50 yards from each goal line and divides the football field into two equal zones, one for each team.

umpire
A football official who stands near the line of scrimmage and ensures that the rules are properly followed.

players' area
Area where players wait for their turn to enter the game.

player
An athlete trained in all the offensive and defensive techniques in the game of football.

head linesman
An official whose duties include recording yardage gained or lost, positioning balls and signaling stoppages.

field judge
An official who makes calls on the field for penalties and other procedural aspects of the game.

goal line
The line, dividing the end zone from the field of play, which must be crossed to score a touchdown.

lace
A long string that is used to tie the seams of the football tightly together.

football
An oval leather ball filled with compressed air, used in the game of football to score points.

seam
The stitching that holds two pieces of the covering of the football tightly together.

back judge
An official whose duties include tracking time between plays and monitoring receivers and defense players.

goal
Frame with two goalposts and a crossbar. Player must kick the ball between the goalposts to score points.

vendor
An employee trained to sell goods and refreshments at a concession stand in a football stadium.

popcorn
Corn kernels that have been heated until they burst open.

beverage
An alcholic or non-alcoholic drink sold at football events.

umbrella
A device used to provide shade to a vendor during a football game.

customer
A football game attendee who buys refreshments at the concession stand.

concession stand
An outlet where refreshments can be purchased, including popcorn and drinks.

stand
A small stall where various goods and refreshments are sold at a stadium during the course of a football game.

basketball arena
A sporting facility with a basketball court, which consists of two baskets and regulation boundary lines.

backboard
The elevated and flat-faced board located behind a hoop that is used for bank shots, layups and other techniques.

basket
The basketball hoop and net. Players score points by throwing the ball into the basket.

three-point line
A curved line that marks the area beyond which players can score three points instead of two with a basket shot.

restraining circle
One of three jump-ball circles, which other athletes cannot enter during a jump ball.

players' bench
Area where players sit when they are not playing, but are available when needed to sub into the game.

stands
The area of a basketball court where spectators sit to watch the game.

backstop
Structure made up of a basketball hoop and net, a backstop and the support framework.

billboard
A large structure designed to display advertising or information related to the sport.

free throw line
A line parallel to the end line, behind which a shooter stands to take a free throw.

free throw circle
The circle which the free throw line bisects on the basketball court.

center circle
The center area of the court, where the game starts with a jump ball, when two players jump for the ball.

net
A flexible mesh attached to the rim of the basket that slows the ball as it passes through.

support
A post that provides the structural framework that holds up the backboard and basketball net.

backboard
A rigid board used for bank shots, layups and other techniques.

rim
A circular hoop through which the ball must pass to score points.

officials
The people who are charged with overseeing the game and applying the rules.

referee
An official who observes the game carefully, applies the rules and settles disputes.

team physician
A doctor trained in sports medicine who is employed by the team to treat the players.

coach
A person trained to provide technical guidance, strategy and mentorship to athletes during training and competition.

basketball
An inflated ball with eight pieces of material stitched together. Players shoot it through a hoop to score points.

rib
The indention on a basketball that helps players grip the ball and indicates where it is sewn together.

basketball
An inflated ball with eight pieces of material stitched together. Players shoot it through a hoop to score points.

sideline
A line along the side of the basketball court that marks the out-of-bounds area.

player
An athlete trained in all the offensive and defensive techniques of the game of basketball.

press photographer
An individual who is trained as a photographic journalist. They attend all types of sporting events.

Basketball moves

The various actions used by basketball players to pass and move the ball down the court to outwit the opposite team.

layup
A two-point shot where the player jumps up and bounces the ball off the backboard into the basket with one hand.

hook shot
A one-handed shot where the player swings his arm in an arc above his head and releases the ball.

holding
A technique used when controlling the ball. The player holds the ball with one hand to avoid being charged with traveling.

dribbling
When a player advances the ball down the court by bouncing it continuously with one hand.

pump fake
A common basketball move when a player signals a break in one direction, then goes another.

thumb
The part of the baseball glove that covers and protects the thumb.

baseball glove: bottom view
A view of the bottom side of a baseball glove. It is stitched together with plastic or leather materials.

strap
Intersecting strips of leather that form the web of the baseball glove and connect the fingers to the thumb.

palm
Central area of the baseball glove that covers the hollow of the hand.

lace
Thin strip of material that is strung through the eyelets and used to tighten the baseball glove on the hand.

finger
The part of the baseball glove that covers and protects a finger.

cross section of a baseball
A cutaway of a baseball showing the inner layers of the ball's core.

yarn ball
A section of yarn threads found inside a baseball.

cork center
The most inner layer of a baseball, which is made of cork.

baseball glove: top view
This large, leather glove is used to catch the ball during play.

stitches
Threads used to hold the layers of a baseball together.

bat
Club that is used in the game of baseball to hit the ball in order to score points. Maximum length 42 inches.

cover
The outer fabric casing of a baseball.

baseball field (baseball diamond)
A diamond-shaped field where the game of baseball is played.

billboard
A large structure designed to display advertising or information related to the sport.

player
An athlete trained in the various techniques common to baseball.

foul line
The line that marks the border of the playing field. When a baseball crosses this line, a foul is called.

umpire
An official who supervises the game of baseball, enforces the rules and makes judgment calls on plays.

third base
The third station a batter runs to. The last base before home plate.

third base coach's box
The area where the third base coach stands to advise runners whether to stop or continue running.

dugout
A partially closed area occupied by baseball team's coaches, manager and substitute players during gameplay.

entrance gate to field
The opening through which players, coaches, officials and spectators enter and exit the baseball field.

baseball
A hard ball covered with two white pieces of leather stitched together.

on-deck circle
A designed area in the foul territory where the player who is next at bat, or on deck, waits their turn.

stairs
A series of steps in the stands of the baseball stadium that allow fans the ability to enter and exit.

stands
The area in a baseball stadium where spectators sit to watch the game.

second base
The second station a batter runs to; marked by a cushion on the ground.

pitcher
Player who throws balls to batter on opposing team and tries to strike them out with deceptive pitches.

pitcher's mound
A raised hill of earth where the pitcher stands to throw the ball to the batter.

first base
First station the batter runs to after hitting the ball, marked by a cushion on the ground.

first base coach's box
The area where the first base coach stands to advise runners whether to stop or continue running.

backstop
A barrier that prevents foul balls, bats and other items from flying into the stadium's stands.

batter
The player who is at bat. They attempt to hit the ball over the fence or into a strategic area on the baseball field.

home plate
The marker on a baseball field beside the batter. Pitches are thrown over it and runners cross it to score a point.

catcher
Person behind batter who catches the pitch, throws it back to pitcher and signals the type of pitch to throw.

catcher's box
The area of the baseball field where the catcher is positioned in order to catch and return baseball pitches.

batter's box
The area where the batter stands when at bat. It is usually marked by a rectangular chalk line.

volleyball court
A rectangular area divided by a high net and marked with boundaries, where the game of volleyball is played.

right attacker
An offensive position on the right side of the attack zone, who makes attack hits to score points.

center attacker
An offensive position in the center of the attack zone, who counters attacks from the opposing team.

left attacker
An offensive position on the left side of the attack zone, who makes attack hits to score points.

vertical side band
A heavy strip of vertical, white tape that marks each end of the volleyball net.

right back
A defensive position on the right side of the back zone, who makes digs on short balls.

umpire
An official who observes the game carefully, applies the rules and settles disputes.

scorekeeper
An official who keeps track of the match score by recording points when scored.

net
A mesh material stretched across the center of the court. The players must hit the ball over the net.

players' bench
A sitting area for players and other personnel, located on the sidelines of the court.

back
The upper part of a piece of furniture on which a person sits, which provides support for their back.

volleyball
An inflated ball used in the game of volleyball, usually made of pieces of leather stitched together.

post
An upright structural component of the net that is used to support the frame of the net and keep it taught.

towel
A piece of absorbent material that is used to dry a wet person and to mop up sweat.

coach
A person trained to provide technical guidance, strategy and mentorship to athletes during training and competition.

players' bench
Area for substitute players and coaches to sit, watch the game and plan strategy.

water bottle
A container with a top that holds drinking water.

attack zone
The area between the attack line and the net, where attackers are usually positioned.

seat
The lower part of a piece of furniture on which a person sits.

white tape
A heavy white tape covering the top and bottom cables of the net. The cables suspend the net from the posts.

referee
An official who observes the game carefully, applies the rules and settles disputes.

left back
A defensive position on the left side of the back zone, who makes digs on short balls.

attack line
A line 10 feet from the net that separates the attack zone from the back zone on the volleyball court.

sideline
A line along the side of the volleyball court that marks the out-of-bounds area.

center back
A defensive position in the center of the back zone, who recovers long balls and blocked balls.

billboard
A large structure designed to display advertising or information related to the sport.

end line
The line at the end of the volleyball court that marks the out-of-bounds and serving area.

linesman
An official who watches the lines of the court to ensure off-side calls and violations do not occur.

back zone
The area at the end of the volleyball court, between the attack line and the end line.

free zone
The area surrounding the volleyball court, which must be at least 6.5 feet wide.

beach volleyball court
The playing area, with a surface of sand,
where the game of beach volleyball
is played.

umbrella
A device that provides
shade from the sun or cover
from the rain.

cooler
A specially designed
container that keeps
drinks and food chilled.

players' chairs
Seats for players.

first referee
The head referee,
responsible for calling
plays, resolving disputes
and overseeing the game.

referee's chair
A high seat for an
umpire.

stand
A support frame to hold
a net and keep it taut.

net
A mesh partition
placed in the center
of a volleyball court in
order to divide play into
two areas.

beach volleyball
An inflated ball used in the
game of beach volleyball,
usually made of pieces of
leather stitched together.

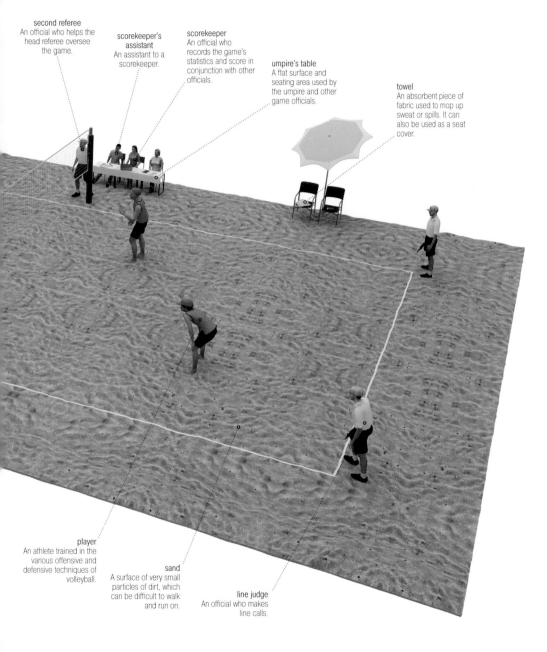

second referee
An official who helps the head referee oversee the game.

scorekeeper's assistant
An assistant to a scorekeeper.

scorekeeper
An official who records the game's statistics and score in conjunction with other officials.

umpire's table
A flat surface and seating area used by the umpire and other game officials.

towel
An absorbent piece of fabric used to mop up sweat or spills. It can also be used as a seat cover.

player
An athlete trained in the various offensive and defensive techniques of volleyball.

sand
A surface of very small particles of dirt, which can be difficult to walk and run on.

line judge
An official who makes line calls.

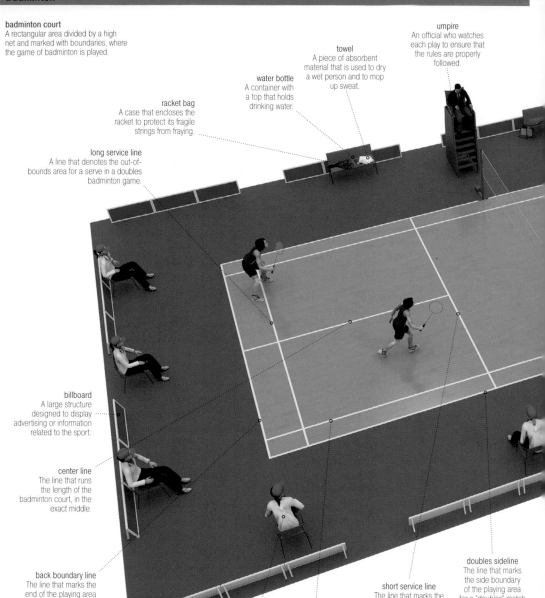

badminton court
A rectangular area divided by a high net and marked with boundaries, where the game of badminton is played.

umpire
An official who watches each play to ensure that the rules are properly followed.

towel
A piece of absorbent material that is used to dry a wet person and to mop up sweat.

water bottle
A container with a top that holds drinking water.

racket bag
A case that encloses the racket to protect its fragile strings from fraying.

long service line
A line that denotes the out-of-bounds area for a serve in a doubles badminton game.

billboard
A large structure designed to display advertising or information related to the sport.

center line
The line that runs the length of the badminton court, in the exact middle.

back boundary line
The line that marks the end of the playing area on a badminton court.

linesman
An offficial who watches the lines to ensure that out-of-bounds and line violations do not occur.

singles sideline
A line that denotes the out-of-bounds area in a singles badminton game.

short service line
The line that marks the front boundary of the service area on a badminton court.

doubles sideline
The line that marks the side boundary of the playing area for a "doubles" match of badminton.

players' bench
A seating area on the side of the court for athletes.

shuttlecock
A small, aerodynamic device, also known as a "birdie," which is hit back and forth across the net in badminton.

racket
A device used to hit a shuttlecock in badminton.

badminton racket
A device made up of a handle and a hoop with strings stretched across it.

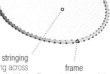

handle
The grip at the end of the racket where the player holds it.

shaft
Hollow central tube of a badminton racket that helps to keep the racket as lightweight as possible.

stringing
The interlaced string across the hoop of the racket that serves as a hitting surface for the shuttlecock.

frame
The metallic hoop of the badminton racket. The stringing is attached to the frame.

player
An athlete trained in the offensive and defensive techniques of the game of badminton.

shuttlecock
A small, aerodynamic device, also known as a "birdie," which is hit back and forth across the net in badminton.

alley
The area on the side of a badminton court between the doubles and singles sidelines.

service judge
An official who monitors the serve to ensure that all the rules are properly followed.

net
A mesh material stretched across the center of a badminton court. The players must hit the shuttlecock over the net.

crown
The cone of light feathers or plastic mesh on the shuttlecock that help make it aerodynamic.

cork tip
The rounded base of the shuttlecock, traditionally made of cork, which always turns to face the direction it is hit.

net
A mesh material stretched across the center of the court. The players must hit the shuttlecock over the net.

tennis court
A rectangular area divided by a low net and marked with boundaries, where the game of tennis is played.

alley
The area on the side of a tennis court between the doubles and singles sidelines.

service line
The line that runs parallel to the net in the tennis court that marks the end of the forecourt.

cameraman
Person who operates a camera.

player's bench
A sitting area for players and other personnel, located on the sidelines of the court.

chair umpire
A procedural official who sits in a tall chair adjacent to the court to view the game's action from above.

tennis racket
A device used to hit a ball in tennis.

ball boy
Person who runs to fetch foul balls and net balls from the court during the game of tennis.

billboard
A large structure designed to display advertising or information related to the sport.

stairs
A series of steps in the stands of the tennis court that allow fans the ability to enter and exit.

stands
The area where spectators sit to watch the game of tennis.

linesman
An official who watches the lines to ensure that out-of-bounds and line violations do not occur.

baseline
The line that marks the end of the tennis court.

foot fault judge
A game official responsible for monitoring whether a line violation occurs during serves.

doubles sideline
The line that marks the side boundary of the playing area for a "doubles" match of tennis.

service judge
A game official responsible for monitoring the serves of players.

singles sideline
The line that marks the side boundary of the playing area for a "singles" match of tennis.

net
A mesh material stretched across the center of the tennis court. The players must hit the ball over the net.

right service court
The right quadrant of a tennis court, where an even-score serve must fall.

center service line
The line that runs down the center of the tennis court to divide the forecourt into two zones.

backcourt
The area of the tennis court between the baseline and the service line.

tennis player
An athlete trained in the offensive and defensive techniques of the game of tennis.

tennis ball
A rubber ball used in the game of tennis. Filled with compressed air, it has great shock-absorbing qualities.

tennis ball hopper
Basket designed to hold tennis balls for court play. It is usually located near center court by the net for convenience.

reporter
A writer who records and recaps the details of the game in the form of news articles and other media.

left service court
The left quadrant of a tennis court, where an odd-score serve must fall.

tennis ball
A rubber ball used in the game of tennis. Filled with compressed air, it has great shock-absorbing qualities.

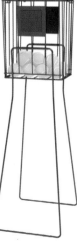

tennis racket
A device made up of a handle and a hoop with strings stretched across it.

table tennis court
The space where table tennis is played; includes the table and the area surrounding it.

camera
Recording device that captures the sights and sounds of the game. It can come in a variety of sizes and styles.

cameraman
A person who operates a camera.

racket
A wooden device made up of a handle and a flat, oval hitting surface, used to hit the ball in table tennis.

racket
A flat, oval hitting surface with a handle; used to hit the ball in table tennis.

face
The rubber surface of the racket. It is dimpled or smooth to provide better angling rotations on the ball.

blade
The flat, oval part of the racket that is used to hit the ball. It is made of a hard and durable yet thin slab of wood.

handle
The grip at the end of the racket where the player holds it.

table tennis ball
Small, hollow ball that is hit back and forth across the net in table tennis. Very light and strong.

umpire
An official who watches each play to ensure that the rules are properly followed.

table tennis ball
Small, hollow ball that is hit back and forth across the net in table tennis. Very light and strong.

scorekeeper
An official who keeps track of the scores in table tennis.

scoreboard
The board where the score is displayed as the game progresses.

billboard
A large structure designed to display advertising or information related to the sport.

net
A mesh material stretched across the center of the tennis table. The players must hit the ball over the net.

tennis table
A wooden, rectangular table with a net stretched across the middle. This is the playing surface for table tennis.

player
An athlete trained in the offensive and defensive techniques of the game of table tennis.

stadium
The specialized outdoor facility used for track and field sports.

javelin throw
An event that involves throwing a light spear the furthest.

high jump
A field event where athletes attempt to clear a high bar.

shot put
A field event that involves the launching of a heavy object, called a shot, as far as possible.

lawn
The grass field inside a track. It must be routinely groomed to meet regulations.

track
The collection of lines where runners race.

safety cage
A series of thick panels set up on a track field to protect spectators from throws.

pole vault
A track and field event in which athletes use a large pole to attempt to spring over a crossbar.

crossbar
The part of a pole vault that athletes must clear during their jumps.

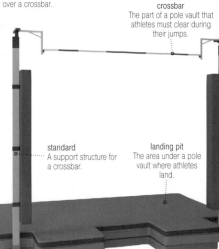

finish line
The line, on a track, that marks where a race ends.

standard
A support structure for a crossbar.

landing pit
The area under a pole vault where athletes land.

hurdle
A frame placed intermittently along a track to provide an obstacle for runners.

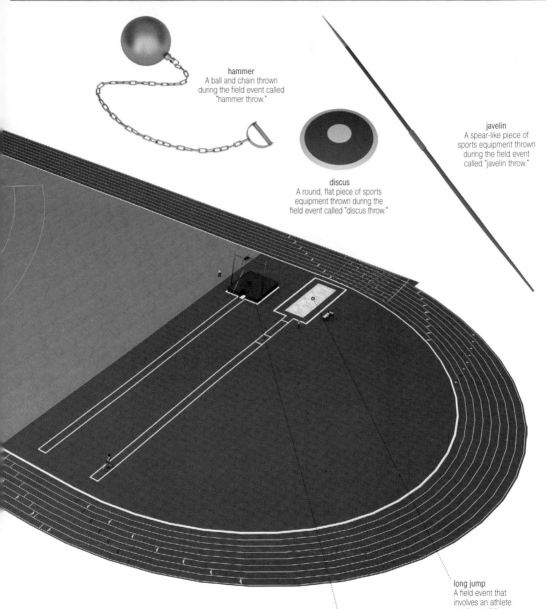

hammer
A ball and chain thrown during the field event called "hammer throw."

discus
A round, flat piece of sports equipment thrown during the field event called "discus throw."

javelin
A spear-like piece of sports equipment thrown during the field event called "javelin throw."

starting blocks
A device in which a track runner places his or her feet before a race starts.

pole vault
A field event that involves an athlete throwing a long, flexible pole over a crossbar.

long jump
A field event that involves an athlete running and then jumping as far as possible into a sandpit.

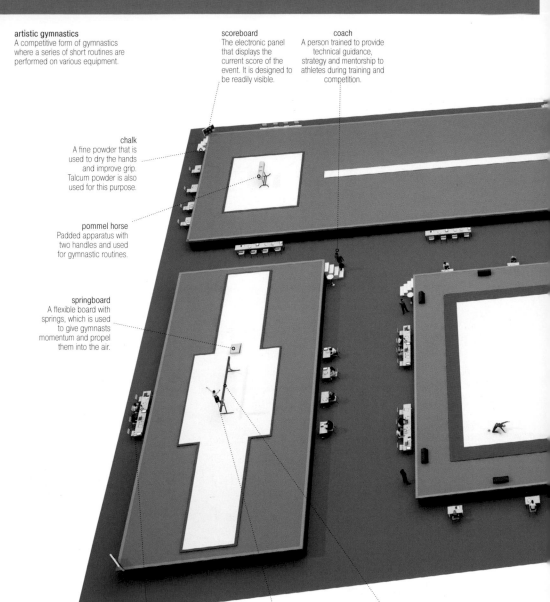

artistic gymnastics
A competitive form of gymnastics where a series of short routines are performed on various equipment.

scoreboard
The electronic panel that displays the current score of the event. It is designed to be readily visible.

coach
A person trained to provide technical guidance, strategy and mentorship to athletes during training and competition.

chalk
A fine powder that is used to dry the hands and improve grip. Talcum powder is also used for this purpose.

pommel horse
Padded apparatus with two handles and used for gymnastic routines.

springboard
A flexible board with springs, which is used to give gymnasts momentum and propel them into the air.

judges
Scorekeepers in the judging area who are responsible for awarding points and overseeing gameplay.

gymnast
An athlete who is trained in gymnastics and performs routines on beams, bars, vaults and rings.

balance beam
Long, elevated bar on which gymnasts perform various routines, including handsprings, round-offs and cartwheels.

vault
Apparatus used by gymnast to propel and bounce off. It can also be a prop in routines.

parallel bars
An apparatus with two parallel, horizontal bars, used to perform aerial maneuvers.

uneven parallel bars
An apparatus with two uneven, parallel bars, to swing on, bounce off and perform routines.

rings
Round hoops that are suspended in the air and can be used by gymnasts to perform routines.

spring floor
A floor specially constructed to provide some bounce for gymnastic and dance routines.

stairs
A small series of risers that allow gymnasts and officials to step up to enter the event platform.

Artistic gymnastics equipment
The apparatuses used in gymnastics routines: stands, bars, beams and vaults.

uneven bars
Gymnastic apparatus with two uneven, parallel bars; used by gymnasts to swing, bounce and perform routines.

upper bar
The higher of the two uneven bars.

lower bar
The lower of the two uneven bars.

guy cable
A thick support cable attached to the adjusting tubes of uneven bars to provide structural integrity.

adjusting tube
A long, hollow shaft that can be raised or lowered and is used to support uneven bars.

parallel bars
Gymnastic apparatus with two parallel, horizontal bars; used to perform aerial maneuvers and other routines.

wooden bar
One of two long, horizontal pieces of wood placed atop an adjustable support to create parallel bars.

vault
Padded apparatus used by gymnast to propel and bounce off. It can also be a prop in routines.

adjustable support
A mechanism, located near the base of parallel bars, that can be used to lower or raise each bar end.

base
The support structure of parallel bars or other objects.

chalk bowl
A bowl with a fine powder, such as talcum powder or chalk, used to dry the hands and improve grip.

neck
The left end of a pommel horse.

saddle
The central part of a pommel horse.

pommel
One of two metal handles fitted on the saddle of a pommel horse and used to perform maneuvers.

pommel horse
Gymnastic apparatus used to perform balance and swinging maneuvers, as well as launches.

horse
The body, or main part, of a pommel horse.

croup
The right end of a pommel horse.

base
The support structure of a pommel horse or other object.

height adjustment
A part, on the base of a pommel horse, that can be used to alter the horse's height.

anti-slip shoe
A rubber part located on the bottom of a pommel horse's base to keep the pommel horse stationary.

springboard
A board used by acrobats and gymnasts to propel themselves into the air.

balance beam
Long, elevated bar on which gymnasts perform various routines, including handsprings, round-offs and cartwheels.

vaulting horse
Large, sawhorse-type, padded apparatus used by a gymnast to jump, bounce, swing or propel them selves into the air.

gymnast
An athlete who is trained in gymnastics and performs routines on beams, bars, vaults and rings.

rhythmic gymnastics
A style of gymnastics that involves performing body movements with a ball, hoop, ribbon, clubs or rope.

stairs
A small series of risers that allow gymnasts and officials to step up to enter the event platform.

chalk
A fine powder used to dry the hands and improve grip. Talcum powder is also used for this purpose.

difficulty judge
Judge who considers the degree of difficulty of the routine, based on a variety of factors within the routine.

technical execution judge
The official who evaluates how well the gymnast executes the routine and awards points accordingly.

scoreboard
The electronic panel that displays the current score of the event. It is designed to be readily visible.

artistic execution judge
A scoring judge who is trained to score the artistic merits of a gymnastic routine.

spring floor
A floor specially constructed to provide some bounce for gymnastic and dance routines.

gymnast
An athlete who is trained in artistic or rhythmic gymnastics.

ball
A round prop used in rhythmic gymnastics to bounce, roll, balance and catch.

loudspeaker
A device that amplifies sound to make it audible in a large space.

meet referee
The highest-ranking judge, charged with overseeing the other judges and all aspects of judging at the event.

coordinator judge
A scoring assistant who transfers, records and edits the various scores in conjunction with the other judges.

golf cart: front view
The front view of the small, motorized vehicle used to transport golfers and equipment around a golf course.

roof
The canopy that extends across the top of the golf cart to protect passengers from bad weather.

back
The backrest that supports the back and spine of the driver of a golf cart.

tire
A rubber wheel that rotates on an axis and helps propel the golf cart forward or backward.

seat
A cushioned area where the driver sits to operate the golf cart.

golf cart: back view
The back view of the small, motorized vehicle used to transport golfers and equipment around a golf course.

club
Device used to hit the ball in golf, which comes in various designs, including putters, drivers and irons.

steering wheel
A circular device in a vehicle, which the driver turns to change direction.

strap
A strip of flexible material attached to the back of a golf cart that is used to secure a golf bag in place.

cup holder
A device in a vehicle where a drinking container can be placed while driving.

golf bag
The sack used to carry golf clubs, with various compartments to store the clubs and accessories.

storage compartment
An area on the front dashboard of a golf cart where miscellaneous items can be placed.

armrest
A padded support for a person's arm to rest on while driving or riding in a golf cart.

basket
A small cargo area on the golf cart behind the seats and between the golf bags, which provides storage.

golfer
An athlete who specializes in golf. Golfers are trained to drive and putt balls.

golf bag
The sack used to carry golf clubs, with various compartments to store the clubs and accessories.

golf club
A piece of sports equipment used in the sport of golf to drive or putt a golf ball into a cup in as few strokes as possible.

zipper
A closure made up of teeth that interlock, used to seal the various pouches of the golf bag to secure items.

golf glove
A specialized hand covering worn by a golfer when using a golf club.

golf shoes
Footwear with cleats worn by golfers on a golf course.

golf ball
The ball used in the sport of golf. It is dimpled and has a solid core.

pocket
A storage area on the side of a golf bag that is used to store golf accessories, such as tees and scorecards.

stand
Frame for a golf bag, which can be used to support it for ease of access during gameplay.

golf course
The outdoor playing area specifically designed for the sport of golf.

green
An area of smooth, shorter grass around the tee. This marks the area where players usually putt.

grass
The terrain of a golf course.

water hazard
A small pool of water located in the middle of a golf course, which golfers must attempt to avoid.

caddie
An individual responsible for carrying the bags and supplies of a golfer around a golf course.

cart path
A small road that runs throughout a golf course.

hole
The small cup on a golf course green. Golfers attempt to hit balls into the hole.

removable flag pole
A pole, with a pennant, inserted in a hole to mark the hole's location. It can be easily inserted or removed.

golfer
An athlete who specializes in golf. Golfers are trained to drive and putt balls.

hand-pulled cart
An equipment bag used by a golfer to carry golf clubs around a golf course.

electric golf cart
A small motorized vehicle used to travel along a golf course.

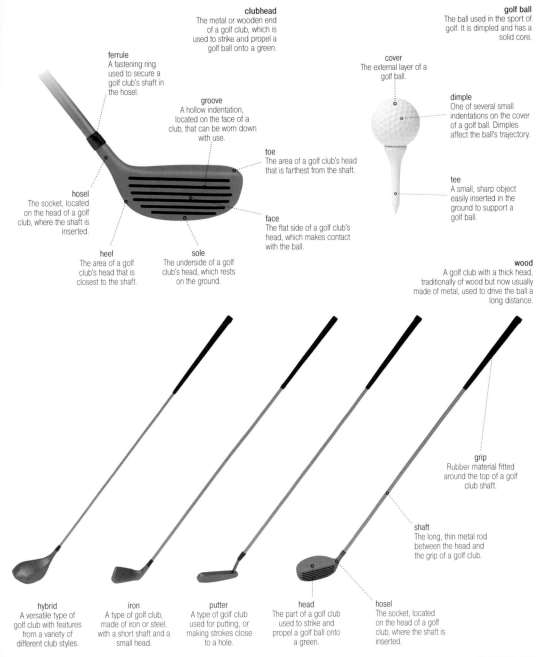

clubhead
The metal or wooden end of a golf club, which is used to strike and propel a golf ball onto a green.

golf ball
The ball used in the sport of golf. It is dimpled and has a solid core.

ferrule
A fastening ring used to secure a golf club's shaft in the hosel.

cover
The external layer of a golf ball.

groove
A hollow indentation, located on the face of a club, that can be worn down with use.

dimple
One of several small indentations on the cover of a golf ball. Dimples affect the ball's trajectory.

toe
The area of a golf club's head that is farthest from the shaft.

hosel
The socket, located on the head of a golf club, where the shaft is inserted.

tee
A small, sharp object easily inserted in the ground to support a golf ball.

face
The flat side of a golf club's head, which makes contact with the ball.

heel
The area of a golf club's head that is closest to the shaft.

sole
The underside of a golf club's head, which rests on the ground.

wood
A golf club with a thick head, traditionally of wood but now usually made of metal, used to drive the ball a long distance.

grip
Rubber material fitted around the top of a golf club shaft.

shaft
The long, thin metal rod between the head and the grip of a golf club.

hybrid
A versatile type of golf club with features from a variety of different club styles.

iron
A type of golf club, made of iron or steel, with a short shaft and a small head.

putter
A type of golf club used for putting, or making strokes close to a hole.

head
The part of a golf club used to strike and propel a golf ball onto a green.

hosel
The socket, located on the head of a golf club, where the shaft is inserted.

boxing ring
A square arena, surrounded by elastic ropes, where boxers fight.

water bottle
A container with a top that holds drinking water.

corner pad
The padded material covering the posts in the corners of the boxing ring, which prevent injuries.

headgear
A protective helmet worn on a boxer's head in order to absorb shock and protect him from cranial injuries.

referee
Official in the boxing ring with the two fighters, who can break up the fight and send the boxers to their corners.

trainer
Personal assistant to the boxer, who provides physical care and advice to improve the athlete's technique.

timekeeper
An official responsible for keeping track of the time of each boxing round.

stairs
A small series of risers that allow boxers and officials to step up to enter the boxing ring.

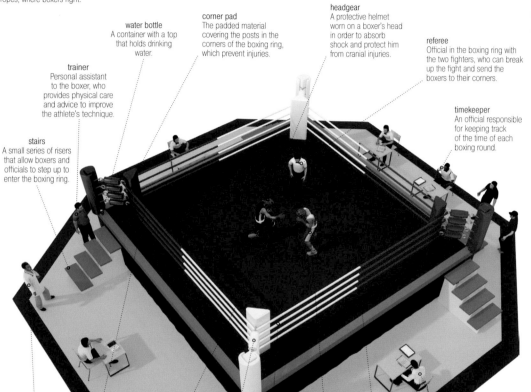

physician
Doctor who treats flesh wounds that can occur during the rounds of a boxing match.

judge
One of the scorekeepers in the judging area, who is responsible for awarding points and overseeing gameplay.

corner
An area of a boxing ring where fighters take breaks between rounds.

boxing glove
The mitt or padded covering used to protect the hands during a boxing match.

turnbuckle
Also known as a stretching screw, this is a mechanism used to adjust the tension of a boxing ring's ropes.

rope
Material that encircles the exterior of the boxing ring. It is used to keep the boxers from falling out of the ring.

boxer
One of the two athletes who square off to fight in a ring according to set rules.

canvas
Covering stretched over the floor of a boxing ring to break falls.

mouth guard
A small, plastic case designed to protect the teeth of a boxer.

heavy bag
A suspended weighted bag used by boxers to practice punching techniques.

shock-absorbing spring
A spring device designed to absorb the impact of jarring punches made against the bag.

stand
Supporting frame that forms the base for the punching bag and holds it in place, with the help of an extended arm.

chain
Links of metal that are connected to each other to form a strong, flexible support for the punching bag.

freestanding heavy bag
A punching bag mounted on a stand, used by boxers to practice technique.

punching bag
A stuffed and weighted bag, usually made of leather, that boxers use for training and to practice their technique.

stitching
Strips of leather or other material that are used to sew the seams of a punching bag together.

base
The foundation that supports and holds the punching bag in place.

rubber foot
A protective rubber coating that prevents the hard steel feet of the punching-bag structure from scratching the floor.

boxing gloves
Padded mittens worn by boxers to protect their hands while fighting in a boxing match.

strap
A flexible strip of material that is used to fasten the glove tightly around the user's hand.

laces
Thin strips of material that are strung through the eyelets and used to tighten the boxing glove on the hand.

speed bag
A bag hung from a platform that boxers use to train, by punching quickly and in succession.

weight room
A space with weight-lifting equipment where weight lifters and athletes go to exercise.

stationary bicycle
An exercise machine with handlebars, pedals and a seat, which simulates bicycle riding for a cardiovascular workout.

elliptical machine
An exercise machine with pedals that simulates walking, running or stair climbing, without pressure on joints.

wall bars
A series of bars fixed to a wall, used for various gymnastic exercises, including chin-ups and pull-ups.

treadmill
An exercise machine with a moving surface that allows the user to walk or run in place.

rowing machine
An exercise machine with a sliding seat that simulates rowing.

bench
A piece of furniture on which people can sit to rest.

mirror
Reflective surface, usually made of glass, which reflects a clear image of objects placed in front of it.

towel
An absorbent material that is used to dry a wet person and to mop up sweat.

potted plant
An ornamental indoor house plant growing in a pot of earth.

abdominal bench
A piece of equipment where the user lies on an incline to do sit-ups to strengthen abdominal muscles.

dumbbells
Short bars with weights at each end, often used in pairs.

barbell
A long metal bar to which weights can be attached for weightlifting.

weight bench
A piece of equipment used by a weight lifter to lie on and lift weights.

plate tree
A metal structure where weight plates are hung when not in use.

barbell
A long metal bar to which weights can be attached for weightlifting.

plate
A disk that can be attached to the end of the bar for lifting purposes. They come in different weights.

bar
A metal pole that connects the plates, which the user grasps to lift the weights.

grip
Where the user grasps the pole; covered with a textured material to prevent slippage.

collar
A metal device that fits against each side of the plate to hold it in place.

barbell plates
Disks that can be attached to the end of barbells for lifting purposes. They come in different weights.

weight machine
An exercise machine that uses gravity, pulleys, levers and wheels to provide weight training for the user.

locker
A small closet or container where clothes and personal belongings can be locked away while exercising.

clock
A timekeeping device, either mechanical or electronic, that measures seconds, minutes and hours.

stack machine
An exercise machine that uses gravity, weights and pulleys for the user to exercise arm muscles.

entry door
The entrance into the fitness center, through which clients and employees come and go.

vending machine
Machine that holds drinks and other products for sale, which can be purchased directly by inserting coins or cash.

reception
A counter where a fitness center employee can make appointments and sell goods.

table and chairs
Furniture where people can sit down, relax and enjoy a break after workouts.

calf machine
An exercise machine where the user raises bars using their calves.

leg abduction machine
An exercise machine where the user pushes against paddles with their upper legs, to strengthen thigh muscles.

cable crossover machine
An exercise machine that uses cables, weights and pulleys for the user to exercise various arm muscles.

disinfectants
A chemical spray that kills bacteria and is used to clean exercise surfaces, benches and other objects.

shelving
A piece of storage furniture on which objects such as disinfectants and paper towels can be placed.

paper towel
Absorbent, disposable towel made of paper and used to wipe up sweat, dirt and spills.

pec machine
An exercise machine where the user pushes against various weights to strengthen the pectoral muscles.

barbell
A long metal bar to which weights can be attached for weightlifting.

leg extension machine
An exercise machine where a person uses their legs to lift bars with weighted padding, to strengthen leg muscles.

wastebasket
A small container designed to hold items that have been thrown away, like used paper and tissues.

reception area
The area in a fitness center where people are greeted and admitted and appointments are made.

bottled water
Drinking water sold in small containers for easy access and portability.

locker
A small closet or container where clothes and personal belongings can be locked away while exercising.

flower vase
An open container used to hold cut flowers in water.

door
A swinging or sliding barrier to a room, house or compartment that can be opened or closed.

laptop computer
A portable computer on which sales information and other data can be recorded.

lock
A device to keep a door securely fastened; usually opened with a key.

desk
A piece of furniture with a flat top that is used as a work surface.

cleaning area
The area where cleaning products, such as disinfectants and paper towels, are stored.

disinfectant
A chemical spray that kills bacteria and is used to clean exercise surfaces, benches and other objects.

shelf
A piece of furniture on which objects such as disinfectants and paper towels can be placed.

wastebasket
A small container designed to hold items that have been thrown away, like used paper and tissues.

bench
A piece of furniture on which people can sit to rest.

paper towel
Absorbent, disposable towels that come in a roll with tear-off sheets.

towel
An absorbent material that is used to dry a wet person and to mop up sweat.

fixed dumbbells
Short bars in different sizes
with non-adjustable weights;
often used in pairs.

cable crossover machine
An exercise machine that uses cables,
weights and pulleys for the user to exercise
various arm muscles.

electronic console
A device on the
stationary bicycle where
users can choose
program settings and
exercise preferences.

handlebars
The grips on a
stationary bicycle, which
are held by the user
while exercising.

stationary bicycle
An exercise machine with
handlebars, pedals and a seat,
which simulates bicycle riding for
a cardiovascular workout.

frame
The structural component
of the stationary bicycle that
supports and connects the
other parts.

saddle
The part of the
stationary bicycle where
the user sits, which can
often be adjusted for
maximum comfort.

pedal
The part on which the
foot pushes to simulate
pushing the pedal of a
moving bicycle.

anti-slip feet
A protective rubber
coating over each
end of the stand that
prevents the machine
from slipping.

stair-climber
An exercise machine that
simulates climbing stairs, for a
cardiovascular and leg-muscle
workout.

height adjustment
The component on the stationary
bicycle exercise machine that
raises or lowers the seat.

treadmill
An exercise machine with a moving surface on a conveyor belt, which allows user to walk or run in place.

electronic console
A device on the treadmill where users can choose program settings and exercise preferences.

display
The screen where the user can see the program settings for the treadmill.

grip
A handle used to hold for support while mounting, dismounting and exercising on the treadmill.

running surface
A platform on a conveyor belt that keeps moving, allowing the person to run or walk in place at varying speeds.

base
The framework of the treadmill, which supports the running surface and the console.

barbell plates and tree
Heavy disk weights that can be attached to barbells to increase the lift load, on a stand built to hold them.

rowing machine
An strengthing machine with a sliding seat that simulates rowing.

handle
The grip the user holds onto with their hands while using the rowing machine.

footrest
A pad with a strap where the foot is placed while using the rowing machine.

display
The screen where the user can see the program settings for the rowing machine.

anti-slip foot
A thick rubber device on the base of the rowing machine that prevents it from slipping.

adjustable dumbbell
A short bar with a weight at each end, used to exercise different muscles.

frame
The main structure that provides support for the various parts of a rowing machine.

strap
A strip of material that holds the foot in place on the rowing machine.

resistance adjustment
An adjustable dial that can be used to increase or decrease the resistance of the rowing machine.

sliding seat
The place where the rower sits, which moves back and forth to simulate rowing and stimulate muscles.

weight machine
An exercise machine that uses gravity, pulleys, levers and wheels to provide weight training for the user.

handle
The grip on a weight machine, which the user grasps with their hand.

frame
The structural component of the weight machine that supports and connects the other parts.

cable
A thick wire rope that attaches the weights to the handles.

weight stack
A series of small weights that can be used to increase or decrease the amount the user lifts.

foam roller
The padded bar where a user's leg is secured when lifting weights on a weight machine.

seat
A padded area of the equipment that the person sits on while exercising.

weight adjustment
An adjustable pin device that goes between different weights to secure and vary the weight load.

weight bench
A piece of equipment used by a weight lifter to lie on and lift weights.

stand
A steel structure that holds the barbell stationary in between a weightlifter's lifts.

adjustable backrest
The place where the user positions their back, which can be adjusted to various inclines to work different muscles.

abdominal bench
A piece of equipment where the user lies on an incline to do sit-ups to strengthen abdominal muscles.

barbell
A long metal bar to which weights can be attached for weightlifting.

height adjustment
A clenching device that is used to adjust and secure the height of the weight bench stand.

foam roller
The padded bar where the user's leg is secured while lifting heavy weights on the weight bench.

seat
The place where the user sits when lifting weights on the weight bench.

stack machine
An exercise machine that uses gravity,
weights and pulleys for the user to
exercise arm muscles.

pec machine
An exercise machine where the user
pushes against various weights to
strengthen the pectoral muscles.

barbell stand
A steel structure that holds
the barbell stationary in
between a weightlifter's lifts.

leg extension machine
An exercise machine where a person uses
their legs to lift bars with weighted padding, to
strengthen leg muscles.

tanning bed
An enclosed bed with flourescent lamps that emit utraviolet rays to produce a suntan.

fluorescent lamps
Glass tubes that produce light through an ultraviolet radiation process.

on/off button
The power button that starts and stops the tanning bed.

exercise ball
A large, lightweight, inflatable plastic ball used in various fitness routines.

rubber hand grip
A ring-like device used to strengthen the wrist and fingers by squeezing, twisting and pulling on it.

hand grips
A device that is squeezed to strengthen hand muscles.

yoga mat
A small, rectangular piece of foam or fabric that yoga practitioners use.

aerobics step
A small, elevated platform that is used to step up and down in aerobic workouts.

shoulder stand
Inverted position with legs in the air that uses gravity to condition and strengthen the whole body.

standing leg lift
A stretching exercise where one leg is lifted to the side of the body: develops balance and strength.

push-up
An exercise where the person lies on their front and lifts their body by pushing down on their hands.

scissors
Exercise where the legs crisscross like scissors to build abdomen and leg strength.

forward bend
A stretching exercise where the upper body is suspended from the waist; develops strength and flexibility.

side lunge
A stretching exercise where one leg is bent to one side and the other is straight on the other side.

bra top
An exercise top for women with a built-in bra.

sweatpants
Loose, warm pants made of breathable fabric with a drawstring waist.

sneakers
Canvas shoes that help the athlete's feet grip the mat and prevent slipping.

seated forward bend
Stretching exercise where the head and back are bent forward while sitting; helps flexibility.

shoulder stand scissors
Strengthening exercises done with legs and hips inverted.

forward lunge
A leg-stretching exercise where one leg is bent in front and the other leg is behind, bent or straight.

Skateboarding
A sport where the athlete rides a short, narrow board with wheels and performs jumps and turns.

mountainboard
A skateboard with large wheels and straps to secure the feet; used for rough terrain and steep slopes.

grip tape
Material with a rough, non-sliding surface that helps the skater's shoes stay on the skateboard.

binding
The device that attaches the skateboard to the user's shoe.

wheel hub
The core of the wheel and where the wheel attaches to the truck's axle.

truck
The device that connects the wheels to the board and allows the wheels to spin. It includes the axle and baseplate.

deck
The long wooden board on a skateboard; usually made from layers of wood laminated together.

tire
The rubber that encircles the rim of the wheel, which provides traction against the driving surface.

skateboard
A short, narrow board with wheels attached; the user rides standing up.

grip tape
Material with a rough, non-sliding surface that helps the skater's shoes stay on the skateboard.

wheel
A circular, rotating device that spins on an axis and allows the skateboard to go forward or backward.

deck
The long wooden board on a skateboard, usually made from layers of wood laminated together.

pads
Protective materials that are placed over a skateboarder's various joints in order to protect them during skating.

elbow pad
A piece of safety equipment with a hard outer covering that protects the elbow.

poles
Slender sticks used as guiding devices by skaters. They provide leverage to push and propel in flat or hilly spots.

helmet
A specially designed helmet worn by skaters that is used to protect the head from injuries.

Ramp
An inclined structure designed for skateboarding or skating tricks and performances.

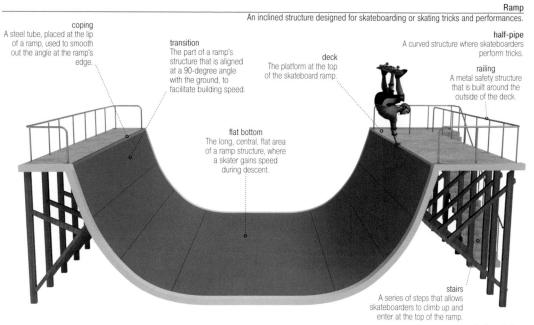

coping
A steel tube, placed at the lip of a ramp, used to smooth out the angle at the ramp's edge.

transition
The part of a ramp's structure that is aligned at a 90-degree angle with the ground, to facilitate building speed.

deck
The platform at the top of the skateboard ramp.

half-pipe
A curved structure where skateboarders perform tricks.

railing
A metal safety structure that is built around the outside of the deck.

flat bottom
The long, central, flat area of a ramp structure, where a skater gains speed during descent.

stairs
A series of steps that allows skateboarders to climb up and enter at the top of the ramp.

In-line skates
Specialized footwear fitted with wheels and secured with lacing or binding.

off-road in-line skates
Skates that have a large wheel in the front and another at the back; used for skating on rough terrain.

binding
The device that tightly fastens the skate to the user's boot.

heel brake
A piece of rubber used to apply pressure to the skating surface to slow down or stop.

boot
A shoe that supports the foot and ankle that is worn by the skater and attached to the skate.

wheel
A circular, rotating device that spins on an axis and allows the skate to move forward or backward.

binding
The device that holds the skate on the user's leg.

frame
The part of the skate that supports the wheels and connects them to the boot.

laces
Lengths of string used to join two sides of a boot together to hold it tightly to the foot.

frame
The part of the skate that supports the wheels and connects them to the boot.

wheel
A circular, rotating device that spins on an axis and allows the skate to move forward or backward.

mountain bicycle
A bicycle designed for rough terrain, with thick, wide tires and multiple gears to negotiate steep inclines.

handlebars
The steering element on a mountain bicycle's frame, which is held by the rider to provide directional control.

front brake lever
Adjustable lever, usually on the handlebars of a bicycle, which is used to apply braking pressure on the front tire.

shifter
A switch that can be used to change gears, found on the handlebars of the mountain bicycle.

rear brake lever
Adjustable lever on the the handlebars of a bicycle, which is used to apply braking pressure on the rear tire.

front fork
A two-prong metal tube attached to either side of the wheel hub on a bicycle.

front brake
A device used to apply pressure to the front wheel of the mountain bike, to slow its motion.

hub
The main rotating casing for the axle, which allows free movement of the tire around the axle rod of the bicycle.

tire
The rubber that encircles the rim of the wheel, which provides traction against the driving surface.

rim
The circular frame that supports the bike tire. It comes in a wide variety of different spoke sizes and types.

spoke
One of many rods that connect the hub of the tire to the rim, to provide advanced weight support on a bicycle.

seat
The part of the mountain bike where the biker sits, which can often be adjusted for maximum comfort.

frame
The main supporting structure, to which the tires and rims connect.

road-racing bicycle
A variety of bicycle designed for racing, with thin rims, lightweight frame and speed gears.

rear brake
A device used to apply pressure to the rear wheel of the mountain bike, to slow its motion.

rear derailleur
A mechanism on a bicycle that shifts the chain from one gear to another.

chain
A length of metal links that connects the crankset and the pedals to the back wheel, to propel the bicycle.

front derailleur
A bicycle sprocket, located above the pedals, used to change a bike's gears.

pedal
The part on which the foot pushes to turn the gears of the bicycle and propel it forward.

stand
A specialized drop-down device that is used as a support to keep the bike upright and stationary.

crankset
A large, central gear on the bicycle with sharp teeth that engage with the bicycle chain to change gears.

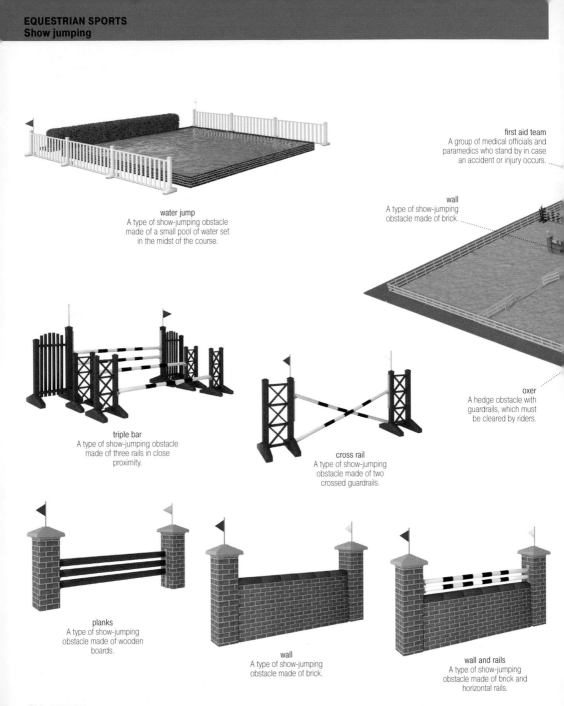

first aid team
A group of medical officials and
paramedics who stand by in case
an accident or injury occurs.

wall
A type of show-jumping
obstacle made of brick.

water jump
A type of show-jumping obstacle
made of a small pool of water set
in the midst of the course.

oxer
A hedge obstacle with
guardrails, which must
be cleared by riders.

triple bar
A type of show-jumping obstacle
made of three rails in close
proximity.

cross rail
A type of show-jumping
obstacle made of two
crossed guardrails.

planks
A type of show-jumping
obstacle made of wooden
boards.

wall
A type of show-jumping
obstacle made of brick.

wall and rails
A type of show-jumping
obstacle made of brick and
horizontal rails.

show-jumping course
The outdoor obstacle course specifically designed for show-jumping events.

planks
A type of show-jumping obstacle made of wooden boards.

audience
A large group of spectators.

water jump
A type of show-jumping obstacle made of a small pool of water set in the midst of the course.

combination
A series of obstacles placed close to each other to create one large obstacle.

rider
An athlete trained to ride a horse.

jury
A panel of judges, who officiate and observe the techniques of riders.

brush and rails
A type of show-jumping obstacle made of a rail placed just before a small, leafy hedge.

rails
Long, horizontal poles positioned as obstacles in a show-jumping course.

oxer
A hedge obstacle with guardrails, which must be cleared by riders.

English saddle
A heavy support apparatus fixed
and secured atop a horse's back
for a show-jumping rider to sit
comfortably.

cantle
The back edge of a saddle,
which projects upward to
define the back of the seat.

pommel
The part of a saddle that
curves upward in front of
the rider.

seat
The area of a saddle, between
the pommel and cantle,
designed to comfortably seat
a rider.

stirrup leather
A strip of leather that
projects outward and
downward from a saddle
in order to support a
stirrup.

stirrup
The metallic frame, used
as a place to rest the foot,
attached to the side of a
saddle.

arch
The top of a stirrup. A
rider's foot rests just below
the arch.

girth
A strap used to secure a
saddle atop a horse's back.

rider
An athlete trained to ride
a horse.

riding helmet
Headgear for a rider.

saddle pad
A thick layer of fabric
placed between a saddle
and a horse's back.

riding jacket
A jacket with special
features for riders.

saddle
A support apparatus
fixed and secured
atop a horse's back in
order for a rider to sit
comfortably.

girth
A strap used to secure a
saddle atop a horse's back.

coronet boot
A protective casing of
leather placed around a
horse's hooves to prevent
injury.

jodhpurs
Long, tight-fitting pants
worn by riders.

stirrup
The metallic frame, used
as a place to rest the foot,
attached to the side of a
saddle.

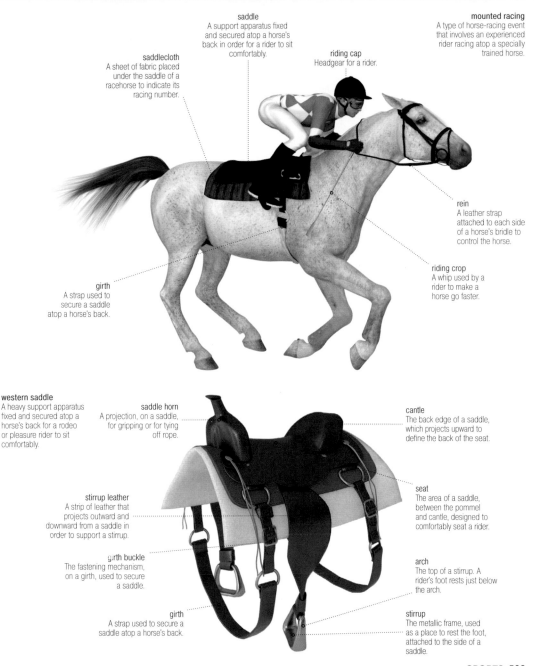

saddle
A support apparatus fixed and secured atop a horse's back in order for a rider to sit comfortably.

mounted racing
A type of horse-racing event that involves an experienced rider racing atop a specially trained horse.

saddlecloth
A sheet of fabric placed under the saddle of a racehorse to indicate its racing number.

riding cap
Headgear for a rider.

rein
A leather strap attached to each side of a horse's bridle to control the horse.

riding crop
A whip used by a rider to make a horse go faster.

girth
A strap used to secure a saddle atop a horse's back.

western saddle
A heavy support apparatus fixed and secured atop a horse's back for a rodeo or pleasure rider to sit comfortably.

saddle horn
A projection, on a saddle, for gripping or for tying off rope.

cantle
The back edge of a saddle, which projects upward to define the back of the seat.

seat
The area of a saddle, between the pommel and cantle, designed to comfortably seat a rider.

stirrup leather
A strip of leather that projects outward and downward from a saddle in order to support a stirrup.

girth buckle
The fastening mechanism, on a girth, used to secure a saddle.

arch
The top of a stirrup. A rider's foot rests just below the arch.

girth
A strap used to secure a saddle atop a horse's back.

stirrup
The metallic frame, used as a place to rest the foot, attached to the side of a saddle.

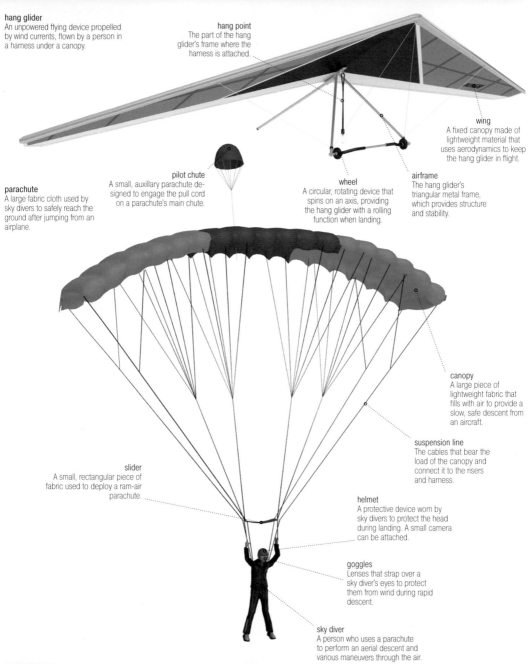

hang glider
An unpowered flying device propelled by wind currents, flown by a person in a harness under a canopy.

hang point
The part of the hang glider's frame where the harness is attached.

wing
A fixed canopy made of lightweight material that uses aerodynamics to keep the hang glider in flight.

pilot chute
A small, auxillary parachute designed to engage the pull cord on a parachute's main chute.

parachute
A large fabric cloth used by sky divers to safely reach the ground after jumping from an airplane.

wheel
A circular, rotating device that spins on an axis, providing the hang glider with a rolling function when landing.

airframe
The hang glider's triangular metal frame, which provides structure and stability.

canopy
A large piece of lightweight fabric that fills with air to provide a slow, safe descent from an aircraft.

suspension line
The cables that bear the load of the canopy and connect it to the risers and harness.

slider
A small, rectangular piece of fabric used to deploy a ram-air parachute.

helmet
A protective device worn by sky divers to protect the head during landing. A small camera can be attached.

goggles
Lenses that strap over a sky diver's eyes to protect them from wind during rapid descent.

sky diver
A person who uses a parachute to perform an aerial descent and various maneuvers through the air.

engine compartment
The central housing area in which the powerboat's engine is encased. It serves to protect the engine.

seat
A cushioned area where the driver sits to operate the powerboat.

powerboat
A boat that is propelled by some form of engine.

windshield
A transparent screen that is mounted in front of the driver's seat to deflect wind currents at high speeds.

hull
The rear of the boat; usually reinforced to increase its strength and durability and prevent damage.

power racing catamaran
A boat designed to reach great speeds and launch off water waves, with an aerodynamic design.

seat back
Also known as a back rest, this is the part of the seat that supports the paddler's back.

whitewater raft
An inflatable boat designed to navigate in rapids and fast-flowing water currents.

ring
A small circular device on the boat, through which rope can be strung to secure it for mooring purposes.

handle
This is a component on the front of the boat that can be used to pull, grab or tether the vessel.

seat
The place in a whitewater raft where the paddler sits.

paddle
A pole with a wide blade at one or both ends, used to propel and steer a small boat through the water.

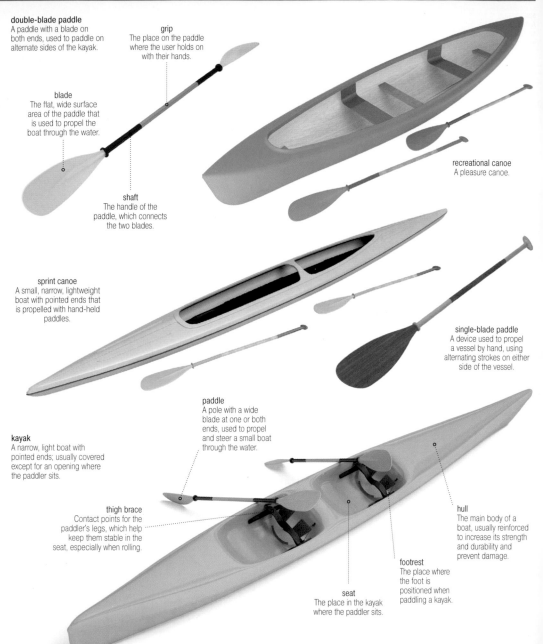

double-blade paddle
A paddle with a blade on both ends, used to paddle on alternate sides of the kayak.

grip
The place on the paddle where the user holds on with their hands.

blade
The flat, wide surface area of the paddle that is used to propel the boat through the water.

recreational canoe
A pleasure canoe.

shaft
The handle of the paddle, which connects the two blades.

sprint canoe
A small, narrow, lightweight boat with pointed ends that is propelled with hand-held paddles.

single-blade paddle
A device used to propel a vessel by hand, using alternating strokes on either side of the vessel.

paddle
A pole with a wide blade at one or both ends, used to propel and steer a small boat through the water.

kayak
A narrow, light boat with pointed ends; usually covered except for an opening where the paddler sits.

thigh brace
Contact points for the paddler's legs, which help keep them stable in the seat, especially when rolling.

hull
The main body of a boat, usually reinforced to increase its strength and durability and prevent damage.

footrest
The place where the foot is positioned when paddling a kayak.

seat
The place in the kayak where the paddler sits.

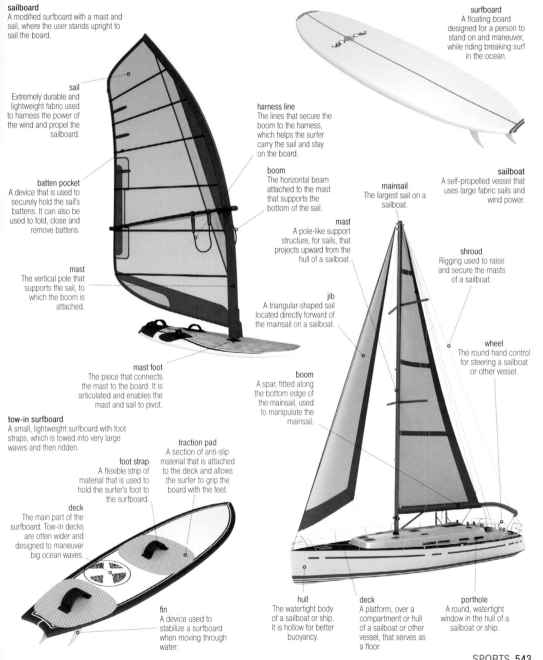

sailboard
A modified surfboard with a mast and sail, where the user stands upright to sail the board.

surfboard
A floating board designed for a person to stand on and maneuver, while riding breaking surf in the ocean.

sail
Extremely durable and lightweight fabric used to harness the power of the wind and propel the sailboard.

harness line
The lines that secure the boom to the harness, which helps the surfer carry the sail and stay on the board.

boom
The horizontal beam attached to the mast that supports the bottom of the sail.

mainsail
The largest sail on a sailboat.

sailboat
A self-propelled vessel that uses large fabric sails and wind power.

batten pocket
A device that is used to securely hold the sail's battens. It can also be used to fold, close and remove battens.

mast
A pole-like support structure, for sails, that projects upward from the hull of a sailboat.

shroud
Rigging used to raise and secure the masts of a sailboat.

mast
The vertical pole that supports the sail, to which the boom is attached.

jib
A triangular-shaped sail located directly forward of the mainsail on a sailboat.

wheel
The round hand control for steering a sailboat or other vessel.

mast foot
The piece that connects the mast to the board. It is articulated and enables the mast and sail to pivot.

boom
A spar, fitted along the bottom edge of the mainsail, used to manipulate the mainsail.

tow-in surfboard
A small, lightweight surfboard with foot straps, which is towed into very large waves and then ridden.

traction pad
A section of anti-slip material that is attached to the deck and allows the surfer to grip the board with the feet.

foot strap
A flexible strip of material that is used to hold the surfer's foot to the surfboard.

deck
The main part of the surfboard. Tow-in decks are often wider and designed to maneuver big ocean waves.

fin
A device used to stabilize a surfboard when moving through water.

hull
The watertight body of a sailboat or ship. It is hollow for better buoyancy.

deck
A platform, over a compartment or hull of a sailboat or other vessel, that serves as a floor.

porthole
A round, watertight window in the hull of a sailboat or ship.

water polo pool
A pool for a sport that involves two teams competing to force a polo ball into the opposing team's goal.

goal judge
An official responsible for confirming scored points.

goal
A net that serves as a scoring area. If a ball goes into the goal, a point is scored.

goal line
A boundary that marks a goal's threshold.

water polo player
An athlete trained in the various offensive and defensive techniques of water polo.

mid-pool line
A boundary in water polo that shows when a player is halfway from the goal.

referee
An official who observes the game carefully, applies the rules and settles disputes.

water polo ball
The ball used in the sport of water polo. It is designed to be easily grasped with a single hand.

cap
Protective headgear worn by a water polo player.

timekeepers
An official responsible for
keeping track of the time
of each quarter of play.

secretaries
Administrative officials,
who oversee water
polo procedures.

water polo player
An athlete trained in the
various offensive and
defensive techniques of
water polo.

five-meter line
A boundary in water
polo that shows when a
player is 5 meters (16.5
feet) from the goal.

goalkeeper
The water polo player
responsible for protecting
the goal from opponents.

players' bench
A seating area where
players can rest, plan
or watch the water polo
match.

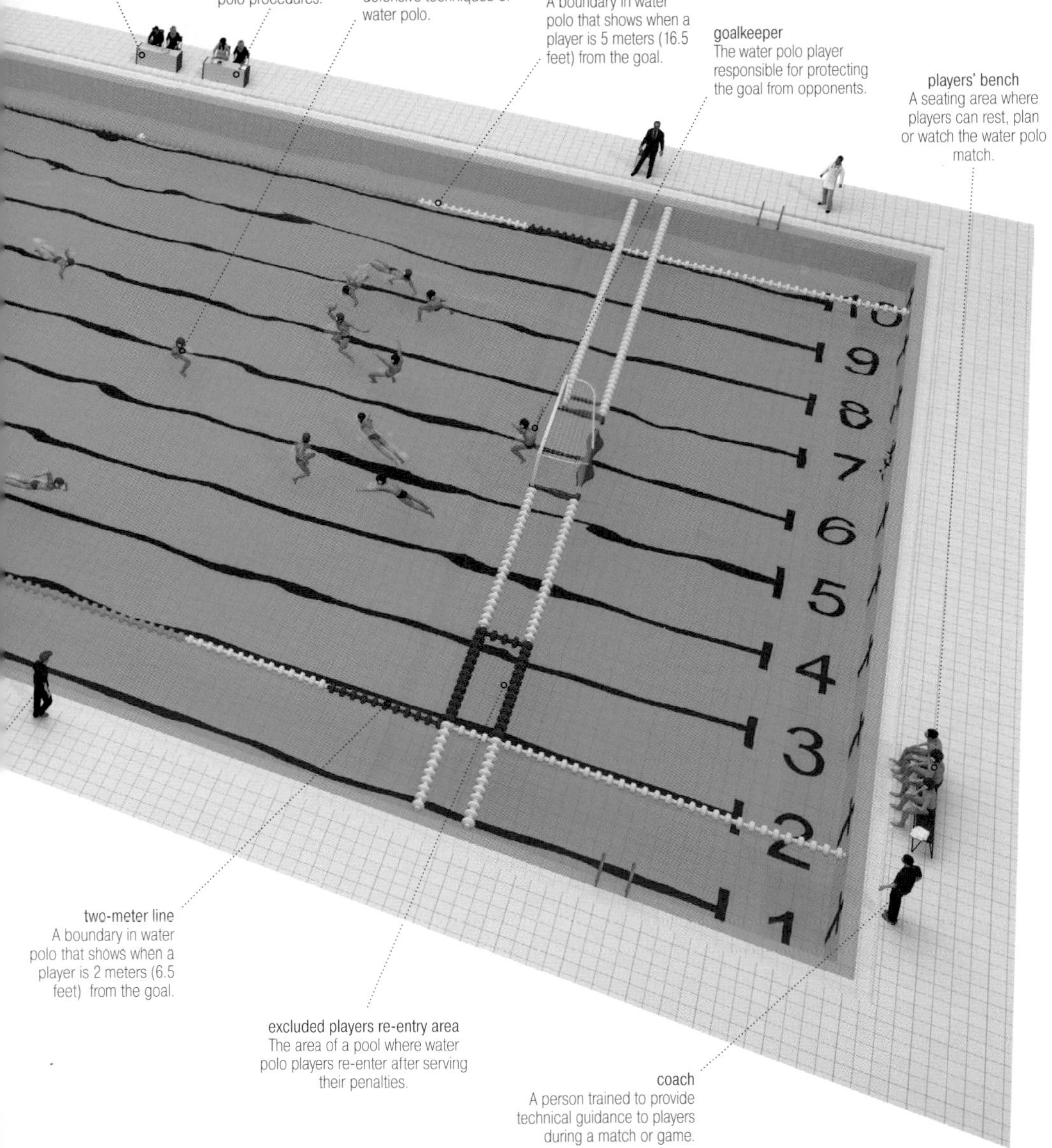

two-meter line
A boundary in water
polo that shows when a
player is 2 meters (6.5
feet) from the goal.

excluded players re-entry area
The area of a pool where water
polo players re-enter after serving
their penalties.

coach
A person trained to provide
technical guidance to players
during a match or game.

Olympic-sized pool
A swimming pool that is the same dimensions as the pools used for Olympic competitions.

lane
The zone designated to each swimmer in a competition, usually marked by rope coils, ribbons or flagging.

backstroke turn indicator
Flags used to alert swimmers doing backstrokes that the pool wall is approaching and it is time to turn.

stroke judge
An official who monitors the swimmers' movements to ensure they are appropriate for the stroke category.

lane rope
A coil or rope used to separate swimming lanes and keep swimmers on track in their designated lanes.

lane marking
The line on the bottom of the pool and the surface coils that mark the separation of swimming lanes.

lane rope
A coil or rope used to separate swimming lanes to keep swimmers on track in their designated lanes.

goggles
Lenses that strap over a
swimmer's eyes to keep them
dry and improve visibility.

swim cap
A tight-fitting cap that
keeps hair dry and out
of swimmer's eyes.

turning judge
An observer who watches
the turning technique of a
designated swimmer to ensure
they do not turn improperly.

starting block
An elevated stand located
at the end of the pool, used
by swimmers to propel
themselves into the water.

chief timekeeper
An official who collects
the times recorded by
the lane timekeepers.

referee
An official who observes
the game carefully,
applies the rules and
settles disputes.

starter
An official who gives
the signal with a flag
for starting a race in
competitive swimming.

starting block
An elevated stand located at the end
of the pool, used by swimmers to
propel themselves into the water.

lane rope storage reel
A device used to wind up and
temporarily store the lane rope when it
is taken off the pool.

handrails
Bars to grasp when entering or leaving
the pool, which give support and
prevent slips and falls.

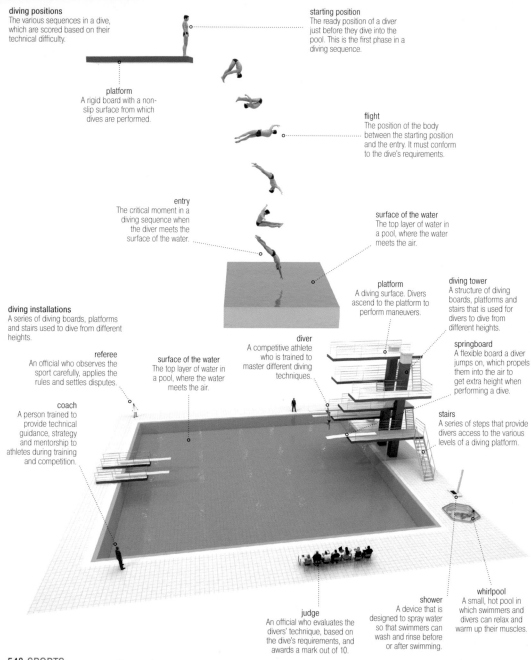

diving positions
The various sequences in a dive, which are scored based on their technical difficulty.

starting position
The ready position of a diver just before they dive into the pool. This is the first phase in a diving sequence.

platform
A rigid board with a non-slip surface from which dives are performed.

flight
The position of the body between the starting position and the entry. It must conform to the dive's requirements.

entry
The critical moment in a diving sequence when the diver meets the surface of the water.

surface of the water
The top layer of water in a pool, where the water meets the air.

platform
A diving surface. Divers ascend to the platform to perform maneuvers.

diving tower
A structure of diving boards, platforms and stairs that is used for divers to dive from different heights.

diving installations
A series of diving boards, platforms and stairs used to dive from different heights.

diver
A competitive athlete who is trained to master different diving techniques.

springboard
A flexible board a diver jumps on, which propels them into the air to get extra height when performing a dive.

referee
An official who observes the sport carefully, applies the rules and settles disputes.

surface of the water
The top layer of water in a pool, where the water meets the air.

stairs
A series of steps that provide divers access to the various levels of a diving platform.

coach
A person trained to provide technical guidance, strategy and mentorship to athletes during training and competition.

judge
An official who evaluates the divers' technique, based on the dive's requirements, and awards a mark out of 10.

shower
A device that is designed to spray water so that swimmers can wash and rinse before or after swimming.

whirlpool
A small, hot pool in which swimmers and divers can relax and warm up their muscles.

compressed-air cylinder
A cylindrical container designed to safely store compressed air.

harness
Straps used to fasten various scuba gear to the body of a diver.

air hose
A part that carries air from the tank to the face mask.

first stage of regulator
A component mounted to a cylinder valve and used to reduce pressure.

scuba diver
An individual fitted with specialized equipment to dive underwater for extended periods.

emergency regulator
An alternate regulator to provide a small amount of oxygen in an emergency.

hood
An elastic cap placed over the head of a diver to seal the wetsuit.

weight belt
A part, fitted around the waist, that contains lead weights in order to counteract buoyancy.

mask
Protective face gear worn by a diver.

wetsuit
A specialized rubber suit worn by divers.

second stage of regulator
Also known as the demand valve, this is a regulator that has two tubes for the passage of air.

fin
A special piece of footwear worn by a diver to provide better underwater propulsion.

inflator
A mechanism to fill objects, such as diving buoys, with air.

diving glove
A specialized hand covering for a diver.

fins
Flat rubber devices that are worn on the feet and used to increase speed for swimmers.

foot pocket
The place where the user tucks their foot, to firmly secure the fin to their body.

lens
A small sheet of tempered glass, designed to withstand pressure, that allows the diver to see underwater.

frame
The plastic structure that forms the shape of the diving mask.

mask
Protective eyeware used to keep eyes dry and provide better visibility underwater.

blade
The wide surface area of the fin that is used to propel the swimmer.

strap
A flexible strip of material that stretches to exert pressure and fastens the mask to the head.

nose pocket
A piece of plastic or other material on the diving mask that covers the nose to prevent water intake.

snorkel
A respiration device with a long, hollow tube, which provides air to swimmers who are just below the water surface.

splash guard
Protective covering that is used to prevent surface water from entering the breathing hole on a snorkel.

mouthpiece
The lower part of the snorkel, which is placed in the mouth in order to breathe air through the tube.

tube
The hollow apparatus on a snorkel that is used to convey air while swimming underwater.

purge valve
A mechanism used to release water and saliva from a snorkel.

clip
The fastening that holds the snorkel and the mask together, providing a strong connection near the face.

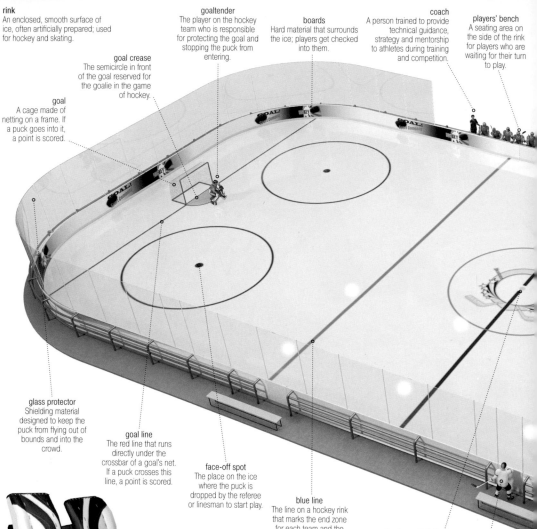

rink
An enclosed, smooth surface of ice, often artificially prepared; used for hockey and skating.

goaltender
The player on the hockey team who is responsible for protecting the goal and stopping the puck from entering.

boards
Hard material that surrounds the ice; players get checked into them.

coach
A person trained to provide technical guidance, strategy and mentorship to athletes during training and competition.

players' bench
A seating area on the side of the rink for players who are waiting for their turn to play.

goal crease
The semicircle in front of the goal reserved for the goalie in the game of hockey.

goal
A cage made of netting on a frame. If a puck goes into it, a point is scored.

glass protector
Shielding material designed to keep the puck from flying out of bounds and into the crowd.

goal line
The red line that runs directly under the crossbar of a goal's net. If a puck crosses this line, a point is scored.

face-off spot
The place on the ice where the puck is dropped by the referee or linesman to start play.

blue line
The line on a hockey rink that marks the end zone for each team and the boundary for off-side calls.

center face-off circle
The place where the puck is dropped at the start of the game, the start of each period and at other times.

goaltender's pads
Wide, reinforced material that protects the goaltender's legs from the impact of pucks, and helps block shots on goal.

puck
A circular, hard, black rubber device used to score goals in hockey and designed to move easily across ice.

offending player
A player who has been given a penalty during the game and must sit out of the game for a period of time.

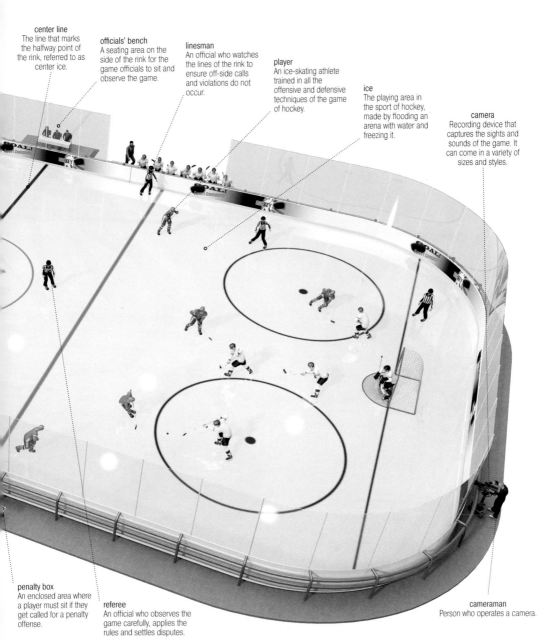

center line
The line that marks the halfway point of the rink, referred to as center ice.

officials' bench
A seating area on the side of the rink for the game officials to sit and observe the game.

linesman
An official who watches the lines of the rink to ensure off-side calls and violations do not occur.

player
An ice-skating athlete trained in all the offensive and defensive techniques of the game of hockey.

ice
The playing area in the sport of hockey, made by flooding an arena with water and freezing it.

camera
Recording device that captures the sights and sounds of the game. It can come in a variety of sizes and styles.

penalty box
An enclosed area where a player must sit if they get called for a penalty offense.

referee
An official who observes the game carefully, applies the rules and settles disputes.

cameraman
Person who operates a camera.

helmet
A hard and padded protective head covering worn by athletes to prevent cranial injuries.

vent
An opening on an ice hockey helmet that allows heat from the head to escape during intense play.

hockey player
An ice-skating athlete trained in all the offensive and defensive techniques of playing the game of hockey.

chin strap
A flexible strip of material fastened under the chin to keep the helmet on the hockey player's head.

glove
A protective hand covering worn by a hockey player.

hockey skates
Reinforced boots that protect and support the feet and ankles, attached to short, curved blades.

player's stick
A long, thin stick with a curved end, used to hit the puck in the game of hockey.

tongue
A flap of material underneath the laces on the boot, over which the laces cross to hold the boot on the foot.

blade
The runner attached to the skate's boot, with a sharpened edge that helps skaters glide, stop and turn on ice.

lace
Length of string used to join two sides of a boot together to hold it tightly to the foot.

shaft
The long, straight handle of the hockey stick, held by the player to manipulate the stick.

toe
The front part of the skate boot, where the toes are encased by hard plastic, leather or other material.

blade
Curved end of the hockey stick that hits the puck. The curve helps to raise it off the ice.

edge
The sharpened surface on the metal blade of the hockey skate that makes contact with the ice.

figure skates
Reinforced boots with blades that allow skaters to glide over the ice; usually fastened by laces.

figure skater
An athlete who performs spins, jumps and dance moves in elaborate routines on figure skates.

hook
A small, circular part located on a skate boot to secure the laces.

tongue
The part of a skate, or other footwear, that is under the laces.

blade
A sharp, flat metal part, fitted to the bottom of a skate, that allows the skate to glide over ice.

dress
The costume worn by a female figure skater, designed to enhance the artistic and thematic impact of a routine.

sole
The bottom front part of footwear, which covers the bottom front part, or sole, of the foot.

edge
The part of a skate blade that makes contact with the ice.

heel
The rear part of footwear, which covers the back, or heel, of the foot.

boot
The part of a skate that fits the foot and is insulated.

toe pick
Saw-like teeth, located on the blade of a figure skate, used for jumping and footwork.

lace
String used to tighten skates or other footwear.

lining
A layer of fabric inside a skate boot to provide warmth.

boot
The upper part of the skate, which encloses the skater's foot and ankle.

shell
The lightweight, aerodynamic casing of a bobsled.

sled
A racing sled with runners, steering and brakes, used by two or more athletes to race down an icy course.

rear runner
A fixed steel blade under the back of the sled that helps the bobsled glide over the ice.

front runner
A movable steel blade under the front of the bobsled that is attached to the steering and controls the direction.

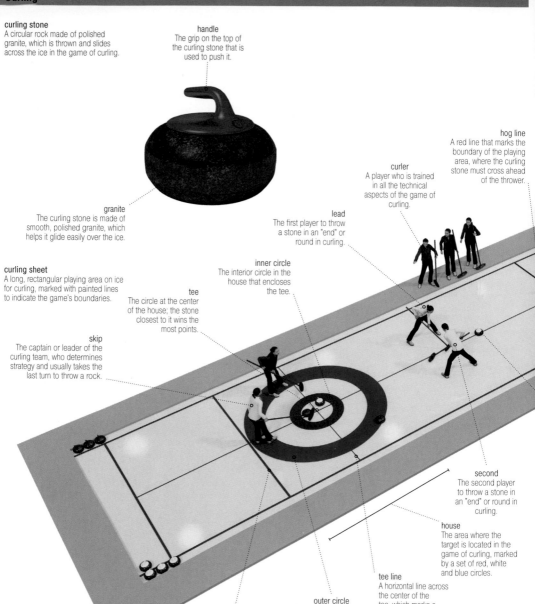

curling stone
A circular rock made of polished granite, which is thrown and slides across the ice in the game of curling.

handle
The grip on the top of the curling stone that is used to push it.

hog line
A red line that marks the boundary of the playing area, where the curling stone must cross ahead of the thrower.

curler
A player who is trained in all the technical aspects of the game of curling.

granite
The curling stone is made of smooth, polished granite, which helps it glide easily over the ice.

lead
The first player to throw a stone in an "end" or round in curling.

curling sheet
A long, rectangular playing area on ice for curling, marked with painted lines to indicate the game's boundaries.

inner circle
The interior circle in the house that encloses the tee.

tee
The circle at the center of the house; the stone closest to it wins the most points.

skip
The captain or leader of the curling team, who determines strategy and usually takes the last turn to throw a rock.

second
The second player to throw a stone in an "end" or round in curling.

house
The area where the target is located in the game of curling, marked by a set of red, white and blue circles.

tee line
A horizontal line across the center of the tee, which marks a boundary for sweeping opponents' rocks out.

back line
The line at the far end of the house that marks the boundary of the playing area on a curling rink.

outer circle
The exterior circle that encloses the inner circle and the tee.

lateral line
A line that marks the boundary of the playing area of the ice sheet. Stones must be kept in bounds.

center line
A line that runs down the middle of the ice; the stone is thrown close to this line.

sheet
In curling, the long, rectangular playing area on ice, marked with painted lines to show the game's boundaries.

brush
A broom used to sweep the ice to change the direction or increase the speed of the curling stone.

curling brush
A broom used to sweep the ice to change the direction or increase the speed of the curling stone.

vice skip
The player who helps the skip with strategy and usually throws third in an "end" or round.

handle
The place at the top of the broom where the curler grips the broom to manipulate it.

curling stone
A circular rock made of polished granite, which is thrown and slides across the ice in the game of curling.

pad
The part of the brush that comes into contact with the ice and sweeps.

alpine skier
Athlete who navigates down steep, snow-covered slopes on skis.

ski boots
Rigid, padded footwear designed to support the feet and ankles and fasten to skis with bindings.

strap
A flexible strip of material that is used to fasten the top of the ski boot tightly to the skier's leg.

upper shell
The upper section of the ski boot, in which the lower leg and ankle is encased.

buckle
A strapping mechanism used to firmly secure a ski boot to the foot.

adjustable catch
An adjustable buckle that can be used to tighten the ski boot on the skier's foot.

lower shell
The lower section of the ski boot, in which the foot is encased.

ski goggles
Protective eyewear used to prevent ice, snow, wind and sun glare from damaging the eyes while skiing.

strap
A flexible strip of material that stretches to exert pressure and fastens the goggles to the head.

lens
The see-through material on the goggles that aids visibility and protects the eyes from wind and snow.

frame
The plastic structure that forms the shape of the ski goggles.

grip
The handle at the top of the ski pole, where the skier's hand holds the pole.

ski poles
Two lightweight poles used by the skier for balance and propulsion.

strap
Loop of flexible material attached to the grip of the ski pole and worn around the wrist.

ferrule
The pointed tip of the ski pole that is used to grip into snow and give traction support to a skier.

cross-country skis
Two long, flat pieces of material, fitted to ski boots, for travel over flat, snow-covered terrain.

bindings
The device that attaches the boot to the ski. It can be easily fastened or unfastened.

tail
The back end of the ski, which is designed to cut through the snow and absorb shock.

basket
A disk near the tip of a ski pole that prevents the pole from sinking too deep in the snow.

front ski bindings
The front portion of the binding fasteners, used to secure and fasten a skier's feet into the ski boots.

waist
The central part of the ski, directly in front of the ski bindings.

boot
An insulated piece of footwear that is fastened to the snowboard with a binding.

binding
The device that attaches the snowboard to the user's boot. It can be easily fastened or unfastened.

snowboard
A wide board used to slide downhill on snow and ice: the user rides standing up, as on a surfboard.

shovel
The front end of the ski, which juts upward to cut through the snow and create a path for the rest of the ski.

deck
The main part of the board, designed to allow the snowboarder to glide and maneuver along the snow.

LEISURE AND ENTERTAINMENT

plush block
A small fabric cube stuffed with soft material; young children use it for stacking and playing.

interactive toy
An electronic toy, usually made of plastic and sometimes with wheels, that has buttons that light up and play music when pressed.

blocks
Small fabric cubes, sometimes stuffed with soft material, with shapes, letters or numbers on their surfaces.

activity gym
A play structure with dangling toys for infants and babies.

mobile
Colorful toys that rotate over an infant's crib, out of their reach.

stuffed animal
A small, soft figure filled with stuffing; children use it to play and cuddle.

dollhouse
A toy that replicates the structure of an actual house on a smaller scale.

doll
A small figurine with a human-like appearance; young children use it as a toy.

balcony
An area on the outer portion of the dollhouse meant to replicate an outdoor terrace.

shelves
A small piece of furniture that mimics tradtional bookshelves.

room
An area designed to mimic an actual room, usually containing small furniture pieces.

toy train
A small plastic toy designed to closely mimic the appearance of a real-life train.

toy fire truck
A small plastic toy designed to closely replicate the appearance of a real-life fire truck.

train set
A wooden toy set featuring train track pieces as well as a train engine and train cars.

building blocks
A set of wooden, three-dimensional shapes used by young children to construct a variety of simple structures.

tricycle
A small, three-wheeled vehicle, similar to a bicycle, used by young children who cannot balance on a bike; also called a trike.

handlebars
The part that is held by the rider to maintain balance and steer to change directions.

basket
A container in which a variety of objects can be placed and transported.

seat
Where the child sits when pedaling and steering the tricycle.

pedal
Where the feet are placed to mechanically generate movement.

rocking toy
A simple toy that is designed in such a way that young children can sit atop it and rock back and forth.

handle
Where the child places their hands to hold onto the toy, for balance and security.

seat
The fabric component that the child sits on when rocking back and forth.

rocker
The curved foundation that allows the rider to rock back and forth.

child's bicycle
A type of bicycle that is used for both training and entertaining young children. It has no pedals.

handlebars
Where the rider places their hands to balance themselves and steer the bicycle.

hopper ball
An inflated ball that small children can sit atop and bounce along the ground.

seat
The child sits on the seat to pedal and direct the bike.

frame
The structural component of the bicycle, which connects the seat to the wheels and handlebars.

wheel
A circular, rubber part of the balance bike that is responsible for grounding the bike and propelling it forward.

play climber
A structure equipped with slides and climbing areas; usually found at a park, but often small enough to fit in a backyard.

sandbox
A small wooden structure that is filled with several inches of sand so that young children can dig or build structures.

handle
Where the child places their hands to hold onto the ride, for balance and security.

kiddie pool
An inflatable structure that can hold several inches of water. Small children use it for swimming and splashing.

spring rider
A playground structure with a spring base; young children ride it to rock in any direction.

seat
Where the child sits.

spring
The foundation of the spring rider, which allows the child to tilt back and forth and side to side.

footrest
Where the child places their feet to secure their weight as they ride.

swing set
A structure with one or more swings for children to play on.

top rail
The structural component from which the swings are suspended.

post
The swing set's foundation, which supports the crossbar and swings.

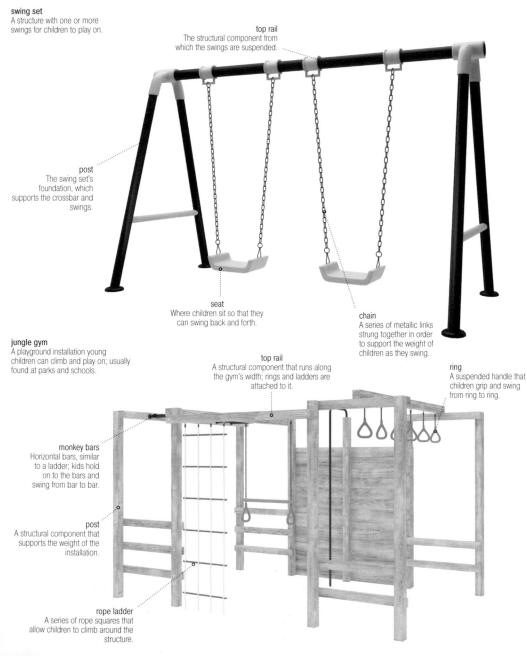

seat
Where children sit so that they can swing back and forth.

chain
A series of metallic links strung together in order to support the weight of children as they swing.

jungle gym
A playground installation young children can climb and play on; usually found at parks and schools.

top rail
A structural component that runs along the gym's width; rings and ladders are attached to it.

ring
A suspended handle that children grip and swing from ring to ring.

monkey bars
Horizontal bars, similar to a ladder; kids hold on to the bars and swing from bar to bar.

post
A structural component that supports the weight of the installation.

rope ladder
A series of rope squares that allow children to climb around the structure.

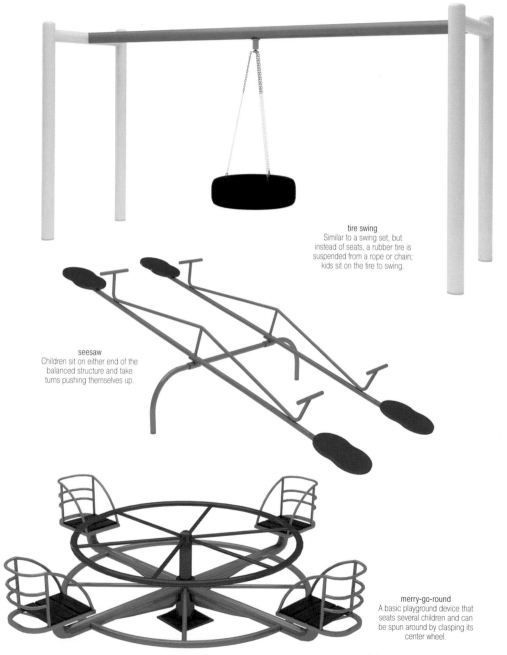

tire swing
Similar to a swing set, but instead of seats, a rubber tire is suspended from a rope or chain; kids sit on the tire to swing.

seesaw
Children sit on either end of the balanced structure and take turns pushing themselves up.

merry-go-round
A basic playground device that seats several children and can be spun around by clasping its center wheel.

amusement park rides
Also called midway rides, these are large machines that children and adults ride for entertainment.

roller coaster
A ride consisting of a track with steep drops; people ride in small cars up and down the track.

waterslide
A long, winding plastic structure that both children and adults can slide down and be ejected into the pool.

swimming pool
A large, water-filled structure that holds thousands of gallons of water, used for recreational swimming.

fence
A metallic structure that runs along the perimeter of an amusement park so that access to the park can be controlled.

climber
A structure with slides and climbing areas upon which young children can climb and play.

sandbox
A small wooden structure that is filled with several inches of sand so that young children can dig or build structures.

swing set
A structure for kids to play upon, typically with one or more hanging swings.

swing ride
An amusement park ride consisting of chairs suspended from a top that rotates very quickly, swinging the chairs out.

car
A road vehicle with four wheels and powered by an engine; it is used to transport one to five passengers.

entrance
The area of the amusement park where patrons enter and exit the park. It is often located near the parking lots.

ticket office
An area where visitors can purchase entry to the park or midway tickets.

Chess

A board game that relies heavily on strategy. Its gameboard has 64 squares over which the chess pieces are moved.

black square
One of the 32 dark squares on the surface of a chess board. Different chess pieces can move along the squares in different ways.

chessboard
The component that players move their pieces along in order to capture the opposing player's pieces.

white square
One of the 32 light squares on the surface of a chess board. Different chess pieces can move along the squares in different ways.

chess piece
The figures used in chess.

pawn
Considered a weak piece; it moves forward only one square at a time and captures pieces diagonally.

knight
This piece is able to jump over other pieces, but it can only move in an L-shaped pattern.

rook
This piece can travel any distance, but only in vertical or horizontal directions.

bishop
This piece can travel any distance, but only in diagonal directions.

king
This is the most important piece. If the king is captured the game is over.

queen
In terms of offensive capabilities, this is the most powerful piece. It can moved in any direction as far as desired.

Checkers

A strategic board game played by two players who take turns moving pieces to take their opponent's pieces.

white square
The area of the checkerboard where pieces are not used in a typical game of checkers.

checkerboard
The component that players move their pieces along in order to capture the opposing player's pieces.

black square
The area of the checkerboard where pieces may be moved diagonally in an attempt to conquer the opponent's checkers.

checker
A circular game piece used to capture the opponent's game pieces. These pieces can only be moved diagonally.

Backgammon

One of the oldest board games in the world, this game involves two players moving pieces according to dice rolls.

point
The area of the backgammon board upon which players progess their pieces in order to reach the final quadrant.

checker
A circular game piece used to capture the game pieces of an opponent.

bar
The raised area between the two tables; pieces are placed here after they have been captured.

die
A small cube with dots on each side, ranging from one to six dots; it is rolled to determine moves of backgammon pieces.

bowling
A game in which players roll bowling balls down a narrow wooden lane in order to knock down as many pins as possible.

score screen
A television-like device where players' turns and scores are displayed.

ball return
A mechanized system that returns bowling balls to players after they have taken their turn.

chair
A piece of where bowlers can sit while they await their next turn.

shoe rack
An area of the bowling alley where bowling shoes of a wide variety of sizes are stored between uses.

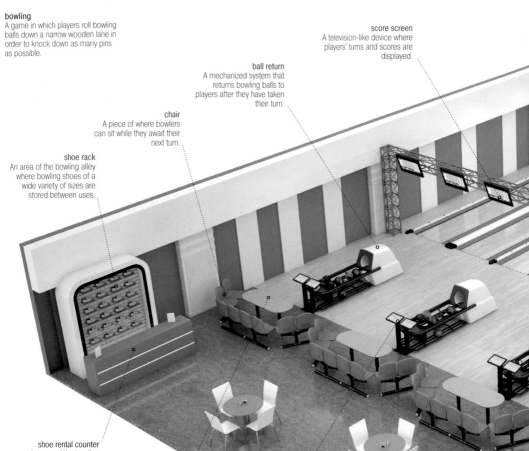

shoe rental counter
An area of the bowling alley where individuals may borrow bowling shoes or purchase concessions.

table
A raised surface at which bowlers can eat or drink between turns.

score console
An electronic interface where players can keep score, adjust settings, clear the pins or raise gutter rails.

pit
The area where the bowling pins are lined up.

rake arm
An electronic mechanism that can be lowered to clear pins after a player's turn.

gutter
A shallow trough down the length of a bowling lane that prevents scoring.

lane
A narrow wooden alley down which players propel balls to knock over pins.

foul line
A line at the edge of a bowling lane that bowlers must not cross.

bowling ball
A dense rubber ball with indentations for the thumb and two fingers.

ball return
A mechanized system that returns bowling balls to players after they have taken their turn.

ball return window
The area of the ball return system that is just wide enough for bowling balls to pass through so they can be positioned on the rack.

track
A metallic railing system along which bowling balls move.

bowling ball
A dense rubber ball, with indentations; it is used to knock down bowling pins.

ball stand
A space that allows players to store different bowling balls for different situations.

lane
A narrow wooden alley down which players propel balls to knock over pins.

bowling ball
A dense rubber ball with indentations for the thumb and two fingers.

bowling pin
A wooden object placed at the end of a bowling lane; it is the ball's target.

pocket
An area of the pool table, used as a target, into which players attempt to propel and sink balls using a cue.

pool cue
A tapered, pole-like device that is used to knock the cue ball against other colored and numbered billard balls.

billiard table
A wooden table with six pockets designed for cue sports. Its surface is covered in felt, which facilitates the balls' movements.

table leg
The structural component of a billard table, which distributes the weight of the table equally.

ball
A small ball, typically striped or solid in color and with a number on the side.

rail
The side component of the billard table, which can be used to execute basic or complex banking shots.

felt
The soft, usualy green fabric over the table's wooden surface; it provides friction against billard balls.

billiards rack
A plastic triangular frame used to organize billard balls into the proper alignment for play.

billiards chalk
A small cube of chalk that is rubbed onto the tips of pool cues in order to provide them with better friction.

snooker table
A table that is designed for playing snooker, a cue sport. It is layered with baize or green felt.

electronic dartboard
An electronic variety of dartboard that is battery powered and can automatically tabulate points during play.

segment score number
A number of points a player scores when they land a dart in that particular wedge.

score display
A digital component of the dartboard that shows the players' scores.

dart
A small, aerodynamically designed projectile that players throw at a circular board, attempting to score points.

bull's-eye
The small circular area located at the center of the dartboard. This is the highest-scoring segment.

triple ring
A small area located between the center and the edge of the board. Points are tripled if a dart lands here.

double ring
A small area at the periphery of the dartboard. If a dart lands here, then points are doubled.

control button
A button that allows players to change game settings, game types or point values.

ARCADE GAMES

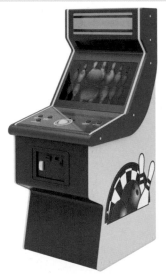

bowling game
A coin-operated arcade video game that offers a virtual bowling experience to its players.

claw crane machine
A coin-operated arcade machine that allows players to manipulate a claw to retrieve a prize.

maze game
A coin-operated video game in which a player must find their way through a virtual maze, avoiding obstacles along the way.

score display
A small digital screen that shows the score of the game.

air hockey table
A gaming device commonly found in arcades; it uses air to levitate a small puck that players hit back and forth.

goal
Hollow slits on opposite sides of the table. Players attempt to push the puck into these slits to score points.

goalie mallet
The small plastic tool that players wield as they shoot or deflect the puck.

face-off spot
A decoration that represents where the puck is dropped during a hockey game.

playing surface
The area where players shoot the puck and attempt to score.

puck return
An area where pucks are returned after a point has been scored so that the next round can begin.

center face-off circle
The area at the very center of the air hockey table, where the puck is dropped for face-offs.

soccer table
Also known as a foosball table, this is a table game in which players use rotational controls to make plastic figurines score goals.

fighting game
A coin-operated arcade video game that is designed to give a virtual combat experience to its players.

table hockey
An electronic two-player arcade game; players pull on handles to control hockey player figures, attempting to outscore an opponent.

light
An electronic component that displays the score and lights the playing surface.

dome
A layer of clear plastic that covers the playing area, preventing the puck from being ejected.

goal
Hollow slits on opposite sides of the table. Players attempt to direct the puck into these slits to score points.

bumper
A plastic shielding that deflects the puck during the course of play.

player
A small plastic figure designed to mimic the appearance of a real hockey player. It is manipulated by rotating controls.

rod
A rotating mechanism attached to plastic figures; players turn the rods to manipulate the figures.

start button
A button that is used to activate the game after inserting coins.

electronic dartboard
A coin-operated arcade video game that allows players to play a game of darts without metal-tipped projectiles.

motorcycle racing game
A coin-operated arcade video game that gives players the experience of a virtual motorcycle race.

two-person shooter game
A coin-operated arcade video game that allows two players to participate in virtual first-person shooting missions.

boxing simulator
A coin-operated arcade video game that provides a virtual boxing experience to its players.

score display
A digital component that shows the scores of participating players.

two-person racing game
A head-to-head arcade game that allows two players to compete against each other in virtual car races.

screen
The optical component that shows the car and race track, providing a visual experience.

control panel
A series of buttons on the dashboard of a racing game that allows players to adjust settings and select game modes.

gearshift
A component that, when pulled, allows players to switch through the various gears of their virtual cars.

brake pedal
A lever pushed with the foot to slow a player's virtual vehicle.

chair
Where players sit in order to play.

accelerator pedal
A lever pushed with the foot to increase the speed of a player's virtual vehicle.

steering wheel
The part that players manipulate to direct their virtual vehicle.

dance pad
A coin-operated arcade system that players dance on according to choreographed patterns.

electronic basketball game
A gaming system that combines physical and electronic elements. Players shoot as many baskets as they can within a minute.

roulette table
The playing area for a casino game that involves betting on the probability of a ball landing on a red or black numbered space.

chip
Also known as a gambling chip, this is a small coin-like piece that represents different amounts of money.

croupier's area
The area of the roulette table where a croupier stands as he manages roulette games and chip exchanges.

layout
The area of the roulette table upon which players can throw dice or place bets by laying chips on numbered spaces.

chip holder
An area where roulette players can safely and securely place their chips while playing.

roulette wheel
The rotational aspect of a roulette table, which is spun to make a small ball land on a red or black space.

craps table
A table commonly found in casino settings that is designed for playing craps.

slot machine
A gaming machine that is operated by pulling a lever to create valuable combinations of symbols, winning money for the player.

casino poker table
A gaming table commonly found in casino settings that is designed for playing poker.

poker table
A type of gaming table that is commonly found in casino settings and that is designed for poker games.

card table
A felt-covered table designed for playing blackjack.

Suits
Refers to one of the four types of cards in a deck: diamonds, hearts, clubs or spades. There are 13 cards of each suit.

hearts
A red suit with a heart-shaped symbol.

diamonds
A red suit with a four-sided symbol.

clubs
A black suit with a clover-shaped symbol.

spades
A black suit with a leaf-shaped symbol.

Face cards and special cards
With regard to points, the face cards are usually the most valuable cards. The joker is often used as a wild card.

jack
The lowest value face card. Its numerical value is 11, so it is stronger than the numerical cards.

queen
The third-highest valued face card. Its numerical value is 12, so it is stronger than every card except the king and ace.

king
The second-highest value face card. Its numerical value is 13, so it is stronger than every card except the ace.

ace
This card can be used as the highest or lowest value card, depending on what type of game is being played.

joker
A card that may or may not be used, depending on what type of card game is being played.

Standard poker hands
The various card combinations that determine who wins a poker hand.

one pair
The lowest value card combination, but it is still stronger than any single card.

two pairs
A poker hand in which a player possesses two differing sets of pairs, two aces and two kings, for example.

three of a kind
A poker hand in which a player possesses three cards that bear the same numerical value.

straight
A poker hand in which a player possesses five cards that are in direct numerical order.

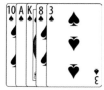

flush
A poker hand in which a player possesses five cards of the same suit.

full house
A poker hand in which a player possesses a combination of both a pair and three of a kind.

four of a kind
A poker hand in which a player possesses four cards with the exact same value.

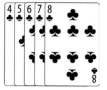

straight flush
A poker hand in which a player possesses five cards that are in numerical order and of the same suit.

royal flush
A poker hand in which a player possesses a five-card straight, ten through ace, of the same suit.

tent
A portable shelter made of water-proof fabric and elastic rods; used when camping.

patio umbrella
A canopy attached to a pole, used outdoors to provide shade or rain cover over objects or people.

pole
A piece that provides structural integrity to the tent's walls.

guy line
A cord that can be staked into the groud in order to firmly secure the structural integrity of the tent.

cooler
An insulated box with a fitted or hinged lid in which perishable goods can be kept cool for a period of time.

lantern
A battery-powered lighting device typically used outdoors, particularly when camping.

hook
A small circular part at the top of the handle; used to hang the lantern up.

handle
The plastic frame that is situated at the top of a lantern and used to hold or carry the device.

floor
The fabric base of a tent, usually made with waterproof materials to protect against the damp ground.

wall
The sides of a tent, constructed with fabric that resists rainfall and snowfall.

globe
The transparent shell that surrounds the inner bulb of a lantern to shield and protect it.

lamp
The actual light source of a lantern. It is battery-powered and can be activated with the push of a button.

seat
The fabric component of a folding camping stool that is pulled taut as the stool is unfolded.

folding camp stool
A collapsible seat that is easy to transport and store; it is made from a metal frame and fabric seat.

on/off button
A small central switch that is pushed to turn the lantern on or off.

leg
The part that provides a stable foundation so that a person can comfortably sit on the chair.

housing
The structural framework of a lantern. It also protects the inner components.

skid-proof foot
A small piece of rubber that wraps around the base of a folding camping stool; it ensures the chair will not slide easily.

backpack
A small fabric bag that is worn on the back.

pocket knife
A small multi-purpose tool equipped with several mini tools, such as a blade, can opener and file.

flashlight
A small, battery-powered device that emits a beam of light when activated.

sleeping bag
A padded fabric bag with a zipper, used to sleep in when camping; it keeps a person warm and comfortable.

thermal jug
A liquid-storage device designed to keep drinks or soups hot for long periods of time.

lounge chair
A wooden seat designed to match the contours of the human body.

rifle
A gun that is specially designed for hunting purposes. This particular rifle is effective at mid-range and long-range shots.

scope
An aiming component that magnifies objects for easy viewing.

magazine
This aspect of the hunting rifle stores ammunition. When the gun is ready to be shot, bullets are fed up from the magazine.

sight
A device that one looks through in order to aim and shoot accurately at a target.

stock
The structural aspect of a hunting rifle that connects its butt with the gun's other components, such as its barrel.

rifle cartridge
The actual bullet that is designed specifically to be used with a rifle. It is aerodynamic.

barrel
The part of a hunting rifle that spins the bullet and propels it through the chamber.

trigger guard
A thin metallic shield that surrounds the periphery of the rifle's trigger so that the gun cannot be accidentally fired.

shotgun
A type of gun that is specially designed for hunting activities. It is a short-range weapon that is common to the hunting of birds.

trigger
The part of a gun that is squeezed by a finger to initiate the shooting mechanisms of the gun.

forearm
The area of a shotgun where the user places their dominant hand in order to steady the gun.

butt plate
The back portion of the rifle's frame. It is positioned against the shoulder.

hammer
A part of a shotgun that will initiate firing when the trigger is pulled.

breech
A structural component of a hunting shotgun that houses the gun's bolt carrier group, magazine port and trigger port.

rib
A sighting aspect of a hunting rifle that allows its operator to adjust the inclination of the rifle's barrel.

barrel
The part of a hunting rifle that spins the bullet and propels it through the chamber.

pistol grip
An area of a shotgun where one places their dominant hand in order to pull the gun's trigger.

trigger guard
A thin metallic shield that surrounds the periphery of the shotgun's trigger so that the gun cannot be accidentally fired.

focusing ring
A ring located near the eyepiece of the binoculars that can be used to manually adjust focus levels.

binoculars
Also known as field glasses, this is an optical instrument that allows users to see distant objects.

eyepiece
The area held up to the eyes so that a person may see through the lenses.

trigger
The part of a gun that is squeezed by a finger to initiate the shooting mechanisms of the gun.

stock
A structural aspect of a shotgun that connects its butt with the gun's other components, such as its barrel.

lens system
The series of lenses located near the eyepiece of binoculars that help to magnify viewed images.

butt plate
The back portion of the rifle's frame. It is positioned against the shoulder.

Porro prism
A reflection prism that is used within binoculars to alter an image's orientation.

central focusing wheel
A rotating mechanism that is used to adjust, alter and manipulate the focus of the binoculars.

body
The structural framework that houses and protects all of the various inner components of the binoculars.

bridge
The plastic connective structure that securely connects both halves of the binoculars.

objective lens
The lens within the binoculars that is characterized as being closest to the object being viewed.

shotgun cartridge
The container that houses the pellets of a shotgun bullet. It can be loaded into the shotgun.

seat
A device common to all fly rods that is designed to give the rod up-locking or down-locking functionalities.

handle
The part of the fishing reel that can be held and turned by a person who is fishing, in order to reel the line.

reel
A mechanism, attached to a fishing rod, used to wind and unwind fishing line.

line spool nut
A small locking instrument that is used to safely secure the position of the rod's bail to its line spool mechanism.

spool
An area of the reel in which fishing line can be coiled and then fed up the rod.

bail
A part designed so that it can instantaneously capture the line whenever the handle is cranked.

fishhook
A small metal tool on which bait, worms or pieces of meat are affixed in order to entice and capture fish.

triple fishhook
A specially designed hook that is used to increase the chances of hooking a fish in the mouth.

leg
A portion of the fishing reel that is responsible for connecting the device's handle with its reel housing.

anti-reverse lever
A component located behind the reel's spool; it allows the user to let out line at controlled speeds.

gear housing
A component of the reeling mechanism that protects several of the mechanism's inner components.

float
A flotation device attached to a fishing line; used to suspend a lure.

bead
The component of the cork float that is responsible for keeping the float in a proper position as it moves through water.

fly fishing rod
A type of angling device used to bait and catch fish using fly fishing methods.

rod
A long, thin pole to which a reel and fishing line are attached; it is used to catch and reel in fish.

keeper ring
A small metallic ring that serves to funnel the fly line to the top of the fishing rod in an organized manner.

float
A flotation device attached to a fishing line; used to suspend a lure.

leader
A structural aspect of a cork float that is responsible for stabilizing its position in both calm and choppy waters.

guide
A small, circular structure comprising plastic or metal that is responsible for feeding the rod's line to its uppermost point.

fly reel
The mechanism of a fishing rod that allows the fly line to be released at a precise and controlled rate.

fly line
The specialized line that is released from the fly reel. It is typically capped with a baited hook.

fishing line
A tough nylon thread that is strung from a fishing rod; it is attached to a baited hook and used to capture fish.

handgrip
The component of a fishing rod that is held by a person who is fishing in order to cast the rod's line.

spool
An area of the reel in which fishing line can be coiled and then fed up the rod.

reel
A mechanism, attached to a fishing rod, used to wind and unwind fishing line.

fishing lure
A baiting device used to attract fish, often made of brightly colored plastic or metal.

OFFICE

cubicles
An area of an office where a small group of employees perform their day-to-day tasks.

file box
A small plastic container that is used to store and organize various documents.

sticky note
A small adhesive sticker that can be placed on an object to label it or provide messages or reminders.

monitor
The visual component of a desktop computer system; it includes a screen for display purposes.

pen and pencil cup
A container that holds writing tools, like pens, pencils, highlighters or markers.

letter organizer
A small piece of desk equipment that allows employees to collect and organize various documents.

partition
A large panel that sections off different workspaces in an office. It allows employees privacy in their work.

letter tray
A small shelf that is used to hold and organize documents and papers.

desk
A piece of furniture with a surface on which a computer, printer and other office equipment can be placed.

desktop computer
A type of computer that features a tower that can be tucked beneath a desk.

mouse
A small, electronic device that can be connected to a desktop computer in order to move its cursor on screen.

telephone
An electronic communication device that can be used to make calls over landlines.

keyboard
A typing apparatus with keys that can be connected to a computer in order to operate it or type.

printer
A common piece of office equipment that is used to produce various paper documents.

task chair
A piece of furniture that employees sit on at a desk.

clock
A battery-powered device that displays the precise, current time.

mobile filing cabinet
A small piece of office furniture on wheels; it is used for storage and can be easily moved.

storage cabinet
Small, hollow square
areas within shelving
that can be used
to store binders,
documents and similar
items.

task chair
A piece of furniture that
employees sit on at
a desk.

headset
An audio-listening device
that can be plugged into
a personal computer so
as not to disturb nearby
employees with audio.

partition
A large panel that
sections off different
workspaces in an
office. It allows
employees privacy in
their work.

monitor
The visual component
of a desktop computer
system; it includes
a screen for display
purposes.

call center
A specially designed facility that
handles a large number of incoming
calls.

desktop computer
A type of computer that
features a tower that can be
tucked beneath a desk.

pen and paper
Writing supplies used for
taking notes or general
writing purposes.

keyboard
A typing apparatus with
keys that can be connected
to a computer in order to
operate it or type.

filing cabinet
A metallic storage unit that is used to
collect and archive documents.

pull
The component of an
extending tray that is
grabbed and held by an
employee in order to open
or close the tray.

drawer
A small metal cabinet
that can be rolled in and
out of its shut position in
order to retrieve pertinent
documents as needed.

label holder
The area of an extending
tray cabinet where a small
notecard can be placed
in order to describe the
cabinet's contents.

desk clock
A small time-telling device that is
designed to be placed on a work
desk or table.

reception
The entrance area of an office, often containing a desk and a receptionist.

storage cabinet
A small, hollow square area within a piece of shelving furniture that can be used to store binders, documents and similar items.

paper
Small white sheets made of pulpwood logs or recycled materials that are used for writing or printing purposes.

binder
A type of folder made of plastic and cardboard; it is used to contain and organize documents.

armchair
A chair designed to support a sitter's back and arms comfortably.

cup
A small piece of ceramic pottery that is used to hold liquids, such as coffee, for drinking purposes.

coffee table
A piece of furniture, usually long and low, designed to be placed in front of a sofa or chairs.

executive armchair
An ergonomic chair that is designed to support a sitter's back and arms for extended periods of time.

armrest
The portion of the airchair that is designed to ergonomically support the human arm. It is covered with a leather cushion.

backrest
An area of the armchair covered with a large leather cushion that is responsible for supporting the back of a sitter.

base
The foundation of the chair; it has wheels for mobility purposes.

seat
A leather cushion located near the middle of the armchair that allows an individual to sit comfortably during work.

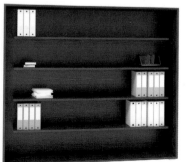

bookcase
A basic piece of furniture that has several rows of thin shelves that can be used to hold documents or books.

wheel
A part located at the bottom of an armchair that is designed to allow the chair to be easily moved.

height adjustment lever
The component of an armchair that can be used to raise or lower the seat's base position.

conference room
A long room designed to facilitate large office meetings or group conference calls.

flip chart
A large surface that can be used to show large images, such as graphs or charts, to a group of people.

binder
A type of folder device made of plastic and cardboard that is used to contain and organize sets of documents.

watercooler
This is a water dispensing device that may be refilled. It dispenses water for drinking.

telephone
An electronic communication device that can be used to make calls over landlines.

file box
A small box made of plastic, metal or wood that is used to store files that may need to be easily accessed at a later date.

executive armchair
A large and sturdy leather chair found in an office; it is designed to ergonomically support the contours of the body.

storage cabinet
A small wooden structure that can be used to store a wide variety of material supplies, such as documents, folders and binders.

laptop computer
A small computer that has the computational power of a desktop computer but with portability.

office chair
An ergonomic chair that is designed to support a sitter's back and arms for extended periods of time.

conference table
The large, rectangular table located in the middle of a conference room where employees sit during meetings.

conference table
A piece of furniture that employees sit at during meetings.

leg
A support attached to the bottom of a piece of furniture; it is used to stabilize the piece or raise it.

top
The surface of a table that is completely flat so as to allow items to be easily and securely placed upon it.

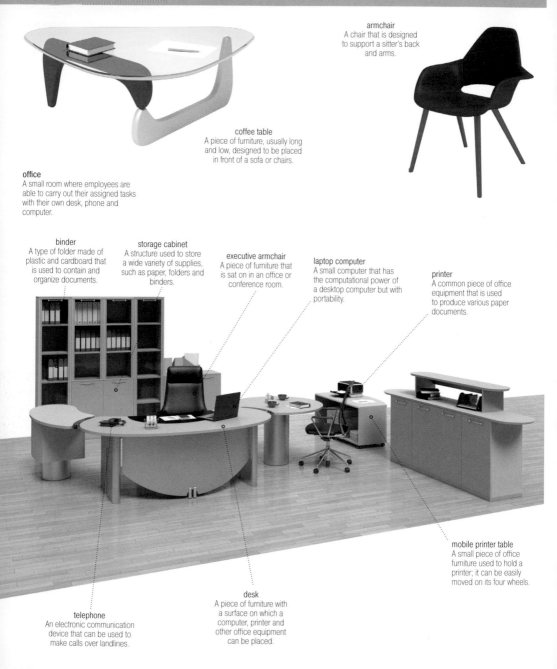

armchair
A chair that is designed to support a sitter's back and arms.

coffee table
A piece of furniture, usually long and low, designed to be placed in front of a sofa or chairs.

office
A small room where employees are able to carry out their assigned tasks with their own desk, phone and computer.

binder
A type of folder made of plastic and cardboard that is used to contain and organize documents.

storage cabinet
A structure used to store a wide variety of supplies, such as paper, folders and binders.

executive armchair
A piece of furniture that is sat on in an office or conference room.

laptop computer
A small computer that has the computational power of a desktop computer but with portability.

printer
A common piece of office equipment that is used to produce various paper documents.

mobile printer table
A small piece of office furniture used to hold a printer; it can be easily moved on its four wheels.

telephone
An electronic communication device that can be used to make calls over landlines.

desk
A piece of furniture with a surface on which a computer, printer and other office equipment can be placed.

break room
An area found within most office settings that allows employees to heat up meals, eat or take coffee breaks.

glass
A small cup used to hold water or other liquids for drinking purposes.

kettle
A piece of kitchenware that can be heated upon a stovetop in order to boil water and brew tea.

plate
A small, flat ceramic surface that is used in office kitchens to hold food for eating purposes.

cup
A small piece of ceramic pottery that is used to hold liquids, such as coffee, for drinking purposes.

drawer
A small wooden cabinet that can be rolled in and out of its shut position; it stores kitchen utensils.

shelf
A small wooden surface that can be used to store various kinds of kitchenware, such as bowls or plates.

counter
A large, flat-topped surface in a kitchen where plates or small appliances are placed.

cooktop controls
Dials that are used to increase or decrease the stove burners' heat.

bowl
A container found in office kitchens that can be used to hold a variety of materials, such as snacks or punch.

cooktop
A type of appliance found in some office settings that is used to heat or cook food.

pull
The component of a kitchen cabinet that can be grabbed and held by hand in order to open or close the cabinet.

filing cabinet
A metallic storage unit that is used to collect and archive documents.

stationary cabinet
A cabinets used to store a wide variety of material supplies, such as documents, folders and binders.

Vending machines

Various types of electronic machines that offer snacks or drinks when coins or bills are inseted.

coffeemaker
A small appliance that brews and dispenses coffee with the push of a button.

coffee hopper
A small piece of ceramic pottery that is used to hold liquids, such as coffee, for drinking purposes.

control panel
An area located on the coffee machine that can be used to select different types of coffee drinks.

drip tray
The part of the coffee machine where cups can be placed to receive coffee; it also collects spilled coffee.

nozzle
The component of the coffee machine that is used to dispense heated coffee into cups.

snack food vending machine
An electronic machine that dispenses a variety of snacks or candies; items can be purchased by inserting money.

coffee machine
A large appliance that is electronically powered and can dispense cups of coffee after money is inserted.

hot and cold beverage vending machine
A vending machine that can be used to dispense hot or cold drinks.

bill acceptor
The area of the coffee machine that is designed to accept dollar bills so that drinks may be purchased.

nozzle
The part of a coffee machine that is responsible for dispensing the coffee.

drink selection keypad
This is the area of a coffee machine where users can select differing types of coffees at varying temperatures.

drip tray
The part of a coffee machine where cups are placed to receive coffee; it also collects spilled coffee.

change return slot
The area of a coffee machine that dispenses cash if the amount of money put into the machine is greater than the coffee's price.

display
A digital component of the vending machine that is designed to convey various types of information, such as pricing or the time.

keypad
An area located on the vending machine that is used to select different drinks at different temperatures.

nozzle
The part of a vending machine that is responsible for dispensing water.

drip tray
The part of a vending machine where cups are placed to receive coffee or water; it also collects spill over.

beverage vending machine
An electronic machine that can dispense a variety of cold drinks after money is inserted.

display
The shelving inside the vending machine, designed to make the products easily visible.

beverage bottle
A plastic container commonly used to hold water, sodas or juices. These drinks can be purchased by inserting money.

bill acceptor
The area of the vending machine that is designed to accept dollar bills so that drinks may be purchased.

keypad
The user interface of the vending machine where buyers can press various buttons to select different drinks.

laptop computer
A small computer that has the computational power of a desktop computer but with portability.

screen
The display component of a laptop, which is responsible for generating the laptop's visual graphics and virtual desktop.

webcam
The camera component of a laptop computer, which allows users to take photos or record video.

keyboard
A typing apparatus built into the surface of a laptop computer, which can be used to generate written communications.

power button
The button of the laptop that is responsible for turning the computer on or off.

ports
An area of a laptop computer where various USB-compatible devices can be inserted to be used in conjunction with the laptop.

touch pad
The area located beneath the keyboard where users can manipulate the cursor with their fingers.

tablet computer
A flat device that performs many of the functions of a laptop but in a smaller size and without a physical keyboard.

power button
The button that is responsible for turning the tablet on and off.

touch screen
The screen component of a tablet, which allows the user to interact with it by touching it with their fingers.

camera lens
A feature of a tablet that serves as a camera and can take pictures, record videos or stream live feeds.

application (app) icon
A small graphic that displays an application's logo. If it is clicked, the application will be opened.

all-in-one computer
A computer that does not require a separate monitor; the hardware is built into the same device as the display.

volume control
A button located on the side of a tablet that is responsible for manipulating the volume levels.

power supply fan
A small, fan-like device located at the back of the computer case, which is used to cool the inner components of the computer.

PSU switch
A small button located at the back of the computer case, which can be used to turn the computer on and off.

power cable connector
The area located at the back of a desktop computer where its power cable may be inserted so as to power the device.

desktop computer
A type of computer that features a tower that can be tucked beneath a desk.

mouse or keyboard port
The area located at the back of a desktop computer where a mouse's connecting cable can be inserted.

case fan
The area located at the back of a desktop computer that allows heat to be released so that the device does not overheat.

USB port
An area located at the back of a desktop computer where a USB flash drive may be inserted for usage.

power button
The button of the desktop computer that is responsible for turning the computer on or off.

network port
The area located at the back of a desktop computer where a network adapter cable can be inserted.

audio jack
An area of the computer cases's frame where a headphone jack can be inserted in order to listen to audio through headphones.

video port
The area located at the back of a desktop computer where a monitor signal cable can be inserted.

expansion slot
The area located at the back of a desktop computer where the cables of peripheral devices can be inserted.

keyboard
A typing apparatus with keys that can be connected to a computer in order to operate it or type.

cordless mouse
A type of computer mouse that connects with its host computer wirelessly.

corded mouse
A small electronic device that can be connected by cable to a desktop computer in order to manipulate its mouse cursor.

graphics tablet
An electronic device that allows messages, pictures or graphs to be drawn onto its display screen.

gaming controller
A type of controller that is designed to be used in conjunction with video game and entertainment consoles.

Printers, copiers and scanners

Three pieces of equipment that are fundamental to any office setting and are often used in tandem.

ink cartridge
A small plastic container that can be inserted into a printer in order to supply it with ink.

plotter
A printer that is used to produce documents on larger-than-normal formats of paper.

laser printer
A printer that uses layers of ink to print high-quality documents.

toner cartridge
A container that is filled with an ink-like substance, designed to be used with a laser printer.

flatbed scanner
An office device that can be used to transfer copies of an original document to a computer.

paper tray
A small component used to organize the sheets of paper as they are fed into the device.

sheetfed scanner
An office device that can be used to transfer copies of an original document to a computer, several sheets at a time.

cover
A rectangular plastic component that facilitates the scanning of documents by pressing them against the scanner.

belt
A component of the scanner that facilitates the movement of the device's scanning equipment.

scan head
The transparent surface that allows documents to be scanned.

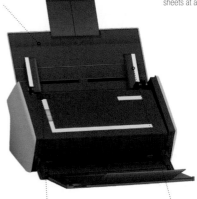

platen glass
A flat surface that documents are placed on so that they can be scanned for reproduction purposes.

control panel
An area that contains buttons that can be used to alter various aspects of the scanner's operations.

power button
The button that, when pressed, turns the machine on and off.

output tray
The component that is used to push scanned copies out of the machine in a neat and controlled manner.

ink-jet printer
A printer that produces documents by converting a file to ink on physical paper.

control panel
An area that contains buttons to select various settings for the machine's operations.

display
The area of the laser printer that provides a visual image of the device's current operational settings.

copier
A piece of office equipment that is used to make duplicates of an original paper document.

memory card
A small device that can store pictures; it can be plugged into printers in order to print its contents.

power button
The button responsible for turning it on and off.

headset
A type of hands-free device common to office settings that employees wear to hear and talk to customers.

headband
A circular piece of plastic that is designed to neatly and securely fasten the headset to the wearer's head.

power button
The button on a smartphone that is responsible for turning the device on and off.

smartphone
An advanced cellular telephone that can also connect to the Internet and perform a wide variety of functions.

receiver
The component of the smartphone device that produces sound and voices during phone calls

earpiece
The component of a headset that audio messages are received through. This part is placed firmly upon the ears.

camera lens
A component of a smartphone device that can take pictures, record videos or stream live feeds.

volume control
A button located on the side of a smartphone that is responsible for controlling the volume level.

touch screen
The screen component of a smartphone, which allows the user to interact with it by touching it with their fingers.

application (app) icon
A small graphic that displays an application's logo. If it is clicked, the application will be opened.

back button
A core button of a smartphone that allows its user to readily return to a previous screen.

microphone
The component of a headset that is responsible for receiving and transmitting audio messages.

cable
A specially designed type of cord that connects the headset to a computer or laptop's audio jack.

menu button
One of the three fundamental control buttons of a smartphone; it allows users to easily access the phone's menu.

home button
One of the three fundamental buttons of a smartphone; when pressed, it returns its user to the device's home screen.

microphone
A type of audio equipment used to be able to communicate orally via a computer.

handset cord
A cable that is used to transfer audio signals to and from a telephone's voice receiver.

display
The component of a telephone that provides a visual image of names and phone numbers.

keypad
The typing element built into the surface of a telephone; it can be used to program caller identifications.

telephone
An electronic communication device that can be used to make calls over landlines.

handset
The component of the telephone that is placed next to the ear and mouth for communication purposes.

push button
Numbered circles on a telephone that, when pressed, are used to dial telephone numbers.

speed dial button
A button located next to a telephone's directory that can be used to instantly dial a programmed number.

webcam
A camera device that can be attached to a desktop computer in order to take pictures or video, or have conferences.

automatic document feeder
The area of a fax machine that holds documents and then sends them through the machine in order to be faxed.

speed dial directory
An area of the telephone that lists a series of important phone numbers, such as for particular departments.

fax
A device that functions as the combination of a phone and printer. Documents may be sent from one location to another.

power button
The button on a fax machine that turns the device on and off.

handset
The component of the fax machine that is placed next to the ear and mouth for communication purposes.

start button
A button located on the top of a fax machine that is responsible for initiating the faxing process.

wireless router
An electronic device that is designed to wirelessly transmit network signals to and from multiple devices.

handset cord
A cable that is used to transfer electronic signals to and from a fax machine's voice receiver.

display
The component of a fax machine that provides a visual image of names and fax numbers.

indicator light
The component of a router that shows the current status of the device's operations by flashing green, yellow or red.

Internet stick
A miniature modem device that can be plugged into the USB port of a laptop or computer to access the Internet.

antenna
The component of a router that is responsible for facilitating the transfer of wireless messages between computer networks.

power button
A component that is used to either engage or terminate the operations of a router.

printing calculator
A small electronic device used to solve arithmetical problems and then print them for archiving purposes.

calculator
A small electronic device powered by batteries or solar power that is used to compute arithmetical problems.

paper roll
The part of the printing calculator that calculations are printed on for archiving purposes.

key
Any of the buttons that have numerical or symbolic values and can be pressed to operate the calculator.

screen
The component of a printing calculator that provides a visual image of the device's current calculations.

shredder
An electronic device that is used to permanently destroy sensitive documents by slicing them into pieces.

lid
A rectangular plastic component of the shredder that helps guide the documents through the cutting head.

pocket calculator
A small electronic device that can be used to compute basic arithmetical problems. The device can fit easily into a pocket.

control button
The button located on a shredder's control panel that can be used to select different settings for the machine's operations.

cutting head
The area of the paper shredder responsible for slicing papers.

external hard drive
A portable storage device that can be attached to a computer via USB to add complementary storage space.

waste basket
The storage component of the shredder that is designed to collect the shredded scraps of paper.

monitor
The visual component
of a desktop computer
system; it includes
a screen for display
purposes.

label maker
An electronic device that can be used
to create and print adhesive stickers.

display
The screen component
of the label maker; it
shows various types of
information, such as the
device's settings.

navigation buttons
A button that allows
users to change
settings and make
typing adjustments.

USB flash drive
A small hard drive device that can
be used to transfer files from one
computer to another.

control button
A button that can be used to
change the devices settings, such
as the type of label or the size of
the type.

keypad
An area where the
letters and words for
the label are input.

case
The plastic structural
frame of a USB
flash drive that is
responsible for
housing the device's
inner components.

connector
The uppermost portion
of a USB flash drive that
is designed to be readily
inserted into a computer
device for data transfers.

cap
The component of a
USB flash drive that
is designed to cover
and protect the drive's
socket region.

digital voice recorder
A small electronic device that
is used to record meetings or
interviews.

display
The screen component
of an audio recorder,
responsible for showing
various types of
information, including
recording time.

control button
A button located on an
audio recorder's control
panel that can be
used to select different
recording settings.

loudspeaker
The component of an
audio recorder that
provides playback of
audio recordings.

e-reader
A small tablet that stores books in
electronic form; users read books
saved onto it.

housing
The plastic frame that surrounds the face of a digital clock. It keeps the clock's components secure.

face
The front screen of a digital clock. The current date and time are shown here.

minutes
The digital display that conveys the current minute. It is on the right side of a digital clock.

digital clock
A battery-powered or electric device that displays the current time and date.

hours
The digital display that conveys the current hour. It is on the left side of a digital clock.

temperature
The area on a digital clock that displays the intensity of heat in a room.

month
The digital display that denotes the current month.

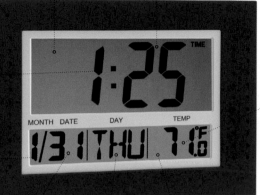

date
The digitial display that denotes the current date.

day of the week
The area that displays the current day of the week, usually in abbreviated form.

additional display
A second and smaller face located directly under the main face of the watch. It conveys dates and temperature.

portable digital audio player
A small handheld audio device into which songs and playlists can be uploaded for listening purposes.

previous button
The switch on a portable digital audio player that can be used to return to earlier songs and playlists.

display
A screen located on a portable digital audio player. It shows the current song that is being played.

on/off button
A switch on a portable digital audio player that can be used to activate or deactivate the device.

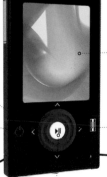

next button
The switch on a portable digital audio player that can be used to cycle between songs and playlists.

earphones
Small earbuds placed within the ear in order to listen to music streaming from the player.

play/pause button
The switch on a portable digital audio player that can be used to both start and stop streaming music.

single-lens reflex (SLR) digital camera: front view
The front view of a device that digitally records images so they can be saved and printed.

data display
The small digital screen that shows a wide variety of data, such as battery level, mode and storage space.

hot-shoe contact
A structural component located on top of the camera that can be used to attach a flash.

accessory shoe
A point where various types of accessories, such as a flash, can be mounted onto the camera.

shutter release button
The button on the upper portion of a camera that opens the camera's shutters to capture a photo.

mode dial
A rotating dial located on the upper portion of a camera that can be used to select different shooting modes.

focus setting ring
A small plastic ring that is manually rotated to change and modify the sharpness of an image.

neckstrap eyelet
A small ring or loop located on the side of a camera; a neckstrap may be attached here.

lens
The transparent device on a camera that turns captured light into images.

camery body
The structural framework that connects and protects all the various components of a camera.

lens aperture scale
A graduated scale that shows the various focus settings on the camera's focus ring.

single-lens reflex (SLR) digital camera: back view
A back view of a single-lens digital camera, showing all parts and components.

viewfinder
The small, transparent opening through which a user looks to view the object to be photographed.

menu button
The button located on the back of a camera that is used to display a list of setting options.

settings display button
The button located on the back of a camera that can be used to alter different camera options.

image review button
The button located on the back of a camera that allows stored images to be cycled through.

erase button
The button on the back of a camera that is used to select and erase pictures.

display
The small LED screen of a camera where recently taken pictures may be reviewed or deleted.

enlarge button
The buttons used during display mode to zoom in or out of an image.

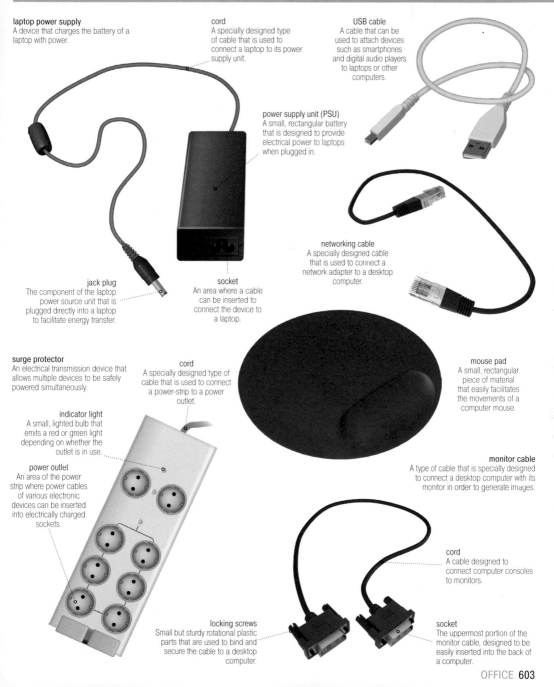

laptop power supply
A device that charges the battery of a laptop with power.

cord
A specially designed type of cable that is used to connect a laptop to its power supply unit.

USB cable
A cable that can be used to attach devices such as smartphones and digital audio players to laptops or other computers.

power supply unit (PSU)
A small, rectangular battery that is designed to provide electrical power to laptops when plugged in.

networking cable
A specially designed cable that is used to connect a network adapter to a desktop computer.

jack plug
The component of the laptop power source unit that is plugged directly into a laptop to facilitate energy transfer.

socket
An area where a cable can be inserted to connect the device to a laptop.

mouse pad
A small, rectangular piece of material that easily facilitates the movements of a computer mouse.

surge protector
An electrical transmission device that allows multiple devices to be safely powered simultaneously.

cord
A specially designed type of cable that is used to connect a power-strip to a power outlet.

indicator light
A small, lighted bulb that emits a red or green light depending on whether the outlet is in use.

power outlet
An area of the power strip where power cables of various electronic devices can be inserted into electrically charged sockets.

monitor cable
A type of cable that is specially designed to connect a desktop computer with its monitor in order to generate images.

cord
A cable designed to connect computer consoles to monitors.

locking screws
Small but sturdy rotational plastic parts that are used to bind and secure the cable to a desktop computer.

socket
The uppermost portion of the monitor cable, designed to be easily inserted into the back of a computer.

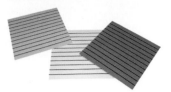

index card
Also known as flashcards, these are small pieces of lined paper that can be used to jot down notes or pertinent information.

sticky note
Small pieces of paper that have an adhesive strip so that they may be stuck to flat surfaces.

window envelope
A kind of envelope that allows a specific and desired portion of its contents to be visible from outside the envelope.

envelope
A type of paper container that is designed to facilitate the mailing or storage of important documents.

flip page
The part of the calendar upon which the dates and months of a year are displayed. It can be rotated to reveal later months.

spiral binding
Small metallic wirings that are used to secure the calendar's flip pages, but are also used to allow the pages to be rotated.

calendar
A series of pages that shows the days, weeks and months of the year.

month
The area of a calendar's flip page where the current month is easily displayed.

JANUARY

SUN	MON	TUE	WED	THU	FRI	SAT
1	2	3	4	5	6	7
8	9	10	11	12	13	14
15	16	17	18	19	20	21
22	23	24	25	26	27	28
29	30	31	1	2	3	4

day
The component of the flip page that conveys the days of the week, Monday or Tuesday, for example.

date
A small square that bears a number that represents a single day of a month on the surface of a calendar's flip page.

cardboard base
The calendar's foundation; it is folded open to allow the pages to be rotated.

sheet of paper
It contain the days and weeks of the year in binder rings to record appointments, deadlines or events.

day planner
A binder that holds a spiral notebook. It is commonly used to organize and record important events and meetings.

divider
Small plastic tabs that come in various colors and are used to separate different collections of documents within binders.

binder
A type of folder made of plastic and cardboard that is used to contain and organize documents.

label
Small, rectangular stickers that can be written on and then attached to documents to identify and categorize them.

divider
A small, colored tab that is used to separate and organize different areas of a personal organizer.

whiteboard
A writing surface that is common to most office settings; one can write on it with a specialized marker that wipes clean.

writing surface
An area that one may write on with a specialized marker that wipes clean.

magnetic bulletin board
A rectangular cut-out of metal that is framed to be hung on walls. Small documents may be attached to it with magnets.

base
The structural component that serves as the foundation of the board. It has wheels for ease of mobility.

caster
Small, circular components of a whiteboard that provide ease of mobility so that the board may be readily moved.

Desk supplies

packing tape dispenser
An apparatus that allows users to dispense and cut sections of packing tape with great control and efficiency.

tape
A roll of adhesive material. This roll is cycled in such a way that its tape can be dispensed and cut.

handle
The component of a tape gun that is grabbed and held in order to tape materials.

staple remover
A small office tool that is used to take staples out of documents or other materials.

tape dispenser
A basic office tool that is designed to hold and easily distribute small or large pieces of tape.

cutting blade
The component of the tape gun that is used to shear strips of tape from the device's tape dispenser.

stapler
An essential office tool that can be used to punch staples into series of documents or into similar materials.

staple
Small pieces of metal that are inserted into a stapler; they are used to attach sheets of paper to one another.

blade
The metal razor component of a pencil sharpener that readily sharpens pencils when they are rotated against it.

pencil sharpener
A device that is designed to sharpen the graphite points of pencils.

set square
A plastic geometrical tool that can be used to measure angles or to solve a wide variety of geometrical problems.

paper punch
A piece of office equipment used to cut small holes into documents so that they can be collected in three-ring binders.

glue stick
A small cylinder of solid adhesive that can be used to fasten different materials together.

box cutter
A small knife-like tool that is specially designed to cut open boxes or containers.

slide lock
A small component of the box cutter that is moved to lengthen the blade and hold it in place.

blade
The metallic razor of the boxcutter that is designed to easily cut into cardboard containers or similar structures.

handle
The component of the box cutter that is grabbed and held in order to cut materials.

correction tape
A special kind of tape that can be placed over a typographical error so as to obscure it and allow it to be written over.

paper clip
Small pieces of metallic wiring that are commonly used to hold documents together.

eraser
A small rubber-like device that is designed to absorb and remove the markings of pencils.

handle
The component of the paper cutter that is held in the hand in order to cut materials.

pushpin
A small tack that can be used to attach papers or documents to walls or boards.

ruler
A small plastic or wooden tool that usually bears measurements such as inches and centimeters.

paper cutter
A device equipped with a sharp-edged arm, used to efficiently slice documents and other papers.

clamp lock
A component of the paper cutter that can be used to make adjustments to the height of the cutter's blade.

paper guide
A sliding component of the paper-cutter that is used to create varying cutting lengths during the device's usage.

base
An area of the paper-cutter device where sheets of paper are placed so that they may be sheared.

wastebasket
A container commonly made of plastic or metal that is used within office settings to collect trash.

comb binding machine
A device common to many office settings that is used to bind and laminate documents to prevent wear.

comb-tightening device
A component of the lamination device that is used to firmly press sheets of paper into a laminated form.

handle
The component of a lamination device that is held by the hand in order to laminate materials.

base
The area of a lamination device where sheets of paper are placed so that they may be laminated.

guide
A small, plastic knob that can be used to make adjustments regarding the size of the sheets of paper it will allow to pass.

scissors
A small cutting tool composed of two blades joined in the middle, which are used with one hand.

date stamp
A small device that has an ink cartridge and is used to imprint specific dates on pertinent documents.

lid
The protective component of an ink pad; it covers the pad so the ink does not dry out or stain other items.

stamp pad
An ink-soaked pad where a stamp is pressed so that its imprint will appear clearly on paper.

ink pad
The component of the ink stamp where the ink supply is stored so that it can be stamped onto objects.

ink pad
A container that holds ink; various kinds of stamps can be pressed onto it to absorb ink.

day-setting band
A component that can be turned in order to create different date combinations.

month-setting band
A component that can be turned in order to create different month combinations.

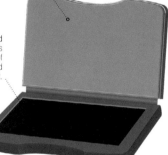

year-setting band
A component that can be turned in order to create different year combinations.

rubber stamp
A stamping device that has a customized rubber surface so that a message may be stamped multiple times.

self-inking stamp
A stamping device that includes ink. When pressed down, the ink is released to print the stamp.

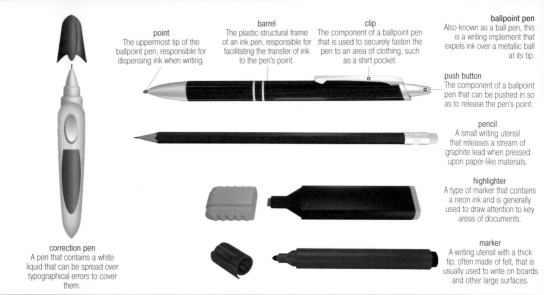

point
The uppermost tip of the ballpoint pen, responsible for dispensing ink when writing.

barrel
The plastic structural frame of an ink pen, responsible for facilitating the transfer of ink to the pen's point.

clip
The component of a ballpoint pen that is used to securely fasten the pen to an area of clothing, such as a shirt pocket.

ballpoint pen
Also known as a ball pen, this is a writing implement that expels ink over a metallic ball at its tip.

push button
The component of a ballpoint pen that can be pushed in so as to release the pen's point.

pencil
A small writing utensil that releases a stream of graphite lead when pressed upon paper-like materials.

highlighter
A type of marker that contains a neon ink and is generally used to draw attention to key areas of documents.

correction pen
A pen that contains a white liquid that can be spread over typographical errors to cover them.

marker
A writing utensil with a thick tip, often made of felt, that is usually used to write on boards and other large surfaces.

Filing

tray
A small plastic piece of office furniture that is used to collect and organize multiple documents.

paper
Small white sheets made of pulpwood logs or recycled materials that are used for writing or printing purposes.

letter tray
A small plastic shelf that is used to collect and store documents.

ring binder
A plastic, folder-like device that has three metal rings that can be used to secure and organize sets of documents.

fastener binder
A plastic container that is specifically designed to house and protect important sets of documents.

rotary file
A small rotational device meant to go on an employee's desk that is used to collect note cards that may be cycled through.

handle
The component of the document case that is grabbed and held by an employee in order to transport documents.

portable expanding file
A document storage device that is designed in a similar fashion to a suitcase, in that it is meant to be easily carried.

binder
A type of folder made of plastic or cardboard that is used to hold and organize sets of documents.

label
A sticker located on the spine of a binder; it is written on in order to identify the contents of the binder.

clasp
A small mechanism located on the frontside of the document case that is designed to securely shut the case.

cover
The protective case on a binder; it envelops the documents on three sides.

file folder
A small, foldable document container that is made of paper and used to organize documents.

spiral binder
A booklet bound by plastic or metal rings, containing covers and note paper.

sheet protector
A plastic folder commonly used in binders to separate different sets of documents from each other.

hanging file
A type of file folder that is placed inside a filing cabinet and hung from rods for easy access.

file box
Small boxes made of plastic, metal or wood and are used to archive files that may need to be readily accessed at a later time.

diacritics

A series of typographical marks that are used to convey varying degrees of accent, stress or tone in a language.

acute accent
A type of accent used in Cryllic, Greek and Latin scripts. It is used in different languages to denote stress.

breve
Also known as a vrachy, this is a diacritic mark that is used to express the appearance of a short vowel.

breve below
Also known as the undertie, this is a diacritic mark that is used to convey the linking of two syllables.

cedilla
A diacritical mark that is found within languages such as French and Portuguese. It conveys a voiceless alveolar sibilant.

cedilla above
A diacritic mark derived from Ancient Greek that is used to convey the occurrence of an /h/ sound before a vowel.

double acute accent
A diacritic mark that is mainly used in the Hungarian language. It is used to denote vowel length.

double grave accent
A typographical mark that is used in the Croatian and Serbian languages; it is used to denote short, falling tones.

grave accent
A diacritic mark that is used for a wide variety of stress purposes in a multitude of languages, such as French, Greek and Welsh.

hook above
This diacritic mark is commonly placed above vowels in the Vietnamese alphabet.

hacek
Also known as a caron, this is a diacritic symbol that is used to indicate the pronunciation of a palatalization.

horn
A diacritic mark that is only found within the Vietnamese alphabet. It is used to create distinct letters.

hook
A diacritical mark that is used to convey the voiceless alveolar affricate sound in the Romanian language.

ring
A diacritic mark that is used in various languages, such as Czech, Danish and Swedish, to denote pronunciation shifts.

macron
A diacritical mark that has been historically used to mark when vowels carry a long stress.

underline
Also known as the macron below, this diacritic used in many languages to convey fricative values.

middle dot
Also known as the interpoint, this is a diacritic mark that is often used to separate distinct words or syllables.

ogonek
A diacritic that is placed under vowels in various European and Native American languages.

under dot
A diacritic mark that is used to express a wide variety of phonetic phenomena.

over dot
A diacritic that is used in various languages to denote pronunciations shifts.

slash
Also known as a stroke, this diacritic is drawn through a letter and is used to denote fricative sounds.

tilde
A typographical grapheme used in many modern languages to denote the usage of a nasalization.

umlaut
A diacritical mark that is used when a vowel is not pronounced as part of a diphthong.

circumflex accent
A diacritic mark that is used in transcriptions between dissimilar languages. It is used to convey accents and pitch.

punctuation marks

Various kinds of typographical symbols that are used to organize and divide words into understandable clauses and sentences.

period
A punctuation mark that is commonly used to close off sentences in many languages.

comma
A punctuation mark that is placed upon the baseline of a text to signal the separation of clauses within a sentence.

semicolon
A punctuation mark that is commonly used to separate two independent clauses.

colon
A punctuation mark that is generally used to signal the appearance of a list. It must be preceded by a complete sentence.

question mark
A punctuation mark that is used to denote the expression of an interrogatory statement.

exclamation mark
A punctuation mark that is used to express the excitement, intensity or fear of an expression.

quotation marks
Punctuation marks that are used to indicate quotations of dialogue or speech within a written text.

hyphen
A symbol that is used to combine words, letters or syllables into a compound word or phrase.

en-dash
A common punctuation mark that is used to convey breaks in diction or the appearance of a parenthetical idea.

em-dash
A symbol that is used to mark information that is not critical to understanding a sentence.

double en-dash
A typographical symbol that is used to signal a break between words without spaces.

slash
A punctuation mark that is commonly used to separate different segments of information.

backslash
Also known as the reverse slash, this is a typographical symbol used in programming languages to separate files and directories.

parentheses
These are punctuation marks used to set apart pieces of text.

square brackets
A punctuation mark that is commonly used to make modifications to a quote.

braces
A punctuation mark that is used in programming languages to convey groups of statements.

chevrons
These punctuation marks are often used as quotation marks in European languages, and can also be used as inequality signs.

ellipsis
A punctuation mark that conveys a portion of text is being intentionally left out.

apostrophe
A symbol that is commonly used in the English language to denote possesion, though it is used as a diacritic in some languages.

double hyphen
A typographical mark that is used to convey a hyphenation at a line break between two words that are usually hyphenated.

interrobang
Also known as the interabang, this is an informal punctuation symbol that is used to express exclamation and interrogation.

tilde
A punctuational grapheme that is mostly used to signal the appearance of an important piece of information.

bullet
Also known as a bullet point, this is a symbol that is used to denote an object within a series of objects.

pound
Also known as the number sign, this symbol is used to designate sequences of numbers.

number sign
A typographical symbol that is used to designate the appearance of a number or series of numbers.

section sign
This typographical symbol is used to designate a paragraph in a series of paragraphs.

pilcrow
This is a typographical character that is used to designate new paragraphs.

at
This is a commonly used symbol that expresses the notion of "at" or "at the rate of." Used often in email addresses.

ampersand
A logogram used to convey the conjunction "and." It was created by combining the Latin "et" into a single glyph.

other marks
Various typographical marks used for inciental purposes, such as footnotes.

prime
A typographical representation that is used to convey the usage of a quotation within a larger quotation.

double dagger
A typographical mark that is used to signal the presence of a third footnote in a longer series of footnotes.

asterisk
A typographical glyph that is commonly used to express linkage to a footnote. It can also be used to censor objectionable words.

asterism
An archaic typographical representation that has historically been used to convey when a small textual break has occurred.

dagger
Also known as an obelisk, this is a typographical glyph that is used in modern times to denote the appearance of a footnote.

double prime
Also known as quotation marks, these typographical marks are used to signal when an individual is being quoted.

vertical line
Also known as the vertical bar, this is a typographical symbol that is commonly used in mathematics to denote various concepts.

degree sign
A typographical representation that is used to indicate temperature or an arc's degree.

hairline
A typographical celement that refers to a portion of a lowercase letter that is thinner than other areas of the letter.

angle of stress
A typographical term used to denote the angle at which a writer is holding their writing instrument.

counter
An area of a typed letter that is left blank during the downpress of a typing machine.

ascender
The area of a letter that is above the mean line.

typesetting
The composition of text created by organizing physical or digital types into particular arrangements.

capital letter height
The height of an uppercase character as it is written.

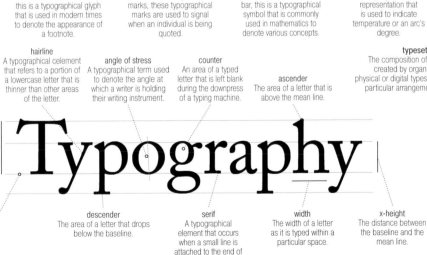

baseline
The area of a typographical space that denotes its lowest point. The bottom points of the longest lowercase letters touch this line.

descender
The area of a letter that drops below the baseline.

serif
A typographical element that occurs when a small line is attached to the end of a stroke in a letter.

width
The width of a letter as it is typed within a particular space.

x-height
The distance between the baseline and the mean line.

TRANSPORTATION

interchange
Any location where multiple roads intersect. Road signs and traffic lights help control traffic at interchanges.

car
A common motor vehicle used for road transportation.

arch bridge
A balanced structure that allows passage over an obstacle.

road marking
Lines painted on a roadway to show lanes.

traffic sign
A posted display with information, such as exit ramps, for drivers.

roadway
A surface made of asphalt where motor vehicles drive.

billboard (back view)
A large outdoor advertisement placed in high-traffic areas.

safety railing
A metal fence or barrier that provides security.

road worker
A person trained to help construct or repair roads.

pedestrian
Any person traveling by foot. Pedestrians must obey traffic laws when crossing streets.

guardrail
A metal barricade along a roadway that acts as a boundary to prevent accidents.

sound barrier
A wall made to absorb loud noise.

road worker
A person trained to help construct or repair roads.

hard hat
A helmet worn by a road worker to protect the head.

roadwork ahead sign
A sign to warn traffic about road construction ahead.

safety boot
Sturdy footwear, with a reinforced steel toe, to protect the foot.

barrier
A warning fence used to keep vehicles out of construction areas.

cross section of road
The materials laid to provide a smooth, durable surface for traffic.

surface course
A coating applied to asphalt to protect it from oxidation, UV rays, traffic and other stressors.

base course
The layer of a roadway directly beneath the binding course.

binding course
The upper layer of a roadway, usually made of tough materials like asphalt or concrete.

speed limit sign
A posted display of the highest speed for cars.

gravel layer
A layer of small, coarse rocks.

sand layer
The lower layer, made of sand, of a roadway.

ditch
A channel designed to drain rainwater from the roadway to prevent flooding.

bank
The raised ground around a roadway.

traffic cone
Cone-shaped markers placed on roads to temporarily redirect traffic.

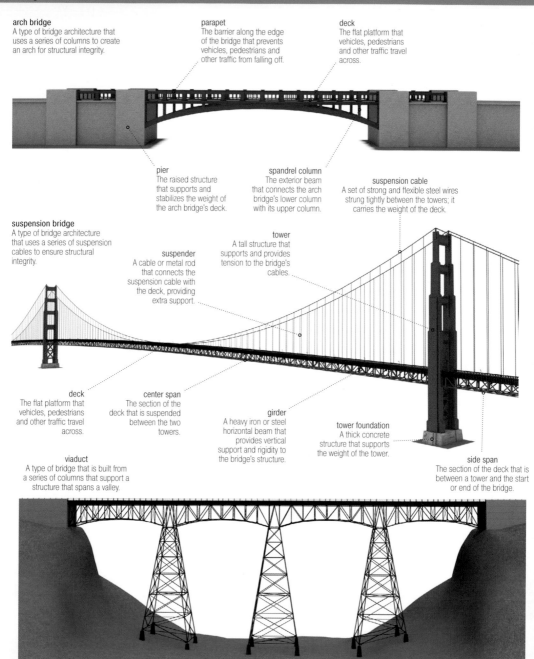

arch bridge
A type of bridge architecture that uses a series of columns to create an arch for structural integrity.

parapet
The barrier along the edge of the bridge that prevents vehicles, pedestrians and other traffic from falling off.

deck
The flat platform that vehicles, pedestrians and other traffic travel across.

pier
The raised structure that supports and stabilizes the weight of the arch bridge's deck.

spandrel column
The exterior beam that connects the arch bridge's lower column with its upper column.

suspension cable
A set of strong and flexible steel wires strung tightly between the towers; it carries the weight of the deck.

suspension bridge
A type of bridge architecture that uses a series of suspension cables to ensure structural integrity.

suspender
A cable or metal rod that connects the suspension cable with the deck, providing extra support.

tower
A tall structure that supports and provides tension to the bridge's cables.

deck
The flat platform that vehicles, pedestrians and other traffic travel across.

center span
The section of the deck that is suspended between the two towers.

girder
A heavy iron or steel horizontal beam that provides vertical support and rigidity to the bridge's structure.

tower foundation
A thick concrete structure that supports the weight of the tower.

viaduct
A type of bridge that is built from a series of columns that support a structure that spans a valley.

side span
The section of the deck that is between a tower and the start or end of the bridge.

overview of gas station
A gas station sells gas, oil and other car essentials. It may also have a car wash.

car
A common motor vehicle used for road transportation.

gas station attendant
A gas station employee who pumps gas and serves customers.

driver
The operator of a car.

service bay
One of several service areas of a gas station.

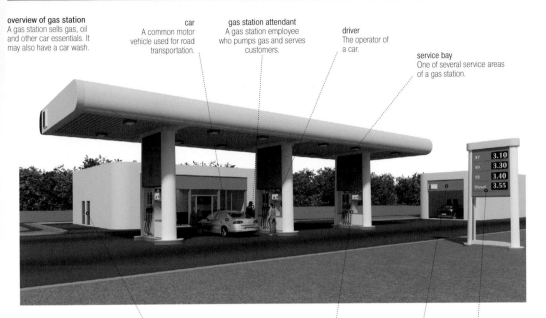

restroom entrance
The doorway into a public washroom.

gasoline pump
A machine at a gas station that fills cars with gas.

car wash
A service area with spray hoses for cleaning cars.

sign
A board with information, such as the price of gas.

gasoline pump
A machine at a gas station that fills cars with gas.

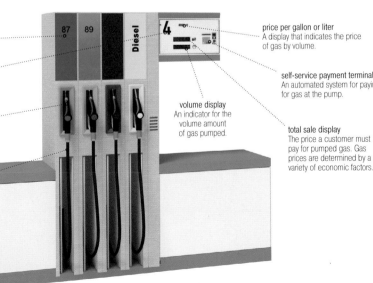

type of fuel
Information on the grade of gas available from the pump.

service bay number
The number given to each service area where gas is pumped.

pump nozzle
The control mechanism used to start or stop pumping.

hose
A flexible tube designed to carry the gas from the station's storage tank to the vehicle's tank.

price per gallon or liter
A display that indicates the price of gas by volume.

self-service payment terminal
An automated system for paying for gas at the pump.

volume display
An indicator for the volume amount of gas pumped.

total sale display
The price a customer must pay for pumped gas. Gas prices are determined by a variety of economic factors.

Car accessories
Various items and tools for cars.

jack
A mechanical device used to
lift heavy loads, such as cars,
so that repairs can be made.

jumper cables
Electrical cables used to start a car with a dead
battery by connecting the dead battery to a
charged one.

fire extinguisher
A portable tank containing
chemicals or foam, which can be
released to put out fires.

bicycle rack
A framework, attached to
the roof or back of a car, for
transporting bicycles.

snow brush with scraper
A tool used to clear snow and
ice from a car.

sun visor
A barrier that can be placed
between the dashboard and
windshield to block the sun.

floor mat
A protective covering placed
inside a car to protect the car's
carpet.

scraper
A tool with an edge that can
be used to clear ice or other
debris from a surface.

ski rack
A framework, attached
to the roof of a car, for
carrying skis.

trailer hitch
A device attached to the frame
of a car so that the car can
tow another vehicle.

roller shade
A covering used to protect the
interior of a car and its passengers
from direct sunlight.

infant car seat
A special seat designed to protect
a baby from injury or death during
a car collision.

booster car seat
A special seat designed to safely
and comfortably seat a young child.

child car seat
A special seat designed to protect
children from injury or death during car
collisions.

emergency warning triangle
A reflective sign to caution other cars when a driver must stop on the side of a highway.

first-aid kit
A collection of supplies and equipment for providing medical care.

reflective vest
A high-visibility piece of clothing worn for safety purposes.

lug wrench
A common tool used to loosen or tighten the nuts, called lug nuts, that secure car wheels to their axles.

Car systems
Various parts that work together to perform a specific car function.

filler cap
A cover that seals and protects a tank's contents.

radiator
A car heat exchanger used for engine cooling.

cooling system
A system of components that circulate air or liquid to prevent the engine from overheating.

grille
A protective vent that is designed to allow air to enter and prevent overheating.

coolant expansion tank
A small tank used to protect a closed liquid system from excessive levels of pressure due to heat.

hose
A flexible tube used to circulate radiator fluid through a car engine.

transmission system
A system of components that transfers the engine's power to an axle and on to the wheels.

fan
A mechanical device, fitted with vanes, that moves air through a ventilation system.

transmission
The mechanism that transfers engine power to an axle.

differential
A gear or set of gears that adjusts the tires' rotation, allowing one wheel to turn faster than the others.

driveshaft
A mechanical rod used for transmitting power from an engine to a transmission.

axle shaft
A mechanical rod used for transmitting torque and rotation from a transmission to a wheel.

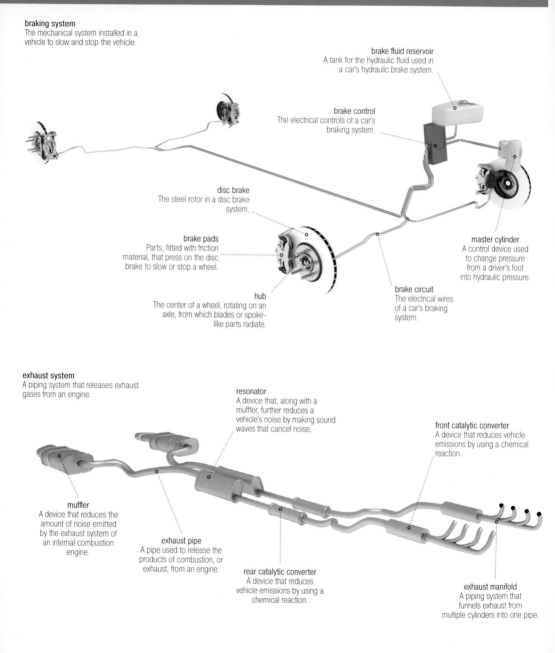

braking system
The mechanical system installed in a vehicle to slow and stop the vehicle.

brake fluid reservoir
A tank for the hydraulic fluid used in a car's hydraulic brake system.

brake control
The electrical controls of a car's braking system.

disc brake
The steel rotor in a disc brake system.

brake pads
Parts, fitted with friction material, that press on the disc brake to slow or stop a wheel.

master cylinder
A control device used to change pressure from a driver's foot into hydraulic pressure.

hub
The center of a wheel, rotating on an axle, from which blades or spoke-like parts radiate.

brake circuit
The electrical wires of a car's braking system.

exhaust system
A piping system that releases exhaust gases from an engine.

resonator
A device that, along with a muffler, further reduces a vehicle's noise by making sound waves that cancel noise.

front catalytic converter
A device that reduces vehicle emissions by using a chemical reaction.

muffler
A device that reduces the amount of noise emitted by the exhaust system of an internal combustion engine.

exhaust pipe
A pipe used to release the products of combustion, or exhaust, from an engine.

rear catalytic converter
A device that reduces vehicle emissions by using a chemical reaction.

exhaust manifold
A piping system that funnels exhaust from multiple cylinders into one pipe.

rear suspension
A system of springs, shock absorbers and linkages that connects a vehicle's rear wheels to allow motion.

shock absorber
A mechanical device designed to smooth out, or dampen, shock impulses.

coil spring
A mechanical device, designed for compressive loads, which compresses or expands as force is applied or removed.

hub
The center of a wheel, rotating on an axle, from which blades or spoke-like parts radiate.

subframe
A structural component found in a car, apart from the larger main frame, used to support parts.

control arm
A hinged suspension link between the chassis and the suspension upright that carries the wheel.

front suspension
A system of springs, shock absorbers and linkages that connects a vehicle's front wheels to allow motion.

upper control arm
An upper hinged suspension link between the chassis and the suspension upright that carries the wheel.

MacPherson strut
A suspension shock absorber that uses the top of a telescopic damper as the upper steering pivot.

hub
The center of a wheel, rotating on an axle, from which blades or spoke-like parts radiate.

subframe
A structural component found in a car, apart from the larger main frame, used to support parts.

sway bar
A suspension device to reduce rolling. It connects opposite wheels through lever arms linked by a torsion bar.

engine
The power source for a vehicle; it is where internal combustion occurs.

engine block
The solid cast-iron structure that encapsulates the engine's various components and facilitates their operation.

pulley
A wheel, fixed on an axle and turned by a belt, used to increase speed or power.

intake manifold
The part of an engine where air intake pipes are fitted.

fan belt
A band used for multiple drives on a car engine.

alternator
A generator, which converts mechanical energy into electrical energy, used to charge a car's battery.

four-stroke engine cycle
An internal combustion engine that completes four separate strokes during its thermodynamic cycle.

intake valve
The engine part that opens to allow the fuel-air mixture into the cylinder.

cylinder
A chamber closed by two valves, where the fuel-air mixture is compressed and ignited.

connecting rod
An articulated shank that, powered by the ignition, transmits thrust from the piston to the crankshaft.

ignition
The moment during the combustion cycle when the fuel-air mixture is ignited within the cylinder head.

burned gases
The gases that fill the combustion chamber after ignition and are expelled at the final cycle.

exhaust valve
The engine part that allows the burned-up fuel-air mixture to be expelled.

intake
The point in the cycle when the piston drops, causing atmospheric pressure to force fuel and air into the cylinder.

crankshaft
A shaft composed of a series of cranks that converts reciprocating motion into rotational motion.

compression
The point in the cycle when the piston rises, compressing the fuel and air up into one of the cylinder heads.

power
The point in the cycle when the compressed fuel and air in the cylinder are ignited by the spark plug.

piston
A moving metal part in the cylinder that is involved in transfer-ring the force of the expanding gases.

exhaust
The point in the cycle when the piston expels the spent fuel by forcing it out through the exhaust valve.

Car interior and exterior
The inside and outside of a car.

rear fascia
A term that describes a car's back-end parts, such as break lights, bumper molding and trunk seal.

trunk seal
Insulated rubber fixed around the opening of a trunk to keep out rain.

brake light
A rear red light activated when the driver applies pressure to a vehicle's brakes. The brake light warns other drivers.

bumper molding
A rigid structure fitted to the front and rear of a car to reduce drag and deflect wind and rain.

grille
A protective vent, located on the body of a vehicle, designed to allow air to enter and prevent overheating.

high beam
A high-power headlight fitted to the front of a vehicle to brightly light the road ahead.

low beam
A regular headlight fitted to the front of a vehicle to light the road directly ahead.

front fascia
A term that describes a car's front-end parts, such as the grille, bumper molding and upper and lower beams.

fog light
Colored lights located on either side of a vehicle for use when visibility is poor.

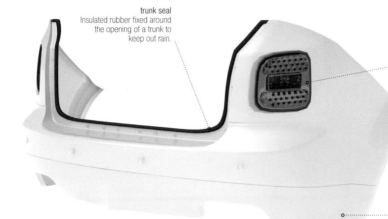

bumper molding
A rigid structure fitted to the front and rear of a car to reduce drag and deflect wind and rain.

turn signal
A flashing light located on either side of a vehicle to indicate a turn or lane change.

bucket seats
Two separate seats, in the front of a vehicle, for the driver and a passenger.

headrest
An upholstered seat part fixed to the top of a car seat. It is ergonomically designed.

seat belt
A restraint used to secure a person in a car seat during a collision or sudden stop.

backrest
The ergonomically designed part of a seat that supports a person's back.

seat adjustments
A system of levers or buttons used to adjust the position of a seat for maximum comfort.

seat
The part of a vehicle where a person sits. The seats are ergonomically designed.

buckle
A locking mechanism used to latch a seat belt and secure a passenger in a vehicle.

rear seats
Two or more seats, fitted in the back of a vehicle, to comfortably seat passengers.

backrest
The ergonomically designed part of a seat that supports a person's back.

headrest
An upholstered seat part fixed to the top of a car seat. It is ergonomically designed.

bench seat
A wide car seat for more than one passenger.

buckle
A locking mechanism used to latch a seat belt and secure a passenger in a vehicle.

seat belt
A restraint used to secure a person in a car seat during a collision or sudden stop.

interior door handle
A part used to open a car door from the inside.

window
An opening, fitted with glass or other transparent material, in the wall of a vehicle.

door
An entrance or exit point that can be opened or closed.

speaker
A device that converts an electrical audio signal into a corresponding sound.

accessory pocket
A recess built into a car interior to hold car items or personal effects.

side mirror
A car mirror positioned to allow the driver to see behind the car. It is used when changing lanes.

molding
A piece of decorative trim that provides protection from scratches.

exterior door handle
A part used to open a car door from the outside.

bracket
A securing device that holds an object. The wiper arm is secured in a bracket.

windshield wiper
A wiping device fixed to the windshield of a vehicle to clear the windshield of rain or snow.

wiper
The contact strip of a windshield wiper.

wiper arm
A support frame for a windshield wiper.

hinge pin
A small rod that permits a part to turn or pivot.

articulation
A joint to attach a windshield wiper to a car.

wiper blade
The moving part of a windshield wiper that provides the sweeping motion for the wiper to clear the windshield.

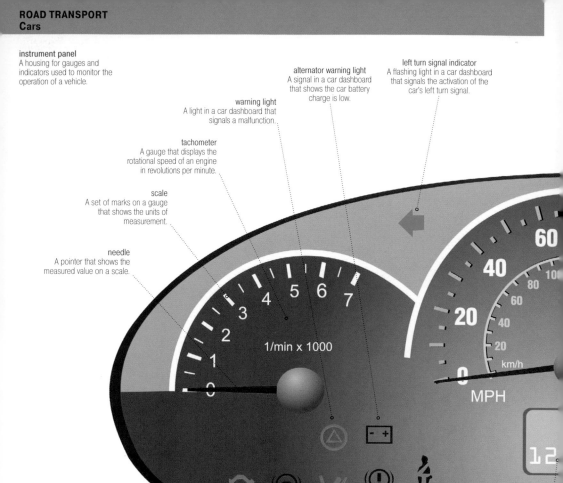

instrument panel
A housing for gauges and indicators used to monitor the operation of a vehicle.

warning light
A light in a car dashboard that signals a malfunction.

tachometer
A gauge that displays the rotational speed of an engine in revolutions per minute.

scale
A set of marks on a gauge that shows the units of measurement.

needle
A pointer that shows the measured value on a scale.

alternator warning light
A signal in a car dashboard that shows the car battery charge is low.

left turn signal indicator
A flashing light in a car dashboard that signals the activation of the car's left turn signal.

malfunction warning light
A signal in a car dashboard that warns when a mechanical malfunction has occurred.

ABS warning light
A signal in a car dashboard that warns when there is an issue with the automatic braking system.

car seat warning light
A signal in a car dashboard that warns when there is an issue with a child safety seat.

seat belt warning light
A signal in a car dashboard that warns when a seat belt is not properly latched.

brake system warning light
A signal in a car dashboard that warns when there is an issue with the braking system.

odometer
A gauge in a car dashboard that displays the distance traveled by the car.

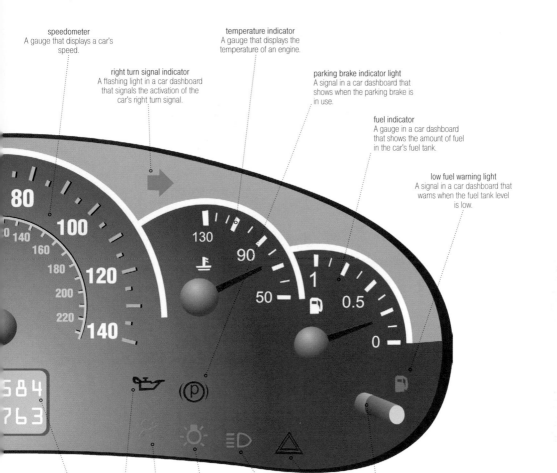

speedometer
A gauge that displays a car's speed.

temperature indicator
A gauge that displays the temperature of an engine.

right turn signal indicator
A flashing light in a car dashboard that signals the activation of the car's right turn signal.

parking brake indicator light
A signal in a car dashboard that shows when the parking brake is in use.

fuel indicator
A gauge in a car dashboard that shows the amount of fuel in the car's fuel tank.

low fuel warning light
A signal in a car dashboard that warns when the fuel tank level is low.

trip odometer
A system that tabulates the distance the car has traveled.

trip odometer reset button
A mechanism used to reset the odometer gauge to zero.

oil warning light
A signal in a car dashboard that warns when oil pressure is low.

hazard light indicator
A signal in a car dashboard that shows when the hazard lights are in use.

high beam indicator light
A signal in a car dashboard that shows when the high beams are in use.

air bag warning light
A signal in a car dashboard that shows the status of the car's airbags.

headlight indicator light
A signal in a car dashboard that shows when the car's headlights are in use.

tires
The wheels of a car,
including parts of the
braking system.

tread
The grooved part of a tire that
makes contact with the road
or ground. Tread wears down
over time.

hubcap
The cover for the center, or
hub, of a wheel.

bolt
A steel fastener with a
threaded end that can be
tightened against a nut or
into a hole.

brake pads
Parts, fitted with friction
material, that press on
backing plates to slow or stop
a disc brake.

shock absorber
A mechanical device
designed to smooth out,
or dampen, shock impulses.

suspension coil spring
A helical device to help
absorb the compressive loads
of a suspension system.

tire
The protective rubber cover
of a wheel. A tire has tread
for better traction.

disc brake
The steel rotor in a disc brake
system.

leaf spring
A long, narrow suspension spring
made of several layers of metal
springs bracketed together.

unibody frame
A car structure that consists of one piece, with the car body and chassis integrated.

roof rail
A metal bar that supports the roof of a car.

pillar
A support for the windshield or window of a car.

wheel well
A recess where a wheel is fitted. A wheel well prevents a buildup of debris, water and other road spray.

floor
The bottom surface of a car. Other components are attached to the floor.

front bumper
A metal bar attached to the front of a vehicle to absorb impact in a collision.

frame rail
A support bar that adds strength to the structure of a car.

spark plug
The part of an engine that transfers electricity to the combustion chamber, creating a spark that ignites the fuel.

hex nut
A six-sided nut that can be tightened to firmly secure the spark plug in place.

body
The framework of the spark plug; it is screwed into the cylinder head.

spark plug terminal
The top of the spark plug; it plugs into a cable connected to the distributor cap.

exhaust manifold
A piping system that funnels exhaust from multiple cylinders into one pipe and out the vehicle.

groove
Small indentations that help keep the current inside the spark plug, preventing short circuits.

gasket
A metal casing that provides a seal between the spark plug and the cylinder head.

side electrode
A metal shank that is welded to the body and encourages heat conduction.

radiator
A car heat exchanger
used for engine cooling.

muffler
A device attached to the
exhaust system of a car
to reduce engine noise.

catalytic converter
A device that reduces vehicle
emissions by using a chemical
reaction.

air filter
A filtration device used to stop
airborne contaminants from
getting sucked into a car engine.

fuel filter
A filtration device designed to
remove dirt and rust particles from
fuel before use in the engine.

oil filter
A filtration device designed to remove
impurities from engine oil.

cabin air filter
A filtration device designed
to remove impurities from air
entering a car interior through
the ventilation system.

battery
A power source, made
of electrochemical cells, that
converts stored chemical
energy into electrical energy.

dashboard
The interior front panel of a car, which contains gauges, buttons and other controls.

ignition switch
The component of the dashboard that is responsible for connecting the vehicle's battery to its starter.

onboard computer
A monitor and hard drive, fitted to the dashboard of a car, which provide data for the driver.

rearview mirror
A car mirror positioned to allow a driver to see behind the car. It is used to safely change lanes.

vanity mirror
A mirror for passenger grooming.

sun visor
A screen fitted above a car windshield to shade the eyes of the driver or passenger.

steering wheel
A round hand control used to turn a vehicle.

instrument panel
A housing for gauges and indicators used to monitor the operation of a vehicle.

audio system
A sound system for playing audio files or the radio.

clutch pedal
A foot control to engage the transmission of a vehicle.

brake pedal
A foot control to engage the braking system of a vehicle.

gas pedal
A foot control to engage the accelerator of a vehicle.

vent
A common installation in cars that provides a continuous supply of cool, warm or neutral air.

windshield wiper
A mechanical device that clears a vehicle's windshield of rain or snow.

panel
The area of a dashboard where gauges and controls are fitted.

glove compartment
A small compartment, usually at the right of the dashboard, that can be used to store various items.

driving mode selector
A button that controls driver options for engine torque, accelerator sensitivity and power steering.

center console
A small compartment between the two front seats that can be used to store miscellaneous objects.

gearshift lever
A hand control to change gears.

parking brake button
A control to engage the parking brake of a vehicle. This control mechanism may be electric in newer cars.

exterior
The outside of a car, which
includes the windshield, wheels,
doors and other parts.

windshield
The front window of a
vehicle.

side mirror
A mirror fitted to both sides of a
vehicle to provide a rearview for
the driver.

cowl
The part of a car body that
supports the area between
the engine and the front of the
instrument panel.

hood
A hinged cover fitted over the
engine of a vehicle.

grille
A protective vent, located
on the body of a vehicle,
designed to allow air
to enter and prevent
overheating.

bumper molding
The decorative and protective
moldings that can be attached
to the front and back bumpers
of a vehicle.

headlight
A light attached to the front
of a vehicle to illuminate the
road ahead.

front fascia
A general term used to
describe a car's front-end
components: grille, headlights,
front bumper and other details.

fender
The part of a car body that
protects each wheel.

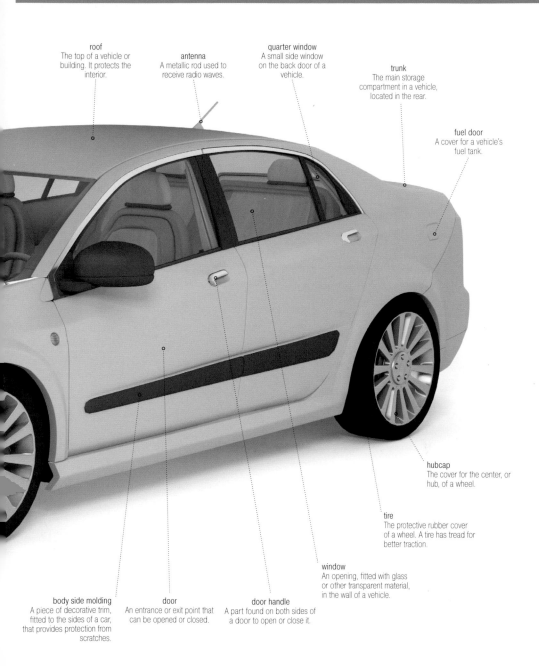

roof
The top of a vehicle or
building. It protects the
interior.

antenna
A metallic rod used to
receive radio waves.

quarter window
A small side window
on the back door of a
vehicle.

trunk
The main storage
compartment in a vehicle,
located in the rear.

fuel door
A cover for a vehicle's
fuel tank.

hubcap
The cover for the center, or
hub, of a wheel.

tire
The protective rubber cover
of a wheel. A tire has tread for
better traction.

window
An opening, fitted with glass
or other transparent material,
in the wall of a vehicle.

body side molding
A piece of decorative trim,
fitted to the sides of a car,
that provides protection from
scratches.

door
An entrance or exit point that
can be opened or closed.

door handle
A part found on both sides of
a door to open or close it.

Types of cars
The body type, category or shape of a car.

electric car
A car that runs on one or more electric
motors. Electric cars can be recharged
at home with electrical outlets.

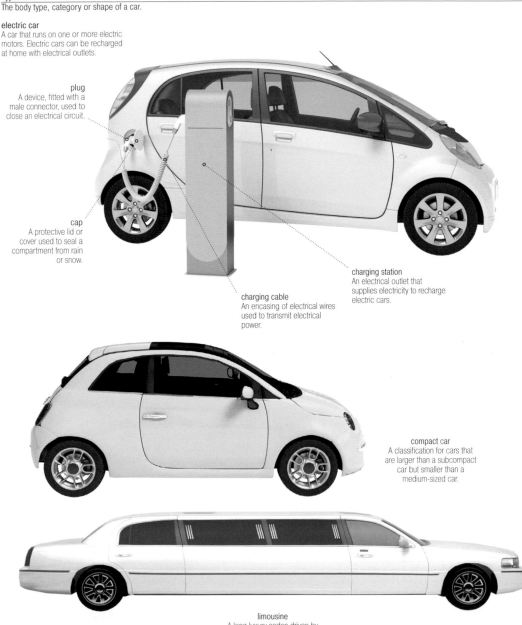

plug
A device, fitted with a
male connector, used to
close an electrical circuit.

cap
A protective lid or
cover used to seal a
compartment from rain
or snow.

charging station
An electrical outlet that
supplies electricity to recharge
electric cars.

charging cable
An encasing of electrical wires
used to transmit electrical
power.

compact car
A classification for cars that
are larger than a subcompact
car but smaller than a
medium-sized car.

limousine
A long luxury sedan driven by
a chauffeur.

convertible
Any car with a retractable or removable roof.

hatchback
A car with a rear door that swings upward to provide access to a cargo area.

crossbar
A fixed rack, on the roof of a vehicle, used for carrying skis, luggage, a roof box or other items.

roof box
A rigid storage container that can be fixed to the roof rack of a car.

mount
A support that securely fastens a rack to a vehicle's roof in order to transport items.

lid
A cover, which protects the contents of a container.

minivan
A van for personal use. Minivans are popular with families.

crossover vehicle
A classification for cars that have the features of both a sports utility vehicle and a passenger vehicle.

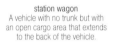

station wagon
A vehicle with no trunk but with an open cargo area that extends to the back of the vehicle.

sports car
A small car made for performance and superior handling.

coupe
A two-passenger car that is shorter than a sedan.

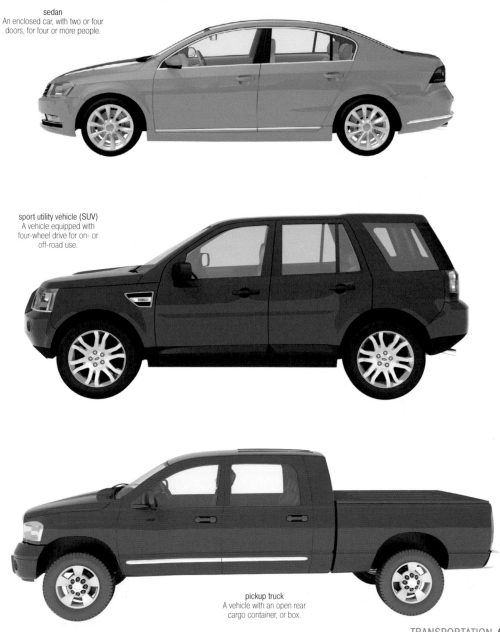

sedan
An enclosed car, with two or four doors, for four or more people.

sport utility vehicle (SUV)
A vehicle equipped with four-wheel drive for on- or off-road use.

pickup truck
A vehicle with an open rear cargo container, or box.

full-size van
A medium-sized vehicle used for making deliveries.

Recreational vehicles
Vehicles designed with living accommodations.

motor home
A recreational motor vehicle with built-in accommodations for camping or road trips.

mirror
A reflective device positioned to allow a driver to see behind the vehicle. It is used to safely change lanes.

windshield
The front window of a vehicle.

hood
A hinged cover fitted over a vehicle engine.

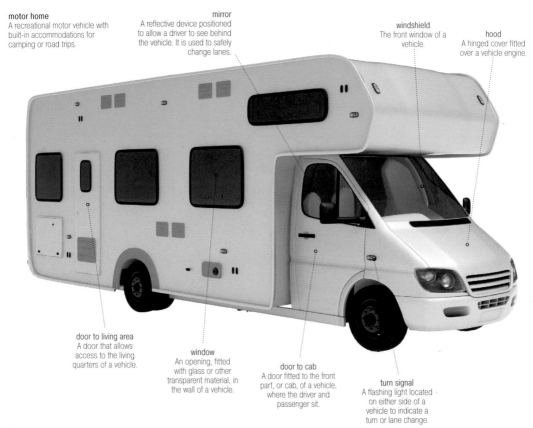

door to living area
A door that allows access to the living quarters of a vehicle.

window
An opening, fitted with glass or other transparent material, in the wall of a vehicle.

door to cab
A door fitted to the front part, or cab, of a vehicle, where the driver and passenger sit.

turn signal
A flashing light located on either side of a vehicle to indicate a turn or lane change.

grab handle
A handrail used when boarding or disembarking a high vehicle.

door
An entrance or exit point that can be opened or closed.

side vent
An opening in the side of a vehicle that allows air to circulate for ventilation.

teardrop trailer
A lightweight, compact trailer with a basic kitchen and sleeping space for two adults.

window
An opening, fitted with glass or other transparent material, in the wall of a vehicle.

storage compartment
A cargo hold fitted to the front exterior of a trailer.

hydraulic jack
A mechanical lift that uses hydraulic force to lift heavy loads.

body
The physical structure of a vehicle. It can be enclosed or partly enclosed.

outlet
The electrical connection for a vehicle. The outlet is used to recharge the vehicle.

stabilizer jack
A steel post that holds a detached trailer in place.

tow bar
The metal frame of a trailer that connects with the tow hitch.

towing hitch
A device attached to the frame of a vehicle for towing.

trailer
An unpowered vehicle, with accommodations, that must be towed by another vehicle.

sport bike
A type of motorcycle optimized for speed, acceleration, braking and cornering on paved roads.

gas tank
A fuel storage tank.

top box
A rear storage container for a motorcycle.

seat
The place where the rider sits. The seat is ergonomically designed.

taillight
A light at the very back of the motorcycle that helps make the rider more visible and indicates braking.

turn signal
A flashing light located on either side of a vehicle to indicate a turn or lane change.

exhaust pipe
A pipe used to release the products of combustion, or exhaust, from an engine.

rim
The outer edge of a wheel, on which a tire is fitted.

tire
The protective rubber cover of a wheel. A tire has tread for better traction.

disc brake
The steel rotor in a disc brake system.

swingarm
Also known as a pivoted fork, this is the main part of the rear suspension of most modern motorcycles and ATVs.

frame
The support structure that provides the framework for the sport bike's body.

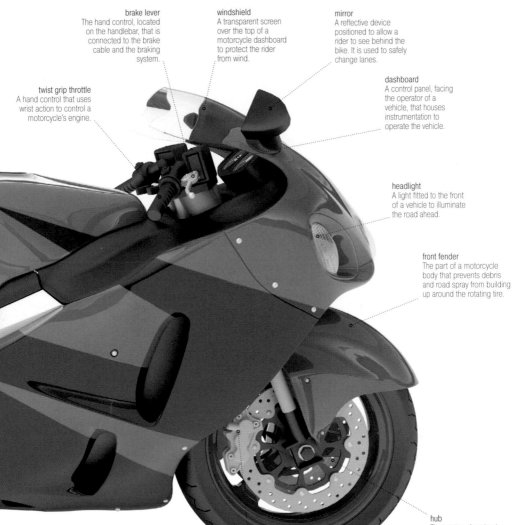

brake lever
The hand control, located on the handlebar, that is connected to the brake cable and the braking system.

windshield
A transparent screen over the top of a motorcycle dashboard to protect the rider from wind.

mirror
A reflective device positioned to allow a rider to see behind the bike. It is used to safely change lanes.

twist grip throttle
A hand control that uses wrist action to control a motorcycle's engine.

dashboard
A control panel, facing the operator of a vehicle, that houses instrumentation to operate the vehicle.

headlight
A light fitted to the front of a vehicle to illuminate the road ahead.

front fender
The part of a motorcycle body that prevents debris and road spray from building up around the rotating tire.

hub
The center of a wheel, rotating on an axle, from which blades or spoke-like parts radiate.

brake caliper
A mechanism that forces the brake pads against the disc brake to slow or stop a motorcycle.

touring motorcycle
A motorcycle, used for long-distance travel, with large fairings and a large windshield for weather protection.

passenger's seat
The place where the passenger sits. It is ergonomically designed.

driver's seat
The place where the operator of a vehicle sits.

windshield
A transparent screen over the top of a motorcycle dashboard to protect the rider from wind.

backrest
The ergonomically designed part of a seat that suppports a person's back.

top box
A rear storage container for a motorcycle.

saddlebag
A bag or compartment attached to the side of a motorcycle.

passenger's grab handle
A handhold for passenger stability or support.

passenger's footrest
A small foot platform for passenger stability or support.

driver's footrest
A small foot platform for driver stability or support.

brake pedal
A foot control used to trigger a mechanical device in order to engage or disengage the braking system.

motor scooter
A lightweight motorbike with a step-through frame and a platform, or deck, for the rider's feet.

off-road motorcycle
An off-road racing motorcycle used in long-distance races.

all-terrain vehicle (ATV)
A four-wheeled vehicle for rough surfaces. A rider sits on and steers an ATV in the same way as a motorcycle.

headlight
A light fitted to the front of an ATV to illuminate the road ahead.

handlebars
The controls consisting of two handgrips.

brake lever
The rod located on a handlebar that connects to the brake cable and the braking mechanism.

handgrip
A handle fitted with friction material.

gas tank
A storage unit to safely store engine gas.

front cargo rack
A framework of bars in the front of a vehicle where cargo can be stowed.

seat
The place where a passenger sits.

rear cargo rack
A framework of bars in the rear of a vehicle where cargo can be stowed.

rear fender
The part of a motorcycle or ATV body fitted over the back wheel to prevent the spray of debris or water.

front bumper
A metal bar attached to the front of a vehicle to absorb impact in a collision.

tire
A circular rubber tread that covers and protects a wheel rim, enabling a vehicle to move.

shock absorber
A mechanical device designed to smooth out, or dampen, shock impulses.

front fender
The part of a motorcycle or ATV body fitted over the front wheel to prevent the spray of debris or water.

footrest
A small foot platform for rider stability or support.

motocross motorcycle
A lightweight motorbike intended for off-road use.

standard motorcycle
A two-wheeled motor vehicle with better gas mileage than that of a car.

brake lever
The rod located on a handlebar that connects to the brake cable and the braking mechanism.

mirror
A reflective device positioned to allow a driver to see behind the vehicle. It is used to safely change lanes.

clutch lever
A handgrip lever designed to engage and disengage a vehicle's transmission.

seat
The place where the rider sits. The seat is ergonomically designed.

handgrip
A handle fitted with friction material.

dashboard
A housing for instrumentation and controls, fitted opposite the rider, for operation of a vehicle.

fuel tank
A storage tank used to safely store engine fuel.

headlight
A light fitted to the front of a vehicle to illuminate the road ahead.

turn signal
A flashing light located on either side of a vehicle to indicate a lane change or turn.

front fender
The part of a motorcycle body fitted over the wheel to prevent the spray of debris and water.

muffler
A device that reduces the amount of noise emitted by the exhaust system of an internal combustion engine.

frame
The support structure for a motorcycle's body.

disc brake
A rotor in a disc brake system.

exhaust pipe
A pipe used to release the products of combustion, or exhaust, from an engine.

V-twin engine
A type of two-cylinder internal combustion engine where the cylinders are arranged in a V-shaped configuration.

front fork
The part of a motorcycle that connects the front wheel and axle to the motorcycle frame.

brake caliper
A mechanism that forces brake pads against a disc brake to slow or stop a wheel.

cruiser motorcycle
A classic or vintage-style motorcycle.

chopper
A type of motorcycle modified from an original design or built from scratch in order to have a unique appearance.

balance bicycle
A training bicycle, with no pedals or chain, used to help children learn balance and steering.

tricycle·
A three-wheeled vehicle, usually with pedals, used by young children.

scooter
A vehicle with handlebars and a platform, or deck, where the rider stands.

BMX bicycle·
An off-road sport bicycle designed for racing and stunt riding.

child carrier
A special belted child seat fixed to the rear of a bicycle.

backpack
A storage bag that can be carried on a person's back.

mountain bicycle
A durable off-road bicycle.

touring bicycle
A bicycle designed for riding on pavement.

tandem bicycle
A bicycle designed for more than one rider.

child bike trailer
A bicycle-towed vehicle used to carry children or other loads.

cruiser bicycle
A common pedal-powered leisure vehicle with two wheels, a frame and handlebars.

lock
A security device used to tether a bike to a fixed object.

rear brake
A brake mechanism for the rear wheel, activated when the cyclist squeezes the rear brake lever.

carrier
A storage rack fixed over the rear wheel of a bicycle.

rear fender
A bicycle body part fitted over the wheel to prevent the spray of debris or water.

mudguard
The curved end fixed to a wheel's rear fender to protect the wheel and rider from the spray of water and dirt.

spoke
The rods radiating from the center of a wheel to the rim.

rim
The outer edge of a wheel, on which a tire is fitted.

tire
The protective rubber cover of a wheel. A tire has tread for better traction.

seat
The place where the cyclist sits. The seat is ergonomically designed.

brake cable
A wire used to connect a brake lever to a bicycle's braking system.

chain
A loop of metal links that transfers pedal power to the drive wheel, propelling the bicycle forward.

chain wheel
A thin metal wheel with teeth, on which a drive chain is fitted.

pedal
A flat piece of metal pushed by the foot to make a bicycle go.

shifter
A lever used to
change gears.

handlebars
The device used
to steer a bicycle.
Handlebars are fitted
with handgrips.

brake lever
The hand control, located
on a handlebar, that is
connected to the brake cable
and the braking system.

frame
The support structure
for a bicycle's body.

fork
The part of a bicycle that
holds the front wheel and
allows the cyclist to balance
and steer.

helmet
Protective headgear for a cyclist
in the event of a collision, crash
or accident.

bicycle multi-tool
A collection of bicycle tools
of various sizes conveniently
stored together.

front fender
The metal part of a bicycle
body, fitted over the front
wheel, that prevents the spray
of debris and water.

front brake
A brake mechanism
for the front wheel,
activated when the
cyclist squeezes the
front brake lever.

double-decker bus
A large motor vehicle with two levels used to carry paying passengers on a fixed route.

route sign
The sign on the front of a vehicle that indicates the route number and destination.

upper deck
The second level of a double-decker bus.

advertising panel
A poster with information about products or services.

grab handle
A handrail used when boarding or disembarking a bus or other high vehicle.

grab bar
A vertical rail fitted on a bus to provide stability and support for passengers.

driver's cabin
The compartment of a bus where the driver sits.

lower deck
The first level of a double-decker bus.

boarding platform
A small deck where passengers board and disembark a vehicle.

mirror
A reflective device positioned to allow a driver to see behind the vehicle. It is used to safely change lanes.

windshield
The front window of a vehicle.

windshield wiper
A mechanical device that clears a vehicle's windshield of rain or snow.

long-distance bus
A passenger bus used for long trips.

passenger door
An entrance or exit point for travelers.

window
An opening, fitted with glass or other transparent material, in the wall of a vehicle.

luggage compartment
The large cargo space onboard a vehicle.

turn signal
A flashing light located on either side of a vehicle to indicate a turn or lane change.

headlight
A light fitted to the front of a vehicle to illuminate the road ahead.

city bus
A large urban motor vehicle used for
public transportation on a fixed route.

minibus
A small bus designed to seat
ten to fifteen passengers.

double-decker long-distance bus
A large passenger motor vehicle,
with two levels, used for long trips.

articulated bus
A long motor vehicle, used for public transportation, that has two rigid sections linked by a flexible joint.

rear rigid section
An unpowered section that is designed to be towed by another section.

window
An opening, fitted with glass or other transparent material, in the wall of a vehicle.

air conditioner
A device used to lower the air temperature inside an enclosed environment, usually through a refrigeration cycle.

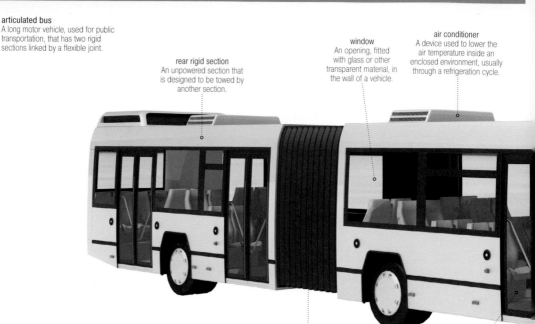

articulated joint
A corrugated cylindrical rubber seal that moves as forces change.

door
An entrance or exit point that can be opened or closed.

bus stop
A designated place where public transportation stops for passengers. Bus stops are common in large cities.

roof
The cover of a structure.

schedule
A posted display of bus arrival and departure times.

bench
A row of seating.

frame
The support structure for a bus stop.

passenger
A traveler other than the bus driver.

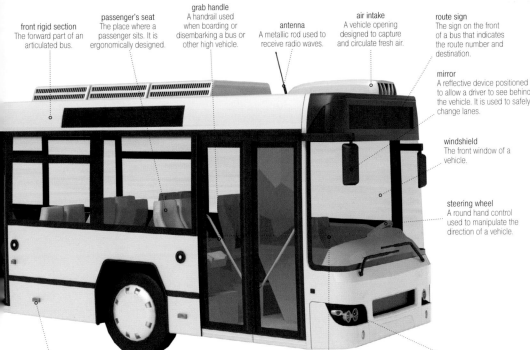

front rigid section
The forward part of an articulated bus.

passenger's seat
The place where a passenger sits. It is ergonomically designed.

grab handle
A handrail used when boarding or disembarking a bus or other high vehicle.

antenna
A metallic rod used to receive radio waves.

air intake
A vehicle opening designed to capture and circulate fresh air.

route sign
The sign on the front of a bus that indicates the route number and destination.

mirror
A reflective device positioned to allow a driver to see behind the vehicle. It is used to safely change lanes.

windshield
The front window of a vehicle.

steering wheel
A round hand control used to manipulate the direction of a vehicle.

turn signal
A flashing light located on either side of a vehicle to indicate a turn or lane change.

driver's seat
The place where the operator of a vehicle sits.

headlight
A light fitted to the front of a vehicle to illuminate the road ahead.

school bus
A large motor vehicle used for student transportation, usually on a fixed route.

semitrailer
A vehicle designed to transport cargo.
It consists of a detachable trailer with
wheels at the back.

cab
The enclosed space
found inside a truck or
vehicle where the driver
and passengers sit.

air horn
A device that uses
compressed air to
make a loud warning
noise for other drivers.

windshield
The front window of a
vehicle.

West Coast mirror
A large mirror designed to
allow a truck driver to see
behind the trailer to safely
change lanes.

door
An entrance or exit
point that can be
opened or closed.

headlight
A light attached to the front
of a vehicle to illuminate the
road ahead.

turn signal
A flashing light located
on either side of a
vehicle to indicate a
turn or lane change.

gas tank cap
A cover for the gas
storage unit.

tank body
The container part of a
tank trailer, designed to
hold liquids or gases.

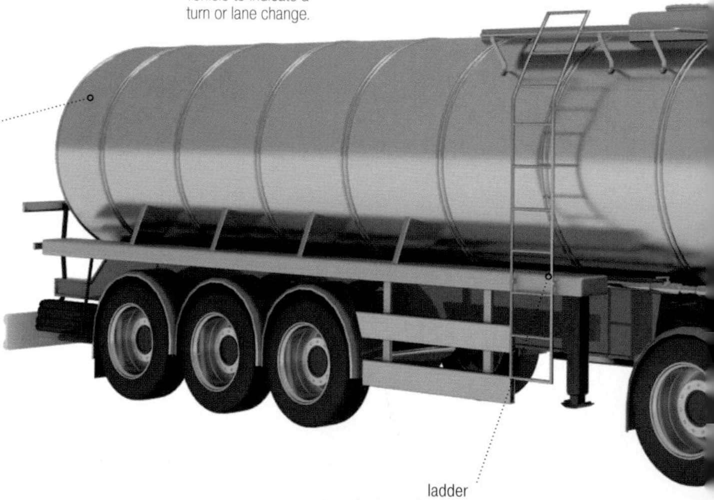

ladder
A vertical or inclined set
of rungs or steps used to
reach high areas.

semitrailer
A large trailer, without a front axle, used to haul cargo. It is attached to the back of a truck.

step
A foot platform that provides access into a cab. It is usually part of a vehicle's ground support.

fuel tank
A storage tank used to safely store engine fuel.

cab
The enclosed space found inside a truck or vehicle where the driver and passengers sit.

tank trailer
A variety of motor vehicle designed to carry liquids or gases in bulk.

West Coast mirror
A large mirror designed to allow a truck driver to see behind the trailer to safely change lanes.

radiator grille
A protective vent, on the body of a vehicle, designed to allow air to reach the radiator and prevent overheating.

headlight
A light attached to the front of a vehicle to illuminate the road ahead.

turn signal
A flashing light located on either side of a vehicle to indicate a turn or lane change.

semitrailer cab
The enclosed space in the truck of a semitrailer where the driver sits.

steering wheel
A round hand control used to turn a vehicle.

speaker
A device that converts an electrical audio signal into a corresponding sound.

gearshift lever
A rod, fitted next to the driver's seat, used to engage and disengage gears.

armrest
A seat feature for passengers to comfortably rest their arms.

sleeper cab
The compartment, attached to the cab of a truck, that is used for resting or sleeping.

clutch pedal
A foot control to engage the transmission of a vehicle.

brake pedal
A foot control to engage the braking system of a vehicle.

gas pedal
A foot control to engage the accelerator of a vehicle.

instrument panel
A housing for gauges and indicators used to monitor the operation of a vehicle.

seat
The place where the driver sits. Seats are ergonomically designed.

dump truck
A truck used to transport loose material such as sand, gravel or dirt for construction purposes.

cement truck
A truck with a revolving drum that mixes cement, sand, gravel and water to form concrete.

truck and tandem trailer
A truck that tows a trailer in addition to its regular load.

semitrailer with sleeper cab
A semitrailer that includes a space in which the driver can sleep.

double drop lowbed semitrailer
A semitrailer with two drops in deck height: one just after the gooseneck and one just before the wheels.

log semitrailer
A long semitrailer that hauls logs.

livestock semitrailer
A large semitrailer used to haul livestock, such as cattle, horses, sheep, pigs and poultry.

van body semitrailer
A large semitrailer used to haul intermodal containers.

tank trailer
A large semitrailer with a container
designed to hold liquids or gases.

automobile transport semitrailer
A semitrailer designed to efficiently
transport passenger vehicles via truck.

truck tractor
A large transport truck used to
tow one or more semitrailers.

box van
A truck with a cube-shaped
cargo area.

police van
A vehicle, fitted with sirens and beacons, used by a police force.

police officer
A member of a police force trained to enforce local and state laws.

fire truck
A vehicle with hoses and water tanks for firefighting.

door
An entrance or exit point that can be opened or closed.

mirror
A reflective device positioned to allow a driver to see behind a vehicle. It is used to safely change lanes.

beacon
A rotating light that signals caution or emergency.

storage compartment
A space to hold cargo.

step
A foot platform that provides access into a cab. It is usually part of a vehicle's ground support.

turn signal
A flashing light located on either side of a vehicle to indicate a lane change or turn.

headlight
A light fitted to the front of a vehicle to illuminate the road ahead.

windshield
The front window of a vehicle.

loading hopper
A loading mechanism that uses a hydraulic paddle to push garbage into the packer body of a truck.

packer body
A storage container used for garbage.

garbage truck
A truck designed to collect waste and then deposit it at a solid waste treatment facility or landfill.

windshield
The front window of a vehicle.

hood
A hinged cover fitted over a vehicle engine.

door
An entrance or exit point that can be opened or closed.

West Coast mirror
A large mirror designed to allow a truck driver to see behind the truck to safely change lanes.

radiator grille
A protective vent, on the body of a vehicle, designed to allow air to reach the radiator and prevent overheating.

headlight
A light fitted to the front of a vehicle to illuminate the road ahead.

armored truck
A vehicle designed to transfer banknotes, coins and other items of value from one location to another.

bulletproof body
A secure space where money, valuables, records and documents can be stored for secure transportation.

gunport
An opening found on the side of a vehicle to allow a gun to be fired.

ambulance
A vehicle for transporting sick or injured people to or from hospital.

armor
A hard protective cover.

run-flat tire
A pneumatic tire designed to stay inflated if punctured.

sliding door
A type of door that moves along a groove rather than turning on hinges.

street cleaner
A vehicle designed to clean streets.

access hatch
A small opening in the wall of a hopper to allow entry.

beacon
A rotating light that signals caution or emergency.

debris hopper
A container designed for the storage of loose bulk materials, such as garbage and debris.

filter
A device used in the hopper of a street cleaner to keep dirt particles in and to let clean air out.

gutter broom
A side brush, on a street cleaner, with a disk of rotating bristles or wires to sweep the streets clean.

extendable gutter broom
A brush, with a disk of rotating bristles or wires, that can move in and out from a street cleaner.

snowplow
A device attached to a vehicle to shovel snow and ice from outdoor surfaces.

snow blower
A rotating spiral blade, attached to a vehicle, that removes snow by lifting it and throwing it aside.

street sweeper
A device attached to a vehicle to clean streets. It can easily be detached.

bulldozer
A crawler equipped with a
substantial metal plate used
to push large quantities of
soil, sand and rubble.

compact excavator
A vehicle used in construction settings
to dig and move dirt or gravel.

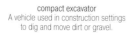

portable concrete mixer
A movable vehicle with a
revolving drum that mixes
cement, sand, gravel and
water to form concrete.

skid-steer loader
A small engine-powered lifting
vehicle with a wide bucket for
heavy loads.

mini road roller
A vehicle used in construction to flatten soil, gravel, concrete or asphalt.

fuel tank
A storage unit to safely store engine fuel.

exhaust pipe
A pipe used to release the products of combustion, or exhaust, from an engine.

drum
A roller used to flatten foundations and road surfaces.

drum support
The support structure that provides the framework for the mini road roller's body.

crawler carrier
A dump body mounted on an undercarriage, which is fitted with tracks for stability and mobility.

dump body
A container used for collecting and dumping loose material from construction sites, such as sand, gravel or dirt.

driver's seat
The place where the operator of a vehicle sits.

tailgate
A hinged opening, at the back of a truck or vehicle, that can be lowered or removed when loading or unloading.

body hoist
Hydraulic pistons that lift the dump body, allowing the material inside to be dumped.

final drive
A wheel with teeth, cogs or sprockets designed to engage with a chain, belt or similar part.

track idler
A type of pulley that doesn't transmit power but that guides or gives tension to a belt or rope.

track
A moving belt that propels a vehicle forward or backward.

wheeled bulldozer
A construction vehicle, with wheels and a metal plate, used to push large quantities of soil, sand and rubble.

road roller
A construction vehicle used to flatten soil, gravel, concrete or asphalt.

backhoe loader
A tractor-like vehicle fitted with a large bucket in the front and a small digger, or backhoe, in the back.

cab
The enclosed space inside a vehicle where the driver sits.

backward bucket
A scoop used for digging and loading.

headlight
A light fitted to the front of a vehicle to illuminate the road ahead.

dipper arm cylinder
A long arm extending from the body of a backhoe loader to its bucket.

bucket
A scoop, mounted on the front of a vehicle, used for lifting and loading.

step
A foot platform that provides access into a cab. It is usually part of a vehicle's ground support.

grader
A construction vehicle with a
long blade used to create a
level surface.

concrete mixer
A revolving drum that mixes
cement, sand, gravel and
water to form concrete.

excavator
A construction vehicle, fitted
with a boom and bucket on
a rotating platform, used to
dig holes.

body
The physical structure
of a vehicle. It can
be enclosed or partly
enclosed.

railing
A fence or barrier made
of rails.

haul truck
An off-highway dump truck
designed for use in high-
production mining and heavy-
duty construction settings.

tire
A circular rubber tread
that covers and protects
a wheel rim, enabling a
vehicle to move.

cab
The enclosed
space inside a
vehicle where the
driver sits.

ladder
A vertical or
inclined set of
rungs or steps
used to reach high
areas.

radiator grille
A protective vent,
on the body of a
vehicle, designed
to allow air to
reach the radiator
and prevent
overheating.

bumper
The metal bar or beam
that is fixed to a vehicle's
front and back ends. It
is designed to absorb
impact in a collision.

tire
A circular rubber tread
that covers and protects
a wheel rim, enabling a
vehicle to move.

haul truck: bottom view
Bottom view of an off-highway dump
truck designed for use in high-
production mining and heavy-duty
settings.

bumper
The metal bar or beam
that is fixed to a vehicle's
front and rear ends. It
is designed to absorb
impact in a collision.

axle shaft
The driving rod for a
rotating wheel or gear.

crankcase
The housing that
protects a crankshaft.

driveshaft
The rotating rod that
provides torque to the
wheels of a vehicle.

transmission
The mechanism that
transfers engine
power to an axle.

round baler
A piece of farm machinery used to make cylindrical bales from cut and raked hay.

rectangular baler
A piece of farm machinery used to make rectangular bales from cut and raked hay.

grain trailer
A vehicle that carries grain and that is towed by another vehicle.

telescopic handler
A vehicle with long lifting forks used to lift and move materials short distances.

safety guard
A series of strong bars fitted over a windshield to protect the driver from falling objects.

beacon
A rotating device designed to attract attention to signal caution or emergency.

mirror
A reflective device positioned to allow a driver to see behind the vehicle.

cab
The enclosed space inside a vehicle where the driver sits.

arm
A programmable mechanism that can lift and lower a load.

fork
One of a pair of long prongs used to transport bales of hay and other large objects.

headlight
A light fitted to the front of a vehicle to illuminate the road ahead.

step
The foot platform that provides access into the cab. It is usually part of the ground support.

harvester
A common piece of farm machinery designed to harvest grain crops.

tractor
A powerful farm vehicle, fitted with large wheels, that pulls other farm vehicles or trailers.

horse trailer
A trailer used to transport horses. It has enough space for horses to fit comfortably.

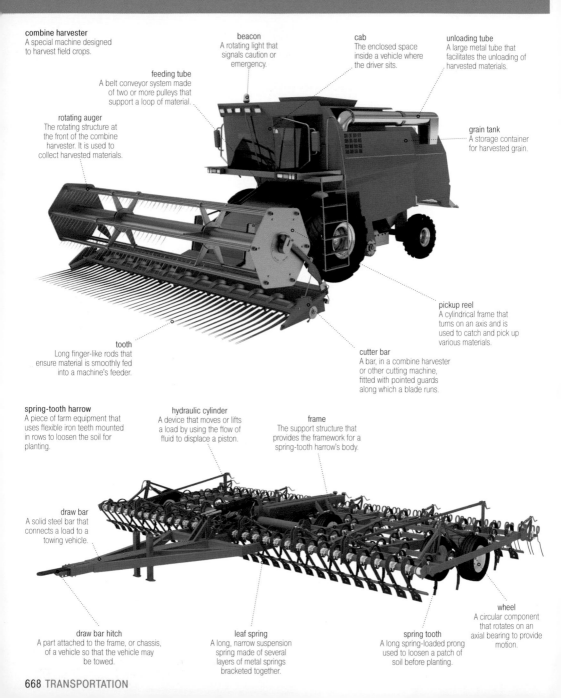

combine harvester
A special machine designed to harvest field crops.

beacon
A rotating light that signals caution or emergency.

cab
The enclosed space inside a vehicle where the driver sits.

unloading tube
A large metal tube that facilitates the unloading of harvested materials.

feeding tube
A belt conveyor system made of two or more pulleys that support a loop of material.

rotating auger
The rotating structure at the front of the combine harvester. It is used to collect harvested materials.

grain tank
A storage container for harvested grain.

tooth
Long finger-like rods that ensure material is smoothly fed into a machine's feeder.

pickup reel
A cylindrical frame that turns on an axis and is used to catch and pick up various materials.

cutter bar
A bar, in a combine harvester or other cutting machine, fitted with pointed guards along which a blade runs.

spring-tooth harrow
A piece of farm equipment that uses flexible iron teeth mounted in rows to loosen the soil for planting.

hydraulic cylinder
A device that moves or lifts a load by using the flow of fluid to displace a piston.

frame
The support structure that provides the framework for a spring-tooth harrow's body.

draw bar
A solid steel bar that connects a load to a towing vehicle.

wheel
A circular component that rotates on an axial bearing to provide motion.

draw bar hitch
A part attached to the frame, or chassis, of a vehicle so that the vehicle may be towed.

leaf spring
A long, narrow suspension spring made of several layers of metal springs bracketed together.

spring tooth
A long spring-loaded prong used to loosen a patch of soil before planting.

air seeder
A planting machine that uses an air delivery system to plant and fertilize seeds.

seed and liquid fertilizer tank
A storage compartment for seeds and fertilizer.

spring-mounted leveling bar
A structural component that uses spring pressure in order to provide leveling power.

serrated disk
A round plate with notched edges or saw-like teeth used for cutting.

rotary hoe
A rotor with blades used for breaking up or tilling soil.

wheel
A rotary part used to press the soil in order to provide successful seed-to-soil contact.

spring tooth
A long spring-loaded prong used to loosen a patch of soil before planting.

leveling blade
A flat edge designed to evenly flatten, or level, soil.

hydraulic cylinder
A device that moves or lifts a load by using the flow of fluid to displace a piston.

frame
The support structure that provides the framework for a disk harrow's body.

disk harrow
A piece of farm equipment used to cultivate the soil before crops are planted.

draw bar hitch
A part attached to the frame, or chassis, of a vehicle so that the vehicle may be towed.

draw bar
A solid steel bar that connects a load to a towing vehicle.

disk
A concave steel plate with a sharp cutting edge for soil penetration.

rotary hoe
A rotor with blades used for breaking up or tilling soil.

roller
A type of gear mechanism that changes a continuous rotation into an intermittent rotation.

fallen rocks
A sign that notifies drivers they are approaching an area where rocks frequently fall onto the roadway.

pavement ends
A sign that notifies drivers that a paved road will soon become a gravel or other non-paved road.

loose gravel
A sign that notifies drivers that the road ahead is an aggregate of stones and coarse sand, called gravel.

no passing zone
A sign that notifies drivers that passing is not permitted in the indicated area of the road.

signal ahead
A sign tha notifies drivers there is a traffic light ahead.

road narrows
A sign that notifies drivers that the road will become narrower ahead.

truck crossing
A sign that notifies drivers there is a hidden or otherwise unexpected intersection where trucks cross ahead.

two-way traffic
A sign that notifies drivers a one-way road will shortly become a two-way road, with traffic in both directions.

advisory speed
A road sign that supplements other speed signs, warning drivers that conditions require a different maximum speed.

metric speed limit
A road sign that displays the maximum allowable speed limit in kilometers per hour.

speed limit
A sign that notifies drivers of the maximum allowable speed limit for the indicated road.

night speed limit
A sign that notifies drivers of the maximum allowable speed limit for the indicated road at night.

divided highway crossing
A sign that notifies drivers they are approaching an intersection with a highway that has a median.

reserved for handicapped parking
A sign that notifies drivers that a particular parking spot is (or spots are) for the sole use of handicapped drivers.

bicycle and pedestrian detour
A sign that notifies pedestrians and cyclists that they must take a detour.

exit closed
A sign that notifies drivers that the designated highway exit is closed.

school zone or area
A sign that notifies drivers they are approaching a school, school crossing and/or school-related activity.

bicycle crossing with share the road warning
A sign that notifies drivers that cyclists frequently use this route and that the road must be shared.

pedestrian crossing
A sign that warns drivers that a pedestrian crossing is on the road ahead.

handicapped crossing
A sign that warns drivers that a handicap crossing is on the road ahead.

obstruction to be passed on left
A sign that warns drivers they are approaching an obstruction in or along the road that must be passed on the left.

obstruction to be passed on right or left
A sign that warns drivers they are approaching an obstruction in or along the road that must be passed on the left or right.

obstruction to be passed on right
A sign that warns drivers they are approaching an obstruction in or along the road that must be passed on the right.

right turn only
A sign that notifies drivers they must turn right at the intersection if they are in the indicated lane.

two-way left turn only
A sign that notifies drivers they are approaching a two-way left-turn intersection and cannot pass or travel through.

intersection lane control
A sign that notifies drivers of the directions they can travel in from the indicated lanes at the intersection.

straight ahead only
A sign that notifies drivers they can only travel straight through the intersection.

truck weight limit
A sign that notifies truck drivers that weight limit restrictions have been placed on the designated section of road.

railroad crossing
A sign that notifies drivers that a train track crosses the road ahead.

HOV lane ahead
A sign that notifies drivers they are approaching a high-occupancy vehicle lane.

left or through
A sign that notifies drivers the designated lane can be used to go straight through an intersection or to turn left.

road ending at T intersection
A road sign that notifies drivers they are approaching a T intersection, also called a three-way junction.

sharp curve to left (arrow)
A sign that warns drivers they are approaching a sharp turn to the left.

sharp curve to left (chevron)
A sign that warns drivers they are approaching a tight turn to the left in the road ahead.

detour
A temporary road sign that notifies drivers they are approaching a mandatory detour.

do not enter
A sign that notifies drivers that vehicles are prohibited from entering the roadway ahead.

wrong way
A sign that warns drivers they are traveling in the wrong direction.

yield
A road sign that notifies drivers they must give way to oncoming or intersecting traffic when entering the roadway.

stop
A traffic sign that notifies drivers they must come to a complete stop before proceeding.

270-degree loop
A road sign that notifies drivers there is a 270° curve, which is a very tight turn, in the road ahead.

curve
A road sign that notifies drivers there is a slight bend or curve in the road ahead.

hairpin curve
A road sign that notifies drivers there is a sharp and potentially dangerous curve ahead.

curve with speed advisory
A road sign that notifies drivers of a curve ahead and the speed limit for that curve.

circular intersection ahead
A sign that notifies drivers of a circular intersection, also known as a traffic circle or roundabout, ahead.

side road (right)
A sign that warns drivers there is a side road intersecting the main road ahead.

winding road
A road sign that notifies drivers that the road ahead has twists and sharp turns.

reverse turns
A road sign that notifies drivers that the road is about to turn left and then sharply turn right.

right curve and minor road
A road sign that notifies drivers the main road will curve ahead and that a minor road intersects the curve.

cross road ahead
A sign that notifies drivers there is a four-way intersection ahead.

limited vehicle storage space
A sign that warns drivers there is limited space between train tracks and a highway intersection.

T intersection ahead
A road sign that notifies drivers they are approaching a T intersection, also called a three-way junction.

merging traffic
A road sign that notifies drivers that two roads merge ahead and that the entering traffic must also merge.

merge
A road sign that notifies drivers that two roads merge ahead and that the driver must also merge.

added lane
A road sign that notifies drivers that two roads merge in a curve and entering traffic has its own lane.

added lane
A road sign that notifies drivers that two roads merge ahead and entering traffic has its own lane.

divided highway ahead
A sign that notifies drivers they are approaching a highway that has a median strip and two or more lanes.

road narrows
A road sign that notifies drivers the right lane will end shortly.

flagger ahead
A sign that warns drivers they are approaching a road worker who is directing traffic in the road ahead.

road works
A road sign that warns drivers there are people working on the road ahead.

cattle crossing
A sign that warns drivers the area
of road ahead is commonly used
by cattle.

trucks rollover warning with speed advisory
A sign that warns truck drivers a curve ahead
must be driven under 35 mph, or they risk
tipping the vehicle.

low clearance ahead
A sign that warns drivers there is an area
of low clearance ahead, specifying the
clearance in feet and inches.

no bicycles
A sign that notifies cyclists that
bicycles are prohibited in the area
indicated.

no pedestrian crossing
A sign that notifies pedestrians they
are not permitted on the indicated
road.

no large trucks
A road sign that notifies truck drivers
they are not permitted on the road
ahead.

no parking
A road sign that notifies drivers that
parking is prohibited in the area
indicated.

no left turn
A road sign that notifies drivers that
left turns are not permitted at this
intersection.

no right turn
A road sign that notifies drivers that
right turns are not permitted at this
intersection.

no left or u turns
A road sign that notifies drivers that
U turns and left turns are prohibited
at this intersection.

no straight through
A road sign that notifies drivers they
cannot drive through the intersection.

no U turn
A road sign that notifies drivers that U
turns are prohibited at this intersection.

slippery when wet
A road sign that warns drivers that
the road can become slippery in wet
conditions.

railroad crossing
A road sign that notifies drivers that a
train track crosses the road ahead.

deer crossing
A road sign that warns drivers of the
possibility of wild deer crossing the road.

tow away zone
A road sign that warns drivers that if
they park in the designated area their
vehicle will be removed.

keep left
A road sign that notifies drivers
that they must stay in the
left lane.

one way traffic
A road sign that notifies drivers that
traffic can only travel in one direction
on the road indicated.

Airport exterior
The outside of an airport, including runways, terminals, airplanes and transport vehicles.

maintenance hangar
A storage building to protect aircraft during repairs or bad weather.

runway
A stretch of pavement used for takeoffs and landings.

road
Paved areas where cars drive.

parking lot
A designated area to leave cars for short or long periods of time.

passenger terminal
A large airport area where travelers prepare to fly and where airplanes arrive and depart.

taxiway
A path that connects runways to ramps, hangars, terminals and other airport facilities.

control tower
A building where air-traffic controllers direct aircraft.

control tower cab
A room where air-traffic controllers direct aircraft.

maneuvering area
The space where aircraft are parked, loaded, unloaded, refueled or boarded.

service road
The paved area where crew load, unload, refuel or repair aircraft.

taxiway line
Painted markings that indicate where aircraft should move.

boarding area
The place where passengers prepare for their flights by checking luggage and going through security.

satellite terminal
An airport area where passengers board and disembark aircraft.

airplane
A flying vehicle with fixed wings that is propelled forward by thrust from a jet engine.

jet bridge
An extendable walkway from a satellite terminal to an aircraft.

Airport interior
The inside of an airport, including check-in desks, baggage areas and secuity checkpoints.

baggage carousel
A rotating machine that delivers checked luggage to waiting aircraft.

baggage cart
A small buggy used for carrying luggage or other loads.

conveyor belt
The moving surface of a baggage carousel where baggage is placed.

wheel
A circular component that rotates on an axial bearing to provide motion.

curtain
Material hung to create a screen.

security checkpoint
The area where passengers and their luggage are checked with metal detectors and X-rays.

metal detector
A device used to detect metal objects concealed by a passenger's clothing.

passenger
An onboard traveler other than the pilot or crew.

security officer
An airport employee who screens and searches passengers for safety purposes.

X-ray machine
A device that uses electromagnetic radiation to create images of objects in passengers' luggage.

X-ray technician
An airport employee in charge of X-ray screening.

hand-held metal detector
A small, electronic device that security personnel use to find metal objects on a person.

bin
A container to hold passenger items as they pass through X-ray.

conveyor belt
The moving surface under an X-ray machine where bins are placed.

check-in counter
The desk at an airport where you show your ticket and identification so that you can be issued a boarding pass.

check-in agent
An airline employee who issues boarding passes to passengers.

baggage cart
A platform set on wheels that helps passengers carry suitcases and bags.

suitcase
A piece of luggage.

conveyor belt
The moving surface where a check-in agent places checked luggage to move it throughout the airport.

desk
A flat work surface where airport workers serve passengers.

passenger
An onboard traveler other than the pilot or crew.

departure area
The place in an airport where passengers prepare for their flights and wait to board.

flight information board
A posted schedule, found throughout an airport, that shows arrival and departure times.

baggage check-in counter
A desk in a passenger terminal for check-in and luggage check.

restroom
A room providing washing and toilet facilities for public use.

coffee shop
A place to buy coffee, tea, snacks and other refreshments.

escalator
A moving staircase that quickly carries people between floors.

self-service check-in kiosk
An automated machine that lets passengers check in and collect their boarding passes.

display
A flat panel that shows data.

document scanner
A device that scans an image or document.

gate agent
An airline employee who takes tickets and helps passengers before they board.

gate
A structure that provides a point of entry or exit. It can be used to provide or deter access.

flight number board
A sign posted for a particular flight.

gate number
The numbered doorway where passengers board a particular flight.

gate agent
An airline employee who takes tickets and helps passengers before they board.

self-service check-in kiosk
An automated machine that lets passengers check in and collect their boarding passes.

passenger
An onboard traveler other than the pilot or crew.

arrival area
The place where arriving passengers collect their baggage and greet family.

suitcase
A piece of luggage.

flight number board
A sign posted for a particular flight.

baggage carousel
A rotating machine that delivers checked luggage to arriving passengers.

passenger
An onboard traveler other than the pilot or crew.

lost baggage desk
A kiosk in a passenger terminal for those who have lost checked luggage.

baggage cart
A platform set on wheels that helps passengers carry suitcases and bags.

baggage claim area
The space where passengers gather after arrival to collect checked luggage.

overview of departure and arrival areas
Travelers constantly move throughout these areas.

departure area
The place in an airport where passengers prepare for their flights and wait to board.

arrival area
The place where arriving passengers collect their baggage and greet family.

security officer
An airport employee who helps enforce the law.

customs officer
A government agent who enforces customs law.

restroom
A room providing washing and toilet facilities for public use.

flight information board
A posted schedule, found throughout an airport, which shows arrival and departure times.

flight information board
A posted schedule, found throughout an airport, that shows arrival and departure times.

frame
A support structure.

screen
An electronic panel that displays text and images.

ARRIVALS 11:34am

DESTINATION	TIME	FLIGHT	GATE	STATUS
NEW YORK	13:12 am	1256	D12	On Time
NEW YORK	11:44 am	656	E34	On Time
NEW YORK	10:46 am	857	A13	On Time
ORLANDO, FL	09:32 am	2584	C27	On Time
ORLANDO, FL	15:17 am	3674	B32	On Time
ORLANDO, FL	17:22 am	1854	A7	On Time
PHILADELPHIA	13:05 am	3110	C22	On Time
PHILADELPHIA	12:14 am	2504	A18	On Time
PHILADELPHIA	11:04 am	654	D29	On Time
PHOENIX	11:37 am	548	E11	Canceled
CHICAGO	07:48 am	1458	D31	On Time
PHOENIX	06:55 am	1684	B38	Canceled
PHOENIX	08:48 am	3561	E17	On Time
NEW YORK	07:14 am	3541	E22	On Time
NEW YORK	09:58 am	2547	D21	On Time

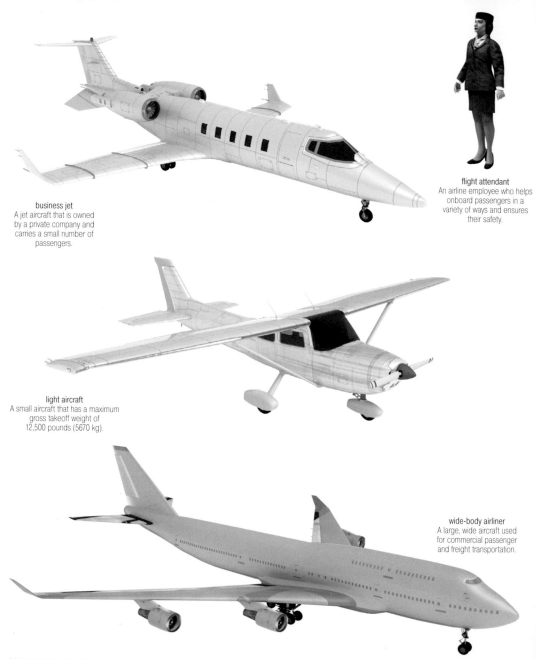

flight attendant
An airline employee who helps
onboard passengers in a
variety of ways and ensures
their safety.

business jet
A jet aircraft that is owned
by a private company and
carries a small number of
passengers.

light aircraft
A small aircraft that has a maximum
gross takeoff weight of
12,500 pounds (5670 kg).

wide-body airliner
A large, wide aircraft used
for commercial passenger
and freight transportation.

fin
A critical component that works with the anti-torque tail rotor to counter the torque of the rotor blades.

driveshaft
The rod that turns the rotor blades.

rotor hub
The central part at the top of a helicopter, where the driveshaft and blades connect.

swashplate
The device that translates input from helicopter flight controls into motion of the rotor blades.

helicopter
An aircraft that uses lift and thrust from rotors to take off and land vertically.

rotor blade
The rotating component that provides the lifting force for a helicopter.

instrument panel
A housing for gauges and indicators used to monitor the operation of a vehicle.

control stick
Also known as the yoke, this is an input device linked to ailerons and elevators. It is used to direct the craft.

flight deck
The pilot's seating area. The seat is ergonomically designed.

skid
The landing supports under a helicopter, usually made of thick steel beams.

boarding step
A step that provides access into an aircraft. It is usually part of the skid.

cabin
The enclosed area with ergonomic passenger seats.

tail skid
A thin metallic strip by the tail rotor that protects the tail in the event of a nose-up landing.

horizontal stabilizer
A horizontal structure that keeps a helicopter level and minimizes drag during flight.

anti-torque tail rotor
A small rotating blade mounted vertically on the tail of a helicopter tail to counter the torque of the rotor blades.

narrow-body airliner
These smaller passenger aircraft only make domestic flights; often called regional airliners.

engine
A type of reaction machine that discharges a fast moving jet to generate thrust.

door
A pressure-sealed entrance or exit.

fin
A fixed vertical stabilizer on the plane's tail assembly.

wing
A type of fin with a surface that produces aerodynamic force to lift and propel an aircraft.

window
An opening, fitted with glass or other transparent material, in the wall of a vehicle.

fuselage
The body of an aircraft. It houses the aircraft's compartments.

landing gear
The supportive undercarriage of an aircraft that allows it to take off, land and taxi.

pilot
A trained person aboard an aircraft who is ultimately responsible for the aircraft's operation and safety.

catering vehicle
A truck with a large cargo area used to
load and unload food and beverages.

box
The storage component
of the catering vehicle. It
can be raised or lowered
and is connected to a
platform.

guardrail
A series of metal railings that
surrounds the platform in
order to prevent accidental
falls.

platform
A raised flat surface that
connects two points.

beacon
A rotating light that signals
caution or emergency.

jet refueler
A tank truck designed to carry fuel to
and from aircraft.

baggage conveyor
A truck fitted with a conveyor belt
designed to move baggage or cargo
on or off aircraft.

mobile closed passenger stairs
A flight of stairs together with
a raised platform that provide
a passageway from one area
to another.

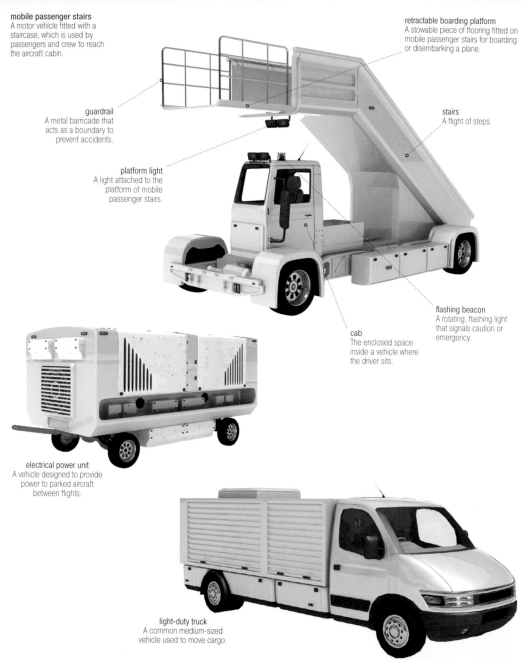

mobile passenger stairs
A motor vehicle fitted with a staircase, which is used by passengers and crew to reach the aircraft cabin.

retractable boarding platform
A stowable piece of flooring fitted on mobile passenger stairs for boarding or disembarking a plane.

guardrail
A metal barricade that acts as a boundary to prevent accidents.

stairs
A flight of steps.

platform light
A light attached to the platform of mobile passenger stairs.

flashing beacon
A rotating, flashing light that signals caution or emergency.

cab
The enclosed space inside a vehicle where the driver sits.

electrical power unit
A vehicle designed to provide power to parked aircraft between flights.

light-duty truck
A common medium-sized vehicle used to move cargo.

escort vehicle
A car used to accompany trucks with large loads or aircraft taxiing from the runway to the terminal.

service vehicle
A type of car used by service technicians. These vehicles are designed for various purposes.

mobile loading platform
A height-adjustable platform to load and unload cargo.

baggage vehicle
A vehicle that moves checked
luggage, mail and cargo between
a satellite terminal and an aircraft.

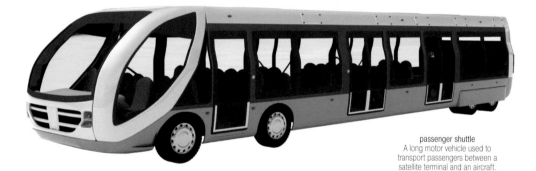

passenger shuttle
A long motor vehicle used to
transport passengers between a
satellite terminal and an aircraft.

monorail passenger shuttle
A type of single-rail tram used
to transport passengers
throughout an airport.

snowplow
A vehicle used to
remove snow and ice.

fire truck
A vehicle with hoses and water tanks
for firefighting.

pushback tug
A low vehicle used to push an
aircraft away from a satellite
terminal.

passenger station
A specially designed building where trains regularly stop to load or unload travelers.

clock
A device that shows the time.

exit
A doorway to leave a room or building.

store
A retail shop that sells a variety of products and goods.

ticket office
Desks or booths where train tickets are sold to travelers.

schedules information board
A posted display of route maps and arrival and departure times.

platform
The raised surface, above a track, where passengers board and disembark trains.

bench
A row of public seating.

stairs
A flight of steps between floors.

escalator
A moving staircase that quickly carries people between floors.

ticket vending machine
A self-service machine that issues tickets to board public transportation.

train
A rail vehicle consisting of a series of railcars along a track. It is used to transport passengers and cargo.

coffee shop
A place to buy coffee, tea, snacks and other refreshments.

train information board
A sign posted for a particular train and route.

commuter train
A long rail vehicle of connected railcars used to transport passengers.

newsstand
A small open booth that sells newspapers, magazines and refreshments.

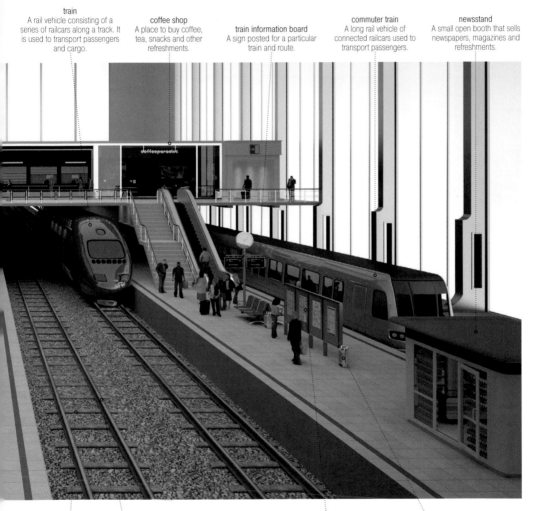

tie
A rectangular wooden or concrete rail support that is laid perpendicular to the rails to connect them.

track
Parallel lines of rail connected by ties set in gravel.

schedules board
A display of arrival and departure times.

trash can
A waste container, which is usually made of metal or plastic.

junction
A place where two or more rail routes meet. Junctions have a lot of train traffic.

water tower
A raised support structure for a water tank. The tank pressurizes a water supply and provides emergency water storage.

locomotive
A railcar that provides the power to drive a train.

hump
A mound that uses gravity to move rail vehicles in a rail yard.

signal
A sign for train drivers that uses the position of a lever to communicate information.

footbridge
A path to walk across a track, waterway, street or other obstacle.

crossing gate
A structure that warns road traffic of an approaching train.

track
Parallel lines of rail connected by ties set in gravel.

barrier lamp
Lights that line the top of the barrier and flash to alert traffic of the lowered barrier and approaching train.

crossing bell
The uppermost component of the crossing gate. It rings loudly to warn drivers and other traffic of an approaching train.

flashing light
A large, bright light that blinks rapidly to warn drivers and other traffic of an approaching train.

barrier
A long bar that is lowered over the roadway to stop traffic when a train is approaching.

crossbuck sign
A traffic sign that is used to notify drivers and other traffic that a train track crosses the roadway.

mast
The structural framework of the crossing gate, from which the barrier is lowered.

conterweight
The heavy weight used to raise the barrier when a train is approaching.

railway switch
A track that can be electronically or manually adjusted to alter the trajectory of oncoming trains.

closure rail
A fixed rail that is used to block one set of tracks from crossing over another set.

power switch machine
An electronic device that can be remotely controlled to alter the position of switch points on a track.

point wire
A metal wire that connects the power switch machine to levers.

switch point
A movable rail that can be activated or deactivated to change an oncoming train's trajectory.

freight car
A common rail vehicle used to transport goods.

gauge rod
A specialized tool that is used to determine the distance between the rails on a track.

Urban rail transit

Various types of local rail systems that transport passengers within and around urban or suburban areas.

articulated streetcar
A vehicle, used for public transportation, that is made of rigid sections linked by pivoting joints.

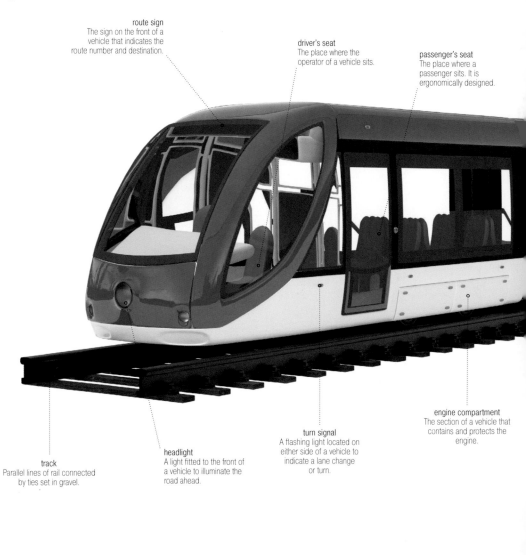

route sign
The sign on the front of a vehicle that indicates the route number and destination.

driver's seat
The place where the operator of a vehicle sits.

passenger's seat
The place where a passenger sits. It is ergonomically designed.

engine compartment
The section of a vehicle that contains and protects the engine.

turn signal
A flashing light located on either side of a vehicle to indicate a lane change or turn.

track
Parallel lines of rail connected by ties set in gravel.

headlight
A light fitted to the front of a vehicle to illuminate the road ahead.

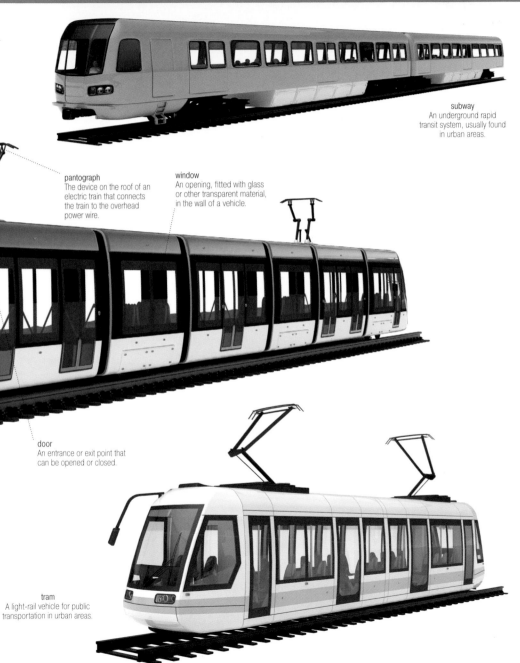

subway
An underground rapid
transit system, usually found
in urban areas.

pantograph
The device on the roof of an
electric train that connects
the train to the overhead
power wire.

window
An opening, fitted with glass
or other transparent material,
in the wall of a vehicle.

door
An entrance or exit point that
can be opened or closed.

tram
A light-rail vehicle for public
transportation in urban areas.

Intercity transport
Large trains that are used to transport people and goods between cities or over long distances.

steam locomotive
A train that consists of a
railcar, with a steam engine,
that pulls other railcars.

chimney
A pipe that provides ventilation
for steam or exhaust from
a boiler, stove, furnace or
fireplace.

driver's cab
The enclosed space inside a
vehicle where the driver sits.

passenger car
A rail vehicle for travelers.

smokebox
The section of a steam
locomotive exhaust system
where smoke and hot gases
pass from the firebox into
the chimney.

cylinder
An arm, attached to a
rotating shaft, used to
convert reciprocating motion into
circular motion, or vice-versa.

tender
A railcar, pulled by a steam
locomotive, used for
holding fuel (wood, coal
or oil) and water.

high-speed train
A type of rail vehicle
designed to move faster than
traditional rail vehicles.

electric multiple unit (EMU) train
A rail vehicle for passengers that
consists of a series of self-propelled
cars that use electrical power.

pantograph
The device on the roof of an
electric train that connects
the train to the overhead
power wire.

headlight
A light fitted to the front of
a vehicle to illuminate the
road ahead.

engine compartment
The section of a vehicle that
contains and protects the
engine.

Locomotives
Railcars that provide the power to pull trains.

ditch light
One of a pair of lights below the main headlight. Ditch lights may flash when the train whistles.

headlight
A light fitted to the front of a train to illuminate the track ahead.

ventilation grille
Slats that allow fresh air to circulate. Ventilation grilles are a common feature of railcars.

driver's cab
The enclosed space inside a vehicle where the driver sits.

engine compartment
The section of a vehicle that contains and protects the engine.

diesel locomotive
A railcar powered by a diesel engine. It is used to transport freight and passengers.

buffer
Shock-absorbing pads, fitted at the ends of railcars, that make contact with the next vehicle.

automatic coupler
A special mechanism used for securely linking railcars or other vehicles.

guardrail
A protective railing for personal support and stability.

side footboard
The steps that provide access into a rail vehicle.

brake
The mechanism to control deceleration, to control acceleration or to keep a vehicle stationary when parked.

truck frame
The support structure that provides the framework for the diesel locomotive's body.

wheel
A circular component that rotates on an axial bearing and provides motion.

battery compartment
A storage unit that contains a battery to power the traction motor during short trips.

fuel tank
A storage unit to safely store engine fuel.

electric locomotive
A railcar powered by overhead lines, a third rail or onboard electricity storage.

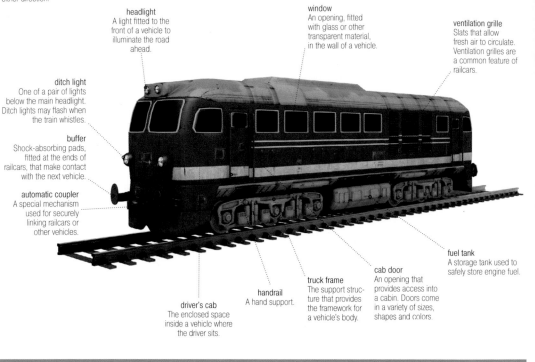

double-ended locomotive
A railcar with controls at both ends so that it can pull in either direction.

headlight
A light fitted to the front of a vehicle to illuminate the road ahead.

window
An opening, fitted with glass or other transparent material, in the wall of a vehicle.

ventilation grille
Slats that allow fresh air to circulate. Ventilation grilles are a common feature of railcars.

ditch light
One of a pair of lights below the main headlight. Ditch lights may flash when the train whistles.

buffer
Shock-absorbing pads, fitted at the ends of railcars, that make contact with the next vehicle.

automatic coupler
A special mechanism used for securely linking railcars or other vehicles.

fuel tank
A storage tank used to safely store engine fuel.

cab door
An opening that provides access into a cabin. Doors come in a variety of sizes, shapes and colors.

truck frame
The support structure that provides the framework for a vehicle's body.

handrail
A hand support.

driver's cab
The enclosed space inside a vehicle where the driver sits.

Freight cars

double-door boxcar
A railcar used to carry different kinds of freight. It can be attached to other railcars by an automatic coupler.

boxcar
A rail vehicle used to carry different kinds of freight. Boxcars can be connected with automatic couplers.

ventilation grille
Slats that allow fresh air to circulate. Ventilation grilles are a common feature of railcars.

fan
A mechanical device, fitted with vanes, that moves air through a ventilation system.

corrugated metal
Galvanized steel with ridges and grooves, known for its strength and relatively light weight.

sliding door
A type of door that moves along a groove rather than turning on hinges.

ladder
A vertical or inclined set of rungs or steps used to reach high areas.

coupler
A mechanism designed to connect railcars or other vehicles.

sliding channel
A slot for a sliding door.

locking lever
A device to secure a closed door.

sill step
A rung that provides access into a boxcar. It is usually part of the boxcar's framework.

wheelset
The wheel and axle assembly on a rail vehicle.

log car
A rail vehicle with a flat, open deck used for logs or other big, bulky loads that can't be carried in closed cars.

auto carrier
A type of rail vehicle used to transport cars and light trucks.

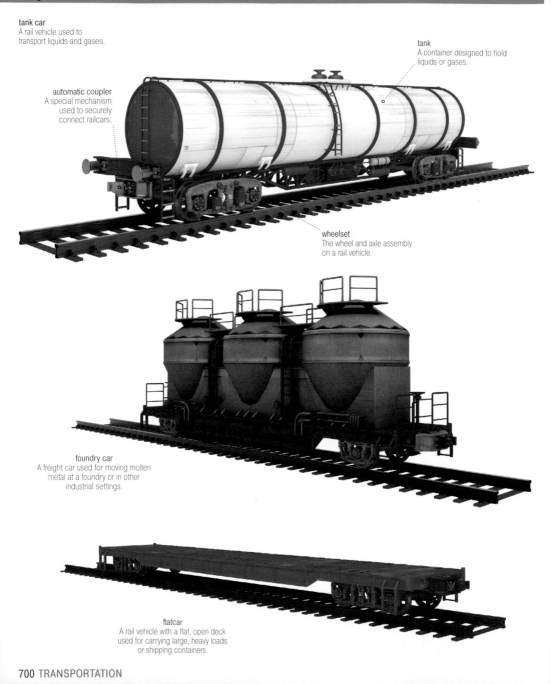

tank car
A rail vehicle used to
transport liquids and gases.

tank
A container designed to hold
liquids or gases.

automatic coupler
A special mechanism
used to securely
connect railcars.

wheelset
The wheel and axle assembly
on a rail vehicle.

foundry car
A freight car used for moving molten
metal at a foundry or in other
industrial settings.

flatcar
A rail vehicle with a flat, open deck
used for carrying large, heavy loads
or shipping containers.

crane car
A rail vehicle fitted with
a crane; it handles freight
and helps with maintenance.

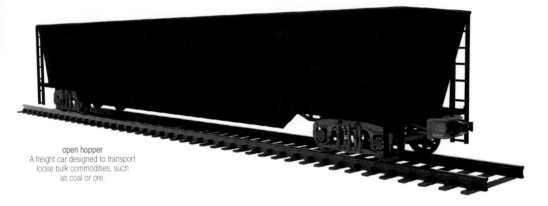

open hopper
A freight car designed to transport
loose bulk commodities, such
as coal or ore.

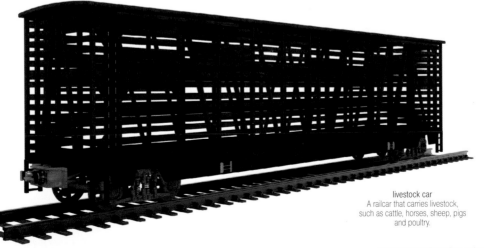

livestock car
A railcar that carries livestock,
such as cattle, horses, sheep, pigs
and poultry.

subway station
A route stop for an underground rapid transit system. Subway stations are generally found in urban areas.

subway map
A diagram that shows the various routes of an underground rapid transit system.

ticket collector's booth
A small housing for a subway attendant to collect fares.

advertisement
A posted display of goods or services for sale.

ticket office
Desks or booths where train tickets are sold to travelers.

city map
A diagram of the layout of a city.

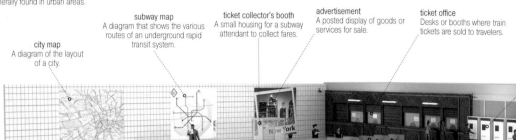

turnstile
A gate designed to allow one person to pass at a time, usually those who insert a coin, ticket or pass.

escalator
A moving staircase that quickly carries people between floors.

tunnel
An underground passage or network of passages dug through a section of earth. Tunnels are used for subways.

stairs
A flight of steps between floors.

subway train
A rail vehicle of connected cars used for an underground rapid transit system, which is usually found in urban areas.

direction sign
A sign in a train's windshield that indicates the train's route or direction.

station name
A posted sign with the name of a particular subway stop, so passengers can orient themselves.

ticket vending machine
A self-service machine that issues tickets to board public transportation.

automatic teller machine (ATM)
A self-service device to withdraw money from your bank account.

coffee shop
A place to buy coffee, tea, snacks and other refreshments.

bench
A row of public seating.

platform
The raised surface, above a track, where passengers board and disembark trains.

safety line
A floor marking that indicates a safe distance from the edge of a platform.

track
Parallel lines of rail connected by ties set in gravel.

port
A coastal location where ships can dock and load or unload passengers and cargo.

transit shed
Large open buildings on a pier that are used to store cargo in transit.

tanker
A merchant shipping vessel for transporting liquids or gases in bulk.

fuel tank
A storage unit to safely store engine fuel.

train
A rail vehicle that consists of a locomotive and a series of connected railcars.

slipway
An onshore ramp to launch vessels.

railroad tracks
Parallel lines of heavy steel rail connected by ties set in gravel.

tugboat
A small vessel that tows ships in a harbor.

gantry crane
A machine, with a hoist fitted on a horizontal beam, that lifts and moves containers, usually in a city port.

customs house
A federal building where cargo is cleared by customs officials.

lighthouse
A tower with a beacon that acts as an aid to navigation.

lantern
A light source.

gallery
A lighthouse lookout deck.

container
A reusable transportation and storage unit used for moving products and raw materials.

container ship
A cargo vessel with large holds to stow storage units, or containers.

container terminal
A port area where ships dock to load and unload container cargo.

tower
A building in the shape of a tall circular structure.

Passenger vessels
Various merchant ships, of various sizes, that carry passengers.

cruise ship
A large pleasure vessel that makes regular port stops for sightseeing.

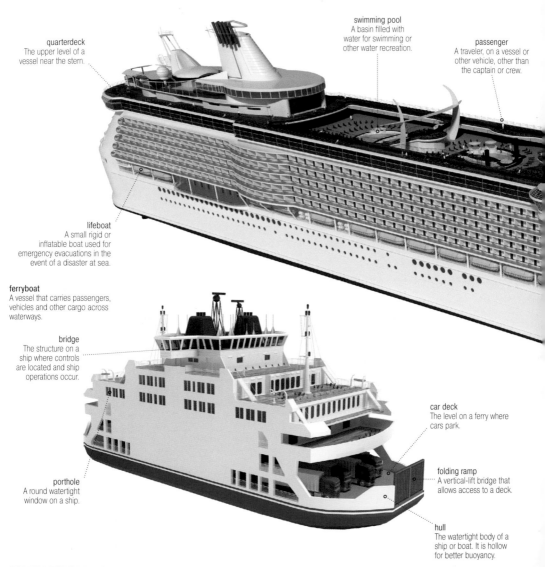

quarterdeck
The upper level of a vessel near the stern.

swimming pool
A basin filled with water for swimming or other water recreation.

passenger
A traveler, on a vessel or other vehicle, other than the captain or crew.

lifeboat
A small rigid or inflatable boat used for emergency evacuations in the event of a disaster at sea.

ferryboat
A vessel that carries passengers, vehicles and other cargo across waterways.

bridge
The structure on a ship where controls are located and ship operations occur.

car deck
The level on a ferry where cars park.

porthole
A round watertight window on a ship.

folding ramp
A vertical-lift bridge that allows access to a deck.

hull
The watertight body of a ship or boat. It is hollow for better buoyancy.

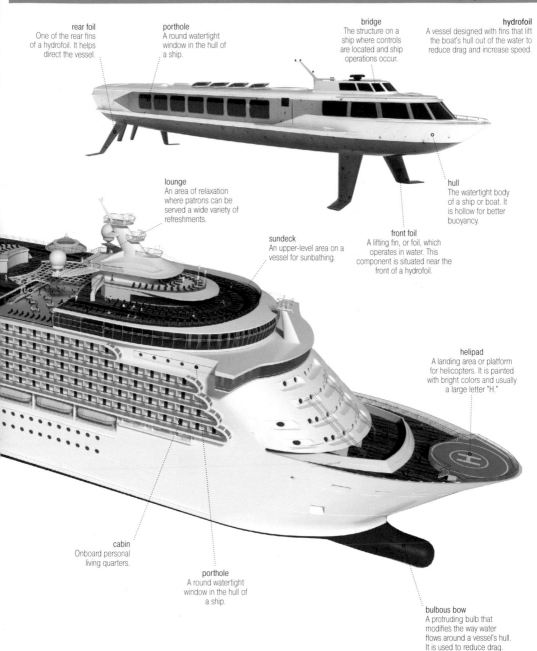

rear foil
One of the rear fins of a hydrofoil. It helps direct the vessel.

porthole
A round watertight window in the hull of a ship.

bridge
The structure on a ship where controls are located and ship operations occur.

hydrofoil
A vessel designed with fins that lift the boat's hull out of the water to reduce drag and increase speed.

lounge
An area of relaxation where patrons can be served a wide variety of refreshments.

sundeck
An upper-level area on a vessel for sunbathing.

front foil
A lifting fin, or foil, which operates in water. This component is situated near the front of a hydrofoil.

hull
The watertight body of a ship or boat. It is hollow for better buoyancy.

helipad
A landing area or platform for helicopters. It is painted with bright colors and usually a large letter "H."

cabin
Onboard personal living quarters.

porthole
A round watertight window in the hull of a ship.

bulbous bow
A protruding bulb that modifies the way water flows around a vessel's hull. It is used to reduce drag.

Ancillary vessels
Vessels that provide support to other vessels.

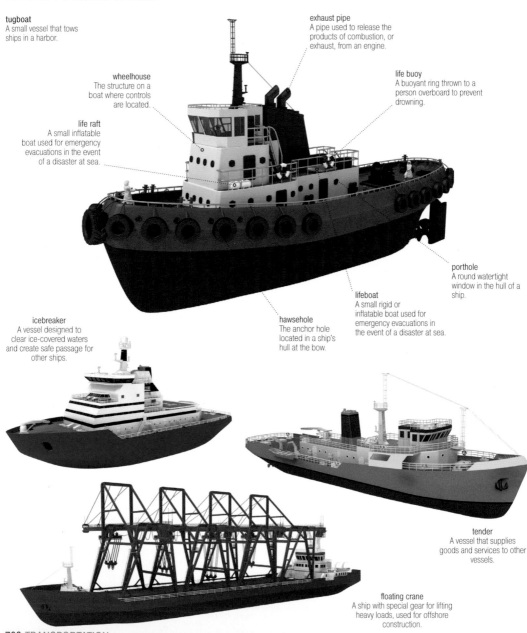

tugboat
A small vessel that tows ships in a harbor.

exhaust pipe
A pipe used to release the products of combustion, or exhaust, from an engine.

wheelhouse
The structure on a boat where controls are located.

life buoy
A buoyant ring thrown to a person overboard to prevent drowning.

life raft
A small inflatable boat used for emergency evacuations in the event of a disaster at sea.

porthole
A round watertight window in the hull of a ship.

icebreaker
A vessel designed to clear ice-covered waters and create safe passage for other ships.

hawsehole
The anchor hole located in a ship's hull at the bow.

lifeboat
A small rigid or inflatable boat used for emergency evacuations in the event of a disaster at sea.

tender
A vessel that supplies goods and services to other vessels.

floating crane
A ship with special gear for lifting heavy loads, used for offshore construction.

Cargo and fishing vessels
Various types of vessels commonly used for the transportation of goods or for commercial fishing.

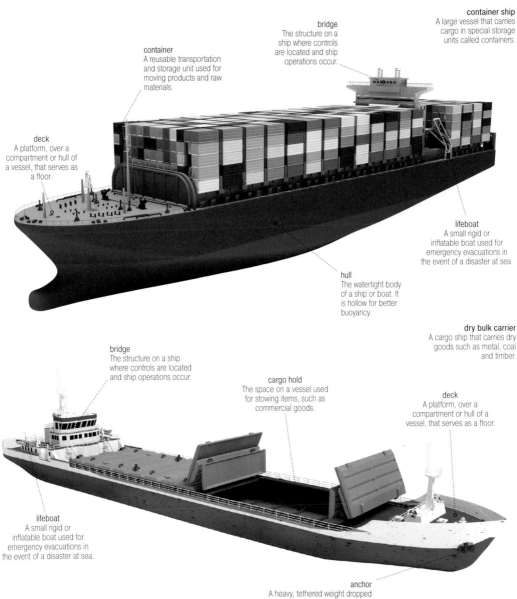

container ship
A large vessel that carries cargo in special storage units called containers.

bridge
The structure on a ship where controls are located and ship operations occur.

container
A reusable transportation and storage unit used for moving products and raw materials.

deck
A platform, over a compartment or hull of a vessel, that serves as a floor.

lifeboat
A small rigid or inflatable boat used for emergency evacuations in the event of a disaster at sea.

hull
The watertight body of a ship or boat. It is hollow for better buoyancy.

dry bulk carrier
A cargo ship that carries dry goods such as metal, coal and timber.

bridge
The structure on a ship where controls are located and ship operations occur.

cargo hold
The space on a vessel used for stowing items, such as commercial goods.

deck
A platform, over a compartment or hull of a vessel, that serves as a floor.

lifeboat
A small rigid or inflatable boat used for emergency evacuations in the event of a disaster at sea.

anchor
A heavy, tethered weight dropped from a vessel onto the sea floor to prevent the vessel from drifting with the current.

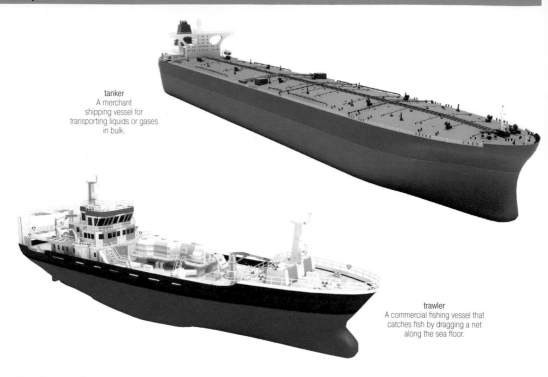

tanker
A merchant
shipping vessel for
transporting liquids or gases
in bulk.

trawler
A commercial fishing vessel that
catches fish by dragging a net
along the sea floor.

Recreational vessels
Vessels of various sizes that are mainly sailed for leisure and entertainment.

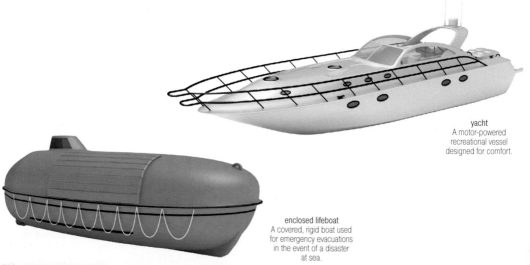

yacht
A motor-powered
recreational vessel
designed for comfort.

enclosed lifeboat
A covered, rigid boat used
for emergency evacuations
in the event of a disaster
at sea.

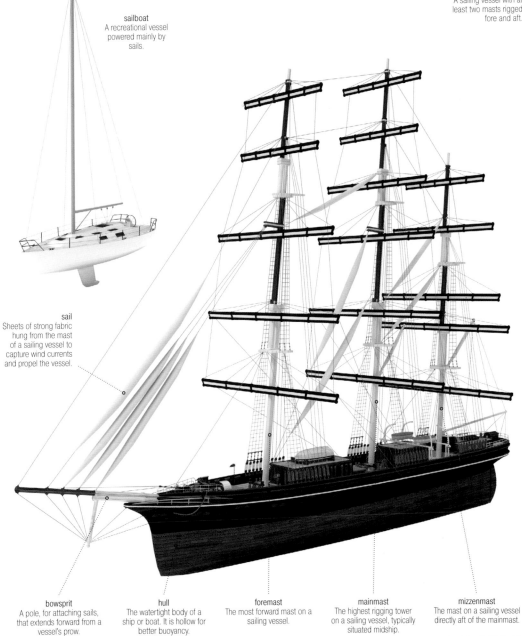

schooner
A sailing vessel with at
least two masts rigged
fore and aft.

sailboat
A recreational vessel
powered mainly by
sails.

sail
Sheets of strong fabric
hung from the mast
of a sailing vessel to
capture wind currents
and propel the vessel.

bowsprit
A pole, for attaching sails,
that extends forward from a
vessel's prow.

hull
The watertight body of a
ship or boat. It is hollow for
better buoyancy.

foremast
The most forward mast on a
sailing vessel.

mainmast
The highest rigging tower
on a sailing vessel, typically
situated midship.

mizzenmast
The mast on a sailing vessel
directly aft of the mainmast.

personal watercraft: front view
A recreational watercraft for one person.

personal watercraft: rear view
The rear view of a type
of recreational watercraft that a user
sits or stands on, rather than inside of.

dashboard
A control panel, facing the
operator of a vehicle, that
houses instrumentation to
operate the vehicle.

handgrip
The handle the rider holds
when driving the vehicle.

seat
The part of a vehicle where
a person sits. Seats are
ergonomically designed.

footrest
A simple contour, located
in the body of a vehicle,
designed for foot placement.

steering nozzle
A jet of water that can be
controlled for propulsion.

SNOW VEHICLES

snowcat
A truck-sized vehicle fitted
with a plow and track so it can
easily drive through snow.

headlight
A lamp attached to
the front of a vehicle
to provide light.

windshield
The front window of a
vehicle.

cab
The enclosed space
where the driver sits.

flashing beacon
A rotating, flashing
light that signals
caution or emergency.

mirror
A reflective device positioned
to allow a driver to see
behind the vehicle. It is used
to safely change lanes.

exhaust pipe
A pipe used to release the
products of combustion, or
exhaust, from an engine.

plow
A device that clears
snow and ice.

track
A moving belt that
propels a vehicle
forward or backward.

auger
A device with blades
to bore through snow
and ice.

windshield
The front panel that protects
the rider from wind.

seat
The place where the
rider sits.

snowmobile: front view
A vehicle with skis and a track
to drive over snow.

headlight
A light attached to the front
of a vehicle to illuminate the
area ahead.

hood
The physical structure of the
top of the vehicle. It can be
enclosed or partly enclosed.

shock absorber
A mechanical device
designed to smooth out,
or dampen, shock impulses.

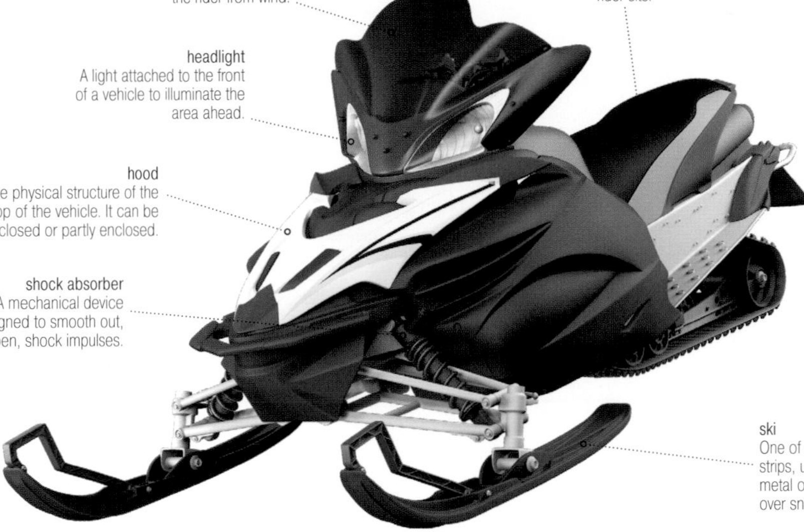

ski
One of a pair of narrow
strips, usually made of
metal or plastic, that glides
over snow.

handgrip
The handle the rider holds
when driving the vehicle.

snowmobile: rear view
A rear visual representation of a type of
land vehicle that is used for winter travel
across the top of snow.

dashboard
A control panel, facing the
operator of a vehicle, that
houses instrumentation to
operate the vehicle.

gas tank cap
A cover for the gas
storage unit.

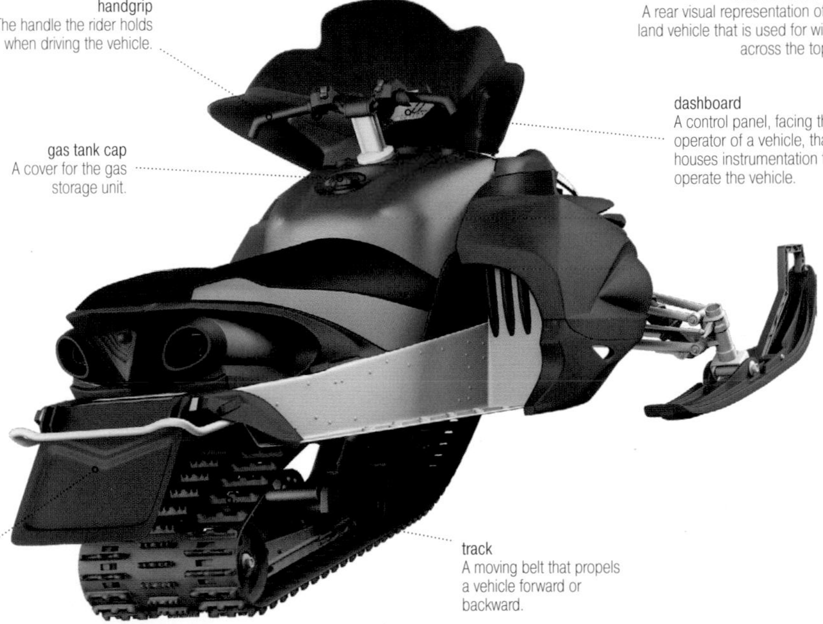

snow guard
A flat, protective cover
plate fitted above a
vehicle track to minimize
snow spray.

track
A moving belt that propels
a vehicle forward or
backward.

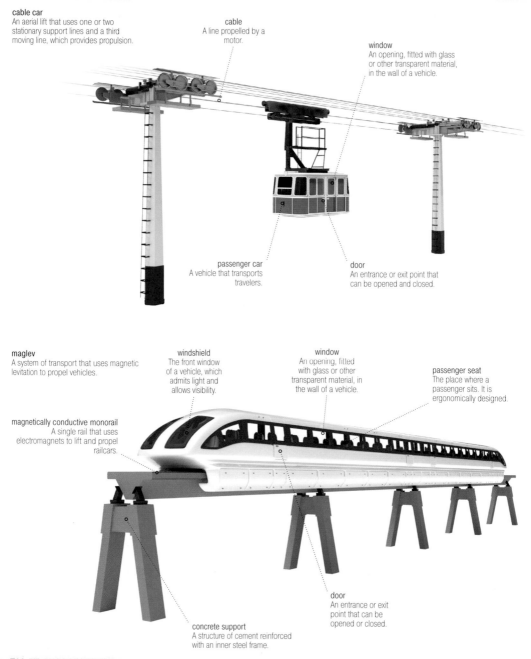

cable car
An aerial lift that uses one or two stationary support lines and a third moving line, which provides propulsion.

cable
A line propelled by a motor.

window
An opening, fitted with glass or other transparent material, in the wall of a vehicle.

passenger car
A vehicle that transports travelers.

door
An entrance or exit point that can be opened and closed.

maglev
A system of transport that uses magnetic levitation to propel vehicles.

windshield
The front window of a vehicle, which admits light and allows visibility.

window
An opening, fitted with glass or other transparent material, in the wall of a vehicle.

passenger seat
The place where a passenger sits. It is ergonomically designed.

magnetically conductive monorail
A single rail that uses electromagnets to lift and propel railcars.

door
An entrance or exit point that can be opened or closed.

concrete support
A structure of cement reinforced with an inner steel frame.

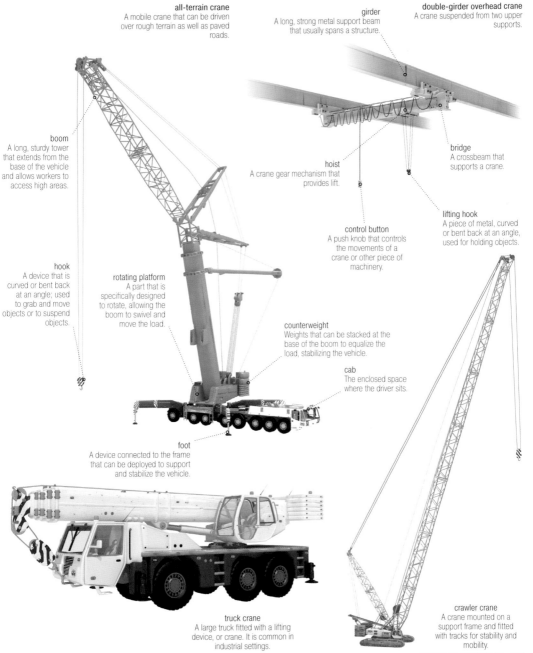

all-terrain crane
A mobile crane that can be driven over rough terrain as well as paved roads.

girder
A long, strong metal support beam that usually spans a structure.

double-girder overhead crane
A crane suspended from two upper supports.

boom
A long, sturdy tower that extends from the base of the vehicle and allows workers to access high areas.

hoist
A crane gear mechanism that provides lift.

bridge
A crossbeam that supports a crane.

hook
A device that is curved or bent back at an angle; used to grab and move objects or to suspend objects.

control button
A push knob that controls the movements of a crane or other piece of machinery.

lifting hook
A piece of metal, curved or bent back at an angle, used for holding objects.

rotating platform
A part that is specifically designed to rotate, allowing the boom to swivel and move the load.

counterweight
Weights that can be stacked at the base of the boom to equalize the load, stabilizing the vehicle.

cab
The enclosed space where the driver sits.

foot
A device connected to the frame that can be deployed to support and stabilize the vehicle.

truck crane
A large truck fitted with a lifting device, or crane. It is common in industrial settings.

crawler crane
A crane mounted on a support frame and fitted with tracks for stability and mobility.

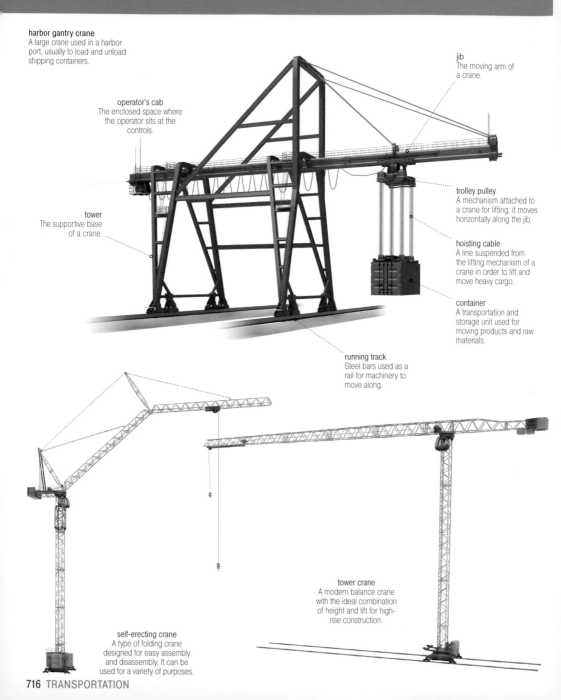

harbor gantry crane
A large crane used in a harbor port, usually to load and unload shipping containers.

jib
The moving arm of a crane.

operator's cab
The enclosed space where the operator sits at the controls.

trolley pulley
A mechanism attached to a crane for lifting; it moves horizontally along the jib.

tower
The supportive base of a crane.

hoisting cable
A line suspended from the lifting mechanism of a crane in order to lift and move heavy cargo.

container
A transportation and storage unit used for moving products and raw materials.

running track
Steel bars used as a rail for machinery to move along.

tower crane
A modern balance crane with the ideal combination of height and lift for high-rise construction.

self-erecting crane
A type of folding crane designed for easy assembly and disassembly. It can be used for a variety of purposes.

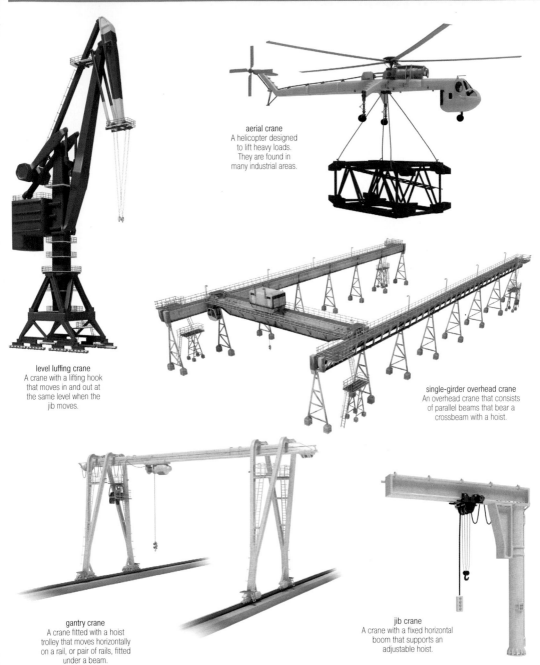

aerial crane
A helicopter designed to lift heavy loads. They are found in many industrial areas.

level luffing crane
A crane with a lifting hook that moves in and out at the same level when the jib moves.

single-girder overhead crane
An overhead crane that consists of parallel beams that bear a crossbeam with a hoist.

gantry crane
A crane fitted with a hoist trolley that moves horizontally on a rail, or pair of rails, fitted under a beam.

jib crane
A crane with a fixed horizontal boom that supports an adjustable hoist.

SCIENCE

periodic table
A tabular representation of the elements organized by their properties.

group
A column of elements.

category
An organization of elements that share similar properties. It is also called a block.

period
A row of elements.

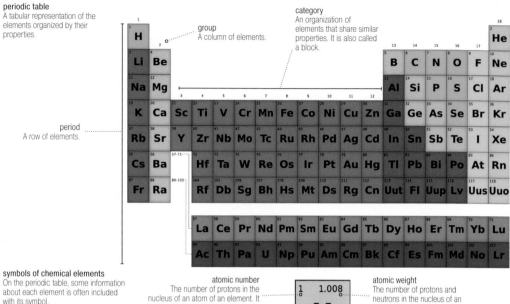

symbols of chemical elements
On the periodic table, some information about each element is often included with its symbol.

atomic number
The number of protons in the nucleus of an atom of an element. It corresponds to the nuclear charge of the element.

atomic weight
The number of protons and neutrons in the nucleus of an atom of an element. It is also called atomic mass.

number of electrons
The number of electrons in the atom of an element.

symbol
The shortened form of the name of an element.

Noble gases
Gaseous elements that are colorless and very unreactive. They comprise group 18.

helium
A colorless, odorless and tasteless noble gas. On Earth, a main source of helium is radioactive decay.

neon
This noble gas refracts light more intensely than its counterparts; it is commonly used in signs.

argon
Its complete outer atomic shell of eight electrons prevents it from bonding with other elements.

krypton
Odorless, tasteless and colorless like other noble gases. It is used with other rare gas in fluorescent bulbs.

xenon
This is one of the few noble gases able to undergo chemical reactions, though these are few in number.

radon
A radioactive noble gas. Emitted from the decay of uranium and thorium. Its half-life can be 3.8 days.

ununoctium
Temporarily named, this element is the heaviest man-made element known. It was first discovered in 2005.

Halogens
Nonmetal elements that are formed in ionic salts. They comprise group 17.

fluorine
Reactive and toxic as a gas, it actually strengthens tooth enamel when consumed in small liquid doses.

chlorine
A strong oxidizing agent used to clean the water supply. Used in World War I for lethal mustard gas.

bromine
A corrosive, toxic nonmetal similar to chlorine. Free bromine atoms damage the ozone layer.

iodine
With a low toxicity rate, it is used to boost contrast in x-rays. It is also proven to greatly benefit the thyroid.

astatine
A rare radioactive chemical resulting from the decay of a few select heavier elements. Its half-life can be 8.1 hours.

ununseptium
Discovered in 2010 and made again since, this highly radioactive element is the second-heaviest man-made element today.

Transition metals
Metal elements that comprise groups 3 to 12.

21 Sc scandium
Exposure to air turns this silver metal a yellowish-pink; easily influenced by weather and diluting acids.

22 Ti titanium
Resistant to chlorine corrosion; ideal for manufacturing, military and spacecraft equipment.

23 V vanadium
A by-product of uranium mining, it is mined almost exclusively in China, Russia and South Africa.

24 Cr chromium
Resistant to corrosion, this hard, brittle metal is used in stainless-steel products.

25 Mn manganese
In nature, it is dependent on other elements such as iron. It is also useful for stainless-steel products.

26 Fe iron
The fourth most common element on the Earth's surface; most has been supplied by meteorites.

27 Co cobalt
A metal from kobold ore with a distinctive blue color. Used in magnetic alloys and disruptive to silver mining.

28 Ni nickel
As with iron, this metal comes from meteorites. It is stable in large pieces and highly reactive in powder form.

29 Cu copper
An extremely conductive, soft and ductile metal used in wiring for electricity and heat. It is reddish-brown in color.

30 Zn zinc
Commonly used as a corrosion protective casting for iron and in batteries.

39 Y yttrium
Found in Ytterby, Sweden, this rare earth element makes electrodes, electrolytes and superconductors.

40 Zr zirconium
A transition metal with a strong resistance to corrosion. Named after the Persian *zargun* for "gold-colored."

41 Nb niobium
Difficult to distinguish from tantalum, this element is used mostly as an alloy for gas pipelines; Brazil is its top producer.

42 Mo molybdenum
Often confused with lead, this element is unique in that it has the sixth highest melting point of all the elements.

43 Tc technetium
A by-product of uranium fission, this element is radioactive in all its forms.

44 Ru ruthenium
A transition metal with similar properties to platinum; it is inert to most chemicals.

45 Rh rhodium
Used as an alloy for both practical and aesthetic reasons, including car engines, white gold and silver.

46 Pd palladium
The softest of the platinum group elements. It is used in hydrogen purification.

47 Ag silver
Historically a currency, second to gold. Today, it is found in solar panels, water filtration and jewelry.

48 Cd cadmium
Once used to alloy plastics, this element is being transitioned out of its primary role due to its toxicity.

72 Hf hafnium
A shiny noncorrosive metal similar to zirconium except it is twice as dense.

73 Ta tantalum
A metal that is unreactive and often substitutes platinum as an alloy for laboratory equipment.

74 W tungsten
Used most commonly in lightbulb filaments. Its name comes from the Swedish for "heavy stone."

75 Re rhenium
The most expensive transition metal due to its rarity and used in jet engine alloys.

76 Os osmium
A hard and brittle transition metal found in platinum ore. Of all the elements it is the densest in free-form.

77 Ir iridium
This hard, brittle transition metal is extremely heat resistant, restisting corrosion up to 3632°F (2000°C).

78 Pt platinum
A dense, malleable and highly unreactive metal, it is greatly valued and considered a noble metal.

79 Au gold
A bright transition metal that is found in free-form. It is resistant to most corrosion and has a high monetary value.

80 Hg mercury
Also known as "quicksilver" because at room temperatures it takes a liquid state. It is used in thermometers.

104 Rf rutherfordium
A radioactive chemical similar to hafnium, though heavier. Its half-life can be 1.3 hours.

105 Db dubnium
First produced and named after Dubna, Russia, its half-life can be 28 hours.

106 Sg seaborgium
A man-made element closely related to tungsten, though heavier. Its half-life is roughly 2 minutes.

107 Bh bohrium
Named for Neil Bohr, this man-made element's stablest isotope has a half-life of roughly 61 seconds.

108 Hs hassium
Named after Hesse, Germany, this man-made element's stablest isotope has a 9.7-second half-life.

109 Mt meitnerium
A man-made radioactive element. Its stablest isotope's half-life is 7.6 seconds.

110 Ds darmstadtium
Named after Darmstadt, Germany, this highly radioactive man-made element has an approximate half-life of 10 seconds.

111 Rg roentgenium
Shares some behaviors with gold, this highly radioactive man-made element's half-life can be 26 seconds.

112 Cn copernicium
A highly radioactive and unpredictable element. Its half-life is only 29 seconds.

Alkali metals

Metal elements that comprise group 1. They are the most reactive of the metals and are known to be soft.

lithium
A soft, silver-white metal, the lightest alkali metal. Lithium citrate is used in mood-stabilizing drugs.

sodium
Sodium stimulates nerves in cells by reacting against potassium.

potassium
An efficient oxidizing alkali metal found in every living organism. It is especially beneficial to cardiac health.

rubidium
A highly combustible, ductile, silver-white metal. Its atomic shell attracts it to other elements.

cesium
An extremely soft alkali metal, it exhibits liquid form at room temperature and is only mildly toxic in this state.

francium
A rare radioactive metal that can decay into astatine or radon. Its half-life is only 22 minutes.

Post-transition metals

Metal elements that are softer than the transition metals.

aluminum
Resistant to corrosion, stronger and a more effective material for aircraft (and domestic uses) than magnesium.

gallium
Its low boiling point, just 84°F (29°C), makes gallium a perfect replacement for harmful mercury in thermometers.

indium
A rare, post-transition metal that can easily fuse with other elements.

tin
This element has the highest number of stable isotopes of the periodic table; combined with copper, it creates bronze.

thallium
A post-transition metal that is toxic in its soluble form. It was previously used in rat poison and insecticide.

lead
The heaviest nonreactive metal, its malleability makes it suitable for batteries, weights, building construction and bullets.

bismuth
Almost as dense as lead but brittle, this post-transition metal's compound is an ingredient in diarrhea medication.

polonium
A metal first discovered by Marie and Pierre Curie, it is highly radioactive in all forms.

ununtrium
Temporarily named, this highly radioactive man-made element is awaiting confirmation since 2003.

flerovium
Unexpectedly revealed similar characteristics to noble gases, though it's still unpredictable and highly radioactive.

ununpentium
Temporarily named, with a 220-millisecond half-life, this radioactive element is still awaiting confirmation.

livermorium
This highly radioactive element has similar properties to oxygen and sulfur. Its half-life is 60 milliseconds.

Metalloids

Elements that share some properties with metal elements but behave like nonmetal elements.

boron
Commonly a brown powder but, in its purest form, it is a semiconducting black crystal used in alloy steel.

silicon
A metalloid of the carbon group that will expand when frozen and resists melting up to 5909°F (3265°C).

germanium
Dependent on other elements, it is mined from sphalerite, zinc ore, and other silver, lead and copper ores.

arsenic
Previously used in pesticides, arsenic is a well-known poison. It is also used to strengthen copper and lead alloys.

antimony
This element reacts strongly with oxygen only if there is heat involved, which is why it is used in bullets.

tellurium
Used in copper alloys. Exposure to this element leads to garlicky breath (one of the minor side effects).

Nonmetals

Elements that are brittle and nonconductive in their solid states, and have low melting and boiling points.

hydrogen
The first and lightest element on the periodic table. It is the most common element in the universe.

carbon
The essential ingredient of life, carbon is found in all living organisms. When compressed, it forms diamonds.

nitrogen
A vibrant part of Earth's atmosphere and human biology, nitrogen is also a crucial ingredient in amino acids.

oxygen
Humans breathe oxygen, a highly reactive element, in order to live. Photosynthesis provides a constant supply.

phosphorus
A highly combustible nonmetal found in two common forms: red and white. Red phosphorus is used in matches.

sulfur
A highly combustible nonmetal formed naturally in volcanic and sedimentary rocks. It is used chiefly in gunpowder.

selenium
Selenium salts are used in multi-vitamins and baby formula. In nature it is dependent on other elements.

Lanthanides

Metal elements that are predominantly silvery white. They are also called rare earth elements.

 57 La lanthanum
A rare, ductile earth element often found in association with cerium and other like elements.

 58 Ce cerium
A rare earth element that oxidizes easily; it reduces fuel emissions and is used in flint for lighters.

 59 Pr praseodymium
A malleable metal with magnetic properties. A small fingernail-sized sample will fully oxidize within a year.

 60 Nd neodymium
A "rare" earth element as common as nickel, copper and cobalt in the Earth's crust. It oxidizes very quickly.

 61 Pm promethium
A radioactive element that is unexpectedly followed by stable elements in the periodic table.

 **62 Sm samarium**
A dense, slightly toxic, silvery metal used in samarium-cobalt magnets, which is permanently magnetic.

 63 Eu europium
An extremely rare metal and only slightly toxic; it oxidizes in both air and water.

 64 Gd gadolinium
Found most often in its salt form, a small dose in alloys greatly improves other solid metals.

 65 Tb terbium
A hard earth metal found in nature only within other minerals.

 66 Dy dysprosium
A rare earth element that is used in control rods within nuclear reactors. It is toxic only in soluble form.

 67 Ho holmium
A highly reactive, rare earth element that rusts easily when combined with water.

 68 Er erbium
A rare earth element that does not oxidize too quickly. Science hints that it can boost metabolism in humans.

 69 Tm thulium
A rare earth element under the lanthanide group. It is used as the radioactive root in portable X-ray machines.

 70 Yb ytterbium
Considered the most rare of the earth elements, in its pure, solid form it is combustible.

71 Lu lutetium
A transition metal that is only resistant to corrosion when dry.

Actinides

Metal elements that are predominantly silvery white. Actinides are radioactive.

 89 Ac actinium
A soft, radioactive metal that is easily oxidized. Its half-life can be 21.7 years.

90 Th thorium
A radioactive actinide metal found in nature. Its half-life can be 14 billion years at most, 25.5 hours at least.

 91 Pa protactinium
A radioactive metal common in expelled nuclear fuel. Its half-life can be 32,760 years.

92 U uranium
A mildly radioactive actinide metal. Its half-life ranges between 69 and 4.5 billion years.

 93 Np neptunium
A radioactive metal of the actinide series that can accumulate in bones.

 94 Pu plutonium
It can accumulate in bones and combusts in solid form. Its half-life can be 80.8 million years.

 95 Am americium
A radioactive actinide metal, named for its close neighbor europium. Its half-life can be 7,370 years.

 96 Cm curium
Named after Marie and Pierre Curie, this radioactive chemical is difficult to produce.

97 Bk berkelium
A low-energy actinide metal that is relatively safe to handle. Its half-life can be 330 days.

 98 Cf californium
A radioactive element used in nuclear reactors. At 51 K (−367°F/-220°C) it develops magnetic properties.

 99 Es einsteinium
Named after Albert Einstein, this radioactive actinide element is a result of the first hydrogen bomb.

 100 Fm fermium
A radioactive actinide that resulted from the hydrogen bomb. Its half-life can be 100.5 days.

101 Md mendelevium
A radioactive actinide. Its stablest isotope is only made in low quantity with a half-life of 51 days.

102 No nobelium
Radioactive and produced only in particle accelerators, its stablest isotope has a 58-minute half-life.

103 Lr lawrencium
The last actinide element, named after Ernest Lawrence. Its stablest isotope's half-life is 11 hours.

Alkaline earth metals

Metal elements that comprise group 2. They are similar to the alkali metals, but are slightly harder and less reactive.

 4 Be beryllium
A rare, light and brittle earth metal found in emeralds; it is formed only through stellar nucleosynthesis.

 **12 Mg magnesium**
This alkaline earth metal is the lightest, and is therefore commonly used in aircrafts and automotives.

20 Ca calcium
In metallic form, calcium reacts with water to produce hydrogen without combusting. It is otherwise unstable.

 38 Sr strontium
Named after Strontian, Scotland, where it was found, this soft silver-white alkaline metal turns yellow when oxidized.

56 Ba barium
A reactive alkali metal, and is therefore never found in nature in free-form.

88 Ra radium
A radioactive metal that oxidizes with nitrogen specifically. Its half-life can be 1,600 years.

molecular formula
A written representation of a molecule that shows the proportions of atoms in the molecule.

structural formula
A representation of the arrangement of atoms in a molecule.

Lewis structure
A representation of how electrons are shared between atoms in a molecule.

C_3H_8

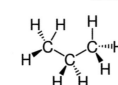

element symbol
The shortened form of the name of an element.

number of atoms
The number of atoms of an element that are present in a molecule.

single bond
A bond between two atoms that results from the sharing of a pair of electrons.

double bond
A bond between two atoms that results from the sharing of two pairs of electrons.

element symbol
The shortened form of the name of an element.

valence electron
An electron that is involved in bonding.

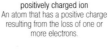

H^+

H^-

positively charged ion
An atom that has a positive charge resulting from the loss of one or more electrons.

negatively charged ion
An atom that has a negative charge resulting from the gain of one or more electrons.

skeletal formula
A simple representation of a complex organic molecule. The vertices and the open ends of a line indicate a carbon atom.

Natta projection
A representation of the three-dimensional arrangement of atoms in a molecule.

chemical equation
A written representation of a chemical reaction. Reactants are on the left side of the arrow, and the products are on the right.

forward reaction
One or more products are being produced from the reactants.

equilibrium
The concentrations of products and reactants have reached a point at which they will not change further.

retrosynthetic
One or more reactants are being produced from a product.

reaction in both directions
The reaction can go in both directions.

$CH_4 + 2O_2 \rightarrow CO_2 + 2H_2O$

cholesterol
An organic molecule found in animal cells. It is a lipid and a modified steroid.

atom
The smallest unit of matter.

electron
An atomic particle that has a negative charge.

nucleus
The core of an atom. It consists of one or more protons and neutrons.

proton
An atomic particle that has a positive charge.

nitrogen
An element that makes up 78% of the Earth's atmosphere. It is essential in proteins.

orbit
The space around a nucleus in which electrons are most likely to be present.

carbon dioxide
An organic molecule that is essential to life. It is necessary for photosynthesis.

neutron
An atomic particle that does not have a charge.

carbon
An element that is fundamental to organic compounds. Carbon atoms have a tendency to form long chains and rings with other carbon atoms.

carbon
An element that is fundamental to organic compounds. It has a tendency to form long chains and rings with other carbon atoms.

hydrogen
An element that is fundamental to organic compounds and occurs widely in non-organic compounds.

oxygen
An element that makes up almost 21% of the Earth's atmosphere. It is very reactive.

oxygen
An element that makes up almost 21% of the Earth's atmosphere. It is very reactive.

Kinematics
The study of motion without consideration of the forces involved.

v
velocity
The rate of change of speed and direction of an object.

a
acceleration
The rate of change of velocity, either in speed or direction in relation to time.

g
gravitational acceleration
The acceleration of an object due only to gravity.

f
frequency
The number of times an object passes a fixed point in relation to time.

n
rotational frequency
The number of revolutions an object makes relative to a fixed point in relation to time.

λ
wavelength
The distance between two consecutive points that are in the same phase of a wave.

v
kinematic viscosity
The ratio of absolute viscosity of a fluid to its density.

t
time
The unit for time depends on what is being measured. Wavelength is commonly measured in seconds.

T
period duration
The time it takes for a wave to complete one full cycle.

ω
angular velocity
The rate of change of the rotational angle of a moving object relative to a fixed point.

Mechanics
The study of motion and the forces involved.

m
mass
The amount of matter in an object.

F
force
An interaction between objects that results in a push or pull action.

J
impulse
The change in momentum caused by a force in relation to time.

p
linear momentum
The product of mass and velocity of an object moving in a straight direction.

I
moment of inertia
The amount of resistance to a change in rotational direction.

M
moment of force
The rate of change in angular momentum of an object.

L
angular momentum
The product of mass and velocity of an object moving in a circular direction.

σ
normal tension
The amount of force perpendicular to the plane of an object per unit area.

τ
shear stress
The amount of force parallel to the plane of an object per unit area.

P
power
The rate at which work is done, commonly measured in watts.

W
work
A quantity related to the action of a force causing the movement of an object.

ρ
density
The mass of a substance per unit volume.

I
intensity
The amount of power transferred per unit area.

η
efficiency
A measure of how much useful energy is transferred compared with the total input of energy.

S
entropy
A measure of the amount of energy that is unavailable to do work.

F_R
frictional force
The force exerted by an object when another object moves along it.

γ
specific weight
The weight of a substance per unit volume.

V
specific volume
The ratio of the volume of a substance to its mass.

Photometry and optics
The measurement of radiant energy as it is perceived by the human eye.

D
diameter
The diameter of the primary lens of an imaging system.

I_V
luminous intensity
The amount of luminous flux per unit solid angle.

Φ_v
luminous flux
The amount of luminous energy per unit time.

η
luminous efficacy
The measure of how well a source of light produces visible light.

L_v
luminance
The amount of luminous intensity per unit area. It is what the human eye perceives as brightness.

E_v
illuminance
The amount of luminous flux received by a surface.

M_v
luminous exitance
The amount of luminous flux emitted by a surface.

H_v
luminous exposure
The amount of luminous flux received by a surface per unit area.

f
focal length
The distance from the lens of an imaging system to the plane of the image.

Q_v
luminous energy
The measure of radiant energy as perceived by the human eye.

Thermodynamics
The study of the relationships between heat, temperature, energy and work.

λ

thermal conductivity
The amount of heat transferred by an object per unit area.

T

absolute temperature
A measure of temperature in which 0 is the lowest possible temperature. It is commonly measured in degrees Kelvin.

ϑ

Celsius temperature
A measure of temperature that is indicated in degrees Celsius.

Q

heat
The energy transferred from an object of high temperature to an object of lower temperature.

U

internal energy
The sum of the potential and kinetic energy of molecules in a system.

E_{th}

thermal energy
The part of internal energy that increases with the temperature; includes latent and sensible forms of energy.

μ

chemical potential
A form of potential energy that can be transferred during a chemical reaction.

H

enthalpy
The amount of heat in a system in relation to pressure and volume.

Φ_{th}

heat flux
The rate of heat transfer per unit area.

S

entropy
The amount of heat needed per unit temperature for a system to remain at a constant temperature.

C_{th}

thermal capacity
The amount of heat needed to increase the temperature of 1 gram (3/100 oz.) of a substance by one degree.

Electricity
A source of energy associated with electric charges.

Y

admittance
A measure of how easily a circuit allows a current to flow.

I

electric current
A flow of electric charge. It is commonly measured in amperes.

J

electric current density
The flow of electric charge per unit area.

Q

electric charge
A property of matter that causes electrical phenomena. It is commonly measured in coulombs.

U

electric tension
The difference in electric potential between two points. It is also called voltage.

φ

phase shift
The measure of change of a wave from its original form.

R

resistance
A measure of how strongly a circuit resists an electric current.

X

reactance
A measure of how much a circuit reacts against a change in electric current.

Z

impedance
A measure of the combined effects of resistance and reactance. It is commonly measured in ohms.

ρ

specific resistance
A measure of how strongly a substance opposes the flow of an electric current.

B

susceptance
A measure of how easily an electric circuit conducts a change in electric current.

F_L

Lorentz force
The combined amounts of electric and magnetic forces exerted on a charged particle in an electromagnetic field.

E

electric field
The amount of electric force per unit charge.

Ψ

water potential
The potential energy of water.

D

electric flux density
The strength of an electric field of a substance.

P

polarization
The change in distribution of positive or negative charge in the molecules of an object.

α

polarizability
A measure of how easily the electron clouds of a particle become distorted by an external electric field.

Magnetism
A source of energy associated with the magnetic fields of electrical charges.

P

effective power
The amount of power being used in an electrical circuit.

B

magnetic flux density
The amount of magnetic field per unit area.

J

magnetic polarization
The change in density of dipole moments of a magnet.

ϵ

permittivity
A measure of how strongly a substance opposes an external electric field.

M

magnetization
A measure of magnetic moment per unit volume.

Φ

magnetic flux
The amount of magnetic field. It is commonly measured in webers.

C

electric capacity
A measure of a capacitor's ability to store an electrical charge. It is also called capacitance.

S

elastance
A measure of the voltage across a capacitor after it accepts 1 coulomb of electric charge.

L

inductance
The voltage created as a result of a change in electric current.

H

magnetic field strength
A measure of how easily a magnet induces a magnetic field.

S

apparent power
The combined amounts of effective power and power lost due to reactance.

m

magnetic moment
The amount of force a magnet can exert an electric current.

Atomic and molecular quantities
Determining quantities of chemical substances.

n
amount of substance
A quantity that measures the size of particles such as molecules, atoms or electrons. Its unit is the mole.

V_m
molar volume
The volume of a substance per amount of the substance in moles.

M
molar mass
The mass of a substance per amount of the substance in moles.

M_r
relative molar mass
The ratio of the molar mass of a substance to the unified atomic weight unit.

A_r
relative atomic mass
The ratio of the mass of atoms of a substance to the unified atomic weight unit.

Nuclear physics
The study of atomic nuclei and the interactions between them

σ
effect cross section
A measure of the probability that a reaction will occur with a target nucleus.

A
activity
The number of atoms that disintegrate per unit of time.

τ
mean lifetime
The amount of time it takes for the number of atoms of an isotope to disintegrate to 1/e.

λ
disintegration constant
The fraction of the number of atoms that decay per unit of time. It is also called a decay constant.

D
absorbed dose
The amount of energy transferred per unit of mass by ionizing radiation.

H
equivalent dose
A measure of the absorbed dose that takes into account biological effects of ionizing radiation.

$T_{1/2}$
half-life
The amount of time it takes for half of the atoms of an isotope to disintegrate.

J
ion dose
A variable that was formerly used for the measurement of the absorbed dose of ionizing radiation.

Radiometry
The absolute measurement of radiant energy.

H
radiant exposure
The amount of radiant energy received by a surface per unit area.

I
radiant intensity
The amount of radiant energy emitted per unit solid angle.

Φ
radiant flux
The amount of radiant energy emitted, transferred, or received per unit time. It is also called radiant power.

Q
radiant energy
The energy of electromagnetic radiation. It is commonly measured in joules.

L
radiance
The amount of radiant flux leaving or passing through a surface per unit solid angle.

MATHEMATICS
Mathematical symbols

l
length
The distance of the longest line of a two- or three-dimensional object.

b
width
The distance of a side-to-side line of a two- or three-dimensional object.

h
height
The distance from the base to top of a two- or three-dimensional object.

σ
thickness
The thickness of a plane.

r
radius
The distance from the center of a circle to any point on its edge.

d
diameter
The distance across a circle through its center.

s
distance
The distance between two points on a plane.

A
area
The size of the surface of a two- or three-dimensional object.

S
cross-sectional area
The size of the surface enclosed in the cross section of a three-dimensional object.

V
volume
The amount of space inside a three-dimensional object.

Ω
space angle
A measure of how large an area of a three-dimensional object appears when it is subtended by an angle.

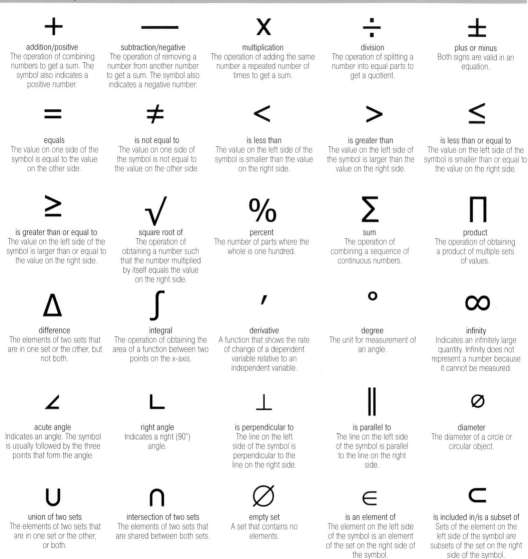

+
addition/positive
The operation of combining numbers to get a sum. The symbol also indicates a positive number.

—
subtraction/negative
The operation of removing a number from another number to get a sum. The symbol also indicates a negative number.

X
multiplication
The operation of adding the same number a repeated number of times to get a sum.

÷
division
The operation of splitting a number into equal parts to get a quotient.

±
plus or minus
Both signs are valid in an equation.

=
equals
The value on one side of the symbol is equal to the value on the other side.

≠
is not equal to
The value on one side of the symbol is not equal to the value on the other side.

<
is less than
The value on the left side of the symbol is smaller than the value on the right side.

>
is greater than
The value on the left side of the symbol is larger than the value on the right side.

≤
is less than or equal to
The value on the left side of the symbol is smaller than or equal to the value on the right side.

≥
is greater than or equal to
The value on the left side of the symbol is larger than or equal to the value on the right side.

√
square root of
The operation of obtaining a number such that the number multiplied by itself equals the value on the right side.

%
percent
The number of parts where the whole is one hundred.

Σ
sum
The operation of combining a sequence of continuous numbers.

∏
product
The operation of obtaining a product of multiple sets of values.

Δ
difference
The elements of two sets that are in one set or the other, but not both.

∫
integral
The operation of obtaining the area of a function between two points on the x-axis.

′
derivative
A function that shows the rate of change of a dependent variable relative to an independent variable.

°
degree
The unit for measurement of an angle.

∞
infinity
Indicates an infinitely large quantity. Infinity does not represent a number because it cannot be measured.

∠
acute angle
Indicates an angle. The symbol is usually followed by the three points that form the angle.

L
right angle
Indicates a right (90°) angle.

⊥
is perpendicular to
The line on the left side of the symbol is perpendicular to the line on the right side.

∥
is parallel to
The line on the left side of the symbol is parallel to the line on the right side.

Ø
diameter
The diameter of a circle or circular object.

U
union of two sets
The elements of two sets that are in one set or the other, or both.

∩
intersection of two sets
The elements of two sets that are shared between both sets.

Ø
empty set
A set that contains no elements.

∈
is an element of
The element on the left side of the symbol is an element of the set on the right side of the symbol.

⊂
is included in/is a subset of
Sets of the element on the left side of the symbol are subsets of the set on the right side of the symbol.

∀
universal quantification
A function is true for all elements of a universal set.

∃
existential quantification
A function is true for at least one element of a universal set.

N
natural numbers
Refers to the set of natural numbers, which are whole numbers that may or may not include zero.

Z
integers
Refers to the set of integers, which are whole numbers that include the natural numbers, their negative counterparts and zero.

Q
rational numbers
Refers to the set of rational numbers, which have a repeating decimal representation.

algebraic numbers
Refers to the set of algebraic numbers. An algebraic number is the root of a polynomial in which not all coefficients are zero.

real numbers
Refers to the set of rational numbers, which includes rational and irrational numbers, but not the imaginary number.

C

complex numbers
Refers to the set of complex numbers, which are a combination of real numbers and the imaginary number.

quaternions
Refers to a four-dimensional extension of the set of complex numbers.

pi
The ratio of the circumference of a circle to its diameter. It represents an irrational number.

simple fraction
A representation of the number of parts in a whole. Simple fractions use only integers.

numerator
The number above the fraction bar. It represents the number of parts of the whole.

fraction bar
The horizontal line that separates the numerator from the denominator.

denominator
The number below the fraction bar. It represents how many parts make up a whole.

e

Euler's number
The base commonly used for logarithmic and exponential functions. It represents an irrational number.

φ

golden ratio
The ratio of two numbers that is the same as the ratio of the larger number to the sum of those two numbers.

i

imaginary number
Refers to $\sqrt{(-1)}$.

Roman numerals

I

one
A symbol that represents the number 1.

II

two
A symbol that represents the number 2.

III

three
A symbol that represents the number 3.

IV

four
A symbol that represents the number 4.

V

five
A symbol that represents the number 5.

VI

six
A symbol that represents the number 6.

VII

seven
A symbol that represents the number 7.

VIII

eight
A symbol that represents the number 8.

IX

nine
A symbol that represents the number 9.

X

ten
A symbol that represents the number 10.

XX

twenty
A symbol that represents the number 20.

XXX

thirty
A symbol that represents the number 30.

XL

forty
A symbol that represents the number 40.

L

fifty
A symbol that represents the number 50.

LX

sixty
A symbol that represents the number 60.

XC

ninety
A symbol that represents the number 90.

C

one hundred
A symbol that represents the number 100.

D

five hundred
A symbol that represents the number 500.

M

one thousand
A symbol that represents the number 1,000.

Circle
A two-dimensional shape whose points are all at an equal distance from its center.

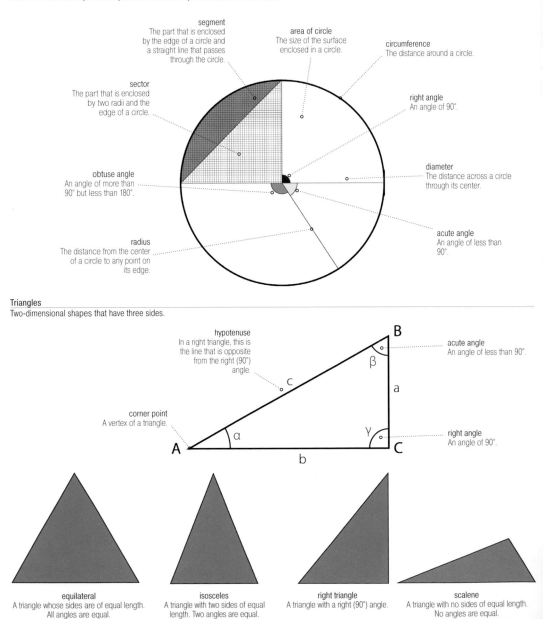

segment
The part that is enclosed by the edge of a circle and a straight line that passes through the circle.

area of circle
The size of the surface enclosed in a circle.

circumference
The distance around a circle.

sector
The part that is enclosed by two radii and the edge of a circle.

right angle
An angle of 90°.

obtuse angle
An angle of more than 90° but less than 180°.

diameter
The distance across a circle through its center.

radius
The distance from the center of a circle to any point on its edge.

acute angle
An angle of less than 90°.

Triangles
Two-dimensional shapes that have three sides.

hypotenuse
In a right triangle, this is the line that is opposite from the right (90°) angle.

acute angle
An angle of less than 90°.

corner point
A vertex of a triangle.

right angle
An angle of 90°.

equilateral
A triangle whose sides are of equal length. All angles are equal.

isosceles
A triangle with two sides of equal length. Two angles are equal.

right triangle
A triangle with a right (90°) angle.

scalene
A triangle with no sides of equal length. No angles are equal.

Polygons
Two-dimensional shapes that have three or more sides.

square
A polygon that has four sides of equal length. All angles are 90°.

rectangle
A polygon that has four sides, with one pair of sides longer than the other pair. All angles are 90°.

rhombus
A polygon that has four sides of equal length. It has no 90° angles.

kite
A polygon that has four sides, with adjacent sides of equal length.

trapezoid
A polygon that has four sides, with one side parallel to the opposite side.

pentagon
A polygon that has five sides.

trapezium
A polygon that has four sides, and no sides are parallel.

rhomboid
A polygon that has four sides, with one side longer than the other pair. It has no 90° angles.

Diagrams
Ways of representing data in graphic form.

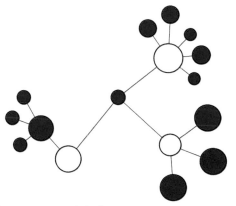

cluster diagram
A diagram that shows relationships between objects or ideas.

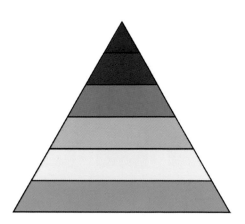

pyramid diagram
A diagram that shows foundational relationships.

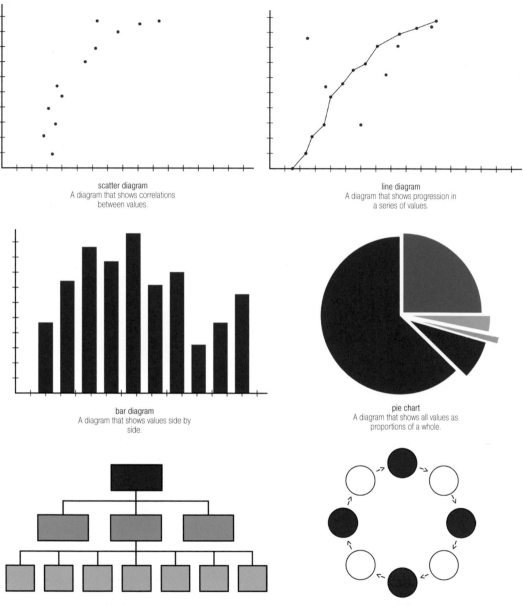

scatter diagram
A diagram that shows correlations
between values.

line diagram
A diagram that shows progression in
a series of values.

bar diagram
A diagram that shows values side by
side.

pie chart
A diagram that shows all values as
proportions of a whole.

tree diagram
A diagram that shows
hierarchical relationships.

cycle diagram
A diagram that shows a logical
progression in a sequence of
events or objects.

Solids
Three-dimensional geometrical objects.

cube
A solid that has six parallel,
square faces. All angles
are 90°.

rectangular cuboid
A solid with six parallel, rectangular
faces. All angles are 90°.

prism
Any solid that has flat faces, straight
sides and the same cross section
along its length.

cylinder
A solid that has two parallel,
circular faces.

rhombohedron
A solid that has six parallel
faces that are rhombi. No
angles are 90°.

pyramid
A solid that has a flat face
with straight sides whose
points meet at one vertex to
form triangles.

tetrahedron
Any solid that has four flat
faces.

cone
A solid that has a circular face
and a vertex.

sphere
A solid whose points on its
surface are all at an equal
distance from its center.

ellipsoid
A solid whose cross sections are
either ellipses or circles.

torus
A solid that is a circular ring and
whose cross sections are circles.

octahedron
Any solid that has eight flat faces.

icosahedron
Any solid that has 20 flat faces.

dodecahedron
Any solid that has 12 flat faces.

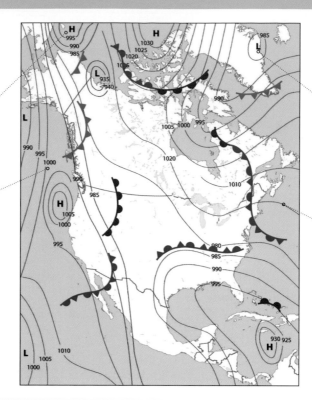

high pressure area
An area with the highest pressure relative to its surrounding regions.

low pressure area
An area with the lowest pressure relative to its surrounding regions.

barometric pressure
The amount of force that is exerted on an area by the weight of the atmosphere above it.

isobar
A line that connects points that have the same atmospheric pressure.

Fronts

The advancing edge of an air mass that has a distinct change in temperature and density.

surface warm front
The leading edge of an advancing air mass that replaces a cooler air mass.

surface cold front
The leading edge of an advancing air mass that replaces a warmer air mass.

occluded front
The edge of air masses where a warmer air mass is forced upward by a cooler air mass.

stationary front
The edge of air masses where neither mass replaces the other.

Precipitation

Any form of water or ice that falls from the atmosphere to the Earth's surface.

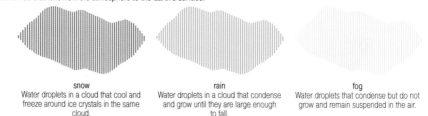

snow
Water droplets in a cloud that cool and freeze around ice crystals in the same cloud.

rain
Water droplets in a cloud that condense and grow until they are large enough to fall.

fog
Water droplets that condense but do not grow and remain suspended in the air.

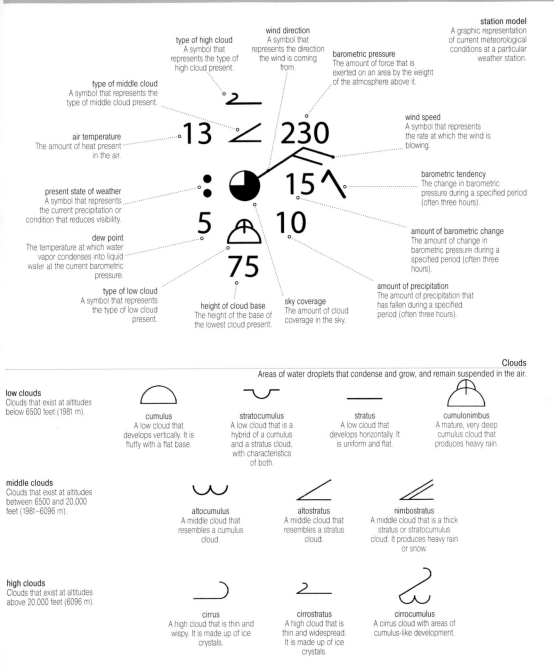

station model
A graphic representation
of current meteorological
conditions at a particular
weather station.

type of high cloud
A symbol that
represents the type of
high cloud present.

wind direction
A symbol that
represents the direction
the wind is coming
from.

barometric pressure
The amount of force that is
exerted on an area by the weight
of the atmosphere above it.

type of middle cloud
A symbol that represents the
type of middle cloud present.

air temperature
The amount of heat present
in the air.

wind speed
A symbol that represents
the rate at which the wind is
blowing.

present state of weather
A symbol that represents
the current precipitation or
condition that reduces visibility.

barometric tendency
The change in barometric
pressure during a specified period
(often three hours).

dew point
The temperature at which water
vapor condenses into liquid
water at the current barometric
pressure.

amount of barometric change
The amount of change in
barometric pressure during a
specified period (often three
hours).

type of low cloud
A symbol that represents
the type of low cloud
present.

height of cloud base
The height of the base of
the lowest cloud present.

sky coverage
The amount of cloud
coverage in the sky.

amount of precipitation
The amount of precipitation that
has fallen during a specified
period (often three hours).

Clouds
Areas of water droplets that condense and grow, and remain suspended in the air.

low clouds
Clouds that exist at altitudes
below 6500 feet (1981 m).

cumulus
A low cloud that
develops vertically. It is
fluffy with a flat base.

stratocumulus
A low cloud that is a
hybrid of a cumulus
and a stratus cloud,
with characteristics
of both.

stratus
A low cloud that
develops horizontally. It
is uniform and flat.

cumulonimbus
A mature, very deep
cumulus cloud that
produces heavy rain.

middle clouds
Clouds that exist at altitudes
between 6500 and 20,000
feet (1981–6096 m).

altocumulus
A middle cloud that
resembles a cumulus
cloud.

altostratus
A middle cloud that
resembles a stratus
cloud.

nimbostratus
A middle cloud that is a thick
stratus or stratocumulus
cloud. It produces heavy rain
or snow.

high clouds
Clouds that exist at altitudes
above 20,000 feet (6096 m).

cirrus
A high cloud that is thin and
wispy. It is made up of ice
crystals.

cirrostratus
A high cloud that is
thin and widespread.
It is made up of ice
crystals.

cirrocumulus
A cirrus cloud with areas of
cumulus-like development.

Precipitation
Any form of water or ice that falls from the atmosphere to the Earth's surface.

light intermittent rain
Light rain is occurring at irregular intervals.

moderate intermittent rain
Moderate rain is occurring at irregular intervals.

heavy intermittent rain
Heavy rain is occurring at irregular intervals.

freezing rain
Rain is freezing on contact with any surface.

light intermittent drizzle
Light drizzle is occurring at irregular intervals.

moderate intermittent drizzle
Moderate drizzle is occurring at irregular intervals.

thick intermittent drizzle
Thick drizzle is occurring at irregular intervals.

freezing drizzle
Drizzle is freezing on contact with any surface.

sleet
Precipitation in the form of small, translucent pellets of ice.

ice crystals
Precipitation in the form of tiny crystals of ice.

intermittent light snow
Light snow is occurring at irregular intervals.

continuous moderate snow
Moderate snow is occurring at irregular intervals.

intermittent heavy snow
Heavy snow is occurring at irregular intervals.

graupel (soft hail)
Precipitation in the form of supercooled water droplets that freeze on falling snowflakes.

haze
Fine particles suspended in the air that reduce visibility.

sandstorm or dust storm
Particles of sand blown by the wind that reduce visibility.

well-developed dust or sand whirl
Particles of sand or dust blown by the wind in a columnar vortex.

drifting snow, low
Snow blown by the wind below eye level that reduces visibility.

drifting snow, high
Snow blown by the wind above eye level that reduces visibility.

fog
Water droplets that condense but do not grow and remain suspended in the air.

lightning visible, no thunder heard
Lightning is visible, so a thunderstorm is suspected.

thunderstorm
A storm with thunder and lightning.

shower of rain and snow, mixed
Period of precipitation in the form of rain and snow.

snow shower
Period of precipitation in the form of snow.

rain shower
Period of precipitation in the form of rain.

funnel clouds or tornadoes
A cumulus or cumulus-type cloud rotating in a columnar vortex.

hurricane
A tropical cyclone that has surface winds of 64 knots or greater.

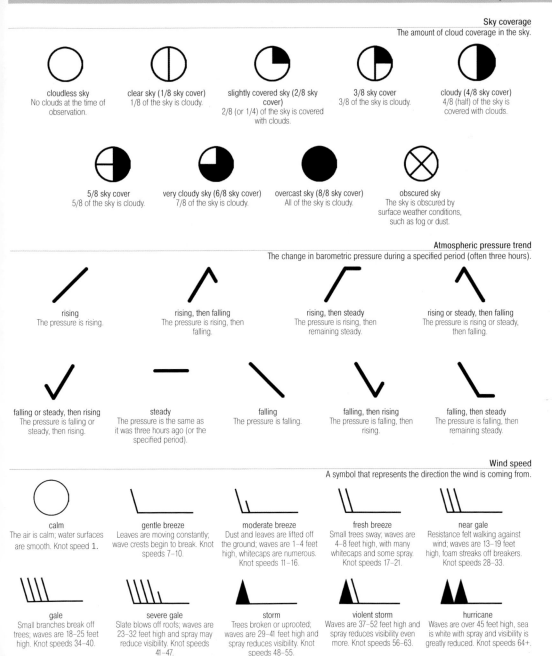

Sky coverage
The amount of cloud coverage in the sky.

cloudless sky
No clouds at the time of observation.

clear sky (1/8 sky cover)
1/8 of the sky is cloudy.

slightly covered sky (2/8 sky cover)
2/8 (or 1/4) of the sky is covered with clouds.

3/8 sky cover
3/8 of the sky is cloudy.

cloudy (4/8 sky cover)
4/8 (half) of the sky is covered with clouds.

5/8 sky cover
5/8 of the sky is cloudy.

very cloudy sky (6/8 sky cover)
7/8 of the sky is cloudy.

overcast sky (8/8 sky cover)
All of the sky is cloudy.

obscured sky
The sky is obscured by surface weather conditions, such as fog or dust.

Atmospheric pressure trend
The change in barometric pressure during a specified period (often three hours).

rising
The pressure is rising.

rising, then falling
The pressure is rising, then falling.

rising, then steady
The pressure is rising, then remaining steady.

rising or steady, then falling
The pressure is rising or steady, then falling.

falling or steady, then rising
The pressure is falling or steady, then rising.

steady
The pressure is the same as it was three hours ago (or the specified period).

falling
The pressure is falling.

falling, then rising
The pressure is falling, then rising.

falling, then steady
The pressure is falling, then remaining steady.

Wind speed
A symbol that represents the direction the wind is coming from.

calm
The air is calm; water surfaces are smooth. Knot speed **1**.

gentle breeze
Leaves are moving constantly; wave crests begin to break. Knot speeds 7–10.

moderate breeze
Dust and leaves are lifted off the ground; waves are 1–4 feet high, whitecaps are numerous. Knot speeds 11–16.

fresh breeze
Small trees sway; waves are 4–8 feet high, with many whitecaps and some spray. Knot speeds 17–21.

near gale
Resistance felt walking against wind; waves are 13–19 feet high, foam streaks off breakers. Knot speeds 28–33.

gale
Small branches break off trees; waves are 18–25 feet high. Knot speeds 34–40.

severe gale
Slate blows off roofs; waves are 23–32 feet high and spray may reduce visibility. Knot speeds 41–47.

storm
Trees broken or uprooted; waves are 29–41 feet high and spray reduces visibility. Knot speeds 48–55.

violent storm
Waves are 37–52 feet high and spray reduces visibility even more. Knot speeds 56–63.

hurricane
Waves are over 45 feet high, sea is white with spray and visibility is greatly reduced. Knot speeds 64+.

subtractive colors
A color obtained by removing a color.

magenta
One of the primary colors in subtractive mixing.

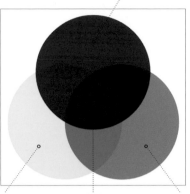

yellow
One of the primary colors in subtractive mixing.

black
The presence of all three primary colors in subtractive mixing.

cyan
One of the primary colors in subtractive mixing.

additive colors
A color obtained by adding a color.

red
One of the primary colors in additive mixing.

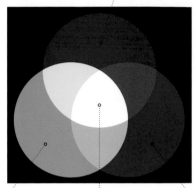

green
One of the primary colors in additive mixing.

white
The presence of all three primary colors in additive mixing.

blue
One of the primary colors in additive mixing.

Color contrasts

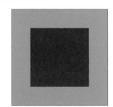

contrast of hue
Displaying the difference between undiluted colors of the color wheel. The farther the colors are from each other, the higher the contrast is.

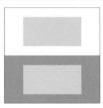

simultaneous contrast
Displaying the difference in how one color appears when it is placed next to another color.

light-dark contrast
Displaying the difference between a light color and a dark color.

saturation contrast
Displaying the difference between a color that is undiluted and the same color that is diluted.

warm-cool contrast
Displaying the difference between a color with red or yellow (warm) and a color with blue or green (cool).

quantity contrast
Displaying the effect of the amount of one color in an image relative to the amount of another color.

complementary contrast
Displaying two colors that are opposite from each other on the color wheel.

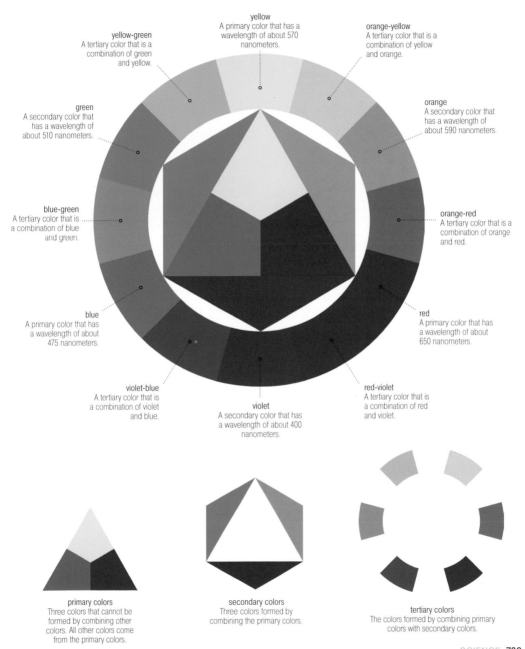

yellow-green
A tertiary color that is a combination of green and yellow.

yellow
A primary color that has a wavelength of about 570 nanometers.

orange-yellow
A tertiary color that is a combination of yellow and orange.

green
A secondary color that has a wavelength of about 510 nanometers.

orange
A secondary color that has a wavelength of about 590 nanometers.

blue-green
A tertiary color that is a combination of blue and green.

orange-red
A tertiary color that is a combination of orange and red.

blue
A primary color that has a wavelength of about 475 nanometers.

red
A primary color that has a wavelength of about 650 nanometers.

violet-blue
A tertiary color that is a combination of violet and blue.

violet
A secondary color that has a wavelength of about 400 nanometers.

red-violet
A tertiary color that is a combination of red and violet.

primary colors
Three colors that cannot be formed by combining other colors. All other colors come from the primary colors.

secondary colors
Three colors formed by combining the primary colors.

tertiary colors
The colors formed by combining primary colors with secondary colors.

flask on stand
A glass container that has a round bottom needs a stand to remain upright.

round-bottom flask
A glass container that is often used in experiments that require heating of a solution.

liquid
The solution that is the site of a chemical reaction.

stand
The stand provides support and stability.

flask with glass tubes
A flask that is sealed with a bottle stopper fitted with glass tubes is commonly used for distillation of liquids.

crucible with cover
A glass container that can withstand high heat. It is commonly used in analytical experiments.

fractional distillation kit
Equipment used to separate a substance into smaller components by heating and distillation.

heating mantle
Equipment that uses gradual heat to warm a liquid.

liquid
The solution that is being heated.

universal heater
Equipment that allows the heating of containers that vary in size and shape.

mantle
A heating element that is insulated to prevent excessive heat from shattering a flask.

heat control knob
This knob allows control of the level of heat in a mantle.

laboratory flask
A glass container that can withstand high heat. It is fitted with glass tubes that collect liquid.

power button
A toggle switch that turns the equipment on or off.

desiccator
A glass container that can be sealed to store substances or objects that may react with the humidity in the air.

graduated cylinder
A glass container that is used for relatively precise measurement of the volume of a liquid.

bottle with drying tube
A glass container that is fitted with a tube. It is commonly used for drying substances.

coil condenser
A glass tube that contains a coil filled with a coolant. The vapor enters the tube and is released as liquid.

dry ice condenser
A glass tube that contains an inner tube filled with dry ice as a coolant.

plastic funnel
A plastic tube that has a wide opening to guide a substance or liquid into a small opening.

glass funnel
A glass tube that has a wide opening to guide a substance or liquid into a small opening.

Erlenmeyer flask
A glass container that allows swirling of a solution without spilling it.

beaker with stirring rod
A glass container that holds a relatively large volume of liquid. A stirring rod is used to stir a solution.

bottle with closure
A glass container that holds a liquid and can be sealed with a closure.

filtering flask
A flask that can be fitted with the tube of a vacuum pump to speed up the filtration of a liquid.

glass water bath
A glass container that provides a hot water bath for heating a solution.

glass tray
A glass container with a large surface area that is often used for drying or staining.

ring stand with clamps
Equipment that can be used for mounting or supporting laboratory glassware.

separatory funnel
A funnel that is used to separate an immiscible liquid from a solution.

barrel
A container that can hold a large volume of a substance.

filter funnel
A funnel that is fitted with a filter to separate particulate matter from the solution being filtered.

test tube with stopper
A glass container that holds a small amount of liquid and can be sealed with a stopper.

electronic pipette
An electronic tool that is used to transfer precisely measured amounts of a substance.

test tube on stand
A glass container that holds a small amount of liquid. A stand is necessary for the tube to remain upright.

beaker with handle
A container that can hold a large volume of a liquid.

wash bottle
A plastic container that can be squeezed to control the pressure of water when rinsing laboratory glassware.

beaker
A container that can hold a large volume of a liquid.

magnetic stirrer/hotplate
Equipment that has a hotplate and uses a rotating magnetic field and a magnetic bar to stir a solution.

temperature probe
The probe monitors the temperature of the solution.

glass beaker
A glass container that holds a relatively large volume of liquid.

hotplate
A plate that covers the heating element.

indicator panel
The panel displays the set temperature or the temperature of the solution.

leg
One of four legs that provide stability to the stirrer.

magnetic stirrer
Equipment that uses a rotating magnetic field and a magnetic bar to stir a solution.

control knob
This knob allows control of the speed of stirring.

bottle with spatula closure
A container that can be sealed with a closure that has a spatula, which is useful for viscous substances.

evaporator
Equipment that allows separating of the components of a solution by heating and distillation.

mixing device
Equipment that uses vibration to mix a solution.

pipette stand
A structure for storing pipettes.

fume hood
Equipment that filters or expels harmful vapors or particulate matter.

note stand
A tool for placing notes for convenient reference.

laminar flow unit
Equipment that provides a working area that is free of contamination.

spatula
A tool that is used to transfer or mix a substance.

mobile base cabinet
Movable equipment that allows storage of laboratory tools.

flask support ring
A tool that is used to support glass containers. It is often mounted on a ring stand.

steam autoclave
Equipment that uses high pressure and steam to sterilize tools and glassware.

electric water bath
Equipment that uses hot water to heat a solution.

thermometer with probe
A thermometer with a probe for monitoring the temperature of a solution.

sound meter
An instrument for measuring the level of sound in decibels.

coarse adjustment knob
This knob allows the stage to be moved up or down to focus on the specimen.

arm
The arm supports the eyepiece and objective lenses.

fine adjustment knob
This knob allows the stage to be moved up or down to focus on the specimen.

stage clip
A clipping mechanism that stabilizes a glass slide to the stage.

base
The base provides support and stability.

microscope
An instrument that is used to magnify the image of an object that is too small to see with the human eye.

eyepiece
The part that the eye looks through. It has is a small amount of magnification.

revolving nosepiece
A disk that can be rotated to adjust the level of magnification. It is also called a turret.

objective lense
Specially designed pieces of glass that are the main source of a microscope's magnification.

glass slide
A small plate of glass on which a specimen is placed.

mirror
A reflective glass that depends on natural light to illuminate a specimen.

pestle and mortar
A pair of tools that are used together for crushing or grinding a substance.

magnifying glass
A tool that enlarges the image of an object or sample for easier viewing.

spray bottle
A tool that is used to spray controlled amounts of liquid.

square magnifying glass
A tool that enlarges the image of an object or sample for easier viewing.

pipette
A tool that is used to transfer precisely measured amounts of a substance.

test tube stirrer
Equipment that uses a rotating magnetic field and a magnetic bar to stir a solution in a test tube.

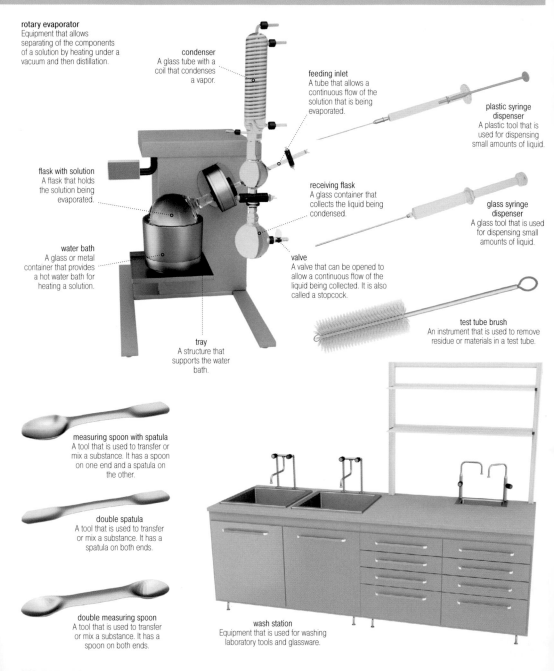

rotary evaporator
Equipment that allows separating of the components of a solution by heating under a vacuum and then distillation.

condenser
A glass tube with a coil that condenses a vapor.

feeding inlet
A tube that allows a continuous flow of the solution that is being evaporated.

plastic syringe dispenser
A plastic tool that is used for dispensing small amounts of liquid.

flask with solution
A flask that holds the solution being evaporated.

receiving flask
A glass container that collects the liquid being condensed.

glass syringe dispenser
A glass tool that is used for dispensing small amounts of liquid.

water bath
A glass or metal container that provides a hot water bath for heating a solution.

valve
A valve that can be opened to allow a continuous flow of the liquid being collected. It is also called a stopcock.

test tube brush
An instrument that is used to remove residue or materials in a test tube.

tray
A structure that supports the water bath.

measuring spoon with spatula
A tool that is used to transfer or mix a substance. It has a spoon on one end and a spatula on the other.

double spatula
A tool that is used to transfer or mix a substance. It has a spatula on both ends.

double measuring spoon
A tool that is used to transfer or mix a substance. It has a spoon on both ends.

wash station
Equipment that is used for washing laboratory tools and glassware.

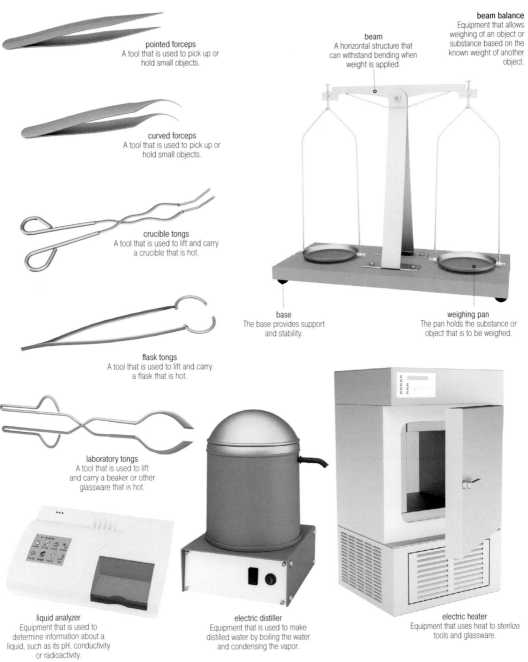

pointed forceps
A tool that is used to pick up or
hold small objects.

curved forceps
A tool that is used to pick up or
hold small objects.

crucible tongs
A tool that is used to lift and carry
a crucible that is hot.

flask tongs
A tool that is used to lift and carry
a flask that is hot.

laboratory tongs
A tool that is used to lift
and carry a beaker or other
glassware that is hot.

beam
A horizontal structure that
can withstand bending when
weight is applied.

beam balance
Equipment that allows
weighing of an object or
substance based on the
known weight of another
object.

base
The base provides support
and stability.

weighing pan
The pan holds the substance or
object that is to be weighed.

liquid analyzer
Equipment that is used to
determine information about a
liquid, such as its pH, conductivity
or radioactivity.

electric distiller
Equipment that is used to make
distilled water by boiling the water
and condensing the vapor.

electric heater
Equipment that uses heat to sterilize
tools and glassware.

glassware dryer
Equipment that blows warm air to dry laboratory glassware.

centrifuge
Equipment that spins samples at high speed to separate its components based on density.

drying peg
Small tubes through which air is dispersed. A glass container is hung on a drying peg to dry.

air channel
The main channel through which air is blown by the motor of the dryer.

digital microscope
A microscope that uses a monitor to display a magnified image. It has no eyepiece.

visual display
The monitor that displays a magnified image of the specimen.

indicator panel
The panel displays the temperature of the air.

power switch
A toggle switch that turns the equipment on or off.

control knob
This knob allows control of the length of time the equipment operates.

control panel
This panel allows adjustment of the properties of the image, such as sharpness.

specimen positioning control
These knobs allow fine adjustment of the position of the specimen.

indicator panel
The panel displays the level of magnification.

field lens
Specially designed pieces of glass that are the main source of a microscope's magnification.

fixed-angle centrifuge
Equipment that spins samples at high speed and a specific angle to separate its components based on density.

position table
The area on which a specimen is placed for viewing.

features of the Moon
The surface structures of the Moon, a natural satellite of Earth.

crater
A basin-like depression on the surface of the Moon. Most craters were formed by impacts.

lake
A large crater that was flooded with lava. It is smaller than a sea.

highland
A rugged region formed by overlapping craters.

sea
A large crater that was flooded with lava. It is also called a lunar mare (plural: maria).

ocean
An extensively sized crater that was flooded with lava.

Phases of the Moon
The different appearances of the Moon as it orbits the Earth.

old crescent
The phase between the last quarter and the new moon. It is also called a waning crescent.

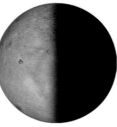
last quarter
The phase between the waning gibbous and the old crescent.

waning gibbous
The phase between the full moon and the last quarter.

full moon
The phase between the waxing gibbous and the waning gibbous.

waxing gibbous
The phase between the first quarter and the full moon.

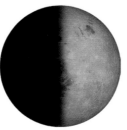
first quarter
The phase between the new crescent and waxing gibbous.

new crescent
The phase between the new moon and the first quarter. It is also called a waxing crescent.

new moon
The phase between the old crescent the new crescent.

solar system
Consists of the Sun and the planets that orbit it.

Jupiter
The planet that is fifth from the Sun. It is the largest planet in the solar system.

spicule
An emission of gas from one of the layers of the Sun. It is short-lived.

Mercury
The planet that is closest to the Sun. It is the smallest planet in the solar system.

Uranus
The planet that is seventh from the Sun. It is the third-largest planet in the solar system.

Earth
The planet that is third from the Sun. It is the fifth-largest planet in the solar system.

Moon
The only natural satellite of the Earth.

Sun
The large star that is the center of the solar system. It is the largest object in the solar system.

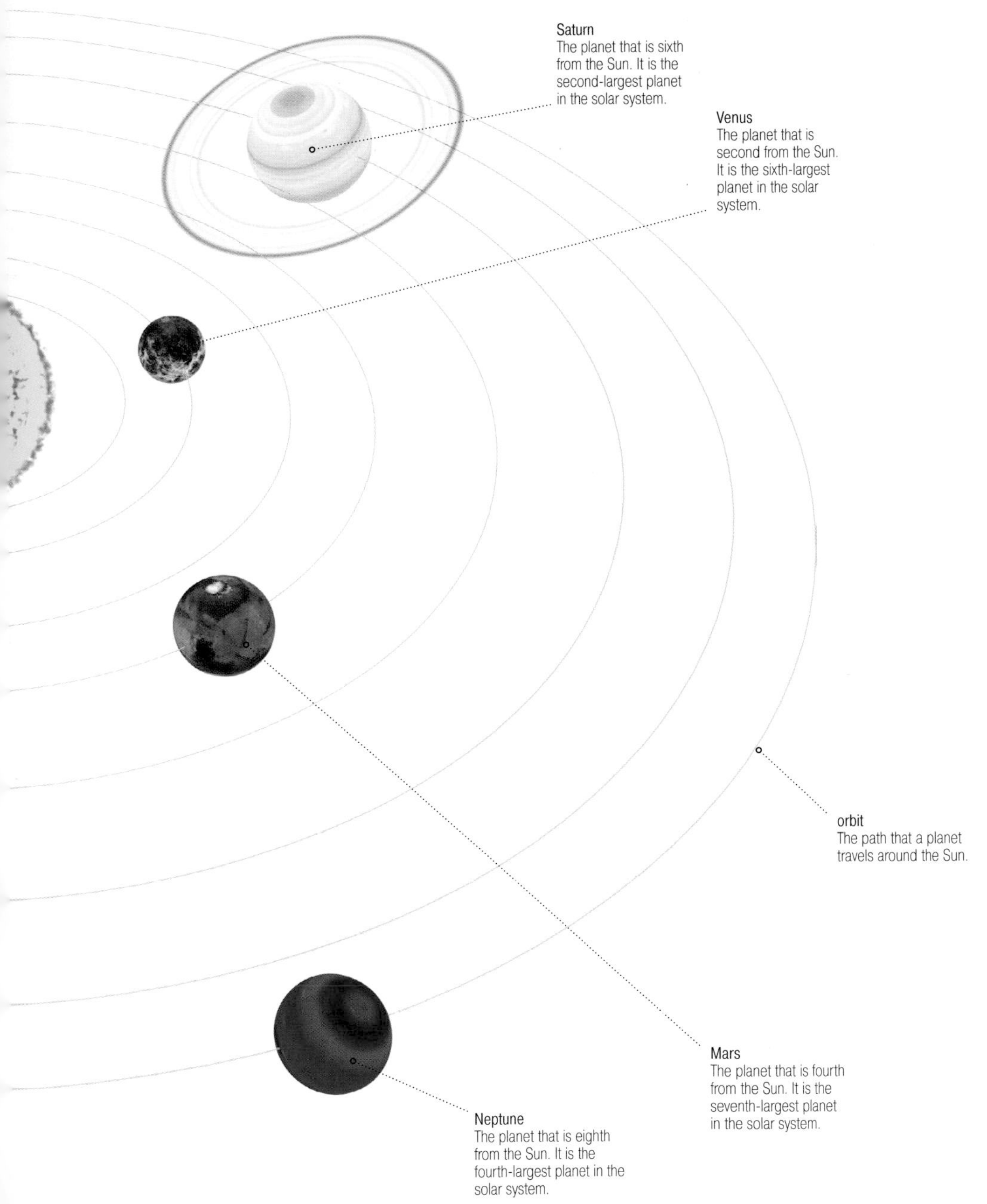

Saturn
The planet that is sixth
from the Sun. It is the
second-largest planet
in the solar system.

Venus
The planet that is
second from the Sun.
It is the sixth-largest
planet in the solar
system.

orbit
The path that a planet
travels around the Sun.

Mars
The planet that is fourth
from the Sun. It is the
seventh-largest planet
in the solar system.

Neptune
The planet that is eighth
from the Sun. It is the
fourth-largest planet in the
solar system.

seasons of the year

Periods of the year that are marked by particular weather conditions and day durations.

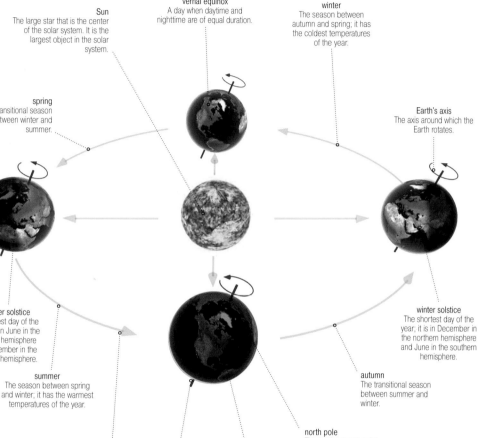

Sun
The large star that is the center of the solar system. It is the largest object in the solar system.

vernal equinox
A day when daytime and nighttime are of equal duration.

winter
The season between autumn and spring; it has the coldest temperatures of the year.

spring
The transitional season between winter and summer.

Earth's axis
The axis around which the Earth rotates.

summer solstice
The longest day of the year; it is in June in the northern hemisphere and December in the southern hemisphere.

winter solstice
The shortest day of the year; it is in December in the northern hemisphere and June in the southern hemisphere.

summer
The season between spring and winter; it has the warmest temperatures of the year.

autumn
The transitional season between summer and winter.

north pole
The northernmost point of the Earth.

Earth's orbit
The path that Earth travels around the Sun.

autumnal equinox
A day when daytime and nighttime are of equal duration.

south pole
The southernmost point of the Earth.

structure of the Earth
The inner layers of Earth, the planet on which we live.

upper mantle
The upper part of the largest layer of the Earth's interior. It is mostly solid rock.

crust
The outermost layer of rock around the Earth.

lower mantle
The lower part of the largest layer of the Earth's interior. It is mostly solid rock.

inner core
The outer part of the Earth's center. It is liquid and contains mostly iron.

outer core
The outer part of the Earth's center. It is liquid and contains mostly iron and nickel.

volcanic eruption
A volcanic eruption occurs when magma and gases are ejected from the vent of a volcano.

eruption cloud
The cloud of ash, gases and rock fragments that form from a volcanic eruption.

eruption column
The pillar of ash, gases and rock fragments that are ejected directly above a vent.

lava fountain
Lava that is forcefully ejected from a vent.

volcanic bomb
A rock that is formed when a blob of lava is ejected into the air and solidifies before falling to the ground.

crater
A basin-like depression over a vent.

dike
A sheet of magma that is perpendicular to the underlying rock that feeds a laccolith or a sill.

side vent
A small opening through which a volcanic eruption occurs.

main vent
The main opening through which a volcanic eruption occurs.

lava flow
Molten rock that reaches the Earth's surface.

fumarole
A hole in the Earth's surface that releases steam and gases.

laccolith
A domed sheet of magma parallel to the underlying rock.

lava layer
A layer of lava that has solidified.

magma
Molten rock under the Earth's surface. It can contain dissolved gases.

magma chamber
An area of the mantle that contain magma.

ash layer
A layer of ash and rock fragments that are held in place by solidified lava.

sill
A sheet of magma parallel to the underlying rock.

ground water
Water that fills the cracks and crevices of rock under the Earth's surface.

radio telescope
A telescope that operates in radio frequencies and can obtain data from objects such as satellites.

receiver
A component that detects and amplifies radio frequency waves.

steerable parabolic reflector
A component that helps focus radio waves into the receiver.

observatory
A facility with powerful observation tools that is used in various areas of study, such as astronomy or meteorology.

parabolic reflector
A dish-like structure that focuses radio waves into the receiver through the steerable parabolic reflector.

rotating dome
The roof of the observatory that protects optical equipment. It can be rotated to view different parts of the sky.

dome shutter
The part of the dome that is opened for viewing the sky.

support structure
A structural component that bears the weight of the parabolic reflector and provides stability.

rotating track
A mechanism that allows the telescope to rotate on a vertical plane.

circular track
A mechanism that allows the telescope to rotate on a horizontal plane.

laboratory
The area where radio signals are analyzed.

telescope
A device that allows viewing of distant objects from Earth.

finderscope
Allows a viewer to align the telescope to the desired area of view. It has lower magnification than the main tube.

dew shield
Protects the lens from condensation buildup.

door
The entranceway into the observatory.

eyepiece
The part that the eye looks through. It positions images for an optimal field of view.

main tube
The part that contains objective lenses for magnifying an image. This is also where light enters the telescope.

focusing knob
This knob allows moving of a mirror to focus light on an image.

cradle
A support structure that secures the main tube of the telescope to its base.

azimuth fine adjustment
This knob allows fine movement of the main tube on a horizontal plane.

counterweight
A weighted part that balances the telescope.

altitude fine adjustment
This knob allows fine movement of the main tube on a vertical plane.

tripod
A structure that stabilizes the telescope.

photovoltaic arrays
These contain photovoltaic cells that convert sunlight into electricity to power the station.

remote manipulator system
A robotic system that allows crew to perform various tasks remotely, such as moving supplies or supporting astronauts in space.

International Space Station
A satellite that provides a livable environment in space. It is used for various fields of research.

European experiment module
A module developed by Germany. It is used for experiments on the effects of space flight on the human body.

U.S. centrifuge module
This module was intended to be used for artificial gravity experiments, but it now serves as an exhibit in Japan.

mating adapter
A component that connects modules and spacecrafts with the station.

truss structure
The structural component of the station that contains mounts for modules and various equipment.

Japanese experiment module
A module developed by Japan. It is the largest module on the station and is used for various experiments.

radiator
Components that expel excess heat that develops when solar energy is converted and distributed to power the station.

Russian module
A module developed by Russia. It is used as a living area and provides some support system functions.

U.S. habitation module
This was intended to be the main living area of the station, but it is now being used for ground-based research.

U.S. laboratory module
A module developed by the United States. It is used for various experiments.

space probe
A crewless spacecraft that is controlled remotely to explore space.

antenna
Typically transmits information to a larger spacecraft, which later relays the information to Earth.

space shuttle
A spacecraft that is used to transport astronauts or objects outside the Earth's atmosphere.

equipment
The part of the space probe that contains most of its instruments.

orbiter
The part of a space shuttle that is designed to be flown back to Earth.

solar panel
Contains multiple photovoltaic cells that convert sunlight into electricity to power the probe.

external fuel tank
Contains liquid oxygen and hydrogen to propel the orbiter for the first 8.5 minutes of flight.

solid rocket booster
Contains propellants to provide thrust for the orbiter for the first 2 minutes of flight.

Moon landing
A spacecraft arriving on the surface of the Moon.

lunar rover
A four-wheeled vehicle that is designed for use on the Moon's surface.

landing module
A spacecraft that is released from a larger space shuttle to transport astronauts to the Moon's surface.

Earth
The planet that is third from the Sun. It is the fifth-largest planet in the solar system.

surface of the Moon
The Moon's terrain consists of mostly old, cratered highlands and large craters that were flooded with lava.

crater
A basin-like depression on the surface of the Moon. Most craters were formed by impacts.

astronaut
A person who is trained to travel in and operate a spacecraft.

space telescope
A massive observational device that is sent into space and is remotely controlled.

aperture door
Protects the optic components of the telescope.

sunshield
Allows the telescope to remain cold by shading it from the Sun.

space launcher
A vehicle that is used to transfer astronauts or objects outside the Earth's atmosphere.

fairing
Protects the payload from pressure and heat during launch.

solar panel
Contains multiple photovoltaic cells that convert sunlight into electricity to power the telescope.

payload
The part of a launch vehicle that carries astronauts, spacecrafts or objects.

electronic boxes
These contain the computer systems that direct the functioning of the telescope and the sending of information.

third stage
When the third stage runs out of fuel, it is detached and leaves the payload, which may contain a spacecraft.

equipment section
An area where various equipment and support systems are stored.

high-gain antenna
Transmits information to communications satellites, which relay the information to controllers on Earth.

fine guidance system
A system that helps the telescope orient on its target.

handrail
These help astronauts to move around the telescope during maintenance.

spacesuit
A specialized garment that protects an astronaut from the environment in space.

second stage
When the second stage runs out of fuel, it is detached and leaves the third stage and the payload.

life support system
Maintains appropriate levels of gases for breathing.

life support system controls
Allows an astronaut to adjust pressure and oxygen levels.

first stage
The largest part of the launch vehicle. When it runs out of fuel, it is detached and leaves the other stages of the vehicle.

helmet
Maintains appropriate levels of pressure.

solid rocket booster
Contains propellants to help provide thrust for the launch vehicle for the initial part of the flight.

solar shield
Protects from radiation.

glove
Protects the hands while allowing some dexterity.

rocket engine
An engine that uses propellant to thrust a launch vehicle through the atmosphere.

protection layer
Protects from impacts with small rock particles.

ENERGY AND INDUSTRY

solar panel
A device that generates energy by using several rows of photovoltaic cells, which convert light into current.

stand
The structural component of a solar panel that positions the panel at a precise angle.

electrical wire
An electrical cord, which transfers electricity from a solar panel's photovoltaic cells to an electrical storage device.

photovoltaic cell
The part of a solar panel that converts solar energy into electrical current.

frame
The structural component of a solar panel that supports the weight of the panel's photovoltaic cells.

hydroelectric dam
A power generator that uses water moving through a dam to create electricity.

headbay
The water supply area of a hydroelectric dam. The headbay can be man-made or natural.

top of dam
The uppermost portion of a hydroelectric dam, where a road is often found.

intake tower
The part of a hydroelectric dam where water enters to generate electricity.

shore
An area of land along a body of water.

road
A paved area for cars. A road allows cars to pass over the dam.

power plant
The part of a hydroelectric dam that generates electricity from the gravitational force of falling water.

afterbay
The area of a hydroelectric dam where excess water settles after passing through the dam.

car
A motor vehicle driven on roads.

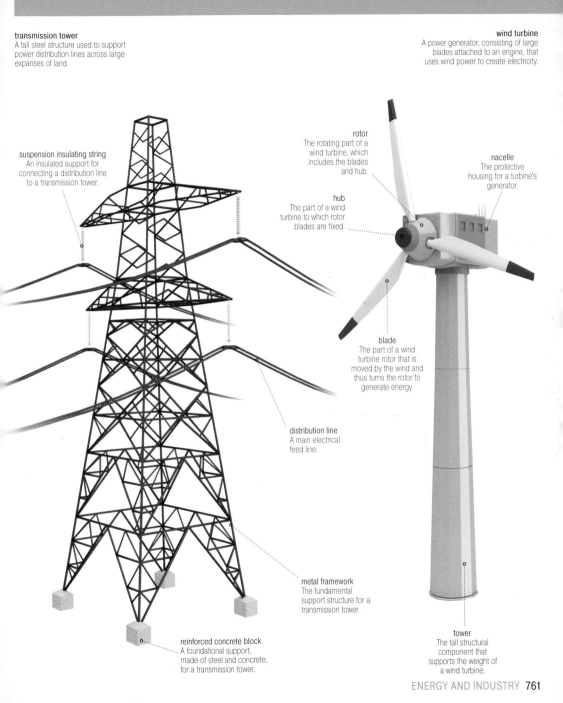

transmission tower
A tall steel structure used to support power distribution lines across large expanses of land.

wind turbine
A power generator, consisting of large blades attached to an engine, that uses wind power to create electricity.

rotor
The rotating part of a wind turbine, which includes the blades and hub.

suspension insulating string
An insulated support for connecting a distribution line to a transmission tower.

nacelle
The protective housing for a turbine's generator.

hub
The part of a wind turbine to which rotor blades are fixed.

blade
The part of a wind turbine rotor that is moved by the wind and thus turns the rotor to generate energy.

distribution line
A main electrical feed line.

metal framework
The fundamental support structure for a transmission tower.

reinforced concrete block
A foundational support, made of steel and concrete, for a transmission tower.

tower
The tall structural component that supports the weight of a wind turbine.

nuclear power plant
A thermal power station that uses a nuclear reactor to convert atomic energy into electricity.

administrative building
A facility where the day-to-day business affairs of a nuclear power plant are conducted by staff.

generator building
The part of a nuclear power plant that houses the electrical generators.

transmission tower
A structure that transfers electrical power from a nuclear power plant to a load center.

reactor building
The part of a nuclear power plant that houses the nuclear reactors.

heat sink
A large mass of water that acts as a safety feature for a nuclear power plant by cooling excess heat.

fuel storage tanks
Storage units, located on the perimeter of a nuclear power plant, to safely store gas reserves.

auxiliary reactor building
A facility for various secondary nuclear power plant operations, such as heating, sewage treatment and water demineralization.

steam turbine
A specialized type of turbine that is designed to generate rotational energy through the use of steam.

stator
A row of fixed vanes that help direct steam to the blades of a steam turbine.

blades
The parts of a steam turbine that are rotated by flowing steam and thus create rotational energy.

inner casing
The inner metal shell of a steam turbine that houses and protects the interior parts.

cooling tower
A heat rejection device that cools circulating water in a nuclear power plant.

rotor
The rotary part of a turbine that receives energy from steam.

shaft
The rod, used to drive a machine, that receives rotary power from a turbine.

outer casing
The outer metal shell of a steam turbine.

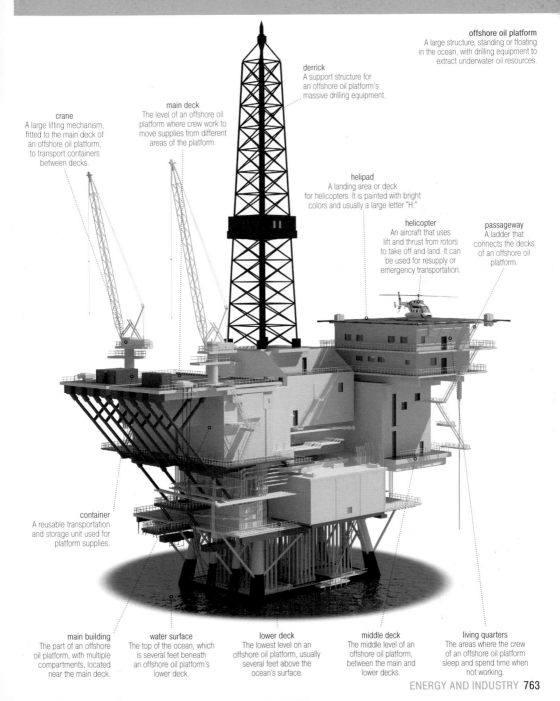

offshore oil platform
A large structure, standing or floating
in the ocean, with drilling equipment to
extract underwater oil resources.

derrick
A support structure for
an offshore oil platform's
massive drilling equipment.

crane
A large lifting mechanism,
fitted to the main deck of
an offshore oil platform,
to transport containers
between decks.

main deck
The level of an offshore oil
platform where crew work to
move supplies from different
areas of the platform.

helipad
A landing area or deck
for helicopters. It is painted with bright
colors and usually a large letter "H."

helicopter
An aircraft that uses
lift and thrust from rotors
to take off and land. It can
be used for resupply or
emergency transportation.

passageway
A ladder that
connects the decks
of an offshore oil
platform.

container
A reusable transportation
and storage unit used for
platform supplies.

main building
The part of an offshore
oil platform, with multiple
compartments, located
near the main deck.

water surface
The top of the ocean, which
is several feet beneath
an offshore oil platform's
lower deck.

lower deck
The lowest level on an
offshore oil platform, usually
several feet above the
ocean's surface.

middle deck
The middle level of an
offshore oil platform,
between the main and
lower decks.

living quarters
The areas where the crew
of an offshore oil platform
sleep and spend time when
not working.

oil tank farm
A specially designed industrial facility used to temporarily store and then distribute oil.

oil tank
A storage unit for oil resources.

aboveground pipeline
Pipes, fitted above ground, used to transport oil to and from oil tanks.

center girder
A beam designed to stabilize the roof of an oil tank during incidences of suction or high wind.

outer girder
A beam surrounding the outside of an oil tank to protect the tank from winds.

roof platform
A secure, flat surface that allows workers to make observations and repairs.

manhole
A circular cement cover that allows access to an oil tank.

stairs
A flight of steps.

overflow drain
A conduit that allows excess oil to overflow and drain.

deck leg
A structural support for features such as overflow drains.

access hatch
The space where workers gain access to the roof platform of an oil tank.

shell
The outer protective cover around the cylindrical part of an oil tank.

floating roof
The top protective cover of an oil tank, which floats on the surface of the oil.

beam pump
An oil-well pump that collects oil by creating force with an oscillating lever, or walking beam.

counterweight
A weight, fitted on a crank arm, to reduce the amount of energy needed to lift the polished rod connected to a beam pump.

pitman arm
A rod that connects a crank arm to the equalizer beam of a beam pump.

equalizer bearing
A machine part used to firmly secure the equalizer beam to the walking beam in a balanced manner.

equalizer beam
The part of a beam pump that balances the weight of the walking beam.

saddle bearing
A machine part used to support the walking beam at a point at the top of the samson post.

walking beam
An overhead oscillating lever that pivots near its center to transmit force from a connecting rod to a pump rod.

wrist pin
A crank bearing used to connect a crank arm to a pitman arm.

horse head
The part of a beam pump that is connected to the walking beam and positioned so the polished rod is directly over the wellhead.

reducer sheave
A gear that helps lower the speed of a beam pump's motor, or prime mover.

ladder
A vertical or inclined set of rungs or steps used to reach high areas.

brake
A mechanical device used to stop the operation of a beam pump or other machine.

polished rod
A cable that connects a horse head with a wellhead.

wellhead
The fittings, such as seals, at the surface of an oil well.

prime mover (motor)
The original source of power for a machine.

belt guard
A strong metal enclosure that protects a beam pump's conveyor belts from being damaged by the elements.

high-mount extension
A raised platform to keep a gearbox clear of debris.

crank arm
One of two parts that connects the motor crankshaft to a pitman arm.

gearbox
A protective housing for a machine's gears.

samson post
Three or four legs of rolled steel that support a walking beam.

drilling rig
A mobile tower with drilling equipment, which bores through rock to find resources such as oil or gas.

crown block
The part of a drilling rig that houses various pulleys used to manipulate the drill line.

derrick
A support structure for a drilling rig's massive drilling equipment.

hoisting equipment
The part of a drilling rig that suspends and maintains the drill bit.

traveling block
An arrangement of pulleys and levers through which a drill line is threaded. It can lift millions of pounds.

working platform
A secure surface, on a drilling rig, that allows workers to make repairs and adjustments.

swivel
A mechanical device that allows a drilling rig's kelly drive to rotate, while simultaneously securing the rig's traveling block.

kelly
The heavy steel part, suspended from the swivel, used to turn the drill bit on a drilling rig.

pin
A threaded part that connects a drill collar and a drill bit.

pin shoulder
The extended edge of a pin, which provides a strong contact point for a drill collar and a drill bit.

shirttail
The support part, consisting of legs, of a roller cone bit.

leg
One of the upper support parts of a roller cone bit to which a cone is fitted.

air passage
The area where air escapes from the back of a cone to the center of the bit.

roller cone bit
A drill bit fitted with cutters, or cones; it bores through rock to find resources such as oil, gas or water.

cone
The cutting part fitted to a roller cone bit.

gauge insert
The cutting surface, usually made of tungsten carbide, of a cone.

rotary table
The part of a drilling rig that allows the drill to cut at precise intervals around a fixed axis.

drill floor
The foundation that supports and balances the weight of a drilling rig.

impervious rock
Rock that oil, gas and water are unable to pass through.

drill collar
The protective casing that holds a drill bit.

water
A transparent liquid made of one oxygen and two hydrogen atoms.

oil
A viscous liquid, used as a fuel source, that can be found in reservoirs throughout the earth's crust.

gas
A mixture of hydrocarbons, used as a fuel source, that can be found in reservoirs throughout the earth's crust.

bit
A large, hard piece of metal designed to drill deep into the earth's crust to extract oil and gas.

oil and gas field
A cross section of the earth showing the shallow layers of the earth's crust, where oil resources are likely to be found.

impermeable rock
A portion of the earth's crust that houses rock formations too difficult to penetrate with modern industrial machinery.

gas
A mixture of hydrocarbons, used as a fuel source, that can be found in reservoirs throughout the earth's crust.

oil
A viscous liquid, used as a fuel source, that can be found in reservoirs throughout the Earth's crust.

fault
A geological phenomenon that occurs when shifting tectonic plates cause a discontinuity in a rock formation.

water
A transparent liquid made of one oxygen and two hydrogen atoms.

grain of sand
A sand particle found in the layers of oil and water in the earth's crust.

oil
A viscous liquid, used as a fuel source, that can be found in reservoirs throughout the earth's crust.

close-up detail of oil and gas field
A detailed representation of the oil, sand and water found in a natural gas and oil reservoir.

octane
A constituent of gas that is categorized as a hydrocarbon of the alkane series. It is flammable.

water
A transparent liquid made of one oxygen and two hydrogen atoms.

hydrogen
A chemical element that is the simplest, lightest and most common.

carbon
A chemical element found in petroleum, as well as in more compounds than any other element.

survey ship
A specialized ship designed with sensors, which locate oil reservoirs beneath the ocean floor.

acoustic projector
A sonar device that projects sound waves toward the ocean floor to obtain measurements of distance.

acoustic receiver
A sonar device that detects and interprets the sound waves of an acoustic projector.

offshore oil field
A marine location where specially designed ships scan the ocean floor for oil resources.

water surface
The top of the ocean, where a ship's waterline is located.

water
A transparent liquid made of one oxygen and two hydrogen atoms.

fault
A geological phenomenon that occurs when shifting tectonic plates cause a discontinuity in a rock formation.

oil
A viscous liquid, used as a fuel source, that can be found in reservoirs throughout the earth's crust.

gas
A mixture of hydrocarbons, used as a fuel source, that can be found in reservoirs throughout the earth's crust.

caprock
A hard, drill-resistant layer of rock commonly found over weaker layers of oil- or gas-bearing rock.

sound waves
Longitudinal pressure waves in any elastic material, such as water.

fossil fuel creation
The naturally occurring processes, near bodies of water, that cause underground oil and gas reservoirs.

ancient rain forest
An old, dense evergreen forest notable for its annual rainfall and biodiversity.

plants die, are buried and decay, forming peat
The result of dead plants gradually accumulating and being covered by sediment.

peat is buried, compressed and heated
A geological phenomenon occurs when peat is buried by sediment and altered physically and chemically over time.

stagnant seabed
An area on the ocean floor with minimal or no current.

organic-rich mud
A portion of sediment, beneath a seabed, with abundant organic and mineral resources.

oil or gas
A layer of oil or gas beneath the seabed.

coal
The end result of plants decomposing and becoming compacted over thousands of years.

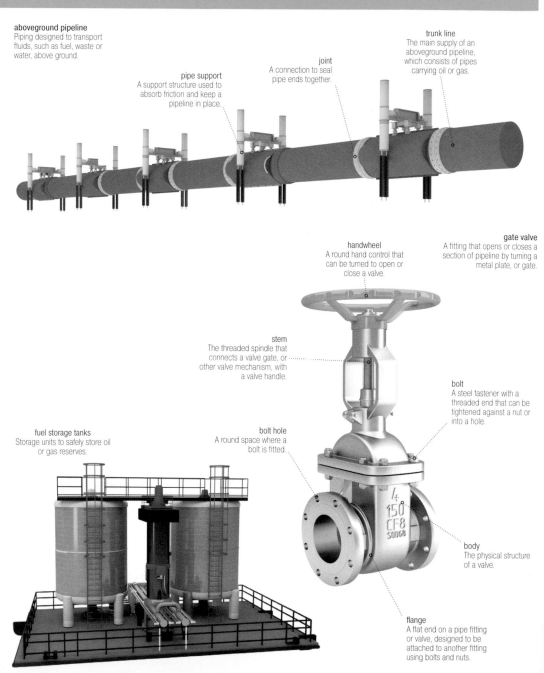

aboveground pipeline
Piping designed to transport fluids, such as fuel, waste or water, above ground.

pipe support
A support structure used to absorb friction and keep a pipeline in place.

joint
A connection to seal pipe ends together.

trunk line
The main supply of an aboveground pipeline, which consists of pipes carrying oil or gas.

handwheel
A round hand control that can be turned to open or close a valve.

gate valve
A fitting that opens or closes a section of pipeline by turning a metal plate, or gate.

stem
The threaded spindle that connects a valve gate, or other valve mechanism, with a valve handle.

bolt
A steel fastener with a threaded end that can be tightened against a nut or into a hole.

fuel storage tanks
Storage units to safely store oil or gas reserves.

bolt hole
A round space where a bolt is fitted.

body
The physical structure of a valve.

flange
A flat end on a pipe fitting or valve, designed to be attached to another fitting using bolts and nuts.

shrink chamber
The part of a shrink wrap machine where wrapped items are heated.

work surface
A flat area where objects are placed for wrapping.

control panel
A board with buttons and switches to operate a machine.

shrink wrap machine
An industrial machine used to tightly wrap large quantities of material with clear film, so they can be transported.

main frame
The structural component that supports the weight of a machine.

power cord
An electrical supply cable.

cart
A small vehicle, fitted with wheels, that carries a load.

shrink film reel
A roll of clear wrapping material for a shrink wrap machine.

caster
A small wheel attached to the base of a machine or other device.

baseplate
A foundation that uniformly distributes a machine's weight.

reel dispenser
The part of a shrink wrap machine that helps unroll a section of clear wrapping material.

fabric-cutting machine
An industrial machine that efficiently cuts and shapes large amounts of fabric.

binding machine
An industrial machine that secures large amounts of documents together quickly and efficiently.

embroidery machine
A common industrial textile machine used to quickly and efficiently create patterns on fabric.

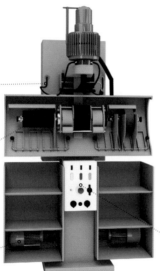

shoe-making machine
A piece of industrial equipment designed for the mass production of shoes.

power cord
An electrical supply cable.

grinding wheel
A rotating wheel of rough material used to sharpen or smooth a workpiece.

motor
An electrical power source to run a shoe-making machine or other device.

control panel
A board with buttons and switches to operate a machine.

press brake
An industrial machine used for bending metal sheets and plates.

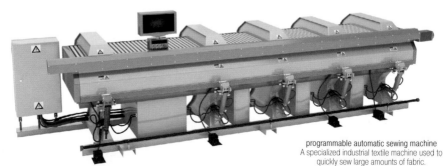

programmable automatic sewing machine
A specialized industrial textile machine used to quickly sew large amounts of fabric.

lathe
An industrial machine that is used to shape sheets of metal.

cross slide
The part that advances and reverses the compound rest, thereby adjusting the cutting tool's position.

tool post
The part of a lathe that holds various cutting tools.

dead center
The part, fitted in the tailstock of a lathe, that supports and centers a workpiece.

chuck
A clamping device that centers and holds a workpiece.

tailstock
The part that secures the dead center, which supports and centers a workpiece.

spindle
The hole through the headstock where bar stock is placed to be turned.

tailstock handwheel
A round hand control that advances and reverses the dead center of a tailstock.

headstock
The part, fixed to the ways of a lathe, that holds the rotating spindle.

half-nut lever
A lever, located on the right side of an apron, used for advancing the carriage when threading on a lathe.

bed
The heavy steel frame of a lathe.

apron
The part attached to the front of the carriage, with controls for the carriage and cross slide.

quick-change gearbox
A set of controls mounted to the front of a lathe bed, to engage or disengage the leadscrew.

carriage handwheel
A round hand control used to move the carriage of a lathe along the ways.

way
One of a pair of precision-machined guide rails for the saddle of a lathe to travel along.

saddle
The top casting of the carriage on a lathe.

carriage
The part of a lathe that acts as a mounting for cutting tools and that moves along the lathe ways.

feedscrew
A long driveshaft that moves a lathe carriage at a relatively slow rate for machining.

chip pan
A large rectangular sheet with a raised edge, located under the bed of a lathe to catch metal shavings.

leadscrew
A long driveshaft that moves a lathe carriage at a faster rate for threading.

guillotine cutter
An industrial tool with a blade that lowers to cut material.

handle
The part of a guillotine cutter that is held in order to cut material.

upper blade
A sharp steel cutting edge fitted on the knife of a guillotine cutter.

knife
The upper part of a guillotine cutter, which can be raised and lowered for cutting.

frame
The structural foundation of a guillotine cutter, which evenly distributes the cutter's weight.

lower blade
A sharp steel cutting edge that a guillotine cutter's knife cuts against.

hydraulic press
A device that uses a hydraulic cylinder to create a large compressive force for metalworking.

stand
A mounting for a guillotine cutter or other object.

milling machine
A machine tool designed to produce a precise part by moving the part past a rotating cutter at a desired angle.

spindle
A vise-like part that holds and rotates a workpiece or tool in a milling machine.

control panel
A board with buttons and switches to operate a machine.

regulating wheel
A hand control used to adjust the machine's spindles and, in turn, the workpiece.

lever
A rod that acts as a hand control to adjust a milling machine's position or gears.

protective cover
A safety device fitted over the cutters of a milling machine.

motor
An electrical power source to run a milling machine or other device.

grinder/sharpener
A device fitted with rotating stones, used to quickly sharpen or smooth a workpiece.

driveshaft
A rod driven by a motor or other prime mover that provides mechanical energy to turn a grinding wheel or other device.

power switch
A device to turn a machine's electrical power on or off.

protective cover
A device fitted over a grinding stone to prevent flying debris.

tray
A flat surface with a raised edge, used to catch a dropped workpiece.

welder
A machine used to heat metal parts so they can be attached, or welded, together.

flange
A flat end, on a fitting, designed to be attached to another fitting using bolts and nuts.

grinding wheel
A rotating wheel of rough material used to sharpen or smooth a workpiece.

access panel
A door or plate for technicians to work on a machine's inner parts.

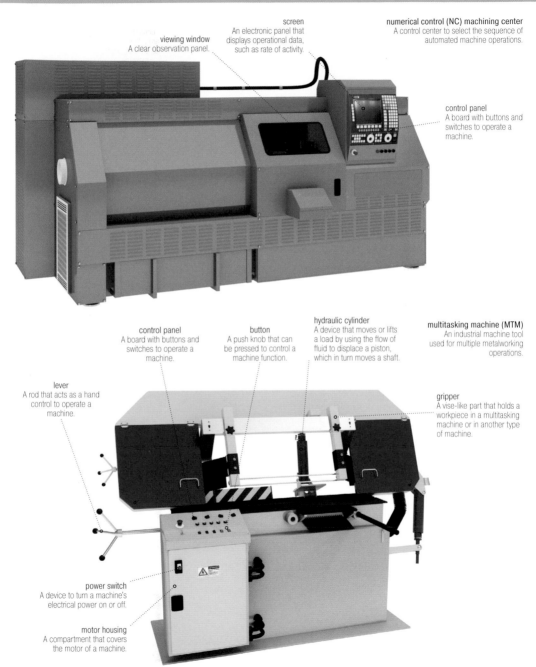

screen
An electronic panel that displays operational data, such as rate of activity.

viewing window
A clear observation panel.

numerical control (NC) machining center
A control center to select the sequence of automated machine operations.

control panel
A board with buttons and switches to operate a machine.

control panel
A board with buttons and switches to operate a machine.

button
A push knob that can be pressed to control a machine function.

hydraulic cylinder
A device that moves or lifts a load by using the flow of fluid to displace a piston, which in turn moves a shaft.

multitasking machine (MTM)
An industrial machine tool used for multiple metalworking operations.

lever
A rod that acts as a hand control to operate a machine.

gripper
A vise-like part that holds a workpiece in a multitasking machine or in another type of machine.

power switch
A device to turn a machine's electrical power on or off.

motor housing
A compartment that covers the motor of a machine.

cut-off saw
An industrial cutting machine with a rotating abrasive blade to cut metals.

protective cover
A safety device fitted over the blade of a cut-off saw.

handle
The part of a cut-off saw that is held in order to lower or raise the blade when cutting.

motor
An electrical power source to run a cut-off saw or other device.

blade
A sharp steel cutting edge.

power switch
A device to turn a machine's electrical power on or off.

handle
The part of a cut-off saw that is held in order to advance or retract the table.

carriage
The part the frame fitted with tracks, that allows the table to be advanced toward the blade.

cradle
A support structure for a cut-off saw.

wheel
A circular component that rotates on an axial bearing and provides motion.

table
A flat work space where material is placed.

mobile floor crane (engine hoist)
A specially designed industrial machine capable of lifting, lowering or moving heavy objects.

boom
The lifting arm of a crane.

sheet-metal shear
A specialized piece of equipment with blades to cut sheets of metal.

hydraulic cylinder
A device that moves or lifts a load by using the flow of fluid to displace a piston.

frame
The structural component of a mobile floor crane that provides a sturdy and balanced foundation.

metal-cutting machine
A specialized piece of industrial textile equipment used to cut large sheets of metal.

multipurpose mixer
An industrial food machine used to mix and stir liquids and solids.

splashguard
A cover fitted over a multipurpose mixer to contain splatters.

main body
The support structure of a multipurpose mixer.

attachment
A tool fitted to the rotor of a multipurpose mixer to mix ingredients.

bowl
A hollow, semicircular container for ingredients.

bowl support
A securing device for the bowl of a multipurpose mixer.

filler
A machine used in food processing plants to efficiently and accurately measure and dispense portions of food products.

bowl cutter
A type of meat processing machine used to chop various types of meat.

belt conveyor
A machine that moves food products along an assembly line in a food processing plant.

part of conveyor system
An industrial machine that uses a conveyor belt to move products from one processing area to another.

alarm
A flashing red light, accompanied by sound, that alerts workers of a conveyor system malfunction.

control panel
A board with buttons and switches to operate a machine.

tunnel
An enclosed section where products pass for further processing.

tunnel curtain
Hanging material, often made of rubber, that covers the opening of a tunnel and acts as a barrier.

outfeed track
One of a pair of rails that feeds products along parts of a conveyor system for further processing.

confectionery coating machine
A candy manufacturing machine used to cover food products in sugar.

drum
The container that holds and continuously spins the food products.

emergency stop switch
A device designed to immediately cut power to a machine in the event of an accident or mistake.

gearbox
A protective housing for a machine's gears.

milk processing machine
An industrial machine that collects raw milk in a tank and then churns the milk.

on/off switches
Buttons designed to be pushed to start or stop a machine.

drum tilt lock
A security device that locks the drum in place during operation.

motor compartment
A protective housing for a motor.

portioning and forming machine
An industrial food processing machine
that cuts various food products, such
as meat, into desired shapes and
quantities.

food slicer
An industrial machine that efficiently
cuts large quantities of food into
precise portions.

food mill
A food processing machine that can
mash and sieve ingredients.

conveyor system feeder
An industrial device used to move food
products or other materials onto a conveyor
belt system.

rib
A reinforcement groove that runs over the top of a hard hat.

hard hat
Rigid headgear that is designed to protect a worker's head from falling objects and other hazards.

peak
A lip that protrudes from the front of a hard hat to act as a visor.

face shield
A visor designed to protect the face from debris, such as metal shavings.

suspension
The securing band of a hard hat.

earplugs
Small, thick pieces of foam placed in the ears to prevent hearing damage from loud noise.

ear protectors
A set of ear covers designed to prevent hearing damage from loud noise.

safety boots
Boots with steel toes and with soles constructed of nonslip material.

toe guard
Thick, protective covers for toes placed over the ends of shoes or boots.

dust mask
Protective face gear that is designed to prevent the user from breathing in dust and other small particles.

cup
The dome-like structure designed to fit securely over the nose and mouth.

safety goggles
Protective eyewear that covers and surrounds the eyes.

headband
The elastics attached to a dust mask to secure the mask to the face.

exhalation valve
A small opening located on the front of a dust mask for the wearer to release exhaled breath.

safety glasses
Eyewear designed to protect the eyes from debris, such as metal shavings.

full-face respirator
An artificial respiration device that is secured to the face and prevents the user from breathing in hazardous materials.

facepiece
The structural component of a full-face respirator that fits snugly on the face.

visor
The thick, transparent shield of a full-face respirator that acts as a protective screen for the face.

head harness
The bands attached to the facepiece of a full-face respirator.

half-mask respirator
A device that protects the wearer from inhaling harmful fumes.

cartridge
A small cylindrical part that contains a filter. It is fitted in front of the inhalation valve.

inhalation valve
An opening fitted with a filter, designed for air intake.

filter cover
A plastic casing that secures a full-face respirator's filter.

exhalation valve
An opening designed for the wearer to release exhaled breath.

INDEX

D